DATE DUE

DE 11			
OC 6 99			

DEMCO 38-296

On the Limits of the Law

On the Limits
of the Law

The Ironic Legacy of Title VI
of the 1964 Civil Rights Act

Stephen C. Halpern

The Johns Hopkins University Press
Baltimore and London

© 1995 The Johns Hopkins University Press
All rights reserved.   Published 1995
Printed in the United States of America on acid-free paper
04 03 02 01 00 99 98 97 96 95   5 4 3 2 1

The Johns Hopkins University Press
2715 North Charles Street
Baltimore, Maryland 21218-4319
The Johns Hopkins Press Ltd., London

ISBN 0-8018-4896-2
ISBN 0-8018-4897-0 (pbk.)

Library of Congress Cataloging-in-Publication Data will be found
at the end of this book.
A catalog record for this book is available from the British
Library.

FOR TAMAR

The face of all the world is changed, I think,
Since first I heard the footsteps of thy soul.

Elizabeth Barrett Browning

Contents

PREFACE

SINCE *Brown v. Board of Education* in 1954, the campaign for racial justice in the United States has increasingly—almost reflexively—relied on legal reform and ideas about legal rights as the primary tools for remedying racial problems. This book examines that dependence on the law and concepts of legal rights by analyzing the history of Title VI, a major provision of the 1964 Civil Rights Act. Title VI prohibits racial discrimination in programs receiving federal funding. It has been enforced most extensively against public educational institutions and systems allotted federal dollars. Like all case studies, however, this book strives to illuminate more than the subject of its immediate focus.

The history of Title VI is important not merely because of the failure of the measure to deliver what it promised or what some hoped it would. Equally important, that history illustrates the consequences of reducing a complicated social and racial problem to a question of law and legal rights. There is an unanticipated and typically unrecognized price that the legal system exacts when we lay a complex social issue at its doorstep. When a problem is analyzed through the lens of the law and is resolved through the application of legal rights, the legal process itself limits both the questions asked and the solutions considered.

In translating a social problem into the "language" of the law, lawyers must frame their analysis in terms of contrived concepts, issues, questions, and remedies that the legal system recognizes and deems legitimate. In that translation, as in any translation, there are constrictions and distortions. Framing a social problem as a legal issue produces a transformation of the issue itself—a reconceptualization of the problem, yielding unique questions and concerns that first become the focus of the legal debate and subsequently tend to dominate public discussion. When racial problems are reformulated as questions of legal rights, the resulting dialogue does not capture the complexity and subtlety of those problems or permit consideration of the fullest range of remedies for them. Inevitably, the demands and limits of the legal process alter the public discourse about and understanding of vital racial issues.

My purpose is not to disparage the racial progress made through legal reform. Rather, it is to recognize that although the establishment of legal rights has long been the dominant tactic used to achieve racial equality, it is a limited strategy. It is not a substitute for sustained political dialogue, organization, and action. Indeed, this study demonstrates that legal "victories" can have perverse and insidiously negative consequences.

I became politically aware during a time of growing public consciousness about racial injustices and growing committment to use law to remedy those injustices. The temper of that time shaped me and, in part, I suspect, moved me to study law and political science and, ultimately, to write this book. Title VI and the civil rights lawsuits initiated to realize its goals arose out of a confidence in the capacity of law and litigation to end American racism. Like many others, I once shared that confidence and exulted in the change that seemed possible through legal action. Consequently, for me, writing a book that stresses the limits of civil rights law and litigation has been disconcerting. I am an author made uneasy by the theme at the heart of his book.

In reaching the conclusions that I do, I have had to ask myself: Does the assessment I advance undermine that continuing struggle for racial justice? Do my conclusions diminish the heroism of lawyers and judges whom I have long admired? Will my arguments strengthen the hand of those who remain unsympathetic to the plight of African Americans and to efforts to address their needs? In considering these questions, I would emphasize several points, both to calm my own fears and parry the inevitable criticism of others. First, I argue not that Title VI has been without benefit but rather that, like many other historic civil rights measures, including *Brown* itself, it has been much less far-reaching than both liberals and conservatives alike are inclined to acknowledge. Second, to chart future strategies to solve the daunting racial problems that remain, it is essential that one have an understanding of the limitations of past efforts. Third, it is decidedly the task of the scholar to seek to provide such understanding.

Issues of race and law have been intertwined throughout the history of the United States in paradoxical ways. From the beginning, the law has played a central role in legitimating and perpetuating racial injustice. On the one hand, provisions written into the Constitution, federal and state statutes that bolstered slavery, and Supreme Court decisions that rationalized the subjugation of blacks provided the nation with a framework for sustaining racial oppression. On the other hand, legislation containing the spread of slavery, legal arguments advanced by abolitionists, constitutional amendments enacted to protect the rights of blacks, civil rights legislation in the nineteenth and twentieth centuries, and legal attacks on segregation in this century provided the nation with a framework for combating racial oppression.

The racial issue at the root of the legal controversies analyzed in this book is the unequal public education provided to African Americans. That inequality has always been a central feature of this nation's system of racial subordination. When the Court took the full measure of that problem in *Brown,* it announced that black Americans had a constitutional right to what the high tribunal called "equal educational opportunity." This book tries to understand the evolution and consequences of the efforts to use the legal system to realize that right.

ACKNOWLEDGMENTS

FEW THINGS IN LIFE ARE more agreeable to an author than writing acknowledgments. Confronting that task signifies that the hard work is finally completed. So it is with relish that I undertake the gratifying job of noting my indebtedness to friends, colleagues, and family.

My colleague Stefan Fleischer read an early draft of this volume, providing detailed and invaluable counsel. On many occasions after that first reading, Steve commented on subsequent revisions and helped me clarify my thoughts as I labored to prune and refine the work. Henry Taylor, director of the Center for Applied Public Affairs Studies at the State University of New York at Buffalo, invited me to be in residence at the Center during the spring of 1992 to work on this project. The opportunity to be relieved of teaching responsibilities and to enjoy the intellectual vibrancy that pervades the Center facilitated and improved the book. Discussions with Henry during that semester and since, and my continuing affiliation with the Center, have brought me great professional satisfaction and deepened my understanding of racial issues. Scott Henderson, one of the ablest graduate students I have had the pleasure to work with, read entire drafts of the manuscript on two occasions, advancing suggestions that made the text shorter and clearer. He helped with an uncommon graciousness and intelligence, well beyond the call of duty.

Wayne McIntosh, Shep Melnick, Joe Stewart, and Ken Tollett all reviewed the manuscript for publication, offering much-needed recommendations for improvements. The final version of the book is considerably different and doubtless better for the many suggestions they made. I am especially indebted to Ken Tollett, who, after reading a draft of the manuscript for Johns Hopkins University Press, continued to offer encouragement and counsel on a regular basis right up until the week of my final submission. Whenever I was stymied, I could call Ken or ask him for comments on revisions and somehow come away with a sharper understanding of what I was studying and a clearer sense of what I had to do to improve the work. I have also been greatly influenced by Elias Blake, who has a deep understanding of the African American struggle for educational opportunity and who generously shared his insights with me. In a similar way, I am indebted to J. Clay Smith, one of the nation's leading civil rights scholar-activists. Though I have never met or spoken with Derrick Bell, I feel obliged to acknowledge him. Bell's creative, path-breaking work, more than that of any other scholar, has shaped my thinking about the limits of litigation. By personal example, Stanley Feingold at the City College of New York, and J. Woodford Howard Jr. at the Johns Hopkins University, made me appreciate the noble role that a teacher and scholar can play. In completing the most challenging professional endeavor I have ever undertaken, I want to acknowledge my gratitude and debt to both of them.

At the State University of New York at Buffalo, I have been assisted by a cadre of exceptional students: Kelly Ann Argy, Antoinette Bonsignore, John Carberry, Tony Delmonte, Jim Fehrman, Christine Garvey, Michelle Melton, Michelle Murray, Lisa Parshall, Robin Stanton, Jennifer Smith, Amy Verdisco, Ric Weber, and John Yakovou have all worked as research assistants. Elliot Lichtman, a brilliant and dedicated civil rights lawyer affiliated with the former firm of Rauh, Silard, and Lichtman, helped facilitate my access to the voluminous files in the *Adams* litigation. In preparing the manuscript, I also had the good fortune of working with a superb typist—Joyce Farrell. At the Johns Hopkins University Press, Miriam Kleiger has done the most thorough and careful copyediting job imaginable, improving the book in countless ways. Finally, I recognize the profound debt I owe my family. They have nurtured me through this book. I treasure them. My sons, Greg and Jake, both of whom attended an inner-city public school in Buffalo, have probably taught me as much about school desegregation and race in America as any book or scholar has. For my wife, Tamar, an exquisite partner, no words or book dedication could adequately reflect how she has contributed to the completion of this effort, nourished my spirit, and enriched my life.

ON THE LIMITS OF THE LAW

I

RACE, LITIGATION, AND THE LEGAL RIGHTS FIXATION

> My friend, I remember when I shared your never-say-die
> enthusiasm. But now I am no longer certain that such
> earnest commitment is a help to our people. . . . In fact,
> I fear that your efforts to effect change through unthinking
> trust in the law and the courts place you not on the side of
> black people, but rather in their way.
>
> Geneva Crenshaw, a fictional character
> in Derrick Bell's *And We Are Not Saved*

HERALDED AS "ONE OF THE legislative milestones in modern American history" and as "the most far-reaching civil rights measure" ever enacted in the United States, the 1964 Civil Rights Act was a watershed event in American law and politics.[1] Its passage was in many ways a culmination of the struggle by the black civil rights movement to use legal reform to achieve racial equality. The history of the enforcement of Title VI of the 1964 act, one of the law's most far-reaching provisions and the main subject of this volume, teaches powerful lessons about the limits of the law.

Title VI prohibits discrimination on the basis of race or national origin in programs receiving federal financial assistance and authorizes federal agencies disbursing monies to terminate funding to programs that discriminate. Its most critical language provides that "[n]o person in the United States shall, on the ground of race, color or national origin, be excluded from participation in, be denied the benefits of, or be subjected to discrimination under any program or activity receiving Federal financial assistance" (42 U.S.C. § 2000d). In the words of Hubert Humphrey, the Senate's primary supporter of Title VI, spending federal tax dollars in support of programs that discriminated on the basis of race offended the "moral sense of the Nation."[2] When Congress subsequently passed civil rights legislation barring discrimination in federally funded programs on the basis of gender, physical or mental disability, and age, it modeled those provisions on Title VI.

Title VI has been used most prominently by the federal government in its attempt to eliminate racial discrimination and segregation in schools.[3] In addition, constitutional litigation, based on the Fourteenth Amendment's equal protection clause, also continued to be used to achieve those ends. Consequently, since 1964 there has been a two-track legal system for combating racial discrimination in schools: enforcement of Title VI administratively by the executive branch, and enforcement of Fourteenth Amendment constitutional guarantees by the judicial branch. The two branches have not operated independently of each other; rather, there has been a constant interplay between them. That interplay occurred because bureaucrats enforcing Title VI, initially in the Department of Health, Education, and Welfare and later in the Department of Education, adopted the judiciary's constitutional standards for measuring racial discrimination in schools under the Fourteenth Amendment to determine what constituted racial discrimination for purposes of Title VI.

Additional and prolonged interaction between the judicial and executive branches began in 1970, when the NAACP Legal Defense and Educational Fund initiated litigation that imposed wide-ranging judicial controls on federal officials enforcing Title VI. Much of this volume analyzes that landmark litigation. Spanning more than two decades, it shaped the day-to-day enforcement of Title VI and eventually mushroomed to regulate the federal government's enforcement of civil rights laws not only on behalf of African Americans but also on behalf of Hispanic Americans, women, the elderly, and the disabled.

THE HISTORY of Title VI chronicles the persistent attempt to use legislation, law enforcement, and litigation to end racial inequality in public education. Reliance on those legal initiatives has distorted our vision and understanding of the issue of equal educational opportunity and limited the measures taken to realize that goal. Using Title VI, this book critically examines the American predisposition to redress racial inequities through civil rights laws and litigation.

In both constitutional litigation and the enforcement of Title VI there was a poor fit — indeed, a gross mismatch — between the legal questions and remedies considered by those attempting to equalize educational opportunities for African Americans, and the reforms needed to accomplish that goal. The legal measures aimed at ending racial inequality in education did not address (and likely are not capable of addressing) the issues that perpetuate that inequality. Civil rights activists and lawyers have failed to recognize this problem. Legalistic strategies based on the Constitution and on Title VI failed to recognize, for example, that racial segregation is only a part, perhaps even an insignificant part, of the problems confronting African Americans in schools. Indeed, the legal concepts of racial segregation and racial discrimination are inadequate analytical tools for understanding the most significant barriers to educational achievement and opportunity for African Americans.

Relying on legal measures to combat racial inequalities in education has had profound negative consequences. First, the legal approach transformed the educational questions raised in the struggle for equal educational opportunity, displacing them with "legal" questions often unrelated to educational issues. Second, the legal approach conceived of the hardships visited on African Americans in narrow conceptual and remedial terms — as violations of "legal rights" best remedied by creating and enforcing new legal protections. Third, the legal rights strategy divorced the black struggle for access to education from its historical roots and objectives in earlier periods. Finally, that strategy failed to respond to the new educational inequalities caused by the transformation of American cities in the post–World War II era.

LITIGATION AS THE CENTERPIECE OF THE CIVIL RIGHTS STRUGGLE

Civil rights organizations resorted to litigation to control the administration of Title VI for much the same reason they had relied on litigation in the era before *Brown v. Board of Education:* they lacked the power to accomplish their goals through the political process. I question the effectiveness of using litigation as a surrogate for political power. Judges cannot compel society to do what it lacks the political will to do, yet that is precisely the aim of much of the litigation analyzed in this volume. The litigation strategy asks too much of the courts and the legal process and too little of ourselves as citizens of a democratic political order. It is a strategy doomed to frustrate and fail. Moreover, a "second wave" of civil rights litigation, focusing on the rights of women, the disabled, Hispanic Americans, and to a lesser extent the elderly, has deflected attention and resources from the black civil rights movement.

In their efforts to use litigation to control the enforcement of Title VI, black civil rights groups became victims of their own success. As lawyers for groups representing women, Hispanics, and the disabled tried to "piggyback" on the court victories won by lawyers representing blacks, their legal initiatives complicated and imperiled the legal successes initially won under Title VI on behalf of blacks. Moreover, the courts seemed unable or unwilling to establish priorities or otherwise distinguish between the legal claims advanced by the different groups that resorted to litigation to control the enforcement of federal civil rights laws. Litigation proved itself repeatedly to be an awkward and even inflexible tool. Once legislation had created categories prohibiting discrimination in federal programs on the basis of race, gender, national origin, and disability, the legal process compelled the courts to treat all the protected groups and their respective claims equally. As a result, blacks' gains and opportunities were diminished, because by treating all minorities similarly, courts tended to underplay if not ignore the uniquely debilitating effects of racism.[4]

Resorting to the legal process to resolve a social issue transforms the way in which we think about that issue and what we do about it. Addressing the problem of unequal educational opportunity through litigation affected outcomes in subtle yet significant ways. Litigation influenced how the federal government defined racial discrimination in schools and what remedies it proposed for that discrimination. Litigation produced a new focus, indeed, a new agenda of concerns, concentrating on secondary and tertiary issues often only tangentially related to educational equality and opportunity.

In translating issues that essentially concern public educational policy into legal questions, lawyers are not free to define and conceive of problems as they or their clients might wish. Rather, they are captives of the process and system within which they work. They must frame the questions they pose for courts in terms of preordained legal concepts and categories that the law recognizes but that often are ill suited for understanding and remedying educational problems. When educational and related social issues are reformulated as legal questions, the legal process transforms the very issues under consideration. Hence, in the litigation focusing on the enforcement of Title VI procedural and managerial issues, rather than substantive educational concerns, dominated. In elementary and secondary education, both in the constitutional litigation and under Title VI, there was an emphasis on achieving racial integration, but virtually no concern beyond that for the quality and character of the educational experience of black students. In the major Supreme Court case involving desegregation in higher education, in 1992, the Court focused on the abstract issue of a student's free choice in selecting a college or university, but displayed little concern for the limited access blacks had to state universities or for the impact the Court's decision might have on the educational needs of blacks.

The tendency of the legal process to transform the way in which we think about an issue is little appreciated. Though Tocqueville noted more than a century and a half ago the American propensity to turn social and political questions into legal issues, we have shown little understanding of the consequences that flow from that propensity. Analyzing how the use of litigation and the legal system transforms the way in which we define and remedy racial problems is especially important, because all of the major racial questions addressed by our society since midcentury have been framed as "legal" issues and have more often than not been the subject of litigation. Racial discrimination in educational institutions — the major subject addressed through Title VI — is no exception.

The central role that litigation has played in determining the impact of Title VI is ironic because Congress passed the measure, in the words of a 1964 White House report, "to remove school desegregation efforts from the courts where they had been bogged down for more than a decade."[5] As the White House report suggested, the effort to implement *Brown* through litigation had failed. Proponents of Title VI hoped that civil rights legislation giving executive agencies the power to terminate federal funding would provide an effective alternative to lawsuits. The history of Title VI, therefore, cannot be understood without linking that history to the *Brown* case, the unsuccessful efforts from 1954 to 1964 to implement *Brown,* and the legal and political efforts before 1954 aimed at overcoming the historic denial of education to American blacks. The civil rights movement's dependence on litigation derived, in part, from entrenched myths celebrating the "rule of law" in American society. In racial matters, that myth was enhanced by the *Brown* decision, which fueled an increasing dependence on "the law" to end racial discrimination not only in education but in other areas as well.

The commitment of civil rights activists to litigation continued even after the historic civil rights legislation of the 1960s. Viewed in this context, the attempt to use litigation to control the enforcement of a major civil rights provision such as Title VI is not surprising. Over the last half century, courts have come to be viewed as having special interest and expertise in matters of race and civil rights. In turn, leaders of civil rights organizations and their lawyers have become preoccupied with — I am tempted to say, addicted to — the "fix" of litigation. That preoccupation has had costs.

The Limitations of Relying on "Legal Rights"

Though this book evaluates the use of litigation to control the enforcement of Title VI, the analysis extends beyond previous studies focusing solely on the efficacy of civil rights litigation.[6] For numerous reasons, understanding the history of Title VI requires examining more than the role that lawsuits played in shaping the provision and influencing its impact. First, Title VI created a legal right not by judicial fiat but by a historic legislative enactment. Second, as noted, Title VI was legislation enacted out of a recognition that a decade of school desegregation litigation following *Brown* had failed. Third, Congress designed Title VI to remedy that failing, basing the provision on the premise that racial discrimination in federally funded schools and other institutions could best be eliminated not by litigation but by the administrative action of agencies enforcing a federal law. Consequently, the history of Title VI is the product not of court actions and judicial power alone, but of legal initiatives advanced by all three branches of government.[7] The core idea behind those initiatives was the belief in a "legal right" that protected blacks against "racial discrimination" in public schools.

That we sought to improve the education blacks received in schools by creating a "legal right" is significant. Writing of the exalted role of legal rights in the black struggle, Patricia Williams argues that African Americans believed in rights in a "mythologic sense — as a pantheon of possibility": "Blacks believed in rights so much and so hard that we gave them life where there was none before; held unto them, put the hope of them unto our wombs, mothered them . . . ; we nurtured rights and gave rights life."[8] Like the commitment to litigation, the devotion to legal rights has not been without its costs.

A major limitation of the legal rights approach to racial issues derives from the need to define the rights that exist. A "right" has been defined as a "power, privilege, demand or claim possessed by a particular person by virtue of law."[9] One drawback of using the law to remedy racial inequality in public education stems from the difficulty of defining the precise "power, privilege, demand or claim" that blacks should be able to assert. Though Title VI forbids "racial discrimination," Congress did not define that term. It was left to the federal courts and to executive branch officials enforcing Title VI to identify the parameters of the legal right blacks had to equal, nondiscriminatory treatment in public schools. There are formidable conceptual and political problems associated with defining that right, and in the course of their legal initiatives to frame an answer, federal bureaucrats and judges settled on simplistic definitions that reflected little attempt to understand or resolve the complexities of achieving equal educational opportunity.

Title VI played a critical role in linking the right to be free from racial discrimination in school to the legal obligation to mix children of different races in schools. Over time, the goal of adjusting the percentages of black and white children in schools — the "racial body count" approach — dominated the effort to protect the "rights" of black children. Conceiving of the legal right in that way offered, at best, a partial and inadequate framework for addressing the educational needs of those children.

Desegregation in higher education was also a focus of litigation under Title VI. Central to that litigation was the controversy, in nearly a score of states, over the status and future of publicly supported historically black colleges and universities. Those institutions, of course, had their origins in a period when states prohibited blacks from attending institutions of higher education with whites. As had occurred in the desegregation of elementary and secondary schools, when the Supreme Court entered the dispute over the historically black institutions it conceived of the rights at issue in narrow, legalistic ways that ignored fundamental educational considerations and offered limited options to improve the educational opportunities of blacks.

The Loss of Focus on the Goals of the Crusade for Black Education

Attempting to resolve racial and educational problems by establishing legal rights is but one way of addressing those problems. Indeed, the twentieth-century legal campaign against "racial discrimination" in schools was part of a long-enduring political struggle by blacks, spanning at least two centuries, to gain access to education. Noting the perseverance of blacks in this regard, one historian observed that it "is difficult to understand how a people systematically kept in densest ignorance for generations could have such a keen and almost unanimous understanding of the power of the written language."[10]

Historically, whites denied blacks education in order to maintain white dominance. Denying blacks education perpetuated their subordinate position and limited their role in the social and economic order. The historian Leon Litwack writes that whereas most slaveholders eventually overcame their fear of religious worship among slaves, "only a very few . . . dared to extend such toleration to teaching blacks to read and write."[11] Indeed, states enacted laws against teaching slaves those skills to preclude them from reading abolitionist literature and to prevent slave insurrections.[12] For slave owners, perpetuating black illiteracy became "essential to the internal security of their society."[13]

In the decades following emancipation, the crusade by blacks to educate themselves was part of a political movement that reflected their "intent to restructure and control their lives" and to resist "racial and class subordination."[14] Those flourishing efforts by blacks to get an education produced new measures by southern whites to deny them that opportunity. In the postbellum period there was a deliberate attempt, led by southern planters, to ensure that blacks received no education or minimal education. Those efforts succeeded. Between 1880 and 1900, though there was a 25-percent increase in the number of black children of school age in the South, the percentage who attended public school decreased.[15]

James Anderson, who has written the definitive history of black education in the South following the Civil War, notes that though the ex-slaves tried to build an educational system that would "defend and extend their emancipation," forces that they could not control consigned their children to a system of vocational education that perpetuated their political and economic subordination. Postbellum fear of and opposition to education for blacks reflected historic white anxieties. Educating former slaves, whites believed, would produce political instability, increase competition between white and black laborers, and yield greater political participation and voting power for blacks. These very possibilities, feared by whites in the nineteenth century, moved black lawyers in this century to mount their legal assault on the South's public educational system.[16]

In explaining why the NAACP Legal Defense Fund focused its legal challenges on educational inequality, Charles Houston stressed the link between education and political and economic power. Speaking in 1935, Houston emphasized that "education . . . is preparation for the competition of life" and that a "poor education handicaps an individual in that competition." Addressing the black lawyers group, the National Bar Association, in that same year, Houston was even more outspoken: "[I]nferior education makes [Negroes] less able to stand competition with whites for jobs" and made it harder for "young Negro men and women [to be] courageous and aggressive in defense of their rights."[17]

Hence, for generations before the decision in *Brown* and the passage of Title VI, the aim of the black struggle for education was to use education to achieve greater economic and political power and end the stranglehold of white domination. *Brown* and Title VI must be seen as part of that struggle. What is remarkable about the history of the constitutional litigation after *Brown* and also about the saga of Title VI, is how divorced those legal initiatives ultimately became from the aims of that historic struggle. Today, no one argues that school desegregation litigation or the enforcement of Title VI bears any significant relationship to the ability of blacks to win, through education, greater political or economic power. Those legal initiatives have become irrelevant to that struggle.

The Irrelevance of the Legal Rights Strategy to the Contemporary Urban Dilemma

The failure of the law to link educational issues to larger political and economic forces has been evident in recent decades in the law's failure to address the educational problems confronting blacks in American cities.[18] Between 1940 and 1980, structural transformations altered American society and the lives of the majority of African Americans. Yet, in both constitutional litigation and the enforcement of Title VI, there were few attempts to cope with those changes and the new race-based educational inequalities they produced. These structural transformations involved long-term demographic, geographic, and economic patterns; ultimately, these changes reconfigured the landscape of America's cities, creating much of the structure and attendant ills associated with what became known as the "inner city."

One of the greatest transformations since 1940 has been the change in where African Americans live. In that year, the South was still home to three of every four African Americans. Nationwide, half of all African Americans still lived in rural areas.[19] Beginning in the early 1940s and continuing through the late 1960s, a "great migration" of African Americans occurred. It began in response to the job opportunities generated by the exigencies of wartime production. Whereas the ten largest wartime production centers saw a 19-percent increase in their white population, they experienced a 49-percent increase in their African American population, as nearly a million African Americans journeyed to cities in hopes of securing employment in the defense industry. More significant still, African Americans, unlike whites, tended to stay in cities in the decades after the war.[20] While the production demands of World War II precipitated the great migration of African Americans, the mechanization of cotton harvesting spurred a continued exodus from the rural South by making the cotton industry less labor intensive and thereby eliminating the need for the sharecropper system, the foundation for African American economic subsistence in that region.

The demographic shifts produced by the postwar African American migration were momentous. Between 1940 and 1970, more than 5 million African Americans moved from the South to the North. By 1970, no more than half of all African Americans lived in the South, and only a quarter of those who remained lived in rural areas.[21] By the 1970s, then, significant numbers of African Americans lived in areas and under circumstances quite unlike those in which most African Americans had lived when the Supreme Court decided *Brown*.

As African Americans entered northern cities in record numbers, a second profound transformation began: the rapid suburbanization of America's metropolitan areas. Of the almost 13 million homes built between 1948 and 1958, 85 percent were built in the suburbs. Between 1950 and 1970, the suburban population doubled from 36 million to 72 million.[22] Suburbia, however, was not open to everyone. Both the Federal Housing Administration (FHA) and the Veterans Administration (VA) mortgage programs discriminated against African Americans, supporting the economic and racial segregation of suburbia.[23] Even where federal discrimination did not block blacks from moving into suburbs, private prejudice — perpetuated by the real estate and banking industries and local neighborhood associations — guaranteed that suburbs would have a homogeneous complexion.

By 1980, whites and African Americans increasingly inhabited two separate worlds and educated their children in school systems that reflected that separateness. In addition to living in two separate worlds, whites and African Americans lived (and continue to live) in two very unequal worlds. That inequality resulted from yet another transformation that coincided historically with the effort to enforce *Brown* and Title VI — the decline of the economic base of the American city.

Perhaps nothing crippled central cities in recent decades as much as the loss of basic manufacturing industries. This process, known as deindustrialization, had tragic consequences for cities and the workers who lived in them. Beginning in the early 1970s, a variety of factors caused corporate profits to fall from the high levels of the 1950s and 1960s. Industrial corporations sought to increase their profits, or at least keep them from falling any further. Because new technologies and transportation allowed production to be decentralized and/or internationalized, many manufacturers either moved their production facilities to areas where costs were lower (usually less well-developed countries), or divested themselves entirely of their manufacturing interests.[24] As a result, by the early 1980s, in cities across the land, once-mighty factories were deserted, and their closings caused unemployment and fiscal crises of unprecedented proportions. Central cities, historically home to thousands of thriving manufacturing concerns, became industrial ghost towns unable to attract new businesses, support high-quality schools, or even meet their municipal payrolls. But what do these transformations and the emergence of the inner city have to do with the *Brown* decision, Title VI, and other legal attempts to effect equality in educational opportunity?

The legal quest for equal educational opportunity for blacks in the decades following World War II coincided with the transformations in the American city outlined above. What is striking about both the legal initiatives under the Constitution and those under Title VI is that they failed to address the impact these transformations had on the education of the nation's black children. By 1990, for example, more than 4 million black children, approximately 60 percent of the national total, attended public schools in central cities. In the face of the postwar urban transformation and the disastrous conditions it produced for black Americans living in inner cities, the legal struggle against racial inequality in public education continued to focus on narrow concerns. In the enforcement of Title VI, as we shall see, litigation focused not on the substantive rights protected by the provision, but on the procedures for processing complaints of discrimination filed with the federal government. In constitutional adjudication, the litigation focused on eliminating segregation in schools situated within the confines of city boundaries. Indeed, desegregation remained the focus of the law even after the public school populations in many cities became so overwhelmingly nonwhite that finding white children with whom to integrate became a serious logistical problem. My point is that the questions posed and the remedies considered in the legal process did not respond to the structural changes in cities that had transformed the lives of millions of blacks, producing a new range of devastating social problems for them and a new kind of educational inequality based largely on race.

In a major review article, Dorothy Strickland and Carol Ascher, two distinguished educational scholars, identified the following factors as contributing to the poor academic achievement of black children: low wages and joblessness among black men, the high percentage of black children living in female-headed households, inappropriate academic evaluation and placement, linguistic differences between whites and blacks, cultural differences and deprivation, poverty, and poor schools.[25] Other factors affecting the academic performance of black children may include their poor physical health, inadequate prenatal care and the poor health of pregnant mothers, high rates of teenage pregnancy, instability in the home, the social isolation of the black poor from other classes, the physical deterioration of urban neighborhoods, the lack of contact between poor minority children and exemplary role models, limited parental involvement in and control over schools, and high student-teacher ratios.

A review of the factors noted by Strickland and Ascher or of the other factors I have mentioned highlights the incongruity between the impediments that limit black children's academic performance and the remedies contemplated within the legal system. The mismatch between the obstacles confronting inner-city children in schools and the issues considered in the legal debate over racial inequality in education is dramatic. Few, if any, of the factors that have an impact on educational achievement are governed by "legal rights" or are readily translatable into an issue of "racial discrimination." Yet, despite the chasm between the factors that influence educational achievement and the factors that dominate the legal discourse, legal initiatives have for decades remained a major strategy used by those who sought to achieve equal educational opportunity for African Americans.

The poor fit between the reforms necessary to address educational needs and the reforms possible through a focus on legal action and legal rights is important. It suggests that the legal struggle to improve schools for blacks through constitutional litigation or Title VI cannot succeed. To the degree that those legal initiatives continue to make any contribution, it is an insidious one. Both civil rights litigation and the administrative enforcement of Title VI have functioned, in significant measure, to offer the illusion of progress and change, while simultaneously ensuring that the existing social and educational order will not be much disturbed.[26] In that way, civil rights reforms have served a fundamentally conservative function. Legal "victories" are held out as evidence that ours is a perfectible regime if we are persistent and creative enough in pursuing that perfectibility. In this view, if civil rights legislation, law enforcement, and litigation have not yet fully eradicated racial inequalities in our schools, that means either that we must rededicate ourselves with renewed zeal to pursuing such legal reforms, or, more troubling, that African Americans themselves are the cause of their own misfortunes.

Thus far, I have identified four consequences resulting from our dependence on legal initiatives to achieve equal educational opportunity for blacks: (1) the tendency of litigation and the legal process to transform educational issues into legal questions that are often unrelated to educational concerns; (2) a predisposition to understand and resolve the problems of African Americans in terms of "legal rights"; (3) a reorientation of the black struggle for education away from its historic objective — the use of education to enhance blacks' political and economic power; and (4) a failure to address the new educational inequalities produced by the emergence of the postindustrial city. Because of my interests and background, I concentrate on the first two consequences. Nonetheless, the third and fourth factors are important, because they reveal the tendency of the legal process to recast the terms of debate about an issue and to abstract that debate from the historical and social roots of a problem. Consequently, the legal movement to help blacks gain access to education and, thereby, to greater power in America, drifted off course. It became dominated by a new agenda of issues generated by the legal debate itself. More significantly, the redefinition of the issues produced by that debate served the interests of the larger white society more than it did the mass of African Americans. Similarly, that same legal movement failed to address the prodigious social forces that created and dominated the urban environment in which nearly two out of every three black children now live and attend school.[27]

TITLE VI, THE LEGAL RIGHTS STRATEGY, AND THE LARGER LESSONS ABOUT RACE

That Title VI sought to combat a racial problem is scarcely an incidental part of its history. The racial issues at the core of the provision help explain why the effort to enforce it produced the unprecedented legal and political conflict it did. No issue in all of American history touches so raw a nerve as does race. Acknowledging our national obsession with race, and our inability to heal the wounds that divide us by color, helps us to make some sense of the uncommon history of Title VI. Therefore, though the bulk of this book focuses on the dynamic between federal administrators, judges, and lawyers vying to control the enforcement of that provision, one cannot divorce the legal battles that engaged those groups from the subject matter of the statute.

Writing of the disappointing results of civil rights laws and litigation, Derrick Bell observed:

Today, while all manner of civil rights laws and precedents are in place, the protection they provide is diluted by lax enforcement, by the establishment of difficult-to-meet standards of proof, and, worst of all, by the increasing irrelevance of antidiscrimination laws to race-related disadvantages. . . .

How are we to assess the unstable status of a struggle that all but the most perversely pessimistic predicted would end in triumph many years ago? Even those most deeply involved in this struggle are at a loss for a rational explanation of how the promise of racial equality escaped a fulfillment that thirty years ago appeared assured.[28]

By analyzing the struggle to enforce a major civil rights provision such as Title VI, we can try to understand how we arrived at the predicament Bell laments.

2

THE KENNEDY LEGACY
AND LEGISLATIVE HISTORY

> If an American, because his skin is dark, cannot eat lunch
> in a restaurant open to the public; if he cannot send his
> children to the best public schools available; if he cannot
> vote for the public officials who represent him; if, in short,
> he cannot enjoy the full and free life which all of us want,
> then who among us would be content to have the color of
> his skin changed and stand in his place?
> President John F. Kennedy, in a radio and
> television broadcast on 11 June 1963

TWO THEMES EMERGE FROM THE historical context that produced Title VI. The first is that the provisions of the 1964 Civil
Rights Act must be seen as measures intended to forestall racial violence. That point is substantiated in reviewing the legislative history
of the 1964 act and the events that prompted its passage. It is worth
emphasizing because we tend not to acknowledge the fear of violence
just beneath the surface of the tenuous racial peace in the United
States or appreciate that our resort to civil rights legislation and litigation and our commitment to notions of "legal rights" are driven by
our desire to provide peaceful, establishmentarian options for the
redress of racial grievances.

The second theme is that though Title VI was a civil rights measure of enormous power, Congress restrained that power by imposing a panoply of procedural requirements that circumscribed what
the law might accomplish. Those procedural constraints were necessary to win congressional passage of the provision. There is in the
United States a long tradition of fear of the national government,
especially in racial matters. Consequently, to counterbalance the
new authority the national government would have under Title VI,
Congress imposed elaborate procedural restrictions intended to pro-

tect against overzealous enforcement. As we shall see, by so doing Congress set the stage for much of what followed: issues of procedural rights and protections played a central role throughout the history of the struggle to enforce Title VI.

Political support for improving the lot of black Americans was stronger in the early and middle 1960s than at any other time since the Civil War. That support was critical in passing Title VI and the 1964 Civil Rights Act. Powerful whites and large numbers of middle-class whites seemed to recognize that continued oppression of blacks, at least in the South, could be disastrous for the nation. Whites appreciated that substantial numbers of blacks were angry with their lot. Blacks seemed more conscious of, and bitter and vocal about, their position in American society than at any other time in the nation's recent history. In the spring of 1963, protests by blacks and sympathetic whites spread across the South like a conflagration. Demonstrations, marches, picketing, freedom rides, and sit-ins dominated the nation's consciousness and news media. During the ten-week period from mid-April 1963 to the end of June, the Justice Department counted 758 racial disturbances caused either by black protests or by white reactions to them.[1]

Violence or the fear of violence was an integral part of these events. In April 1963 William Moore, a Baltimore mailman hiking to Jackson, Mississippi, on a one-man civil rights crusade, was shot to death near Attalla, Alabama. Approximately a month and a half later, Medgar Evers, a black civil rights activist and leader of the NAACP in Jackson, Mississippi, was murdered. During the summer of 1963 racial tension did not abate. There was continuing unrest in Cambridge, Maryland; Danville, Virginia; Birmingham, Alabama; and Jackson, Mississippi; plus the shocking bombing of a Baptist church in Birmingham, which resulted in the deaths of four black children.

Most of the incidents in the spring and summer of 1963 arose from blacks' demands that public facilities such as restaurants, parks, swimming pools, and theaters be desegregated. Often, these incidents involved mass arrests and violent confrontations. In April 1963, in Birmingham, the site of the most appalling confrontations, police used fire hoses and dogs to assault and beat back demonstrators. The turbulent events of what came to be called "the long, hot summer" culminated in the August 1963 mass march on Washington of nearly a quarter of a million people, led by the Reverend Martin Luther King Jr.

The protests against segregation were manifestations of a movement whose roots went deeper than resentment of seating restrictions at lunch counters and on buses. In black culture and in the work of black political organizations and leaders, there were signs of a growing, profound discontent. The black scholar and activist Pauli Murray characterized the events of the spring of 1963 in this way: "[N]egroes have confronted the nation with what has been described as a 'massive insistence' upon drastic changes in the social structure. . . . They have abandoned their traditional role of patience; they have rejected tokenism and gradualism; they are saying, 'One-hundred years of fractional citizenship is enough: We want full citizenship now.'" Shortly before the tumultuous events of the spring of 1963, a group of scholars, lawyers, and activists met at the Notre Dame Law School to discuss civil rights. In the statement released at the end of their meeting, the group concluded that "the crisis of America's race relations had become almost unbearably intense."[2]

An important message seemed to be getting through to increasing numbers of liberal and moderate whites. They began to recognize that the struggle over the status of blacks was a high-stakes struggle with potentially grave consequences for all Americans, whether black or white. As a result of the maelstrom of events in the first half of 1963, the white establishment came to understand that if it failed to address the grievances of blacks, widespread civil disorder, lawlessness, and racial violence could ensue. Walter Lippmann, not given to hyperbole, surmised that "a revolutionary condition exists" and counseled, "We cannot count upon nonviolence persisting in the face of brutal and illiterate resistance. The outstanding danger is not that there may be rioting and brawling. For these can be suppressed. The outstanding danger is a loss of confidence by the Negro people in the good faith of white people."[3] As Lippmann's words suggest, blacks held considerable power in the unfolding national drama, a power rooted in ambivalent feelings among whites. The power of blacks derived simultaneously from white sympathy for the civil rights movement and white fear of the consequences should the movement fail.

Although a political conservative himself, Lippmann, like so many liberals, looked to national legal reform as the answer to racial strife. So did the Kennedy administration. The South's brutal response to civil rights protests galvanized northern white sympathy for the civil rights cause. Indeed, in May 1963 television brought home unforgettable images of police using dogs, fire hoses, and cattle prods against peaceful demonstrators in Birmingham. That incident, graphically presented to millions on network news shows, heightened the drama of the struggle and energized the national coalition that emerged to win passage of the 1964 Civil Rights Act. President Kennedy noted that the outcry following the mistreatment of civil rights demonstrators in Birmingham was a major factor causing him to submit a civil rights bill to Congress in June 1963.[4] That bill, though subsequently modified in major respects in congressional deliberations (as shown in appendix B, below), eventually became the Civil Rights Act of 1964.

Writing of the importance of the Birmingham incident, Arthur Schlesinger observed, "Birmingham and the Negroes themselves gave [Kennedy] the nation's ear." Hanes Walton concluded that "it was clearly the Birmingham demonstrations and subsequent events that forced a reluctant government to take sides." A public opinion groundswell provided the political foundation for new civil rights legislation. Polls taken between March and July of 1963 showed a 1,200-percent increase in the number of Americans who believed that black civil rights was the most urgent issue facing the nation. This public mood, Gary Orfield concluded, helped lift the question of equal rights to the top of the congressional agenda for the first time in the twentieth century.[5]

In one of the first responses to the Birmingham crisis, numerous members of Congress introduced bills demanding that the federal government end its financial support for segregated schools. Those bills contained the root idea of what was ultimately to become Title VI. In the House, fifty-three congressmen introduced such bills, a typical one being the proposal by Congressman Gill (D.-Hawaii) that future federal education grants go only to desegregated schools. Even before the administration assembled its civil rights bill, Congressman Adam Clayton Powell of New York had scheduled hearings on congressional proposals.[6]

Out of the dramatic events of 1963 emerged a historic, though fleeting, national consensus for racial reform. Mandating separation of the races in public facilities blatantly violated the ideology of equality in America. The stark, explicit, and physical character of the discrimination — compelled by law — made it easier to win support for the black cause and to rally people to its banner. In the struggle over segregation, good and evil were readily, indeed dramatically, discernible to most white northerners. Nor would the abolition of segregation affect them directly; that kind of racial domination was alien to northerners. Additionally, much of the civil rights movement in the South was premised on the principle of nonviolence and was, in the best sense of the word, a Christian movement, organized and led by black clergy who conceived of their cause as rooted in scriptural teachings.

When some southern communities responded to demonstrating blacks and whites with savage police methods, bombings of churches, and the murders of civil rights workers, it was not difficult for many white nonsoutherners of diverse political leanings — and some moderate southerners — to discern the justice of the civil rights drive. A chorus of white governmental officials, journalists, academics, and lawyers implored white America to embrace the Negro cause. Following the murder of Medgar Evers in June 1963, an editorial in the *New York Times* voiced that sentiment when it exclaimed, "[E]very family, every home, every community is in the front lines of the crusade for decency to which Mr. Kennedy has summoned America."[7]

The disturbances of the spring and summer of 1963 were simultaneously frightful and stirring. They were frightful because they revealed the brutishness of American racism and because, in the unnerving, physical confrontations they produced, there was an ever-present fear of violence. They were stirring because they focused the nation on the immorality of our racial policies and produced a sense that, after a century of neglect, reform of those policies was a national imperative. These factors produced a psychological and political bond between blacks and a broad coalition of whites in the North and South, manifested in the array of labor unions, religious fellowships, fraternal and professional associations, and national political associations that eventually supported the 1964 Civil Rights Act.

The Leadership Conference on Civil Rights was, in the 1960s, the national umbrella organization for the civil rights movement. Writing of the efforts of the conference to organize groups in support of the administration's civil rights bill, Beryl Radin observed that the conference had "managed to pull together — at least for that moment — otherwise disparate and dissenting groups within the American society."[8] The coalition of groups favoring new civil rights legislation included such new, activist civil rights groups as the Student Non-Violent Coordinating Committee (SNCC) and the Congress on Racial Equality (CORE), as well as the more traditional NAACP and National Urban League. In addition, a range of women's organizations, religious groups, and labor organizations joined the call for strong federal civil rights legislation.

There was, however, a disquieting side to the relationship between blacks and sympathetic whites. White sympathy, at some level, could be traced to fear that racial violence would spread.[9] Pauli Murray warned that though 85 to 95 percent of blacks did not believe in nonviolence, they remained willing to go along with nonviolent tactics as long as these appeared to produce results. "If [nonviolence] fails," she warned, "we are in for serious national bloodshed."[10] The Kennedy administration saw civil rights laws and litigation as an antidote to violence. When he first proposed his 1963 civil rights bill Kennedy acknowledged that the "fires of frustration and discord [were] burning in every city." Again, in his 11 June address to the nation, Kennedy warned that unless Congress acted to provide legal redress for the wrongs inflicted on blacks, "their only remedy is in the street." In the absence of legal remedies, he noted, "redress is sought in . . . demonstrations, parades and protests, which create tensions and violence — and threaten lives."[11]

Continuing that theme in the written message to Congress that accompanied his civil rights bill, Kennedy observed that if Congress failed to enact the bill, blacks would be increasingly likely to seek vindication of their "rights" through "organized direct action" that could have "potentially explosive consequences." In that event, Kennedy foresaw "continued racial strife, causing the leadership on both sides to pass from the hands of responsible and reasonable men to purveyors of hate and violence, endangering domestic tranquility."[12] Advancing a similar worry, Attorney General Robert Kennedy argued that the nation needed new civil rights laws to move the problems, in the words of a national news magazine, "from the streets into the courts." Writing of the pressures on the administration, Arthur Schlesinger observed that "the President felt he would lose control over an increasingly dangerous situation unless he exerted leadership."[13]

Even Martin Luther King Jr. warned of the threat of violence. In September 1963, when a dynamite blast in a Birmingham church killed four black girls during Sunday school services, rioting, sporadic gunfire in black neighborhoods, and multiple fires ensued. Before peace returned, two black youths lay dead and scores of blacks and whites had suffered injuries.[14] To restore order, Governor George Wallace called out three hundred state troopers and five hundred national guardsmen. En route to Birmingham from Atlanta, King said that he would "plead with my people to remain nonviolent in the face of this terrible provocation." In a telegram to Kennedy, King urged the president "to use everything within your constitutional power to enforce the desegregation orders of the courts." "I'm convinced," said King, "that unless some immediate steps are taken by the Federal Government to restore a sense of confidence in the protection of life, limb and property, my pleas will fall on deaf ears and we shall see in Birmingham and Alabama the worst racial holocaust the nation has ever seen."[15]

The racial incidents of the spring, summer, and fall of 1963, and the public rhetoric they produced, formed the backdrop against which Congress considered the 1964 Civil Rights Act. In convening a subcommittee (generally referred to as Subcommittee Number 5) of the House Judiciary Committee to consider the Kennedy administration's 1963 civil rights bill, Chairman Emanuel Celler of New York observed:

> The twenty million Negroes must be reckoned with. They have power. We white leaders must not let the twenty million Negroes be led by demagogues and fanatics and extremists. That power must be molded and led by men of reason not men of rancor. Congress must help supply the format of leadership, with strong progressive laws. . . . Otherwise, we shall share the blame for unconfined and dangerous strife and disorder. Much evil will result unless we act and act quickly, for time is of the essence. Might must not triumph over right, riot over reason. The bullet should not replace the ballot.[16]

Emphasizing similar themes, Celler's New York colleague John Lindsay commented "that every American must be warned that some of the local violence we have seen in various parts of the United States is just a token of what might come . . . in every State of the Union."[17]

In its debate on the bill, the Senate also discussed the frustration and impatience in the black community and the violence that both could breed. Senator Paul Douglas of Illinois entered into the *Congressional Record* statements by Black Muslim leader Malcolm X, who in August 1964 announced that he intended to form and lead a black nationalist movement. "There will be more violence than ever this year," Malcolm X promised. "White people will be shocked," he warned, "when they discover that the passive little Negro they had known turns out to be a roaring lion." He added, "[W]hites had better understand . . . while there is still time" that the "Negroes at the mass level are ready to act."[18] Oregon's Senator Wayne Morse admonished his colleagues to recognize "that unless we give full constitutional rights to Negroes, we cannot stop the issue from going to the streets of America." Speaking of the resolve of blacks on this matter, Morse commented that "tens of thousands of colored people . . . have developed a martyrdom complex" that made them, he concluded, "ready to die for their conviction."[19] Attorney General Robert Kennedy had contributed to these perceptions when he observed that there was a "revolution" going on within the black leadership as power moved from Martin Luther King Jr. to others who had no "confidence in the system of government we have" and who believed that "the way to deal with the problem is to start arming young Negroes and sending them into the streets."[20]

Even those in Congress who opposed the civil rights bill recognized that violence was a political factor. Yet those opponents, most notably Congressmen Rivers and Dorn of South Carolina, urged that Congress not enact legislation out of a fear of violence. Rivers warned that blacks were being "led into revolutionary methods by . . . arrogant, militant leaders," that "violence begets violence," and that "revolutionary methods only fan the passions already at white heat." While fearing that a "mob of a few hundred at the local level today could become a chanting, screaming mob of a million people," Dorn warned his colleagues against "appeas[ing] the agitators and mob violators, because if you reward them with this bill, they will be back." By contrast, Will Maslow of the American Jewish Congress argued that action by Congress would "do more to stop the violence than 100 different police measures."[21]

A reading of the legislative history makes this much plain: Violence, both the fear of its outbreak and its actual use, was a key factor that impelled Congress to enact the 1964 act. As I noted at the outset of this chapter, resorting to legal reform and action to forestall violence is a powerful, enduring, but little appreciated aspect of American civil rights history. I shall return to this theme in the concluding chapter and epilogue. For present purposes, it is sufficient to note that at the conception of what was to become the 1964 Civil Rights Act, there was a strong impetus to resort to civil rights laws and litigation to forestall racial violence. This placed blacks in an atypically strong position from which to make demands and extract concessions from whites. The country had seen nothing like it before in this century and is not likely to see blacks wield that kind of power again anytime soon.

THE BASIC APPROACH: THE CONTROL OF FEDERAL MONIES

Title VI sought to ensure that federal monies did not support activities, institutions, or programs that discriminated on the basis of race or national origin. Prior to the passage of the provision, there had been many controversies focusing on the conditions that Congress might attach to federal financial assistance. By 1964, Congress's authority to establish reasonable conditions on the use of federal funds was well established.[22]

During the 1940s, in an effort to make the best of the constitutional doctrine of "separate but equal," the NAACP Legal Defense Fund sought equal federal expenditures for black and white schools. In *Oklahoma v. U.S. Civil Service Commission* (1947), the Supreme Court affirmed the authority of Congress to establish the terms under which federal monies are disbursed.[23] Presidential concern about federal funding of racially discriminatory programs arose as early as March 1953, during the Eisenhower administration, when the popular, middle-of-the-road Republican president observed, "[W]herever Federal funds are expended for anything, I do not see how any American can justify, legally or logically or morally, a discrimination in expenditure of those funds as among our citizens."[24]

Of course, the *Brown* decision in 1954 focused even greater attention than ever on the use of federal funds — especially in southern school systems. In 1955, attempting to capitalize on *Brown*, the NAACP Legal Defense Fund requested that the government withhold federal aid from educational institutions violating the Supreme Court's decree.[25] Harlem's congressman, Adam Clayton Powell, repeatedly but unsuccessfully sought in the 1950s to add nondiscrimination amendments to appropriation bills providing federal aid for housing, education, and other matters.[26]

In its famous confrontation over the desegregation of schools in Little Rock, Arkansas, in 1958, the Supreme Court declared that, under *Brown,* the "Fourteenth Amendment forbids states to use their governmental powers to bar children on racial grounds from attending schools where there is state participation through any arrangement, management, *funds* or property."[27] If states could not constitutionally provide "funds" to segregated schools, it was difficult logically, legally, or morally to permit the federal government to do so. Though the constitutionality of providing federal funds to programs that discriminate has never been the subject of an express holding by the Court, the language in the Little Rock case suggests that the core principle of Title VI was linked to the Fourteenth Amendment guarantee entitling all citizens to the equal protection of the laws.

Further support for the principle of nondiscrimination in the use of federal funds came from the U.S. Commission on Civil Rights. The commission, an advisory body established by Congress in 1957 to assess civil rights problems, urged the withholding of federal funds to segregated colleges late in the Eisenhower administration and then again in the early stages of the Kennedy presidency.[28]

The use of federal funds for leverage in the black civil rights struggle had enormous potential. Following World War II, the federal government had dramatically expanded its aid to the states. Between 1952 and 1962, Washington's financial assistance to state and local governments tripled, increasing from $2.6 billion to $7.9 billion annually.[29] By 1960, states and localities received 14 percent of their income from federal grants in aid. In some states, including several southern states, the figure reached 32 percent.[30] In 1960, in the eleven states of the former Confederacy—states in which 99 percent of black children attended segregated schools—the federal government disbursed $63 million.[31] Moreover, each year the dollar amount of federal aid to education was increasing.[32]

The Leadership Conference on Civil Rights and the National Urban League, as well as other organizations, urged President Kennedy to issue an executive order that would prohibit those receiving federal money from discriminating on the basis of race. Although the administration rejected this course of action, it did, in response to the persistent urgings of Congressman Powell, take two tentative steps to deal with the discriminatory use of federal dollars. As a first step, the administration's secretary of health, education, and welfare, Abraham Ribicoff, inserted a nondiscrimination clause into contracts with colleges receiving federal money under the National Defense Education Act (NDEA). Under that clause, summer teacher training institutes funded by the NDEA would not be located at any institution that refused to operate the institutes on a nondiscriminatory basis.[33] Subsequently, Ribicoff actually withheld federal funds from some schools. The second step involved a program of federal aid to "impacted areas." Under that program, school districts received compensatory federal aid to offset the loss of local property taxes caused by the presence of federally owned land or schools operated by the Department of Defense. The administration decided to withhold such federal aid from school districts that required the children of military personnel living on federal bases to attend segregated schools.[34] Instead, it would fund desegregated schools on the military bases.[35] The impact of this action was limited because the lawyers for the Department of Health, Education, and Welfare (HEW) determined that they had no authority to take similar action with respect to military personnel who lived off-base and had to send their children to segregated schools.[36]

After the administration took these two steps, Attorney General Robert Kennedy publicly speculated in October 1962 that the withdrawal of federal subsidies, grants, loans, and contracts could be used to persuade southern states to alter their racial practices. But when in February 1963 President Kennedy submitted his initial civil rights message to Congress calling for the enactment of a civil rights law, that message did not contain a prototype of Title VI, that is, a provision prohibiting discrimination in federally funded programs. The administration's February 1963 civil rights bill was innocuous: it was notable for containing a weak voting rights provision and for proposing a continuation of the U.S. Commission on Civil Rights.

At the time he submitted the bill, Kennedy observed that executive orders banning discrimination in certain federal programs had proven beneficial. Various executive orders, Kennedy noted, banned discrimination in the sale, lease, or use of buildings owned or built by the federal government, in homes guaranteed under home financing programs run by the Federal Housing Administration and the Veterans Administration, in employment by the federal government, and in federally financed merit systems for state employees.[37] Executive orders also barred discrimination by contractors on construction sites financed by federal funds, and discrimination in the armed forces.[38] Finally, the president noted that his Committee on Equal Employment Opportunity had imposed nondiscrimination requirements in all federal contracts. These actions, Kennedy said, documented that the executive branch had moved to ensure that federal monies did not support programs that discriminated.

Notwithstanding the progress that Kennedy cited, the executive orders dealt with only a small proportion of federal funds. In April 1963, the idea of a complete legislative ban on the disbursement of federal monies to programs that discriminated resurfaced when the U.S. Commission on Civil Rights recommended that the president seek authority to suspend federal assistance on a statewide basis to states such as Mississippi "until [such states] comply with the Constitution and laws of the United States."[39] However, neither Congress nor the president displayed much interest in acting on that proposal. Indeed, according to Gary Orfield, Congress "summarily defeated anti-discrimination amendments on two education bills after five minutes of debate on one and ten on the other."[40] The administration showed no greater stomach for such a reform. At a news conference on 17 April 1963, Kennedy indicated that he did not support the recommendation of the civil rights commission. First, he stressed that without legislative authorization he had limited power to terminate funds, and then he seemed to imply that it might not be a good idea, in any case, for Congress to give him that power: "I would think it would probably be unwise to give the President of the United States that kind of power because it could start in one State and for one reason or another it might be moved to another State which was not measuring up as the President would like to see it measure up in one way or another."[41] The implication was that, in Kennedy's view, a president could use the power to withhold federal funds arbitrarily, unfairly, and for political reasons.

Kennedy ultimately altered his position because of the racial tension that erupted during the spring of 1963. In his address to the nation in June 1963, he called for a new civil rights law, stronger than the one he had proposed in February 1963. Yet the power on which he intended to rely to improve the education that blacks received was the provision of the administration's newly proposed civil rights bill that authorized the attorney general to initiate lawsuits to compel desegregation. In his speech, Kennedy made no mention of requiring the nondiscriminatory use of federal funds. When he presented his 1963 civil rights bill to Congress a week later, however, one of the seven major titles dealt with discrimination in federally assisted programs. Kennedy added the provision, according to presidential aide Theodore Sorensen, at the suggestion of congressional leaders.[42]

The seven titles in the bill dealt with (1) protecting voting rights; (2) providing for nondiscriminatory access to public accommodations; (3) desegregating schools by authorizing the attorney general to initiate civil actions; (4) establishing a community relations service to ease racial tension; (5) extending the term of the U.S. Commission on Civil Rights; (6) prohibiting federal funding to programs that discriminated on the basis of race; and (7) establishing a commission on equal employment opportunity.[43] In his message to Congress, the president referred specifically to the concept ultimately embodied in Title VI: "[S]imple justice requires that public funds, to which all taxpayers of all races contribute, not be spent in any fashion which encourages, entrenches, subsidizes or results in racial discrimination." Implicitly recognizing how awkward a tool litigation could be in some circumstances, the president noted that where federal funds are used to support programs that discriminate, "it should not be necessary to resort to the courts to prevent each individual violation."[44]

The administration introduced identical civil rights bills in the House and Senate. The Senate bill was referred to the Judiciary Committee, chaired by Senator Eastland of Mississippi. Eastland, with the support of his fellow southern senators Strom Thurmond and Sam Ervin, stymied action on the bill in the upper chamber. In the House, New York's Emanuel Celler, chair of the House Judiciary Committee, arranged for Subcommittee Number 5 to hold hearings on the bill during the violent and fateful summer of 1963.

During the House hearings, administration officials suggested that without legislation specifically barring the disbursement of federal funds to programs that discriminated, the president had questionable authority to withhold such monies. In the absence of an express legislative authorization, administration officials maintained, the president's power turned on the wording of each statute providing federal funding.[45] In answering a question from a member of a House sub-committee as to why HEW continued to make federal funds available to segregated school districts, HEW secretary Ribicoff replied, "Congressman, you people control the purse strings. You vote us the money and say, 'Give it out.' As far as I am concerned, our Department listens to the voice and instructions of the Congress of the United States. . . . this is a congressional problem and not an administrative problem. You can determine under what conditions the money is paid out."[46] The administration's position did not go unchallenged in the legislative hearings. John Roche and Joseph Rauh of Americans for Democratic Action, Roy Wilkins of the NAACP, and John Pemberton of the American Civil Liberties Union, among others, maintained that the president did not need congressional authorization but had the unilateral authority via executive order to withhold funds from programs that discriminated.[47]

Unwilling to accept the political risk and confront the controversy that would ensue if he issued an executive order, the president opted to seek congressional authorization. In contentious civil rights matters, as we shall see time and again, elected officials, bureaucrats, and judges alike are loath to take firm, clear stands protecting civil rights. Moreover, when they do act they are inclined to look to other officials and other branches for political cover, to share the burden and blame involved in taking such action. Not only did Kennedy want the cover of an explicit congressional authorization to withhold federal monies, but he rejected the idea that the civil rights bill "require unconditionally" that federal funds be withdrawn from programs that discriminated. The administration argued that unconditionally requiring termination would "only penalize those who least deserve it, without ending discrimination."[48]

The Kennedy bill did not even contain an outright prohibition on discrimination in federal programs. It merely provided that no law offering federal financial assistance could be construed as *requiring* the government to provide that assistance, if the program or activity receiving the money discriminated on the basis of race, religion, or national origin.* Under this proposal, in cases where a program or activity receiving federal funding discriminated, the law through which the government provided the monies could not be used as a

---

*For the original administration version of Title VI (entitled "Nondiscrimination in Federally Assisted Programs") and all subsequent revisions made during the congressional process, see appendix B.

basis for requiring the government to disburse the funds. The bill did not mandate that the government withhold funds where discrimination occurred or, for that matter, require it to take any action where discrimination existed. Indeed, it did not explicitly authorize terminating federal funds to programs that discriminated or declare that individuals had the right to be free of racial discrimination in federally funded programs. It was a weak and limited provision, justifiably criticized as such by civil rights lobbyists.

In the course of considering and substantially strengthening the administration's measure, Subcommittee Number 5 addressed issues that bedeviled those enforcing Title VI in subsequent years. It tried unsuccessfully, for example, to develop standards for administrators to use in deciding when illegal discrimination warranted terminating federal funds. It also explored making the withholding of federal funds mandatory rather than discretionary.

The version of the bill that emerged from the subcommittee went far beyond the original administration proposal.* The subcommittee's draft, containing eight major amendments that both strengthened Title VI and made it more complicated, dealt with the principle of nondiscrimination in federal funding through four separate provisions.[49] The first provided that "notwithstanding any inconsistent provision of any law . . . no person shall be excluded from participation in, be denied the benefits of, or be subjected to discrimination under any program receiving federal financial assistance because of race, color, religion or national origin."[50] In direct and forthright language, this provision gave each individual the right to be free of discrimination in federally funded programs. It marked the first time Congress attempted to impose a national requirement of nondiscrimination in almost all programs financed by Washington.

The second section in the subcommittee's draft of the bill authorized each federal agency to develop rules and regulations to carry out the requirements of the statute, and to achieve compliance with the statute's requirements by either instituting a civil action, terminating, refusing to grant, or refusing to continue federal assistance, or employing any other means authorized by law. The provision required that each agency, before resorting to any of the above measures to secure compliance, attempt to convince recipients of federal dollars to comply with the requirements voluntarily. This second sec-

---

*For a detailed analysis of the transformation of Title VI during the congressional process, including the precise changes wrought by Subcommittee Number 5, see appendix B. The draft that emerged from the subcommittee is designated as Version 2.

tion of the bill that emerged from Subcommittee Number 5 was significant because Congress enacted this section into law, changed in only minor ways. The third section of the subcommittee proposal provided that any requirement promulgated pursuant to the statute could be enforced in federal district court. A final section provided for the right of judicial review of an agency's actions.[51] There was irony in the subcommittee's strengthening of the administration's proposal on Title VI, for the president and his brother had maintained that they had initially resisted including a provision on federal funding in their bill because they believed that there would be overwhelming congressional opposition to such a provision.[52]

Subcommittee Number 5 strengthened not only Title VI but also several other titles of the bill. Indeed, it so transformed President Kennedy's proposed measure that both Celler and the administration withheld their support from the subcommittee's version and, in cooperation with southern moderates, redrafted the subcommittee version and submitted a modified and weaker draft to the full Judiciary Committee.[53] In the process of that redrafting, however, the subcommittee's transformation of Title VI of the bill remained largely untouched. That Celler, the administration, and moderate southerners did not bother to undo the subcommittee's significant changes to Title VI suggests that they did not view it as a powerful or controversial part of the legislative package. Making only three minor changes, the full Judiciary Committee accepted the subcommittee's recommendations on Title VI.* The full Judiciary Committee reported out

---

*The changes made by the full Judiciary Committee to the bill reported by Subcommittee Number 5 were as follows:

1. The subcommittee bill provided that Title VI applied to "each federal department and agency which is empowered to extend federal financial assistance to any program or activity, by way of grant, contract, loan, *insurance, guarantee, or otherwise.*" (For the full text of the language of Title VI produced by the subcommittee, see version 2 in appendix B.) The full committee struck the italicized words. House Report No. 914, 88th Cong., 1st sess., pp. 85–86. Since virtually all forms of federal insurance and guarantees occurred in contracts, and since the word *contract* remained in the full committee's version, this omission was not significant.

2. The full committee struck the paragraph expressly authorizing the government to enforce Title VI by initiating lawsuits in federal district court. Nonetheless, the full committee's version retained the provision that authorized the government to enforce Title VI by terminating funds *or* "by any other means authorized by law." The latter phrase implicitly contemplated the right of the Justice Department to sue recipients in federal court, at least in school desegregation cases, pursuant to Title IV of the bill focusing on school desegregation.

3. The subcommittee version provided that Title VI could be enforced "by the termination of or refusal to grant or to continue assistance upon an express finding that there

the bill for consideration by the entire House on 20 November 1963, two days before Kennedy's assassination.

Once the House passed the bill, the bill's Senate supporters urged immediate consideration of the House bill by the whole upper chamber, fearing that a hostile Senate Judiciary Committee, dominated by southerners, would squelch the proposal. The course of the Senate's consideration of the bill showed that to be a realistic worry. The Senate Judiciary Committee began hearings on the 1963 civil rights bill in July 1963, but the bill met such intense opposition from southerners on the committee that its chair, James O. Eastland of Mississippi, decided, one month later, to adjourn hearings. At that point, the Senate Judiciary Committee's consideration of the administration bill ended.[54] Nonetheless, some noteworthy things did occur before Eastland's abrupt ending of the hearings. Shortly after the bill was introduced, Senator Ribicoff of Connecticut and Senator Keating of New York offered a significant amendment to Title VI. They objected that the bill did not impose on those administering federal programs an affirmative obligation to act to end discrimination, that it depended too heavily on cutting off funds, that it did not authorize executive officials to institute civil actions to eliminate discrimination, that it did not grant the right of judicial review to a recipient when an agency withheld money, and that it did not authorize a private right of action by individuals who suffered discrimination in federally funded programs.[55] To address these objections, on 20 August 1963 Keating and Ribicoff moved to amend Title VI and submitted written recommendations for those changes. The Ribicoff-Keating amendment proposed the following:

- Discrimination would be prohibited in every program or activity receiving federal funds.
- If discrimination existed, the executive official administering the

---

has been a failure to comply with . . . [the requirement of nondiscrimination]." *Civil Rights Act of 1963*, 88th Cong., 1st sess., H.R. 7152, 2 Oct. 1963. The full committee changed that language to authorize "the termination of or refusal to grant or to continue assistance *under such program or activity to any recipient* as to whom there has been an express finding of a failure to comply." House Report No. 914, p. 8; my emphasis. This addition was an attempt to clarify the scope of the funding that could be terminated: it specified that the termination applied to the programs or activities in which there had been an express finding of discrimination. The scope of the funds that could be terminated under Title VI proved to be an issue that the Supreme Court decided nearly two decades later, and that, in turn, prompted a protracted congressional struggle focusing on the rewriting of that language.

program would be required either to terminate funds or to ask the attorney general to institute a civil suit.

- The attorney general would be explicitly authorized to initiate civil actions to end discrimination.
- If an agency terminated funds, the recipient would have the right of judicial review to challenge that decision.[56]

The Justice Department agreed to redraft Title VI in light of the Ribicoff-Keating criticisms, and three days after receiving the proposal from the two senators, Attorney General Kennedy appeared before the Senate Judiciary Committee with a revised version of Title VI that met most of the criticisms advanced by the two men.[57]

Testifying before the Senate Judiciary Committee on 23 August 1963, Kennedy stressed that the revisions advanced an unequivocal policy prohibiting discrimination in federally supported programs. The administration's revised Section 601 read: "No person shall, on the ground of race, color, religion, or national origin, be excluded from participation in, be denied the benefits of, or be subject to discrimination under any program or activity receiving Federal financial assistance."[58] With one minor exception, this was the very language enacted into law by Congress almost a year later. The next redrafted section authorized each agency to bring suit to enforce its rules and regulations, or, if it was deemed more effective, to terminate funding. A third redrafted section provided for the right of judicial review where an agency terminated funds, another provision that ultimately became a part of the law Congress enacted.[59]

The reforms prompted by the Ribicoff-Keating objections simultaneously strengthened the bill as a civil rights measure and addressed southern fears. The changes strengthened the bill by including a direct prohibition on discrimination, imposing an affirmative obligation on federal agencies to act to eradicate illegal discrimination, and expressly authorizing the termination of funding. The reforms addressed the concerns of southerners, because Ribicoff and Keating stressed the need to de-emphasize the termination of funds and the need for a provision granting the right of judicial review to recipients when an agency did terminate assistance.

Providing for the right of judicial review was crucial in assuaging the fears of southerners. Fear that the administration's bill placed an undue emphasis on terminating funds seemed implausible, however, as the bill did not even specifically grant the power to terminate funds. In any case, as in the hearings before the House Judiciary Committee's Subcommittee Number 5, the administration was on the defensive before the Senate Judiciary Committee, scrambling to satisfy those on the political Right who feared and opposed the measure and those on the Left who wanted it strengthened. What happened to the Title VI provision in the abbreviated Senate Judiciary Committee hearings in July and August 1963 was, in microcosm, what followed throughout the remainder of the legislative process. There were efforts to add language strengthening and expanding the protections provided in Title VI, and there were offsetting measures, typically procedural in character, intended to counterbalance those changes.

After Eastland adjourned the Senate Judiciary Committee hearings in July 1963, the Senate did not return to the 1964 Civil Rights Act until after the House passed the measure in February 1964. A record-setting seventy-five days of Senate debate took place. Finally, a compromise agreement between the Senate leadership and the attorney general produced a slightly modified version of the House bill, enabling supportive senators to shut off debate on 10 June 1964 and win approval of the bill in the upper chamber.[60] Notwithstanding the considerable impact that Title VI eventually came to have on school desegregation, the Kennedy and Johnson administrations viewed it as a relatively unimportant part of the civil rights bill.[61] Instead, "[t]he [Kennedy] Administration continued to view expansion of the Attorney General's authority [to initiate lawsuits] as the key to school desegregation." Nicholas Katzenbach, who worked for Robert Kennedy at the Justice Department in 1963, expected that Title VI was one of the provisions intended to be "traded away" by the administration because "it had the most symbolic significance to the South and the least practical significance of anything in the bill."[62]

Despite the administration's deflated view of the value of Title VI, the potential impact and reach of the provision was enormous.[63] For example, in 1965 Title VI would have regulated almost $18 billion in federal aid that flowed through twenty-two different government agencies and departments.[64] In 1964, in HEW alone, Title VI would regulate 128 programs through which the department provided $3.7 billion for education, public health, and welfare assistance.[65] Payments to private individuals and institutions were more than $500 million.[66] Derrick Bell, deputy director of the Office for Civil Rights in HEW during the Johnson administration, surmised that "in some respects this short section of the . . . bill [Title VI] may be the most effective. It hits where it hurts — in the pocketbook. It makes discrimination an expensive luxury."[67] Bell was right — and wrong. Title VI could hit and hurt; however, before it could have that effect, those enforcing it had to meet the statutory requirements that Congress imposed to regulate how the provision would be implemented.

THE PROVISIONS REGULATING THE ENFORCEMENT OF TITLE VI

The critical terms that Congress wrote into Title VI and that affected how the provision would be enforced are listed below (an analysis of each of them follows):

- Administrators enforcing the law against violators could choose either to terminate their federal funding or to enforce Title VI by "other means authorized by law."
- The "rules, regulations or orders of general applicability" developed to enforce Title VI had be to approved by the president.
- Funding agencies had to pursue "voluntary compliance" before they could terminate funds. Only after it had determined that a recipient would not voluntarily comply with Title VI could an agency commence administrative enforcement proceedings leading to possible termination of funds.
- Before the government could terminate funds, the recipient had the right to be notified and to have a hearing before an administrative law judge to determine whether, in fact, it was discriminating.
- Following an agency's decision to terminate assistance, there was a required stay of thirty days, during which time the agency had to provide a written report to the appropriate oversight committees in both houses of Congress, detailing the grounds for its decision.
- The termination of funding was limited in scope to the particular funded program found to be discriminating.
- Where an agency decided to terminate funds after hearings by an administrative law judge, recipients had the right of judicial review in federal court.

The Granting of Discretion to Administrators Enforcing Title VI. Those involved in the legislative battle over Title VI recognized that the impact of the provision would be determined by the discretionary choices of the officials administering the law. Civil rights leaders criticized the administration's desire to make the withholding of funds from recipients who discriminated discretionary, and not mandatory. Title VI provided that "compliance with any requirement adopted pursuant to this section *may* be effected" by terminating funds *or* "by any other means authorized by law."[68] When Congress passed Title VI, it was not altogether clear what that latter option might entail. As it turned out, the provision in the statute that permitted that choice had enormous consequences.

Most civil rights partisans believed that politicians who had discretionary choices were not likely to use that freedom to protect black civil rights. They noted ruefully that President Kennedy did not choose to use his discretionary authority unilaterally to mandate Title VI through executive order. Consequently, they were unhappy with the option the statute gave to agencies because they had little confidence that, given a choice, those enforcing Title VI would select the politically more difficult option — terminating financial assistance.[69] Civil rights activists testifying in the House before Subcommittee Number 5 urged that once an agency made a finding that discrimination existed, the agency should be required to terminate funds. Roy Wilkins, arguing for "mandatory" withholding of funds, asserted that given the long-term failure to end discrimination on the basis of voluntary, discretionary actions, "we always shy away from 'discretionary' in these areas." James Farmer, of the Congress on Racial Equality, took the same position.[70]

Others criticized the power given to administrators to terminate funding, not out of concern that administrators would choose not to use the sanction, but rather out of a fear that unaccountable bureaucrats would wield that power arbitrarily against the South.[71] Typical of these comments was the remark of Congressman Dorn (D.-S.C.), who observed that there "is no end to where this type of power could lead . . . in the hands of unelected, empire-building government bureaucrats."[72] Senator Gore of Tennessee, a southern moderate who had voted for the 1957 and 1960 Civil Rights Acts, also expressed reservations about Title VI because he believed that the withholding of funds could be used as a political reprisal.[73] Congressman Elliot (D.-Ala.), voicing similar objections, concluded that Title VI "would place in the hands of a president an extreme and dangerous power to withhold tax dollars from our taxpayers."[74] President Kennedy's own statement to that effect at his press conference in April 1963 was often used against the administration.[75]

Even Congressman Celler, chair of the House Judiciary Committee and staunch supporter of Title VI, conceded that one "wouldn't want to have this tremendous power involving so many billions and billions of dollars to be in the control of someone who would turn the spigot on or off with whim or caprice."[76] In questioning HEW secretary Celebrezze, Celler explained his concern about the discretionary power that administrators would have under Title VI:

> I can see what is bothering some of the members and it bothers me somewhat, too. Great powers are given to you and there is fear expressed directly or indirectly that you might abuse your power. . . . Therefore, since that power is given, this committee in its wisdom might feel that there should be some standards to govern your action. Some criteria might be added to this bill that would not only help you in your determination as to whether or not there was discrimination. . . . It would also be a governing force, a restraint upon a Secretary of Education and Welfare *[sic]* to prevent him from acting capriciously, and arbitrarily.[77]

In a subsequent exchange with Celebrezze during the subcommittee's hearings, Celler asked the HEW secretary to submit to the subcommittee "some sort of guidelines under which you would have to operate with reference to Title VI."[78] As best as can be determined, HEW never submitted such standards.

The House subcommittee's version of the bill authorized the government to seek injunctive relief and provided that the requirements of Title VI imposed by "rule, regulation, order, agreement or otherwise" could be enforced in U.S. district courts by a civil action. The bill reported out by the full Judiciary Committee, however, deleted those two provisions and simply authorized enforcing Title VI by terminating funds or "by any other means authorized by law,"[79] the language ultimately enacted into law. Thus, the final language in the statute left unclear what role litigation initiated by the government or by private plaintiffs might play in enforcing the requirements of Title VI.

Senator Ribicoff maintained that the words "any other means authorized by law" did not confer any new authority on federal agencies. Rather, he argued, this language authorized agencies to achieve compliance with Title VI through the law that created them or the particular statutory aid program involved, or through Title IV of the 1964 Civil Rights Act. Title IV authorized the attorney general to institute legal action against a school board or institution of higher education after receiving a written complaint that the board or institution was unlawfully discriminating.[80] For Ribicoff, the option of enforcing Title VI by "any other means authorized by law" was significant because it provided an alternative to terminating funds:

> This alternative is designed to permit the agency to avoid a fund cutoff if some other means of ending discrimination is available. This will enable the agency to achieve compliance without jeopardizing . . . its basic program objective by terminating or refusing aid. Perhaps the best example of this relates to school lunches or other assistance to segregated schools. Cutoff of the lunches or other assistance will obviously impose a severe hardship upon students. . . . The way to avoid such a hardship will be for the Attorney General to institute a desegregation suit under Title IV rather than to terminate the assistance.[81]

This enforcement option proved to be a crucial feature of the statute, beginning in 1969, when the Nixon administration chose to emphasize and rely almost entirely on that method of enforcing Title VI.

The House report accompanying the civil rights bill specifically referred to the value of enforcing school desegregation through litigation initiated by the attorney general. That approach, according to the report, took the onus off private litigants and made it the "responsibility of the Federal Government to protect constitutional rights."[82] Senator Pastore of Rhode Island noted that enforcing Title VI by means of litigation instituted by the attorney general could be appropriate where a particular program in a state discriminated and all other programs operated on a nondiscriminatory basis. It would be foolish, he suggested, to "cut off assistance to one hundred people because one person was being discriminatory." In Pastore's view, the "by any other means" provision "encourages agencies to find ways to end discrimination without refusing or terminating assistance."[83]

The Requirement That Title VI Regulations Be Approved by the President. Congressman John Lindsay of New York proposed an amendment that "directed" each agency providing federal funds "to effectuate the provisions of" Title VI by "issuing rules, regulations or orders of general applicability" and that required that those rules, regulations and orders be approved by the president. Noting the wide latitude and power that the statute gave to administrators enforcing it, Lindsay argued that it was important for the president "to put his stamp of approval" on proposed rules and regulations.[84] Lindsay's amendment sought to check the discretion of agency bureaucrats and to make the president accountable for enforcement policies.[85] This issue was the subject of some controversy during the Johnson administration, when HEW issued its 1965 Title VI desegregation "Guidelines." The Guidelines, which governed the enforcement of

Title VI in southern school districts, were not approved by the president, and the absence of presidential approval became a legal and political issue.

The Requirement That Agencies Pursue "Voluntary" Compliance before Terminating Funds. Under Title VI, an agency cannot terminate funds "until the department or agency concerned has advised the appropriate person or persons of the failure to comply with the requirement and has determined that compliance cannot be secured by voluntary means."[86] This provision was significant because it required that before an agency could terminate funds, it had to discuss the alleged violation with the entity receiving the monies and determine that it could not get the offending agency to comply voluntarily with Title VI. Hubert Humphrey explained, "Termination of assistance, however, is not the objective of the title. I underscore this point—It is a last resort, to be used only if all else fails. . . . This fact deserves the greatest possible emphasis: cut off of Federal funds is seen as a last resort, when all voluntary means have failed."[87]

Having required that efforts be made to achieve voluntary compliance, Congress did not elaborate on what those efforts should entail. It did not, for example, say what steps agencies had to take before concluding that compliance could not be achieved through voluntary means, or for how long agencies were obliged to persist in discussions about "voluntary" compliance, or what standards governed how an agency could "determine" when voluntary compliance was unachievable. These issues left considerable discretion in the hands of those administering Title VI, and became major concerns during the Nixon administration.

The Requirement That a Finding of Failure to Comply Be on the Record before Funds Are Terminated. The statute provided that funds may be terminated where "there has been an express finding on the record after opportunity for hearing, of a failure to comply with" Title VI.[88] This requirement meant that before an agency could terminate funds, there had to be an administrative hearing and an "express finding" of noncompliance by an administrative law judge, based on a record developed at the hearing.[89] The amendment, passed unanimously, meant that a finding of noncompliance had to be based on a written record—a record that would be reviewed by a court if the recipient challenged the finding under the statute's judicial review provision.

The Requirement That Agencies File Written Reports with the Appropriate Congressional Committees and Then Wait Thirty Days before Terminating Funds. Requiring that before an agency cut funding to a program it file a report with the committees of Congress responsible for funding the program provided congressional oversight and a further check against arbitrary enforcement. Requiring a thirty-day delay after the filing of the written report, and before the cutoff of funds began, also offered a final opportunity to pursue voluntary compliance.[90]

The Requirement That Termination Be Limited to the "Particular Political Entity" and the "Particular Program" Found in Noncompliance. This requirement was intended to lessen fears that Title VI would be used to cut off federal funds to an entire state or a significant part of a state because of a finding of noncompliance in one program. As noted earlier, the U.S. Commission on Civil Rights had urged such a sweeping tactic, and President Kennedy, at his April 1963 news conference, had rejected it. Hubert Humphrey explained that the restriction on the withholding of funds was "designed to limit any termination of Federal assistance to the particular offenders in the particular area where the unlawful discrimination occurs."[91] As an example, Senator Ribicoff stated that if there were one hundred school districts in a state, and one of those districts discriminated, the funds would be cut off to only that one district. In another illustration, Senator Pastore explained that if there were a finding of discrimination in a federally funded program of aid to dependent children, the federal government would not cut off funds for the building of a road. He explained, "The action must be confined to the specific program in which discrimination exists, and then only within the particular jurisdiction where the discrimination takes place."[92]

The Granting of the Right of Judicial Review. Of all the safeguards written into Title VI, the right to judicial review of an agency decision received the most attention.[93] The original administration bill did not provide for such review. The House Judiciary Subcommittee version of the bill contained a provision granting the right of judicial review, and that provision was enacted into law. Congressman Celler asked civil rights lawyer Joseph Rauh to prepare a legal memorandum on the issue of judicial review of decisions under Title VI. Rauh concluded that a plaintiff who sought judicial review, even in the absence of a specific provision in the statute granting that right, would have standing to sue. Nonetheless, Rauh saw "the political practicality of a statutory provision spelling out judicial review."[94]

Years later, Rauh led civil rights lawyers seeking judicial review of HEW's alleged failure to enforce Title VI. In passing the judicial review provision, however, Congress acted from a far different motive: fear that the power to terminate funds might be used excessively. Ironically, the major legal challenges to the enforcement of Title VI in subsequent years sought judicial redress not against administrators overzealously enforcing Title VI, but against administrators who neglected to enforce the measure and failed to terminate funds in spite of protracted noncompliance.

ADMINISTERING TITLE VI: A STATUTORY OVERVIEW

The panoply of procedural safeguards in Title VI reflected extended discussion and concern in Congress about the need for such protections. Hubert Humphrey, among many others who urged passage of the bill, emphasized the procedural protections at each stage of the enforcement process. Those protections, Humphrey stressed, ensured against arbitrary and politicized enforcement of Title VI. At one point in the Senate debate, Abraham Ribicoff actually enumerated the elaborate list of safeguards, checks, and limitations governing the enforcement process. That list included the following:

- Agencies had to promulgate the requirements of Title VI by rule, regulation, or order of general applicability.
- The rule, regulation, or order had to be approved by the president.
- Before an agency enforced Title VI by terminating funds or by other means authorized by law, it had to advise the recipient of its noncompliance, and determine that compliance could not be achieved by voluntary means.
- An agency could terminate funds only after there was a hearing in which recipients could present their case, and only after an administrative law judge issued an "express finding" of noncompliance on the basis of the record developed at the hearing.
- Federal agencies had a choice between two enforcement methods that could be used to achieve compliance — withholding financial assistance, or achieving compliance by "any other means authorized by law."
- Enforcing Title VI by "other means authorized by law" meant having the attorney general sue a school or school district under Title IV; or, if a nondiscrimination clause was part of a recipient's contract with the federal government, suing to enforce the

contract; or, in the absence of a contract, suing to enforce compliance with the agency's own regulations.

- In cutting off funds, the following requirements had to be followed: (1) The cutoff had to be limited to the program or activity that discriminated. (2) The head of the agency or department terminating the monies had to file a written report with the appropriate committees of Congress. (3) There had to be a mandatory holding period of thirty days between the filing of the report to Congress and the effective date of the termination of funding.[95]
- An aggrieved party had the right of judicial review.[96]

It would be hard to overestimate the significance of the procedural protections Congress placed in the statute. Though Congress granted the federal government broad, and indeed unprecedented, power in Title VI, it encumbered those who would have to wield that power with a multitude of procedural requirements that impeded the utility and potency of the provision. That was the price that had to be paid for the grant of the power in the first place.

When one reviews the evolution of the language of Title VI, one sees that Congress, and not the president, was responsible for shaping the important contours of the provision. The initial Kennedy administration version was weak and sketchy. The most significant transformation of that proposal occurred in the House judiciary subcommittee known as Subcommittee Number 5. Its version was the first to contain an outright prohibition on discrimination in federally funded programs, to impose an obligation on all agencies to enforce that prohibition, and to explicitly authorize the termination of funding. Subsequent congressional deliberations and revisions focused almost entirely on the need for procedural protections to control those who would be enforcing Title VI and to limit the impact the provision would have.

Procedural protections and issues loom large in the history of the litigation to enforce Title VI. If, as is often said, it is difficult in the law to distinguish procedure from substance, in civil rights law enforcement there may well be a tendency for procedure to overwhelm substance. That happened in the enforcement of Title VI. As we shall see, beginning in 1969 procedural issues played such a dominant role in the legal struggles over the enforcement of Title VI that the substance of the statute seemed a secondary and remote concern. What is striking is that both Congress and the president avoided the critical issue in Title VI — defining racial discrimination in schools or elsewhere. There was, for instance, no congressional debate about the long-term substantive goals of the provision in public education or elsewhere. Rather, a review of the origins and legislative history of Title VI reveals a focus on the need to come to terms with the political repercussions of authorizing the termination of funds. That need produced a measure riddled with procedural restrictions on the legal right granted. As to the substance and content of the right to be free of discrimination in federally funded programs, there was conspicuously little discussion by either the president or Congress as to what that right would mean.

3

THE JOHNSON YEARS:
Implementing and Redefining the Right
to Equal Educational Opportunity

TWO DEVELOPMENTS DOMINATED THE ENFORCEMENT of Title VI during the Johnson administration. The first was the synergistic relationship that developed between federal courts and the administrators in the Department of Health, Education, and Welfare who enforced the provision. The conscious cooperation between the judicial and executive branches was noteworthy for several reasons. It demonstrated that even after the passage of Title VI, litigation in federal courts would continue to play a powerful role in the development of policies to address racial discrimination in schools, and that federal courts enforcing the Fourteenth Amendment and federal bureaucrats enforcing Title VI would have to share power in defining and combating racial discrimination in schools. The unusual relationship between the federal bench and bureaucracy that developed between 1964 and 1968 produced the first major successes in ending the near-complete segregation of southern schools that had persisted for a decade after *Brown v. Board of Education*.

The second development was the redefinition of the goals of *Brown* and of the legal right protected by it. As noted in chapter 1, *Brown* culminated a centuries-old effort by blacks to overcome the denial of educational opportunity. Emphasizing the significance of education in mid-twentieth-century America, the Supreme Court framed the legal question in *Brown* in terms of a right to "equal educational opportunity." The "question presented," the Court said, was whether segregated facilities "deprived the children of the minority group of equal educational opportunities?"[1] Though the Court decided that it did, what the "right" to equal educational opportunity meant and what remedies it required remained unclear until the efforts to enforce Title VI during the Johnson era.

By the time Lyndon Johnson left office, there had been a redefinition or at least a substantial clarification of the right established in *Brown*. That change was a direct result of the enforcement of Title VI by the Johnson administration — an effort that transformed the legal and political debate on race and schools for decades. This recasting of the meaning of *Brown* occurred in three discrete steps.

First, the Department of Health, Education, and Welfare developed annual "Guidelines" for the enforcement of Title VI that imposed specific numerical goals for southern school districts, focusing on the percentage of black children who had to be enrolled in schools with whites. The Guidelines presumed that school districts had a legal obligation not merely to stop segregating students, but to achieve racial integration in schools. That represented a new and profoundly important understanding of the legal rights at issue in the struggle to achieve equal educational opportunity for blacks. Second, in *United States v. Jefferson County Board of Education,* in 1967, the U.S. Court of Appeals for the Fifth Circuit, the circuit court with the widest experience in school desegregation cases, endorsed the approach of and the requirements in HEW's Guidelines.[2] Third, in a landmark decision by the Supreme Court in 1968, in *Green v. County School Board of New Kent County, Virginia* (a case also linked to the enforcement of Title VI), the Court ruled that the ultimate test of compliance with *Brown* was the achievement of racial integration in schools.[3]

The changes that occurred as a result of the enforcement of Title VI during the Johnson years grew out of the failed efforts to enforce *Brown* through litigation in the decade before the passage of Title VI. In 1963, the school year immediately preceding the passage of Title VI, nearly 99 percent of black children in the eleven states of the former Confederacy still attended segregated schools.[4] In the following year, 97.7 percent of those children still attended all-black schools.[5] In Alabama, Mississippi, and Louisiana in 1964, less than 1 percent of black schoolchildren attended schools with whites. Of the 4,094 school districts in the southern and border states in 1964, more than half, educating more than 3 million black schoolchildren, remained fully segregated.[6] From May 1954, when the Supreme Court decided *Brown,* through April 1965, when HEW began its first efforts to enforce Title VI, only 142 of the nation's 27,000 school districts had been desegregated by court orders.[7] Only a handful of schools had integrated faculties. Commenting one decade after *Brown,* Thurgood Marshall observed, "What makes one uneasy, of course, is the truly awesome magnitude of what has yet to be done."[8] If Marshall was uneasy, so, too, was the Supreme Court.

Frustrated with the lack of progress in desegregation, the Supreme Court declared in 1963 that "*Brown* never contemplated that the concept of 'deliberate speed' would countenance indefinite delay in the elimination of racial barriers in schools." The following year, just six weeks before Congress passed Title VI, the Court declared that there "has been entirely too much deliberation and not enough speed in enforcing the constitutional rights" announced in *Brown*.[9]

Title VI was intended, Gary Orfield observed, "to make litigation unnecessary." G. W. Foster, consultant to HEW in the period following the passage of Title VI, viewed the provision as "a golden opportunity for taking the intolerable pressure of the school cases off the federal judges by introducing a powerful new force for school integration."[10] Notwithstanding the expectations of Orfield, Foster, and others, litigation in federal courts continued to play an influential, if not decisive, role in school desegregation in the years following the passage of Title VI.

Lyndon Johnson signed the Civil Rights Act of 1964 on 2 July 1964. It became effective in January 1965, after Johnson's landslide electoral victory in November 1964 against Barry Goldwater. There was little effort to prepare for the enforcement of Title VI until after the election.[11] In December 1964, HEW announced regulations under Title VI imposing conditions on the $4 billion in federal aid to education to be dispensed by the Johnson administration. The seventeen southern and border states received a total of $350 million for elementary and secondary school programs.[12]

Though the regulations did not contain standards by which to judge violations of Title VI, one procedural regulation did have a significant substantive influence on the measure's enforcement. That regulation linked the criteria federal courts imposed for school desegregation under the Fourteenth Amendment to the criteria HEW imposed on school districts under the nondiscrimination requirement of Title VI. Linking the two legal standards was a critical policy decision, ensuring that courts would be entangled in the administrative enforcement of Title VI. The effect of the regulation was that districts under a federal court order automatically qualified for federal financial assistance if they attested to their willingness to abide by the court order, regardless of the requirements of the order or the actual level of compliance with it. Consequently, districts subject to a final court order avoided having the sanctions of Title VI applied against them.[13]

In January 1965, a month after HEW announced its regulations, the Office of Education informed all state departments of education and all school boards throughout the country that to receive federal monies for the 1965–66 school year they would have to pledge in writing that they would not discriminate. The state departments of education had until March 1965 to submit replies. An official of the Office of Education announced, "We don't want to take money away from anyone. But each new application for a grant will have to include a satisfactory statement that segregation is being abolished or it will simply not be approved."[14]

By March 1965, each of the state departments of education in the seventeen southern and border states had signed assurances that it would not channel federal funds to schools that discriminated. During the early part of March 1965, the Office of Education received several hundred assurances each day from school districts.[15] A front-page article in the *New York Times* that month began, "A wave of public school desegregation has begun moving across the South, propelled by what one Southern educator this week called 'that great equalizer . . . the Yankee dollar.'"[16] In April 1965, HEW unveiled its first set of "Guidelines" for the enforcement of Title VI and mailed those Guidelines to each school district in the nation.[17]

THE 1965 HEW GUIDELINES

Although many southern school superintendents were indignant about Title VI, some wanted to know what the federal government would require them to do to qualify for federal funding. That interest intensified after Congress passed the Elementary and Secondary Education Act (ESEA) in April 1965.[18] The first general federal aid-to-education act ever enacted by Congress, ESEA provided Title VI enforcers with a big carrot — more than $1.3 billion in federal aid distributed according to a formula weighted to favor economically depressed counties and, therefore, especially likely to benefit southern school districts. Under Title I of the ESEA, more than seventeen thousand school districts across the nation received federal funds for special educational programs for disadvantaged children.[19]

Yale law professor Alexander Bickel concluded that the passage of the ESEA caused Title VI to "become the main instrument for accelerating and completing the desegregation of southern public schools." The U.S. Commission on Civil Rights agreed that Title VI "heralded a new era in school desegregation" that "promised speedier and more substantial desegregation" than had been achieved in "district-by-district litigation." Given the infusion of federal monies made available through the ESEA, the commission concluded, "most school systems would be placed at a serious disadvantage by termination of Federal assistance."[20]

HEW's Guidelines, announced the same month that Congress passed the ESEA, were the agency's first attempt to establish requirements for compliance with Title VI. The department needed the Guidelines to accomplish the task it confronted. By April 1965, five hundred districts had submitted plans, most of which Commissioner of Education Keppel considered inadequate. There was a need for the Guidelines because it was impossible to negotiate with hundreds of districts without national standards, because many districts were holding back in their negotiations to see how serious the administration intended to be in enforcing Title VI, and because straightforward, written standards would be more defensible if challenged in court.[21]

Under the Guidelines, a school district could certify its compliance with Title VI by any one of three methods:

- It could execute an "assurance of compliance" form certifying that race, color, or national origin was not a factor in student, faculty, or staff assignments; that school facilities and services were not segregated; and that no vestige of segregation remained. This method of compliance was intended to be used primarily in the border states by school districts with little history of de jure school segregation.
- It could submit a final order of a federal court, attest to its willingness to comply with that order, and report on its progress in complying. This provision essentially restated the policy announced in the HEW regulations in December 1964.
- It could submit a desegregation plan approved by the U.S. commissioner of education.

HEW's 1965 school Guidelines were straightforward. First, the agency required that southern school districts demonstrate a good faith start by desegregating at least four grades by the fall of 1965 — the first grades of elementary school and junior and senior high school, and the last grade of high school. All twelve grades, faculties, and transportation facilities had to be desegregated by the fall of 1967. Second, though there were no requirements for desegregating faculties during the 1965–66 academic year, faculty members at black and white schools had to meet to plan for the eventual desegregation of teaching staffs. An Office of Education official explained, "Our main concern this year is to desegregate the kids. We will get to the teachers after that."[22] Third, school activities and programs had to be desegregated. Fourth, and most important, the Guidelines accepted freedom-of-choice plans, attendance zones drawn on a nonracial basis, or some combination of those two options as acceptable methods for desegregating. Under freedom-of-choice plans, rather than assigning students to a school on the basis of geography or some other factor, the district gave students the "choice" to select the school they wanted to attend. Consequently, for black children to attend formerly all-white schools, black parents had to initiate a request to have their children admitted to those schools.

After a decade of minimal progress under *Brown,* the Guidelines reflected a continued commitment to gradualism in desegregating southern schools. Having meetings to talk about faculty desegregation was not path-breaking, and making freedom of choice an acceptable desegregation method gave the South what it wanted. Orfield wrote that freedom of choice became a "powerful fallback position" for those resisting change:

> Once it became obvious that [freedom of choice] would produce substantial integration only in communities with relatively good race relations, those opposed to any integration took up the cause of freedom of choice, denouncing anything else as "forced integration" and righteously promising to enroll in the white schools all the Negro students who chose to come. In more than 100 districts with approved freedom-of-choice plans, community attitudes were so strong that not a single Negro student chose to enroll in any white school. In hundreds of other districts only an insignificant fraction of Negro pupils challenged the system of racial separation. The fear and apathy pervading Negro communities in areas with a poor racial climate transformed the freedom-of-choice plan from a mechanism for integration to a means of legalizing segregation.[23]

Almost two-thirds of all voluntary desegregation plans that the Office of Education accepted in 1965 were freedom-of-choice plans.[24]

With the issuance of the December 1964 HEW regulations for Title VI and the April 1965 Guidelines, there developed a two-track system to end illegal school segregation — one track governed by judicial standards developed in the course of school desegregation litigation, and another governed by administrative standards developed by HEW in the course of enforcing Title VI. Judicial authority to establish desegregation requirements derived from courts' authority to construe the requirements of the equal protection clause of the Fourteenth Amendment. HEW's authority to impose desegregation requirements derived from the provisions of Title VI prohibiting discrimination on the basis of race in programs receiving federal financial assistance.

Under this two-track system, it became apparent that many school boards preferred to desegregate by dealing with southern federal judges rather than with Johnson administration bureaucrats. James Quigley, assistant secretary of HEW in charge of enforcing Title VI, observed that school boards found it "politically more comfortable" to be forced to desegregate by court order.[25] In Louisiana, for example, twenty school districts chose to precipitate a lawsuit rather than submit a desegregation plan to HEW, because they believed that this approach would require less integration while still enabling them to receive federal funds.[26] Often, court orders contained desegregation requirements differing from those mandated in the Guidelines.[27] Discussing such discrepancies, the *Shreveport Journal* observed in July 1965, "The local school boards prefer a court order over the voluntary plan because HEW regulations governing the voluntary plans or compliance agreements demand complete desegregation of the entire system, including students, faculty, staff, lunch workers, bus drivers, and administrators, whereas the court ordered plans can be more or less negotiated with the judge."[28] Indeed, resistance to the HEW Guidelines was greatest in Louisiana, where ultimately there were thirty-two court orders entered, affecting 86.5 percent of the school districts in that state.[29]

Opposition to the Guidelines also took an unusual twist in Alabama. Soon after HEW issued its 1965 Guidelines, a number of Alabama districts decided to desegregate all twelve grades for the 1965–66 academic year. In August 1965, and then again in September, Governor George Wallace sent a telegram to each of the superintendents of those districts emphasizing that they were not obliged to adopt desegregation standards "beyond the maximum requirements of court precedents."[30] Subsequently, the Alabama legislature enacted a law declaring the Guidelines "null and void" and prohibiting any school official from entering into agreements to comply with them.[31]

Any discrepancy between the judicial and HEW standards encouraged districts to resist the Guidelines and to search for ways around them. It also necessitated clarification of the legal status of the Guidelines. The status of the Guidelines was an issue, in part, because of the unusual circumstances surrounding their promulgation. Recall that Title VI required that each federal agency develop enforcement regulations that would not become effective until signed by the president.

HEW officials promulgated the 1965 Guidelines through an irregular, if not bizarre, procedure: The Guidelines were published in the *Saturday Review* by G. W. Foster, a law professor and consultant to the department, as a memorandum explaining Title VI and the standards that should govern southern school desegregation. The magazine's editors prefaced the publication of Foster's memorandum with these words: "The following memo is designed to provide specific guidelines to school authorities seeking to meet the terms of Title VI. . . . Mr. Foster's memo has no official status and does not bind the Office of Education in any fashion. Yet there is no doubt that it reflects directly the thinking of the officials charged with the responsibility for enforcing Title VI."[32] The article, initially distributed throughout the South informally, gradually assumed the status of acknowledged HEW standards. As a result of the peculiar circumstances surrounding the promulgation of the 1965 Guidelines, their legal status, in the words of one commentator, fell "somewhere within the realm of the unknown."[33]

The Guidelines came under attack from southerners for several reasons. First, they were not regulations signed by the president as required by the statute. Second, there were discrepancies between some court orders and the HEW standards. Third, and most significantly, the Guidelines constituted an unprecedented threat to the South. The administration's resort to Guidelines with specific and graduated desegregation goals over a three-year period suggested that the executive branch might be serious about enforcing Title VI as a new and potentially powerful desegregation weapon.

Notwithstanding southern fears about the Guidelines, northern liberals attacked them as weak. New York's William Fitts Ryan, congressman from the upper west side of Manhattan, concluded that the Office of Education "was not stringent enough" in enforcing Title VI under the 1965 Guidelines. Robert Sherrill, writing in the *Nation,* concluded that the "Guidelines were, in short, a farce: a blank map to nowhere." The U.S. Commission on Civil Rights reported that, despite its threats to withhold and defer monies, HEW had certified 98 percent of the 4,823 districts in the seventeen southern states as qualified to receive federal funds.[34]

That the president did not sign the Guidelines or in any other way officially endorse them is interesting. As discussed in chapter 2, above, Congress had required that Title VI regulations be approved by the president in order to make agencies accountable to the president and the president accountable to the public.[35] Internal HEW disagreements and the desire to shield Lyndon Johnson explain the peculiar way in which Foster's memorandum evolved into the Guidelines.[36]

There was a deliberate attempt to avoid injecting the president into controversies about Title VI and to spare him the political liabilities associated with enforcing the provision. Consequently, by the informal way in which it adopted the Guidelines, HEW tried to take the political heat off the president and off itself.[37]

JUDICIAL SUPPORT FOR THE 1965 HEW GUIDELINES

A significant judicial interpretation of the status of the 1965 Guidelines came in *Singleton v. Jackson Municipal School District* (known as *Singleton I*), decided in June 1965 by the U.S. Court of Appeals for the Fifth Circuit.[38] The case produced complicated legal proceedings that confirmed, among other things, the cumbersome, costly, and time-consuming nature of judicial attempts to desegregate.

In March 1963, black parents sought an injunction to desegregate public schools in Jackson, Mississippi. After the district court dismissed the complaint, ruling that the plaintiffs had failed to exhaust administrative remedies, the Fifth Circuit reversed the decision and ordered that the plaintiff's motion for injunctive relief be heard and resolved quickly.[39] On remand, the district court ordered that the Jackson school board file a desegregation plan by a specified date. On that date, in July 1964, less than two weeks after President Johnson had signed the 1964 Civil Rights Act, the board filed a freedom-of-choice plan, ultimately approved by the district court, that would desegregate one grade per year, beginning with the first grade in September 1964. Still unsatisfied, the plaintiffs appealed a second time to the Fifth Circuit, contending that the plan was too vague and that it desegregated at too slow a pace. The Justice Department intervened, certifying that the issues raised were of "general importance" and posed questions "bound to affect the resolution of desegregation controversies elsewhere in the state and throughout the South."[40]

By the time the Fifth Circuit heard the second appeal, HEW had announced its Guidelines. The court seized the opportunity. Judge Wisdom, writing for the court, stated that he considered it to be in the best interests of all concerned if the Jackson school board met the standards established in the Guidelines:

> We attach great weight to the standards established by the Office of Education. The judiciary has of course functions and duties distinct from those of the Executive department, but in carrying out national policy we have the same objective. There should be a close correlation, therefore, between the Judiciary's standards in enforcing the national

policy requiring desegregation of public schools and the executive department's standards in administering the policy. Absent legal questions, the United States Office of Education is better qualified than the courts and is the more appropriate federal body to weigh administrative difficulties inherent in school desegregation plans.[41]

The Guidelines, as noted earlier, recommended that four grades be desegregated beginning in September 1965, and set the fall of 1967 as the final date for the desegregation of all grades. In the *Singleton* decision, the court, embracing the standards of the Office of Education, ordered the Jackson school board to submit a plan to desegregate at least four grades for the 1965–66 school year and directed it to revise its plan to conform to the requirements of the Guidelines. A month later, in July 1965, in *Price v. Denison Independent School District,* the Fifth Circuit reiterated and expanded its holding in *Singleton.*[42]

Writing of the HEW Guidelines, the *Price* court declared that "these executive standards, perhaps long overdue, are welcome."[43] After extolling the HEW standards, the court of appeals noted that the desegregation plan, promising desegregation of one grade per year, that the district court had accepted in *Price* was inconsistent with HEW's standards requiring that four grades be desegregated in the 1965–66 academic year. In *Price,* the Fifth Circuit held, in effect, that HEW's standards under Title VI were identical to the constitutional requirements under the Fourteenth Amendment. For good measure, the court attached the full statement of the HEW Guidelines as an appendix to its decision. Yet another endorsement of the HEW Guidelines by the Fifth Circuit occurred a few months later, in January 1966, in another decision in the *Singleton* case, *Singleton II,* where the court again measured the required pace of school desegregation by using HEW's standards.[44] The import of the *Singleton I, Singleton II,* and *Price* decisions was considerable, given that the Fifth Circuit had more experience dealing with school desegregation than did any other court in the nation.

After years of getting no support in southern school desegregation from the other branches of government, the Fifth Circuit seemed eager to embrace the executive branch's Guidelines. During the summer of 1965, as the new school year approached, many of the most intransigent school districts seemed resigned to complying with Title VI. On 23 August 1965, the *New York Times* reported that approximately four hundred of the five thousand school districts in the seventeen southern and border states had elected to forego federal monies rather than desegregate.[45] By 29 August, that figure was reported to be 170.[46] By mid-September, HEW secretary John Gardner claimed that only eighty school districts had taken no steps to comply with the act and that the vast majority of southern school districts had submitted desegregation plans that met the requirements of the Guidelines.[47] Critics contended, however, that though progress had occurred in "moderate" states such as Tennessee and Texas, progress in the "Deep South" was minimal.

The 1966 HEW Guidelines

Shortly after becoming commissioner of education in January 1966, Harold Howe wrote to the state superintendents of education in the seventeen southern and border states to advise them that his office was preparing revisions to the 1965 Guidelines. He also advised Douglas Cater, a special assistant to President Johnson, that he had sent out those letters and wanted to discuss the revisions with Cater. He described the revisions as "fraught with difficult policy decisions." Two days later, F. Peter Libassi, the HEW secretary's special assistant for civil rights, also wrote to Cater to advise him that HEW was revising the Guidelines and adding requirements that had "far-reaching implications."[48] Libassi indicated that he wanted to talk with Cater about the proposals. Following those discussions, in March 1966, HEW announced its 1966 Guidelines. In discussing these Guidelines before a House appropriations subcommittee that month, Howe explained that the 1965 Guidelines had been used by HEW to negotiate desegregation plans with individual school districts throughout the South. In 1966, he stressed, the emphasis would shift "from negotiation to performance."[49]

In the 1966 Guidelines, HEW changed the requirements for freedom-of-choice and faculty desegregation plans. "The single most substantial indication as to whether a free-choice plan is actually working," the 1966 Guidelines read, "is the extent to which Negro or other minority group students have, in fact, transferred from segregated schools."[50] Hence, under the 1966 Guidelines, the test of the validity of a freedom-of-choice plan was whether it actually produced racial integration in schools. Against that backdrop, HEW developed a scale detailing the normal rate of progress toward desegregation which it expected school districts to achieve and against which they would be judged.

The performance scales contained sliding desegregation requirements for the 1966–67 year depending upon a district's rate of progress during the previous year. The Guidelines recommended that districts with 8 to 9 percent integration in the 1965–66 school year should attempt to double that in the 1966–67 academic year, that districts with 4 to 5 percent integration in 1965–66 should try to triple that figure in the following year, and that those with less than 4 percent integration (primarily districts in Mississippi, Louisiana, Alabama, Georgia, South Carolina, and Arkansas) should make a "substantial" effort to catch up with the leading desegregated districts.[51] In no instance, however, did the Guidelines require that more than 20 percent of the black children in a school district be in desegregated schools.[52] Whereas the 1965 Guidelines required only that schools "plan" to desegregate faculties, the 1966 Guidelines mandated that some desegregation of professional staffs actually take place.[53]

CRITICISM OF THE 1966 GUIDELINES

Like the 1965 Guidelines, the new Guidelines evoked opposition from many quarters — from the South, from civil rights leaders, and from liberal northern politicians. On the Left, critics claimed that HEW had caved into the South's insistence on continued "gradualism" in desegregating schools. The Southern Regional Council, a human relations organization, rejected the approach the Guidelines advanced:

> By building gradualism into its Guidelines by the use of minimum percentages, the U.S. Office of Education perhaps unwillingly allowed attention to shift from the illegitimacy of dual schools and the need to end them. Instead, Southern officials haggle over whether "ten percent is too much," while continuing segregated patterns. . . . The Guidelines still presuppose a dual system of schools, drawn as they are from the prevailing notion of *allowing Negro children to attend White schools.*[54]

Jack Greenberg of the NAACP Legal Defense Fund agreed, maintaining that desegregation was "going at a snail's pace." He complained that his organization had been referring cases involving discrimination in schools to HEW and that the department's inaction on those matters forced him to conclude that the government "obviously is not going to implement its own legislation." As to the pace of desegregation, Roy Wilkins, executive director of the NAACP, remarked that "any slower pace would be standing still."[55]

Most of the criticism of the 1966 Guidelines from southerners was directed at the provisions dealing with freedom-of-choice plans. "No single policy decision," Orfield concluded, "was to subject the Office of Education to more sustained and heavy abuse."[56] The political fall-out following the announcement of the new Guidelines was such that HEW secretary John Gardner wrote a lengthy explanatory letter to each member of Congress and state governor, attempting to mollify critics and justify the new HEW standards.

In his letter, Gardner stressed that the Guidelines did not require school districts to balance the races in schools or to achieve "instantaneous desegregation" of faculties. On faculty desegregation, he explained that the Guidelines offered "considerable flexibility" and required only "that a reasonable beginning be made and that reasonable progress be achieved beyond what was achieved last year." Responding to the objection that the percentages in the Guidelines imposed "racial balance" in schools, Gardner said that the percentages were just an "administrative guide" for measuring progress toward desegregation where freedom-of-choice plans had been adopted.[57]

Notwithstanding the secretary's efforts, Orfield estimated that four out of five members of Congress from the South believed that HEW had exceeded its authority in issuing the new rules.[58] Indeed, Jack Greenberg acknowledged that most court orders then in effect fell "far short" of the standards in the Guidelines. Consequently, several civil rights groups recommended that districts under court order be required to meet the tougher standards in the Guidelines.[59]

CONSERVATIVE CRITICS agreed that the Guidelines went beyond what the federal courts required.[60] No court decision, for example, had decreed anything like the percentage goals imposed by the Guidelines. Critics maintained that in mandating the percentages of students who had to be in desegregated schools, HEW had exceeded its authority under Title VI. Governor Godwin of Virginia, for example, went to see HEW secretary Gardner shortly after the agency announced its new Guidelines and lambasted the Guidelines as requiring "racial balance."[61] Godwin and others claimed that the requirements for faculty desegregation constituted interference with employment relationships and therefore exceeded HEW's authority.[62]

More than a month after HEW issued the Guidelines, and three days before the deadline for districts to indicate their intent to comply with them, only one district in seven had done so. For the first time in the controversy over HEW's enforcement of Title VI, the 1966 Guidelines prompted discussion about the unfairness of imposing desegregation requirements on the South while doing little about de facto segregation in the North. Consequently, after HEW announced its 1966 Guidelines, Congressman Whittener of North Carolina introduced an amendment to Title VI that was intended, among other things, to negate HEW's authority to require racial balancing in schools and to prohibit HEW bureaucrats from "perform[ing] quasi-judicial functions."[63]

Congressman Landrum of Georgia, in a letter to HEW secretary Gardner and in congressional debate on Whittener's amendment, argued that the 1966 Guidelines were illegal:

> I find nothing in Title VI of the Act and nothing in the legislative history of the Act requiring such drastic and precipitous new regulations and guidelines as have been issued. Moreover, Title IV of the Civil Rights Act of 1964, Section 401, paragraph (b) specifically states: "Desegregation means the assignment of students to public schools and within such schools without regard to their race, color, religion, or national origin, but desegregation shall not mean the assignment of students to public schools in order to overcome racial imbalance." Clearly, therefore, one must reach the conclusion that the regulations issued . . . are in direct violation of [that paragraph].[64]

Congressman Selden of Florida, echoing Whittener's objections, declared that "the guidelines are beyond the law. They are outside the law. They are a law unto themselves."[65] Georgia's Congressman Calloway argued that in the congressional debates on Title VI there was a clear distinction between requiring "desegregation" (the assignment of students to schools without regard to race) and requiring "racial balancing" (the achievement of a predetermined racial mix in schools). In passing Title VI, he argued, Congress had intended to accomplish only the former.[66] Congressman Fountain of North Carolina spoke of "shocking administrative abuses" in the enforcement of Title VI and reminded his colleagues that Congress required that Title VI be implemented through rules, regulations, and orders approved by the president — a requirement that had been "effectively evaded — if not deliberately violated."[67]

The debate over the Whittener Amendment contained references by congressional representatives to the "unbelievably callous attitude" of HEW officials, the "illegal, high handed and tyrannical action" of the Office of Education, that office's "almost dictatorial powers," and the "harsh and belligerent attitude" reflected in the government's enforcement of Title VI. There were also denunciations of HEW's decisions to terminate or defer funds to specific districts.[68]

Southern representatives and educational officials objected particularly to the idea that they might have to do more than establish freedom-of-choice plans. In an August 1966 letter to Congressman

Calloway of Georgia, Secretary Gardner explained HEW's policy on freedom of choice:

> Let me address myself to the question of whether a free-choice plan offered in good faith operating freely would be accepted even if it resulted in no desegregation. The answer would be "no."
>
> Desegregation is the goal. A district may seek to achieve that goal through a free-choice plan, but if the plan doesn't achieve the goal, then other means must be tried.[69]

Under federal court rulings, argued Congressman Fountain, it was "extremely unlikely that an otherwise valid free-choice plan would be found to violate the requirements of Title VI simply because it did not result in a large enough amount of actual integration to satisfy the Commissioner of Education." Nonetheless, Fountain stressed that HEW had notified at least seventy school districts operating under free-choice plans that they might lose federal funds unless they transferred more black students to predominantly white schools.[70]

In debate over the Whittener Amendment, southerners denounced Commissioner of Education Harold Howe and warned northerners that they, too, could suffer from Howe's excesses in pursuing integration. Congressman MacGregor of Minnesota warned that, if Congress did not pass the Whittener Amendment, it would be approving a policy that would destroy the neighborhood school. Congressman Martin of Alabama declared that he did "not want to turn the future of my children or your children or the children of millions of Godfearing, law-abiding, freedom-loving Americans over to the social experimental laboratories of Commissioner Harold Howe." Congressman O'Neal of Georgia, also attacking Commissioner Howe, declared that Howe had "set himself up as a little Caesar" whose "Bible is an unconstitutional set of Guidelines which flout the intent of Congress" and whose "weapon is the threat of withdrawal of federal funds."[71]

Ultimately, in responding to these objections, the House adopted by a vote of 220 to 116 an amendment that required a hearing before HEW could delay or defer federal funds to districts suspected of violating Title VI. In the Senate-House Conference Committee, the provision was changed to impose a maximum period of deferment of ninety days.[72]

Anger over the 1966 Guidelines and Commissioner Howe resulted in action in September 1966 by Congressman Emanuel Celler. Celler, the liberal New York congressman whose Judiciary Committee had overseen the passage of the 1964 Civil Rights Act in the House, announced that there would be an investigation into the methods used by the federal government to achieve integration.[73] The call for the investigation was unusual because, in addition to Celler, several other nonsoutherners, including Republican congressman H. Allen Smith and Democratic congressman B. F. Sisk, both of California, and Senate majority leader Mike Mansfield of Montana, were among those expressing concern about the issue.

JUDICIAL SUPPORT FOR THE 1966 GUIDELINES

In December 1966, after nearly a year of intensifying controversy about the validity of HEW's Guidelines and of the agency's enforcement of Title VI under the Guidelines, a three-judge panel of the U.S. Court of Appeals for the Fifth Circuit handed down its decision on the legality of the Guidelines. That decision, *United States v. Jefferson County Board of Education,* was a landmark decision in school desegregation law. The case involved twelve Alabama and Louisiana school districts with cases then pending before the Fifth Circuit. The districts had a combined student population of 155,000, including almost 60,000 black children, but in 1965, under existing court-ordered desegregation plans, only 110 of those black children attended schools with whites. Nor was there any faculty desegregation in any of these school districts.[74]

In a strongly worded and wide-ranging opinion written by Judge Wisdom, the circuit's most distinguished jurist, the court held that the 1966 Guidelines were within HEW's scope of authority under Title VI. It was lawful, Wisdom ruled, for HEW to develop standards for freedom-of-choice plans and faculty desegregation that imposed an affirmative duty on school boards. HEW's standards, the court wrote, provided the "best system available" for uniformly applying Title VI, and the "best aid" to the courts in evaluating progress. Moreover, the court held that the Guidelines would be accorded "great weight" in future school desegregation litigation.[75]

The scope of the holding in *Jefferson* was most unusual. Appended to Wisdom's opinion was a sample or model court decree containing general requirements for the pace of desegregation, examples of annual progress reports to be submitted by districts under court order, and procedures for creating freedom-of-choice plans, constructing new schools, and desegregating faculties and staffs.[76] The requirements in the model decree, Wisdom emphasized, borrowed heavily from the HEW Guidelines and would apply in all school desegregation cases in the Fifth Circuit. On appeal, the entire Fifth Circuit court of appeals, making only minor modifications, affirmed the decision of the three-judge panel.[77] A "comment" in the *Harvard Law Review* compared the breadth of the Fifth Circuit's ruling in *Jefferson* to the holding in *Miranda v. Arizona,* the landmark U.S. Supreme Court decision earlier in 1966 that expanded the rights of defendants in criminal cases.[78]

THE REDEFINITION OF THE RIGHT TO EQUAL EDUCATIONAL OPPORTUNITY

What is so critical about the HEW Guidelines and the Fifth Circuit's decision in *Jefferson* is that they helped produce a new understanding of the right established in *Brown.* The Supreme Court had announced in that decision that black children had a constitutional right to equal educational opportunity. That was the "legal right" that constituted the great victory in that case. The evolution in policy from the Guidelines to *Jefferson,* and ultimately to the Supreme Court's decision in the *Green* case, established that the right that black children enjoyed was the right to sit beside white children in school. The implicit assumption was that placing black children in school with white children would guarantee equal educational opportunity for the black children. As a legal principle, perhaps it made sense. As an educational policy it did not.

It is always easy, it must be conceded, to judge others harshly in retrospect. Nonetheless, surely it should have been evident to many, even in 1967, that one could not overcome generations of poverty, intimidation, psychological stigmatization, economic and social subordination, and calculated educational neglect by giving black children the "legal right" to sit next to white children in school buildings. I do not mean to denigrate the significance of that change, but only to suggest that even the slightest understanding of why children learn and achieve academically should have made reformers question whether that change alone could realistically produce what *Brown* promised — equal educational opportunity.

Two prominent authors did recognize the pitfalls of an approach that relied almost exclusively on racial integration. Kenneth Clark, whose research on the adverse psychological effects of segregation on black children was so closely linked to the *Brown* decision, warned of the limits of a legal rights strategy that hinged on racial body counts. In 1965 — the very year that federal bureaucrats began enforcing Title VI by relying on racial mixing — Clark cautioned that "the educational crisis in the ghettos is not primarily, and certainly not exclusively, one of inequitable racial balance in schools." The "inferior

quality of the education" black children received was just as delete-
rious as segregation. "One thing is clear," said Clark, "and that is that
meaningful desegregation of urban ghetto public schools can occur
only if all of the schools in the system are raised to the highest standards, so that the quality of education does not vary according to
income or the social status of the neighborhood." For Clark, integration and high-quality education were "interdependent," and both
had to be pursued. "One is not possible," he insisted, "without the
other."[79] Starting in the Johnson years, the law began to lead down
only one path — racial mixing — ignoring a range of powerful societal
forces whose adverse impact on the education of black Americans
was equal to, if not greater than, that of segregation.

Charles Silberman, in his 1964 classic *Crisis in Black and White,* also
argued that racial integration alone would not produce equal educational opportunity for blacks. Silberman maintained that blacks and
liberal whites alike had become "prisoners of their own rhetoric,"
focusing exclusively on desegregation and failing to press for other
changes geared to the educational needs of black children. Though
Silberman acknowledged that integration was "the greatest moral
imperative of our time," he insisted that it required more than "the
mere mixing of Negroes and whites in the same classroom, or in the
same school." To attempt to deal with the educational needs of black
children by focusing exclusively on integration was "to violate the
Commandment which prohibits the worship of false gods: it is to
sacrifice the children for the sake of an abstract principle." In language that paralleled Clark's reservations, Silberman insisted that
meaningful integration "will not be possible until the schools in Negro neighborhoods . . . are brought up to the level of the very best
schools in each city; until the schools do their job so well that children's educational performance no longer reflects their income or
their social status or their ethnic group or color."[80]

What the nonlawyers Clark and Silberman make clear is that the
legal right to attend a desegregated or racially integrated school addressed only part of the change that needed to occur. Desegregation
was not an educational panacea. Other equally important public educational reforms were also needed — reforms not easily cast in terms of
legal rights or readily subject to judicial resolution. Yet such political
reforms were largely ignored in the legal campaign against racial discrimination in schools. As we shall see, a similar shortsightedness and
lack of concern for educational considerations prevailed again in later
years, in the effort to desegregate black colleges and universities.

HEW's AND THE COURTS' MUTUAL DEFERENCE

The Reasons for Judicial Deference

The *Price, Singleton,* and *Jefferson* cases establish that courts during the Johnson years, particularly in the Fifth Circuit, gave great weight to the HEW Guidelines. Where courts deferred to the HEW desegregation standards, they advanced the following reasons for doing so:

- Courts acting alone had limited capacities to produce desegregation.
- There was a need to mount a coordinated attack on racial discrimination, based on uniform national standards.
- HEW officials had invaluable expertise in matters of educational policy and administration.
- Courts should defer to the will of Congress as reflected in Title VI.

The Limited Capacity of Courts Acting Alone

Some federal judges were exasperated with the dilemmas posed by judicial control of school desegregation. In an unusually direct expression of that frustration in a 1966 school desegregation case, Albert Tuttle, the Fifth Circuit's chief judge, wrote:

> This is the fourth appearance of this case before this court. This present appeal, coming as it does from the order of the total court entered nearly eighteen months ago . . . points up the utter impracticability of a continued exercise by the courts of the responsibility for supervising the manner in which segregated school systems break out of the policy of complete segregation into gradual steps of compliance and towards complete compliance with the constitutional requirements of *Brown*. [81]

Tuttle's comment speaks to several difficulties that confronted both the Supreme Court and the circuit courts in southern school desegregation cases.

Appellate courts were often unable to control the decisions of district courts. That failure was especially significant because in the *Brown* case the Supreme Court delegated to district courts the responsibility for monitoring school desegregation throughout the South. As Tuttle's comment intimates, the independence and occasional intransigence of district courts could cause years of delay as cases moved up and down the judicial hierarchy. The costs to black plaintiffs, in time and legal expenses, often seemed excessive when compared to the actual results achieved by appellate court "victories."[82] One law review comment linked the creative, wide-ranging remedy propounded in *Jefferson* to the resistance of some district courts:

> There is little doubt that the court's broad remedy was designed in part to eliminate the prior practice of several district courts of construing the Court of Appeals' desegregation opinions so narrowly as to defeat their purposes. The procession of appeals and remands occasioned by these battles between the district courts and the Fifth Circuit was, of course, a major cause of the procedural delays which constituted a great obstacle to the effective implementation of *Brown*. [83]

Judge Wisdom declared in his opinion in *Jefferson* that Title VI "was necessary to rescue school desegregation from the bog on which it had been trapped for years." Lauding the advantages of administrative enforcement of Title VI, he said that "the HEW Guidelines offer, for the first time, the prospect that the transition from a *de jure* segregated dual system to a unitary integrated system may be carried out effectively, promptly, and in an orderly manner."[84] Wisdom discussed at length the limited capacity of courts to bring about school desegregation in the South. "There are natural limits to effective legal action," he stated.[85] These were limitations, in Wisdom's view, that derived from the traditional organization and structure of the judicial process.[86] He noted the delays in implementing appellate court rulings, the burden on black plaintiffs in bringing lawsuits, the limited effectiveness of judicial sanctions for noncompliance, and the inability of courts to render advisory opinions or to remedy problems beyond the scope of the immediate case. The contempt power, he also observed, was ill-suited for use as a judicial weapon in school desegregation, and the case-by-case method had not produced prompt or uniform national desegregation standards.[87]

Wisdom's analysis suggested that there was a discrepancy between the tasks before federal courts in southern school desegregation cases, and the functional capacities and powers of courts. The courts, Wisdom concluded, needed help. "[A]cting alone" they had "failed."[88] The *Jefferson* court, among others, was looking for help. That the *Jefferson* panel eagerly sought the assistance of HEW is evidenced by the panel's initiative in making HEW's Guidelines an issue in the case. The Guidelines were not an issue raised in the pleadings or the trial. Indeed, the cases consolidated for decision in *Jefferson* had been tried in district courts and had appeals pending in the Fifth Circuit even before HEW promulgated its 1966 Guidelines.[89] The *Jefferson* court raised the question of the legal status of the HEW Guidelines, *sua sponte,* in its written request to counsel for supplemental briefs addressing the following questions:

> (a) To what extent, consistent with judicial prerogatives and obligations, statutory and constitutional, is it permissible and desirable for a federal court (trial or appellate) to give weight to or to rely on H.E.W. guidelines and policies in cases before the court?
>
> (b) If permissible and desirable, what practical means and methods do you suggest that federal courts (trial and appellate) should follow in making H.E.W. guidelines and policies judicially effective?[90]

The Need for Uniform National Standards for Attacking Racial Discrimination

The independence and discretion of district court judges produced a variety of desegregation approaches and standards. Those judges, by and large, determined the extent of desegregation required, the remedies or types of plans to be adopted, and the time frame within which compliance was to occur.[91] These realities led Judge Wisdom to lament, writing for the three-judge panel in *Jefferson,* that in the 128 school desegregation cases decided by district courts in the Fifth Circuit up to that time there was a "lack of clear and uniform standards."[92]

The lack of uniformity in desegregation standards was itself a cause of delay and a burden on appellate courts because it necessitated frequent appeals to clarify legal requirements. Problems of consistency and uniformity in federal courts' school desegregation rulings were exacerbated by the possibility that school districts under court order and districts submitting desegregation plans to HEW might also be subject to different standards.

In *Singleton I, Singleton II,* and the *Jefferson* case, the Fifth Circuit recognized the undesirable consequences should courts develop less demanding desegregation requirements than HEW. In such circumstances "school boards may turn to federal courts as a means of circumventing the HEW requirements for financial aid," and if "judicial standards are lower than HEW standards, recalcitrant school boards in effect will receive a premium for recalcitrance."[93]

HEW's Expertise in Educational Policy and Administration

Judges deferred to HEW's policies for reasons other than the belief that administrative enforcement had greater functional capacities and flexibility than did litigation. They praised the supposed expertise of HEW administrators, who were presumed to be more knowledgeable than judges about the educational issues associated with desegregation. In *Singleton,* that sentiment was expressed by the observation that "absent legal questions, the United States Office of Education is better qualified than the courts and is the most appropriate federal body to weigh administrative difficulties inherent in school desegregation plans."[94] Judge Brown, in *Price,* expressing relief that HEW had developed its Guidelines, characterized the standards as "long overdue" and "welcome," and indicated that many, both on and off the bench, felt a "great anxiety" in school desegregation cases in which the federal judge was "in the middle of school administrative problems for which he was not equipped."[95] In a similar vein, Judge Wisdom remarked in *Jefferson* that "most judges do not have sufficient competence — they are not educators or school administrators — to know the right questions, much less the right answers." By contrast, he referred to officials in HEW's Office of Education who were "experts in education and school administration" and had "day-to-day experience with thousands of school systems." He concluded, "Judges and school officials can ill afford to turn their backs on the proffer of advice from HEW."[96]

That federal judges should defer to HEW's supposed expertise in matters of educational policy and administration is surprising. Federal courts in the South, more than any other governmental institutions, had the most experience in overseeing school desegregation and dealing with the administrative and educational problems associated with that process. It was, in part, out of a recognition of that special judicial expertise that HEW officials decided to base the agency's Guidelines in large measure on the policies promulgated by federal judges. Indeed, Wisdom's elaborate and elegant opinion in *Jefferson* was evidence that Fifth Circuit judges had a sophisticated grasp not only of the legal and educational problems of school desegregation but also of the vast scholarly literature on the subject.

It was ironic for the federal courts to defer to the expertise of a federal agency whose first real experience with school desegregation problems came in the spring of 1965. Moreover, what is known about the situation within the Office of Education during this period hardly suggests that the agency's efforts to enforce Title VI were the result of an efficient, organized, and well-considered process. The Equal Educational Opportunities Program, the unit within the Office of Education responsible for enforcing Title VI, had done little to prepare itself for that task. It had virtually no budget for Title VI enforcement, and was in internal disarray.[97] Indeed, the first report of the White House Task Force on Civil Rights noted that Congress had not supplied the Office of Education with sufficient funds to investigate violations of and achieve compliance with Title VI.[98]

In August 1966, on the eve of the new school year under the 1966 Guidelines, Peter Libassi, a civil rights official in HEW, wrote that he anticipated that as many as two-thirds of southern school districts would not meet the requirements of the Guidelines, and noted that the "Office of Education does not have the staff or resources to deal effectively with so large a number of inadequate performers."[99] In 1967, the Office of Education had only forty-one field workers to "police" the actions of 2,200 school districts. Indeed, speaking of his department's enforcement of Title VI, HEW secretary John Gardner remarked, "We were plunged into a situation where we had no experience."[100]

In *Price,* Judge Brown wrote that after passage of the 1964 Civil Rights Act, the administration of school desegregation was "largely where it ought to be — in the hands of the executive and its agencies."[101] He suggested that the judiciary should confine itself to issues raising justiciable and not operational questions. Yet constitutional and operational considerations were inseparable. Any effort to desegregate schools would inevitably have an impact on how schools operated. Judge Wisdom had himself found the "means" and "ends" in school desegregation inseparable when he declared in *Jefferson* that the only desegregation methods that were constitutional were those that produced the desired end result — actual desegregation.[102] One could not divorce the legal requirements in school desegregation from educational, operational, and administrative considerations. Judges overseeing school desegregation were necessarily educational administrators of a sort and could not really have it otherwise. In short, the administrative and educational issues about which the Office of Education ostensibly possessed expertise could not readily be distinguished from the "justiciable" legal issues that fell to judges to decide. The *Price* case was as good an illustration of that as any.

In *Price,* black plaintiffs challenged the adequacy of a school desegregation plan for Dennison, Texas, that desegregated one grade per year. After the district court found the plan adequate, the court of appeals, taking note that the 1965 HEW Guidelines required that four grades per year be desegregated, ordered that the school board comply with the HEW standards. Hence, the issue in *Price* was the pace at which a formerly de jure segregated system had to be transformed into a unitary school system operating on a nonracial basis.

Surely such a restructuring posed bona fide issues of educational administration for which professional educators might have a special insight and competence. Just as surely, however, the pace of desegregation had repeatedly come before federal courts and had been properly considered and decided as a constitutional issue.[103] In much the same vein, the debate over freedom-of-choice plans posed legitimate questions of educational, operational, and constitutional import.

When an issue of educational administration poses a constitutional question, the constitutional requirements, as the courts define them, control. "Absent legal questions," Judge Wisdom qualified in the *Singleton* decision, the Office of Education was the more appropriate body "to weigh administrative difficulties" in school desegregation cases.[104] What Wisdom recognized in his qualifying phrase is that "administrative difficulties" and other "educational" issues may have legal implications requiring that judges, and not educators, decide them.

The courts were, however, apparently unwilling or unable to delineate how to determine where deference to HEW on "administrative" and "educational" matters ended, and where the judicial obligation to assert constitutional requirements began. Without such an elaboration, it remained for courts to articulate on an ad hoc basis where that line lay. However one conceived of the functional and constitutional division of authority between courts and HEW, this much was clear: Those southern federal judges who for years had struggled to desegregate schools without much support from Congress or the president welcomed the political support of the executive branch and, indirectly, of the Oval Office itself.

Moreover, as an administrative agency, HEW made contributions in areas in which administrative agencies do have far greater capacity and experience than do courts. HEW developed annual, quantifiable goals for desegregation in southern school districts and began to develop a system, however crude, for monitoring progress toward those goals. These were the first steps in a transition to a new phase in the civil rights era—a phase that centered not on the articulation and pronouncement of new legal rights, but on the development of a national bureaucratic system to enforce rights.

The Need to Defer to the Will of Congress

In its *Jefferson* decision, the Fifth Circuit maintained that in making its decision it deferred not only to HEW but also to Congress. Through Title VI, Wisdom said, Congress had expressed its dissatisfaction with the slow pace of school desegregation "inherent in the judicial adversary process." "We read Title VI," he stated, "as a congressional mandate for change — change *in the pace and method of enforcing desegregation.*"[105] Accordingly, Wisdom declared that the judiciary had a "duty to cooperate with Congress" and to assist agencies charged with implementing the 1964 Civil Rights Act so as not "to destroy or dilute the effectiveness" of the congressional policy: "When Congress declares national policy, the duty the two other coordinate branches owe to the nation requires, that, within the law, the judiciary and the executive respect and carry out that policy."[106]

It is noteworthy that Wisdom defended the extraordinary scope of the ruling in *Jefferson* by maintaining that its requirements derived from the policies of "the politically representative branch of government."[107] When making controversial, landmark decisions, high appellate courts like to advance that claim to add legitimacy to their decisions. In *Jefferson,* therefore, Wisdom in part justified the court's deference to HEW on the basis of the judicial obligation to cooperate with the congressional policy established in Title VI. The passive and deferential judicial role that Wisdom assumed vis-à-vis HEW did not go uncriticized. It led Judge Cox to remark, in dissent on the *Jefferson* panel, that the court was "abdicating" its constitutional responsibilities to HEW and Congress.[108]

Returning the Favor: HEW's Deference to the Courts and to Judicial Standards

If the Fifth Circuit went out of its way to acknowledge and laud the efforts of HEW in helping to combat racial discrimination in schools, HEW was no less deferential in acknowledging the special role and expertise of the courts. In enforcing Title VI, HEW was keenly sensitive to the policies announced in court decisions. Wanting to protect and insulate their enforcement program from political attacks, HEW officials were especially concerned that Title VI regulations be "immune to the very serious political damage to the enforcement program that would arise from a defeat in the courts."[109] The Johnson administration's desire to protect itself against legal attack had two immediate consequences. First, judicial precedents were the most important standards HEW officials consulted in devising the Guidelines. Second, the administration gave the Justice Department overall authority to coordinate various agency regulations for Title VI because of that department's experience and expertise in the legal questions surrounding southern school desegregation.[110]

HEW emphasized that the rulings of federal courts in school desegregation cases determined the agency's Guidelines and enforcement decisions. Testifying before Congress, Commissioner of Education Keppel stressed that the first items on his desk every morning were judgments from the U.S. Court of Appeals for the Fifth Circuit. Underscoring that point before a House appropriations subcommittee in March 1967, HEW secretary John Gardner stated that, in enforcing Title VI, "court cases must serve as our guide," for "I must move at every step in conformity with what . . . the courts regard as appropriate."[111]

HEW reviewed and relied on court rulings in preparing and later defending the controversial 1966 Guidelines. Officials within the Office of Education initially wanted the Guidelines to require that a minimum of 20 percent of a district's minority children attend desegregated schools. However, HEW rejected that requirement because the Justice Department and HEW's general counsel both objected that any specified minimum percentage would probably not be upheld by the courts.[112]

When Secretary Gardner wrote his explanatory letter clarifying and defending the 1966 Guidelines to all the members of Congress and all state governors, he specifically referred to the judicial basis of the most disputed provision — the requirement that freedom-of-choice plans actually produce racial integration. Gardner noted that in reviewing the adequacy of free-choice plans HEW "adopted the objective criteria applied by the Courts in similar situations"; he added that one such criterion was the level of racial integration achieved after the students had exercised their choices.[113]

By maintaining that HEW guided its decisions by judicial standards and by characterizing those standards as "objective," Gardner sought to insulate the agency's decisions from political attack by taking advantage of the belief that courts based their standards not on partisan or political considerations, but rather on the impersonal, impartial, neutral demands of the law. Hence, federal judges lauded HEW's "expertise" in writing the Guidelines, and HEW officials, in turn, extolled and relied on the "objective" policies of the courts.

THE COURTS' ULTIMATE CONTROL OVER SUBSTANTIVE STANDARDS

The central role of litigation and judicial standards in the enforcement of Title VI was evident even at the height of Title VI's power in the Johnson years. Realizing that court victories on constitutional doctrine in school desegregation would be translated into new administrative standards for HEW's enforcement of Title VI, civil rights groups appreciated that litigating was their "only real opportunity for broad influence" over HEW's enforcement policies.[114] Consequently, during the period when the executive branch's enforcement of Title VI was most vigorous, litigation continued to be a decisive force in guiding policy in school discrimination cases.

Even in *Singleton I, Singleton II,* and the *Jefferson* case, the strongest judicial endorsements of HEW's policies, the courts left no doubt that HEW standards should not be taken as always and necessarily equivalent to constitutional requirements, or as determinative of them. In *Singleton I,* the court emphasized that the 1965 HEW Guidelines established only "*minimum* standards" that might in certain circumstances be insufficient to meet the constitutional requirements established by the Supreme Court or the Fifth Circuit.[115] In *Jefferson,* writing for the three-judge panel, Judge Wisdom noted that the central issues in school desegregation cases involved not questions about whether federal financial assistance should be withheld, but questions about constitutional rights and obligations. Moreover, he stressed that courts would also make independent determinations about the lawfulness of HEW's decisions under Title VI. "Our approval of the existing [1966] Guidelines and the deference owed to any future Guidelines," Wisdom declared, "is not intended to deny a day in court to any person asserting individual rights or to any school board contesting HEW action."[116]

There were slight differences between the requirements of the model court decree in *Jefferson* and those of the HEW Guidelines. Lawyers for the school board in *Jefferson* argued that complete and uncritical adoption of the Guidelines would have constituted an abdication of the judicial function. Wanting to convey the impression that it had engaged in its own independent assessment of the validity of the Guidelines, the court may have deliberately avoided adopting the totality of HEW's requirements. By doing that, it made itself less vulnerable to the charge that it relied uncritically on the determinations of federal administrators enforcing Title VI.[117]

Outside of the Fifth Circuit, there was also emphasis on the need for courts to retain independent judgment and power in reviewing HEW standards. In *Kemp v. Beasley,* decided in the Eighth Circuit just a few months after *Singleton I,* Judge Gibson expressed reservations about excessive judicial reliance on HEW's standards:

It is for the courts, and the courts alone to determine when the operation of a school system violates rights guaranteed by the Constitution. The constitutional right of plaintiffs to attend a nonsegregated
school is not dependent upon federally financed programs, but is an
inherent right that is completely separate and apart from the executive function of regulating and financing schools.

. . . [T]he courts should endeavor to model their standards after
those promulgated by the executive. They are not bound, however, and
when circumstances dictate, the courts may require something more,
less or different from the H.E.W. guidelines.[118]

Again, in *Clark v. Board of Education of Little Rock School District,* a case
decided after the 1966 Guidelines appeared, Gibson advanced a similar position. The court, he said, had "great respect" for the expertise
of HEW and found its Guidelines most useful. However, to adopt the
Guidelines as an "absolute polestar," he concluded, would be to ab-
dicate to HEW the power to determine constitutional rights and
duties in the area of school desegregation.[119] In both *Kemp* and *Clark,*
Gibson emphasized that school desegregation problems varied significantly from district to district and that constitutional resolutions
of those problems should vary accordingly. Whereas Wisdom intimated that it was impractical to delegate to district courts the primary responsibility for overseeing school desegregation, Gibson suggested that in some situations courts were perhaps better equipped to
fashion remedies than were administrative agencies because courts
could more flexibly tailor desegregation plans to the particularities of
individual school districts, thereby producing plans more likely to be
workable and effective.[120]

Gibson's view, conforming to the reasoning in *Brown II,* dealing
with the implementation of school desegregation, suggested the continuing value of keeping primary responsibility for desegregation in
the hands of federal district court judges. The differences between
Wisdom and Gibson, to be sure, were fine ones. Nonetheless, the
Fifth Circuit did seem more eager than the Eighth to relinquish to
HEW the responsibility of managing school desegregation. That difference could well have been the result of the different problems in
the two circuits. The Fifth Circuit, encompassing such states as Georgia, Mississippi, Louisiana, and Alabama, was the site of the most
intense and persistent efforts to evade school desegregation;[121] by
contrast, the Eighth Circuit consisted of North Dakota, South Dakota, Nebraska, Minnesota, Iowa, Missouri, and Arkansas. Wisdom's frustration with adjudication and its limitations likely derived

from the special problems courts confronted in the Deep South.[122]

Whereas the courts insisted that they had the authority to review the school desegregation policies of HEW, the reverse was not true for two reasons. First, school desegregation cases typically raised constitutional questions, and the constitutional requirements took precedence over statutory requirements under Title VI. In an Eighth Circuit case comparing the standards of HEW and those of federal courts, the court pointedly remarked, "[W]e must keep in mind that we deal here with constitutional rights and not with those established by statute."[123] Indeed, if districts voluntarily decided to forego federal funds rather than comply with Title VI, HEW could take no action against them under the statute. Such districts could be compelled to desegregate only when there was a judicial finding of a constitutional violation. The second reason that HEW was precluded from reviewing courts' school desegregation decisions was that the HEW Guidelines accepted the final school desegregation order of a federal court as proof of compliance with Title VI.

Indeed, the question of disparity in standards between the executive and judiciary was a central concern in both the *Singleton* and the *Jefferson* litigation. Although the Fifth Circuit, and to a lesser degree the Eighth Circuit, demonstrated a sensitivity to this problem and a desire to avoid such disparities and the problems they might cause, not all other circuit courts did the same. Discrepancies between court decisions and HEW standards repeatedly posed problems in the Fourth Circuit. David Seeley, who led the civil rights effort in the Office of Education during the Johnson administration, complained in writing in July 1965 to John Doar, then assistant attorney general in the Justice Department's Civil Rights Division, that the Fourth Circuit was accepting inadequate school desegregation plans from districts under court orders. He asked Doar if there would be any way "to get these court orders remedied in a routine almost automatic basis." Reflecting on that problem, Radin concluded that even though it was a recurring issue as the Guidelines changed, Seeley's request "was quite impossible given the formal deference to the courts."[124]

It wasn't feasible for HEW to insist that the antidiscrimination requirements under Title VI were greater and more demanding than those imposed by the Fourteenth Amendment. Even if HEW could have argued persuasively that federal judges were misconstruing the constitutional requirements in particular cases, there was no way for HEW officials to advance that argument because they were not parties to the litigation. Moreover, though integrationist federal judges were pleased to have HEW as an ally, they remained jealous of their prerogatives and power. The most dramatic example of that occurred as a result of a series of cases coming from Macon County, Alabama.

Alabama, the state that was perhaps more intransigently opposed to school desegregation than any other, refused to comply with the HEW Guidelines. It capped its resistance by passing a law that not only negated the 1966 Guidelines but also declared that any statements by school boards in the state assuring HEW of compliance with Title VI were null and void. In the first case from Macon County in 1967, *Alabama NAACP State Conference of Branches v. Wallace et al.*, the court declared the state statute unconstitutional because it conflicted with the requirements of federal law.[125] In the second, *Lee v. Macon County Board of Education,* the court permanently enjoined the state board of education from discriminating on the basis of race and required the board to take affirmative measures to disestablish the dual school system in all ninety-nine school districts throughout Alabama.[126] As part of its decision, the court ordered certain school districts to adopt desegregation plans meeting specific requirements. Among the plans submitted was one from the Lanett City school system. The court subsequently approved that plan, and the city provided HEW with a written assurance that it was in compliance with the court's order.

Given HEW's policy of accepting final court orders as demonstrating compliance with Title VI, the court, by imposing a court order for all districts in the state, appeared to preempt a significant role for HEW. However, HEW interpreted its regulations as meaning that it would accept a final court order as demonstrating compliance with Title VI only where school districts were named as defendants.[127] In the Macon County cases, the governor and state officials, not particular school districts, had been named as defendants. Consequently, HEW held a hearing, and when it found that the Lanett City school system was not complying with the court-ordered plan, it terminated federal funding.[128] In a strongly worded opinion in a third Macon County case, a three-judge panel enjoined HEW from terminating funds, ruling that HEW could not engage in administrative review or supervision of a court order requiring desegregation. Permitting HEW to terminate the funding of school systems under court order would be an abdication of the court's authority to enforce compliance with its own decrees.[129] HEW could only inquire into the school district's compliance with the court order and then bring any evidence of noncompliance to the attention of the court. In dicta, in the first Macon County case, the three-judge panel commented that "as courts attempt to cooperate with executive and legislative policies, so too, the Department must respect a court order for the desegregation of a school or school system."[130]

The problem that surfaced in the Macon County cases remained an issue in many school districts and became more important as more school districts came under court order. In the 1965–66 school year 155 school districts filed court orders with the Office of Education to qualify for federal funding.[131] By the 1970–71 academic year, approximately four hundred southern school districts demonstrated their compliance with Title VI by filing final court orders with the Office of Education.[132] A leading civil rights official in HEW at the end of the Johnson administration concluded that districts under court order were making very slow progress because there was "no machinery now in existence for monitoring compliance with court orders for school desegregation."[133] This problem reflected the way in which authority over the monitoring of school desegregation in the South had been divided between the courts and HEW during the Johnson administration.

Conclusions

The relationship between HEW and the federal courts during the Johnson administration cannot be understood without examining the problems each branch was having in coping with its own responsibilities. The responsibility for enforcing Title VI was thrust upon the Office of Education, an office that had not been involved in drafting the provision and had done very little to ready itself to enforce it. When Congress passed the legislation, there was little to indicate that the office could do an effective job of enforcement.

Officials in HEW's Office of Education had historically enjoyed close and cordial relations with the leaders of state educational establishments. Professional educators frequently moved back and forth from the federal agency to the state and local educational bureaucracies. Relations between Washington and the localities were collegial. Thus, within the traditional leadership of the Office of Education there was very little interest in or incentive for the enforcement of a law that could result in local educational institutions' losing federal funds.

Another constraint on HEW's enforcement of Title VI was lack of resources. The scope of the enforcement task was enormous. In the seventeen southern and border states alone there were some fifty-one hundred school districts. Initially, there was not even a separate budgetary allotment for the enforcement of Title VI.[134] Though courts repeatedly referred to the special expertise and resources of the Office of Education, in those early years the office was poorly staffed and in constant turmoil, and its enforcement efforts were often chaotic, inefficient, and mismanaged. The turmoil came from both within and outside of the agency. Writing of the external forces constraining the Equal Educational Opportunities Program (EEOP), Alan Wolk observed, "[EEOP] was never able to fully get off the ground, because it was constantly stymied by a myriad of forces . . . it was not only engaged in a running battle with the opponents of civil rights . . . but also had to contend with: the demands of civil rights entities; the inquiries of Congressmen who were concerned about efficient methods of administration; differences of opinion with the Justice Department; and the watchful eye of the White House."[135]

To realize the mandate of Title VI, those responsible for its enforcement developed enforcement standards from judicial rulings. This borrowing of judicial standards was an effective strategy.[136] First, notwithstanding the frustrations of courts between 1954 and 1964, they were the governmental institutions with the broadest experience in dealing with racial discrimination in schools. Second, HEW bureaucrats wished to move with some dispatch to enforce Title VI beginning in September 1965. To do so, they needed to develop policies quickly so that they could begin negotiations with school districts in the spring of 1965. Judicial standards were readily available — one needed only to read the cases. Third, and most important, appropriating the "objective" constitutional standards of courts gave HEW policies the imprimatur of legality, adding badly needed legitimacy, credibility, and authority to HEW's fledgling efforts to enforce Title VI.

HEW's standards, the department repeatedly emphasized, were little more than the requirements of the Constitution as federal judges had interpreted those requirements. HEW officials realized that federal courts were a good ally, and the agency had few allies in beginning the politically touchy task of enforcing Title VI. And, by and large, federal courts delivered their support when states and school districts challenged the department's authority. Time after time, the Fifth Circuit intervened, in Wolk's phrase, to give HEW's school desegregation efforts "a boost." For example, the decision in *Jefferson*, Wolk concluded, "buttressed EEOP's sagging program."[137] Moreover, in meetings with angry southern educators HEW officials could claim that their hands were tied — that court decisions and hence, indirectly, the Constitution itself, required HEW to be as insistent as it was.[138]

In *Jefferson,* the synergistic power of the bench and bureaucracy's working together was apparent. The day after the decision by the three-judge panel, the implications of the case for HEW's enforcement were evident. Administration officials greeted the decision with "undisguised elation." HEW secretary John Gardner, jubilant over the court's endorsement of HEW's policies, called it a "very very constructive decision" that went "right down the line" in backing HEW's policies, and that should "lay to rest" doubts about the legality of HEW's efforts. One HEW official stated that the decision would have the salutary effect of "finally persuading southern school districts that there is no turning back, that they cannot any longer avoid the inevitability of desegregation." Another official commented that as long as the struggle "was being waged by Commissioner Howe and the Office of Education alone," there were "many people who persuaded themselves that we would either abandon the field or be defeated. Now we have backing in the courts."[139]

Peter Libassi, Gardner's special assistant for civil rights, characterized the decision as "very significant . . . not just another school case decision," and noted that HEW would no longer be as patient with recalcitrant school districts.[140] He reported that in December 1966 HEW had initiated hearings to terminate funds to more than one hundred school districts and that over the first three months in 1967 HEW planned to initiate enforcement proceedings under Title VI against another one hundred to three hundred school districts.[141] Two days after the decision, taking further advantage of the momentum offered by the three-judge panel in *Jefferson,* Secretary Gardner announced new Guidelines that required "significant progress" in faculty desegregation beyond what had been accomplished in the 1966–67 academic year.[142]

In his pioneering work on the district judges responsible for implementing *Brown,* Jack Peltason concluded that because federal courts were insulated from the political process they could "take the heat" on school desegregation, thus functioning, in effect, as scapegoats. Those community officials who needed some individual or institution to blame could point to the federal judge and claim that the judge made them desegregate.[143] To some degree, HEW used a similar strategy to gain political cover from the courts. It tried not to expand the scope of Title VI's prohibition on discrimination beyond those actions that courts had held violated the Fourteenth Amendment. Hence, the cutting edge of administrative enforcement under Title VI paralleled the contours of evolving constitutional doctrine.

In assessing the relationship between the courts and HEW, a *Yale Law Review* "comment" observed:

> At least under present HEW policy, the Office of Education's ability to attack discrimination will only grow and evolve as the constitutional requirements themselves do. . . . The result of course is that future changes in HEW standards to permit attacks on the worst examples of racial imbalance or the elimination of freedom-of-choice as a legitimate desegregation plan will only occur if courts hold such phenomena and practices unconstitutional. Until the courts strike down the free choice plan, the Office of Education will not move, and once the courts so hold, the Office of Education has no choice but to act accordingly.[144]

The circularity of the process was evident. Courts first developed standards for defining what constituted illegal racial discrimination in schools under the Constitution, and what remedies could be imposed for such violations. HEW said that it based its policies for enforcing Title VI on those judicial precedents. When school districts advanced legal challenges to HEW's policies, the courts upheld HEW's policies as consistent with judicial rulings. Occasionally, judicial support came at critical junctures, as with the holding in *Singleton I* validating the first Guidelines. That decision came at an especially propitious moment: June 1965, just before the frantic negotiations in the summer of 1965 in which HEW sought desegregation plans from hundreds of southern school districts.[145]

Timing was also important in *Singleton II*, which again contained a strong endorsement of the Guidelines. It was more than mere coincidence that HEW announced its 1966 Guidelines just weeks after the Fifth Circuit handed down *Singleton II* in January 1966, and then issued new Guidelines for the following year within days of the decision by the three-judge panel in *Jefferson*. Following the issuance of the 1966 Guidelines, as noted earlier, there was intense controversy about HEW's requirements with regard to freedom-of-choice plans and faculty desegregation. When the Johnson administration decided to reissue the 1966 Guidelines for the following year, the *New York Times* commented on the political comfort the *Jefferson* case provided: "Administration officials say they would not be surprised if the new 1967 guidelines caused a similar storm [to that of the previous year]. But they do not appear particularly concerned. The reason is that on Thursday, the United States Court of Appeals for the Fifth Circuit . . . upheld the legality of the Guidelines."[146]

The end result of HEW's enforcement of Title VI during the Johnson years was ironic. The enforcement of a law intended as a substitute for litigation became heavily dependent on and linked to the
standards advanced in litigation. Concerned about the continuing
central role of courts in school desegregation, the White House Task
Force on Civil Rights in 1966 warned in its first report that though
judicial proceedings "can play an important role in enforcement . . .
litigation cannot be made a substitute for the administrative proceedings prescribed by Congress as the primary device for enforcing Title
VI."[147] Courts provided both important substantive standards for
Title VI and crucial validation of HEW's own enforcement policies.
The "comment" in the *Yale Law Journal*, noted earlier, concluded that
Jefferson was a "benediction by the courts of the Office of Education
and an anointing of the guidelines with the holy oil of judicial approval."[148] That observation, however, captures only part of the dynamic. The relationship cut both ways. The courts gained as much
as they gave.

Exclusive judicial management of and responsibility for school
desegregation after *Brown* proved a bedeviling experience for federal
courts. The problems have been noted — the inability of appellate
courts to "control" district courts, the expense and delay to plaintiffs,
the individualized nature of remedies, the lack of uniform judicial
standards, the damage to the prestige of courts because of local opposition to desegregation, and, most conclusively, the negligible school
desegregation achieved between 1954 and 1964. These difficulties were
acute in the Deep South states covered by the Fifth Circuit — the circuit that provided the most ringing endorsements of HEW policies.
Those endorsements stemmed from the frustrating experiences and
dismal performance that resulted from attempts to achieve school
desegregation in the Fifth Circuit through litigation. HEW's entrance
was a welcome one, seen as something of a rescue mission by some
judges who had sought unsuccessfully to desegregate schools through
judicial decree.

The courts, especially in the Fifth Circuit, seemed decidedly interested in ensuring that HEW helped them shoulder the burden of managing the desegregation process.[149] During the mid-1960s, the federal
bench and bureaucracy were engaged in a cooperative and mutually
beneficial strategy, sharing the political onus of managing a social
transformation that was of profound magnitude, and to which there
was intense local and regional opposition. Both the courts and HEW,
each recognizing the political liabilities associated with racial change,
attempted on occasion to give the other the "credit" for devising the

policies that compelled an end to the dual system in the South.

Legitimacy has been defined as governmental power "exercised both with a consciousness on the government's part that it has a right to govern *and* with some recognition by the governed of that right."[150] With respect to both aspects of this definition, the legitimacy of governmental action on school desegregation during the Johnson administration was in question. The white majority in the South had grave doubt as to whether either the courts or HEW had a "right to govern" in school desegregation. That doubt placed the courts and HEW on the defensive, causing them to seek opportunities to cooperate with one another to bolster their authority and precarious political position in their respective struggles to end segregated schools. Simultaneously, as noted, each was also occasionally interested in holding the other responsible for the policies that compelled that result. This odd, awkward, but creative and functional alliance between the branches produced the first significant progress in school desegregation to occur in the South after years of litigation, resistance, inaction, and failure. That accomplishment is rightfully recognized as a historic breakthrough. Nonetheless, there was a little-appreciated price paid for that success.

The enforcement of Title VI during the Johnson years produced a profound change in the underlying legal right in question. As noted at the beginning of this chapter, that change occurred in a three-step process that included the development of the HEW Guidelines, the Fifth Circuit's endorsement of the Guidelines in the *Jefferson* litigation, and the Supreme Court's reformulation, in 1968 in the *Green* case, of the ultimate objective of school desegregation. Faced with the obdurate defiance of the South and the negligible success of the effort to implement *Brown* through litigation, the Office of Education began its efforts as perhaps any bureaucracy might. Bureaucracies need and search for relatively simple, straightforward indicators by which to measure their progress. Accordingly, in enforcing the right protected under Title VI, the Office of Education developed objective, quantifiable measures by which to evaluate compliance with the law and its own success in producing that compliance. The fundamental measure was the level of racial integration achieved in schools—a strategy I call the "racial body count" approach.

The court decision that produced the most influential and complete discussion of this new criterion was the decision by the three-judge panel in the *Jefferson* case. That opinion makes it plain that impatience with the slow pace of change in the South helped produce the new, quantifiable standards. "[T]he clock has ticked the last tick for tokenism and delay in the name of 'deliberate speed,'" Judge Wisdom ruled in *Jefferson*. In an obvious rebuttal to school officials who claimed that they satisfied their constitutional obligation by adopting freedom-of-choice plans, even if those plans did not produce desegregation, Wisdom declared: *"The only school desegregation plan that meets constitutional standards is one that works."*[151] To determine whether the plan "worked" in any given school, one would, in effect, count the number of black and white faces in that school.

Jefferson turned on basic definitional issues — how one defined what was "illegal segregation," and how one remedied that illegality. It was a landmark case because the Fifth Circuit endorsed the idea, initially advanced in the 1966 HEW Guidelines, that southern school districts had an affirmative obligation to end de jure segregation and that courts would measure whether districts had met that obligation by looking at the level of racial integration achieved in schools. In its *en banc* affirmance in *Jefferson,* using language later adopted by the Supreme Court in *Green,* the Fifth Circuit wrote:

> The Court holds that boards and officials administering public schools in this circuit have the affirmative duty under the Fourteenth Amendment to bring about an integrated, unitary school system in which there are no Negro schools and white schools — just schools. Expressions in our earlier opinions distinguishing between integration and desegregation must yield to this affirmative duty we now recognize. In fulfilling this duty it is not enough for school authorities to offer Negro children the opportunity to attend formerly all-white schools. The necessity of overcoming the effects of the dual school system in this circuit requires integration of faculties, facilities, and activities, as well as students. To the extent that earlier decisions of this Court . . . conflict with this view, the decisions are overruled.[152]

The distinction between "desegregation" and "integration," the *en banc* court noted in *Jefferson,* first appeared in dicta in *Briggs v. Elliot,* a district court case decided in 1955, six weeks after the Supreme Court's ruling in *Brown II.*[153] *Briggs* interpreted the latter decision as forbidding racial segregation and discrimination, but as not requiring integration:

> [The Supreme Court] has not decided that the federal courts are to take over or regulate the public schools of the states. It has not decided that the states must mix persons of different races in the schools or must require them to attend schools or must deprive them of the right of choosing the schools they attend. What it has decided, and all it has

decided, is that a state may not deny to any person on account of race the right to attend any school that it maintains. The Constitution, in other words, does not require integration. It merely forbids [segregation].[154]

In rejecting the *Briggs* dicta, the Fifth Circuit in *Jefferson* repudiated the idea that Title VI and the Constitution required only that states eliminate the barriers that prevented or forbade racial integration.[155] Rather, *Jefferson* held that the law compelled more, that it imposed an affirmative legal duty on school districts to integrate.

At issue in *Jefferson* were the very meaning of *Brown* and the way to measure compliance with *Brown*'s requirements. Indeed, in its *en banc* decision the *Jefferson* court picked up the emphasis on "equal educational opportunity" in *Brown I* by observing that "if Negroes are ever to enter the mainstream of American life, as school children they must have equal educational opportunities with white children."[156] After *Jefferson,* the right to equal educational opportunity—both under the Constitution and under Title VI—required school districts to ensure that children of different races attended school together. In turn, that meant that courts and districts began using statistical measures of the racial balance in schools as the paramount criterion in evaluating whether a district met its legal obligations. It was the 1966 HEW Guidelines that first advanced this approach. *Jefferson* reinforced and validated the approach for the Fifth Circuit. In *Green,* the Supreme Court essentially endorsed the underlying rationale of the Guidelines and of the *Jefferson* ruling.

Green itself grew out of the efforts to enforce Title VI. The school district in *Green,* which had initially resisted all efforts to desegregate, ultimately relented by adopting a freedom-of-choice plan in 1965 so as to continue receiving federal financial assistance. After three years, no white student had chosen to attend a formerly black school, and 85 percent of the black students still attended all-black schools. In language drawn verbatim from the *en banc* decision in *Jefferson,* the Supreme Court held that school officials must "fashion steps which promise realistically to convert promptly to a system without a 'white' school and a 'Negro' school, but just schools."[157] Thus, the Court imposed an "affirmative" duty on school districts to integrate, largely because freedom-of-choice plans had proven so popular with southern school districts and so ineffective in ending racial segregation.[158]

Green "marked a major turning point" in constitutional doctrine on school desegregation.[159] It resolved the issue implicitly raised in the 1966 HEW Guidelines and discussed at length in the Fifth Circuit's

Jefferson decision: Did the Fourteenth Amendment merely prohibit segregation, or did it require integration? For the first time the Supreme Court, in *Green,* approved of determining whether school boards had met their legal obligations not by evaluating whether the process of assigning students to schools was "pure" (i.e., was not determined by racial considerations) but by examining the resulting level of racial integration actually achieved in schools. *Green* advanced "the theory that achieving racial integration was the only acceptable evidence that the process had been purified."[160] School systems, the Court ruled, must dismantle the state-imposed dual system "at the earliest practicable date," and must "convert to a unitary system in which racial discrimination [is] eliminated root and branch."[161] There was an unmistakable edge, almost a note of urgency, to the Court's language and tone in *Green.* The case sounded the death knell of the doctrine of desegregating "with all deliberate speed."[162] Seizing the Court's ruling in *Green,* the Johnson administration renewed its call for southern states to complete the desegregation process. In the HEW Guidelines, the administration established September 1969 as the final deadline for total desegregation in most southern districts, save those with black majorities, which were given until September 1970.[163]

The enforcement of Title VI between 1965 and 1968 is widely and rightfully recognized as having produced historic breakthroughs in the dismantling of the system of racial segregation in southern schools. It is far less appreciated, however, that the judicial and administrative policies that effected that change narrowed our thinking about what the law should require in order to achieve racial equality in public education. The legal right won in *Brown* imposed an obligation on states to ensure that public school systems provided black children with educational opportunities equal to those of whites. The operational definition of that legal right that emerged from the judicial-administrative dialogue described in this chapter was based on the dubious assumption that simply permitting black children to attend school in the same building as whites would achieve that goal.

4

THE NIXON-FORD YEARS:
Litigating against the Political Backlash

THE NIXON-FORD YEARS PROVED to be a critical period in the struggle over the enforcement of Title VI. During that period, the relationship between the courts and HEW took a dramatic turn, redefining yet again the way in which the government conceived of the rights protected by Title VI. Indeed, the litigation initiated between 1968 and 1976 affected Title VI for the next decade and a half. By producing a focus on the procedural rights and managerial issues associated with enforcement, the litigation during the Nixon-Ford era altered the debate over and the impact of Title VI. In addition, the controversies over Title VI during the Nixon-Ford period became inextricably embroiled with the enforcement of civil rights laws protecting women, Hispanics, the disabled, and the elderly. These groups emulated the black movement and its reliance on litigation, and ultimately eclipsed it.

As noted in the previous chapter, by the time Richard Nixon entered the White House in 1969 a significant shift in school desegregation policy had occurred. That policy shift, originating with the HEW Guidelines during the Johnson era, measured the success of desegregation by the levels of actual integration achieved in schools. It provided the backdrop to the 1968 presidential campaign and the early Nixon administration decisions on Title VI. To better understand the litigation over Title VI during the Nixon-Ford era, one must appreciate the impact that the provision had on southern school desegregation during the Johnson period.

Enforcing Title VI brought desegregation in localities that had become infamous battlegrounds for civil rights: Selma, Alabama; Philadelphia, Mississippi; Americus, Georgia; and other staunchly segregationist areas in Alabama, Louisiana, and the Black Belt counties of Georgia, South Carolina, and Virginia. To understand the crucial role played by Title VI in effecting these breakthroughs, one need only compare the progress in desegregating schools for ten years under *Brown* with the progress under Title VI in the Johnson years. Consider, for example, the desegregation progress in the seventeen southern and border states after the passage of Title VI: In the 1964–65 academic year, the first year of enforcement under Title VI, 11 percent of black children in those states attended schools with whites. In 1965–66, that percentage rose to approximately 16 percent; and the following year, it rose again to approximately 24 percent.[1] That was as much progress in desegregation in the southern and border states in three years as there had been under *Brown* in the previous ten years.

Progress was even more dramatic in the eleven states of the former Confederacy, where progress under *Brown* had been meager. In the 1962–63 school year, less than 1 percent of black schoolchildren in the eleven states of the former Confederacy went to school with white children. That percentage inched up to a little over 1 percent in the 1963–64 academic year. During 1964–65, the first year after Congress passed Title VI, that percentage reached 2.25 percent, almost double what it had been the previous year. Consequently, in the first year following passage of Title VI, almost as much desegregation was achieved in the Deep South as had been achieved there in the entire decade following *Brown*. For the 1965–66 school year, the percentage more than doubled again, reaching 6.01 percent. The figure for the 1966–67 academic year was 16.9 percent.[2] Hence, in the heartland of southern resistance, during the first three years under Title VI sixteen times as much desegregation was produced as had been produced under *Brown* during the previous decade.

Between 1964 and 1967, Title VI had produced historic breakthroughs against the previously impregnable walls of segregation in southern schools. Though the vast majority of southern children still remained in segregated schools after the first three years under Title VI, the barriers of segregation had begun to fall. By the end of 1966, the Johnson administration had terminated funds to thirty-two school districts. Under the weight of these terminations and the collaboration between the executive and judicial branches, the first meaningful steps toward southern desegregation at the elementary and secondary school levels occurred.[3]

Nixon's Southern Strategy

In 1968, Richard Nixon grounded his bid for the White House on a "southern strategy" in which he courted the white South by criticizing the racial reforms that had been imposed by federal courts and HEW. Primary among those reforms was school desegregation, especially where it involved efforts to bus children. Rowland Evans and Robert Novak wrote of candidate Nixon, "He left the solid impression . . . throughout the South that as soon as he took the oath of office, President Nixon would fix everything. No one knew exactly how, but the conviction was rampant that by fiat, by new legislation or by packing the courts with strict constructionists, Nixon would make the South whole."[4]

During the 1968 Democratic presidential primaries, Governor George Wallace of Alabama garnered considerable public support by emphasizing his hostility to school desegregation. In an obvious reference to the enforcement of Title VI, Wallace declared that if he were president, he would "bring all these briefcase-toting bureaucrats in the Department of Health, Education and Welfare to Washington and throw their briefcases in the Potomac River."[5]

In the November general election, Nixon pitched his message to attract Wallace voters, making it plain that, if elected, he would slow down school desegregation. Writing of Wallace and Nixon in 1968, Gary Orfield observed,

> Both George Wallace and Richard Nixon emphasized desegregation in their campaigns. Wallace roused southern audiences with his passionate attack on HEW bureaucrats. . . .
>
> [Nixon] said it was "dangerous" to use the threat of federal aid cutoffs to "force a local community to carry out what a federal administrator or bureaucrat may think is best for that local community."[6]

By repeatedly supporting freedom-of-choice plans, Nixon implied that he would change the enforcement of Title VI. His support for freedom of choice, however, was necessarily vague because both the Supreme Court in *Green* and HEW in its Guidelines had determined that adopting a freedom-of-choice plan was not, by itself, sufficient to meet a school district's legal requirements under the Constitution or Title VI. Though *Green* and the Guidelines left Nixon little room to advance a blanket endorsement of freedom of choice, he emphasized that there were good freedom-of-choice plans and poor ones, and insisted that local communities could develop freedom-of-choice plans acceptable to federal bureaucrats and judges.[7]

In a television interview in Greensboro, North Carolina, less than two months before the election, when a reporter asked Nixon what he thought of freedom-of-choice plans, the candidate replied, "I tend to look with, I would say, great concern, uh, whenever I see federal agencies or whenever I see the courts attempting to become, in effect, local school boards. I think the decision in the local areas should be made primarily by people who are more familiar with those problems."[8]

Though the constitutional requirements established by the Court in *Green* limited Nixon's options and forced him to adopt a cautious, vaguely worded policy in support of freedom of choice, there was much greater flexibility and discretion available to him in devising the administration's policy on terminating funds under Title VI. Recall that there were no mandatory statutory requirements, specific administrative regulations, or court decisions establishing when HEW was obliged to terminate assistance to a recipient violating the civil rights provision. Title VI left that decision to the discretion of the executive branch, that is, to the agency providing the funds. Because no agency head would cut off funds without consulting with and receiving the approval of the White House, in practical terms it was the president who controlled whether and when to terminate monies under the civil rights provision.

When asked during a campaign visit to the South whether withholding money under Title VI was a "valid weapon," Nixon responded:

> I think that the use of that power on the part of the Federal Government to force the local community to carry out what a federal administrator or bureaucrat may, what he may think is best for that local community, I think that is a doctrine that is a very dangerous one. . . . I believe that the Supreme Court decision was a correct decision, the *Brown v. Board of Education,* but on the other hand when you go beyond that and say that it is the responsibility of the Federal Government and the federal courts to, in effect, act as local school districts in determining how we carry that out, then to use the power of the federal treasury to withhold funds in order to carry it out, then I think we are going too far.[9]

EARLY NIXON ENFORCEMENT DECISIONS AND POLICIES

The Johnson administration initiated administrative proceedings leading to a possible cutoff of funds in 634 school districts and actually ordered federal funds terminated to about 125 districts.[10] As noted previously, the HEW Guidelines called for all but a few districts in the South to desegregate no later than the fall of 1969. From the moment he won the election, Nixon was under heavy pressure from southern politicians who had supported his candidacy to delay the achievement of that goal. The message came to Nixon from Republican state chairmen and Republican officeholders, and it came through his deputy counsel, Harry Dent, a former chief administrative assistant to Senator Strom Thurmond. Thurmond himself played a central role in pressing Nixon to reevaluate the entire school desegregation program:

> Thurmond appealed to Nixon to halt the fund-cutoff process immediately and take a long look at the entire school desegregation process. Thurmond and other powerful southerners of both parties really wanted, first, a complete end to cutting off funds and, second, a lifting of the "terminal desegregation" deadlines, which in most cases set a 1969–70 deadline for starting desegregation.[11]

Nixon did not wait long to keep his campaign pledge on Title VI. In his first year in office, he made several decisions that had a profound impact on school desegregation and the enforcement of Title VI. Those decisions, in turn, precipitated the extraordinary *Adams* litigation that, in many ways, constitutes the central subject of the rest of this study, for *Adams* dominated the school desegregation efforts under Title VI for nearly two decades.

The Initial Mississippi Delays

Within its first weeks in office, the administration decided to delay an order by Johnson's outgoing HEW secretary, Wilbur Cohen, terminating funds to five Mississippi school districts. Under political pressure from the South and after personal consultation with Nixon, Robert Finch, the new HEW secretary, announced a sixty-day stay in the implementation of his predecessor's order. Finch made it plain that he did not believe that terminating funds was a desirable way to achieve school desegregation. Speaking about racial integration in schools, he said, "You can't do it with a sledge hammer, and you can't do it overnight—without tearing a community to pieces." Referring to Title VI, he declared that "the worst thing you can do is just lopping off funds and closing down schools."[12]

In a lengthy, highly publicized interview he gave to *U.S. News and World Report* a month and a half after Nixon's inauguration, Finch indicated that he would not insist on quick progress in school desegregation under pain of loss of federal funds. The article—entitled "New Approach to Integration?"—highlighted the administration's caution. Maintaining that terminating federal dollars often hurt black children more than whites, Finch stated that he saw his role as that of a broker committed to more sophisticated approaches to desegregating schools than merely withholding federal funds.[13] One HEW official, a leader of the agency's desegregation effort, said that the *U.S. News and World Report* interview was widely read and often referred to by southern school officials negotiating with HEW: "It was bad from our point of view. I'd swear every time I walked into a superintendent's office he'd wave a copy of that article in my face."* On the impact of Finch's public remarks, another HEW official stated, "[T]hose statements have set us back tremendously. . . . They're just killing us down South. Everybody believes there's going to be a change. As a result, they don't even want to talk to the people in our regional offices. They want to come to Washington. The problem is, they can get away with it."[14] Finch's stated reluctance to terminate funds was a precursor of what was to come — a formal announcement, in July 1969, making that reluctance the official enforcement policy of the administration.

The July 1969 Mitchell-Finch Policy Statement on Title VI

To understand the Nixon administration's July 1969 policy statement, announced jointly by Attorney General Mitchell and HEW secretary Finch, it is necessary to recall key provisions of Title VI. Agencies could effect compliance with Title VI either by terminating funds or "by any other means authorized by law." The primary "other means" available was referral of the case by the funding agency to the Justice Department, with a recommendation that the department initiate a civil action against the offending recipient. Whether the granting agency chose to terminate or to litigate, the statute requires that "no such action shall be taken until the department or agency concerned has advised the appropriate person or persons of the failure to comply . . . and has determined that compliance cannot be secured by voluntary means."[15]

The Nixon administration's Title VI policy was based on a careful reading of these provisions, a sophisticated understanding of the mechanics of the statute, and a desire to send a signal to southerners that the administration intended to relieve the pressure on them to desegregate. First, the July 1969 policy statement de-emphasized the termination of funds, declaring that the administration intended to

---

*Here and throughout the remainder of this book, where direct quotes appear without citations they are drawn from personal interviews with individuals who were assured that their identity would not be divulged.

minimize the number of cases in which it used that remedy. Instead, the administration announced, it was committed to making greater efforts to convince school districts to comply voluntarily and, where that failed, to enforcing Title VI through lawsuits initiated by the Justice Department. Second, whereas HEW had previously established the beginning of the 1969–70 academic year as the deadline for the desegregation of southern schools, the Nixon administration announced that it had no target date. To insist on an across-the-board deadline, the administration declared, would be to establish an "arbitrary" policy that was "too rigid to be either workable or equitable."[16] Third, the administration announced a major Title VI school desegregation initiative in the North, the West, and the Midwest.

Ben C. Dawkins, a federal district court judge in Louisiana who was overseeing school desegregation in numerous Louisiana school districts, had an unusual reaction to the Mitchell-Finch statement. In June 1969, HEW had proposed a plan covering thirty-seven Louisiana school districts required to complete desegregating before the fall. Negotiations between HEW and the districts about the acceptance of HEW's plan were under way and, according to some officials, were close to fruition when Finch and Mitchell issued their announcement.

In a statement published in the *Shreveport Times* the same day as the Mitchell-Finch announcement, Judge Dawkins expressed his gratitude to the administration for making the policy change. Noting that he had received five thousand letters opposing HEW's plan in past weeks, the judge characterized the plan as "outrageous" and surmised that the new policy would "give considerably more elbow room than was available before." Though Dawkins acknowledged that it would be inappropriate for him to discuss the plans for any particular district, he did say that "in general we can state without reservation that the new policies issued today give all of us — federal courts, school boards, parents of school age children . . . a sort of new breath of fresh air to replace the virtually intolerable situation all of us were faced with."[17]

The response from northern liberals and the civil rights community was predictable. New York's Republican senator, Jacob Javits, characterized the statement as "an invitation to the eight hundred school districts still to be desegregated . . . to further defer a long overdue historic change." Minnesota's Walter Mondale said that the resulting delay would be "both tragic and unnecessary," and Michigan's Philip Hart, "the conscience of the Senate," said that though he had "never made the charge that President Nixon made a deal with the South to

win the nomination . . . events are beginning to speak for themselves."[18]

Roy Wilkins of the NAACP said that the Mitchell-Finch policy
statement was "almost enough to make you vomit."[19] Joseph Rauh,
the vice-chairman of the liberal Americans for Democratic Action
and general counsel to the Leadership Conference on Civil Rights,
characterized the policy as "a sellout of civil rights." In a statement
issued by its chairman, the Reverend Theodore Hesburgh, the U.S.
Commission on Civil Rights criticized the decision to shift from cutting federal monies to litigating in federal court, calling it a "major
retreat in the struggle to achieve meaningful school desegregation."[20]
Charles Bullock and Harrell Rodgers, scholars of civil rights enforcement methods, characterized the new policy as "a blueprint for failure," which held out "faint hope that meaningful progress would [be]
achieved under the new procedure." Commenting on the administration's July 1969 policy statement, they observed that the new policy
"deemphasized the technique that had proven best at achieving school
desegregation in recalcitrant school districts (HEW fund cutoffs),
and adopted a technique that had proven bankrupt before, the individual negotiations with school boards backed by litigation brought
by the Department of Justice."[21]

Approximately a month after the announcement of the administration's new policy, in an unusual action taken at the direction of the
president, Secretary Finch wrote to the chief judge of the U.S. Court
of Appeals for the Fifth Circuit asking the court to delay ordering
thirty-three Mississippi school districts to desegregate. After the
administration won its delay from the Fifth Circuit, the NAACP
Legal Defense Fund (LDF) appealed. On that appeal, for the first
time since 1954, LDF lawyers and government lawyers were on opposing sides in a school desegregation case, and also for the first time
since *Brown*, the federal government appeared in court to argue for
slowing the pace of school desegregation. With its July 1969 statement, its delaying of enforcement actions in Mississippi, and its letter to the Fifth Circuit, the administration consolidated its political
position on school desegregation.

The Firing of Leon Panetta and Its Aftermath

Following the administration's decision to seek delays in school
desegregation in Mississippi, there was an unprecedented, public
revolt within the Justice Department's Civil Rights Division. Sixty-
five of the division's one hundred attorneys signed a petition charac-

terizing the administration's actions as "inconsistent with clearly defined legal mandates" and as evidence of "a disposition on the part of responsible officials of the federal government to subordinate clearly defined legal requirements to non-legal considerations."[22] When Nixon saw the item in his daily "News Summary" he was irate, demanding of Robert Haldeman, his chief of staff, "Get their names! Have their resignations on my desk by Monday."[23]

One highly visible head did roll. The administration dismissed Leon Panetta, director of the Office for Civil Rights (OCR). OCR was in the Department of Health, Education, and Welfare, having been established in 1967 to oversee the enforcement of Title VI throughout the department. Panetta, a liberal Republican from California, had fought a quiet internal battle within the administration on Title VI enforcement since his appointment. In his first few months in office, he had cut off funds to southern school districts that had not filed acceptable desegregation plans.[24] Panetta's battle with the administration ended in February 1970, when Nixon announced Panetta's resignation. Shortly thereafter, Nixon's commissioner of education, James E. Allen, was also forced to resign because, apparently, he also disagreed with the administration's school desegregation policies. At a news conference held after he left, Allen commented that the "Administration's concern is with meeting the minimum requirements of the Civil Rights Act."[25]

After his dismissal from OCR, Panetta declared his "consternation at the tendency of this administration to sell everything, including its stand on civil rights, for political profit."[26] He observed, "It takes the complete leadership of the President and the Secretary [of HEW] to say we're not going to back away [on Title VI enforcement]." Presidents Kennedy and Johnson had exerted leadership, he declared, "and the South got the message," but in the Nixon administration "the message has never been clear."[27] The political value of firing Panetta was not lost on Nixon, who told his domestic policy adviser, John Ehrlichman, that firing Panetta was "worth dozens of speeches and statements about integrating the schools."[28]

On the day Nixon appointed Panetta's successor, Stanley Pottinger, 125 members of the OCR staff (more than one-third of the total) sent a letter to the president expressing their "bitter disappointment" at the ouster of Panetta and at the administration's enforcement policies.[29] The letter called on the president to exercise the "moral leadership that we feel is now essential to avoid a reversal of the nation's longstanding commitment to equal opportunity."[30] When the White House received the letter, the president's press secretary, Ronald Ziegler, issued a strongly worded statement declaring that the president intended to control the enforcement of Title VI and the enforcement officials in OCR. One long-time OCR official commented, "When Ziegler announced that those people over there [at OCR] better do what the president says or heads will roll — well that's a frightening thing to a bureaucrat who is of a certain age and who may have difficulty getting a new job. After that, the bottom fell out of the program."

By 1970, the issues of race and school desegregation had evolved as national issues, and the way the nation thought about these problems was different than it had been during the Johnson years. Both southerners and northern liberals pointed with increasing frequency to racial segregation in the North and to the unfairness, if not hypocrisy, of focusing school desegregation efforts solely on the South. Moreover, Nixon and his aides downplayed the need for government to do more to protect the civil rights of blacks. In January 1970, Nixon aide Daniel Patrick Moynihan wrote to the president suggesting that the alienation and disaffection within the black community was so great that "the time may have come when the issue of race could benefit from a period of 'benign neglect'" since the "subject has been too much talked about." Moynihan suggested that the administration pay greater attention to the problems of Mexican Americans, American Indians, and Puerto Ricans. At the bottom of the memorandum Nixon scribbled, "I agree."[31]

Nixon seemed to be personally in charge of his administration's school desegregation polices. In a meeting at his San Clemente home in July 1970, he explained what he saw as the political liabilities of school desegregation to a small group of top advisers, and then directed them to "quit bragging about school desegregation. We do what the law requires — nothing more."[32] When an aide to John Ehrlichman wrote to Ehrlichman that in Dallas and Richmond he had received complaints of "over enforcement" of civil rights laws, Nixon scrawled angrily to Ehrlichman in the margin of the memo, "I want you personally to jump Richardson + Justice + tell them to *knock off this crap*. I hold them personally accountable to keep their left-wingers in step with my express policy — do what the law requires and not *one bit* more."[33] Nixon's biographer Stephen Ambrose remarked, "Above all, Nixon wanted 'as low a profile as possible' on desegregation." Ambrose, an even-handed and at times admiring biographer, explained further that

Nixon's defenders pointed out, rightly, that there was more desegregation during his Administration than under any other President. But, obviously, this was because the laws had been put on the books in 1964 and 1965 and the courts had ruled that they had to be enforced. Nixon had to be hauled kicking and screaming into desegregation on a meaningful scale, and he did what he did, not because it was right but because he had no choice.[34]

THE SUPREME COURT'S DIRECTIVES IN ALEXANDER, SWANN, AND MILLIKEN

The Nixon administration policies on Title VI produced a different kind of relationship between HEW and the courts than had existed in the Johnson period. Though the Fifth Circuit granted the administration's request for a delay in desegregating thirty-three Mississippi school districts, that decision and the administration's "go-slow" policy met with a resounding and unanimous rejection by the Supreme Court in October 1969 in *Alexander v. Holmes.* The Court moved with dispatch to decide the Mississippi case, hearing it just two weeks after the term started and then handing down its decision six days later.

In a unanimous, tersely worded opinion written by Warren Burger, the man Richard Nixon himself had nominated as chief justice, the Court declared that the case was of "paramount importance" and that the "continued operation of segregated schools under a standard of 'all deliberate speed' for desegregation is no longer constitutionally permissible." "[U]nder explicit holdings of this Court," Burger wrote, "the obligation of every school district is to terminate dual school systems *at once* and to operate now and hereafter only unitary schools."[35] *Alexander* contradicted Nixon administration policy and a widely publicized statement by the president, only a month earlier, characterizing those who advocated immediate desegregation as "extremists."[36] *Alexander,* coming on the heels of the *Green* decision the previous term, reinforced the Court's insistence that there be genuine, immediate progress in desegregating southern schools.

The Court's message in *Alexander* could not be misread. It was a rebuke to the administration. Though Nixon could not control the Supreme Court, he could control the federal government's lawyers, and in the wake of *Alexander* he was intent on doing just that. In his memoirs, he explained that he was "determined to ensure . . . that the many young liberal lawyers in HEW and in the Justice Department's Civil Rights Division would not treat this decision as a carte blanche for them to run wild through the South enforcing compliance with extreme or punitive requirements they had formulated in Washington."[37]

Though it was a rebuke, *Alexander* was also a perfect political solution to the dilemma that Nixon faced with regard to school desegregation. By the end of 1969, there was no realistic possibility that the South would be permitted to continue to require segregation in schools. No president could allow the South to do that. What *Alexander* afforded the administration was what so many politicians needed, wanted, and exploited in the battle over school desegregation: a court order that left them no choice but to insist on desegregation and that enabled them to hold a federal court to blame. Harry Dent confirmed the political value of *Alexander* by noting that the "southern reaction [to *Alexander*] was one of placing blame on the Court and recognizing that Nixon had tried to be helpful."[38] The decisions in *Green* and *Alexander*, however, did not end southern opposition to school desegregation or resolve all the legal uncertainties about it. As evidence of that continuing opposition and uncertainty, in the ten months between December 1969 and September 1970 the Fifth Circuit heard 166 appeals in school desegregation cases.[39]

In *Swann v. Charlotte-Mecklenburg Board of Education*, decided in April 1971, the Court noted that the "problems encountered by the district courts and courts of appeals make it plain that we should now try to amplify guidelines, however incomplete, for the assistance of school authorities and courts." In its unanimous opinion in *Swann*, the Court reaffirmed the policy advanced in *Green* and *Alexander* that balancing the racial composition of the student population in schools was a signal part of the desegregation process. Accordingly, the Court ruled that school districts had "broad power" to establish "a prescribed ratio of Negro to white students reflecting the proportion for the district as a whole." Though the Court noted that there was no constitutional right to have the racial balance of a school reflect the districtwide racial composition, it did rule that "the racial composition of the whole system is likely to be a useful starting point in shaping a remedy to correct past constitutional violations" and that it was within the power of district courts to use that measure to fashion their remedies.[40]

Where there had been a history of de jure segregation in a district, the Court ruled that there was "a presumption against schools that are substantially disproportionate in their racial composition" when compared to the racial composition of the entire school district.[41] In such districts, the school board had the burden of showing that student assignments were "genuinely nondiscriminatory." The Court ruled that to facilitate desegregation, it was permissible to alter school attendance zones, to pair and group noncontiguous zones, and to use bus transportation. Emphasizing the "broad remedial powers" of district courts, the Court declared that desegregation remedies might be burdensome, "administratively awkward, inconvenient, and even bizarre in some situations."[42]

Whereas the Court's unanimous decisions in *Green* in 1968, *Alexander* in 1969, and *Swann* in 1971 reaffirmed and expanded the affirmative obligation to achieve integrated schools, the Court's five-to-four decision in 1974 in *Milliken v. Bradley* severely limited school desegregation in urban school districts, where the overwhelming majority of the nation's black children attended school. In Detroit, as in many other large cities, the majority of schoolchildren were black, and there were many separately governed neighboring suburban systems that were overwhelmingly white. After finding that segregation existed in Detroit and that the state had contributed to that segregation, the district judge in *Milliken* had designated fifty-three of the eighty-five surrounding suburban districts as the "desegregation area" and ordered a desegregation plan for that entire metropolitan area. In affirming that decision, the Sixth Circuit remarked, "[A]ny less comprehensive a solution than a metropolitan area plan would result in an all-black system immediately surrounded by practically all-white suburban school systems."[43] In one of the most controversial decisions in the history of school desegregation litigation, the Supreme Court reversed the decision.

Chief Justice Burger, writing for the sharply divided Court, argued that there was no basis for extending the remedy to outlying suburban districts. Unpersuaded that the state had played a role in contributing to segregation in suburban Detroit, Burger argued that black plaintiffs in Detroit had a constitutional right to attend a unitary school system in their own district, and that any remedy had to be limited to that district. To hold otherwise, he claimed, would dramatically and unjustifiably extend the constitutional right in school desegregation cases. In a searing dissent, Justice Marshall declared, "[I]n the short run, it may seem to be the easier course to allow our great metropolitan areas to be divided up each into two cities—one white, the other black—but it is a course, I predict, our people will ultimately regret."[44] *Milliken* was a turning point. It was one of the first non-unanimous Supreme Court decisions in a school desegregation case, and the first time that the Court had overruled a desegregation decree in the three years since its *Swann* decision endorsing the broad remedial powers of district courts.[45]

Because the plaintiffs in *Milliken* tried to get the Court to link the remedy for racial segregation in Detroit to a metropolitan desegregation plan that included the suburbs, *Milliken* dramatically confronted the new racial inequalities in education that pervaded virtually all major cities in the decades following World War II. That the Court refused to acknowledge that the state was responsible for the concentration of black students in city school systems and for the existence of nearly all-white suburban districts attests to the capacity of courts to employ legal concepts that ignore social realities and that abstract issues in litigation from their social context. In America's greatest cities, by the end of the decade in which the Court decided *Milliken,* even the limited educational goal that had emerged from the late 1960s — racial integration — was endangered. By 1980, in many of the nation's largest cities, including New York, Los Angeles, Baltimore, Washington, D.C., and Chicago, whites represented a numerical minority of the total public school population and lived in highly segregated neighborhoods, raising serious impediments to achieving racial integration in schools.

The controversy surrounding the Nixon administration's enforcement of Title VI and the Court's decisions in *Alexander, Swann,* and *Milliken* also highlight how thoroughly the racial body count approach dominated the legal campaign for educational opportunity for blacks. The legal strategy intended to achieve equal educational opportunity increasingly focused on mechanical issues associated with achieving racial balance in schools. It ignored considerations having to do with the quality of the education provided to black children, the desperate conditions of urban life facing increasing numbers of those children, and the need to conceive of access to education as part of a strategy for achieving greater political and economic power for African Americans.

Though *Green, Alexander, Swann,* and *Milliken* set the larger context within which OCR enforced Title VI, the litigation affecting Title VI most directly in the Nixon-Ford era came not from the Supreme Court or the Fifth Circuit, but quite unexpectedly, from a federal district court in Washington, D.C. There, in October 1970, in *Adams v. Richardson,* volunteer attorneys representing the NAACP Legal Defense Fund challenged the legality of the administration's Title VI enforcement policies. That challenge, to the surprise of all involved, spawned two decades of landmark civil rights litigation over Title VI, ultimately affecting virtually all of the federal government's civil rights enforcement efforts, and shifting the focus of the legal debate even further away from educational issues.

THE START OF THE *ADAMS* LITIGATION

The Issues Initially Raised

How long could HEW wait in its attempt to persuade school districts to comply with Title VI "voluntarily" before it was obliged to either terminate funds or refer a case to the Justice Department? That was the initial central question in *Adams*.[46]

Representing the plaintiffs was the firm of longtime Washington civil rights activist Joseph Rauh. Rauh, first in his class at Harvard Law School, former law clerk to Justices Brandeis and Frankfurter, and founder and former president of the liberal Americans for Democratic Action, was a venerable civil rights lawyer and social activist. Rauh wrote the historic civil rights plank of the 1948 Democratic Party platform that proved to be a model for much of the national civil rights legislation during the next two decades. In 1964, he represented the Mississippi Freedom Democratic Party, a group that challenged the seating of the all-white, regular Democratic Party at that year's Democratic National Convention. And for forty years he was the general counsel to the Leadership Conference on Civil Rights. Often described as "the personal embodiment of American Liberalism," Rauh was a leading supporter of the major civil rights legislative proposals in the 1950s and 1960s and had helped draft the 1964 Civil Rights Act.[47] After Congress enacted those measures, Rauh observed that "what our generation has done is bring equality in law. The next generation has to bring equality in fact."[48] The *Adams* case, at least in its origins, was an attempt to use litigation to do just that.

Rauh was well connected in Democratic Party circles. Photographs in his Connecticut Avenue law office showed him in the company of Democratic Party luminaries, including Democratic presidents, going back to the 1940s. Nonetheless, Rauh insisted that partisan politics had nothing to do with his decision to bring the *Adams* lawsuit. As if to underscore that point, at the news conference called after the filing of the suit in October 1970 Rauh implied that Title VI had never been enforced effectively. With the confidence characteristic of seasoned civil rights litigators, he concluded, "[I]f the courts say it hasn't been enforced, that is going to be important."[49] Hence, from the outset of the litigation there were high hopes about the capacity of courts to correct failings in the enforcement of Title VI.

Rauh's firm, working closely with the NAACP Legal Defense Fund and covertly with disaffected HEW bureaucrats, alleged that HEW's failure to terminate funds after protracted, unsuccessful negotiations with school districts constituted a "calculated default" in enforcing

Title VI.[50] The *Adams* plaintiffs alleged that since March 1970, when Stanley Pottinger had replaced Leon Panetta as director of the Office for Civil Rights, OCR had stopped enforcing Title VI in southern elementary, secondary, and higher education. For example, whereas HEW had terminated funds to forty-six school districts between the summer of 1968 and the summer of 1969, it terminated funds to a lone school district in the 1969–70 academic year.[51] HEW's abdication of its responsibilities, the plaintiffs in *Adams* contended, was the direct result of the Mitchell-Finch policy statement in July 1969. The plaintiffs argued that the administration's policy, emphasizing greater efforts to achieve voluntary compliance through negotiation, was a subterfuge for its real objective: to cease enforcing Title VI entirely, for political reasons.

HEW's comptroller general, the plaintiffs noted, estimated that the time HEW took to negotiate with school districts to coax them into voluntarily complying with Title VI ranged from fifteen to forty-eight months and averaged thirty-three months.[52] That should not be permissible, the plaintiffs insisted, for it effectively gutted Title VI of meaning. The plaintiffs sought injunctive and declaratory relief compelling HEW to act to meet its enforcement obligations under Title VI.

HEW argued that it was enforcing Title VI. HEW secretary Elliot Richardson, alluding to the significant increase in the numbers of students attending desegregated schools, charged that it "is ironic that, during the school year in which the nation has registered its greatest desegregation progress, a lawsuit has been filed charging the department with failure to carry out its responsibilities in this field."[53] In responding to the complaint, government lawyers argued that federal courts should not dictate how the executive branch should enforce Title VI:

> It is practically impossible for any court to provide for comprehensive direction of the future administration of HEW's enforcement responsibilities under Title VI. To do so realistically would require a judicial determination regarding resource allocation within HEW, setting priorities as between Title VI enforcement in education and Title VI enforcement in other areas, arbitrary setting of time limits on the negotiating of voluntary compliance and a myriad of other matters . . . [I]ssues regarding determinations of this type are not appropriate for judicial control.[54]

What jurisprudential and practical considerations limit a court's power to review and control the enforcement of a civil rights law by a federal agency? How can a court determine whether a federal agency is enforcing a civil rights law in good faith; and if the court concludes that the agency is not acting in good faith, what measures may it take to remedy that? In his initial decision in *Adams,* Judge John Pratt of the federal district court for the District of Columbia provided a beginning framework for considering those questions; for all its boldness and assertiveness, it revealed much about the limits of judicial power to control the enforcement of civil rights laws.

The District Court Decision

Judge Pratt found that the plaintiffs had documented a failure by HEW to enforce Title VI during the Nixon administration. During the Johnson years, HEW had initiated approximately six hundred administrative enforcement proceedings against school districts accused of noncompliance with Title VI. During the Nixon administration's first year, the rate at which HEW initiated Title VI enforcement proceedings dropped somewhat. Thereafter, it dropped dramatically. From March 1970, the month that Stanley Pottinger succeeded Leon Panetta, through February 1971, HEW instituted not one administrative enforcement proceeding.

The impact of the Nixon administration's policies was even more dramatic with respect to fund terminations. Forty-four school districts had had their funding terminated during the 1968–69 school year, almost exclusively as a result of administrative proceedings commenced by the Johnson administration and inherited by the Nixon administration. There was only one cutoff ordered in the 1969–70 academic year, and none ordered from that time to the date of Pratt's initial order in November 1972.

Pratt conceded that negotiations with school districts could take time and that HEW had some discretion to continue negotiations rather than commencing administrative enforcement proceedings leading to the possible termination of funds. He concluded, however, that such discretion was not unlimited. Where a substantial period of time had elapsed, during which attempts to achieve voluntary compliance had not been made or had proven unsuccessful, Pratt ruled that HEW's discretion to seek voluntary compliance had ended. In those situations, ruled Pratt, HEW had a duty to effectuate the goals of Title VI by either determining, through an administrative proceeding, whether a recipient was discriminating, or by referring the matter to the Justice Department for litigation so that a determination could be made by a court.[55] Pratt's order established the agenda for the legal and political fights over Title VI for the next fifteen years. It included the following provisions: (1) an order regarding desegregation of higher education in ten states; (2) an order to begin enforcement proceedings in connection with violations of Title VI; (3) an order requiring HEW to ensure that school districts receiving federal money were in compliance with the Supreme Court's decision in *Swann;* (4) an order requiring HEW to monitor school districts under court order; and (5) an order requiring HEW to issue reports of its compliance with Pratt's orders and to process complaints within a specific time frame.

The Order Regarding Desegregation of Higher Education in Ten States. Between January 1969 (the month Nixon became president) and February 1970, HEW had concluded that ten southern states were operating segregated systems of public higher education, in violation of Title VI. These were states that had long operated historically black colleges and universities, dating back to the era when states barred blacks from attending colleges and universities with whites. Five of these states ignored HEW's request for a desegregation plan and never submitted one, and the other five submitted plans that HEW found unacceptable. When Pratt decided *Adams* in November 1972, HEW had not yet taken any formal action under Title VI, even though between eighteen and thirty-six months had elapsed since the states had submitted the plans. Pratt enjoined HEW, within 120 days of his order, to either commence Title VI administrative enforcement proceedings against the ten states or "to utilize any other means authorized by law, in order to effect compliance with Title VI."[56]

The Order to Commence Enforcement Proceedings in Connection with Violations of Title VI. In the 1970–71 school year, HEW determined that 113 school districts had either reneged on previously approved desegregation plans or had otherwise violated Title VI. It referred 8 of the 113 districts to the Justice Department and initiated administrative enforcement proceedings against seven others. As to the remaining ninety-eight districts, Pratt noted that HEW knew that seventy-four remained out of compliance with Title VI and yet the agency had not begun enforcement proceedings against them. Pratt ordered HEW to begin enforcement proceedings against those seventy-four school districts within sixty days or to use any other means authorized by law to effect compliance with Title VI.[57]

The Order Requiring HEW to Ensure That School Districts Receiving Federal Money Were in Compliance with Swann. After the Supreme Court decided *Swann* in April 1971, HEW identified many southern school districts that were not under court order and that had one or more schools composed mostly of minority students. For example, even though HEW knew of eighty-five districts that had one or more schools with at least a 20-percent disproportion between the percentage of minority students in the school and the percentage in the entire school district, and even though the Court in *Swann* ruled that there was "a presumption against schools that are substantially disproportionate in their racial composition," HEW did not require any of those eighty-five districts to justify or explain the racial breakdown in those schools.[58] Pratt ruled that continued financial assistance to those eighty-five districts violated Title VI, and that HEW had a duty to require each of those districts to explain why there was a racial disproportion in its schools.

Pratt also noted that HEW had mailed letters to ninety-one school districts in the summer of 1971 notifying them that under *Swann* further steps to desegregate might be required. Of those ninety-one districts, HEW had received acceptable desegregation plans from thirty-seven, had given notice to three for administrative hearings, and had found *Swann* inapplicable to another nine. That left forty-two remaining school districts out of the original ninety-one that HEW deemed to be in presumptive violation of *Swann*. Despite that presumption, HEW was still reviewing those districts when Pratt handed down his decision in November 1972. Pratt ordered that unless the presumption was overcome by information provided by the districts, HEW had sixty days either to commence enforcement proceedings or to begin to use other means authorized by law to effectuate compliance with Title VI.

The Order Requiring HEW to Monitor School Districts under Court Order. Approximately 640 school districts under court order to desegregate in the seventeen southern and border states received money from HEW, among them some of the largest school districts in the South. As previously noted, where a school district was under a desegregation order of a federal court, HEW accepted that order as evidence of compliance with Title VI. Judge Pratt ordered HEW, to the extent that its resources permitted, to monitor the compliance of school districts under court order and to report its findings to the court.

The Order Requiring HEW to Issue Reports of Its Compliance with the Court's Orders and to Process Complaints within Specified Time Frames. Pratt ordered HEW to provide the plaintiffs' attorneys with periodic reports of its activities in connection with each aspect of his order. He ordered that the reports contain

- A description of each complaint or any information received by HEW relating to racial discrimination in educational institutions
- The reasons for any failure by HEW to determine the validity of a complaint within 120 days in higher education and 90 days in elementary and secondary education
- HEW's findings for each complaint
- The reasons for any failure by HEW to commence enforcement proceedings within ninety days of making a finding of racial discrimination

Hence, Pratt's order mandated specified periods of time within which HEW had to determine the validity of complaints of racial discrimination under Title VI; and where HEW found a violation, Pratt gave the agency ninety days to achieve voluntary compliance through negotiations. After that ninety-day period, HEW was compelled either to commence administrative enforcement proceedings or to act to enforce Title VI by other means authorized by law.

The reporting requirement obliging HEW to provide the plaintiffs' attorneys with an account of its progress in complying with the decree was significant. Recognizing that HEW's enforcement of Title VI would raise continuing problems between civil rights lawyers and HEW, Pratt imposed a remedy that was prospective in character and that provided some way for the plaintiffs to monitor HEW's future compliance with Title VI and his orders. The reports would provide the plaintiffs continuing data about HEW's performance, and an opportunity to assess and criticize HEW and to initiate further litigation if needed.

The *Adams* decision was another judicial rebuke to the Nixon administration. To make matters worse for HEW, Pratt awarded attorneys' fees to Rauh's law firm, making it more likely that they would be able and inclined to bring future legal challenges. "The heart of the matter," declared Rauh, "is that the Court has held that cutting off funds is not discretionary as Secretaries Finch and Richardson have maintained."[59] The government appealed.

The government's argument on appeal emphasized that HEW's discretion in enforcing Title VI was comparable to the prosecutorial discretion of the attorney general and hence was beyond the authority of courts to review. The U.S. Court of Appeals for the District of Columbia, sitting *en banc,* affirmed Pratt's decision unanimously. In rejecting the government's position, the court observed that HEW's decision to rely on voluntary compliance was "particularly significant in view of the admitted effectiveness of fund termination proceedings in the past to achieve the congressional objective."[60] The only modifications the court of appeals made in the district court's order was in lengthening slightly the time frames that applied to reviews of desegregation plans in higher education. Explaining that decision, it declared itself "mindful that desegregation problems in colleges and universities differ widely from those in elementary and secondary schools, and that HEW admittedly lacks experience in dealing with them. HEW must carefully assess the significance of a variety of new factors as it moves into an unaccustomed area."[61]

Recognizing the unique characteristics of higher education, the court of appeals noted that desegregation in higher education should be handled on a statewide basis and that a major objective should be "to provide more and better trained minority group doctors, lawyers, engineers and other professionals."[62] The court elaborated:

> A predicate for minority access to quality post-graduate programs is a viable, coordinated state-wide higher education policy that takes into account the special problems of minority students and Black colleges. As *amicus* points out, these Black institutions currently fulfill a crucial need and will continue to play an important role in Black higher education.[63]

The amicus to which the court referred was the National Association for Equal Opportunity in Higher Education (NAFEO), an organization formed in 1969 and composed of the presidents of 110 predominantly black colleges and universities. NAFEO officials and the organization's lawyers played a key role in desegregation in higher education in the years following Judge Pratt's initial order.

In prevailing at the district court and the court of appeals, Rauh and his legal team had overcome a substantial initial hurdle. They had convinced Pratt, a moderate Republican jurist and one not predisposed to dramatic and novel uses of judicial power, that HEW could not keep its own house in order and that it was proper for the court to issue detailed orders dictating what HEW was to do in enforcing Title VI. The result was an unusual and elaborate court order intended to curb and correct the Nixon policy announced in July 1969.

Aggressive and unorthodox though Pratt's intervention was, one must appreciate that it was entirely procedural in character. Indeed, the court of appeals noted that the district court order did not resolve substantive questions about racial discrimination "but merely requires initiation of a *process* which, excepting contemptuous conduct, will then pass beyond the District Court's continuing control and supervision."[64] There was nothing in Pratt's order that directly controlled the substance of the enforcement process — HEW's decision about whether a violation existed or about the remedy that should be imposed for violations. On the contrary, Pratt's decision did not have anything to do with defining racial discrimination in federally funded programs or with the measures that Title VI required recipients of federal funds to take.

Implications of the Adams Suit

When the lawyers from Joseph Rauh's law firm filed suit to challenge the Nixon administration's Title VI enforcement policy in 1970, none of them could have predicted the range and complexity of the issues that would ultimately confront executive branch officials, the courts, and civil rights groups and their lawyers as an outgrowth of that legal challenge. Few of the legal and political problems targeted by the *Adams* complaint in 1970 were resolved by the time Jimmy Carter became president in January 1977. Many remained unresolved when Ronald Reagan left office more than a decade later. Indeed, the legal questions raised by the *Adams* complaint in 1970 dominated the struggle over the enforcement of Title VI until 1990. It is impossible to separate the enforcement of Title VI in educational institutions from the course and requirements of the *Adams* litigation. The story of Title VI from 1973 to 1990 is the story of that litigation. Unpredictable from its inception, the *Adams* litigation grew in scope to encompass the civil rights protections of virtually every significant minority constituency. It represents the most ambitious and enduring effort ever mounted to use litigation to ensure the effective enforcement of federally protected civil rights. Spreading its tentacles chaotically and with astonishing rapidity, it required persistent efforts by judges and litigants alike to keep it and the issues it raised under control.

The Suit by the Women's Equity Action League

The first unexpected consequence of Judge Pratt's initial order came not from the actions of the NAACP Legal Defense Fund but from the actions of another civil rights organization, one devoted to protecting the rights of women. In November 1974, the Women's Equity Action League (WEAL), a national women's legal defense organization, filed suit in federal district court in Washington, D.C., against HEW and the Department of Labor for failing to enforce Title IX of the 1972 Education Amendments Act and Executive Orders 11246 and 11375 — provisions prohibiting gender discrimination.[65] WEAL's lawsuit dealt primarily with the enforcement of sex discrimination laws in elementary and secondary schools and institutions of higher education.

The plaintiffs' attorneys in the *WEAL* suit were associated with the Center for Law and Social Policy, a public interest law firm in Washington, D.C. The legal issues raised in the *WEAL* case and the motivation to take the action were inspired by the NAACP Legal Defense Fund's victory in *Adams*. When the District of Columbia court of appeals unanimously affirmed Judge Pratt's initial order in *Adams*, lawyers at the Center for Law and Social Policy decided to bring an action modeled on *Adams* that alleged a calculated default by HEW in the enforcement of the gender discrimination provisions of federal laws. One of the attorneys close to the *WEAL* case explained:

> Many women's groups were upset that there had been no enforcement of the executive orders. Many complaints were filed [with HEW] and little was done about them. Then in 1973 the *en banc* decision in *Adams* came down from the Court of Appeals. That became our basis for believing that we could do the same for women. . . . After all that is the way the law works. At that time Title IX had been passed, but there were no [Title IX] regulations and no Title IX enforcement had been begun. Complaints had been filed but there was no processing of them.

Though WEAL initiated its suit as an independent legal action, the *WEAL* case eventually became inextricably intertwined with *Adams*. The *WEAL* suit marked the first of many instances in which the *Adams* litigation became linked to questions about the enforcement of civil rights laws in ways that neither the *Adams* plaintiffs nor the government were able to predict or control.

Judge Pratt's March 1975 Supplemental Order

Pratt issued his opinion in *Adams* in November 1972, his first order in the case in February 1973, and a supplemental order in 1975.[66] The supplemental order provided the first glimpse of the difficulties associated with trying to compel a federal agency, via court order, to alter the way in which it enforced a law. That order also indicated how tenacious and aggressive Rauh and his colleagues would be in taking advantage of the leverage provided by Pratt's initial order and by Pratt's receptivity to their arguments. Just as important, the supplemental order significantly expanded the scope of Pratt's involvement in and regulation of HEW's enforcement of Title VI. In his supplemental order, Pratt concluded that documentation presented by the *Adams* plaintiffs revealed 125 additional southern districts in which one or more schools had a racial composition that was substantially disproportionate to the overall racial composition of the school district. Pratt ordered HEW to contact those schools and to give them sixty days to explain or rebut that racial disproportion.

Two parts of the supplemental order dealt with HEW's failure to enforce aspects of Pratt's initial 1973 order. First, with respect to thirty-nine of the eighty-five districts identified in Pratt's first order as being in presumptive violation of *Swann*, HEW had not reached a final decision as to whether Title VI had been violated. Pratt ordered HEW, within sixty days, to take action against those districts by either commencing enforcement proceedings or by referring the matter to the Justice Department. Second, Pratt's initial decree also ordered HEW to inform federal courts, to the extent that the agency's resources permitted, about the noncompliance of districts under court order. HEW had brought such information to the attention of the Justice Department but not to the attention of the courts involved. The supplemental order compelled HEW, within 120 days, to bring information about violations of court orders to the attention of the courts that had issued those orders.

Part F of the supplemental order contained the most far-reaching and controversial requirement in the litigation to that point. In Part F, Pratt found that, aside from the school districts expressly identified for specific action in the initial *Adams* order, HEW had not initiated a single administrative enforcement proceeding. Under HEW regulations, the department was required to make a "prompt investigation whenever its own compliance review, or complaint or other information indicated possible noncompliance with Title VI."[67] Observing that HEW had too often delayed in investigating and resolving complaints that alleged violations of Title VI, and had relied too heavily on voluntary and protracted negotiations,[68] Judge Pratt established timetables within which HEW had to resolve complaints of violations of Title VI from any of the seventeen southern and border states. The timetables were as follows: (1) HEW had 90 days from the receipt of a complaint of racial discrimination to determine whether the district was in compliance with Title VI. (2) Whenever HEW determined that the district was not in compliance, the agency had an additional 90 days within which to secure voluntary compliance. (3) Where voluntary compliance was not achieved by the end of that second 90-day period (that is, within 180 days of the receipt of the complaint), HEW had to commence enforcement proceedings or take other actions authorized by law to enforce Title VI.

By successfully going back to Judge Pratt for a supplemental order, the plaintiffs demonstrated their capacity to monitor HEW's compliance with Pratt's orders and, on the basis of that monitoring, to present information to the court to justify further judicial intervention. By imposing time frames prospectively for all of HEW's investigations of complaints of racial discrimination from the seventeen southern and border states, the supplemental order dramatically expanded the court's supervision of the department. It was one thing for Pratt to compel HEW to act in regard to specific cases that HEW had failed to bring to a timely resolution. It was another matter for him to mandate enforcement procedures for all complaints of racial discrimination that HEW handled in a region of the nation, never indicating when and under what circumstances the court's control would end. That widened, future-oriented judicial supervision of OCR gave civil rights lawyers the opportunity to monitor the enforcement of Title VI throughout the South and to return to Judge Pratt's courtroom if HEW failed to meet the requirements he imposed.

Compelling HEW to initiate enforcement actions within detailed time frames for all complaints of racial discrimination in seventeen southern and border states meant that the court had become deeply embroiled in the enforcement of Title VI. How to enforce a law, and whether and when to impose its sanctions, is a matter that goes to the heart of the discretionary power that administrative agencies typically enjoy. For a federal judge to attempt to control that discretion in a major civil rights provision across one-third of the states in the nation was unprecedented. The administration, bridling under the requirements of Part F of the supplemental order, ultimately returned to Judge Pratt in hopes of being freed of its strictures.

THE ADMINISTRATION GOES ON THE OFFENSIVE

The June 1975 Proposals to Consolidate OCR's Regulations

An important legal requirement used by both the plaintiffs and Judge Pratt to justify Part F was the regulation mandating that HEW make a "prompt investigation" whenever a compliance review, report, or complaint indicated a possible violation of Title VI. The Office for Civil Rights, the unit within HEW established to enforce Title VI and other civil rights laws, was responsible for complying with that regulation. In June 1975, less than three months after Pratt issued the supplemental order containing Part F, HEW secretary Weinberger announced a proposed consolidation of the regulations governing the enforcement of civil rights statutes, a change that would have eliminated HEW's obligation to investigate all complaints.[69] He contended that OCR's enforcement responsibilities had grown dramatically since the passage of Title VI, stretching the agency's resources and making it impossible and unwise for the unit to investigate each complaint.

Because Title VI covered approximately sixteen thousand public school districts, three thousand institutions of higher education, and some thirty thousand institutions and agencies delivering health and social services, its enforcement alone was an enormous task. Yet by 1975, that task constituted only a small portion of OCR's overall mandate. Added to OCR's Title VI tasks were its enforcement responsibilities under Title IX of the Education Amendments of 1972, Sections 799A and 845 of the Public Health Service Act, Section 504 of the Rehabilitation Act of 1973, and Executive Order 11246.* In proposing to alter the regulation requiring OCR to investigate every com-

---

*Title IX of the Education Amendments of 1972 prohibited discrimination on the basis of sex in federally funded educational programs and activities. Modeled after Title VI, it applied to approximately sixteen thousand public school districts and twenty-seven hundred institutions of higher education.

Section 799A of the Public Health Service Act, covering approximately fifteen hundred institutions, prohibited the awarding of federal grants, contracts, or other forms of assistance under Title VII to schools of medicine, osteopathy, dentistry, veterinary medicine, optometry, podiatry, and pharmacy unless the secretary of HEW had received satisfactory assurances that the institution was not discriminating in admissions on the basis of sex.

Section 504 of the Rehabilitation Act of 1973, also modeled after Title VI, prohibited discriminating on the basis of physical or mental handicap in any program or activity receiving federal funds. It reached all federally assisted programs and activities, and its universe was coterminous with that of Title VI.

Executive Order 11246 prohibited discrimination on the basis of race, color, national origin, religion, or sex by government contractors or by contractors performing under federally assisted construction contracts. Though this provision was largely administered by the Department of Labor's Office of Federal Contract Compliance, enforcement responsibilities with respect to educational institutions, medical and health institutions, social services facilities, certain nonprofit organizations, and state and local public agencies holding federal government contracts had been delegated to HEW. Under Executive Order 11246, OCR's responsibility covered nearly nine hundred institutions of higher education and some thirty-five hundred contractors.

plaint of racial discrimination, Secretary Weinberger emphasized that when that regulation became effective in 1967, OCR's responsibility had covered only Title VI and Executive Order 11246.

Weinberger proposed the change to get out from under Part F of Judge Pratt's supplemental order. OCR officials argued that Part F made the agency "almost totally complaint-oriented" in enforcing Title VI in the southern and border states, squandering the agency's resources, producing an ineffective Title VI enforcement strategy, and diverting resources from the agency's efforts to enforce other civil rights statutes.[70] HEW's proposed new regulation did not even mention the word *complaint*. It provided only that any person or organization wishing to provide "information" regarding possible noncompliance with Title VI could do so by communicating with OCR's director in writing.[71] OCR would be obliged only to acknowledge each submission of information and would thus be free to determine what action, if any, to take.

The administration's move to eliminate OCR's obligation to investigate each complaint met with uniform and unified opposition by the U.S. Commission on Civil Rights and a broad coalition of 130 civil rights groups, dubbed the Ad Hoc Coalition. Explaining that opposition, one OCR official commented:

> Nobody had the least bit of confidence in us. There was a general belief that our enforcement of Title VI was bankrupt. . . . The June 1975 regulation, giving the agency discretion to choose what it investigated, was the only sensible way for OCR to manage its resources. If we brought in an objective consultant and asked him, it would be clear that we need the discretion to choose where and how to allocate the resources. But no one trusted us to do that in good faith.

Though the Ad Hoc Coalition publicly maintained a unified front, some individuals raised questions privately about whether Part F of the supplemental order, focusing exclusively on complaints of racial discrimination, diverted resources from the enforcement of civil rights provisions other than Title VI. Cynthia Brown, a former OCR employee who was active in the Ad Hoc Coalition, complained that the groups, "who were working together for the first time, were especially annoyed at what they saw as OCR attempts to play one type of group off against another."[72] Over the course of the *Adams* litigation that issue arose repeatedly, as anxiety about competition among the groups that make up the civil rights community did not abate.

The attempt to revise the Title VI regulations in June 1975 was an effort by OCR officials to regain control of their agency from Judge

Pratt. The effort failed. The political outcry by civil rights groups and by congressional representatives caused HEW to rescind the proposed regulations. As of that moment, the civil rights lobby had prevailed in the political struggle to continue to require OCR to investigate every complaint of racial discrimination that it received. Nonetheless, controversy over that requirement persisted as an issue in the *Adams* litigation for years.

OCR's Claim of Insufficient Resources, and Advocacy Groups' Legal Response

The struggle over the investigation of complaints took a dramatic and unexpected turn in October 1975. In that month, OCR's Dallas regional office, which received one-third of all the complaints of racial discrimination in the nation,[73] sent letters to complainants who had alleged civil rights violations other than racial discrimination, stating that because of the demands of the *Adams* orders, OCR had to postpone investigating their complaints. The letters did not say when OCR would resume those investigations. For example, a Hispanic complainant who alleged discrimination based on national origin in a school district received a letter with this explanation:

> We had anticipated conducting a review of the [Beeville Independent School] District in the near future. However, the Federal Court Order in the case *Adams v. Weinberger* has necessitated allocation of a major portion of the Region VI OCR staff resources to the task of resolving problems of race discrimination. Because of the volume of those cases on hand, it will be impossible for us to investigate your complaint at this time.[74]

OCR sent similar letters from its Chicago regional office. Predictably, those letters triggered further litigation. The roots of that litigation went back to November 1974.

As noted earlier in this chapter, in November 1974 WEAL filed suit against HEW in federal district court in the District of Columbia, alleging that the department had failed to enforce federal civil rights laws prohibiting discrimination based on gender. In January 1976, in response to OCR's new policy in the Dallas regional office, the plaintiffs in *WEAL* moved, as part of that lawsuit, to enjoin HEW's regional offices from refusing to investigate Title IX gender discrimination complaints. Given OCR's actions in its Dallas and Chicago regional offices, WEAL had little choice but to seek such an injunction.

Not surprisingly, within days of WEAL's motion for an injunction the Mexican American Legal Defense and Education Fund (MALDEF) moved to intervene in the *WEAL* suit. MALDEF, represented by lawyers from the Washington firm Arnold and Porter, alleged that the letters from HEW's regional offices indefinitely postponing investigations of complaints of discrimination based on national origin amounted to "an illegal and unconstitutional use of a court order to discriminate against Mexican Americans."[75] MALDEF, like WEAL, sought to enjoin HEW from delaying those investigations and to compel it to comply with the regulation requiring it to review promptly all complaints of discrimination. What all the parties to the various lawsuits failed to acknowledge was that notwithstanding that regulation, OCR had never really investigated every complaint. Though the leaders of civil rights groups knew this, they did not want to legitimate that practice by explicitly granting OCR the option to investigate only some complaints. The reason for that was simple. They were wary of officially giving OCR such discretion because of what they perceived to be the hostile attitude of the Nixon and Ford administrations to the enforcement of civil rights.

In the *MALDEF* and *WEAL* suits, civil rights lawyers used the long-unenforced regulation as leverage to eliminate OCR's discretion to select the complaints it would investigate. WEAL and MALDEF hoped to assure equal priority among OCR's various constituencies — that is, to give complaints of discrimination based on gender and national origin the same priority given to complaints of racial discrimination. Their legal moves raised the stakes and widened the focus of the *Adams* litigation.

By 1975, *Adams* no longer involved only judicial regulation of the timely and lawful disposition of complaints alleging racial discrimination under Title VI — a complex and controversial issue in its own right. By the letters it sent out in the Dallas and Chicago regions, OCR had linked the questions about Title VI raised in *Adams* to OCR's handling of complaints of discrimination in other areas. After the WEAL and MALDEF legal actions responding to those letters, what Judge Pratt decided about Title VI in *Adams* became tied to every other aspect of OCR's enforcement activities. The government, by insisting that it could not enforce the requirements of *Adams* in the Title VI area without affecting enforcement in other areas, underscored the interconnectedness of OCR's enforcement of civil rights protections for different minority groups. In light of that interconnectedness, reforms in the enforcement of Title VI could not be considered in isolation from their impact on the enforcement of other civil rights statutes, a realization posing novel and difficult questions.

How should OCR's resources be allocated among its various enforcement responsibilities? What criteria should determine that allocation? How adequate were OCR's resources to meet its legal responsibilities? These questions, normally answered unilaterally by executive branch officials, were resolved in *Adams* through litigation.

The government itself was responsible for this transformation of the *Adams* litigation. When OCR advised those complaining of discrimination based on gender and national origin that their complaints could not be investigated because of *Adams,* it had to know that those letters would prompt objection, produce further legal action, and require a reevaluation of *Adams* and of OCR's policy for investigating complaints and allocating resources. Having precipitated a controversy by the letters it sent out, the government sought to capitalize on the controversy as part of its motion to amend Part F of Judge Pratt's supplemental order — the part imposing time frames for handling complaints of racial discrimination in the seventeen southern and border states.

The Government's Motion to Amend Part F of Pratt's Supplemental Order

In March 1975, HEW moved before Judge Pratt to amend Part F to permit the agency to operate under its own alternative enforcement plan rather than the time frames required in Part F. In proposing to substitute its own plan for Part F of the supplemental order, OCR again sought to wrest control from Pratt. It argued that having to allocate its resources to investigate every complaint of racial discrimination within the court's time frames left it unable to do much else in the seventeen southern and border states. In effect, OCR maintained that resources that could be devoted to protecting other civil rights had to be sacrificed so that OCR would not be in contempt of Part F.

Martin Gerry, acting director of OCR in 1975, emphasized that to comply with Part F, OCR had been forced to reassign personnel and resources from other units and regions of HEW to the Elementary and Secondary Education Division of the Dallas regional office and to postpone or cancel much-needed civil rights enforcement. The agency's proposed enforcement plan sought to "redistribute staff time among multiple objectives so that the interests of no minority group are neglected." Urging Judge Pratt to accept OCR's plan and revoke Part F, Gerry stressed that the agency had multiple constituencies and limited resources, and that "unless OCR's available resources [were] apportioned in an impartial and balanced manner, it [would] be impossible for [it] to serve the competing interests of all its civil rights beneficiaries."[76]

The premise of OCR's motion was that its enforcement plan would yield greater and more equitable civil rights protection than the court-ordered scheme mandated by Part F, which required investigating each Title VI complaint within a specified time period. Agency officials claimed that Part F concentrated too much of OCR's resources on individual rather than systemic patterns of discrimination—"on matters which by their nature often impact on a relatively few people." Peter Holmes, the OCR director who preceded Gerry, explained that "the time required to investigate and resolve these individual complaints can dominate and eventually supplant enforcement efforts designed to eliminate systemic forms of race and sex discrimination often directly affecting hundreds of thousands of students."[77]

In responding to the government's motion, the plaintiffs argued that OCR had failed to establish that it lacked the resources to investigate all complaints in a timely fashion. Even if the government did not have the resources both to comply with Part F and to meet its other civil rights responsibilities, said the plaintiffs, the proper remedy was for OCR to seek funding from Congress to meet all its legal obligations, rather than asking the court to sanction its failure to comply with the law.

The issue reduced itself to whether OCR or Judge Pratt would determine what the agency's enforcement strategy and priorities would be. Law enforcement agencies typically have wide discretion in such matters. Invariably, they do not have the resources to perform fully all of their enforcement responsibilities all of the time. Moreover, political factors also influence enforcement priorities. Finite resources and political considerations, therefore, compel agencies to establish priorities determining the speed, care, vigilance, and vigor with which they enforce legal requirements. Judicial regulation of these matters goes to the heart of administrative power and prosecutorial prerogatives.

JUDGE PRATT'S JUNE 1976 ORDER: A NEGOTIATED SETTLEMENT FOCUSING ON PROCEDURE

In April 1976, thirteen months after the government filed its motion to amend Part F, the motion was still pending before Judge Pratt. Whereas Pratt had imposed timetables and procedural requirements for the handling of complaints of racial discrimination in his initial order in 1973, and in his supplemental order in 1975, he did not impose his own solution in responding to the government's motion to amend Part F. Rather, he facilitated a settlement among the parties and then reduced the terms of that settlement to a court order.

Pratt called top OCR officials and lawyers for the NAACP, WEAL, and MALDEF to his chambers in April 1976 to inform them that unless they reached a resolution among themselves regarding OCR's processing of complaints, he would take matters into his own hands and impose a solution. Summarizing the conference with Pratt and the ensuing discussions among the parties, a lawyer for the LDF wrote that Pratt "directed the parties to try to settle the resources issue. While indicating his belief that an order should remain over HEW's head, he also manifested some sympathy with HEW's lack of resources plea. If the parties were unable to settle, Judge Pratt asserted, he would cut the Gordian knot. Thereafter, all parties have engaged in weekly comprehensive settlement discussions."

Uncertainty in the minds of litigants produces settlements, and at this stage of the *Adams* litigation both the government and the plaintiffs had reason to feel uncertain about what Pratt might do if he did cut the Gordian knot. On the one hand, in his original and supplemental orders Pratt had demonstrated his willingness to impose a detailed enforcement regimen on OCR. In doing so, he embarrassed the agency and stripped it of the authority to manage its own operations. If OCR officials did not reach a negotiated settlement with the plaintiffs, they risked a continued loss of power over their unit, and further litigation, judicial intervention, and political embarrassment.

On the other hand, in April 1976 civil rights leaders believed that Pratt was less inclined to impose a judicial solution favorable to them than he had been at the time of his original order in 1973, and again in his supplemental order two years later. Pratt was neither an activist judge nor a champion of civil rights. The *Adams* decisions were atypical actions for him — actions he justified because of the blatantly politicized enforcement policies of the Nixon administration.

By 1976, there was a new president in the White House, Gerald Ford, for whom race was a less salient political issue than it had been for his predecessor, and there was a new director of OCR, Martin Gerry, in whom Pratt had expressed confidence. In his chambers during the April 1976 conference, Pratt stated that the deliberate recalcitrance in OCR that had existed during the Nixon years was gone. Hence, civil rights lawyers believed that the judge was less inclined than he had been in the past to issue an order controlling how OCR should enforce various civil rights laws. In short, both the government and the civil rights groups had incentives to reach a negotiated solution.

During the course of the settlement discussions, some representatives of the civil rights groups felt that the administration deliberately tried to create tension among the groups lobbying for OCR's resources. Gerry, who was especially interested in the rights of the disabled, was critical of the priority given complaints of racial discrimination in the *Adams* litigation. OCR, as Gerry put it, had "a lot of problems with Judge Pratt's order . . . because it created a preferential order among clients" that "gave one group more rights than others." OCR's "argument" with Pratt, Gerry said, was that it wanted "to create a balanced national approach" so that every kind of complaint was "on an even footing."[78]

Lawyers for the various civil rights groups, sensitive to the possibility that the administration might be attempting to play one against the other, tried to settle their differences in private discussions among themselves in order to present a united front to OCR. The lawyers met with one another informally as frequently as they met with government representatives, conferring prior to virtually every negotiating session with the government.

The groups did have different issues that they wished to press in the negotiations. The women's groups were especially interested in the procedural rights of complainants. Lawyers representing the NAACP Legal Defense Fund were interested in what OCR's obligations would be in enforcing Title VI in programs funded by the Emergency School Assistance Act, a major program providing federal aid to education. Mexican Americans were concerned about the degree to which any settlement would orient OCR's enforcement to investigating complaints rather than to performing compliance reviews. Compliance reviews were systemwide investigations initiated by OCR to determine whether civil rights violations existed in a school district. Lawyers for MALDEF believed that their clients would be best protected by maximizing the number of compliance reviews OCR conducted.

Reflecting on groups' differing capacities to bring complaints and to invoke civil rights laws, OCR director Gerry observed that he thought it "very important . . . to emphasize . . . that groups complain differentially. Some groups . . . complain very quickly and in large numbers, very vociferously and fairly sophisticatedly. Other groups don't."[79] The lawyers from WEAL and the LDF were the most forceful both in the negotiations with the government and in the separate discussions among the lawyers for the various civil rights groups. MALDEF's lawyers from Arnold and Porter, working on a *pro bono* basis, had a limited role in the *Adams* litigation. By contrast, lawyers from Joseph Rauh's firm, representing the LDF, and lawyers from the Center for Law and Social Policy, representing the women's groups, had a long-term interest and involvement in *Adams,* as well as greater resources with which to pursue their interests.

The lawyers for all parties, including the government, met for approximately eight weekly sessions to forge the settlement agreement. They produced a document that Pratt signed as a court order in June 1976. It established, among other things, brisk timetables for the processing of new and backlogged complaints regarding racial, sexual, and national origin discrimination; timetables for the completion of compliance reviews in all of the above areas; and an enumeration of the specific information required for a "complete complaint." It also provided for a variety of procedural rights for complainants, including the right of access to files.

The timetables and procedures that were agreed to included the following:

- After providing written notice of its receipt of a complaint, OCR would within the next ninety days make a written finding as to whether a violation had occurred.
- If OCR concluded that a violation of law had occurred, it would during the next ninety days seek voluntary compliance and corrective actions through negotiations. If by the end of the ninety-day period corrective action had not been achieved, OCR would initiate enforcement action within the next thirty days, either by commencing administrative proceedings or by other means authorized by law.
- Time frames for completing compliance reviews were established that paralleled the timetables for handling complaints.
- OCR would develop an annual enforcement proposal, spelling out its yearly goals and priorities and how it planned to allocate its resources. There was to be comment by the public on the proposal before OCR published its final plan.
- HEW would provide the civil rights groups with computer printouts every six months, detailing the actions OCR had taken on complaints and compliance reviews.

In a press conference the day after HEW announced the June 1976 order, Martin Gerry stated that though its requirements technically applied only to the seventeen southern and border states in the original *Adams* dispute, OCR voluntarily agreed to apply the terms of the order nationally. It would also apply them to the enforcement of Section 504 of the Rehabilitation Act, even though there was no interest group representing disabled persons as a formal party to the litigation.

Judge Pratt had facilitated the June 1976 settlement by compelling the lawyers representing OCR's various constituencies to sit down with agency officials and hammer out an enforcement strategy, at least with respect to the procedures for enforcing the civil rights provisions for which OCR was responsible. Previous to that, OCR had been whipsawed by individual organizations, representing blacks, women, and others, that either initiated or threatened to initiate separate legal actions. The resulting ad hoc judicial intervention had left the unit with little opportunity to devise a rational, comprehensive enforcement strategy.

Pratt recognized the need for a comprehensive review of OCR's work. Reluctant to impose his own solution to the complicated mesh of legal, administrative, and political issues posed by the government's motion to amend Part F and by the intervention of both WEAL and MALDEF, he convinced the parties that they would be better off reaching accommodations among themselves. On the day he announced the settlement, Pratt remarked that the negotiated agreement was "something that could only have been worked out by people with an intimate knowledge of the problem. . . . It seemed to me that if I were to do it I would be using a meat axe when something a lot more refined was required. I didn't have the background or anything else tailor-made on order which could meet the problems."[80]

In *The End of Liberalism,* what Theodore Lowi called "interest group liberalism" was said to operate on the very premises and through the very processes at work in the June 1976 settlement in *Adams.* In *Adams,* as in Lowi's interest group liberalism, the private parties gathered together under the auspices of the public authority (in *Adams,* the court) and achieved a negotiated resolution of their problems. Without the court's guidance or intervention regarding the substance of an agreement, the parties in *Adams* reached a settlement that subsequently received the imprimatur of the court when Pratt incorporated its terms into a court order.

Transforming the agreement into a court order increased the legal stakes and sanctions in the event of noncompliance. If the terms agreed upon had constituted only a private agreement, and the plaintiffs believed that the government was not complying, they would have had to initiate a new lawsuit against the government. With the

settlement announced as a court order, however, if the plaintiffs concluded that the government was not living up to the terms of the
agreement, they could return to Judge Pratt and ask him to take
action to enforce the order without starting a new lawsuit. A civil
rights lawyer explained:

> The fight that the agreement be a court order was important. . . .
> First, it means the plaintiffs can move for contempt of court if OCR
> fails to enforce adequately. It explicitly places the court's imprimatur
> on the agreement. A court order as opposed to a regulation establishes
> that this is the way it must be done. Regulations are, to an extent, vol-
> untary actions an agency takes. A court order suggests that there has
> been a problem — an inadequacy in the agency's enforcement efforts —
> and the court is compelling specific corrective actions.

The June 1976 order helped justify internal changes within OCR.
Those who managed the agency argued that the order compelled
them to change the way in which they carried out their responsibilities. One high-ranking HEW official, discussing the leverage the order gave OCR director Martin Gerry to justify bureaucratic reforms,
stated:

> Gerry was helped by the June 1976 order vis-à-vis his staff. He could
> come down hard on [OCR's staff], suggest changes and criticize past
> procedures, all the while saying that the court Order leaves him no
> choice but to change things and to compel his staff and the regional
> offices to change.
>   We must speed up the processing of the cases, he could argue, not
> because I insist and believe we should, but because the court Order
> requires that we do. This helped minimize staff resistance to change,
> because Gerry could argue, "We are under the gun — under the court
> Order."

The June 1976 agreement provided leaders of OCR not only with
leverage within their own bureaucracy but also with political cover to
fend off external political pressure. One HEW official explained:

> We'll get a little mileage out of it [the June 1976 order]. We can say to
> recipients: "We can't risk non-compliance with Judge Pratt's order." It
> is a backstop. Thank God for Judge Pratt. We can say, "Don't forget,
> we don't have a choice here, we are under court order."
>   It is similar to the 1950's and 1960's when there were those in the
> South who wanted to move against segregated educational facilities,
> but couldn't. They needed the 1964 Act so that they could then argue

that the law requires that we do thus and such. "We don't want to, but the law forces us. We would love to give you another year, but Judge Pratt didn't give us any choice."

Another high OCR official explained, "[W]e can hide behind the court order to an extent" by saying "to the complaining Congressmen or educational administrator: 'Sure, we'd love to negotiate, but our ninety days are up, and we are under court order to move.'"

Armed with the 1976 court order, OCR officials could also better argue for additional personnel and resources — needed, they insisted, to meet the requirements of the order. In letters from Gerry to HEW secretary David Mathews in November 1976, and from Mathews to Office of Management and Budget (OMB) director James Lynn in December 1976, OCR sought 299 additional positions. Both Gerry and Mathews cited the requirements of the June 1976 order to justify the request.

By intervening as he did, Pratt prompted a resolution to the crisis precipitated by the government's insistence that it could not simultaneously comply with the requirements of *Adams* in the area of racial discrimination and enforce civil rights laws in other areas as well. Although the civil rights lawyers, the government, and even the court touted the June 1976 order as a "comprehensive" resolution, that characterization of the settlement was misleading. The original and root problem that prompted the *Adams* litigation — the lack of political will to enforce Title VI — had not been confronted, let alone resolved. As a surrogate for that political will, the *Adams* plaintiffs sought to substitute a legal compulsion to act. The implicit assumption was that what politics prevented from happening, litigation could compel. Yet, the legal compulsions imposed in the June 1976 agreement were quite limited.

The agreement dealt with managerial issues. It provided a scheme for allocating OCR's resources and processing its complaints. The core components of the agreement dealt with the need for bureaucratic regularity in the enforcement of civil rights laws. What emerged in the agreement was founded on the idea that apolitical, procedural changes focusing on administrative efficiency and managerial rationality could counteract the political considerations that had overwhelmed and paralyzed OCR early in the Nixon administration. The *Adams* litigation had helped to transform the focus of the debate over Title VI. Rather than concentrating on what OCR did about racial inequality in schools or elsewhere, *Adams* centered on how OCR did what it did — on the procedures it used to enforce the law.

THE *ADAMS* PLAINTIFFS' MOTION FOR FURTHER RELIEF IN HIGHER EDUCATION

The June 1976 order dealt exclusively with elementary and secondary education. Significant issues in higher education still remained to be decided by Pratt. OCR's involvement in higher education dated back to the 1960s.

In May 1969, a report issued by a respected southern organization, the Education Reporting Service of the National Association of State University and Land Grant Colleges, found a high level of segregation in state colleges and universities and an underrepresentation of blacks at the collegiate level. The report found that whereas blacks constituted 11 percent of the American population they made up only 5 percent of the students on college campuses, and nearly all of those black students were at historically black institutions. Similarly, a survey of eighty traditionally white institutions found that less than 2 percent of the student body was black.[81] Though there were some efforts to enforce Title VI in higher education between 1964 and 1969, it was not until the 1969–70 academic year that HEW began to investigate ten states that had traditionally operated dual systems of higher education to determine if those states were violating Title VI. In his letter to the ten states in 1969, Leon Panetta declared "that the persistence of racially identifiable institutions supports the conclusion that [a state] is not in compliance with the requirements of the law." Panetta emphasized that in eliminating the racial identifiability of institutions, the states could not "close or downgrade" historically black institutions, or place "a disproportionate burden upon black students, faculty or institutions."[82]

In January 1970, Eloise Severinson, OCR's Atlanta regional director, wrote to William Friday, president of the University of North Carolina at Chapel Hill, detailing the agency's first guidelines for compliance with Title VI in higher education. Severinson wrote that white colleges and universities that had been segregated under law had an affirmative duty to overcome the effects of past discrimination by recruiting black students and faculty members and providing more financial help to black students.[83] From 1970 to the time of Judge Pratt's first order in *Adams,* in February 1973, little of significance had happened in desegregation in higher education.

In his order, Pratt required OCR to obtain desegregation plans for public institutions of higher education in the ten states to which Panetta wrote letters in the 1969–70 academic year. In June 1973, at roughly the same time that the court of appeals handed down its affirmance of Judge Pratt's decision, the Legal Defense Fund distributed its first set of proposed criteria for desegregation in higher education, providing copies to both OCR and Judge Pratt. When OCR received preliminary plans from nine of the states in November 1973,[84] it rejected the plans because they did not contain specific timetables and goals for changing the racial enrollment patterns that prevailed.

"Letters of guidance" sent to the states by OCR director Peter Holmes in 1973 and 1974 paralleled the standards that the LDF had suggested in June 1973. By filing the *Adams* suit and then by distributing criteria for desegregation in higher education, the civil rights lawyers influenced the substantive content of the standards involved in enforcing Title VI. OCR's letters of guidance were startling in the level of control, regulation, and oversight asserted over the state systems of higher education. Predictably, the requirements in those letters became the subject of a protracted legal and political struggle. That struggle culminated in a Supreme Court decision in 1992, almost two decades after the initial skirmishes between the states and OCR. One such letter sent by OCR to Mississippi, the state involved in the 1992 Supreme Court case, is examined below.

In his 1974 letter to Governor Waller of Mississippi, seeking modifications in the plan submitted by that state, OCR director Holmes noted that the agency was not acting on its own, but rather that it sought a desegregation plan from Mississippi that complied with Judge Pratt's initial order.[85] This statement demonstrates yet again that, whenever they could, OCR officials used *Adams* to justify their enforcement efforts. Holmes's reference to Judge Pratt is all the more striking because Pratt's order said not one word about the standards by which to evaluate the adequacy of desegregation plans in higher education. In a fourteen-page memorandum accompanying his letter to Waller, Holmes explained that a desegregation plan had to contain specific commitments by the state to desegregate, had to delineate the cost of each part of the plan, had to discuss and justify the rate at which each aspect of the plan would be implemented, and had to commit the state to providing comprehensive, semiannual program reports.[86]

According to OCR, Mississippi had to revise its plan to address the following issues:

- *The impact of academic decisions on future segregation:* Addressing this issue involved a commitment to determine the impact on desegregation of any decisions to add, expand, or delete academic programs; to construct new facilities or close existing ones; to create new institutions or close existing ones; or to modify admission standards.

- *The allocation of resources to the black and white institutions:* Because historically black institutions had fewer resources than their white counterparts, OCR required that Mississippi develop a statewide plan specifying how it intended, by the 1976–77 academic year, to equalize the resources at the black and white institutions. OCR called for equalization of resources in such areas as the number and quality of facilities; the level of per capita expenditures; the quality of programs, services, and staff; the number and quality of degree offerings; the number of library holdings; and the number and quality of faculty members.
- *The educational roles assigned to the black and white institutions:* The revised plan required of Mississippi had to contain a statement of each institution's role that would enable traditionally white institutions to attract black students, and traditionally black institutions to attract white students.
- *The duplication of curricula and programs:* In the past, black and white institutions in the same geographic area duplicated program offerings so that whites could attend the white school and blacks the black school. OCR required Mississippi to take steps to end such duplication.
- *Student recruitment:* OCR required that, whereas it was important to preserve students' freedom to select an institution, it was "fundamental" that Mississippi identify and describe the specific steps that it would take to encourage the recruitment of "other race" students at the historically white and black institutions.
- *Retention of black students:* OCR required the state to take all "reasonable steps" to reduce the drop-out rate of black students at the four-year institutions and to identify the specific measures that it would take, including the initiation of compensatory course offerings and counseling services.
- *Programs to desegregate faculties and staffs and increase the number of black faculty and staff members:* OCR required Mississippi to develop statewide plans to desegregate faculties and staffs and to increase the numbers of black faculty and staff members.[87]

Each of the governors of the nine states that had submitted plans to OCR in November 1973 received a letter from OCR similar to that sent to Governor Waller of Mississippi, requesting revised state desegregation plans. The first revised desegregation plans in response to OCR's letters of guidance came in February 1974. In April 1974, the lawyers for the plaintiffs in *Adams* submitted to HEW detailed written critiques of the revised state plans for five states. Later that month, OCR concluded that the plans it had received were inadequate and wrote again to each of the states specifying what they had yet to do. In June 1974, OCR accepted the revised plans offered by eight states.

The LDF viewed the plans accepted by OCR as inadequate, contending that they did not meet OCR's own criteria established in its letters of guidance. It claimed that OCR had made a political decision to accept virtually anything submitted in response to the letters of guidance. Rather than take legal action immediately, LDF officials decided that they would await the first reports by the states reviewing the implementation of the plans.

In January and March 1975, LDF lawyers critiqued all of the state reports, filed documents with OCR suggesting the standards to use in judging compliance with Title VI, and began planning to go back to court. The LDF returned to court by filing a Motion for Further Relief in Higher Education in August 1975. In that motion, the LDF argued that the eight state plans accepted by OCR did not comply with Pratt's February 1973 order and with the requirements under Title VI advanced in OCR's November 1973 letters of guidance. The Motion for Further Relief in Higher Education marked the first time in the *Adams* litigation that the plaintiffs dealt with a substantive desegregation issue.

During the early summer of 1975, OCR discovered that the LDF intended to return to Judge Pratt to allege that the agency had accepted inadequate plans and that it had not obtained compliance with even the limited commitments that the states had made in those plans. As a result, in late July and early August 1975, just as the LDF was preparing to file its Motion for Further Relief, OCR sent letters to the states informing them that they had not done what they had said they would do to comply with Title VI, and elaborating what each state had to do within a specified period. OCR gave each state a fixed number of days to take the appropriate measures. With that action, the dispute over desegregation in higher education became intensely political. North Carolina and Maryland essentially said that they would not comply with OCR's recommendations. When OCR indicated that it was going to initiate administrative enforcement proceedings against Maryland that could lead to the termination of federal funds, Maryland sued HEW. That lawsuit, *Mandel v. HEW*, is discussed in the next section of this chapter. Thus, it was in this highly charged environment, in August 1975, that the plaintiffs made their critical legal and strategic move: filing their Motion for Further Relief in Higher Education.

HEW had accepted state plans, the plaintiffs claimed, that amounted to little more than "plans to plan for desegregation" and that would neither increase black enrollment at the predominantly white institutions nor establish programs at the predominantly black institutions to rectify their second-class educational status.[88] Urging Judge Pratt to step in again, the plaintiffs geared their Motion for Further Relief to arguments that had resonated with the judge before — allegations that HEW had overstepped the bounds of lawful administrative discretion and had engaged in a deliberate abdication of its responsibilities:

> HEW has accepted proposals from the affected states that contain no commitments to take specific action at specific times to eradicate the vestiges of their dual system. Instead, the states have submitted . . . plans that contain no more than commitments to conduct unspecified studies of indefinite duration on problems associated with achieving meaningful desegregation. . . . This departmental policy clearly oversteps that area of its activities where agency discretion must be permitted to function free of judicial oversight. It reflects a rather calculated determination to thwart the desired aims of Congress under Title VI.[89]

HEW confronted directly the issue of its discretionary authority. No one really knew, it argued, what specific actions would desegregate institutions of higher education. The plaintiffs' criticisms, the government insisted, were "attempts to impose on HEW the plaintiffs' view of how the *Adams* order and Title VI should be enforced and do not give the due respect necessary to the agency's implementation of its own program."[90] HEW urged, as it had from the outset of *Adams,* that assessing how educational institutions are to be desegregated under Title VI was a determination it, and not the plaintiffs, could best make. That argument was a more formidable one with regard to the Motion for Further Relief in Higher Education than it had been at the start of *Adams* because, following Pratt's 1973 decision, OCR had taken concrete steps to enforce Title VI in higher education. It had pressed for and received written commitments from the states and, after reviewing and hearing the plaintiffs' reactions, had approved those plans. It had also commenced enforcement proceedings against Maryland for failing to implement desegregation plans. These facts established a crucial difference between the plaintiffs' initial suit against HEW and their Motion for Further Relief.

In their initial suit, the plaintiffs had asked Pratt to review OCR's failure, over substantial periods of time, to take any action at all to bring the states into compliance. By contrast, in the Motion for Further Relief the plaintiffs asked Pratt to review whether the particular measures OCR had taken to achieve desegregation in higher education were legally adequate. Hence, in their Motion for Further Relief in 1975, the plaintiffs asked Pratt, for the first time, to review the validity of HEW's decisions on substantive legal issues. In opposing the motion, HEW emphasized that very point: The motion required the court to review not the procedure by which OCR enforced Title VI, but the "substance of the method chosen for enforcement."[91] Pratt was not eager to do that. Were he to do so, he would have thrust himself directly into the middle of the emerging debate about desegregation policies for public colleges and universities throughout the South.

To respond to the substance of the plaintiffs' claims would have placed Pratt in an awkward position. It would have required him to review the legal sufficiency of the plans that HEW decided to accept from each of eight states and, if he disagreed with those decisions, to challenge the authority and expertise of HEW officials, justifying his position in each instance. He was not comfortable with that prospect. In higher education as in elementary and secondary education, the legal standards for determining what was an adequate desegregation plan were at the heart of the controversies over Title VI. Yet in 1975 there was much less judicial experience and legal precedent to rely upon and learn from in desegregating colleges and universities than there had been at the elementary and secondary school levels a decade earlier.

Deciding the plaintiffs' Motion for Further Relief was further complicated by the division within the black community on the future of the historically black colleges. Though the NAACP Legal Defense Fund was closely involved in the *Adams* litigation from the outset, many influential blacks in the South, including many black educators, were not enthusiastic about desegregating the historically black colleges. Black educators remembered, warily, that desegregation at the elementary and secondary school levels, also produced by the LDF's initiatives, had cost many blacks their jobs. Moreover, the black colleges had played an invaluable historical role as the only institutions in the South providing higher education to blacks. Many blacks, including many in the black establishment, had a special pride in those institutions and feared that desegregation would destroy them. Consequently, the National Association for Equal Educational

Opportunity, the organization of the presidents of black colleges, submitted an amicus brief opposing the Motion for Further Relief.

Desegregating institutions of higher education in the South raised broad social and educational issues for the region. In each state, the desegregation plans contained provisions establishing goals to increase the percentage of black high-school graduates who matriculated at the state's institutions of higher education, including the state's professional schools. Restructuring blacks' access to public higher education necessarily would restructure blacks' access to the middle class and the professions. To the extent that access to higher education is a conduit to future success, achievement, opportunity, influence, and power, the stakes involved in desegregation in higher education were portentous. Recall that the District of Columbia circuit court, in its affirmance of Judge Pratt's initial decision, had commented that the "most serious problem" facing blacks in higher education in the South was the lack of statewide planning to increase the number of black doctors, lawyers, engineers, and other professionals, and that such planning had to take "into account the special problems of minority students and black colleges."[92]

The complexity and sensitivity of the controversy surrounding the higher-education part of the *Adams* litigation made Judge Pratt reluctant to review the legal adequacy of each state desegregation plan. That was, of course, precisely what the LDF lawyers asked him to do in the Motion for Further Relief in Higher Education. When Pratt announced the June 1976 settlement in *Adams* discussed above, the Motion for Further Relief in Higher Education was still pending before him. After announcing the settlement on the other issues, Pratt turned to Elliot Lichtman, the attorney from Joseph Rauh's firm who did much of the work on *Adams*. Hinting at the difficulties associated with the desegregation of the black colleges and at his desire to avoid the issue, Pratt said:

> [W]e have your pending motion with respect to black colleges which is, I can tell you a matter of real concern. If you people want to withdraw that motion, I think you ought to think about it. In the present climate of opinion, I don't know whether that would fly. . . . We have an *amicus* brief, as you know, from the Association of Black Colleges [NAFEO] which is not so much a legal document, but it is a real cry from the soul.[93]

In making these comments, Pratt sent an unmistakable signal, indicating that he was not inclined to act favorably on the plaintiffs' Motion for Further Relief in Higher Education, and all but requesting that Lichtman withdraw the motion. Pratt's words revealed that the concerns raised by NAFEO had given him cause to think twice about how to proceed in desegregation in higher education. His description of NAFEO's amicus brief as a "cry from the soul" revealed his understanding of the anguish some blacks felt about the prospect of losing historically black colleges in return for the "progress" of desegregation.

Elliot Lichtman and the staff lawyers at LDF were undeterred. Within twenty days of that court appearance, in July 1976, Lichtman filed a memorandum requesting that Pratt decide the Motion for Further Relief. Pratt did not decide that motion for another six months, until a new president was in the White House. Whereas the resolution of the Motion for Further Relief in Higher Education fell largely on the shoulders of the next presidential administration, the impasse in desegregating the Maryland state university system during the Nixon-Ford years suggested that difficulties would lie ahead in this area.

MARYLAND'S SUIT AGAINST HEW

Early in the Nixon administration, Maryland was one of the ten states that OCR determined to be operating a segregated system of higher education and that OCR asked to develop a desegregation plan. In October 1969, Maryland submitted its first plan, and four months later, in January 1970, OCR rejected that proposal. When Maryland submitted its revised plan in December 1970, Nixon's Title VI policy of delay was well established. Consequently, OCR did not reject Maryland's revised plan of December 1970 until March 1973 — two years and four months after receiving it and, not coincidentally, a month after Pratt's first *Adams* order. In February 1974, Maryland presented HEW with its third desegregation plan. That was just short of five years after OCR had determined that Maryland was violating Title VI and ordered it to submit a plan. In June 1974, HEW accepted Maryland's plan, and the state's efforts to implement it proceeded uneventfully until August 1975, when OCR concluded that Maryland had failed to fulfill the commitments it had made in the plan.

OCR contended that the state had not kept its commitment to enhance its four predominantly black colleges or to foster racial desegregation by eliminating the duplication of educational programs at neighboring black and white institutions. As part of its plan, Maryland was to turn Morgan State College, a historically black institution, into a university, and to make it the leading campus studying urban problems. OCR charged that instead, the state cut back the urban program at Morgan and allowed a competitive program to start at the state's flagship institution, the University of Maryland at College Park.[94]

After months of fruitless negotiations between OCR and state officials, OCR director Gerry wrote Governor Mandel of Maryland in December 1975, advising him that OCR was referring the case for the administrative enforcement hearings required to terminate funds.[95] A month later, in *Mandel v. U.S. Department of Health, Education, and Welfare,* Maryland sued to enjoin HEW from starting those hearings.[96] In March 1976, Judge Northrup, in the U.S. district court in Baltimore, enjoined OCR from commencing enforcement proceedings against Maryland's university system, holding that OCR had not made adequate efforts to achieve voluntary compliance through negotiations and had not identified with sufficient specificity the university programs receiving federal funds in violation of Title VI. The court ordered HEW to halt administrative proceedings until the agency analyzed each statutory aid program through which federal funds were distributed to the university system, determined which programs were not in compliance, and made a good faith effort to achieve voluntary compliance in each separate program in which HEW alleged there was noncompliance.[97]

The stakes in *Mandel* were substantial, and OCR had little choice but to appeal the decision. The elaborate procedural requirements prescribed in *Mandel* could very likely have prevented OCR from complying with the timetables in the *Adams* order of June 1976. Recall that in the original *Adams* case, Judge Pratt concluded that OCR did not have unlimited discretion to pursue voluntary compliance. Indeed, Pratt identified Maryland as a state in which OCR had negotiated over voluntary compliance for too long. In *Mandel,* after OCR initiated enforcement proceedings pursuant to Pratt's order, Judge Northrup ruled that OCR had failed to make an adequate "good faith effort" to achieve voluntary compliance before commencing enforcement proceedings.

The requirements of Judge Pratt in *Adams,* combined with those of Judge Northrup in *Mandel,* offered confusion as to when to commence enforcement proceedings. *Adams* imposed brisk, definitive, quantitative timetables for investigating complaints and negotiating settlements. *Mandel* required innumerable individualized investigations and negotiations in each federally funded program and held, in effect, that more than two years of negotiations about voluntary compliance was insufficient. Most striking was the conflict between the two cases about whether Title VI required OCR to engage in program-by-program compliance reviews or statewide reviews. The *Mandel* court held that a statewide approach was "not conducive to compliance by voluntary means and in all likelihood, contrary to congressional non-vindictive intent."[98] The District of Columbia court of appeals in *Adams*, by contrast, concluded that integration in higher education "must be dealt with on a statewide rather than a school-by-school basis."[99]

HEW officials were also discouraged that the district court in *Mandel* allowed the recipients to bring a legal challenge to OCR's enforcement initiatives prior to exhausting administrative remedies. After *Mandel*, school districts became aware that HEW's administrative enforcement proceedings under Title VI could be stopped by initiating legal action during those very proceedings. Indeed, in 1976 school districts in Seattle, in Michigan, and in Texas did just that. One exasperated HEW lawyer declared that the *Adams* and *Mandel* cases had created "an administrative nightmare" and that OCR "simply can't go on like this."

THE *BROWN V. WEINBERGER* CASE:
ADAMS IN THE NORTH

In *Brown v. Weinberger*, filed in July 1975, the plaintiffs contended that there was a deliberate HEW policy not to enforce Title VI in thirty-three northern and western states. Basically, they alleged that whereas the enforcement of Title VI in the South came to a halt in 1969, enforcement in the North had never really begun. The *Brown* case, like the case initiated by WEAL discussed earlier in this chapter, was modeled on the original *Adams* case and was an unanticipated consequence of the success of that litigation. Filed by Joseph Rauh's law firm and by William Taylor, director of the Center for National Policy Review at the Catholic University Law School,[100] the *Brown* suit had the support of the NAACP and the NAACP Legal Defense Fund. Lawyers from the Puerto Rican and Mexican American legal defense funds, alleging discrimination based on national origin, were co-counsel in the case.

The plaintiffs in *Brown v. Weinberger* asked the court to impose in the northern and western states the same timetables for the investigation of Title VI complaints that had been imposed in the 1975 *Adams* supplemental order on the southern states. To emphasize the significance of the delays in enforcing Title VI, the plaintiffs cited the Supreme Court's holdings in *Green* and *Alexander*, declaring the need to end segregation in public schools without further delay. Much of the data used to support the plaintiffs' allegations in *Brown v. Weinberger* came from information OCR had filed with the plaintiffs as a result of the reporting provisions of the *Adams* orders. In July 1976, six months before Jimmy Carter took office, U.S. district court judge John Sirica decided *Brown v. Weinberger*. Sirica ruled, much as Judge Pratt had found in the South, that HEW had deliberately failed to comply with the requirements of Title VI in thirty-three northern and western states. The legal pressure on OCR tightened.

CONCLUSIONS

By the end of the Nixon-Ford years, the Office for Civil Rights had grown dramatically. When Congress first passed Title VI, the job of enforcing it had gone to a small, informal group of twenty-five people in HEW's Office of Education. The Johnson administration later shifted the responsibility for enforcing Title VI to OCR, housed in the Office of the Secretary at HEW. At the end of the Johnson administration, however, it still remained a small unit with a budget of $4.8 million. By 1975, OCR had almost one thousand employees and a budget of $24.3 million.[101]

The Contrast between Johnson and Nixon

In the Nixon-Ford era there was a shift in the relationship between HEW and the courts. During the Johnson years the courts and HEW had cooperated in an almost calculated fashion, supporting one another in developing the law on racial discrimination in educational institutions. During the Nixon years, however, prompted by Nixon's enforcement policies, and by civil rights groups' attempts to use the courts to combat those policies, the courts and HEW became adversaries.

During the Nixon-Ford era, civil rights lawyers attempted to gain, through the *Adams* litigation, what black civil rights groups could not win through the political process. Yet, there was a different objective in *Adams* than in previous litigation campaigns. Through test cases, civil rights lawyers had traditionally sought to establish innovative legal doctrines creating new legal rights. The *Adams* litigation, however, was not an attempt to convince courts to establish new legal rights, but an attempt to persuade them to supervise and control an executive agency's policies regarding enforcement of existing civil rights protections.

By the time of the first *Adams* order in 1973, the nation had moved into an era in which the requirements of the civil rights laws "on the books" were fair, equitable, and just. The great political and legal controversies focused on how those laws would be implemented — on what Joseph Rauh called "equality in fact." In addition, by 1973 the nation had moved into an era in which civil rights questions no longer occupied center stage in our domestic politics as they had during the early 1960s. In the late 1960s and early 1970s the Vietnam War became the transcendent American political issue. More important, the black struggle was no longer the *only* civil rights cause.

In the 1970s political movements to improve the status of women, Hispanics, the elderly, and the physically and mentally disabled achieved national visibility and legitimacy, much as the black civil rights movement had attained that status in the previous decade. These movements by groups that, like blacks, had been historically discriminated against had an adverse impact on the black cause. The uniqueness and compelling moral underpinnings of the black cause were diminished by a recognition that blacks were one of many groups that could justifiably allege that they had been historically mistreated. This second wave of the civil rights movement, therefore, deflected attention from issues of race and displaced the primacy the black civil rights struggle had once enjoyed.

The Proliferation of Litigation Aimed at Controlling HEW's Civil Rights Enforcement

To a striking extent, the problems that arose in implementing the *Adams* order of February 1973 were resolved through further litigation. Litigation generated more litigation for numerous reasons. First, each of the parties affected by the *Adams* decision — the government, the educational institutions, and the civil rights groups — had access to lawyers and hence had low start-up costs if they wanted to litigate. Second, the government, the regulated institutions, and the civil rights groups are what Marc Gallanter has called "Repeat Players."[102] Each of them had a substantial, long-term stake in court decisions shaping OCR's policies, and had the capacity to use litigation to achieve their strategic goals. Third, the educational institutions often used litigation as a tactical maneuver, not to win legal victories but to delay action, divert the energies of OCR, dissipate the resources of civil rights groups, and thereby improve their own bargaining position. Fourth, more than ten thousand educational institutions were covered by Title VI. This made possible, indeed inevitable, many individualized legal skirmishes in implementing new enforcement policies. *Mandel,* for example, was only one such skirmish. Finally, civil rights groups' resort to the legal process was a direct by-product of their political weakness. If they had possessed the political power to achieve their goals they would not have had to resort to legal action, at least not as frequently.

This analysis suggests that powerful, long-term forces that first manifested themselves in the Nixon-Ford era ensured continuing litigation over the enforcement of Title VI for administrations to come. The ease, frequency, and skill with which civil rights groups and educational institutions could litigate led many in OCR to believe that the agency had lost control of its own fate. One OCR lawyer explained:

> Before I joined government I was inclined to think of this all-powerful federal government that has all these resources and can do whatever it wants to do. Sometimes I feel as though we are an embattled, small contingent against powerful forces waiting to pounce on us . . . besieged by clever lawyers on all sides . . . looking over our shoulders, ready to pounce on us in court each step of the way.

Shortly before he left office, David Mathews voiced a similar lament when he observed that it "is inevitable, no matter which way [OCR officials] decide a case, it's going to go to litigation."[103]

The proliferation of litigation during the Nixon-Ford era meant that OCR was, indeed, less and less in command of its enforcement policies and its own future. It became a federal agency stripped of its authority to control its own destiny. By the time Jimmy Carter entered the White House in January 1977, OCR had become the object of an elaborate and tenacious legal tug-of-war in which the agency appeared to be the captive of well-armed and aggressive legal combatants using the courts to control its major policies. That circumstance remained largely unchanged for the next decade and a half.

Politics and the Control of Administrative Discretion

During the Nixon era, civil rights leaders, southern educators, and elected officials all distrusted OCR. Southern political and educational officials still smarted from the treatment they had received during the Johnson administration. The *Adams* case made them anxious that wholesale terminations of funds would again be in the offing. By contrast, civil rights lobbyists and lawyers believed that every administration, including Johnson's and surely Nixon's, was inclined to subordinate the enforcement of Title VI to political considerations. To the extent that OCR officials had discretion in devising the agency's enforcement policies, many civil rights activists believed that those officials would use their discretion to minimize the impact of Title VI.

Civil rights leaders' and southern politicians' and educators' distrust of OCR officials caused all of these groups to resort to the same tactic — to seek to control the discretion of those officials through litigation. For instance, *Mandel* limited OCR's discretion by fragmenting the enforcement process into innumerable, discrete steps and by imposing burdensome procedural requirements on OCR at each step. Similarly, the *Adams* litigation limited OCR's discretion by forcing it to adopt an enforcement agenda controlled not by OCR, but by the accumulated allegations of individual complainants.

The obligation to investigate every complaint within the time frames imposed by Judge Pratt meant that OCR could not concentrate on those complaints that it determined were serious, well-documented, and important, and that, if resolved, were likely to have the greatest impact in reducing discrimination. It is unusual for a law enforcement agency not to have that discretion. Most agencies enforcing legal requirements enjoy broad discretionary power over their enforcement strategy and priorities and the allocation of their resources. They typically enjoy wide discretion in determining how to enforce the law so as to maximize the protection afforded by it. The problem is that discretion also makes possible the opposite result.

Discretion permits an agency deliberately to avoid cases and issues of consequence, and instead to concentrate on insignificant and politically inoffensive matters, thus rendering itself and the laws it enforces ineffectual. Always skeptical of the national political establishment, the civil rights groups believed that this was precisely what OCR would do if left to its own devices — especially in a Republican administration. The dilemma was a simple if exasperating one. OCR needed discretion over its enforcement strategies, priorities, and resources if Title VI was to be effective and its protections maximized. Yet, that very discretion gave OCR officials the power to make choices that could cripple Title VI and limit its impact.

By the end of 1976, court decisions had minimized OCR's discretion in two basic respects. They had established the agency's obligation, first, to investigate all complaints, and second, to resolve them within specified time frames. The termination of funds, however, remained, as always, an unpopular and politically risky act for OCR to recommend and for presidents to approve. Whatever a president's commitment to America's black community, any chief executive will be reluctant to halt the flow of federal dollars to state and local educational institutions.

The Emphasis on Procedural Rather than Substantive Matters

Judicial review of substantive decisions by OCR under Title VI could occur in three ways. First, courts could review the standards OCR used to define unlawful discrimination. Second, courts could review whether OCR had applied the legal standards properly, that is, whether the agency had erred in determining whether unlawful discrimination existed in a given factual circumstance. Third, where OCR found illegal discrimination and required remedial actions by recipients, courts could review the legal validity of OCR's decisions to impose, accept, or reject certain remedial measures intended to correct the violations found.

It is a simpler task, politically and intellectually, for lawyers to ask judges to determine the *procedural* standards by which an agency must investigate complaints of illegal discrimination than it is for them to ask judges to determine the *substantive* standards by which to define, measure, and remedy that discrimination. Procedural standards for Title VI could be more clearly articulated and precisely applied than could substantive standards. Less discretion was involved in determining whether enforcement procedures had been violated. Because timetables for the handling of disputes were quantifiable standards, it was an easy task—indeed, a mechanical one—to determine whether they had been violated. Much the same is true of procedures requiring OCR to investigate all complaints, to provide complainants access to their files, to publish an annual operating plan, to gather and review public comments about a proposed operating plan, and to forward summaries of complaints to lawyers for the *Adams* plaintiffs. It is relatively easy intellectually to determine whether the agency has complied with such requirements. In addition, these procedural requirements did not raise politically sensitive and controversial issues for the agency.

The greater willingness of courts to review the procedural dimensions of OCR's work was not lost on the *Adams* plaintiffs. With the exception of the Motion for Further Relief in Higher Education, all of their initiatives during the Nixon-Ford years involved challenges to the procedures by which HEW enforced Title VI. In the first *Adams* decision in 1973, in the 1975 supplemental order, in the June 1976 order, and in *Mandel*, the courts imposed elaborate procedural obligations. Even in the Motion for Further Relief, the issue that the plaintiffs took to Pratt did not require him to review or establish the validity of substantive standards for Title VI. What the plaintiffs alleged was that the states had failed to comply with OCR's own criteria.

However ingenious and capable the *Adams* plaintiffs' legal attacks on OCR were (and they were indeed ingenious and capable), the ultimate significance of Title VI does not depend on the procedural rights it protects. Rather, it depends on substantive rights — on the standards that OCR employs in defining and remedying racial discrimination. These substantive concerns remained largely unaffected by the litigation examined in this chapter.

Indeed, the litigation begun in the Nixon years transformed the core controversies over Title VI. As the litigation focused increasingly on procedural issues and rights and on the management of the agency, there seemed to be less and less focus by both the government and its critics on the underlying objective of the provision — the elimination of unlawful discrimination. The focus on procedure and management was driven, in significant measure, by what civil rights lawyers determined it was possible to win through litigation. Consequently, the concentration on issues of peripheral importance resulted, in part, from the need to frame the legal attack in ways likely to yield some kind of positive response from the courts. Civil rights litigators, and the organizations they represent, like to win and to be able to claim a victory. The lawyers framed the issues in *Adams* accordingly. That strategic mindset, inherent in almost any litigation sponsored by a civil rights organization, ultimately had an insidious effect. It trivialized both the law and the litigation, and left substantive educational questions unaddressed and unresolved.

Judicial Review of OCR's Discretion
and the Separation of Powers

The legal challenge to the Nixon administration's default in enforcing Title VI posed questions about the proper scope of judicial power over administrative agencies. Once Judge Pratt was persuaded of OCR's calculated failure to enforce Title VI, he had little choice but to assume an unusual degree of power over the administration of the agency if he wanted to remedy that problem. Did the unusual control Pratt exercised over OCR — a control intended to compel the agency to enforce the law and comply with its legal obligations — amount to judicial usurpation of the executive function?

There is no simple standard delineating the point at which requirements imposed by courts on administrative agencies violate norms about separation of powers. Each instance must be judged on its own facts. Nonetheless, when courts control the allocation of an agency's resources, impose detailed procedures for its investigations, and set stringent timetables for achieving basic tasks under the relevant statutes, judges and not agency officials are determining critical administrative policies, and the distinction between the executive and judicial branches becomes blurred.

When courts exercise such power over an agency's enforcement of a law, however derelict the agency may be, it is incumbent upon the courts to articulate the principles governing their own power to intervene. There can be no doubt that Judge Pratt had the authority to regulate OCR's policies and priorities, and that in light of the agency's performance he was justified in doing so. He was obliged to do something. In the face of an abdication of responsibility by an agency, the critical questions are, what range of practical options are available to judges, and what legal principles govern and limit what they may do?

The judicial opinions during the Nixon-Ford era in *Adams* provided ad hoc, operational answers to immediate problems. They did not offer general principles or conceptual explanations justifying and exploring the limits of what a judge could do when confronted with an agency systematically derelict in enforcing the law. On the one hand, any set of principles or conceptual understandings would have to give courts broad authority to review an agency's administrative policies. On the other hand, in all but the most grievous and persistent examples of an agency's failure to meet its law enforcement obligations, courts should probably leave the responsibility for devising enforcement policies and allocating resources with the agency itself.

It is neither proper nor practicable for judges, in effect, to be the highest administrative officials of OCR or any other federal agency. Such judicial intervention, moreover, cuts two ways. Though it permitted Judge Pratt in *Adams* to impose policies that might help achieve the goal of Title VI, it also permitted Judge Northrup in *Mandel* to impose policies that hindered that goal. Delineating the line of authority between courts and administrative agencies requires that one develop a sense of what the proper limits of judicial intervention should be, without first considering whether that intervention is likely to deliver what one considers politically agreeable administrative policies.

OCR's politically inspired abdication of responsibility was inde-
fensible, and created the jurisprudential problem discussed above.
For the agency's exasperated critics, there was something attractively
fast, simple, and just in using courts to impose extensive control over
an irresponsible and lawless agency. The excessive politicization of
the law enforcement process by the executive branch led, in the *Adams*
litigation, to the excessive politicization of—and perhaps to over-
reaching by—the judicial branch. Excesses of power by one branch,
however, should not be remedied by excesses of power by another.

Although courts had justification to intervene to remedy OCR's
bankrupt enforcement policies, judicial review did not and could not
entirely displace administrative power. While the courts did exercise
extensive control over the agency, they had to do so in a way that left
largely untouched many of the essential characteristics, powers, and
prerogatives associated with the administrative process. In truth,
there was no other choice. Courts cannot run agencies. Like it or not,
in the long term we must depend on the integrity of the administrative process, not the power of the courts, to ensure the lawful and
effective enforcement of laws—Title VI or any other. Practicalities, if
nothing else, make it so, simply because only an infinitesimal fraction of any agency's administrative decisions can ever be subject to
judicial review.

Furthermore, however tight a stranglehold the courts may place on
an agency, clever and politically inspired administrations, if intent
upon subverting those controls, will be able to do so. During the
Nixon-Ford era, the administration made several attempts to wrench
control of OCR from Judge Pratt: first, Secretary Weinberger's June
1975 proposal to consolidate OCR's regulations, then OCR's allegations that the resources needed to comply with *Adams* precluded it
from enforcing other civil rights laws, and finally the government's
motion to amend Part F of Judge Pratt's order. In the face of an administration's desire to enforce a law so as to frustrate its intended
purpose, litigation may not be an effective weapon. However, litigation can be used politically to admonish, goad, and embarrass an
agency into acting responsibly. Perhaps this was the *Adams* litigation's
primary contribution during the Nixon-Ford period.

Some of the negative consequences of using a litigation strategy to
realize the goals of Title VI had begun to emerge by the end of the
Nixon-Ford years. The litigation developed an agenda and priorities
of its own. It raised a proliferating array of secondary and technical
issues about such questions as the separation of powers, OCR's allocation of resources, and the procedures for investigating complaints.

The issue of primary substantive importance — the use of Title VI to equalize educational opportunity — was displaced as the central subject of debate and discussion. Though that goal was the reason for bringing the litigation in the first place, it became overshadowed by a host of legal questions that were raised by the litigation itself and that were far removed from educational considerations. In addition, during this period those enforcing Title VI continued to focus almost exclusively on the South, and on desegregation as the critical educational reform. The disintegration of urban public school systems throughout the nation, and the devastating impact that this had on the education of African Americans, drew scant attention in the legal debate. When the Supreme Court did get a chance to address that question in *Milliken,* it ignored the political forces that operated to create separate systems for urban minorities and suburban whites. By the time Jimmy Carter became president, the legal debate about racial discrimination in schools, both in the *Adams* litigation and before the Supreme Court, was becoming eerily irrelevant to the underlying problems that the litigation was ostensibly intended to remedy.

5

CARTER:
Litigation and the
New Civil Rights Priorities

SEVERAL THEMES EMERGED IN THE enforcement of Title VI
during the Carter years. First, the *Adams* litigation increasingly turned
the focus of OCR to managerial and procedural issues associated
with the investigation of complaints of discrimination. Substantive
issues having to do with the character and effect of racial discrimination in schools continued to take a back seat to considerations of managerial efficiency and procedural regularity in the enforcement of the
law. Second, in the realm of desegregation, OCR turned its attention
away from elementary and secondary schools — its historic focus — to
desegregation in higher education. That reorientation of OCR's focus
was also a by-product of *Adams* because it derived, in part, from a
shift in the emphasis of civil rights litigators. They changed their
focus to higher education because there were limited opportunities to
win legal victories in *Adams* at the elementary and secondary school
levels. Third, the record of enforcement during the Carter years suggests that enforcement of Title VI under a liberal Democratic president was not, in its national effect, strikingly different from enforcement under Republican administrations.

OPTIMISTIC EARLY SIGNS

With the Carter presidency, some observers saw the possibility
of returning to an enforcement of Title VI that resembled the record
in the Johnson period. During his campaign, Carter often emphasized that his daughter attended an integrated public school with a
black majority, and referred to Title VI as "the best thing that ever
happened to the South."[1]
Carter did well in black communities in the presidential primaries,

carrying 96 percent of the vote in Chicago's heavily black Seventh Ward, for example, in the Illinois presidential primary.[2] He enjoyed strong ties to the powerful civil rights leadership community in Atlanta, including the King family. Even the pageantry at the 1976 Democratic National Convention suggested a return to civil rights themes. After Carter's acceptance speech, Coretta Scott King joined Democratic Party luminaries on the podium, and, hands clasped and held aloft, all those on the stage, joined by those in the auditorium, sang "We Shall Overcome."

The early signs from the Carter administration with respect to Title VI encouraged civil rights supporters. In July 1977, as a prelude to his address before the national convention of the National Urban League, the president issued a strongly worded and well-publicized directive to all executive departments and agencies committing his administration to the enforcement of Title VI. "Title VI," the directive declared, "writes into law a concept which is basic to our country—that the government of all the people should not support programs which discriminate . . . no matter how important the program, no matter how urgent the goals." The memorandum directed that all agency heads "*will* enforce Title VI" and should "exert firm leadership" to ensure that their agencies implemented the civil rights provision.[3] "There are no exceptions to this rule," the president ordered.[4]

Shortly after Carter issued the directive, the Justice Department sponsored a conference devoted to the enforcement of Title VI. Clarence Mitchell, director of the Washington bureau of the NAACP, Arthur Fleming, chairman of the U.S. Commission on Civil Rights, and Texas congresswoman Barbara Jordan, among others, spoke to the assembled group. In a speech to the Leadership Conference on Civil Rights, Vice President Walter Mondale said that, by his actions, President Carter intended to signal that the "administration will not support with tax dollars discrimination of any form."[5] Not only did the rhetoric of the new administration contrast sharply with the tone set during the Nixon-Ford era, but so, too, did the appointment of the key personnel charged with enforcing Title VI.

Carter's appointment of Joseph Califano, a former adviser to Lyndon Johnson on domestic and social affairs, as HEW secretary heightened expectations that the enforcement of civil rights would be a priority in the Carter years.[6] Those expectations increased further when Califano hired F. Peter Libassi, former deputy director of the U.S. Commission on Civil Rights and the first director of HEW's Office for Civil Rights in the Johnson administration, to conduct a study of how to improve OCR's effectiveness.

The new HEW secretary declared that the Nixon and Ford administrations had inadequately protected the civil rights of racial minorities, women, and the disabled.[7] In a much publicized news conference held within a month of Carter's inauguration, Califano promised that he would cut off federal funds to any school or school district that violated federal laws prohibiting racial discrimination.[8] The Chicago public school system, the secretary announced, had been notified that it faced a cutoff of $100 million in federal funds because of an inadequate bilingual program and because of its disproportionate assignment of black teachers to predominantly black schools.

Califano explained that his statement about cutting off funds and his announcement about Chicago were intended to "restore the integrity of HEW's civil rights program." He viewed these actions as "the first steps in rekindling the commitment of the Department of Health, Education and Welfare under President Carter to forceful and fair enforcement of the civil rights laws passed by Congress." Though Califano explained that he had "no desire ever to cut off funds to any school district or other educational institution," he noted that "the way to ensure compliance with civil rights laws is to make clear that we will order fund cutoffs if we must."[9]

The secretary also noted that he was reviewing possible funding terminations in six small school districts in Texas and Arkansas. Termination of funding to those districts had been ordered during the previous administration, yet HEW had never implemented those orders. By 1977, the written records in those six cases were one to four years old.[10] With much publicity, Califano ordered reviews of those cases to determine whether the original decisions were still valid.

In selecting the people who would have direct responsibility for enforcing civil rights, Carter looked to the black civil rights movement. He appointed David S. Tatel director of OCR. Tatel, a nationally prominent civil rights lawyer, had worked on civil rights cases in Mississippi in the 1960s while a law student and went on to become director of the Lawyers' Committee for Civil Rights under Law. Carter appointed Cynthia G. Brown as deputy director for compliance and enforcement, a newly created position. Having worked first in OCR during the Johnson administration and then with several civil rights organizations in Washington, including the Lawyers' Committee for Civil Rights under Law and the Children's Defense Fund, Brown had spent a lifetime in the field of civil rights, was well known in Washington liberal circles, and enjoyed the respect of leaders from the major national civil rights organizations. Carter selected Norman Chachkin, a former lawyer with the NAACP Legal Defense Fund and the

Lawyers' Committee for Civil Rights under Law, as OCR's associate director for policy, planning, and research. As part of his work at the LDF, Chachkin had been co-counsel for the plaintiffs in the *Adams* case and had needed to get a written waiver of a possible conflict of interest from the LDF before joining the administration.

In the Justice Department, Drew S. Days replaced J. Stanley Pottinger as assistant attorney general of the Department's Civil Rights Division — another appointment heralded by national civil rights groups. Days, a prominent black civil rights lawyer, had worked since 1969 for the NAACP's Legal Defense Fund. In appointing Tatel, Brown, Chachkin, and Days, the Carter administration sent a strong message to the black civil rights community.

The Disenchantment Begins

OCR's Motion to Consolidate Adams *and Related Cases*

Despite the rhetoric and the promising appointments early in the Carter administration, the relationship between the administration and civil rights groups soon became adversarial. The *Adams* litigation was the source of that acrimony. In May 1977, in a motion in the *Adams* case, the LDF accused the administration of ignoring a provision in Judge Pratt's 1973 order requiring HEW, "without unreasonable delay," to enforce Title VI by desegregating state-run vocational schools and schools for the handicapped in the South. In filing the motion, Joseph Rauh noted that though Secretary Califano and the leading officials of OCR were his friends, he could not ignore their failure to comply with the order. The motion asked for a new court order directing HEW either to compel the schools to desegregate by June 1978 or to cut off all federal support for their programs.[11] Also in May 1977, Pratt directed the parties to start discussions to settle the *WEAL* case — the case alleging a systematic failure by the government to enforce the laws barring discrimination based on gender in federally funded programs.

In June 1977, a month after LDF filed its motion on the vocational schools and schools for the handicapped, and after Pratt urged the parties to settle the *WEAL* case, OCR responded with its own legal initiative. It moved before Judge Pratt that the *Adams, Brown,* and *WEAL* cases be consolidated and that it be given until August 1977 to present its own comprehensive plan to enforce all the antidiscrimination laws under its jurisdiction. In an argument indistinguishable from the claims advanced by OCR during the Nixon-Ford years, the agency's new leaders maintained that the resources needed to comply with the orders in the three cases precluded them from enforcing anti-discrimination laws intended to protect the disabled, the aged, and Native Americans.[12]

Claiming that it could not keep pace with the time frames and other requirements imposed in the June 1976 *Adams* order, OCR asked the court to modify Part F of Judge Pratt's 1975 order (the part establishing timetables for the processing of complaints) and to substitute for Part F OCR's own annual operating plan. The agency declared that the *Adams, WEAL,* and *Brown* cases posed the question of how OCR's limited resources should be "equitably assigned among multiple enforcement responsibilities."[13]

In an affidavit filed in support of OCR's motion in June 1977, OCR director Tatel asserted that he was unable to achieve needed reforms in OCR's operations because the agency's priorities are "in large part dictated by present or potential court orders."[14] The crux of the controversy, Tatel argued, was no longer whether OCR fulfilled its statutory obligations, "but rather how the details of this responsibility are to be fulfilled."[15] To develop a rational, balanced, and effective enforcement program, Tatel maintained, OCR had to be relieved of the burdens imposed by the various court orders. Asserting that he would be "seriously hampered" in leading OCR if he were "bound by the mistakes and constraints of the past," Tatel declared that he could not "plan systematically if we must respond to each group's attempts to compel OCR to commit the bulk of its resources to enforcement of a particular law, or to enforcement in a particular set of institutions in a particular manner."[16]

OCR proposed to file with the court a comprehensive annual enforcement plan detailing how it planned to allocate its resources for the next several years. If the court did not give it that opportunity, OCR argued, its "limited resources . . . will continue to be allocated and consumed by the duty to comply with individual and uncoordinated court orders, thereby frustrating the efforts of the new administration to develop a balanced enforcement program which fairly, equally and uniformly enforces all anti-discrimination laws within HEW's jurisdictions."[17] Though the June 1976 order was the result of good faith negotiations by well-intentioned people, OCR stressed, it had imposed unforeseen burdens on the agency.

When agency officials said that they wanted to develop "a balanced" enforcement program, among other things, they meant one that relied both on complaints and on compliance reviews. Compelling them to use almost all of their resources to investigate complaints precluded them from expending adequate resources on compliance reviews — a more effective method, they maintained, for discovering and remedying illegal discrimination. Compliance reviews, they argued, were particularly effective in protecting the poor and undereducated, who historically did not file complaints.[18] For this reason, OCR's proposed annual operating plan projected using only 55 percent of the agency's resources for investigating complaints, leaving almost half of its resources for compliance reviews and other measures.[19] By maintaining that if OCR were able to allocate its resources as it saw fit, it would be able to maximize the impact of civil rights laws, Tatel and Califano were advancing precisely the argument urged by the previous Republican administrations.

The Carter administration's June 1977 motion asking to be relieved of the obligations of Judge Pratt's orders highlighted the confusion and complexity caused by the proliferation of lawsuits against the agency. To appreciate the significance of that motion, one must place it in the context of what had already transpired in the litigation. The initial *Adams* litigation, brought in 1970, had charged that HEW had failed to enforce Title VI against educational institutions in the seventeen southern and border states. The *WEAL* suit, filed in 1974, alleged that HEW had failed to enforce Title IX, which prohibited discrimination based on gender in federally assisted educational programs. The *Brown* case, filed in 1975, the northern version of the *Adams* case, alleged that OCR had failed to enforce Title VI vis-à-vis educational institutions in thirty-three nonsouthern states. Within a year of the June 1976 court order in *Adams* imposing time frames for resolving all complaints of discrimination filed with OCR, the National Federation of the Blind intervened in *Adams,* accusing HEW of failing to enforce Section 504 of the Rehabilitation Act of 1973, which prohibited discrimination against disabled individuals. Against that backdrop of proliferating lawsuits, OCR filed its June 1977 motion.

One cannot understand OCR's efforts to extricate itself from *Adams* during the Carter administration without understanding the power of HEW secretary Califano. A shrewd strategist with well-honed political skills, Califano enjoyed a special status as a former presidential aide to Lyndon Johnson and as one of Washington's most astute, influential, and politically connected lawyers. He had the kind of experience that made him a consummate Washington insider. He had worked for prestigious law firms in New York and Washington — Dewey, Ballantine in New York; and Arnold and Porter, as well as Williams and Connolly, in Washington. Interspersed with the private practice of law, he had done stints of government service in various high-level positions in the Department of Defense, ending up as a special assistant to the president from 1965 to 1969. From 1970 to 1972 he had been general counsel to the Democratic National Committee. Califano was everything that Jimmy Carter was not, and it doubtless was difficult for a one-term governor from Plains, Georgia, to second-guess the political instincts and preferences of a strong-willed, seasoned Washington veteran such as Califano. In contrast with HEW secretary Robert Finch, during the Nixon years, Califano's reputation and personal tenacity permitted him, in the words of one of his aides, "to be his own man and not permit much White House intervention with his staff or the development of HEW policies."[20]

Califano was the moving force behind OCR's effort to consolidate the various lawsuits that had become enmeshed with the *Adams* litigation. OCR's motion reflected his desire to be relieved of the pressure of responding to competing orders in the *Adams, WEAL,* and *Brown* cases. He emphasized to top OCR officials that he did not want HEW run by civil rights lawyers bringing suit against the department, and he directed these officials to get the agency relieved of the constraints imposed by Pratt's orders. One attorney explained that everyone knew that there had to be a new accommodation reached:

> All of a sudden you were finding yourself in Sirica's court room [the *Brown v. Weinberger* case], in Pratt's court room [the *Adams* case], in Waddie's court room [the *WEAL v. Weinberger* case] and everybody was going to come out with a court order against the Department because we were not complying with the requirements of the court order of 1976. It was like a guy paying alimony to three or four wives. We just didn't have the money. The net result was the need to consolidate these cases and come up with one order which we could live with.

One former civil rights lawyer working for OCR complained of the chaotic effect the litigation seemed to have on the agency:

> The litigants were moving in on us from lots of different directions. They were giving us no time to get control of the place. The women's groups wanted court orders, the Mexican American groups wanted court orders, the handicapped groups wanted court orders, the blacks wanted court orders. And if you add all those court orders up, they added up to about 150 percent of our resources.
>
> They were moving too fast on us and not giving us any breathing space and demanding more than we had at the time . . . that is why we pursued a consolidation of all of the cases.
>
> We wanted one judge to see in one set of pleadings what we were facing. Every individual case, when looked at by itself, appeared to be rea-

sonable, but when you added them all up it wasn't, and since they were all separate cases it was hard to make that case to each individual judge.

So Norman Chachkin and Cynthia Brown, instrumental in bringing the *Adams* case, prepared arguments to extricate OCR from Part F of Judge Pratt's 1975 order establishing timetables for the processing of complaints and to substitute instead OCR's own annual operating plan. OCR's motion to rescind the requirements of Part F and to consolidate *Adams, Brown,* and *WEAL* led to a bitter fight between civil rights lawyers who remained on the outside and those who had joined the new administration. Brown and Tatel spent many a difficult evening and weekend in heated sessions with the opposing civil rights lawyers — their former compatriots. There was much finger pointing and hostility. David Tatel testified for two days in a fiercely contested deposition conducted by his former ally Joseph Rauh. The plaintiffs in the *Adams* and *Brown* cases, represented by lawyers from the Legal Defense Fund, and the plaintiffs in the *WEAL* case, represented by lawyers from the Center for Law and Social Policy, filed briefs opposing OCR's motion to consolidate, arguing that the motion should not be granted because OCR had failed to seek adequate personnel to carry out earlier court orders, because it overestimated the time needed to process complaints, and because it continued to do a poor job of enforcing civil rights laws on behalf of all groups.

Pratt's Denial of OCR's Motion to Consolidate, and the Ensuing Negotiations

In October 1977, Judge Pratt denied OCR's request to consolidate the three civil rights lawsuits and refused to free the agency from his previous orders requiring it to resolve, within specified time limits, complaints of race and gender discrimination in school systems and colleges in the seventeen southern and border states. Though Pratt expressed sympathy for OCR's contention that it did not have the resources to do all that it was legally required to do, he indicated that the agency had been slow in filling vacant positions and had not done enough to gain additional resources. It was HEW's responsibility, Pratt ordered, to acquire the necessary resources to carry out its legal duties.[21] Accordingly, Pratt ordered the government to "take all steps necessary to secure resources adequate to comply with the Order and statutes at the earliest feasible moment," to advise the Office of Management and Budget, within thirty days, of the resources it needed, and then to work with OMB to obtain those resources.[22]

The immediate effect of Pratt's decision was to thrust the plaintiffs in the various lawsuits, yet again, into negotiations with OCR to hammer out the differences among themselves and to reach a new comprehensive settlement. If OCR could neither impose its own solution via a new and revised court order from Pratt nor comply with the specifics of existing court orders, it had to achieve a new accommodation with the civil rights groups. The negotiations to produce that accommodation extended from October through December 1977, involving lawyers representing the LDF, MALDEF, WEAL, and the National Federation of the Blind.

As expected, there continued to be major disagreements about how OCR should allocate its resources and what it should be able to accomplish. There were, for instance, repeated disagreements about how many compliance reviews OCR could perform, and OCR officials insisted that, given their resources, they would not be able to meet Pratt's timetables for complaints and still do many compliance reviews. In the negotiations leading to the June 1976 settlement, OCR officials had overestimated what the agency could accomplish. In the 1977 negotiations they insisted that they could not achieve the 1976 goals and conservatively estimated what they could do. Ambitious estimates would risk causing the agency to be out of compliance with yet another court order in the future.

In many respects, however, the most significant negotiations occurred not between the civil rights groups and the government, but among the various civil rights groups. Each group had an interest in the bargain struck with OCR because it would affect both how the agency allocated its resources and what enforcement methods it used. The two most powerful groups in the negotiations were the NAACP Legal Defense Fund and the Women's Equity Action League. Tensions between the lawyers representing those two groups also tended to be greatest. Those tensions derived, in part, from the general superiority of the legal and bargaining position that the LDF enjoyed. The LDF was the most powerful group in the negotiations because it was the only group that had won anything in court — the initial Pratt decision, the unanimous *en banc* decision by the District of Columbia court of appeals, and Pratt's 1975 supplemental order. WEAL, the Mexican American Legal Defense and Education Fund, and the National Federation of the Blind had all made allegations about OCR's wrongdoing that mirrored what the LDF had alleged, but none had obtained a finding by a court validating those allegations.

An attorney for the LDF explained the relationship between the WEAL and LDF lawyers in this way:

We had some respect from Pratt which he didn't give them. They had never gotten orders from Pratt. He had dismissed their suit early on. We had timetables, they didn't. They resented our superior bargaining position. The women also realized that we were in the superior position in that if they did not come to a resolution with OCR we, representing the blacks, could say to Pratt: "Well, look we have a court order and our court order is not being complied with, therefore give us relief on this matter or that matter and we don't care what you do with those other folks."

We were the only ones that had anybody in potential contempt. . . . There was the possibility that in those circumstances that Pratt would say, "Well, these people do have an order and OCR hasn't delivered what it is required to deliver under that court order. I'm going to now require them to do what I asked them to do three years ago and the other people can just wait on line."

The lawyers representing the LDF occasionally assured the lawyers for the women, the Mexican Americans, and the disabled that they would not reach a bilateral settlement with the government and leave the others to cut their own deals. WEAL lawyers recognized that many of OCR's leaders had first been drawn to civil rights work during the black civil rights struggle, and the WEAL litigators sometimes believed that the sympathies of OCR's leadership did not carry over with equal zeal to the women's rights movement. Several of the WEAL litigators also believed that Judge Pratt did not consider the gender discrimination issue important, never giving the WEAL attorneys or their lawsuit their due respect.

Also exacerbating relations between WEAL and LDF was the social and economic status of the women who tended to file complaints with OCR. Those women tended to be white, middle-class, educated professionals who were good at the formalities of lodging and presenting complaints. Accordingly, investigating complaints was a productive, if not preferred, method for remedying gender discrimination. Consequently, WEAL wanted OCR to spend a greater proportion of its resources investigating complaints than did the representatives of the LDF.

Within OCR, there were similar tensions between those committed to remedying racial discrimination and those committed to remedying gender discrimination. Some OCR bureaucrats who had come to work for the agency because of their prior involvement in civil rights work during the racial struggles of the 1950s and 1960s resented OCR's growing interest in the 1970s in discrimination against white, middle-class professional women. OCR officials tried to use LDF lawyers to "control" WEAL representatives—the latter often assuming the most hard-nosed bargaining positions with the agency. At one point in the negotiations, one of the lawyers for the LDF turned to one of the lawyers for WEAL and reportedly declared, "If you don't come up with a realistic goal for what OCR should do in enforcing Title IX we will make our own settlement."

Groups representing the disabled had entered the litigation in 1977—seven years after the filing of the complaint in *Adams* and four and a half years after Pratt's first order. They were represented by lawyers from one of Washington's most prestigious firms, Covington and Burling. While technically representing the National Federation of the Blind, these attorneys sought relief generally on behalf of all disabled persons. Because OCR's enforcement of laws affecting disabled people had not been before the court prior to 1977, there was uncertainty as to how Pratt would react to the concerns of the disabled, and to yet another group making demands on OCR's resources through the mushrooming *Adams* litigation. The government emphasized the problems with regard to the disabled by stating in its motion papers that the plaintiffs alleging racial and gender discrimination sought "activities far in excess of the Department's capabilities" and that meeting those demands would "require the Department to ignore new responsibilities under recently enacted civil rights legislation protecting the handicapped."[23]

Hispanics, represented by MALDEF, wanted to maximize reviews by OCR of the adequacy of bilingual educational programs. They were concerned that if Pratt compelled OCR to comply with the June 1976 order requiring that it investigate and resolve all complaints within the established timetables, OCR would be unable to perform as many bilingual compliance reviews as it otherwise could. WEAL's lawyers, pressing their own priorities, stressed that Title IX policies needed to be developed with regard to such issues as dress codes for schoolchildren, rules regulating hair length, and especially, criteria for equal treatment for men and women in intercollegiate athletics.

The contrasting and somewhat incompatible priorities of the groups produced delicate negotiations among their lawyers, who remained eager to cooperate rather than compete with one another, if that was possible. A lawyer for WEAL explained, "Our consistent position was that you must enforce for all groups" and that "[y]ou can't play us off against one another." Where disagreements did occur, the civil rights lawyers sought to resolve them privately. To that end, before negotiating sessions with OCR officials the groups hammered out a unified position in their own meetings, telephone conversations, and exchanges of statements.

HEW favored a single round of negotiations with all parties, rather than separate negotiations with each group. Consequently, the strategic interests of both the individual groups and the government converged in the fall of 1977. All the parties to the litigation wanted to negotiate a comprehensive enforcement scheme for OCR. Those negotiations came to fruition in December 1977.

The December 1977 Settlement of Adams and the Related Cases

There were eight major provisions to the settlement achieved in the *Adams, Brown,* and *WEAL* suits. As with previous settlements, Judge Pratt ultimately issued an order containing the terms of the agreement. The order dealt with time frames for the resolution of complaints, time frames for OCR's catching up on its backlog of complaints, the procedural rights of complainants, and the contents of OCR's annual operating plans and biannual reports.

Many of the provisions of the December 1977 order, including the time frames for the investigation of complaints, paralleled the requirements in the June 1976 order. Nonetheless, several new procedural innovations emerged. The 1977 order established the requirements for a complete written complaint of illegal discrimination and contained a schedule requiring OCR to eliminate its backlog of complaints within two fiscal years. Further, it required OCR to interview the complainant and witnesses and gave the complainant the right to rebut adverse evidence, to receive a copy of HEW's letter of findings and of correspondence between the agency and the institution alleged to have discriminated, and to be informed of the remedy being sought by the department. Though there were time frames established for the completion of compliance reviews initiated by OCR, the number of compliance reviews initiated was left to the agency's discretion.

In the press conference announcing the December 1977 settlement, Secretary Califano stated that the most important part of the settlement was the flexibility and discretion it gave OCR with regard to compliance reviews. Compliance reviews were the most effective way to remedy discrimination, he emphasized, because they often assisted individuals who were poor and uneducated, and who did not know what their rights were or how to go about enforcing them.[24] Califano indicated that OCR had conducted compliance reviews with less frequency since *Adams* because it had needed to devote so much of its resources to resolving complaints.[25]

Notwithstanding Califano's claims, it is hard to see what OCR won in the December 1977 settlement. The most onerous judicially imposed burden, the obligation to investigate every complaint within the time frames, remained in place. When Pratt denied OCR's motion to consolidate, he eliminated any real possibility that in the subsequent negotiations with the rights groups, OCR could get out from under the burden of investigating all complaints within the mandated time frames.

THE ADMINISTRATION'S FOCUS ON MANAGERIAL ISSUES IN CIVIL RIGHTS ENFORCEMENT

The December 1977 order proved valuable to OCR in justifying its need for more personnel. Contemporaneously with the negotiations leading to the December 1977 settlement order, OCR was negotiating with the Office of Management and Budget for more staff positions. Those positions were imperative, OCR maintained, to comply with the *Adams* orders, avoid a contempt citation, and meet the demands being pressed by the civil rights groups. Secretary Califano used the December 1977 court order, and the requirements of the *Adams* litigation, in his negotiations with OMB and the White House to justify additional personnel for OCR. He argued that the various groups of plaintiffs would be more inclined to settle and to forego further litigation if OCR could demonstrate that it was making headway in getting the personnel it needed to meet the time frames and eliminate its backlog of complaints.

Both OMB and White House officials were reluctant to ask Congress for the money. When Califano went to the final meeting with OMB officials at the White House, he emphasized the requirements of the new court order and the plaintiffs' aggressiveness and success in using litigation to embarrass OCR. Califano insisted that the administration had no choice but to request funds for more OCR personnel. In January 1978, a month after the parties reached their agreement in *Adams,* OMB asked Congress for funds for nearly nine hundred new employees in OCR.[26] The total number of personnel in OCR increased from roughly one thousand in 1977 to approximately seventeen hundred in 1979.[27]

The December 1977 order's focus on issues of organizational management and efficiency was consistent with the direction that the administration had itself initiated. Early in the Carter administration, there had been several actions suggesting that the administration's effort in civil rights would focus on management issues and the organizational restructuring of OCR. In April 1977, the General Accounting Office (GAO) issued a report criticizing the management of OCR for, among other things, the lack of internal coordination among OCR's different divisions in Washington, D.C., and the lack of coordination between OCR's national and regional offices. Noting that OCR could not even determine how many complaints of discrimination based on race, gender, or national origin it had received, that it lacked systematic information about the status of complaints lodged with it, and that it did not know how much staff time was spent on an average complaint or whether there was any correlation between staff time and the successful resolution of a complaint, the study concluded that OCR needed "a comprehensive and reliable management information system" to provide basic data and to improve the agency's efficiency and effectiveness.[28]

The GAO initiated the review at the request of Senator Birch Bayh (D.-Ind.), who described its findings as "truly appalling" and wrote to Califano noting his "incredulity" that OCR did not have a management information system. The acting director of OCR at the time acknowledged that there had been "a management problem" under previous administrations, and emphasized that the Carter administration had established a task force to reorganize the agency and establish a "coherent rational process" within OCR.[29]

In light of the GAO's report and Senator Bayh's criticisms, when Cynthia Brown and David Tatel came to OCR in 1977 they sought to systematize record keeping and the flow of work and information, both within each region, and between each region and Washington. That effort culminated in September 1978, when the administration announced a new organizational hierarchy and structure for OCR. In keeping with its emphasis on organizational efficiency, the restructuring created a management division in Washington to review the work of the regional offices and established the Office of the Deputy Director for Management and Administration, as well as several other new management divisions.[30]

To provide systematic information about the number and kind of complaints filed with OCR and the progress of the efforts to investigate and resolve them, the administration required all OCR investigators to send in monthly status reports on every complaint they were investigating. The administration needed these management reforms to cope with the *Adams* timetables. One longtime OCR employee explained, "Things used to fall through the cracks. No one really kept record of the tracking of complaints either in the regions or in the headquarters. It was often unclear what stage a complaint was in before *Adams*. With *Adams,* one finds a greater centralization of information and power in Washington OCR headquarters as a result of the need to monitor the processing of complaints in the regions."

Systematically gathering and analyzing information enabled OCR officials to determine how efficiently the OCR staff resolved complaints of discrimination. Early in the Carter administration, OCR adopted a policy assigning each of its investigators a quarterly "case closure goal." Regional managers broke down the quarterly objectives into monthly goals, with each investigator assigned a goal as to the number of new and backlogged complaints he or she should try to close. As a result of this system, OCR officials boasted that the agency had tripled its "productivity," as measured by the number of complaints resolved. OCR's 1978 annual operating plan acknowledged the importance that it placed on processing and resolving complaints expeditiously: "Major emphasis in fiscal year 1978 will be placed on increasing complaint handling efficiency. Efforts will focus on revised complaint handling procedures, policy articulation, orientation and training, and new approaches to resolving complaints. The expected result is a 30 percent reduction by the end of fiscal year 1978 in the average time required to conduct complaint investigations."[31]

OCR, an agency that had led a social revolution in the late 1960s by enforcing Title VI under a Democratic administration, was preoccupied with management efficiency in the processing of complaints under another Democratic administration a decade later. A profound change in OCR's organizational goals and culture had occurred. By the late 1970s, OCR had been transformed into an agency primarily interested not in combating racial discrimination in schools or anywhere else, but in maximizing the cost efficiency with which it utilized its resources and negotiated settlements of complaints of discrimination. There was a direct connection between the focus on organizational efficiency and the *Adams* litigation.

The speed with which investigators closed cases, the tracking of the status of cases, the processing of complaints, and the gathering and managing of information about OCR's work were the issues emphasized by OCR in the *Adams* era. Managerial efficiency became the primary organizational objective. The enforcement process became the focus of both the reforms initiated by the Carter administration and those mandated by the *Adams* court orders. Moreover, it was a focus on process conspicuously divorced from a concern about whether and how that process had an impact on racial justice or equal educational opportunity. During the Carter years, as after the first *Adams* order in the Nixon-Ford period, the substantive concerns at the heart of Title VI—racial discrimination in educational institutions—remained conspicuously peripheral to the litigation, the litigators, and the agency itself. Institutionalizing the proper bureaucratic form was accomplished at considerable expense.

One of the most important issues raised in the *Adams* era was to what extent the emphasis on efficiency and on the settlement of complaints may have increased either findings of no violation by OCR investigators or settlements whose terms did not completely meet the requirements of the law. After the 1977 settlement, OCR was under pressure both to eliminate the backlog of old cases and to process and resolve new complaints within the time frames. Those concerns explain why the agency began evaluating personnel in terms of how many cases they closed each month. Reluctantly and privately, OCR officials expressed concern about the effect these pressures had on the quality of OCR's investigations and settlements.

No provision of the December 1977 order sought to monitor the quality of OCR's investigations or settlements. William Taylor, a lawyer prominently involved in *Adams,* conceded that there had been insufficient discussion among civil rights attorneys, as well as HEW officials, as to the possibility of "sell-out settlements." In the period immediately following the December 1977 settlement, a long-time ranking OCR official estimated that the agency was finding discrimination in roughly 20 to 25 percent of the complaints lodged. In the past, the same official suggested, OCR had found discrimination in a much higher percentage of complaints. Concerned about the impact of the *Adams* order, he lamented:

> I don't feel we have accomplished a heck of a lot. The lower rate of findings of discrimination and the superficial nature of investigations makes me think that. We narrowed the investigation to exactly what the complainant wrote. Investigators were not to look at anything else. Our previous policy had been that whenever we got a complaint against a school district we would investigate not only the complaint but . . . the large volume of data that we collected every year from that school district to see whether there were any other problems or factual evidence suggesting a broader scope of inquiry. That kind of thing slows you down.

The organizational pressures that encouraged findings of no violation or inadequate and even unlawful settlements of complaints were not counteracted by the ability of civil rights groups to monitor OCR's actions. Though the attorneys for these groups received detailed reports of OCR's work in investigating complaints, the reports contained voluminous quantities of information, and the groups did not have the resources to monitor that information in a careful and systematic way.

One former high-ranking OCR official, with the agency from 1969 to 1977, stated that the "biggest scandal" in OCR involved the investigation of complaints. He did not recall one instance in those eight years in which there was an administrative enforcement hearing to terminate funds in connection with the investigation of a complaint. During that period, he estimated, there must have been fifteen to twenty thousand complaints filed:

> How can this be? How can regional offices go through so many complaints and not find one that warrants going through enforcement proceedings? That doesn't make any sense to me. This has been going on for ten years. It's not just this [the Carter] administration. I think some of the complainants are off the wall, but not all. Some of them fall victim to poor investigations, some of the complaints may be "resolved" in ways that may not be fair or even legal. We should be skeptical of the low proportion of complaints that are ever moved very far in the enforcement process.

As noted earlier, the procedural and managerial orientation of the *Adams* litigation involved a deliberate choice taken for reasons of legal strategy. In getting judges to oversee the enforcement of Title VI, civil rights lawyers recognized that it would be much easier to get them to address questions of administrative procedure than it would be to convince them to overturn the substance of an agency's decision. Accordingly, the LDF lawyers handling the *Adams* case relied on a legal strategy that limited the extent to which Judge Pratt and the District of Columbia Circuit would have to establish or review substantive Title VI policies.

CONGRESSIONAL RESTRICTIONS ON TITLE VI: THE ESCH AND EAGLETON-BIDEN AMENDMENTS

In 1974, Congress attached the Esch Amendment to the Equal Opportunities Act of 1974. The amendment provided that "[n]o court, department, or agency of the United States shall . . . order the implementation of a plan that would require the transportation of any student to a school other than the school closest or the next closest to his place of residence which provides the appropriate grade level and type of education for such student."[32] The Senate added a provision indicating that nothing in the amendment was intended to restrict the authority of federal courts to order busing or otherwise remedy unconstitutional discrimination in school districts.[33] In 1977, Congress passed what became known as the Eagleton-Biden Amendment — an amendment to the 1964 Civil Rights Act. This measure, signed by President Carter in December 1977, provided that "[n]one of the funds contained in this Act shall be used to require, directly or indirectly, the transportation of any student to a school other than the school which is nearest the student's home, except for a student requiring special education, in order to comply with Title VI of the Civil Rights Act of 1964."[34]

Congress passed the Eagleton-Biden Amendment to prevent HEW from using Title VI to require school systems to bus children. Debate in both the Senate and the House established that, whereas Congress intended the amendment to limit HEW's authority under Title VI to order busing, the measure did not prevent the Justice Department from initiating litigation seeking busing as a remedy under the Constitution or prevent federal courts from imposing that remedy.[35] The effect of the amendment was such that, where OCR concluded that busing was necessary for compliance with Title VI, and the school district would not voluntarily agree to bus, OCR had no choice but to refer the case to the Justice Department for litigation.

Prior to the Esch and Eagleton-Biden Amendments, when OCR determined that Title VI required busing in a school system the agency could either commence administrative enforcement proceedings leading to the termination of funds, or refer the case to the Justice Department for litigation. By means of those amendments, Congress eliminated that option wherever OCR viewed busing as a remedy. In other words, the amendments eliminated HEW's authority to do precisely what Title VI was intended to do — replace litigation with administrative determinations of discrimination that punished offenders by terminating their federal funds. Senator Eagleton explained that the amendment applied "where HEW, acting solely on its own administrative authority and acting without any judicial determination of unconstitutionality, administratively seeks to impose its own formula as to the racial mix or racial balance of a given school district."[36]

Senator Biden, too, focused on his reservations about HEW's authority under Title VI:

The issue is, can an administrative agency, the Department of Health, Education and Welfare, absent a finding, by any court order in this nation — absent a finding, absent a court order, absent a court ruling that there is a constitutional violation — can an administrative agency make a determination that in their judgment there is, in effect, a constitutional violation; and that, therefore, unless a school district or a series of school districts entered into a plan suggested by or sanctioned by HEW, that district or those districts will have their federal funds withheld?[37]

In advancing his argument, Biden attacked the basic idea behind Title VI — that a determination of discrimination should be made via an administrative process:

. . . [T]hose of you who are going to vote with the Senator from Massachusetts are making one decision: That you think, absent a court order, a bureaucrat downtown or out in the district can make a judgment that there is constitutional violation that exists. I say to you that the only person who should be able to make that decision is a duly constituted federal court. It is not for some bureaucrat to say, "We think you violated the Constitution; therefore, we make the judgment that unless you comply with our order, you do not get any federal money."[38]

The congressional debate questioned the very rationale for Title VI and the authority it granted to agencies to withhold monies where the agency determined that recipients had discriminated. Congress had enacted Title VI out of a recognition that relying on judicial determinations of discrimination and on judicial remedies had proven ineffectual. The Eagleton-Biden Amendment was the death knell for Title VI in elementary and secondary education because it eliminated the enforcement mechanism that made Title VI effective: the termination of funds after administrative proceedings. The Nixon administration had used the discretion provided in Title VI to refer cases for litigation rather than for administrative enforcement. The Eagleton-Biden Amendment, however, made that approach mandatory in elementary and secondary education. It compelled HEW, in dealing with questions of student segregation, to fight racial discrimination by the method that had proven ineffectual, that is, by litigating.[39]

The Carter administration was ambivalent about the constitutionality of the Eagleton-Biden Amendment. OCR director Tatel wrote a lengthy memorandum to the Justice Department arguing that the amendment was unconstitutional. Rebuffing Tatel, the Justice Department appeared in court to defend the amendment, arguing that though it was unwise, it was not unconstitutional: The question presented, said the administration, was "whether Congress, which has through the 1964 Civil Rights Act provided judicial and administrative procedures to remedy segregation by race in schools and school districts receiving federal funds, may *require* resort to the judicial avenue in circumstances where busing is sought to be required for unconstitutional segregation." Taking the position that what the Esch and Eagleton-Biden Amendments changed was not the prohibition on funding segregated districts, but only the means by which that mandate is carried out, the Justice Department insisted that the measures, however ill-advised, were valid attempts by Congress to establish the remedy for enforcing Fifth and Fourteenth Amendment guarantees.[40]

When the bill containing the Eagleton-Biden Amendment came before President Carter for his signature, the U.S. Commission on Civil Rights advised the president that the provision conflicted with the federal government's obligation, under the Fifth Amendment and the 1964 Civil Rights Act, not to fund racially discriminatory activities. Though he expressed misgivings about the amendment, saying that it might "raise new and vexing constitutional questions, adding further complexities to an already complex area of the law," Carter signed the measure.[41]

In December 1977, on the very day Carter signed the Eagleton-Biden Amendment into law, the NAACP Legal Defense Fund filed *Brown v. Califano,* a lawsuit intended to enjoin HEW and the Justice Department from enforcing the amendment. The LDF argued that the amendment negated court orders in *Adams,* inhibited school desegregation in violation of the *Swann* decision authorizing busing, and unconstitutionally required HEW to provide federal aid to segregated schools. In arguing before Judge Sirica in a Washington, D.C., federal district court in April 1978, Joseph Rauh asked the court to declare the amendment unconstitutional and to require HEW to re-open its enforcement of Title VI in the seventeen districts in which it had previously determined that busing was required to achieve compliance with Title VI.

In July 1978, Judge Sirica ruled that Congress could prohibit HEW from requiring school districts to bus to achieve desegregation as long as HEW could continue to ask the Justice Department to sue any district that HEW believed could be desegregated only by busing.[42] On appeal, in February 1980, Judge Bazelon, writing for the District of Columbia circuit court of appeals, affirmed Sirica's decision and ruled that the statute was not unconstitutional because it preserved a remedy to achieve compliance with Title VI, namely, Justice Department lawsuits.[43] Noting that the court's finding of constitutionality assumed that Congress intended the Justice Department to act promptly on cases referred to it by HEW, Bazelon left open the possibility that if the Justice Department failed to prosecute those referrals expeditiously, the statute could later be held unconstitutional *as applied*. "We are clearly gasping," a prominent civil rights lawyer offered, "but we are not yet dead." He explained:

> We are eager to find out more about the procedures by which Justice handles HEW referrals and we have gone so far as to send out notices for depositions. In response to that, Justice has gone into court and asked for a protective order arguing that the case challenging Eagleton-Biden is over and moving that we not be permitted to depose individuals on the question of Justice's handling of cases referred to it by HEW. You can't take depositions, they say, in a case which is over. . . . We would like to proceed to gather more information on . . . Justice's handling of HEW Title VI referrals. And I think that awareness on the part of the Justice Department, that we continue to be interested, may help prod them on with some of the investigations they have been conducting.

HEW–JUSTICE DEPARTMENT RELATIONS UNDER THE EAGLETON-BIDEN AMENDMENT

After the Eagleton-Biden Amendment became law, OCR played the role of a fact finder for the Justice Department, investigating complaints or conducting compliance reviews, producing a file and then giving that information to the department's lawyers. If it found a violation, HEW was obliged to refer the case to the Justice Department, because school desegregation in large cities typically required busing beyond the school nearest a student's home, thereby triggering the Eagleton-Biden prohibition.

A veteran OCR attorney characterized a typical northern school desegregation case involving possible violations of Title VI in this way:

> Residential segregation exists. As the black community grows and expands school districts adopt and utilize optional zone plans. Anyone in this optional zone can go to this school or any other school. The school district uses crowding as the excuse. These are white protection mechanisms. The whites tend to utilize the transfer option and the

blacks do not as a rule. This is the northern version of free choice. We can do nothing about this sort of thing now [after Eagleton-Biden]. The limitations of Eagleton-Biden are devastating to the Title VI enforcement in the North.

Where OCR investigated racial discrimination in assigning students to schools, the school districts understood that HEW could not order busing or terminate funds and that if OCR found a violation of Title VI, the case was going to end up in the Justice Department. That understanding affected the willingness of school boards to negotiate seriously with OCR. One congressman, long familiar with HEW's enforcement of Title VI, remarked:

> Now if the school board officials know that at the end of the road OCR is simply going to ship its case to Justice it makes no sense for them [school board officials] to lay themselves bare and provide information which will then get fed over to Justice and be used against them should Justice litigate. In such circumstances, serious negotiations with HEW are not likely. School officials are not apt to engage in meaningful and substantial discussions. It would be silly for them to do so. Some systems might just, because they don't want problems. But when you are talking about the bigger systems, when you are talking about systems able to afford lawyers, it is silly for them to sit down and lay themselves open. . . . The consequence is that you are slowly, through Eagleton-Biden, eliminating an area of enforcement in civil rights, an area of negotiations, another arm that could be applied in this process and essentially you are bringing it all under Justice and the court system.

In OCR's new limited role, the agency's relationship with the Justice Department was unsteady. When HEW had enforced Title VI through administrative action leading to the possible termination of funds, it used its own lawyers and retained exclusive control over the enforcement process. Its lawyers controlled the critical decisions determining whether there was a violation and, if there was one, what remedial measures were necessary. After the Eagleton-Biden Amendment, that was no longer true. The Justice Department determined what to do with cases once OCR had referred them to the department for violations of Title VI, and the department's lawyers did not view themselves as obliged to initiate litigation in cases referred by OCR or even to accept the legal positions that OCR lawyers had advanced in their discussions with the school district. One OCR official described the awkward situation in this way: "We say to a school system you are not in compliance. Then we send their case over to the Justice Department and Justice doesn't sue. We're stuck out on a limb and that has happened in a number of student assignment cases." The Justice Department explained such administrative awkwardness by saying that it was not interested in using its resources in federal courts on small issues and cases, but rather needed to reserve its resources for big, precedent-setting cases.

During the Carter administration, Justice Department lawyers in several instances sent cases referred by OCR back to the civil rights unit with directives, in effect, for OCR to resume negotiations with the school districts. Consequently, cases referred to the Justice Department by OCR were, on occasion, like tennis balls popping back and forth between the two agencies, with neither taking effective action. In these situations OCR was in a weak bargaining position vis-à-vis the school districts because the implication of referring a case to the Justice Department in the first place was that OCR had determined that further negotiations would be fruitless. When the Justice Department referred the matter back to HEW without initiating litigation, that rebuff diminished OCR's leverage with the recipient in the second, unexpected round of negotiations between the two.

Occasionally, the Justice Department encouraged OCR to accept settlements offered by school boards although the agency had rejected the terms of the proposed settlements prior to referring the case to the Justice Department. Where OCR would not accede to suggestions from the Justice Department, cases often remained in limbo for extended periods with no meaningful enforcement steps taken by either agency. Recall that the *Adams* time frames did not apply once the formal enforcement process began — that is, after OCR sent a notice of an administrative hearing or referred a case to the Justice Department. That was a significant limitation in the extent to which the litigation controlled the enforcement of Title VI.

By the end of the Carter term, in part because of the Eagleton-Biden Amendment, segregation in elementary and secondary schools, once an issue central to OCR's work, had become a marginal concern. To be sure, OCR still conducted compliance reviews. But it did so largely because of the political need to demonstrate at least some symbolic interest in the subject. One OCR official explained:

> The reason we still conduct compliance reviews is from a public standpoint. It is not viable to withdraw from this issue. The Department couldn't announce that it is withdrawing from all student assignment cases because that is saying that the problem [of segregation in schools]

doesn't exist. What we do say is that we are going to do something because the problem does exist but in terms of what happens from an enforcement standpoint, we must depend on Justice [the Justice Department]. If you are willing to admit that fund termination is no longer a viable tool, and you couple that with Eagleton-Biden, you're handcuffed.

The situation in Chicago in 1980 provided yet another explanation for the meager activity by the federal government on student assignment questions. There was ample evidence demonstrating racial discrimination in the assignment of students to schools in that city. Attorneys in the Justice Department as well as in OCR were convinced of that. In June 1980, that case was before Attorney General Benjamin Civiletti for decision. As one OCR official summarized the case, the real problem in Chicago was remedy:

It is all there. The wheel-in wagons [used as classrooms], the drawing of school boundary lines, the schools side by side, a half a mile away — one white, one black. You name it, the case is there — the evidence is nailed down.

The question in Chicago really is remedy with a system that is approaching 90 percent minority students in the public school population. It's going to be a case for an affirmative finding and what are you going to do? Are you going to settle for 10 percent white in each of the schools . . . and if you're going to do that, are you going to increase white flight? And you will end up with, "Where am I going to get the whites from?"

OCR's New Focus on Desegregation in Higher Education

Pratt's Order Requiring HEW to Develop Desegregation Standards for Higher Education

Though enforcement of Title VI in student assignment questions at the elementary and secondary school levels languished during the Carter administration, enforcement in higher education emerged as a pivotal issue for OCR. Recall that LDF lawyers sought further relief in higher education from Judge Pratt in August 1975, claiming that the state desegregation plans submitted to and accepted by OCR did not comply with Pratt's orders or with the legal requirements of Title VI as set out in the letters of guidance the agency sent to the states in November 1973.

It took almost a year and a half to get a decision from Judge Pratt on LDF's Motion for Further Relief in Higher Education. In January 1977, the logjam broke in a curious and political way. Several days after the election in November 1976, when it was clear that the Republicans were leaving office, Martin Gerry, the OCR director leaving office with the Ford administration, made a presentation to the Southern Education Foundation, a group that had provided financial support for the higher-education portion of the *Adams* litigation. Gerry advanced detailed criticisms of the plans that OCR had accepted, concluding that they were little more than plans to plan for desegregation. Jean Fairfax, the LDF official monitoring desegregation plans for higher education, was in the audience that day, taking careful notes on Gerry's comments.

Guided by Fairfax's notes on Gerry's criticisms of the state plans, Elliot Lichtman, an attorney from Joseph Rauh's law firm, deposed Gerry in January 1977 and elicited testimony from him specifying the inadequacies of the plans OCR had accepted. The deposition constituted nothing less than sworn testimony by the director of OCR that the office was not complying with its own standards and with Judge Pratt's orders. With only seven days left in the Ford administration, the timing of the deposition was critical. Gerry's deposition testimony, ultimately submitted to Pratt as part of the Motion for Further Relief in Higher Education, persuaded Pratt that the plans were, indeed, inadequate.

Pratt heightened the pressure on OCR in April 1977 in his second supplemental order in higher education. In that order, he held that the desegregation plans that HEW had accepted in June 1974 from the states involved in *Adams* were inadequate. He ruled that the plans failed to meet the requirements that HEW had itself specified and that they had not produced sufficient desegregation to comply with Title VI.[44] Pratt required HEW, within 90 days of the date of his order, to develop comprehensive, written criteria specifying the ingredients of acceptable statewide desegregation plans in higher education, and he ordered the six remaining *Adams* states to submit new plans within 60 days of their receipt of HEW's criteria.* Pratt further ordered HEW to accept or reject the states' plans within 120 days of receiving them.

The basis for Pratt's second supplemental order was Gerry's depo-

*Of the ten states initially involved in the higher-education portion of *Adams,* Louisiana and Mississippi became parties in litigation initiated by the Justice Department. Maryland, which claimed in the *Mandel* case that HEW had failed adequately to pursue voluntary compliance, had an appeal pending before the Fourth Circuit. Pennsylvania was engaged in settlement negotiations with HEW.

sition. Pratt noted that Gerry conceded "lack of progress and the need to obtain specific commitments" from the states, and that Gerry further acknowledged the problems in the admission, recruitment, and retention of "other race" students at the historically black and white schools, in the duplication of program offerings among the institutions, in the role and enhancement of historically black institutions, and in the racial composition of the faculties.[45]

Demonstrating yet again his concern for the impact that desegregation might have on the historically black colleges, Pratt reminded HEW of the language that the court of appeals had used in its affirmance of his initial decision when it emphasized the need to take "into account the special problems of Black colleges" because they "fulfill a crucial need and will continue to play an important role in Black higher education." Mindful of that admonition, Pratt added:

> The process of desegregation must not place a greater burden on Black institutions or Black students' opportunity to receive a quality public higher education. The desegregation process should take into account the unequal status of the Black colleges and the real danger that desegregation will diminish higher education opportunities for Blacks. Without suggesting the answer to this complex problem, it is the responsibility of HEW to devise criteria for higher education desegregation plans which will take into account the unique importance of Black colleges and at the same time comply with the congressional mandate.[46]

Pratt's statement of the problem was prophetic, for the very issues he raised dominated the political and legal struggle surrounding desegregation under Title VI for the next decade and a half. In the short term, Pratt's order produced the long-awaited desegregation criteria from OCR.

HEW's Desegregation Standards for Higher Education

The LDF wanted OCR to develop comprehensive guidelines for desegregation in higher education, paralleling the Guidelines for elementary and secondary education developed by HEW during the Johnson years. Approximately seven years had passed since the filing of the *Adams* complaint in 1970, and roughly four years had passed since the District of Columbia court of appeals had unanimously affirmed Judge Pratt's initial decision. Though those victories were impressive, transforming those legal triumphs into swift and effectual action had proven to be difficult. Indeed, the absence of comprehensive desegregation criteria in higher education, four years after Pratt's initial order, was but one example of the exasperatingly slow pace of progress under *Adams*. Pratt's January 1977 order to establish such standards seemed yet another decisive legal victory for the plaintiffs. Once again, a Pratt order offered hope to the LDF and their litigators. It also produced a new set of extended negotiations between OCR officials and civil rights lawyers over the desegregation criteria. One civil rights lawyer characterized the process in this way:

> We met a number of times with the staff of OCR without the acting director and we made compromises. Then we were told that we had to clear this with the acting director and then he got into the act and then the guidelines got watered down somewhat and then they said this has to be taken to the General Counsel's office to see what they think about it and then we negotiated with the General Counsel. . . . When we saw eye to eye with him then he said, "I've got to show this to the Secretary." When he came back from the Secretary, he said that the Secretary won't accept even this and we're going to have to reduce it further. The next series of negotiations essentially involved eroding our original agreements through a process of seeking agreement from many many layers of the bureaucracy. In the meantime, the black college presidents were filing a brief against us because they were disgruntled and nervous about the whole process and then, of course, we had to deal with other southern educators who also were intensely opposed. What OCR did at that point was to hold a series of rather large meetings in May and June of 1977. This involved a process of testing all the waters. What came out of all these deliberations and consultations was a set of proposals which were substantially compromised from what we had initially proposed to OCR in February 1977.

OCR officials, too, felt frustrated by the need to clear agreements reached by the plaintiffs with authorities outside the civil rights unit. Yet, they had no choice. HEW secretary Califano monitored the negotiations closely, dispatching his own personal aide to all negotiations and insisting on the power to withhold final authorization. Prior to issuing their desegregation guidelines, OCR officials also met on a number of occasions with representatives from NAFEO, the association of presidents of historically black colleges and universities.

HEW issued its "criteria" in February 1978. According to those standards, Title VI required the traditionally white and black institutions "to provide an education to all citizens without discrimination or segregation" in "a unitary system free of the vestiges of state imposed racial segregation."[47] The HEW criteria established goals and timetables for upgrading the historically black institutions, increasing the number of blacks enrolled in institutions of public higher education in each state, increasing the number of black faculty members and administrators at state institutions, and increasing the number of blacks on the governing boards of the white institutions.

The five-year plans outlined in the criteria involved a two-pronged desegregation process that would integrate the black colleges into state systems of higher education, both racially and programmatically. The first prong concentrated on increasing black enrollment at white schools, while allowing the historically black colleges to retain their traditional character. The second prong—the one that concerned black educators—called for enhancing the academic role of the historically black colleges and increasing the white enrollment at those schools.

By establishing that states had an affirmative duty to eliminate all the vestiges of the de jure system of segregation, the criteria adopted concepts developed by the Supreme Court, especially in the *Green* case, in overseeing desegregation at the elementary and secondary school levels. That was noteworthy for several reasons. It indicated that just as HEW had tried to support its Guidelines in elementary and secondary education in the 1960s by relying on standards developed by federal courts, it was trying to rely on judicial concepts again, a decade later, in desegregation in higher education. However, because there was little case law exploring the issue of desegregation of colleges and universities, there remained considerable uncertainty as to whether and how the legal principles developed by courts for elementary and secondary schools applied in the milieu of higher education. Higher education was different from elementary and secondary education in basic ways. There were standards for admission to the schools, attendance was not compulsory, and student choice in selecting an institution was an accepted part of the process. Complicating matters further were the thorny issues of academic freedom raised by university administrators, black and white, who felt that through desegregation they could lose educational control over their institutions.

In accordance with the District of Columbia Circuit's affirmance of Pratt's initial decision in *Adams,* the criteria directed HEW to require statewide desegregation plans. The criteria contained numerical goals and timetables in several areas, referring to those numbers as "benchmarks." To blunt the expected political criticism, the criteria contained this qualifying language: "These goals are not quotas. The Department is opposed to arbitrary quotas. Failure to achieve a goal is not sufficient evidence, standing alone, to establish a violation of Title VI. In addition, the Office for Civil Rights upon showing of exceptional hardship or special circumstances by a state, may modify the goals and timetables."[48]

The criteria recognized the "unique importance" of the historically black colleges and universities (HBCUs), noting that those institutions had trained 80 percent of all black college graduates and that, even as late as the mid-1970s, 40 percent of all blacks graduating from college each year attended those schools. Nonetheless, HEW did not exempt those institutions from the constitutional requirement to desegregate. To the contrary, the criteria emphasized that the black and white institutions were "subject to the same constitutional and congressional mandate to provide an education to all citizens without discrimination or segregation." The criteria did provide, however, that increased enrollment by whites in the black colleges must be preceded by steps "to strengthen the role of traditionally black institutions and give them new vitality by setting up new courses and programs and eliminating areas where they merely duplicate other schools."[49]

The criteria required that desegregation plans define the mission of each institution on a basis other than race and specify the steps that would be taken to strengthen the role of the historically black colleges. The desegregation plans had to include commitments to increase the resources provided to the traditionally black institutions for physical plant, program offerings, research equipment, and student and staff services. In addition, each state had to eliminate unnecessary program duplication at the historically black and white institutions serving the same area, give priority to establishing new undergraduate, graduate, or professional degree programs at historically black colleges, and achieve the goals of the desegregation plans no later than the close of the 1981–82 academic year.

To achieve the above goals, the desegregation criteria required that states

- specify annual numerical goals for increasing the numbers of white students at the historically black institutions;
- adopt the goal that the proportion of black high-school graduates entering state institutions of higher education should equal the proportion of white high-school graduates entering such institutions, and commit themselves to reducing the existing disparity in those proportions by at least 50 percent by the 1982–83 academic year;

- specify goals regarding the annual percentage increase in the number of blacks enrolled in the traditionally white four-year institutions;
- adopt the goal that the proportion of black state residents entering graduate or professional schools in the state equal the proportion of white state residents entering those schools; and
- take all reasonable measures, through the use of financial aid and compensatory education programs, to reduce the rate of black college drop-outs and the disparity between the college graduation rates of whites and blacks.[50]

Reviewing the provisions of the 1977 desegregation criteria gives one a sense for the profound changes in the state university systems HEW envisioned. The criteria called for changes not merely in the racial makeup of student bodies, faculties, staffs, and governing boards — profound changes in their own right — but for transformations in educational programs throughout the state at the undergraduate, graduate, and professional levels. By seeking to equalize the percentage of black and white high-school seniors who attended the state universities, the criteria, at least indirectly, contemplated the need for educational changes at the elementary and secondary school levels. The criteria contained the government's most ambitious statement ever of the *educational* goals to be achieved in the desegregation process in higher education.

OCR officials were in an unenviable political position in developing and implementing the criteria. They continued to be dogged by the poor reputation the agency had acquired during the Nixon-Ford era. Moreover, during the Carter years they had been obliged to please a demanding and politically sensitive secretary who insisted on running his own agency, free of the demands of civil rights lawyers and litigation. Notwithstanding that insistence, OCR continued to be pressed by lawyers for the LDF who remained skeptical about the agency's commitment to civil rights, by NAFEO representatives who trusted neither OCR, the LDF, nor the states, and by the states themselves, which jealously guarded their prerogatives to run their state university systems.

In announcing the criteria, Secretary Califano indicated that they would apply not merely to the six states involved in the *Adams* litigation but to all of the southern and border states. Consequently, the criteria applied to some 260 publicly supported colleges enrolling 1.1 million students, of whom nearly 50,000 were students at historically black colleges. Hoping that the new standards would eliminate future

legal challenges to HEW's enforcement of Title VI in higher education, Califano observed that such tactics were unnecessary in the
Carter administration.[51] Despite his tenacity, the priority he placed
on extricating HEW from the grip of *Adams,* and the credibility and
credentials of his civil rights staff, Califano could neither extricate
HEW from the litigation nor quiet the fears and criticism of civil
rights activists.

Following Califano's announcement of the higher-education criteria in July 1977, the LDF responded that though it was pleased that
HEW had finally announced the standards, it remained unhappy
with them. John Silard, the lawyer from Rauh's firm who did most of
the negotiating with HEW for the LDF, said that he was "disap-
pointed that HEW had given the states another five to ten years to
finish a reform which should have been completed many years ago
under Supreme Court rulings and federal law."[52] Jean Fairfax, of the
LDF staff, observed that whereas the criteria established "strong,
very specific language" about enhancing the historically black colleges, she, too, believed that OCR was giving the states too much
time to desegregate.[53]

The *Adams* plaintiffs received and commented extensively on drafts
of the desegregation criteria developed by HEW. NAFEO leaders,
though consulted in the development of the criteria, were not confi-
dent that OCR, LDF, or the southern states were reliable partners.
In many ways, the most awkward and strained relationship was between NAFEO and LDF officials — people presumably motivated by
similar goals. NAFEO leaders were suspicious of the LDF lawyers,
believing that the LDF had disregarded the concerns of those in the
black colleges by plunging into the *Adams* litigation without adequately consulting NAFEO leaders or thinking through the consequences LDF's "integration" model would have for the historically
black institutions. Though Elias Blake Jr., the president of Clark College and a leader in NAFEO, had been belatedly approached by the
LDF lawyers to testify as an expert witness in the *Adams* case, his relationship with those lawyers was an uneasy one.

Herbert Reid, a veteran civil rights lawyer and professor at the
Howard University Law School, had submitted an amicus brief on
behalf of NAFEO to Judge Pratt and to the court of appeals in the
Adams case. Reed's brief emphasized the dangers that the *Adams* litigation posed to the historically black institutions. As OCR prepared to
implement its criteria in 1978, there was continued apprehension in
NAFEO.

If the LDF was unhappy with the criteria and NAFEO was anxious about them, southern states were no more welcoming. In Virginia, for example, where two-thirds of the black students enrolled in the state's fourteen state colleges attended just two of those colleges — the two historically black colleges — Governor Godwin declared that the standards "reduced higher education in Virginia to a federal numbers game."[54] In Georgia, where three of the state's thirty-two colleges were historically black institutions, one member of the state board of regents observed that the criteria would enhance the black schools at the expense of the white institutions, and that the priority given the black colleges would "starve the white institutions out."[55]

Desegregating institutions of higher education was a prominent political issue throughout the South. In the deliberations that produced the HEW criteria, OCR negotiated with state governors, state commissioners of education, state boards of regents, and university presidents. The negotiations received a high level of attention and priority within HEW. On occasion, they involved both the HEW secretary and members of the White House staff. Moreover, the issue also received a good deal of attention from the media in each state, making desegregation in higher education the most politically controversial area of school desegregation during the Carter administration. One OCR official explained: "The negotiations with the institutions of higher education involved the Office of the Secretary directly. There was very little that was done that did not have direct oversight by the Secretary."

Another OCR official elaborated on some of the special difficulties OCR faced from the academic community:

> The academic community can make a big blow up. It has the skills to make a big stink. Everyone in the hierarchy is an alumni of something. This is not so true at the elementary and secondary level. In addition, of course, the academics were always able to charge that the desegregation standards, in effect, seriously jeopardized the academic freedom of individual faculty members and administrators to determine within their own institution what priorities and allocation of resources there would be.

In February 1978, after HEW issued the final version of the criteria, the *Adams* plaintiffs moved for an order suspending federal aid to the six *Adams* states. As always, their action prompted OCR, defensively, to take action. Later that month, Califano announced that OCR had accepted the desegregation plans submitted by Arkansas, Oklahoma, and Florida, and the community colleges of North Carolina, and had rejected the plans submitted by Virginia, by Georgia, and by North Carolina's four-year institutions.[56] Califano said that if the states whose plans HEW had rejected did not produce satisfactory plans within forty-five days, the agency would start administrative enforcement proceedings against them that could result in the loss of millions of dollars of federal funds.

Under its previous policies, HEW had deferred all new applications for federal funds from institutions against which it had begun administrative enforcement proceedings. Califano indicated, however, that under a new Carter administration policy he would defer applications for future funding only if the funds to be awarded would contribute to continuing segregation in the affected institutions. Moreover, in no instance, the secretary promised, would student financial aid be affected. This new policy supposedly tailored deferrals to the underlying civil rights problem that the department sought to remedy. Though it did that, it also blunted the immediate impact of administrative hearings on alleged violators. Moreover, it was hard to avoid the perception that for all the administration's tough talk, its new policy amounted to a retreat from past practice, or at least a public recognition that it had to proceed cautiously and defensively in threatening to withhold federal monies from state universities. That skittishness was not lost on Joseph Rauh, who, characterizing the new policy as a capitulation, proclaimed, "It's time to stop playing patty-cake with people who violate the law."[57] President Carter, who kept a low public profile in desegregation in higher education, commented, cryptically, "I don't deplore nor do I disagree with the action HEW has taken. But it is in direct compliance with the federal court order."[58]

The Confrontation with North Carolina

In March 1978, HEW received and accepted desegregation plans from Georgia and Virginia. Now North Carolina, perennially the toughest state on desegregation in higher education, remained the only *Adams* state that had not submitted an acceptable plan under the HEW criteria.

The forty-five-day deadline Califano had set when he announced HEW's acceptance of the Arkansas, Oklahoma, and Florida plans came and went, and North Carolina had not submitted a plan HEW would accept. At the expiration of that period, in March 1978, Califano announced that HEW would commence administrative enforcement proceedings against the state.[59] He emphasized, as the department invariably did, that under the time frames in Judge Pratt's court order, it had no choice — it was legally obligated to act.

It was obvious that a dual system remained in North Carolina, Califano insisted, because 91 percent of the students at the traditionally white schools were white, and 90 percent of the students at the traditionally black schools were black. But HEW's claims against North Carolina went well beyond the racial segregation of students. Significant segregation still persisted on the faculties at the traditionally white and black institutions. Although blacks constituted 11 percent of all faculty members in the university system, at the eleven traditionally white schools only 2 percent of faculty members were black. OCR also found that faculty members at the historically black schools had weaker academic credentials than did their counterparts at the traditionally white schools, that blacks were underrepresented on the governing boards of the traditionally white colleges in the state, and that the black institutions generally had weaker academic programs and did not attract many white students.[60] Califano also explained that North Carolina's sixteen state university campuses contained unconstitutional vestiges of the system of de jure segregation: the state provided a greater number and variety of degree programs at the predominantly white institutions, employed faculty members at lower academic rankings and salaries at the black schools, and provided those schools with inferior facilities.

In keeping with HEW's new policy on deferring future funding applications, Califano wrote to Governor James Hunt of North Carolina that HEW "will begin to defer — in a carefully targeted and limited fashion — consideration of future application for HEW funds from the University system if those new funds would contribute to continuing segregation in [the University of North Carolina] system."[61] Califano emphasized that if there had been such a deferral in the previous fiscal year, OCR would have reviewed $68 million in HEW funds that went to public institutions of higher education in North Carolina, and he estimated that about $10 million might have been identified as contributing to continued segregation.[62]

North Carolina's response to Califano's announcement was defiant. Governor Hunt announced that the state was prepared to do without Washington's money, declaring, "[W]e are going to pursue our right to run public education in this state." In a press conference, William C. Friday, long-time president of the University of North Carolina at Chapel Hill, couched his objection in carefully chosen words that framed the issues in dispute in terms of educational policy questions instead of race. "[W]e will not agree to any plan that takes from the university its responsibility to make educational decisions," stated Friday.[63] The chief remaining obstacle between the state and Washington involved plans to end the duplication of programs at the predominantly white and black campuses. That problem involved disagreements about enhancing the black colleges so as to draw more white students to them, and, conversely, about the need to attract more black students to white campuses.

On 11 May 1978, after extended negotiations that received much public attention, HEW provisionally accepted a desegregation plan from North Carolina. The major components of the agreement included commitments to give priority consideration to creating new programs at the five traditionally black institutions, to equalize the salaries of black and white faculty members over a five-year period, and to boost the total number of blacks in the freshman class at the primarily white colleges from the current total of about 950 a year to 2,360 by 1982 — a 150-percent increase over a five-year period.

OCR accepted North Carolina's plan provisionally because it was not fully satisfied with what the state proposed to do with respect to the future of the historically black colleges and universities. Consequently, it gave the state another six months to complete the part of the plan devoted to those institutions. Following the announcement of the provisional agreement, there was once again a temporary halt to the battle between the state and the federal government. That pause, however, was not long-lived.

HEW's desegregation criteria required that, over a five-year period, the state universities reduce by half the difference between the proportions of white and black high-school graduates who enrolled at the historically white campuses. As noted, for North Carolina that requirement meant a 150-percent increase from the 950 black freshmen at the white institutions in 1978 to 2,360 black students in 1982. In mid-August 1978, Friday announced revisions in the part of North Carolina's plan intended to increase the number of minority students entering the traditionally white institutions. Friday, referring to the 150-percent goal as neither "realistic or feasible however desirable it may be,"[64] stressed that the university would not comply with that requirement. He insisted that it was an unattainable goal barring a major relaxation of admission standards — an option unacceptable to the university. Instead, he proposed a 32-percent increase over the five-year period. As for strengthening the historically black institutions, Friday argued that the university could not decide a priori that new programs and resources must go to those institutions without a comprehensive assessment of the educational needs of the state. Once again, the parties were on a collision course.

A strong-willed lawyer who had spent his entire academic career at

Chapel Hill, Friday had been president of the university for more than two decades. He had been the moving force in bringing Chapel Hill into the ranks of the nation's elite research universities. For him, not surprisingly, the major issue was academic freedom — the state's control over its institutions of higher education. The university's board of governors also saw it that way. After it endorsed Friday's proposal on minority enrollment, the chairman of the board declared that the HEW criteria "violate the integrity of the university and constitute an unjustified infringement on the right of this board and this university . . . to remain free from improper interference by outside forces and agencies." In language reminiscent of defiant statements opposing elementary and secondary school desegregation a decade earlier, the board's chairman proclaimed, "[T]his university does not belong to HEW nor to Judge Pratt and the District Court over which he presides in Washington D.C. It is the university of this state and it belongs to the people of the state of North Carolina."[65]

Notwithstanding Califano's statements, at the time of his appointment, about enforcing civil rights laws and even terminating funds, he seemed to back off as the situation in North Carolina headed for collision:

> To say to a major school system we will cut all your funds unless you meet these standards has aspects of cutting off your nose to spite your face. . . . You need a penalty that's related to the offense or an incentive that is related to what we want people to do to make these things work — and these atomic bomb penalties don't work. I'll use them if that's all I've got but I want them related to the offense.[66]

One White House strategist indicated that the Carter administration was in an awkward position, saying, "We have a political problem from both sides. A tough line with the university hurts Mr. Carter with the white power structure; an easy line risks alienating black and civil rights communities." An editorial in the *New York Times* concluded that "it looks as if the Carolina-Califano battle is going to hurt Jimmy Carter no matter what happens."[67]

Notwithstanding the supposed stakes for Carter, the conflict was ultimately forged and controlled by the North Carolina board of regents (pressed by President Friday) and by HEW secretary Califano (pressed by his civil rights staff). On Califano's staff, David Tatel, among others, threatened to resign if HEW backed off. One high OCR official explained that OCR held fast, in part, because of the actions of the Legal Defense Fund lawyers:

Everyone is patting us on the back for bringing North Carolina to a hearing in higher education, but that didn't happen until the plaintiffs went back into court to file for a contempt citation. OCR was going to back off again and negotiate some more with North Carolina. Finally, the plaintiffs said this has got to stop so they found their way back into the courtroom for a contempt citation because we were out of the *Adams* time frames with respect to North Carolina. Our negotiations had extended beyond the 120 day time frame established in the order. It was in response to that action by the plaintiffs that OCR ultimately filed before an administrative law judge for enforcement proceedings. Had the plaintiffs not gone back to court, we would have negotiated with North Carolina forever.

The experience in North Carolina again emphasizes that LDF could not directly influence substantive decisions on civil rights issues, but rather relied on litigation to compel OCR to initiate the enforcement process. Litigation, if nothing else, could be used to forestall HEW's interminable footdragging and compel it to act.

It was not until June 1979, after the *Adams* plaintiffs brought their motion, that HEW concluded that North Carolina's plan was inadequate. The following month, formal hearings to consider withholding funds from the state began before an administrative law judge. Each side presented voluminous documents and nearly two score witnesses. In the middle of the administrative enforcement process, however, North Carolina responded with its own legal initiative, trying to blunt the immediate effect of that proceeding. In a North Carolina federal district court, it filed suit to enjoin HEW from deferring its federal funds while the proceeding was under way. In a decision in the fall of 1979, the court did enjoin HEW from deferring funds until the agency had made a final administrative determination on North Carolina's compliance with Title VI. As one civil rights lawyer explained, this had a direct impact on the continuing administrative enforcement efforts:

> What we saw in North Carolina then is what we had seen in respect to Mississippi and Louisiana in that if you take the immediate bite of deferral away you do eliminate an important and crucial incentive for the educational institution to come into compliance. The response on the part of the defendant then is to filibuster. North Carolina hired civil liberties lawyer Chuck Morgan to handle their case [the administrative proceeding]. There has been an attack on the criteria, on the plaintiffs, and a million objections and a million witnesses. Lawyers know how to slow things down and they've been very good at it in this case.

When Jimmy Carter left office in January 1981, the administrative proceeding against North Carolina was still under way.

THE ISSUES IN DESEGREGATION IN HIGHER EDUCATION

Desegregation Standards

As the District of Columbia court of appeals observed in affirming Judge Pratt's first order in *Adams,* there was little judicial or administrative experience in desegregating colleges and universities, and there was a need, therefore, for HEW and federal courts to proceed cautiously in that area. During the Carter years, it became evident that this was a wise observation.

In desegregating institutions of higher education, there was uncertainty about what constituted violations of Title VI and what remedies could be imposed to correct those violations. For example, there was no agreement about whether either Title VI or the Fourteenth Amendment imposed an affirmative obligation on states to achieve a certain mix of black and white students on campuses. Though the HEW criteria sought to alleviate the imbalance in the racial mix at white and black public colleges, they made no mention of how a state or a judge might know when that mix was adequate under Title VI or the Constitution.

Repeatedly expressing its anxiety and consternation about the goals of desegregation, NAFEO announced in July 1978 that it intended to monitor the progress of the six states under the *Adams* order to ensure that the plans focused on the "educational needs of blacks, rather than on mechanical, numerical schemes which do not take into account the end results to be accomplished."[68] Leaders of NAFEO insisted that equalizing educational opportunities; enhancing the programs, faculties, and facilities of black colleges; ending the duplication of programs; and ending inequality in access to public higher education were the essential elements in desegregation. One official of NAFEO, critical of the LDF and its conception of desegregation in higher education, declared:

> The Legal Defense Fund has always had a concept of desegregation which has involved the moving around of bodies. They are uninterested in education as such. They brought this notion of body ratios of blacks and whites to the desegregation of colleges and universities. Don't tell me that the movement of bodies in elementary, secondary or higher education is going to help black children do better. Our definitions are bad; LDF's definition of integration is off base.

The Controversy over the Survival of the Black Colleges

The most important contribution of *Adams* during the Carter years was the HEW criteria's explicit recognition that Title VI required black colleges to be strengthened and enhanced. That meant providing the programs and resources to enable those colleges to become full educational partners in the state university systems in their states. During the Carter years, OCR and LDF officials often cited the establishment of Florida's new school of architecture at predominantly black Florida A&M as an example of the kind of enhancement required by Title VI and the HEW criteria. By contrast, they cited the decision not to establish the new School of Veterinary Medicine at North Carolina A&T as a badly missed opportunity.

The black colleges filled a special role historically in the drive for educational opportunity for American blacks. With the possible exception of the black churches, these schools rank as perhaps the most venerable and influential black institutions in American history. Most of the nation's black leadership was educated in those colleges. In 1976, a critical year in the negotiations leading to desegregation standards, more of those blacks with bachelors degrees had received their education at the country's one hundred or so black colleges than at more than two thousand other, "white" institutions of higher education. Recall that Judge Pratt, in his April 1978 opinion, emphasized that desegregation plans under Title VI should take into account the unequal status of the black colleges and the danger that desegregation could diminish educational opportunities for blacks by destroying those colleges. Harold Howe, a vice president at the Ford Foundation and former commissioner of education during the Johnson administration, asked, "Is it fair or reasonable for whites to say to blacks, who have maintained these colleges through years of ingenuity and sacrifice, that since the whites have recently been good fellows and dropped their segregation laws, the blacks should be good fellows and forget their colleges?"[69]

Black educators feared that the white institutions would not be able to provide for the remedial academic needs of many black students and that desegregation would diminish the pool of outstanding minority students applying to the historically black institutions. There was also a fear, voiced less publicly, that desegregation would have an adverse effect on the black educators who ran and controlled the historically black institutions. Others argued that minority students at the black colleges benefited from the black role models on the faculty, a benefit that might be jeopardized if those institutions lost their racial identity.

A range of black interest groups were involved in desegregation in higher education. There was the LDF, representing the plaintiffs in the *Adams* dispute. There were individuals who worked for and were affiliated with the Institute for Services to Education, a nonprofit organization based in Washington, D.C., devoted to improving opportunities for blacks in higher education. Those individuals included Elias Blake, the president of the institute and former president of Clark College; Leonard Haines, Blake's close associate and protégé, who was working on a Ford Foundation grant to evaluate the *Adams* litigation; and Kenneth Tollett, an attorney at Howard University's Institute for the Study of Educational Policy. Blake, Haines, and Tollett were influential scholar-activists who saw in the *Adams* litigation the chance to remake southern public higher education with an eye to providing much greater access to higher education for blacks.

Another group with a crucial stake in desegregation was NAFEO. Its leaders argued that melding the black and white institutions was inadvisable because it would eliminate the special identity and contribution of the black colleges. Yet leaders of the historically black colleges, dependent on governors and state legislatures, had to be wary when advancing any criticisms. Students, as always, seemed less reluctant to express their concerns publicly.

In May 1978, students on the campuses of black colleges in eight southern states protested the effort to desegregate their schools. The president of the National Organization of Black University and College Students said that he feared that the *Adams* litigation would destroy the black colleges. He worried that the predominantly white institutions would siphon off students from the black colleges to fill their goals under the HEW criteria, rather than attempting to increase their black enrollment by seeking students who would not otherwise be able to go to college.[70]

The LDF was in a sensitive position. It insisted, somewhat defensively, that enforcing Title VI in higher education would not destroy the black colleges but would instead ensure, for the first time, their full participation and equal funding. Jean Fairfax, who spearheaded the LDF's efforts in higher education, emphasized that though the fear that black colleges would be undermined was "well founded," the HEW criteria protected those institutions by requiring states to provide more resources than ever to them. Moreover, she maintained that the responsibility of providing remedial education for poorly prepared black students should not fall primarily on the black colleges, but should be borne to a greater degree than in the past by the traditionally white institutions.

OCR, the LDF, and Judge Pratt all seemed to be walking a tightrope, maintaining that desegregation must occur and yet that it must not eradicate the historically black college. One long-time OCR official expressed an understandable exasperation: "My job is a loser. It is a very difficult situation fraught with anxiety. If a plan works it is conceivable that the identity of the black institutions will disappear and that is not something that the greater share of the black community wants to see. Yet, there can't be a desegregation plan accepted which doesn't include that possibility." The ambivalent concerns within the black community only exacerbated matters for OCR. Another OCR official explained, "There is great anxiety in the minority community about the need to desegregate these colleges and equalize educational opportunities between the white and black schools. They want that very much. On the other hand, we could have repeats of West Virginia where the two black institutions are now 85 percent white with white presidents."

In May 1978, a NAFEO task force headed by the organization's counsel, Herbert Reid, published a report concluding that "the state desegregation plans that were accepted have redefined the missions of the traditionally black college in ways that do not reflect the historically and currently unique role of those institutions."[71] Criticizing both the states and HEW for misunderstanding the mission of the colleges and for accepting desegregation plans that (in violation of Judge Pratt's order) placed a disproportionate burden on the black colleges, the report broached the possibility that the two laudable goals — desegregating, and maintaining the "core blackness" of the black colleges — could well be irreconcilable.[72] That predicament was highlighted during the Carter years as a result of a decision by a federal district court in Tennessee.

In February 1977, shortly after Judge Pratt ordered HEW to devise standards for desegregation in higher education, the district court for the Middle District of Tennessee handed down a landmark desegregation decision.[73] The case, *Geier v. Blanton,* had a long history. More than a decade earlier, the University of Tennessee, a predominantly white state institution, had announced plans to build an extension center in Nashville. A young black woman had filed suit in federal court to block the project, charging that the expansion initiative preserved the state's dual system of higher education by perpetuating segregation at Tennessee Agricultural and Industrial State University (Tennessee A&I), a historically black institution in Nashville.

Though Judge Frank Gray Jr. denied her request for an injunction against the construction project, he did find that Tennessee was operating a racially discriminatory system of higher education and that the state had an affirmative duty under the Constitution to dismantle it. Over the next several years, Judge Gray rejected as inadequate the desegregation efforts that the state made. In February 1977, after nearly nine years of litigation, Gray concluded that Tennessee officials were not going to produce a constitutionally satisfactory desegregation plan. He ruled that the expansion of the predominantly white University of Tennessee at its Nashville campus had forced a competition for white students between that institution and Tennessee A&I and had impeded the dismantling of the dual system. Gray ordered the merging of the black institution and the University of Tennessee branch *under the governing authority of the former.*

Prior to Judge Gray's ruling, no court had ever ordered a state to disestablish its racially separate system of higher education and to merge what were once historically black and traditionally white institutions. Though such mergers had taken place in the past without court intervention, in no previous merger was the predominantly black institution made the governing institution. The *Chronicle of Higher Education,* stressing the wide-ranging implications of Gray's decision, concluded that all sides in the litigation acknowledged that the consequences of his order were "profound."[74] The battle over Title VI and the *Adams* litigation during the Carter years must be viewed against the backdrop of Gray's ruling. All concerned—OCR, LDF, NAFEO, elected state and federal officials with an interest in the subject, and the educators and students at the white and black institutions—had to recognize that the issues in the *Geier* case would eventually have to be resolved in all twenty states operating historically black institutions. That day was still to come when Jimmy Carter left the White House in 1981.

The Controversy over Educational Governance

The HEW criteria directed the states to submit to OCR, ninety days prior to adoption, "proposals for any major change in the operations of the state system which may directly or indirectly affect or impede the achievement of desegregation goals." University administrators resented this provision. North Carolina's William Friday protested that the provision made OCR an "approving body" for academic programs:

We cannot place ourselves in a position in which considerations of race and considerations of historical institutional racial identity, are the dominant and compelling factors in making educational decisions. The Board of Governors must insist upon the freedom to carry out our responsibilities to govern and administer the university on the basis of the best informed and soundest educational judgment that we can make.[75]

OCR officials privately complained that educators at the traditionally white schools exploited the cry of academic freedom to protect themselves against the dislocations and possible loss of status, power, perquisites, and jobs that might accompany desegregation. As one bureaucrat put it, the primary pressure that OCR bureaucrats experienced from both black and white educators was "a concern for what is going to happen to me and to my operation in the new system." The greatest fear of these educators was that to avoid program duplication at the white and black schools, some programs would be moved from one school to another, affecting individual job locations, job security, and careers. Such changes, affecting people's professional status and advancement, produced anxiety among educators and skittishness among politicians.

Desegregation in Higher Education and the Transfiguration of the South

Some black educators insisted that the desegregation controversy required not merely desegregation but a kind of de novo review of how state university systems functioned and who they served. They stressed that desegregation, rather than focusing on racial mixing in student bodies, should involve restructuring statewide systems of higher education to better meet the needs of all the citizens of the state. They believed that the *Adams* litigation offered an opportunity to address questions of equity in access to public higher education, and a much-needed stimulus to reform the way in which state universities served varying constituencies and, in particular, underserved the black community. Both LDF and NAFEO hoped that the *Adams* litigation would compel states to examine basic questions: What populations are served by the existing organization of public higher education? What populations are not well served? And what can be done to reduce inequalities in access to undergraduate, graduate, and professional schools?

The educational issues involved in desegregation in higher education during the Carter administration need to be contrasted with those in question in the landmark cases dealing with blacks in higher education in the years before *Brown v. Board of Education*. Those cases dealt with the admission of individual blacks to state law schools, professional schools, and graduate schools. What was significant in higher education in the late 1970s was that the litigation focused not on the admission of a few highly qualified blacks to previously all-white schools, but rather on the dismantling of a total structure of racist admission standards and on the re-evaluation of a wide range of other educational practices at all public colleges and universities throughout the South. The stakes were enormous for hundreds of thousands of potential college-going blacks and for the region as a whole.

Consider the importance and breadth of the issues involved. They touched on such questions as giving blacks greater influence in the governance of the traditionally white institutions; revising admission standards; ensuring that the white institutions admitted greater numbers of blacks; equalizing the percentage of the white and black populations admitted to state undergraduate, graduate, and professional schools; improving the retention rates and remedial educational programs for black students; providing parity in salary for black faculty and staff members; and establishing equitable funding and enhanced educational offerings for the historically black institutions.

By altering the patterns of access to higher and professional education, desegregation in higher education seemed to have the potential to redistribute power in the South. Greater access to public higher education for blacks meant greater access to positions of power and influence.[76] One southern black leader explained:

> What is at issue here is the development of another class of educated people. We are interested in making quality institutions of public higher education accessible to blacks in a way that they simply never have been before. That is apt to have enormous repercussions. Even though a lot of [black] students who will be admitted to those institutions will not be able to maximize those opportunities because of their own disadvantaged backgrounds, perhaps 25 percent will. So we're talking roughly about a million people going to college and university in the South who would not normally have been there in the past. And out of those million you can believe that 250,000 of them will enter the "system." Then there will be the consequences that will flow from their new positions and from what they, in turn, will be able to give to their children and their children's children.

Not only would dismantling the segregated system of higher education in the South enlarge the cadre of black leadership, but the new generation of college-educated blacks, because of the more open social environment they would enter, would have opportunities unavailable to their predecessors, strengthening even further the power of blacks in the region. In past generations, the students who graduated from black colleges graduated into a segregated system. By contrast, black college graduates in the 1970s and 1980s were more likely to work in the larger, integrated social system. Some NAFEO officials maintained that black leadership in the South was weak because racial segregation had ensured that the professional experiences of black leaders was limited to the restricted situations open to blacks in a segregated society. Consequently, when these leaders had to get things done that required a broader experiential background in the dominant white culture, they often were not knowledgeable about how to proceed.

Some blacks believed, for instance, that when major white institutions raided the faculties of the historically black institutions to take their best teachers, it was a good thing, because it widened the opportunities of the faculty members, increased their power and influence as educators, and forced the black institutions to appreciate what they needed to do to retain high-quality faculty members. Previously, talented black faculty members had had no place to go but the historically black institutions. As one black faculty member explained: "My first job was head of a department at the age of twenty-three at Clark College. Now I wasn't prepared for that and I shouldn't have had it. The only reason I had it was because it was in a subsystem and the only thing I could look forward to was moving up in the subsystem."

Black educators who took this view of the social ramifications of desegregation in higher education conceived of the *Adams* litigation as a way of restructuring publicly supported southern higher education. *Adams* and the HEW criteria established a framework in which the black institutions, which had once been separate and apart from the rest of the educational system, could be re-evaluated to determine how to enhance and integrate them as fully functioning components of that system. By the same token, *Adams* and the criteria required re-evaluating the role of the white institutions and their programs, function, and funding. Finally, one could not realistically increase black access to state institutions of higher education without taking some measures to improve the quality of public education blacks received at the pre-collegiate level. The complexity, scope, and political sensitivity of these tasks was daunting.

HEW's criteria for desegregation in higher education were potentially much more far-reaching than were the HEW Guidelines for elementary and secondary education in the 1960s. The latter dealt only with racial integration. The former sought nothing less than to restructure access to public higher education for blacks throughout the South and to reconsider the distribution of program offerings on the various campuses of each state system. Even marginal educational reform initiatives enjoying a considerable base of support within state university systems and on individual campuses are notoriously difficult to implement. Far-flung, statewide reforms in public higher education, engineered by litigation and law enforcement, suffered much greater vulnerabilities. State university bureaucracies have a prodigious capacity to absorb the assaults of reformers and to withstand, unscathed, calls for fundamental change. The *Adams* litigation would test that capacity.

As a statement of goals, the criteria for desegregation in higher education advanced laudable and ambitious objectives. The problem was that achieving those objectives required an educational revolution in each state, and there was insufficient political support in the nation and hence within the administration to compel the states to achieve those goals. Consequently, HEW had neither the political will nor the clout to achieve what the criteria mandated. Litigation, through *Adams* or otherwise, could not alter that reality. The result was predictable.

OCR officials recognized that the states viewed extensive federal intervention in and reorganization of state systems of higher education as improper and that the states had the political muscle to fight such interference over extended periods of time. In negotiations with state educational officials, OCR representatives emphasized that the HEW criteria provided ample flexibility to meet the legitimate educational concerns of state officials. As one OCR official explained: "We don't intend to impose our notions on the states. We are not doctrinaire."

For example, under a desegregation plan two institutions offering an early childhood program in the same service area might have to restructure the offerings on each campus to avoid continued duplication. OCR stressed that there were no absolute answers to such problems and that states would have great flexibility in resolving them. For instance, Georgia's Armstrong College, a traditionally white institution, had a focus in business administration, and Savannah State, a black college, focused on early childhood education programs. Georgia reversed those priorities in its plan, and OCR, in approving the plan, noted that control over the programs on specific campuses would continue to be determined largely by state university officials. That experience reflected the general pattern.

CONCLUSIONS

The Carter administration's record on Title VI must be assessed in the context of the national political climate that prevailed from 1976 to 1980. By the late 1970s, the fervor over the struggle for racial equality in American life that had erupted in the Kennedy and Johnson years had subsided. Also gone was the antagonistic, racially divisive rhetoric of the Nixon administration. In the minds of politicians and the public alike, racial discrimination had become a minor domestic issue rather than the central domestic priority. In the late 1970s, economic worries prompted by double-digit inflation, soaring interest rates, and a national gasoline shortage dominated domestic politics.

Economic anxieties not only displaced racial issues as a priority but also highlighted the price whites might pay for racial reforms. Hence, the Supreme Court's decision in the *Bakke* case in 1977 fueled a prolonged and bitter national debate about affirmative action that drew attention to how the financial well-being of working-class and middle-class whites might be imperiled by measures intended to help blacks.[77] The altered national priorities of the late 1970s affected public opinion on racial matters. In 1970 a national survey found that three out of four whites believed that blacks experienced discrimination. In 1977, a similar survey found that only one in three whites believed that racial discrimination was still a problem.[78] A Carnegie Foundation study published in 1978 concluded that "many [whites] believed the nation's debt to black people has been so fully paid that whites themselves are becoming the victims of reverse discrimination."[79]

In late 1979, in a series of special articles devoted to the national mood on black civil rights, the *New York Times* reported what it characterized as "a toughening mood" on racial issues among whites who would never join a racist organization, did not believe they were prejudiced, and had supported black demands in the 1960s. Though survey data continued to show an improvement in the attitudes of whites in terms of their support for the ideal of racial equality, there was increasing evidence that whites were not willing to support the actions proposed to implement that ideal. Hence, during the Carter years, support for busing to achieve school desegregation, support for affirmative action to achieve employment equality, and support for publicly supported housing in suburban communities all met with considerable white opposition. In 1979, the NAACP warned of a "spirit of meanness that is sweeping the nation"—a spirit that the National Urban League characterized as the "new negativism."[80] Changed attitudes on our racial problems manifested themselves in the academy as well.

James S. Coleman, the University of Chicago sociologist whose massive study on educational opportunity in the mid-1960s had been widely used to support school desegregation, announced in the fall of 1978 that it was a "mistaken belief" that black students learn better in an integrated classroom. Contrary to the findings that he had reached in the previous decade, Coleman reported that new research suggested that school desegregation had not improved academic performance for disadvantaged children.[81] Also reflecting a new way of thinking about race in America was the aptly titled work *The Declining Significance of Race,* by William Wilson, a prominent black sociologist at the University of Chicago, who argued that the plight of blacks was best understood not in terms of racial discrimination but rather in terms of class and economic subordination.[82]

The Carter White House

During the Nixon years, both the president and the secretary of HEW publicly advanced a negative attitude toward Title VI, and enforcement of the statute languished. In the Carter administration, surprisingly, after a few initial, rhetorical flourishes from the president, there was no strong leadership or high priority given to civil rights enforcement from the White House. The president neither gave speeches preaching racial justice nor sought new civil rights legislation. Rarely was the White House a factor in determining the policies governing the enforcement of Title VI.

While controversies associated with enforcing Title VI against the Chicago public school system coincided with the 1980 primary elections, the administration permitted both HEW and the Justice Department to determine for themselves, unimpeded by the White House, the actions that should be taken. It was only in the North Carolina dispute in higher education that the White House kept directly informed and involved in the enforcement process. Even there, Secretary Califano prevailed as the dominant policy maker. Though the White House monitored the situation, it did not dictate decisions, or reverse or revise HEW policy.

In contrast to Lyndon Johnson, who determined that Title VI

should be vigorously enforced against elementary and secondary schools only in the South, and Richard Nixon, who determined that there should be a retreat on Title VI, Jimmy Carter adopted a hands-off policy on the enforcement of the provision. The immediate beneficiary of the vacuum created by the neutral stance of the White House was Secretary Califano. It was Califano who seems to have imposed whatever political constraints there were on the enforcement of Title VI during the Carter years. He probably was more independent than any HEW or Department of Education secretary before or since.

Aware that Califano wanted to know a great deal about OCR's activities, OCR director David Tatel made no major moves without consulting him. Tatel's most difficult assignments involved efforts to convince Califano to permit OCR to take enforcement actions in Chicago and North Carolina, the two most politically sensitive cases during the Carter administration. Tatel spent hours closeted with Califano in one-on-one working sessions to convince the secretary to permit OCR to move in those two instances. Unlike other assistant secretaries and office directors who reported to Califano, Tatel had an adversarial relationship with Califano. That was as much a function of the positions the two men held as it was a function of their views on Title VI. The task of the OCR director is to safeguard the integrity of the statute and its objective — making sure that expenditures of federal funds for educational institutions are nondiscriminatory. The secretary earns political points for his boss, the president, by giving money away, not withholding it.

Monitoring Compliance and Negotiating Differences

Under Judge Pratt's court orders during the Carter years, OCR continued to give the *Adams* plaintiffs wide-ranging information about its actions. For example, the plaintiffs received copies of almost all internal OCR memoranda discussing policy issues and, pursuant to Pratt's April 1977 decision, HEW gave the plaintiffs copies of state desegregation plans before HEW decided whether to accept them. As was true during the Nixon-Ford era, access to information increased the scrutiny of OCR's work by the plaintiffs' lawyers. In light of that access, lawyers for the plaintiffs could make suggestions to OCR officials who were reviewing the plans, and those officials occasionally accepted those ideas.

After the initial 1973 decision by Judge Pratt, almost all of the disputes in *Adams* resulted in consent decrees in which an administration agreed to certain things after negotiations with civil rights groups, with Pratt ratifying those agreements by issuing them as court orders. Confrontational legal actions, in the form of new motions and especially motions for contempt, always remained an option for the plaintiffs. OCR officials understood, and civil rights attorneys emphasized, that if the plaintiffs were unsatisfied with the concessions the government made in negotiations, the plaintiffs could resort to legal action before Judge Pratt. As in any legal dispute, the ability of each side to advance credible threats to prevail in court fostered settlement discussions and agreements. The *Adams* plaintiffs enjoyed such credibility because they were represented by outstanding and tenacious lawyers who had proven their ability to convince Pratt of the legal inadequacy of OCR's performance.

OCR officials used Pratt's orders and the possibility of legal action by the *Adams* plaintiffs to OCR's advantage, typically to provide political cover for the agency. As one OCR official explained: "[W]e always cite court orders whenever we are required to do something found in them." The time frames in *Adams,* for example, enabled the director of OCR to justify actions that would otherwise have been politically unfeasible or dangerous. He could say to a complaining congressman or educational official that, though OCR might otherwise have preferred to continue discussions about a dispute over Title VI, a time limit imposed by a court order compelled the agency to end discussions. Hence, in a variety of contexts both within HEW and in dealings with congressional representatives, OMB, and even the White House, officials in OCR could use the court orders to free themselves from supervision by their nominal superiors. In addition to providing political protection, the court orders also enabled OCR to argue more persuasively for resources from Congress. They needed greater resources, OCR officials argued, to avoid violating Pratt's orders and being cited for contempt.

However effective *Adams* may have been in moving OCR to act in some instances, the remedies achieved in the litigation suffered from certain limitations. *Adams* regulated OCR only in terms of timetables for investigating complaints. It did not control OCR's actions once the agency determined that there was a violation and initiated administrative enforcement proceedings. Nor did it govern what the Justice Department did once OCR referred a case to it.

When Shirley Hufstedler became secretary of the newly created Department of Education in May 1980, Joseph Rauh wrote to her to inform her about *Adams* and to acquaint her with the issues in the litigation, which had, at that point, spanned a decade and involved six

HEW secretaries. Rauh's letter was a kind of status report on Title VI at the end of the Carter years. Strikingly, he devoted almost all of his letter to desegregation in higher education, making virtually no mention of desegregation in elementary and secondary schools. By 1980, even Rauh, an advocate of the most aggressive use of Title VI, saw no reason to press the new secretary about OCR's obligations under Title VI to end racial discrimination at the elementary and secondary school levels. That omission evidenced a profound transformation in the use of Title VI. The initial objective of the statute, the rooting out of racial discrimination in elementary and secondary education, was no longer of any real significance to those enforcing Title VI or to the lawyers in the civil rights community monitoring the enforcers. That original focus had been displaced, and a major reorientation toward higher education had occurred. That new focus and reorientation dominated the enforcement of Title VI throughout the 1980s.

The Dominant Themes: Higher Education, Managerial Efficiency, and Procedural Regularity

During the Carter years, there was an emphasis on achieving procedural regularity and managerial efficiency in the enforcement of Title VI. Both the *Adams* litigation and the administration's reorganization of OCR focused on the need for OCR to be efficient and businesslike, conducting its affairs according to well-defined procedures. Often, the concern for procedure and efficiency seemed to overshadow the concern for substance. For example, in the preface to the OCR's 1979 annual operating plan, David Tatel wrote that to comply with the consent order of December 1977 OCR had to increase its "productivity" so that each OCR investigator resolved a minimum of eighteen complaints each year. To do so, Tatel explained, OCR planned to improve management control and complaint processing procedures, strengthen its training of investigators, and improve coordination between the regional offices and the office of HEW's general counsel.[83]

The implications of this list of planned improvements are unmistakable. Complying with *Adams* had come to mean, in large measure, complying with procedural requirements and improving the managerial efficiency of OCR. The substantive impact of the law and of the managerial and procedural reforms seemed to be an almost peripheral consideration. That is not to suggest that the businesslike management of OCR's affairs is insignificant. It is to suggest, however, that managing and processing civil rights violations became so much of a focus, both in the litigation and in OCR's own priorities, that it eclipsed in importance a concern for what all of that managing and processing produced in the way of eliminating discrimination in federally funded programs and achieving the fundamental goal of *Brown v. Board*—equal educational opportunity.

The two themes that dominated the work of OCR during the Carter years—an emphasis on procedural and management regularity and on desegregation in higher education—offered certain political and organizational advantages to the agency. Both afforded OCR an opportunity to shift its primary focus to new goals that were less politically volatile than a continued focus on elementary and secondary school desegregation. Reorienting the agency's focus toward managerial and procedural reforms de-politicized its work. A commitment to managerial efficiency and procedural regularity rankled few in Congress, in state educational establishments, or in the public at large. Moreover, external factors restricted what OCR could do in enforcing Title VI substantively at the elementary and secondary school levels.

The Eagleton-Biden Amendment limited what OCR could do with respect to claims that students were assigned to schools in a racially discriminatory manner. Additionally, demographic factors increasingly limited the practicality of desegregation programs in America's largest cities. When Carter became president, nonwhite children constituted 60 percent of the student population in the nation's twenty largest districts and nearly 70 percent in the ten largest districts.[84] The demographics in large urban public school systems, combined with the Eagleton-Biden Amendment, meant that there was little that OCR could do in enforcing Title VI in elementary and secondary school desegregation—the traditional focus of its activities since 1964.

Enforcing Title VI in higher education offered an attractive change of focus both for OCR and for LDF litigators. Because desegregation in higher education involved young adults rather than children, it was a less emotional issue and there was less hostility to it among the general public. Consequently, though the issues raised in desegregation in higher education were potentially far-reaching, they did not elicit the intensely negative political reactions and national controversy associated with desegregation and busing at the elementary and secondary school levels. Like the desegregation that OCR fought for successfully in the 1960s, desegregation in higher education was largely a southern issue and a product of de jure discrimination in the past. Yet, because a college education and degree were requirements for admission into virtually any professional position, desegregation in higher education had the potential to affect the social and economic power of blacks — the original aim of their historic quest for equal education.

For civil rights lawyers, both the history of discrimination and the contemporary effects of that discrimination were easier to demonstrate in higher education than they were in cases of de facto segregation in the North, or in such "second generation" racial problems as discrimination in student suspensions, educational testing, or tracking in elementary and secondary schools. In addition, the desegregation of colleges and universities had the decided advantage that it was not likely to become a national racial issue pitting black against white. The divisions within the black community itself would help ensure that. Finally, a focus on higher education offered the lawyers at the LDF an opportunity to continue to litigate and win important cases using Title VI as their legal foundation.

During the Carter years, both OCR and the *Adams* plaintiffs adapted to a changed environment. In light of congressionally imposed limitations, the need to avoid powerful political reprisals, and the need to find new goals that were politically and legally feasible, both the civil rights agency and civil rights lawyers reoriented their focus. By doing so, they sometimes advanced the cause of equal education for blacks. In the ambitious HEW criteria for desegregation in higher education, they set out goals that were laudable and wide-ranging but that proved politically unfeasible to implement, notwithstanding *Adams*. In other realms, in their heavy emphasis on managerial reforms and procedural regularities, both OCR officials and civil rights litigators failed to address the substantive issues that might redress the inequalities that blacks increasingly faced, especially the growing number who lived in America's cities and sent their children to urban public school systems.

6

REAGAN:
The Irrelevant Formalism
of the Legal Battles

IN THE LEGAL MEASURES TO control the enforcement of Title VI during the Reagan era, there was both continuity and change. The *Adams* litigation continued to produce an emphasis on managerial reforms and efficiency, and pressure on OCR to settle cases. The difficulties that had developed during the Carter years in referring Title VI violations to the Justice Department persisted. Finally, like its Democratic and Republican predecessors, the Reagan administration argued before Judge Pratt and the U.S. Circuit Court of Appeals for the District of Columbia that the intervention in *Adams* exceeded the judiciary's authority and prevented OCR from doing the most that it could do to protect civil rights.

The major change during 1981–89 was the increasing difficulty of keeping the *Adams* litigation alive. During the Reagan years, more than ever, the plaintiffs were on the defensive in their efforts to sustain the litigation. This was true not so much because of the efforts of the administration but rather because Judge Pratt and the District of Columbia Circuit were becoming increasingly concerned about the expansive scope of the litigation. Those concerns made them more receptive than before to the government's arguments and led to a series of decisions that culminated in a ruling dismissing the case. This dismissal occurred more than twenty years after lawyers for the LDF brought the suit. Fittingly, just as the civil rights lawyers and judges had largely avoided dealing with substantive issues throughout the *Adams* litigation, the court of appeals, when it dismissed the case, did so on the basis of procedural considerations.

During Ronald Reagan's presidency, a heightened distrust and combativeness developed between national civil rights organizations and the administration, resulting in highly publicized and often bitter legal disputes focusing on the enforcement of civil rights laws. These disputes took on an almost surreal quality because the issues in question — at least those relating to the enforcement of Title VI — had a limited impact on people's lives. The disputes were significant, however, in the sense that they enabled each side to stake out a political position, criticize the other side, and play to its own political constituency. In their disputes about legal rights, both the administration and civil rights advocates overdramatized and exaggerated the importance of their disagreements. The legal disputes functioned as the medium through which a largely symbolic, staged political combat occurred.

REAGAN'S CIVIL RIGHTS POLICIES

More than any other presidential administration since Johnson's, the Reagan administration was animated by a political ideology that influenced its civil rights and Title VI policies. Reagan officials challenged long-held liberal positions on civil rights. Bradford Reynolds, assistant attorney general in the Justice Department's Civil Rights Division, was the administration's primary spokesman on civil rights. An accomplished lawyer in commercial litigation and regulatory matters, Reynolds had little experience in civil rights law, a deficiency that he saw as an asset. Boasting that the administration "dared to reexamine some of the relief that has come to be 'accepted practice' in the civil rights community,"[1] Reynolds remarked, "The civil rights community has been basically marching along the same path for a number of years, and nobody has stood up and taken a hard look at where they were going and said, 'Wait a minute, they really are not serving the interests they pretend to be serving.'"[2]

As the administration's point man, Reynolds argued that government should be "color blind" and that goals, quotas, and timetables for hiring minorities and women were "reverse discrimination."[3] He insisted that "race-conscious remedies which require preferential treatment for minorities" or interfere with the functioning of local governments were "not widely supported" and that civil rights enforcement agencies such as OCR were "overly intrusive" in the affairs of state and local governments.[4] The fact that Reynolds published more than ten articles in law reviews and other legal journals during the Reagan years, and that scholars analyzed his writing and thinking, reflects the emphasis that Reagan conservatives placed not only on holding power but also on winning the war of ideas about civil rights.

Under Reynolds's leadership, the Civil Rights Division took numerous steps that affected Title VI and school desegregation. For example, in a school desegregation case before the Supreme Court in the fall of 1982, the division, reversing the position it had taken in lower federal courts, supported the authority of the state of Washington to enact an anti-busing law that prevented school systems from adopting desegregation programs that included mandatory busing.[5] Reversing the position that the United States had advanced in the lower courts, the Reagan-era Civil Rights Division argued the states' rights position before the Supreme Court, insisting that the state had the ultimate authority to regulate educational policy.[6] In another reversal by the Justice Department, in the *Grove City College* case, the administration dropped its defense of the Department of Education's authority under Title VI to terminate federal funds provided to colleges under the Guaranteed Student Loan Program.[7] That reversed the policy advanced under Presidents Nixon, Ford, and Carter.[8]

When Arthur S. Flemming, a moderate Republican who was chair of the U.S. Commission on Civil Rights, criticized the administration's civil rights policies as "regressive," President Reagan fired him. Subsequently, Flemming's successor, Clarence Pendleton, complained publicly of the White House's refusal to cooperate with the commission, and threatened to subpoena documents from executive agencies if the administration did not make the information available.[9] Ralph Neas, executive director of the Leadership Conference on Civil Rights, concluded that Ronald Reagan's was the worst administration on civil rights in half a century.[10] Congressman Donald Edwards of California, who had served on the Civil Rights Subcommittee of the House Judiciary Committee for twenty years, declared at congressional hearings in 1982, "I am here today to express my alarm and fear at the wholesale dismantling of the civil rights enforcement machinery. . . . I can remember only one other time when there has been a concerted effort by the executive branch to undermine civil rights enforcement. That was in the early seventies and the issue was school desegregation, the strategists were HEW [officials]."[11]

Benjamin Hooks, executive director of the NAACP, observed that the Civil Rights Division had "launched an all-out attack on civil rights" that amounted to a "shocking . . . unprecedented, aggressive and unnerving campaign to reverse more than two decades of well-established principles."[12] Clarence Pendleton noted that the U.S. Commission on Civil Rights "view[ed] with increasing alarm the efforts to end federal leadership in promoting equal educational opportunity." Vernon Jordan, the president of the National Urban League, claimed that though Reagan was personally a compassionate man, his policies lacked compassion, increased race and class segregation, and represented a "clear and present danger" to blacks. Combating those policies, he lamented, was especially challenging because the "national consensus for racial justice ha[d] withered."[13]

In September 1982, the heads of thirty-three state civil rights agencies charged that, through budget cuts and appointments to federal civil rights positions, President Reagan had produced "a dangerous deterioration in the federal enforcement of civil rights."[14] That same month, the Washington Council of Lawyers, a prominent nonpartisan group of Washington, D.C., attorneys, issued a 140-page report that concluded that the Reagan administration had "retreated from well-established, bi-partisan, civil rights policies . . . developed during both Democratic and Republican Administrations."[15]

The administration's policies and Reynolds's high-visibility defense of them led to a barely concealed revolt in 1982 among the 390 employees in the Justice Department's Civil Rights Division.[16] The dispute between Reagan appointees and staff lawyers in the Civil Rights Division was reminiscent of similar, but more highly publicized, struggles during the Nixon administration. This time, more than one hundred lawyers in the division signed a letter to Reynolds objecting to the administration's efforts to reverse established federal policy denying tax-exempt status to racially discriminatory private schools.[17]

By 1984, as Reagan prepared to run for re-election, even leading black Republicans publicly expressed dismay and disaffection. J. Clay Smith, a black Republican who had served as acting chair of the Equal Employment Opportunity Commission (EEOC) from 1977 through 1981, explained that Reagan's policies "are not the type of policies that traditional black Republicans can sell to the minority constituency." Clarence Thomas, who replaced Smith at EEOC, criticized the Justice Department for being too belligerent in opposing busing and quotas and for setting "a negative rather than a positive agenda on civil rights." William Coleman, a distinguished black lawyer who had served as secretary of transportation in the Ford administration, declared the Justice Department's policies to be "100 percent wrong, and despicable," and not "consistent with the law, with the Republican Party or with the long-range interests of the country."[18] When the administration announced in its last year in office that it sought to dismiss two hundred school desegregation cases in school districts in Georgia, Alabama, and Mississippi, the co-chairs of the Lawyers' Committee for Civil Rights under Law wrote that Reagan's was "an administration unprecedented in its hostility to Civil Rights."[19]

THE ADMINISTRATION'S EFFORTS TO LIMIT THE SCOPE OF CIVIL RIGHTS PROTECTIONS

The Reagan administration worked assiduously to limit the scope of the coverage of numerous antidiscrimination laws, including Title VI. Those efforts provide the background for understanding developments in the *Adams* case during the Reagan years. Although the administration's attempts to circumscribe the reach of federal civil rights laws were prompted by a dispute over Title IX and not Title VI, that controversy and the ensuing legal and political fights affected the enforcement of Section 504 of the Rehabilitation Act of 1973, the Age Discrimination Act, and Title VI because all of those statutes used virtually identical language prohibiting discrimination in federally funded programs.

Civil rights enforcement by the new Department of Education (created by Congress months before the end of the Carter administration) was at the center of the fight over the scope of the protection of the civil rights laws. The new department assumed responsibility for enforcing federal civil rights laws in educational institutions.[20] Running on a platform advocating the abolition of the department, Ronald Reagan made the very existence of the educational agency a political issue.

From the outset of his tenure as Reagan's first secretary of education, Terrence Bell expressed doubts about his department's role in enforcing civil rights laws. Speaking to state educational officials two months into the new administration, Bell urged that the federal role in administering antidiscrimination laws be reduced and the role of the states increased: "We ought to try to get the federal government, to the extent we can, out of the monitoring and enforcement business."[21] A few months later, he expressed "indignation over certain federal laws and regulations that encroach upon State and local authority."[22] That same month, speaking at the University of Texas, he stated that the "administration is committed to working with States rather than policing them, particularly in such areas as civil rights."[23] Stressing his own career as an educational bureaucrat, Bell said that he knew, firsthand, how federal regulations burdened those running educational institutions.[24] Bradford Reynolds agreed, declaring that universities receiving federal aid were "engulfed" by bureaucrats enforcing civil rights laws, who "harassed" them on the basis of very little evidence.[25]

In the fall of 1981, Bell proposed that OCR no longer consider three federal student loan programs — the Guaranteed Student Loans Program, parent loans, and "Pell" student loan grants — as federal financial assistance to institutions. That meant that receipt of those loans by students at colleges and universities would no longer be a basis for subjecting the institutions to the requirements of Title VI and the other civil rights laws modeled after it.[26] Aid to students under those loan programs, Bell insisted, did not constitute federal financial assistance to institutions because the aid went to students and not to the schools. Margaret Kohn, a lawyer for the National Women's Law Center who had long been involved in the *Adams* litigation, argued that the distinction between aid to a student and aid to a "program or activity" at an institution was an artificial one because schools played an integral role in administering the loan programs and relied on the programs "to survive financially."[27]

Bell moved to curtail the scope of the coverage of the civil rights laws because of controversial efforts by OCR to apply Title IX to athletic programs at colleges and universities. OCR had initiated those efforts because of charges by women's groups that colleges and universities spent disproportionate sums of money on men's sports programs. There was also sentiment within the administration to limit the scope of coverage under Section 504, which dealt with discrimination against disabled persons in federal programs. There is no evidence that concern about the enforcement of Title VI motivated Bell to narrow the coverage of the civil rights laws. However, since the language in Title IX, Section 504, and Title VI was virtually identical, narrowing the coverage of Title IX would narrow coverage under the other provisions as well. It is telling that misgivings about Title VI were not a consideration behind Bell's move, for it shows the weakened force and growing unimportance of that provision and the emergence of gender discrimination and other kinds of discrimination as issues that had eclipsed racial discrimination in political prominence.

In a 2 December 1981 memorandum to Secretary Bell, Daniel Oliver, the Department of Education's general counsel, stated that Justice Department lawyers had concluded that Bell's proposed interpretation of the guaranteed student loan provisions would likely be struck down by the courts. Notwithstanding the Justice Department's opposition, Oliver urged changing the definition of what was considered federal aid to "make a political point concerning the reach of federal jurisdiction," because Ronald Reagan had been elected "to curtail the interference of the federal Government" and because the reach of federal civil rights laws was "highly visible and very symbolic."[28]

In March 1982, acting on Bell's proposal, the administration announced that the Guaranteed Student Loan Program would be excluded from coverage under the civil rights statutes banning discrimination based on gender, disability, and race. This would exclude from coverage under the civil rights statutes several hundred schools whose only federal aid was guaranteed student loans. Later that year, inconclusive and somewhat inconsistent decisions by the Supreme Court and three lower federal courts caused the scope of the coverage of civil rights statutes to remain unclear and unresolved. In an appeal to the Supreme Court in *North Haven Board of Education v. Bell*, the Reagan Civil Rights Division argued that Title IX authorized terminating the funding only of the specific federally funded program or activity that discriminated, and not of the entire institution. In its decision in *North Haven*, handed down in May 1982, the Supreme Court agreed with that interpretation.[29] Within days of the Court's decision, Bradford Reynolds declared that Title IX no longer applied "to an institution as a whole, but only to those federally assisted programs at the institution," and stated that the Justice Department was reviewing how *North Haven* applied to Title VI.[30]

Critics of the administration, such as Mary Berry of the U.S. Commission on Civil Rights and Margaret Kohn of the National Women's Law Center, emphasized that Reynolds had misread *North Haven* and had moved with unjustifiable haste to limit the scope of the civil rights statutes. Berry and Kohn insisted that although *North Haven* held that Title IX was "program-specific," it reserved for future litigation the task of defining what a "program" or "activity" was within the meaning of the civil rights statutes.[31]

Two months after the Court decided *North Haven*, in *University of Richmond v. Bell*, a federal district court in Virginia enjoined the Department of Education from investigating allegations that the University of Richmond discriminated against women in its intercollegiate athletic program because the complainant neither alleged nor introduced evidence that the university's intercollegiate athletic program received federal financial assistance.[32] The court ruled that the government had no authority under Title IX, "absent a showing that the program or activity is the recipient of *direct* financial assistance."[33] Notwithstanding criticism of *Richmond* by the assistant secretary for civil rights in the Department of Education, who warned that the decision would jeopardize civil rights enforcement, Bradford Reynolds endorsed the decision and, over the protests of civil rights groups and the U.S. Commission on Civil Rights, decided that the Justice Department would not appeal.[34]

After the *North Haven* and *Richmond* cases, the law regarding how the existence of a federally funded program at an institution affected that institution's civil rights obligations became hopelessly muddled by two inconsistent court of appeals decisions handed down within four months of one another in 1982. In *Grove City College v. Bell,* the Third Circuit ruled that the federal financial assistance that Grove City College's students received from guaranteed student loans benefited the entire college and subjected the entire institution to the strictures of Title IX.[35] Four months later, the Sixth Circuit reached a contrary conclusion.[36]

Until the conflicting federal court decisions in 1982, OCR assumed that if any part of a school or college received federal aid, the entire institution was subject to federal civil rights laws. Consequently, when students received federal financial aid, OCR held that receipt of that aid made the institution subject to Title VI, Title IX, and the other civil rights statutes. The Supreme Court changed that in *Grove City College v. Bell.*

THE *GROVE CITY COLLEGE* CASE

Background

The *Grove City College* case began in July 1977, when college officials argued that the institution was under no legal obligation to certify its compliance with Title IX. That was true, they maintained, because other than the federal student loan program, which benefited only individual students, the institution received no direct federal financial assistance. The government subsequently terminated aid to the college's students, and Grove City College sued, advancing an argument warmly received by the Reagan administration. It maintained that the presence of 140 students on campus who received federal aid in the form of student loans did not subject the institution to Title IX. Unlike Bob Jones University, which had, in effect, argued for the right to discriminate on the basis of race the previous year, Grove City College, claiming the moral high ground, insisted that it found any kind of discrimination morally repugnant. Rather, according to college officials, they had decided to forego all federal aid, not out of any sinister motivation to be free to discriminate, but to avoid the bureaucratic burdens and financial expense invariably occasioned by federal control.

Though the federal government had opposed the college's position in the district court and the court of appeals, the Reagan administration reversed that position in the Supreme Court. In keeping with the suggestions that Secretary Bell had been making, Reagan's Justice Department argued that only the specific "program or activity" within a college or university that received the federal aid was subject to Title IX. To enforce Title IX more broadly "would mean that if one student paid for his education with one dollar of [federal] funds, the entire school would automatically be subject to [Title IX]."[37] To subject the entire institution to federal regulation under such circumstances would, in the words of the deputy solicitor general, authorize "huge bureaucratic overkill."[38]

Before the Supreme Court, two dozen civil rights organizations submitted amicus briefs opposing the government's position. In an unusual move, a bipartisan group of forty-nine senators and representatives also filed a brief contesting the Justice Department's position. They "strongly urge[d]" the Court "to reject [the] effort to limit the protections afforded by Title IX," arguing that in passing Title IX, Congress had intended "to include entire institutions where students receive federally funded tuition assistance."[39]

The Impact of Grove City College on OCR

The Supreme Court's six-to-three decision in February 1984 in *Grove City College* resolved the uncertainty over the scope of coverage of federal civil rights provisions. The Court ruled that receiving student aid did not make an entire college a "recipient" of federal aid within the meaning of Title IX, but rather that Title IX applied only to the specific educational "program or part thereof" receiving federal funds. Hence, federal monies that supported an institution's financial aid program for students did not permit federal civil rights regulation of the entire institution. Though the Court acknowledged that any federal financial aid program to students could have "economic ripple effects" throughout the institution, it held that Congress did not intend to subject an entire institution to the requirements of Title IX simply because one part of the institution received federal aid.[40]

The impact of *Grove City College* was immediate, and in the view of critics of the decision, considerable. A little more than a week after the decision, OCR announced that it had dropped gender discrimination charges against the University of Maryland's intercollegiate athletic program because the program did not receive federal funding.[41] Within the next three months, OCR closed investigations against Pennsylvania State University, the University of Alabama, Duke University, the University of Washington, and several colleges and universities in Idaho and Mississippi.[42] The assistant secretary for civil rights in the Department of Education, Harry Singleton, wrote to OCR personnel explaining the significance of *Grove City College:*

In reviewing complaints to determine whether or not OCR has jurisdiction over the alleged discrimination, one must first determine
whether funding received by the institution is earmarked or non-earmarked. If the funding is non-earmarked, jurisdiction may be asserted
recipient-wide. If the funding is earmarked, jurisdiction may be asserted over the program of the recipient receiving the earmarked funds.
. . . *The only Department of Education program which has been identified as non-
earmarked is Impact Aid* [aid to areas containing military or other federal
facilities].[43]

Singleton instructed OCR personnel that *Grove City College* applied to
Title VI, Section 504, and the Age Discrimination Act.[44]

After the *Grove City College* decision, to establish jurisdiction over a
matter involving an allegation of discrimination OCR had to trace
the flow of federal monies to determine whether they went to the particular program or activity in which the alleged discrimination occurred. A congressional report on the impact of *Grove City* declared:

The OCR staff was compelled to spend days, and often weeks, to determine whether a particular program or activity received federal financial assistance. Some cases took sixty days to establish jurisdiction.
After such an arduous search was made, the agency often found that it
did not have jurisdiction over the case. If jurisdiction was found after
so many days, the staff was still faced with having to investigate the
discrimination charge within the remaining time allotted [under the
Adams time frames], resulting in a more superficial review and a strong
likelihood of a "no violation" finding or an inadequate settlement.[45]

Before *Grove City College,* OCR did not collect data pinpointing the
flow of federal monies to particular programs and activities within
institutions. Congressman Leon Panetta, former OCR director in
the Nixon administration, testified:

[I]t is virtually impossible to trace funds. If you are going to distinguish between what funds go to this particular program, or what funds
go to that particular program, it is almost impossible, because most of
these funds usually go in a general pot and it is very difficult to trace
them to specific programs that are put in place. . . . [O]nce you have
established discrimination it would be almost impossible, then, to try
to trace the funds so that you could terminate those specific funds.[46]

Advancing similar reservations, David Tatel, OCR director under
Carter, concluded that *Grove City College* produced a "bureaucratic
nightmare" in which the government and recipients alike needed to

"hire teams of accountants to trace the flow of federal funds and armies of lawyers to argue endlessly about what is and what is not a program or activity."[47] Other critics pointed out that *Grove City College* so complicated the threshold question of jurisdiction that it deterred victims of discrimination from even initiating complaints.[48]

In the wake of *Grove City College*, OCR acknowledged that it had dropped investigations in eight hundred complaints. *Grove City* also resulted in lower courts dismissing cases brought by the Justice Department under various civil rights statutes, because the government had failed to detail where and how recipients spent federal monies. The most extreme case occurred in October 1987, in *United States v. Alabama*, which involved the desegregation of the entire Alabama state system of higher education. Citing *Grove City College*, the Eleventh Circuit reversed a ruling in which a district court had found that Alabama had not eliminated the vestiges of its former dual system of higher education and had ordered the state to develop a plan eliminating those vestiges. The Eleventh Circuit ordered a new trial and held that the "complaint and proof must be redrawn to make the requisite showings of which particular programs or activities received federal funding and how these programs were discriminatory."[49]

The Civil Rights Restoration Act: A Four-Year Effort to Achieve a Congressional Override of *Grove City College*

The Supreme Court's ruling in *Grove City College* produced a four-year, politically charged struggle in Congress to nullify the decision. Supporters of the so-called Civil Rights Restoration Act (CRRA) saw their effort as an attempt to restore the original intent of Congress as to the scope of federal civil rights laws, by ensuring that the ban on discrimination in those statutes applied to an entire institution if any part of the institution received federal financial assistance. One of the most prominent and protracted civil rights struggles of the Reagan administration, the campaign to pass the CRRA became a cause célèbre within Washington civil rights and liberal circles. Proponents and opponents of the *Grove City College* decision evaluated its significance in the starkest terms. For example, Congressman Don Edwards (D.-Calif.), chair of the House Judiciary Committee's Subcommittee on Civil and Constitutional Rights, declared that the decision had "resulted in an avalanche of discrimination nationwide."[50] Not to be outdone metaphorically, Bradford Reynolds remarked that the decision had "touched off an avalanche of criticism."[51]

When Congress finally enacted the Civil Rights Restoration Act in 1988, after four long years of legislative wrangling, the new law defined programs or activities receiving federal financial assistance differently for different kinds of institutions. For states and localities receiving federal aid, coverage under the civil rights laws extended to all the operations of the department or agency receiving the funding, or the entity that distributed the funding or to which the assistance was extended.[52] For colleges and universities, the act defined a "program or activity" receiving federal aid in such a way that if any one unit received the funds, the civil rights laws would apply to all of the operations of the institution.[53]

Advocates of the Civil Rights Restoration Act considered it to be among the most important civil rights legislation in years. When it finally passed the Senate in January 1988, by a vote of seventy-five to fourteen, Ralph Neas, executive director of the Leadership Conference on Civil Rights, said that the enactment of the bill was "an overwhelming bi-partisan rejection of the Reagan Administration's efforts to weaken the nation's civil rights laws."[54] House minority leader Robert Michel, following the lead of his Democratic colleagues in the House, called the bill "the single most important piece of civil rights legislation since those landmark bills of twenty years ago."[55] Desperate to declare a victory in the midst of a conservative era that had repeatedly frustrated them, liberals especially overstressed the significance of the new legislation. Following Senate passage of the measure, Senator Kennedy declared, "[T]his is a big day for civil rights in the United States of America"— one that "demonstrated that the cause of civil rights is alive."[56] Kennedy claimed that Vice President Bush, who opposed the CRRA and was seeking the Republican presidential nomination, "is going to have to do a lot of explaining" for the position he took on the bill.[57]

Opponents of the bill were no less restrained than its proponents in their evaluations of what was at stake. Orrin Hatch (R.-Utah), who argued the administration's position on the floor of the Senate, complained that religious groups running social programs with federal monies would be unduly regulated, with the "long arm of the federal government coming in and interfering with religious rights."[58] Strom Thurmond (R.-S.C.) argued that the bill was just another shift of power from the states to Washington — the kind of shift, he said, that was responsible for the huge federal deficit.[59] Not to be outdone by other intemperate appraisals of the measure, pro and con, the Moral Majority insisted that for the purposes of receiving federal money, the law would enable "drug addicts, alcoholics, active homosexuals, transvestites, among others, to claim that they were handicapped."[60] The administration exaggerated only a bit less, when President Reagan asserted that the bill would "vastly and unjustifiably expand the power of the federal government over the decisions and affairs of private organizations, such as churches and synagogues, farms, businesses and state and local governments . . . [and] place at risk such cherished values as religious liberty."[61]

After Congress passed the CRRA, President Reagan, despite urgings from many Republicans that he sign it, vetoed the bill. The administration had fought to expand the exemptions for religious institutions, businesses, and state and local governments receiving federal funds. Reagan's veto message advanced a conservative theme oft echoed in the 1980s: the need to curtail intrusive, burdensome federal regulation. In overblown rhetoric, Reagan maintained that the measure "dramatically expand[ed] the scope of federal jurisdiction . . . diminish[ing] the freedom of the private citizen to order his or her life."[62]

When Congress overrode the veto, the political rhetoric heated up one last time. Ralph Neas called the override "a bipartisan repudiation of the civil rights extremism of the Reagan-Bush Administration." Marcia Greenberger of the National Women's Law Center declared that "women, minorities, the disabled and the elderly once again have laws that will open the door to equal opportunity that has been denied them for the last four years." Judith Lichtman of the Women's Legal Defense Fund, also hailing the congressional override, called it a "clear indication that the American people do not want their tax dollars to support discrimination."[63]

Over a four-year period, leaders of national civil rights groups expended enormous energy lobbying to enact the Civil Rights Restoration Act. Considering its passage one of the most significant civil rights victories won against the Reagan administration, both advocates and opponents of the act characterized it in apocalyptic terms, inflating its importance and overdramatizing the struggle and the stakes. The CRRA and the legal rights it protected were far less important than either its critics or its supporters claimed, because the rights in question never had the potential to effect the pronounced change that both advocates and opponents claimed they did. The struggle to establish those legal rights was noteworthy less for the tangible consequences at stake than for the political posturing, acrimony, and accusations that it provoked. If anything, the protracted struggle to establish the legal protections in the CRRA evidenced the political weakness of the civil rights lobby, for the act did no more than return civil rights protections to where they had been in 1984, when, as the history of the *Adams* litigation shows, all of the major federal civil rights laws in OCR's jurisdiction had already been hobbled.

Groups representing African Americans, women, and the disabled had struggled to sustain the *Adams* litigation in the first place because the federal civil rights statutes had already been politically neutralized. The ultimate sanction for violating those laws—the termination of funds—was not a credible threat under any of the statutes. Hence, long before the Supreme Court's decision in *Grove City College*, political considerations had negated the rights ostensibly protected by those laws. Evaluated against that backdrop, the Court's decision was of little significance, as was the legislation that overrode it. The CRRA did not produce dramatic changes affecting the lives of many people or the operations of many institutions. The clash over the act in Washington took on the character of a pseudo-conflict. It produced civil rights legislation more noteworthy for the rhetoric generated inside the Beltway than for the help it would give to those suffering from discrimination. In the struggle to enact the CRRA, as on so many other occasions, the legislative and litigative controversies about legal rights focused the civil rights struggle on narrow, legalistic issues. That orientation deflected attention away from basic questions and overemphasized the power and significance of legal rights.

The Impact of *Adams* on the Administration and Management of OCR

The Emphasis on Managerial Efficiency

As it had done during the Carter administration, the *Adams* litigation continued to produce an emphasis on managerial reforms, on the processing and settlement of cases, and on referrals to the Justice Department. Reagan officials, like their Carter predecessors, insisted that they managed OCR more efficiently than previous administrations, and made a point of stressing that theme before congressional committees. When Congressman Ted Weiss's Subcommittee on Intergovernmental Relations and Human Resources held hearings in July and September 1985, inquiring into allegations that OCR was failing to enforce civil rights laws, the Department of Education's assistant secretary for civil rights, Harry Singleton, defended the administration's civil rights record almost exclusively in terms of its managerial accomplishments. He underscored that the administration had reorganized OCR (following an earlier Carter reorganization), improved its planning, record keeping, and efficiency, and initiated a system of management by objectives. The result, Singleton boasted, was "a much more streamlined, much more efficient organization, and . . . the statistics show that." Peeved that these managerial achievements went unrecognized and unappreciated, Singleton asserted that "[t]he Education Department has a fantastic record as far as enforcement actions are concerned. All you have to do is look at the statistics. . . . We've eliminated a backlog of cases. We've reduced the average age of complaints from over a thousand days old down to 229."[64]

At hearings of a House appropriations subcommittee, also in 1985, when asked by Congressman Stokes of Ohio what the most important activities of OCR were, Singleton responded, "[T]he most significant activities of our office have been continued improvement in our management and efficiency of operations." When asked why the number of complaints filed with OCR had dropped from roughly thirty-five hundred in 1980 to approximately two thousand in each year from 1981 through 1983, Singleton indicated that he had no idea why that was true, returning again to his primary focus: "[W]hat I am concerned about are the active cases that I have, trying to process them within the time frames that are imposed upon me by the court, managing my office in the most efficient way that I possibly can."[65]

Testifying before the House appropriations subcommittee during fiscal year 1986, Singleton's successor, Alicia Coro, emphasized similar themes, noting, for example, that OCR had begun to use management information systems and other technologies to try "to be up to par with the 20th century" and to "process these investigations faster." Although OCR received more complaints in 1986 than it had received in the previous five years, Coro boasted that the agency had processed and investigated all of them, that the average age of pending cases was down 10 percent from 1985, and that though it had taken five hundred days on average to investigate a complaint in 1982, that average was 176 days at the end of 1986.[66] Even more significant than the government's reliance on such statistics was the fact that leaders of the NAACP Legal Defense Fund accepted and encouraged the idea that OCR should be judged on the basis of its timely resolution of complaints. In his testimony before Congressman Weiss's subcommittee in July 1985, Julius Chambers, then general counsel of LDF, emphasized OCR's continued failure to live up to the *Adams* time frames. In answering a question from Congressman Conyers (D.-Mich.) about what the LDF wanted to achieve, Chambers replied that "the objective" was "to cut red tape and to enable the agency to operate more efficiently."[67]

The *Adams* litigation transformed the way people evaluated OCR. As a result of the litigation, judges, congressional oversight committees, leaders of civil rights organizations, and the parties to the litigation all evaluated the agency in terms of the timely resolution and processing of complaints. Measured by that criterion, the Reagan administration did not do a bad job. The number of complaints in which OCR missed one of the *Adams* deadlines declined from 498 in 1984, to 338 in 1985, to 316 in 1986, to 296 in 1987, to 102 in 1988.[68]

The administration used its claims of efficiency to its political advantage by claiming that its managerial reforms enabled OCR to do its job with fewer resources, justifying cuts in the agency's funding. From 1981 through 1988, the number of full-time employees in OCR decreased from 1,099 to 820, a reduction of more than 25 percent. In constant 1981 dollars, the annual appropriation for OCR also went down, from approximately $47 million in 1981 to $31 million in 1988, about a one-third reduction. Also, in each of those years some of the monies appropriated "lapsed." Lapsed monies are funds appropriated by Congress that an agency does not spend, but returns to the Treasury. Each year between fiscal years 1982 and 1988, OCR failed to spend between 0.4 percent and 6.1 percent of its annual appropriations.[69] OCR officials maintained that it was possible to get along with less because of "improved caseload management" and the greater productivity resulting from the use of sophisticated management information systems.[70]

The Reagan administration's focus on management issues was not surprising. As we have repeatedly seen, from its inception *Adams* had focused every administration on management issues in civil rights enforcement. When Carter came to power, recall that the new leaders of OCR deplored the organizational disarray in the agency and initiated their own management overhaul. Four years later, Reagan's OCR officials followed suit, complaining of the organizational mess they had inherited and initiating their own managerial restructuring.

Some critics were skeptical that management reforms necessarily produced progress in protecting civil rights. Testifying before a congressional committee in 1985, one high-ranking OCR official, Anthony Califa, took a dim view of the management improvements so often touted by the Reagan administration: "There is not much of substance going on. . . . What has been going on has been a lot of filling out of management reports, and indicating how much time you use the computer, and indicating how many copies of your management report you made. There is a lot of that activity, but there is very little civil rights enforcement going on."[71]

By the 1980s, OCR officials considered managerial issues in the enforcement of federal civil rights laws just as important as, if not more important than, the substantive protections themselves. Managerial reforms and organizational restructuring held out a bipartisan attraction because they gave the appearance of action, progress, and energy and because the putative efficiencies presumably saved taxpayers money. Managerial reforms were also less politically contentious and intellectually demanding than the substantive tasks of defining legal rights, assessing when and whether a right had been violated, and determining the appropriate remedy for that violation. The management orientation produced by the *Adams* litigation celebrated form over substance, and by the Reagan years nearly all concerned with civil rights, both in and out of OCR, accepted the need to focus on managerial issues in assessing the agency's work.

The Processing of Civil Rights Complaints and the Pressure for Sellout Settlements

Early Conflict Resolution

During the Reagan years, when OCR received a complaint its first response, even before undertaking an investigation, was to ask the complainant and the federally funded institution alleged to have discriminated to discuss settling the matter. OCR called that kind of mediation Early Complaint Resolution (ECR). During that phase of its work, OCR tried to mediate a settlement between the complainant and the funded institution; and if the parties reached a settlement, no investigation by OCR ever occurred.

In a memorandum written in November 1981, lawyers in the Civil Rights Division of the Justice Department took exception to the ECR process because the guidelines governing settlements reached through that process "do not require that the agreements . . . meet the legal standards set by Title VI."[72] OCR's manual of operations noted that the government's sole objective during the ECR phase was to reach settlements, and that it took no position on the legal merits of these settlements.[73] OCR's "apparent willingness . . . to accept any agreement which results in a withdrawn complaint, regardless of the substance of that agreement," raised a "major concern," the Civil Rights Division warned, because the terms of those settlements could be used as precedents that watered down civil rights requirements in other cases.[74] In advancing a comparable objection, a 1986 report of the House Subcommittee on Intergovernmental Relations and Human Resources concluded that though ECR might save time and money, it "may be illegal, may not protect the rights of complainants, and may jeopardize future litigation involving violations of civil rights laws."[75]

The Processing of Complaints after ECR

Table 1 shows that, of the eight hundred complaints of racial discrimination brought under Title VI and investigated between 1983 and 1988, OCR found no violation in 679 (84.9%). It issued a "violations corrected" Letter of Finding in another 116 (14.5%) of the cases. The agency issued such letters indicating that a violation had been "corrected" where its initial investigation had found a civil rights violation and the recipient of federal funds promised to take specified actions to remedy the violation.[76] These settlements occurred *before* OCR took formal enforcement action, that is, before the commencement of administrative enforcement proceedings leading to the possible termination of funding, and before referral to the Justice Department. In only five complaints, 0.6 percent of the total, did OCR find a violation that ultimately required taking formal enforcement action.[77]

The data regarding compliance reviews reflect a variation in the pattern that emerged for complaints. Of the 281 compliance reviews OCR completed during fiscal year 1983 in all the civil rights areas under its jurisdiction, 196 resulted in a finding of noncompliance — that is, of a violation of a civil rights requirement.[78] Hence, while OCR found no violation in about 85 percent of its complaints between 1983 and 1988, it found violations in about two out of every three compliance reviews in 1983. This confirms that compliance reviews may be a more valuable enforcement activity, at least as measured by the frequency with which they uncover civil rights violations. However, the data for 1983 establish that in handling civil rights violations uncovered in compliance reviews, OCR showed the same predisposition to seek settlements that was seen in its handling of Title VI violations uncovered by complaints.

In every one of the 196 compliance reviews in which OCR found a violation in 1983, the agency reached a settlement with the recipients.[79] Nineteen eighty-three was not an unusual year. From fiscal year 1983 through 1987, OCR conducted a total of 1,231 compliance reviews in all the areas in which it had civil rights enforcement responsibilities. It closed 27 percent of those reviews with a finding of no violation and another 72 percent by reaching a settlement before the time for administrative enforcement proceedings. Consequently,

Table 1.
Disposition of Title VI Race Complaints, 1983–1988

Disposition	Percentage	Number
Finding of no violation	84.9	679
"Violations corrected" letter issued	14.5	116
Enforcement through administrative proceedings	0.6	5
Enforcement by referal to Justice Department	0.0	0
Totals	100.0	800

Source: House Committee on Education and Labor, *A Report on the Investigation of the Civil Rights Enforcement Activities of the Office for Civil Rights, U.S. Department of Education,* 100th Cong., 2d sess., Dec. 1988, 96–97.

OCR concluded 99 percent of the 1,231 compliance reviews completed during 1983–87 without ever initiating enforcement proceedings.[80]

The data with respect to OCR's Title VI compliance reviews follow the same pattern. In fiscal years 1983–88 (through 6 May 1988) there were 158 Title VI compliance reviews. In seventy-one (44.9%) of these, OCR found no violation. In eighty-two (51.9 percent), a settlement was reached and no Letter of Findings was issued. In two instances a settlement was reached after OCR issued the Letter of Findings, and in one case OCR settled a matter after referring it to the Justice Department.[81]

When one looks at all violations of civil rights laws, whether uncovered by investigating complaints or by conducting compliance reviews, the overwhelming significance of "settled" cases remains dramatically apparent. From January 1981 through July 1985, in investigating complaints and conducting compliance reviews OCR found 2,000 violations of civil rights laws. In those 2,000 cases, it issued only 27 notices for administrative hearings leading to a possible termination of funds, and referred only 24 cases to the Justice Department.[82] All of the remaining 1,949 cases in which OCR found violations during that period were settled by the agency without either administrative hearings or referral to the Justice Department. The data establish, therefore, that during the first four years of the Reagan era, OCR settled about 98 percent of the cases in which complaint investigations and compliance reviews had led it to conclude that civil rights laws were being violated.

Discussing the significance of the large number of settlements OCR obtained, one experienced civil rights lawyer observed:

> OCR engages in what I consider to be wholesale conciliation. It brags that over 90 percent of complaints are resolved. But the discrimination is often still there, and I question whether it has really been eliminated. OCR settles very large numbers of cases on extremely good terms for the recipient, requiring that only some, but not all, of the discriminatory practices be eliminated. The corrective action need not be, and in most instances has not been taken, when OCR issues its finding of compliance. The compliance is based on the recipient's promise to implement a corrective plan.
>
> Two problems exist. First, many plans are too lenient, allowing discrimination to continue, and second, OCR does not perform adequate monitoring of the implementation efforts by the recipient, and so many recipients never actually implement the plan.[83]

A December 1988 report by the House Committee on Education and Labor also concluded that OCR did not adequately monitor settlements, noting that after it reached settlements the agency performed on-site inspections only in "exceptional circumstances," satisfying itself in most instances with written reports submitted by recipients. The monitoring of settlements received low priority within OCR, in part because the *Adams* time frames no longer applied once OCR achieved a settlement, and also because spending time on a "closed" matter, rather than investigating and closing "open" complaints, did not improve an OCR investigator's productivity.[84]

THE CONSTRAINTS operating on OCR under *Adams* during the Reagan years continued to create pressures either to find no violation or, where there was a finding of a violation, to settle the matter quickly, and perhaps on terms unfavorable to the complainant. These settlements had advantages for the agency. By considering a case settled, OCR placed that matter beyond the purview of *Adams* and beyond the easy reach and challenge of civil rights lawyers.

The Referral of Title VI Cases to the Justice Department

Referrals to the Justice Department seemed to work no better in the Reagan administration than they had in the Carter administration. There continued to be no guidelines governing the cases that OCR referred, and it was not uncommon for such cases to languish in the Justice Department for years.[85] Indeed, in a letter to President Reagan in 1983, the chair of the U.S. Commission on Civil Rights, Harold Flemming, criticized the administration for referring its dispute with Alabama to the Justice Department. Flemming maintained that Congress had intended federal agencies "generally to enforce Title VI by terminating funds when all efforts to gain voluntary compliance fail."[86]

As in the Carter era, during the Reagan years there were occasions when OCR referred a case to the Justice Department for litigation and the department, after making its own independent review, chose not to initiate legal action. OCR continued to have no policy for dealing with that situation, and no authority to control the Justice Department's decisions. As one high-ranking Reagan OCR official explained the confusion that resulted: "[T]he practice has been totally bewildered [sic] and confused. We [OCR] thought there was a violation on Monday when we sent it over, now on Tuesday they [the Justice Department] say they're not going to handle it. It's Wednesday, the case has been returned to us, and we don't know what to do."[87] Referral to the Justice Department under Reagan, therefore, continued to mean that cases got lost in a kind of no man's land, beyond the reach of Judge Pratt and the *Adams* requirements, and beyond the control of OCR.

The Road to the Unraveling and Dismissal of *Adams*

Defeating Adams *on the Bog of Procedure: The* North Carolina Settlement *and* Adams v. Bell

As discussed earlier, North Carolina sued in federal district court in that state during the Carter presidency to enjoin HEW from deferring federal funds while Title VI hearings against the state were under way. Though the court declined to issue an injunction, it did retain jurisdiction over the matter until the administrative proceedings were completed. Those hearings began before an administrative law judge in July 1980, four months before the presidential election.

The Title VI hearing against North Carolina turned on the adequacy of the state's proposed desegregation plan, particularly on its plans to increase the number of African American students enrolled at the traditionally white institutions and to enhance the educational programs at the historically black institutions. For three-quarters of a year, the parties presented their case to the administrative law judge, amassing a record of some five hundred exhibits and fifteen thousand pages.[88] Contemporaneously, settlement discussions between North

Carolina and HEW continued. When Jimmy Carter left office in January 1981, no settlement had been reached. Negotiations with the Reagan administration proved more fruitful.

In June 1981, Frank Krueger, a Reagan administration OCR official, wrote to Joseph Rauh, chief counsel for the *Adams* plaintiffs, to advise him of the status of OCR's settlement discussions with North Carolina. Krueger informed Rauh that Secretary of Education Bell would decide shortly whether to accept a proposed settlement from North Carolina, and that if Bell accepted the proposal, it would be filed with the North Carolina district court in the form of a consent decree, subject to that court's approval. The Carter administration had refused to submit any settlement to the North Carolina court as a consent decree, seeing that as a way of circumventing administrative oversight of desegregation under Title VI.

Carter's deputy assistant attorney general in the Civil Rights Division, James Turner, noted in July 1979 that "HEW's enforcement of Title VI would be irreparably undermined if a recipient of funds could routinely by-pass statutorily-mandated administrative compliance procedures by . . . filing a lawsuit and then obtaining a substantive consent decree." Turner insisted that the North Carolina dispute could "be settled only by the submission of an acceptable desegregation plan, to be monitored and enforced *administratively* [by OCR], with the [North Carolina] lawsuit dismissed with consent."[89] Indeed, the Nixon, Ford, and Carter administrations had all resisted North Carolina's efforts to get a consent decree embodying the state's desegregation plan for higher education entered in a federal court in North Carolina.[90] The Reagan administration relented and reversed.

In July 1981, within six months of Ronald Reagan's inauguration, the administration settled the North Carolina case, submitted the settlement for the approval of the federal district court in North Carolina, and agreed to formalize the agreement as a consent decree issued by the court.[91] The desegregation plan accepted by the Reagan administration proposed, over a five-year period, to raise black enrollment at the white schools from 7.4 percent to 10.6 percent and white enrollment at the black colleges from 11.2 percent to 15 percent. Secretary Bell noted that the "goals are set with the clear understanding that failure to meet them is not automatically to be deemed failure to comply with the agreement."[92] Bell credited North Carolina's ultraconservative senator Jesse Helms with promoting settlement negotiations.

Concluding that the plan did not meet the legal requirements of Title VI, the U.S. Commission on Civil Rights asked the Department of Education to reconsider its decision.[93] Among other objectionable features, the commission noted that the plan allowed black and white institutions in close proximity to one another to continue to offer academic programs that were virtually the same.[94] Moreover, the commission took exception to the way in which the administration handled the settlement procedurally:

> [B]y submitting the agreement as a consent decree in the U.S. District Court for the Eastern District of North Carolina instead of as a desegregation plan subject to the *Adams* criteria and review by the U.S. District Court for the District of Columbia, the Department of Education and North Carolina, in effect, may avoid scrutiny by the *Adams* court. The consent decree approach sets a Department precedent as a way to circumvent Title VI administrative compliance and court-ordered desegregation requirements.[95]

What remained uncertain was whether there was any legal basis for the *Adams* plaintiffs to raise that objection in litigation.

When North Carolina sued HEW in 1979 to prevent it from deferring funds during the period in which an administrative law judge was holding hearings, it sued only HEW. The *Adams* plaintiffs never intervened in the lawsuit, appearing only as an amicus in that case. Because they were not a party to the action in North Carolina, they could not appeal the consent decree entered between the state and OCR. In June 1981, however, four days after Krueger wrote to Rauh advising him of the status of settlement discussions, Rauh's firm moved before Judge Pratt, as part of the *Adams* litigation, to enjoin Secretary Bell from entering into the agreement with North Carolina and to prevent entry of the judgment in the North Carolina district court. Pratt denied the motion, concluding that reviewing the legality of the Department of Education's settlement with North Carolina was beyond the scope of his initial 1973 decree in *Adams,* which was "directed primarily at the agency and not at the individual states and school districts with which the agency has to deal."[96]

In making his ruling, Pratt's conception of what he had done in the *Adams* case and why he had done it was important. It reflected his own assessment, or perhaps reassessment, of what he had intended to do. The purpose of his initial 1973 decree, Pratt stated, was "to see that the agency complied with its statutory [and] constitutional responsibilities. It was not directed . . . at the *individuals* that are the subject of any action that the agency might see fit to take."[97] For the *Adams* plaintiffs, Pratt's unwillingness to review the North Carolina settlement was a significant loss, so they appealed.

In *Adams v. Bell,* an *en banc* decision handed down in June 1983, the District of Columbia Circuit affirmed Pratt's decision, ruling that the limited scope of his initial *Adams* decree did not give him the authority to review the terms of OCR's settlement with North Carolina. Filled with language that reflected the court's wariness of judicial excesses of power, the *Adams v. Bell* decision construed the scope of *Adams* narrowly, severely restricting its reach and limiting its impact. In reviewing the *Adams* litigation, the court of appeals noted that Judge Pratt had eschewed imposing enforcement standards on OCR and had, instead, "carefully crafted" decrees so as not to "dictate specific compliance criteria" and thereby leave the choice "among lawful criteria" to the department and the states: "The point of [Judge Pratt's] various district court orders . . . was not to specify what the final results of enforcement would be in every detail, nor to decree unalterable requirements for compliance with Title VI, but rather to have the Department initiate the process of enforcement, the process by which the specifics of compliance would then be determined" (165, 166).*

Judge Pratt's 1973 decree, the court of appeals held, was "directed at the Department's lassitude, if not recalcitrance, in fulfilling its responsibilities under [Title VI]" (165). Its "purpose" was to compel the department to initiate enforcement proceedings, not "to supervise or dictate the details of the Department's enforcement program" (165). This limited judicial intervention protected against "an undue exercise of judicial control over the Department" (166).

Lest there be any mistake about the appeals court's view as to the proper relationship between the judiciary and the department in the enforcement of Title VI, the court declared:

> [T]he Department and the states have many ways of implementing Title VI's goals of preventing discrimination in federally aided education. An enforcement proceeding or voluntary settlement may culminate in any one of these possible approaches to compliance; Title VI . . . gives responsibility to the agency and not the courts to choose among possible means of compliance.
>
> Were the district court to read its initial decree to contemplate the relief plaintiffs now seek, that court would encroach upon the role of the institutions responsible for implementing Title VI and constitute this court as a perpetual supervisor of the enforcement actions of the Department and of the desegregation policies of the states. (166)

*In this discussion, page numbers for citations to the *Adams v. Bell* decision are given parenthetically in the text.

Rejecting the plaintiffs' arguments that Pratt had the authority under *Adams* to enjoin Secretary Bell from entering into the settlement with North Carolina, the court declared that such a power "would centraliz[e] judicial control of Title VI implementation in the District of Columbia district court" and that Pratt had "correctly declined to exercise [this] extraordinary supervisory power" (167, 169). The *Adams v. Bell* court concluded that "the effect of the appellants' argument would be to vest in the federal courts of the District of Columbia plenary power to approve or disapprove the Department's Title VI decisions. We should hesitate to arrogate such power to ourselves" (169).

Though it acknowledged that Pratt had reviewed the legal adequacy of settlements between HEW and state systems of higher education in 1977 when he ordered the department to revoke its acceptance of plans from those states (including North Carolina), the *Adams v. Bell* court emphasized that Pratt's review in that instance had occurred before OCR had commenced enforcement proceedings under Title VI. Judicial review at that point, the court insisted, "differ[ed] significantly" from judicial scrutiny of plans "accepted after initiation of administrative enforcement proceedings" (169).

"[O]nce the processes of administrative enforcement and subsequent judicial review are set in motion," the court of appeals insisted, "the role of Judge Pratt's enforcement orders comes to an end" (170 n. 40). Why Judge Pratt could review the adequacy of settlements reached in 1977, before OCR initiated Title VI enforcement proceedings, but could not review the validity of settlements reached after proceedings had begun, is hard to understand. The court offered no legal basis or public policy reason for that distinction, which cannot be justified on the basis of the language of the statute, the legislative history of its judicial review provision, or any case law construing Title VI. Nonetheless, the practical effect of the distinction was clear. The District of Columbia Circuit, like Judge Pratt, never considered whether the settlement with North Carolina met the legal requirements of Title VI, for it deemed that question to be beyond the purview of the *Adams* case. To reach that question, the court insisted, it was necessary for the *Adams* plaintiffs or others to bring a separate action against North Carolina in a federal court in that state.

Judge Skelley Wright, joined by Chief Judge Robinson and Judges Wald and Mikva, wrote a powerful forty-page dissent, arguing that the relief that the *Adams* plaintiffs sought in 1981, in North Carolina, was indistinguishable from the relief Pratt granted in 1977 when he reviewed the adequacy of state desegregation plans and ordered HEW to revoke its acceptance of those plans (185). In both instances, the dissenters argued, the plaintiffs sought the same relief: they wanted the court to order the agency to follow its own requirements for Title VI as set down in the 1977 criteria. Wright noted that the 1981 agreements under review in *Adams v. Bell,* like the earlier agreements that Pratt had invalidated in 1977, were "voluntary compliance agreements reached through 'informal negotiation'" (186). The section of Title VI authorizing judicial review applied to all agency action taken under the provision, Wright declared, and that included formal enforcement actions and voluntary settlements, even where the agency reached those settlements after it had initiated administrative enforcement proceedings (186).

The Import of Adams v. Bell

By interpreting Pratt's initial intervention in *Adams* narrowly, *Adams v. Bell* restricted the scope of future legal relief that could be obtained under *Adams.* It was not feasible for the LDF or the Rauh firm to initiate separate actions in federal courts across the country challenging individual settlements between OCR and school systems receiving federal funds. The opportunity to use *Adams* to monitor desegregation in higher education across the seventeen southern and border states by taking action in a district court in Washington, D.C., was, therefore, a critical strategic advantage to the plaintiffs in *Adams.* After *Adams v. Bell,* they lost that advantage. Under that ruling, the "primary mechanism" for vindicating rights in connection with final agency decisions was a suit against the recipient of funds in the state in which that recipient was located. In his 1977 decision ordering HEW to revoke its acceptance of desegregation plans, Pratt had left open the possibility that in some circumstances *Adams* could be used to challenge the substance of the government's enforcement decisions. *Adams v. Bell* suggested that those circumstances were limited — that *Adams* required little more than that OCR initiate the enforcement process.

Adams v. Bell marked a turning point in the thirteen-year-old *Adams* litigation. Judge Pratt had construed the sweep of the original *Adams* intervention narrowly, and the court of appeals affirmed that reading. Moreover, the tone and temper of the appeals court's decision was perhaps as important as the substance of the decision. In an admonitory style, filled with buzz-words and phrases traditionally used in criticisms of judicial activism, the court communicated its reluctance to see Judge Pratt exercise the kind of "extraordinary supervisory power" the *Adams* plaintiffs wanted him to exercise. That message from the District of Columbia Circuit was a harbinger of what was yet to come in *Adams*.

The Plaintiffs' Motion for Contempt and Judge Pratt's Reaffirmation of the Time Frames

The time frames for the processing of complaints imposed by Judge Pratt continued to be a contested legal issue in the Reagan years. In the two years after the 1977 consent decree reaffirming the basic time frames, HEW improved the speed at which it investigated Title VI complaints and completed compliance reviews. It also made progress in eliminating the backlog of old cases. However, in late 1980 OCR began consistently missing the deadlines set forth in the time frames. In November 1980, 88 percent of OCR's 225 compliance reviews were not on schedule.[98]

Data for 1981 presented to Judge Pratt by the *Adams* plaintiffs indicated that, on average, OCR missed the deadlines for completing compliance reviews 97 percent of the time. As for complaints, OCR missed the *Adams* deadlines for completing its initial investigations in two out of every three cases, and where it found violations, it missed the deadlines for completing settlement negotiations in nearly nine of every ten cases.[99] The plaintiffs also accused Secretary Bell of holding up the issuing of eighty to one hundred Letters of Findings in 1981, in cases where OCR investigators had discovered violations of civil rights laws.[100]

Armed with these and other statistics, and prompted by a deep suspicion of and animosity toward the Reagan administration, the *Adams* plaintiffs moved before Judge Pratt, in April 1981, three months into the new Republican administration, to hold the government in contempt for its failure to comply with the time frames in the 1977 consent decree. After the plaintiffs served him with the contempt papers, Secretary Bell wrote to Senator Paul Laxalt of Nevada, President Reagan's closest friend and ally in the Senate, to advise the senator of the legal action in *Adams* and to request his assistance:

> I am enclosing a copy of a contempt of court complaint that was delivered to my office yesterday. You can see from this complaint that the federal courts may soon be after us for not enforcing civil rights laws regulations. Your support for my efforts to decrease the undue harassment of schools and colleges would be appreciated. It seems that we have some laws that we should not have, and my obligation to enforce

them is against my own philosophy. Hopefully, the new administration and the new majority in the United States Senate can join in an effort to make some long overdue changes and improvements in civil rights laws.[101]

Asking that a high-ranking executive branch official be found in contempt of court was a dramatic legal move by the plaintiffs. The administration met the challenge combatively. It went on the offensive, moving to vacate the remedy at the heart of the *Adams* case: the 1977 consent decree imposing the time frames. Advancing an old refrain — that the time frames unjustifiably dictated how OCR should allocate its resources — the government called for a "re-examination of the whole time frames approach, its workability and productiveness."[102] This was, of course, the very same argument that had been advanced unsuccessfully in the Nixon and Carter administrations.

In March 1982, Judge Pratt ruled that there was still a need for time frames. He concluded that, if he removed the "coercive power of the court" and OCR were "left to its own devices, the manpower that would normally be devoted to this type of thing . . . might be shunted off in other directions . . . and the substance of compliance will eventually go out the window."[103] Nonetheless, rather than issue a contempt citation Pratt wanted the parties to explore whether they could agree on modifications to the time frames that might meet some of the government's objections. He ordered the parties to discuss such modifications over a five-month period, directing that if they did not reach agreement on a new consent decree by 15 August 1982, each party should submit its own proposed order. By that date, no agreement had been reached. In March 1983, Pratt denied the administration's motion to vacate the consent decree of December 1977 and imposed new time frames that, with minor modifications, utilized the basic framework and timetables in the 1977 consent decree. The administration appealed. Like its predecessors, it had always viewed the time frames as an unwarranted intrusion in the operations of an executive agency.

Indeed, in each of OCR's first three annual reports during the Reagan years, the administration had characterized the 1977 decree as the most important factor shaping OCR's operations. Clarence Thomas, who was the assistant secretary for civil rights in the Department of Education before moving to the Equal Employment Opportunities Commission, estimated that OCR devoted 95 percent of its staff time to complying with *Adams*.[104] Thomas's successor as assistant secretary, Harry Singleton, agreed. *Adams*, he declared, "dictated" how

OCR allocated its resources, requiring the agency to use almost all of its staff time to comply with court orders, "significantly curtail[ing] other important compliance enforcement activities."[105]

In their appeal contesting Judge Pratt's March 1983 order reaffirming the validity of the time frames, lawyers for the government launched the most forceful, aggressive, and persuasive legal argument against the *Adams* case yet. Jack Greenberg, director-counsel of the NAACP Legal Defense Fund, believed that the challenge to Judge Pratt's authority was part of a larger administration policy that amounted to a "concerted effort to sabotage the gains made since 1954 by minorities and women pursuant to congressional mandate, Supreme Court decisions and established legal principles."[106] Other liberal critics emphasized that a cadre of young, aggressive, and talented conservative ideologues had come to work as lawyers at the Justice Department in the Reagan administration and had calculatingly initiated legal challenges to undermine activist, liberal judicial decisions. Assailing the *Adams* litigation, the critics believed, was part of that strategy.

The government's brief challenging Judge Pratt's March 1983 order echoed the litany of objections often advanced against activist court decisions. Inveighing against judicial activism, the government stressed that *Adams* raised constitutional considerations about "the proper role of courts in our governmental structure."[107] The government argued that the case should be dismissed because the time frames violated the principle of separation of powers and usurped the management prerogatives of the executive branch, and because *Adams* no longer involved a dispute between "particular injured plaintiffs" and the government.[108] Government lawyers sought to exploit the opinion in *Adams v. Bell* that limited the reach of *Adams* and suggested that the District of Columbia court of appeals was uncomfortable with the power Pratt had assumed in the *Adams* litigation. Skillfully lifting language from the opinion in *Adams v. Bell,* the government argued that the district court had become the "perpetual supervisor" of OCR's enforcement efforts, thereby "effectively reversing the normal relations between the agency and the court."[109]

The administration also raised a standing question, arguing that whereas previous orders in *Adams* had grown out of findings that particular school districts had violated Title VI, the 1983 order continuing the time frames did not derive from violations of the statute by specific recipients of federal funds and did not, therefore, vindicate the rights of any identifiable injured individuals. Rather, the government declared, the *Adams* litigation had "become an endless judicial receivership of the civil rights enforcement functions of two large agencies," determining "how the executive branch will carry out its broadly delegated enforcement responsibilities in the future."[110]

The kinds of complaints lodged with OCR had changed since 1977, and the administration noted that as well. In 1977, it stressed, approximately 8 percent of the complaints OCR received had raised issues involving the rights of the disabled. For fiscal year 1981, that figure had risen sixfold, to 50.9 percent. Pratt's orders, the administration claimed, did not give OCR adequate flexibility to adjust to that change.[111]

The District of Columbia Circuit proved receptive to the government's arguments. In deciding the appeal contesting Pratt's decision to retain the time frames, the court of appeals focused on the question of standing. It concluded that the government had advanced "serious charges" that raised questions "about whether the current litigation constitutes a justiciable case or controversy" and "whether the district court had continued the litigation after the case or controversy initially entertained ha[d] expired."[112] The court said it was "obliged" to consider the standing issue because, while the government's appeal was pending, the Supreme Court had decided *Allen v. Wright*[113] — a decision that had direct application to the *Adams* case.

In *Allen*, parents of children in public school districts undergoing school desegregation in seven states sued the IRS claiming that it had failed to deny, investigate, or rescind the tax-exempt status of private schools that practiced racial discrimination in those districts. The IRS's failure, the parents alleged, violated both statutory and constitutional requirements and adversely affected their children's right to be educated in a desegregated school. After the District of Columbia Circuit decided that the parents had standing, the Supreme Court reversed, ruling that by granting standing in *Allen* the court of appeals had adopted too expansive a view of the role of federal courts.

In considering the appeal challenging Judge Pratt's March 1983 order retaining the time frames, the court of appeals found that the concerns expressed by the Supreme Court in *Allen* "pervade[d]" its deliberations. Quoting extensively from *Allen*, the District of Columbia Circuit explained that it was constrained by that ruling:

> In *Allen v. Wright* the Supreme Court pointedly admonished this court to pay close attention to standing doctrine as the Court has now clarified it in "suits challenging, *not specifically identifiable Government violations of law, but the particular programs agencies establish to carry out their legal obliga-*

tions. Such suits, even when premised on allegations of several instances of violations of law, are rarely if ever appropriate for federal court adjudication". . . . . The Court elaborated this warning, stating:

> "Carried to its logical end . . . [this] approach would have the fed-
> eral courts as virtually continuing monitors of the wisdom and
> soundness of Executive action; such a role is appropriate for the
> Congress acting through its committees and the 'power of the
> purse'; it is not the role of the judiciary, absent actual present or
> immediately threatened injury resulting from unlawful govern-
> mental action.
>
> ". . . When transported into Art. III context, that principle 'that
> the government has traditionally been granted the widest latitude
> in the dispatch of its own internal affairs,' grounded as it is in the
> idea of separation of powers, counsels against recognizing standing
> in a case brought, not to enforce specific legal obligations whose
> violation works a direct harm, but to seek a restructuring of the
> apparatus established by the Executive Branch to fulfill its legal
> duties."[114]

Without reaching the merits of the appeal, that is, without deciding whether Judge Pratt had the authority to continue the time
frames, the court of appeals remanded the case to Pratt for a "ruling
on whether standing and other threshold Article III requirements
are satisfied."[115] Though technically it took no position on the merits
of the standing question in *Adams,* the court's language suggested that
it doubted that the *Adams* plaintiffs still had standing. By stressing
that in *Allen* the Supreme Court had "admonished" the District of
Columbia Circuit "to pay close attention" to standing issues and by
quoting extensively from the Court's opinion denying standing in
Allen, the District of Columbia Circuit seemed to be implying that
Adams was precisely the kind of judicial excess the Supreme Court
had in mind in *Allen.*

The appeals court's remand and its emphasis on *Allen* was another
sign that the *Adams* litigation was faltering. First, Pratt had refused to
intervene and enjoin North Carolina from entering into a settlement
with the Department of Education, thereby preventing the plaintiffs
from centrally monitoring settlements under the rubric of the *Adams*
litigation. Second, the court of appeals affirmed Pratt's decision in
Adams v. Bell, interpreting the scope of *Adams* restrictively and using
language that emphasized that courts should limit their supervisory
authority over executive agencies. Third, in remanding the question
about continuing the time frames, the court of appeals, by its re-

peated references to *Allen* and to ideas about separation of powers, cautioned Pratt to think carefully about whether there was justification for him to continue his judicial regulation of OCR.

Judge Pratt's Dismissal of Adams and the Reversal of That Decision by the Court of Appeals

The court of appeals handed down its remand in September 1984. It took more than three years for Judge Pratt to decide the issue on remand, in part because he permitted extensive discovery addressing the issues of mootness and standing. In December 1987, fifteen years after his first decision, Pratt dismissed the *Adams* case, ruling that the plaintiffs lacked standing to continue to challenge the government's enforcement of Title VI and that the court's prior orders violated the principle of the separation of powers.[116]

To emphasize what he called "the breadth of this extensive and protracted litigation," Pratt noted that *Adams* had ultimately included forty individuals named as plaintiffs, eight individual plaintiff-intervenors, and five plaintiff-intervenor organizations, including the Women's Equity Action League, the National Organization for Women, the National Education Association, the Federation of Organizations for Professional Women, and the National Federation of the Blind. Recall that the *WEAL* and *Adams* suits were being handled simultaneously by Judge Pratt. Pratt denied standing based on the issue of causality, concluding that the discriminatory practices of which the plaintiffs complained had existed long before the 1964 Civil Rights Act and were not caused by the continued grant of federal financial assistance after passage of the act.[117] "I think," one court of appeals judge stated bluntly, off the record, "that what really happened is that Judge Pratt just got tired of being the Czar of civil rights enforcement."

Having accomplished what the three preceding administrations had failed to achieve, the Reagan administration lauded Pratt's dismissal of the case. Wendell Willkie II, general counsel of the Department of Education, declared that Pratt's decision recognized the department's "independent authority to administer the nation's civil rights laws." "After seventeen years," Willkie continued, "the Department welcomes this opportunity to resume full responsibility for the day to day affairs of the Office for Civil Rights."[118] Not surprisingly, the plaintiffs appealed.

The course of the litigation following that appeal, like most everything else about *Adams,* was unpredictable. The initial surprise was the decision by the court of appeals following Pratt's dismissal of the case. Notwithstanding the strong intimations in its remand suggesting that it believed that the *Adams* plaintiffs lacked standing, the court of appeals reversed Pratt on the standing issue. A panel consisting of Judge Sentelle, Judge Re, and Judge Ruth Ginsburg concluded that Pratt was wrong about the causality issue.[119]

Judge Ginsburg, writing for the panel, found that federal funding of programs that discriminate perpetuates discrimination. She concluded that "initiating federal fund termination proceedings [is] highly effective in gaining compliance with federal anti-discrimination laws" and has the "potential to redress in meaningful measure plaintiffs' injury."[120] Once it was decided that the *Adams* plaintiffs had standing after all — the only issue on appeal — one would have expected the matter to have ended there, with the court of appeals reinstating the *Adams* suit. Yet, in a puzzling move, Judge Ginsburg declared that "several fundamental questions remain" because when the court of appeals had remanded the case for Pratt to consider whether and how the *Allen* case applied to *Adams,* it had "left several matters unaddressed."[121]

Ginsburg explained that in the government's appeal contesting Pratt's March 1983 order — the appeal that led to the remand — the government had argued that several recent Supreme Court decisions restricted the authority of federal courts to regulate the law enforcement policies of federal agencies. Because the issues raised by the government's arguments had never been addressed by the court of appeals and "appear[ed] to implicate no issues of unresolved fact," Ginsburg explained, the court would "no longer defer [these] issues raised or suggested in the prior appeal."[122]

Judge Ginsburg did not explain why, in the interest of judicial economy, the court of appeals had not decided those legal issues in 1984, before remanding the standing question to the district court. If the court believed that questions raised by the government were, to use the court's word, "fundamental," and raised no disputed issues of fact, why did the court leave them "unaddressed" in its 1984 opinion? Why did it, instead, address only the standing and mootness issues and remand on those questions, "deferring" fundamental legal issues that, if addressed in 1984, would have led to the dismissal of the case at that point? In short, if there were legal issues in 1984 that, in the court's opinion, fatally flawed the case and necessitated dismissal as a matter of law, it made no sense to remand on the issues of standing and mootness. Inexplicably, that is precisely what the court did. Moreover, in the court's 1984 remand opinion there is no mention that the court was deferring "fundamental" and dispositive legal questions that would be addressed in the event that the district court found that the *Adams* plaintiffs had standing. The first indication of that came five years after the remand, on the appeal of Judge Pratt's decision on standing.

The court of appeals never explained why it was imperative to return to those "unaddressed" issues in 1989. Appellate tribunals are not obliged to answer every issue or argument raised by the parties. Having reversed Pratt's decision and ruled that the plaintiffs had standing, the next most plausible and predictable step for the court of appeals would have been to send the case back to the district court for the litigation to continue. Yet, the court insisted that "previously tendered issues" be addressed again in briefs submitted by the parties. Explaining the reason for the ruling and the issues to be considered in the briefs, Judge Ginsburg declared:

> To determine whether plaintiffs may proceed further in the district court, this court acknowledges the propriety of taking up, in view of current Supreme Court instruction, these previously tendered issues:
>
> (1) Do the statutes plaintiffs invoke authorize an action directly against the federal funding/compliance-monitoring agency? See *Cannon v. University of Chicago*, 441 U.S. 677, 99 S.Ct. 1946, 60 L.Ed.2d 560 (1979); cf. *Council of and for the Blind of Delaware Valley, Inc. v. Reagan*, 709 F.2d 1531 n. 69 (D.C. Cir. 1983) (en banc).
>
> (2) Does the district court have the authority to impose procedural or enforcement requirements (time frames, compliance monitoring, and reporting) supplementing those set out in the governing legislation? See *Vermont Yankee Nuclear Power Corp. v. Natural Resources Defense Council, Inc.*, 435 U.S. 544–46, 98 S.Ct. 1213, 55 L.Ed.2d 460 (1978); *Heckler v. Cheney*, 470 U.S. 821, 105 S.Ct. 1649, 84 L.Ed.2d 714 (1985).
>
> (3) Are current government officer defendants bound by provisions set out in a consent decree negotiated and agreed upon by prior administrations? [4] If they are, what must they show if they wish to be released from, or obtain modification of, those provisions? Cf. *Citizens for a Better Environment v. Gorsuch*, 718 F.2d 1117 (D.C. Cir. 1983), *cert. denied*, 467 U.S. 1219, 104 S.Ct. 2668, 81 L.Ed.2d 373 (1984).[123]

In a footnote, the judge explained further that "fresh and full briefing is in order because standing was the focus of the parties' presentation to this panel and because the law in point is still evolving and variously interpreted."[124]

Ginsburg's explanations raise more questions than they answer. What "current Supreme Court instruction" did Judge Ginsburg have in mind? Of the four questions she posed for further briefing, only the second, dealing with judicially imposed procedural requirements, had been the subject of a Supreme Court opinion (*Heckler v. Cheney*) since the previous briefing by the parties in 1983. There simply was not any significant "current Supreme Court instruction" on "previously tendered issues," at least no such instruction that Judge Ginsburg identified. Indeed, with the exception of *Heckler*, every other case the judge cited in her listing of issues and cases to be addressed anew in briefs had been addressed by the parties in their briefs in 1983.[125] Once the court of appeals determined in 1989 that the *Adams* plaintiffs had standing, there was little new to be raised that had not been analyzed by the parties and presumably considered by the court six years earlier. Moreover, it is scarcely persuasive to maintain that another round of briefing was warranted because, as the court claimed, "the law in point is still evolving and variously interpreted." There is hardly any legal issue of any significance about which that might not be said.

The court's explanation of the need to submit briefs on "fundamental" questions that had gone "unaddressed" earlier is implausible. Though there is no direct evidence to support this, it appears that the court did not want the *Adams* litigation to continue and went to odd and inexplicable lengths to ensure that result. By resurrecting issues previously examined by the litigants and asking for new briefs, the court of appeals gave the government another opportunity to advance its arguments to end the litigation and gave itself another opportunity to reconsider the fate of the *Adams* case. After further briefing in June 1990, the court of appeals resolved the allegedly unaddressed issues in an opinion issued by a panel consisting of Judges Ruth Bader Ginsburg, Douglas H. Ginsburg, and David Sentelle.[126]

Judge Ruth Bader Ginsburg, writing for the court, explained that the issue in the case was whether, in light of the *Cannon* and *Council* cases, the "plaintiffs may maintain a broad-gauged right of action directly against the federal government officers charged with monitoring and enforcing funding recipients' compliance with discrimination prescriptions." She concluded that *Cannon* and *Council* were "pivotal doctrinal developments" that "curtailed the availability of suits directly against federal enforcement authorities for tardigrade administration of antidiscrimination prescriptions." The two cases, according to the panel, required the dismissal of *Adams* because they established that Congress had not authorized a lawsuit such as *Adams* against the federal agency enforcing Title VI.[127]

What sense can one make of the sequence of rulings by the court of appeals, from its 1983 remand on standing hinting that there was no standing, to its 1989 reversal of Pratt ruling that there *was* standing but requesting additional briefing, to its 1990 ruling dismissing the case? Not much. *Cannon* and *Council* had been decided in 1984, when the court remanded on the standing question. If those cases were the significant doctrinal departures that the court, in 1990, insisted that they were, and if the parties analyzed those cases in briefs in 1983, why didn't the court dismiss the case in 1983, rather than remand on the standing question? The court offered no plausible explanation.

Further, the court of appeals did not rule out the possibility that even after its 1990 dismissal of *Adams,* an aggrieved party could still sue a federal funding agency. It acknowledged that it had previously stated, in dicta, that "a private individual could challenge in court HEW's continued funding of a noncomplying district." "We do not," Judge Ginsburg wrote, "gainsay that suggestion."[128] Indeed, she allowed that, in *Council,* the court gave "implicit approbation" for suits against federal funding agencies so long as those suits were, to use the court's awkward terms, "recipient-specific" or "situation-specific." She further conceded that whereas *Council* held that there was no right of action against a federal agency for failing to investigate or respond to complaints, it did not decide whether there was a right of action against an agency that received a "finding" or "holding" that a recipient had discriminated and then failed to act to terminate funding.[129]

When all the jurisprudential verbiage about implied rights of action is laid aside, what emerges from Judge Ginsburg's opinion is the strong hint that the court objected to the kind of power that Judge Pratt had come to exercise in the *Adams* litigation, and ended the case for that reason. The circuit court's opinion, while not saying so directly, is replete with language that supports that inference. The court referred, for example, to the "grand scale action plaintiffs delineate." It noted that "over the past two decades the once contained action expanded to colossal proportions," and had grown "ever larger."[130] It stressed that the litigation had "swelled" to encompass new classes of plaintiffs and new judicially imposed remedies and procedures,[131] and that it had imposed "grand scale relief" involving "across-the-board supervision of the funding and enforcement practices of the agency."[132] In the end, Ginsburg wrote, *Adams* "cast the district court as nationwide overseer or pacer of procedures government agencies use to enforce civil rights prescriptions."[133]

Similar characterizations of *Adams* had been advanced by each administration from the beginning of the litigation in 1970. Neither Pratt nor the District of Columbia Circuit, however, had ever expressed concern in an opinion about the expansive character of the litigation until the District of Columbia Circuit remanded the case to Pratt in 1983 for consideration of the issues of standing and mootness. The concerns of the court of appeals raised questions about the role of the courts and the kind of power they should exercise—especially in reviewing and seeking to control the actions of executive agencies enforcing laws. In the opinion dismissing the case, Judge Ginsburg's language suggests that the court of appeals was troubled by these larger themes in the *Adams* litigation; but the court's opinion and dismissal turned on technical legal issues. The court seemed deliberately to avoid treating the larger and more interesting jurisprudential questions about the proper role of judges and courts, in favor of an analysis of a narrow, procedural point—implied rights of action. Yet, that was consistent with the pattern throughout both the constitutional school desegregation litigation and the *Adams* litigation. Major substantive issues seemed to be repeatedly resolved by courts on narrow, technical, and often procedural grounds that left central policy questions unaddressed.

The State of Higher-Education Desegregation at the End of the Reagan Era

Background: The Adams *Plaintiffs' May 1982 Motion for Further Relief in Higher Education*

During the Reagan years, prior to the dismissal of *Adams,* the *Adams* plaintiffs continued to monitor desegregation in higher education and returned to Judge Pratt to push for continued pressure from him. By 1982, *Adams* regulated public higher education in two groups of states. The first group consisted of the original ten *Adams* states minus Maryland, Louisiana, Pennsylvania, North Carolina, and Mississippi, which all came to be involved in separate litigation in federal courts. Hence, OCR regulated and monitored the desegregation plans of the "first tier" states: Florida, Arkansas, Georgia, Oklahoma, and Virginia. After HEW promulgated its desegregation criteria for higher education in 1977, it received and accepted from those states desegregation plans committing them to achieving certain goals within a five year period.

In addition to the five "first-tier" states, there was another group of six states that OCR investigated in the middle and late 1970s: South Carolina, Delaware, Missouri, West Virginia, Kentucky, and Texas. In their second Motion for Further Relief in Higher Education, filed in 1982, the *Adams* plaintiffs argued that the first-tier states had defaulted on the objectives to which they had committed themselves in their five-year plans, necessitating that OCR commence Title VI enforcement proceedings against those states. As to the second group of states, the plaintiffs argued that OCR had improperly accepted plans that were not statewide for Delaware, Missouri, and West Virginia, and had failed to negotiate adequate and acceptable plans in two other states — Kentucky, and Texas.[134]

In moving for further relief in May 1982, the plaintiffs argued that commencing Title VI enforcement proceedings was "the only mechanism which could render effective the government's otherwise toothless entreaties to the states for compliance measures." With respect to both sets of states, the plaintiffs urged that the court establish a date for commencing enforcement proceedings unless each of the states had achieved "substantial progress" toward desegregation by that date.[135] The plaintiffs took aim at Secretary Bell in advancing their argument:

> With a Secretary who will not commence enforcement proceedings and professes that enforcement of Title VI is "against my own philosophy" [reference omitted], OCR is perceived to be a "paper tiger." The futile and immensely protracted charade of letter writing and meetings between OCR and the states demonstrates that no real desegregation progress will occur without the imposition of an enforcement proceeding deadline. Without such a deadline, there is no credibility to OCR's compliance efforts.[136]

The government responded to this motion as it had to similar motions during previous administrations. It argued that if the court granted the motion it "would necessarily be inserting itself into the administrative process" and undertaking a "sweeping and detailed review of innumerable exercises of administrative judgment necessary to determine the adequacy of state plans."[137] Once again, Judge Pratt was not persuaded by the government's arguments.

In October 1982, Pratt ordered the states to develop new plans and to be in full compliance with Title VI by the fall of 1985. As to the five first-tier states, he concluded that they had each defaulted in major respects in meeting the objectives in their plans and in HEW's desegregation criteria. He ordered each of the first-tier states to submit, no later than 30 June 1983, an amended plan "containing concrete and specific measures that reasonably ensure that all the goals of [their] 1978 desegregation plans will be met no later than the fall of 1985."[138] He further ordered OCR to commence enforcement proceedings no later than 15 September 1983 against any state that failed to submit such a plan. This was, in effect, a final deadline date for the receipt of collegiate desegregation plans.

As to another group of states—Pennsylvania, Texas, and Kentucky—Pratt had found in his second supplemental order in 1977 that the plans that they had submitted and that OCR had approved were inadequate. In responding to the plaintiffs' 1982 Motion for Further Relief, Pratt ordered OCR, within a specified number of days, to commence administrative enforcement proceedings against the three states unless the agency concluded that those states had submitted plans "which fully conform to the HEW desegregation Criteria and Title VI."[139] With respect to a third group of states—West Virginia, Missouri, and Delaware— Pratt held that there was no showing of systemwide racial imbalance in those states and that the plans that OCR had accepted from them complied with Title VI.

Several patterns are evident in Pratt's 1982 order dealing with desegregation in higher education. The plaintiffs did not argue, nor did Pratt rule, that OCR's standards for desegregation under Title VI were inadequate. Nor did Pratt announce any new substantive judicial standards for complying with Title VI. Once again, he embraced and accepted the standards in HEW's criteria. In 1982, all that the plaintiffs alleged, and all that Pratt ruled, was that the states had failed to meet OCR's existing goals and the states' own standards and commitments as set forth in their plans. Hence, though it is true that Pratt continued to intervene in OCR's enforcement of Title VI during the Reagan years, he also continued to avoid reviewing the adequacy of the desegregation standards OCR used. In that sense, Pratt could argue that he was only ordering the states to do what OCR's policies required them to do and what the states said they would do.

OCR received amended plans from all five of the first-tier states during May and June 1983. At the end of June, it sent a letter to each of the states rejecting the state's amended plan, identifying the plan's deficiencies, and requesting a new submission by August 1983. Though OCR threatened those states that it might have to start enforcement proceedings against them, it eventually accepted a desegregation plan from each of them, obviating the need to initiate such proceedings.

Five state desegregation plans expired in December 1985—the plans for the first-tier states Arkansas, Florida, Oklahoma, and Georgia, and the plans for the community colleges in North Carolina. Another five state plans—for Virginia, West Virginia, South Carolina, Missouri, and Delaware—expired in June 1986. When these plans expired, OCR reviewed and evaluated each state's performance. The reviews were completed in March 1987. Rather than send those reviews out as the agency's final findings, OCR sent a draft of each report to the governor of the state covered by the report, so that the governors could have an opportunity to review and comment on the reports.[140] Only after receiving comments from a state's governor did OCR determine whether the state was in compliance with Title VI. Giving each state a chance to review and comment on OCR's draft findings was a remarkably conciliatory gesture and policy, given that all of those states had failed to take the necessary measures for years.

The Disappointing Fruits of Litigation: The Persistence of Unequal Opportunity in Higher Education

In August 1987, Julius Chambers announced that an NAACP Legal Defense Fund report had concluded that the first-tier states had seriously defaulted on the commitments they had made in their desegregation plans. The report noted that in the five first-tier states, black students received a smaller percentage of student aid in the 1986–87 academic year than they had seven years earlier, that they comprised only 6 to 8 percent of graduate students, and that the disparity between the percentage of white and black high-school seniors going on to college had grown larger since the 1970s.[141] Chambers called on Secretary of Education William J. Bennett to commence Title VI enforcement proceedings to compel the states to meet the 1977 desegregation criteria.

Chambers noted that, according to the American Council on Education, black enrollment nationwide had peaked in 1976, when blacks amounted to 9 percent of the college population. The percentage never reached that high in the 1980s, even though the black percentage of the public school population was increasing. Of those in college, a larger percentage of black students than of whites enrolled in two-year as opposed to four-year institutions, a larger percentage dropped out, and a smaller percentage went on to graduate and professional schools.[142]

The picture that emerged, said Chambers, was of a work force increasingly composed of minority people who were "educationally ill-prepared to function at their fullest potential."[143] The failure of the

Adams states to desegregate and, more important, to provide greater access for blacks to state university systems, Chambers concluded, exacerbated that problem. Notwithstanding three cycles of submissions of state plans, all compelled by the *Adams* litigation, the end result of those efforts had not changed things significantly.

Black high-school graduates in the *Adams* states continued to enroll in colleges in significantly lower percentages than whites and in percentages that were lower than the black proportion of the states' overall population. The historically white and black institutions remained overwhelmingly segregated, and the latter institutions remained underfunded. Separate and unequal institutions continued.[144] Of the original ten *Adams* states, six had committed themselves in their plans to achieving parity in the percentage of black and white high-school graduates who went to college. As of April 1987, none of them had met that goal.[145] College enrollment rates for blacks in several of the *Adams* states had actually decreased under the plans.[146] All ten states had set goals for the hiring of black faculty members at the doctoral level. No state had met that goal either. All the states had set goals for hiring faculty members at the nondoctoral level. Only Georgia and Oklahoma had met one numerical goal in that area.[147]

Janell Byrd, an LDF lawyer, noted that though between 1978 and 1985 the percentage of white high-school seniors going on to college had increased in Arkansas from 36 percent to 46 percent and in Oklahoma from 56 percent to 63 percent, the percentage of black high-school graduates going to college remained constant at 36 percent in Arkansas and went down in Oklahoma from 56 percent to 52 percent.[148] LeGree Daniels, the assistant secretary of education for civil rights, testifying for the Reagan administration before a House subcommittee in April 1987, insisted that the goals in the plans were not "quotas" and that "failure to achieve [a goal] is not sufficient evidence standing alone to establish a violation of Title VI."[149]

In February 1988, eleven months before Ronald Reagan left office, the Department of Education announced that Virginia, Delaware, Georgia, Florida, Missouri, and Oklahoma remained in partial violation of the goals and timetables for minority recruitment, faculty hiring, and enhancement of facilities and curriculum. Secretary of Education Bennett, putting the best face on the news, noted the administration's position that the goals in the plans were not quotas, and stated that all of the states had made "significant" and "substantial" progress toward desegregation, and that each had done "all or most of what it committed to do under the plan."[150] Bennett was "heartened," he said, by the progress that the states had made in desegregating, in recruiting minority students, and in enhancing the traditionally black institutions.[151]

Following Bennett's upbeat assessment, the Department of Education asked the governors of the six states that were not in compliance to submit written assurances that they would implement steps to achieve full integration in their state university systems by the end of 1988. As to four other states that the department had also been monitoring—North Carolina, South Carolina, West Virginia, and Arkansas—it did not require them to make any further efforts to desegregate. The LDF announced that requiring no further action from the four states, and imposing only modest additional requirements on the other six states, "effectively excused ten southern states from their affirmative obligation" to eliminate the vestiges of segregation. Elliot Lichtman, the lawyer in Joseph Rauh's firm who had for so long carried the burden of the *Adams* litigation, called the action "a blow to any serious civil rights enforcement" and "a clear, clear indication that they will find everyone in compliance before they leave office."[152]

Conclusion

Though an adversarial relationship between the civil rights lobby and the current presidential administration had become a predictable, almost institutionalized feature of our national politics by 1980, during the Reagan era there was a more than usual combativeness between the two. That combativeness manifested itself most dramatically in the administration's efforts to roll back the coverage of civil rights laws and in the struggle to enact the Civil Rights Restoration Act. The civil rights community viewed Reagan even more suspiciously and fearfully than it had viewed Richard Nixon because the Reagan administration's attack on civil rights laws and their enforcement was grounded in an ideology about the proper role of government. Reagan was a more dangerous and formidable opponent than Nixon precisely because he advanced arguments against civil rights enforcement that were founded on philosophical and ideological considerations and not on short-term political opportunism. Unlike Nixon, the Reaganites did not devise their civil rights positions to facilitate winning an election or white votes. Rather, their objections to civil rights enforcement were more sophisticated and respectable, couched, as they were, in terms of ideas about what was fair and good and what it was proper for government to do. Whether one agreed with the Reaganites or not, their views on civil rights, unlike Nixon's, had a much-emphasized moral and philosophical dimension.

The Reaganites maintained that, as a matter of political philosophy, in civil rights policies and virtually every other realm they sought to reduce the intrusiveness of government and the scope of its power. Thus (if one takes them at their word), the Reaganites believed that when government acted in the civil rights area, as elsewhere, it proved to be inefficient and ineffective. In Reagan's view, the American people did not need courts, law, and government bureaucracies to tell them the right and moral way to treat racial minorities, women, and disabled people. That was the appealing message of little Grove City College standing up to the federal bureaucrats, defiantly rejecting their money and asserting the college's moral independence and superiority over the blustery government bureaucracy that sought to dictate morality. As Ronald Reagan saw it, Americans knew how to treat people fairly, not because of what laws required but because of the values they had learned through family and religion, and in some measure, because of values they understood instinctively, just because they were Americans.

The "Golden City on the Hill" to which Reagan so often alluded was one where people knew and did naturally what it was fair and right to do. In this view, the intrusion of law into relationships between people or between people and government was unnecessary. Moreover, using law in that way was counterproductive because, to the degree that we relied on law to compel us to act fairly, we undermined what we learned and understood more "naturally" through informal, nongovernmental institutions. This was a philosophy that countenanced systematic bigotry and unfairness but did so with a kind face, presented by a telegenic, good-natured, well-meaning, avuncular man who was personally difficult to dislike. Oh, how civil rights lobbyists longed to be playing opposite that almost naturally villainous figure Richard Nixon.

Yet, when one looks at the enforcement of Title VI during the Reagan era, one must not make too much of the administration's conservative ideology and its impact, and especially of the battle over the Civil Rights Restoration Act. There was not much potency left in Title VI and OCR when Ronald Reagan became president. Neither the provision nor the agency was a threat to the Reagan revolution or its goals. Unlike Nixon, Reagan did not have to initiate measures either to thwart those who might use the statute to produce significant social change, or to play to or pay off his political constituency. Reagan inherited a hobbled Title VI and an enfeebled Office for Civil Rights. He had no real need to blunt the force of the statute. That task had already been achieved, and had been administratively and politically institutionalized. In short, by 1981 there was no realistic way of reconfiguring Title VI and its enforcement by OCR so that the provision could effect significant changes in the way in which American public education served blacks. For a brief and unique period in the middle to late 1960s, that is what those enforcing Title VI tried to do. Yet, it was our politics that made this happen — or at least, that permitted it to happen. No matter who had won the election in 1980, there would have been no political base for using the statute to transform the way in which the American educational establishment failed black Americans.

By 1980, Title VI and OCR were little more than a nuisance to federally funded educational institutions. Moreover, legal victories in the *Adams* litigation could not alter the political dynamics that, like some inescapable gravitational force, constrained those who would enforce Title VI in any administration. In short, the Reagan administration did not really have to do much to ensure that business as usual, unimpeded by Title VI, continued in educational institutions receiving federal funding.

By the middle of the Reagan years, probably beginning with the June 1983 affirmance of Judge Pratt's decision not to intervene in the North Carolina settlement, the plaintiffs in *Adams* found themselves increasingly in a defensive legal posture. Thereafter, it became evident that both the District of Columbia court of appeals and Pratt were uncomfortable with the direction the *Adams* litigation had taken. Pratt first became concerned when the women's groups entered the legal struggle. After that, his uneasiness about what he was doing increased. The lawyers for the women's organizations picked up on that uneasiness and characterized Pratt as insensitive to their legal concerns and to them personally. They believed that he did not think they belonged in the *Adams* lawsuit and that he was unhappy that they were in it. I think they are right. *Adams* would likely not have been dismissed had it remained a case focused exclusively on issues of racial discrimination. In the *Adams* litigation, at least, the transformed civil rights movement, albeit unintentionally, had a negative effect on what blacks could do and get for themselves. That important, but politically sensitive, point is one whose implications will be explored in a later chapter.

It is also noteworthy that in the late 1980s, as the Reagan administration rushed to reach settlements with numerous states undergoing desegregation in higher education, there was little effort to challenge the legal adequacy of those settlements. Having focused almost exclusively on procedure, the *Adams* plaintiffs had little basis in the litigation to employ earlier decisions by Pratt or the court of appeals to challenge the substance of settlements. Moreover, in part because the *Adams* litigation had such a procedural focus, there was still little case law providing substantive judicial standards for desegregation in higher education. Also, unlike the Guidelines for desegregation in elementary and secondary education that HEW issued in the 1960s, HEW's criteria for desegregation in higher education never received wide endorsement by federal courts. Finally, once the court of appeals remanded the *Adams* case to Pratt in 1983 on grounds of standing and mootness, the *Adams* plaintiffs were constantly on the defensive. Forced to focus on how to keep the litigation alive, they had little time or legal maneuvering room to challenge the substantive merits of negotiated settlements.

What we saw in Title VI enforcement and in civil rights enforcement generally during the Reagan era was a charade of a struggle by both the administration and its critics. On the one hand, the administration overstated the intrusiveness of civil rights regulation, and the associated dislocations and costs. On the other hand, the civil rights lobby overstated the significance of the change in Title VI enforcement in the Reagan administration, of the administration's efforts to reduce the coverage of the civil rights laws, and of the Civil Rights Restoration Act. The stakes in those disputes were not nearly as momentous as each side alleged. In fact, the fight over the Civil Rights Restoration Act took on the character of an almost staged conflict, involving fairly meaningless stakes — at least for Title VI. It was a struggle noteworthy largely for its inflated posturing and rhetoric and for its irrelevance to the real-life needs of so many millions of poorly educated black children.

Traditional liberals will find this conclusion objectionable, if not heretical. As I am a rather conventional liberal myself, simply advancing these observations makes me feel defensive and uncomfortable. Nonetheless, intellectual candor compels me to ask a tough question: To what extent do the traditional liberal efforts to use civil rights legislation and litigation provide significant assistance to those whose plight liberals claim to champion? Stated for purposes of this chapter, what exactly did blacks win — what and how did they really gain — by the enormous expenditure of political energy that produced the Civil Rights Restoration Act?

What significance could there be to the debate over the scope of a right if everyone recognized that the only meaningful sanction for failure to honor that right — the termination of federal funding — had long ceased to be politically viable for Democrats and Republicans alike? What significance could there be to the debate over racial discrimination in schools if the very agency responsible for combating such discrimination paid scant attention to advancing the legal standards that addressed that discrimination, focusing instead on managerial reforms and the efficient resolution of complaints? What sense was there to struggle to restore a legal right that, at least in terms of racial discrimination, had ceased to have much impact on people's lives? In the struggle to enact the Civil Rights Restoration Act, the value of merely establishing a legal right was overemphasized, and there was virtually no appreciation for the context within which that right would function and be enforced. As occurred time and again in the history of Title VI, the legal right to equal educational opportunity became abstracted from the real-world circumstances in which it would operate and which ultimately controlled the fate and impact of that right.

Though the administrative enforcement of Title VI had little bite left by the end of the Reagan years, there were several states in the higher-education part of the *Adams* litigation that had been referred to the Justice Department for litigation. The most important case that had emerged from that part of the *Adams* litigation was the lawsuit challenging the operation of Mississippi's state university system. That case, *United States v. Fordice,* became the most important higher-education school desegregation case decided by the Supreme Court since *Brown v. Board,* and the most significant recent chapter in the torturous history of Title VI.

7

Fordice:
The Disappointing Legacy
of the Rights Strategy

> I am upset not with your review of the precedents but with
> your sense that you have to defend them or at least defend
> civil rights lawyers' continued reliance on a freedom train
> that has run out of steam.
>
> I'm discussing, not defending.
>
> Wrong! You are defending, and I hear you also admit-
> ting that civil rights litigation, although no longer a pri-
> mary weapon, is necessary "busy work," occupying those
> who feel that "something should be done" even if it is not
> particularly helpful and may be a harmful delusion. Why
> cannot you simply concede that my conclusion is the cor-
> rect one?
>
> Geneva Crenshaw, in Derrick Bell's
> *And We Are Not Saved*

BECAUSE OF THE *ADAMS* LITIGATION, by the late 1980s, in such
states as Alabama, Louisiana, and Mississippi, the struggle to desegregate in higher education began producing decisions in federal
courts. These lawsuits resulted from HEW's, and later the Department of Education's, referral of cases to the Justice Department for
litigation. Although these disputes originated as part of the *Adams*
case, the litigation initiated by the Justice Department produced case
law independent of *Adams*. Throughout the latter part of the Reagan
years, OCR officials, state university officials, and civil rights lawyers
and organizations waited to see which case would get to the Supreme
Court first so that the high tribunal could set national policy on the
legal questions involved in the desegregation of higher education.
That first case, *United States v. Fordice*, came to the Court from Mississippi in 1991.

The basic question in desegregating colleges and universities centered on the measures courts would require states to take to dismantle the former dual systems of higher education. To answer that question, it was necessary to determine what educational policies, practices, and results were required in a "desegregated" system of higher education, and what role, if any, historically black colleges and universities (HBCUs) would play in such a system. When Ronald Reagan left the White House in 1989, there was still surprisingly little scholarship or case law addressing such issues.

In the years following *Brown v. Board of Education,* the Court did address the duty to desegregate in elementary and secondary education. As discussed in chapter 4, above, the Court ruled in the 1968 *Green* case that elementary and secondary school systems had to do more than merely end the practices that had historically produced racial segregation in schools. Under *Green,* school officials had "the affirmative duty" to act "now" to "fashion steps which promise[d] realistically to convert promptly to a system without a 'white' school and a 'Negro' school, but just schools."[1] Merely eliminating the laws that compelled or permitted racial segregation was not enough.

Though in *Green* the Court expressed skepticism that a state could meet its constitutional obligation in elementary and secondary education by offering students "freedom of choice" in selecting their schools, it did not rule that freedom of choice was always unacceptable. Rather, it held that the state had a constitutional obligation to achieve a unitary, nonracial system and that where freedom of choice did not achieve that end, something more was required. What remained unclear until the Court decided *United States v. Fordice* in 1992 was how the rationale and ruling of *Green* applied to desegregation in higher education. Before the Court decided *Fordice,* the three primary cases on that question were the *Alabama State Teachers Association, Norris* and *Bazemore* decisions.[2]

FOR YEARS the major, conflicting precedents in desegregation in higher education were *Alabama State Teachers Association v. Alabama Public School and College Authority* (hereafter cited as *ASTA*) and *Norris v. State Council of Higher Education for Virginia. ASTA* was the first case involving desegregation in higher education decided after *Green.* It was a class action suit brought to enjoin Alabama from constructing an extension of Auburn University, a white school, near the campus of Alabama State, a historically black school. In *ASTA,* the plaintiffs argued that the affirmative duty to desegregate established in *Green* obliged the state to develop new facilities and campuses so as to maximize desegregation. They maintained that developing an extension of a traditionally white school near a historically black college would have the opposite effect.

Emphasizing the tradition of "free choice" for students selecting a college or university,[3] and the free choice for black and white students alike to attend the new extension of Auburn, the district court refused to enjoin construction of the extension. It held that the duty to desegregate in higher education did not extend beyond the obligation to provide nondiscriminatory admissions. The Supreme Court summarily affirmed. Two years later, in 1971, another district court seemed to reach a different conclusion on the same issue.

In *Norris,* faculty members and students at Virginia State College, a black four-year institution near Petersburg, Virginia, sought to enjoin the state from expanding Richard Bland College, a nearby white two-year college, into a four-year institution. Advancing arguments that paralleled those of the plaintiffs in *ASTA,* the plaintiffs in *Norris* contended that expanding Richard Bland College would frustrate Virginia State's efforts to desegregate by attracting white students. The state argued that it had fulfilled its constitutional obligation to desegregate by operating its public colleges and universities on the basis of freedom of choice. The *Norris* court ruled that this was not enough, and enjoined Virginia from expanding Richard Bland College. It held that though the methods needed to desegregate colleges and universities might differ from those used at the elementary and secondary levels, the state's duty was the same. The state had an affirmative duty under *Green* to take the steps necessary to convert to a unitary system and to eliminate racial discrimination root and branch.[4] *Norris,* like *ASTA,* was summarily affirmed by the Supreme Court. Because *Norris* and *ASTA* were contradictory rulings, there was uncertainty about whether a state could meet its obligations under the law by simply offering black and white students the "free choice" to apply to any school in the state university system. That uncertainty increased in 1986 after the Supreme Court's decision in *Bazemore v. Friday.*

The Supreme Court's decision in *Bazemore* involved North Carolina's Agricultural Extension Service, an organization that disseminated information about home economics, agriculture, 4-H, and community development. North Carolina State University administered the extension service. In the home economics and 4-H areas, the extension service established "clubs" to educate people about such subjects. Until 1965, the clubs operated on a segregated basis. After that year, the state began a new policy of "open enrollment"— a policy simlar to the freedom-of-choice concept used to desegregate elementary and secondary schools. The new policy opened all clubs to everyone regardless of race. Notwithstanding that policy, as late as 1980 nearly 40 percent of the 4-H clubs (1,348) remained all white.[5]

The district court found that the racial segregation in the clubs "was the result of the voluntary choice of private individuals" and was not unconstitutional.[6] The Supreme Court agreed. By a five-to-four margin, it ruled that the Constitution did not require more than what the extension service had done to disestablish segregation in the clubs. It was sufficient for the extension service to discontinue its prior discriminatory practices and adopt "a wholly neutral admissions policy."[7] The mere existence of all-white or all-black clubs did not constitute a violation of the equal protection clause. Distinguishing segregation in the clubs from segregation in schools, the court observed that, whereas children must attend school, there was no compulsion to join a club, and that whereas school authorities may assign a student to a school and otherwise regulate a student's choice of a school, "a young person [has] the right to join any club he or she wishes to join."[8] While the concept in *Green* of an affirmative duty to desegregate was a sound doctrine for public schools, the Court ruled, "it has no application to this wholly different milieu."[9] The Court's analysis in *Bazemore* left unanswered the question of whether and how *Green* applied in the "milieu" of higher education. That answer came in *United States v. Fordice.*

THE JURISPRUDENTIAL LEGACY OF *ADAMS:* THE *FORDICE* CASE

The Facts in Fordice

The struggle to desegregate the Mississippi state university system by enforcing Title VI extended over a quarter of a century and was linked directly to the *Adams* case. In 1969, Mississippi was one of the ten states from which HEW requested a higher-education desegregation plan; it was also one of five that ignored that request.[10] Mississippi's failure to desegregate its university system and OCR's failure to do anything about it caused the NAACP Legal Defense Fund, in its complaint in the *Adams* case, to cite Mississippi as one of the states in which Title VI was not being enforced.

In 1973 OCR again contacted Mississippi, advising the state university that it was violating Title VI and requesting that the state submit a desegregation plan.[11] OCR noted, among other things, that because of differences in the range and quality of program offerings at

historically black colleges and universities and traditionally white institutions (TWIs), the former would be "unable to attract significant numbers of white students."[12] Notwithstanding OCR's efforts in
1969 and 1973, it was not until Judge Pratt ordered Mississippi to submit a desegregation plan that the state finally did so, presenting one to
HEW in September 1974.[13] Later that year, HEW rejected the plan
and referred the matter to the Justice Department for litigation.[14]

In January 1975, before the Justice Department had taken any action on HEW's referral, a group of Mississippi citizens brought *Ayers
v. Allain,* * a class action lawsuit on behalf of blacks throughout the
state, maintaining that Mississippi had not met its obligations under the Constitution and Title VI to dismantle its former dual system of higher education.[15] The lead plaintiff, Jake Ayers, was a long-
time civil rights activist in the state. Representing Ayers was Alvin
Chambliss, a native of Mississippi and a graduate of the Howard
University Law School, who worked for a federally funded legal services organization. Chambliss was to spend more than twenty years
of his life on the *Fordice* case, beginning discussions with plaintiffs in
1972, arguing the case before the Supreme Court in 1991, and handling the proceedings on remand in the years following the Court's
decision in 1992. In 1976, shortly after the plaintiffs first brought suit,
the Justice Department intervened in the case, echoing the plaintiffs' allegations.

The Mississippi state system of higher education consisted of eight
institutions, five of which were traditionally white and three of which
were historically black. All of these institutions were totally segregated when the Court decided *Brown v. Board of Education* in 1954. No
black had ever attended a TWI, and no white had ever attended an
HBCU. Total segregation remained in effect until 1962, when, in a
nationally publicized incident, the Fifth Circuit ordered James Mer-
edith admitted to the University of Mississippi.

Between 1962 and 1970, each of the institutions took its first steps to
integrate its student body. Progress beyond token desegregation was
slow, however, especially in attracting white students to the black colleges. In 1986, more than 99 percent of the twenty-six thousand white
students in the state system were enrolled in traditionally white insti-

---

*Ayers v. Allain was the beginning of what I call the *Fordice* case. As the case progressed
over the years, the named defendant changed as the governors of Mississippi changed.
Because of protracted pre-trial proceedings and the complexity and length of the trial, the
first opinion in the case (by the federal district court in Mississippi) was not written until
1987. Inasmuch as the United States government intervened in the case, I occasionally
refer to the case as *United States v. Fordice;* elsewhere I refer to it as *Fordice.*

tutions. Seventy-one percent of all black students were enrolled in historically black institutions.[16] Alvin Chambliss liked to say that higher education in Mississippi was still run like a system of apartheid.[17]

The *Fordice* plaintiffs alleged discrimination in the state university's admissions policies; in the schools' racial composition and the quality of faculties; in the institutional missions for the black and white campuses; in the differential program offerings at the institutions; in program duplication at the black and white schools; and in differential funding and facilities for the HBCUs and TWIs.

Admissions Policies. The statewide board of trustees required incoming freshmen to attain certain scores on the "ACT," a standardized achievement test. The plaintiffs argued that they were denied equal access to the state university because a student's score on the ACT was the sole criterion Mississippi used to determine admission to TWIs. The state did not consider high-school grades and other noncognitive measures in evaluating candidates, even though those who had developed the ACT test recommended that this be done,[18] and even though high-school grades are known to be a better predictor of student success in college than scores on achievement tests.[19]

A score of fifteen on the ACT guaranteed a student admission to the TWIs. Those scoring below fifteen were automatically rejected. It was undisputed that the state had instituted that policy at the TWIs in 1963 to limit black enrollment at those institutions in the wake of efforts to integrate them. The policy worked. In 1985–86, for instance, whereas 70 percent of white high-school graduates scored fifteen or higher on the ACT, only 30 percent of black high-school graduates attained such scores. Hence, the state's sole reliance on ACT scores kept seven out of ten black high-school graduates from gaining admission to Mississippi's five traditionally white institutions.[20]

The Racial Composition and Quality of Faculties. At the three HBCUs the faculties were approximately 70 percent black.[21] At the five TWIs, the faculties were about 3 percent black. At the white institutions in 1986–87, the average salaries of faculty members varied from approximately $26,000 to $31,000. At the black institutions, it ranged from about $23,000 to $27,000. At the TWIs, the percentage of full professors ranged from 26 percent to 43 percent of the total faculty, whereas at the HBCUs it ranged from 11 percent to 23 percent. There were also notable differences in the percentage of faculty members with doctorates. The plaintiffs claimed that the identifiable racial character and the differential quality and salary of the faculties at HBCUs and TWIs were evidence that a dual system continued.

Institutional Missions. After a review that began in 1980, the board of trustees of the state university classified the institutions in the state system into three categories for funding purposes: comprehensive, urban, and regional.[22] Comprehensive institutions offered the widest range and highest level of academic programs and received the most funding. Three traditionally white institutions were the only ones given that designation. Jackson State, an HBCU, was the only institution categorized as "urban," with a mission to serve the city of Jackson. A regional designation meant that the institution had the most limited funding and programmatic offerings. Two of the three black institutions received that designation; two of the five white institutions did as well. The plaintiffs argued that the missions assigned to the institutions perpetuated past discrimination. Mississippi responded that it assigned missions on the basis of educational considerations, not race.

Program Offerings. The missions the state assigned to each institution shaped the program offerings at the campuses.[23] The HBCUs offered only 6.2 percent of the 388 graduate programs offered throughout the state system. Of the 626 different programs offered statewide at the graduate and undergraduate levels, the three HBCUs offered only 129, or approximately 20 percent. That was true although in a 1974 desegregation plan submitted to HEW, Mississippi had committed itself to giving priority to placing new programs at HBCUs. However, of the 107 new programs the state started between 1975 and 1986, it placed only twenty-three at an HBCU. Not one professional degree program in law, medicine, dentistry, or pharmacy was offered at a black institution.

Program Duplication. The *Fordice* plaintiffs argued that a substantial percentage of the programs offered at the HBCUs, at the bachelor's and master's degree levels, were unnecessarily duplicated at the white institutions and that this duplication perpetuated a dual system. As part of that duplication, the state established "branch centers" of the white institutions near HBCUs in the 1950s and 1960s, so that local whites could take college courses without enrolling at the black institutions. Those centers still existed at the time of the *Fordice* lawsuit.

Inequitable Funding. In maintaining a segregated system, the state university's board of trustees historically underfunded the HBCUs.[24] In 1960, for example, the expenditure per student at the HBCUs was approximately half what it was at the TWIs. In 1986, the expenditure per student at the HBCUs remained only about 70 percent of what it was at TWIs. Mississippi argued that the continuing disparities in funding were due to the different educational missions of the institutions, not to racial discrimination. The plaintiffs responded that channeling more money to the comprehensive universities perpetuated the funding inequities of the past under a new rationale.

Mississippi claimed that it had a racially neutral policy for admission to its public colleges and universities and had implemented programs to attract blacks to the traditionally white institutions and whites to the historically black colleges and universities. The state argued that the continued existence of schools with students and faculty of predominantly one race was not a denial of equal protection, and that courts had to evaluate whether it had achieved enough student and faculty desegregation against the backdrop of other competing and legitimate educational objectives.[25]

Public Reactions to the Fordice Litigation

While pending before the U.S. Supreme Court, the *Fordice* case received an unusual level of attention in educational and legal circles, and even from the popular press. When the Court granted a writ of certiorari, a step in the appellate process that typically receives little public attention, that decision and the case itself were the subject of a front-page article in the *New York Times*.[26] About a month later, the *Times* ran another front-page article on desegregation in higher education, characterizing the fate of publicly supported black colleges as "one of the most emotionally charged and complex issues in the South [involving] some of the most vexing contemporary questions about race."[27]

Shortly after the *New York Times* articles appeared, an editorial on the subject appeared in the *Washington Post*.[28] The *Chronicle of Higher Education,* following *Fordice* closely, ran several first-page articles on the case, and the *National Law Journal* featured an opinion article on the case before oral argument.[29] Julius Chambers, general counsel of the NAACP Legal Defense Fund, lent credibility to the widespread attention given the dispute by calling it the most important civil rights case since *Brown v. Board of Education.*[30] Chambers and others believed this because of the impact they thought the decision would have on the future of the HBCUs and on blacks' opportunities to attend college in the nineteen states with state-supported HBCU's.

The HBCUs had amassed an unparalleled record of educational achievement. They had produced more than one-half of the nation's black teachers.[31] In 1989, five HBCUs with engineering schools awarded engineering degrees to approximately 45 percent of the blacks who received engineering degrees in the United States in that year.[32] Almost three out of every ten black college graduates in all of American history have been graduates of HBCUs.[33] Moreover, the HBCUs did not merely enroll black students: they graduated them at an impressive rate. In 1991, the HBCUs, while accounting for approximately 17 percent of all blacks enrolled in higher education, accounted for more than 40 percent of the total number of graduates.[34] HBCUs had also become a critical pipeline feeding black students to the nation's graduate schools. For example, when one looks at the institutions where blacks who earned the Ph.D. degree in 1986–88 had received their undergraduate education, a striking statistic emerges. Seventeen of the top twenty institutions were HBCUs.[35] As one commentator has observed, the HBCUs have been "the principal contributors to black literacy, the principal inspiration to black social organization, and the sole promoters and guardians of Afro-American culture."[36]

The Reversal of the Justice Department's Position

As noted earlier, after Mississippi citizens brought suit against the state, the Justice Department in 1976 intervened in *Fordice* on the side of the plaintiffs. In arguments before the Fifth Circuit, the government maintained that differences between the white and black institutions in facilities, libraries, and the number of academic programs were vestiges of the system of segregation.[37] The government insisted that the difference between the funding and resources provided to Mississippi Valley State, a black "regional" institution, and those provided to Delta State, a white "regional" institution just thirty-five miles away, was "the most striking illustration of the defendant's failure to eliminate the vestiges of the dual system."[38]

Noting that Mississippi Valley had fewer academic programs, a smaller library, and less extensive extracurricular opportunities, the Justice Department argued that "if [Mississippi Valley] is to attract white students from its region it must either be given added resources or some distinctive offerings that will enable it to do so."[39] This argument, dealing with the "enhancement" of HBCUs, was critical to black educators and students, who viewed enhancement as a way of expanding the limited educational offerings at their institutions and the limited state financial support for them.

From the outset of its involvement in *Fordice,* the Justice Department had supported the plaintiffs' argument that to remedy the history of discrimination it was necessary to enhance HBCUs. In its initial brief filed before the Supreme Court, the department reversed its position on that issue. That change produced an unprecedented three-month struggle, led by NAFEO, that culminated in an extraordinary result: the Bush administration's express disavowal, in its reply brief, of the legal position advanced in its initial Supreme Court brief.

In its first brief, the Justice Department acknowledged that there "can be no question that the historically black colleges share the distinctive trait of a shameful history of inadequate funding."[40] However, in contrast to the position it had advanced before the Fifth Circuit, the government rejected the idea that in light of that history, states had a legal obligation to take measures to improve the quality of and increase the level of state support for those institutions:

> Nor do we discern an independent obligation flowing from the Constitution to correct disparities between what was provided historically black schools — in terms of funding, programs, facilities, and so forth — and what was provided historically white schools . . . [S]uch a requirement would be at odds with the overriding objective that there no longer be "a 'white' school and a 'Negro' school, but just schools" [citing *Green*]. The idea is to end duplication, not perfect it by ensuring that separate schools are in fact equal. It would be the height of irony for the resounding mandate of *Brown* that separate schools are inherently unequal . . . to be taken 37 years later, as dictating a focus on whether funding of separate historically black and historically white schools is equal. Indeed, "improved" duplication might well have the perverse effect of encouraging students to attend a school where, other things being more nearly equal, their own race predominates. That odd result is not required by the Equal Protection Clause. . . .
>
> What is not clear is why the Constitution demands that, at this late date, the state turn its energies to redressing an historical imbalance in spending on those institutions, rather than ensuring that each of its young people be free to choose among all that the State has to offer, limited only by ability and not race.[41]

The government's departure from the position that it had advanced throughout the *Fordice* litigation produced a swift and furious negative reaction from black educators and their organizations. Elias Blake, former president of Clark College and consultant to the plaintiffs both in *Adams* and in *Fordice,* wrote a lengthy, impassioned memo to the White House advisory board on HBCUs. The board, set up by President Bush, by executive order, was composed of college presidents and business leaders. Fearful that the government's position would permit states to continue to underfund HBCUs, Blake declared that the government's reversal was "an error of enormous proportions [that] must be somehow corrected."[42] Blake, a well-respected figure within NAFEO and among black southern educators, also made a powerful presentation to the advisory board in which he charged that the position of the United States was founded on the "very dangerous" idea that HBCUs were "expendable."[43]

Following Blake's presentation to the advisory board, James Cheek, former president of Howard University, chair of the advisory board, and longtime personal friend of President Bush, declared that the brief "was inconsistent with the president's executive order on historically black colleges as well as contradictory to every statement [the president] has made" about HBCUs.[44] The advisory board sent Bush a letter noting its "grave and urgent concern" that the Justice Department's position "substantially undermined" HBCUs and the president's stated desire to enhance those institutions.[45] The "best interests" of the nation and of the president, the board declared, "would be well and better served by an aggressive and persuasive submission . . . to the Supreme Court on the historic and continuing role and services of the HBCUs to this country and Mississippi."[46]

Other influential black educators also spoke out. Norman Francis, president of Xavier University, observed that the position advanced in the brief would be "disastrous" for HBCUs.[47] J. Clay Smith, former dean of the Howard University Law School and counsel for NAFEO, commented that the Justice Department's position on funding was an "ominous signal" for the future of HBCUs and one that continued to victimize those who had historically suffered discrimination.[48] In an editorial critical of the Justice Department's brief, the *Washington Post* claimed, "By emphasizing that 'It is the students — and not the colleges — who are guaranteed the equal protection of the laws' and by focusing on free choice, the department [was] implying that if the state wants to let the black institutions slide, it can do so, so long as 'choice is free.'"[49]

J. Clay Smith led a campaign on behalf of NAFEO to publicize the dangers of the government's position for HBCUs and to persuade the government to disavow its position. It was a sensitive task for Smith because his clients, the college presidents comprising NAFEO, were vulnerable politically. As heads of state institutions, all the presidents were accountable to and dependent on state legislatures for their institutions' funding each year, and on state governing boards for their own tenure in office. Understandably, some of the presidents were skittish about pressing the federal executive branch to advance a legal position that would compel states to spend more money on HBCUs. Mounting an effort to reverse the Justice Department's position on funding would inevitably be viewed by state elected officials as a politically hostile act.

Challenging the Justice Department's position on funding was also a sensitive matter for the plaintiffs' lawyers in *Fordice*. Funding was only one of many issues they had raised, and it was not as critical an issue to them as it was to the black educators in NAFEO. More important, the Justice Department, aligned with the plaintiffs against Mississippi from early in the litigation, was an influential ally for the plaintiffs to have in the Supreme Court. Indeed, Solicitor General Kenneth Starr and Alvin Chambliss, the plaintiffs' chief counsel, agreed to share the time allotted the plaintiffs at oral argument. Maintaining a working relationship with Starr was important to Chambliss. Recognizing the valuable but fragile alliance of interests that had been forged with the government, the plaintiffs' lawyers were not eager to join in NAFEO's criticism of the Justice Department's brief.

The NAACP Legal Defense Fund also was not well positioned to campaign against the Justice Department on the funding issue. Though the LDF's general counsel, Julius Chambers, believed that *Fordice* was a historic civil rights case, the LDF had an uncertain relationship with the southern black educators in NAFEO. The desegregation of southern schools at the elementary and secondary levels, led by the LDF's lawyers, had cost many black teachers and principals their jobs. NAFEO's leaders were mindful of that legacy and of the role that the LDF played in it as the leading proponent of desegregation. Indeed, some in NAFEO were resentful that the LDF, from the beginning of its efforts in the *Adams* litigation, had been insensitive to the need to consult with NAFEO. Moreover, to the degree that NAFEO wanted to retain HBCUs as "black" institutions, that goal conflicted with the goal of racial integration for which the LDF had fought so hard for generations.

Some black educators viewed the LDF as committed to desegregation at any cost, even though nearly four decades of desegregation at the elementary and secondary school levels had not produced notable advances in the academic achievement and educational opportunities of black children. For all these reasons, the relationship between NAFEO and LDF officials was an uneasy one. The LDF recognized that enhancement was a question of critical importance to NAFEO, and that LDF lawyers were not the best people to lead the fight against the administration on that issue. Indeed, the LDF's generally adversarial relationship with the administration could have hurt the cause. Consequently, the LDF limited its involvement in the campaign to convince the Bush administration to re-think its legal position on enhanced funding for HBCUs.

The government had filed its initial brief in *Fordice* with the Supreme Court in June 1991. NAFEO's campaign to convince the government to recant its position reached the president personally in early September. As part of a White House conference, President Bush met for a question-and-answer session with fifteen educational writers. Answering questions about HBCUs and the *Fordice* case, Bush remarked that he would not support anything "that would detract from what I think is a very specific and important role for these historically black colleges, and our administration will not be taking new steps to make things more difficult there."[50]

The president's remarks provided an opening for the black educators to act, because, from their perspective, the position that the Justice Department had advanced on funding did make things more difficult for HBCUs. Consequently, the president's advisory board on HBCUs requested a meeting with Bush to discuss their concerns about the Justice Department's position. At that meeting, James Cheek, speaking for the advisory board, told the president that by providing a legal justification for states to continue to limit their support of HBCUs the Justice Department's brief had created a "crisis" for the black colleges. Black educators stressed that the brief was inconsistent with the president's longtime personal commitment to HBCUs and with his administration's policy of enhancement as laid out in an executive order he had issued in support of the black institutions.

Explaining that he was unaware that the Justice Department had filed a brief that might harm the black colleges, Bush expressed sympathy for the concerns of the advisory board and a willingness to help.[51] The meeting between the advisory board and Bush, scheduled as a five-to-ten-minute photo opportunity, turned into nearly a half-hour discussion of the black educators' fears about the government's brief. After the meeting, Robert Goodwin, executive director of the White House initiative on HBCUs, was very conciliatory, just as the president himself had been. Goodwin stated, "There may be a real communication problem on this issue. . . . The president indicated that he does not want to willfully do anything to threaten the viability of HBCUs. He did not realize the situation had that potential."[52]

The White House meeting with Bush was a critical strategic victory for the black educators. It gave them an opportunity to tell the president directly what they believed to be at stake in the Justice Department's brief. Given the visibility of the *Fordice* case and the unusual reversal of policy that the educators sought from the government, a decision authorizing a reversal had to come from either the attorney general or the president himself. The opportunity to spell out their concerns in face-to-face meetings with the president, and later with his White House counsel, provided direct access to the people who had to be persuaded. Moreover, the president's willingness to spend time discussing the matters in detail with representatives of HBCUs, and his willingness to set up a subsequent meeting with the White House counsel, were encouraging signs.

Despite those positive signs, Solicitor General Starr resisted making any changes in the government's brief to meet the criticisms that had been expressed, until a few days before the deadline for submitting the government's reply brief. In the days before the deadline, NAFEO officials met twice with Starr and White House lawyers,[53] the last meeting occurring the day before the deadline. In discussions with administration officials, those pushing for a change continued to emphasize that the government's brief was, as James Cheek put it, "totally at odds with" the Bush administration's stated policy of enhancing the HBCUs through greater federal support.[54] Ultimately, President Bush himself intervened and ordered the Justice Department to disavow the legal position on the funding of HBCUs advanced in its initial Supreme Court brief.[55]

In what the *New York Times* called a "remarkable footnote," the Justice Department retracted and repudiated its previous position.[56] The disavowal was quite remarkable. The government stated in the body of its reply brief:

> [I]t is incumbent on the State of Mississippi to eradicate discrimination from its system of higher education. Over the years, that discrimination manifested itself in a deprivation of equitable and fair funding to historically black institutions, which sought faithfully, and under difficult circumstances, to serve the interests of black students in Mississippi. Those students were deprived of the unfettered choice demanded by the Equal Protection Clause. Indeed, those historic disparities operated to deprive prospective students of all races of the full

range of choices that would have been theirs to enjoy but for the state's discriminatory practices. The time has now come to eliminate those disparities and thereby unfetter the choices of persons who can here-after choose freely among the State's institutions of higher learning.[57]

At the end of this paragraph in the Justice Department's brief, the de-partment placed an asterisk referring to a most unusual notation at the bottom of the page: "[S]uggestions to the contrary in our opening brief . . . no longer reflect the position of the United States."[58] NAFEO had won.

In a campaign that took about one hundred days, NAFEO had turned the United States government around. J. Clay Smith, the architect of the strategy, and the driving force behind it, called the change in the government's position "monumental, as the DOJ [De-partment of Justice] has . . . almost never withdrawn or changed po-sition on such a critical issue in a brief filed before the U.S. Supreme Court."[59] James Cheek, whose personal relationship with the presi-dent had played a pivotal role, observed that he and the presidents of HBCUs "argue[d] pretty hard, and long, and passionately for the change."[60] Being the astute politician that he is, Cheek made sure that the president got the political credit for the change, declaring of Bush, "He's to be commended for understanding what the problem was and what was at stake."[61] Oscar Bronson, president of Bethune Cookman College and chair of NAFEO, explained what his organi-zation believed to be at stake: "Had this position gone before the Supreme Court without clarification, it could very well have spelled the epitaph for the historically black college community. . . . Our great fear was that the states would use . . . it to dismantle black colleges."[62]

Awaiting the Fordice Decision: Doubts and High Expectations

The campaign to reverse the Justice Department's position on funding marked the HBCUs' most effective and visible effort to that date in the controversy over desegregation in higher education. Not surprisingly, that success took the form of a victory by lawyers press-ing for a legal position on what was fundamentally a political issue — the level of state support for historically black colleges and universi-ties. Litigating about enhancement offered the possibility of bypass-ing state politics and of forcing states, by dint of legal obligations in the Constitution or Title VI, to invest more in HBCUs. This ap-proach represented a classic use of litigation to achieve, through the judicial process, what could not be won through the political process.

It was NAFEO counsel J. Clay Smith and the group of law students and lawyers that he mobilized who played the crucial role in causing the Justice Department to reverse its position. With the exception of the amicus brief that NAFEO had filed in the District of Columbia Circuit in the appeal of Judge Pratt's first *Adams* order in 1973, the lawyers for NAFEO had remained relatively uninvolved in the legal actions in *Adams*. By submitting an amicus brief in *Fordice,* maintaining steady and open communications with Alvin Chambliss, the lawyer representing the plaintiffs in *Fordice,* and then leading the campaign against the Justice Department's brief, NAFEO carved out a central place for itself in advance of the most important legal decision ever on desegregation in higher education.

Two weeks before the oral argument of the case in the Supreme Court, Franklyn G. Jenifer, president of Howard University, published a widely circulated opinion essay entitled "The Supreme Court Must Act to Preserve and Strengthen Historically Black Colleges" in the *Chronicle of Higher Education*. Jenifer feared that *Fordice* could lead to the "demise" of HBCUs "throughout the nation":

> The danger is real. It is real if the Supreme Court — capriciously, simplistically, mechanically, or otherwise — decides that providing additional funds for predominantly black colleges and universities would mean endorsing "separate but equal" higher education as a remedy for past discrimination. On that basis, the Court could then rule that since providing separate but equal education is unconstitutional, not only is there no need for extra financial support, but more fundamentally, there is no need for "racially identifiable" (read: "predominantly or historically black") higher-education institutions.[63]

Jenifer argued for maintaining "predominantly" black institutions that did not exclude anyone on the basis of race but that retained their historic focus on the needs of black students. Emphasizing the educational benefits that resulted from that orientation, he noted that though HBCUs enrolled only 20 percent of all black students nationally, they produced 40 percent of all black college graduates. HBCUs were an invaluable educational resource for the nation, Jenifer concluded: "To threaten their identity, their mission, their very existence in the noble name of 'integration' would be a grave disservice."[64]

The stakes in *Fordice* were considerable. If the black colleges prevailed, they could emerge with a decision imposing legal obligations on states to provide them with greater funding and better educational programs. That would help them in their political struggle to obtain resources from often hostile state legislatures. A defeat would enable states that had never been very supportive to scale back aid further or even close some HBCUs altogether. Arthur Thomas, president of Central State University, an HBCU, declared, "States all over America are systematically and openly questioning whether historically black colleges and universities should continue."[65] Douglas Anderson, one of two blacks in the Mississippi State Senate, said, "What you've got going on now is the historically black colleges fighting for their lives."[66] Reinforcing that view, Silas Lee, a sociology professor at Xavier University, declared, "People are fearful that what you're talking about is the elimination of black institutions. It's a subject that is almost like a time bomb."[67]

While *Fordice* was pending before the Supreme Court, OCR was reviewing the adequacy of the higher-education desegregation plans submitted by Kentucky, Maryland, Texas, and Pennsylvania. OCR decided to withhold its decision until the Court's ruling in *Fordice*. In addition, both Louisiana and Alabama were involved in federal litigation that would be controlled by what the Court did in *Fordice*. Legal challenges to state plans that OCR had already accepted might also be possible if the Court rejected Mississippi's efforts and imposed demanding standards for states. The potential educational impact of the case grew as enrollment in publicly supported HBCUs increased by one-third, from about 120,000 in 1987 to 160,000 in 1991.[68]

Fordice reaffirmed how centrally important litigation and ideas about legal rights were in school desegregation policy. Enforcement of Title VI in desegregation in higher education began in a significant way only after lawyers used the *Adams* litigation to compel HEW to initiate enforcement actions. By 1992, there had been more than two decades of litigation in lower federal courts dealing with desegregation in higher education under both Title VI and the Constitution. In *Fordice*, the issue of desegregation in higher education had finally reached the legal pinnacle. The case promised to have a profound influence because, for the first time, the nation's highest court was poised to define the legal rights at issue in desegregation in higher education, under both Title VI and the Constitution.

In November 1991, on the Sunday before the case was heard by the Court, Clay Smith organized a "dry run" moot court intended to prepare Alvin Chambliss for the oral argument before the Supreme Court. Present at that session at Howard University Law School were the counsel for the plaintiffs in the case, black educators, representatives of the LDF, and other lawyers, academics, and students interested in the case. After nearly four hours of questions and answers, and discussion of the legal positions that should be advanced at oral argument, Elias Blake, a nonlawyer, spoke out in frustration.[69]

Why was it, he asked, that in cases such as *Fordice,* when lawyers framed the questions and discussed the arguments that needed to be advanced, they tended to lose sight of the educational issues involved? He reminded the roomful of lawyers that the real sin of segregation and of discrimination against blacks in education was not so much separation by race, but rather the underlying objective of that separation. Mississippi's system of segregation, like that of so many other states, Blake emphasized, was intended to deny blacks access to education and thereby keep them subordinate to whites. That objective was most dramatically manifested in laws that made it a crime to teach a slave to read or write. Mississippi continued to advance that same objective in the 1980s in the way it ran its state university system. Blake lamented that in the legal arguments about such things as "free choice" and eradicating the "vestiges of segregation," the impact of the state's policies on the education of blacks, and the need to find remedies that actually improved blacks' education, often got lost. Blake's point — central to the theme at the heart of this book — haunts me.

Why is it that litigation and an approach emphasizing legal rights so often produce disappointing — or worse, counterproductive — results? Why is it that the very analytical concepts and legal principles that lawyers use to address social problems often miss or fail to consider the underlying factors that produce the problems and that need to be considered to alleviate them?

Blake's observations stressed a basic, but little explored, question about the consequences of using litigation to define and resolve important social issues. We do not understand, or for that matter much appreciate, how the efforts to deal with social problems through the specialized format of litigation influence our thinking about those problems, our construction of critical questions, and our conceptions of appropriate remedial measures. Litigation is a unique process, and like any other process used to consider and resolve problems it has its own internal rules and demands that influence how it defines problems and what it can do about them. These issues are critical in thinking about American racial problems generally, and the enforcement of Title VI specifically, because we have dealt with those problems so extensively — indeed, almost reflexively — through litigation.

As I think back on that long moot court session at the Howard University Law School and on Elias Blake's comments, I am reminded of the extended discussion that day focusing on how Alvin Chambliss should deal with questions at oral argument addressing the issue of the "free choice" of students. On the one hand, the concern about free choice was understandable. As has been noted, the concept of free choice had played an important role in the legal doctrine dealing with school desegregation. Therefore, as a legal consideration, it was relevant.

Civil rights lawyers legitimately feared that though the Court had previously ruled that states had a duty to do more than provide free choice for students in desegregating schools at the elementary and secondary school levels, it might draw a different conclusion when addressing desegregation in higher education. Given that higher education was not compulsory, that admissions standards existed, that different institutions had different strengths and orientations, and that the state did not assign students to schools but instead permitted them to choose the schools to which they applied, there was a basis to worry that the Court might rule that merely giving black students "free choice" to apply to any school in the state system fulfilled the state's legal duty.

On the other hand, focusing the legal debate on free choice was a narrow way of understanding the educational questions raised by *Fordice* and the educational inequalities blacks experienced in Mississippi. Though blacks had the "free choice" to apply to any school in the state, that hardly produced the "equal educational opportunity" that *Brown v. Board* mandated. Indeed, at the heart of the claim that black citizens could bring against Mississippi's state university system was the complaint that, by almost any indicator that compared white and black citizens in the state, there was unequal opportunity to gain access to and enjoy the benefits of the state's university system. For example, a much smaller percentage of black as opposed to white high-school graduates had the opportunity to attend the state university; a smaller percentage of the blacks who were admitted actually graduated; and a smaller percentage of the blacks who graduated went on to the state's professional and graduate schools.

The idea of "free choice" did not help one understand the real dispute in *Fordice*. Rather, "free choice" was little more than an artificial construct that lawyers and judges imposed on the situation to help them frame the issues as a legal question. Racial differences in enjoying the benefits and opportunities offered by Mississippi's state university system derived from problems that went well beyond the issue of a student's so-called free choice.

What was crucial to understand about *Fordice* from an educational standpoint was that because a disproportionate percentage of black students in Mississippi came from impoverished homes and received inadequate preparation at the elementary and secondary school levels, or were not enrolled in a college preparatory track in high school, those students could not realistically be said to have an "equal opportunity" or "free choice" to gain admission to the state university. Indeed, the vast majority never even tried to gain admission. Only 42 percent of black high-school graduates took the qualifying test required of those seeking admission, and of that percentage, only three in ten qualified for automatic admittance on the basis of their scores. By contrast, 80 percent of white high-school graduates took the test, and of that percentage, seven of ten gained admission on that basis. The public black colleges had historically drawn their basic constituency from the ranks of the "unqualified" black students and, with considerable success, had geared their educational missions to those students' needs.

This analysis suggests that the question of a high-school graduate's supposed "free choice" to decide whether and where to attend the state university could not be divorced from questions about differences in the quality and availability of precollegiate preparation for whites and blacks in Mississippi public schools. Indeed, some black educators maintained that the overwhelming majority of white and black children in the state were, in effect, in two different public educational tracks in terms of the level of preparation and opportunity offered them at the precollegiate level. That two-track system, they claimed, perpetuated the subordination of blacks at the end of the twentieth century much as de jure racial segregation had subordinated their ancestors at the end of the previous century. Among other things, the contemporary system precluded the majority of black high-school students from even considering attending the state university. Hence, *Fordice* raised a tangle of complicated and controversial issues about educational equity, addressing whether Mississippi's entire public educational system served the black population of the state fairly. Yet, in the legal discourse — in the briefs, at oral argument, and ultimately in the Supreme Court's opinion — those basic educational and social justice issues were invisible.

Derrick Bell has argued that litigation often disappoints civil rights advocates because the lawyers representing their cause lose sight of their clients' needs and desires.[70] While this no doubt occurs, that failing was not a factor in *Fordice*. Rather, to understand what transformed the educational issues in that case one must understand that the legal system compelled the lawyers to analyze the issues and argue their client's cause in terms of the concepts and principles the law had already developed in related cases. For the law not only has its own language, it has its own analytical constructs for understanding problems. In *Fordice,* the concepts of students' "free choice" and of school "desegregation" were the principal legal constructs that dominated the analysis of the lawyers and judges alike. For litigators to win their case, they had to employ and apply those constructs. They had no choice. They had to use the tools of legal analysis that the law provides and that judges recognize as legitimate. This dilemma, illustrated in *Fordice,* exemplifies how translating a social or educational policy issue into a "legal" question can transform the debate about that issue, abstract it from its social context, and limit the remedies considered.

As lawyers, scholars, and educators awaited the Court's decision in *Fordice,* it was evident that litigation seemed destined, yet again, to play a central role in how the vexatious problem of race and education was dealt with in America. The stakes in *Fordice* were high, in part, because it had become apparent by 1992 that the administrative enforcement of Title VI had not produced the transformation of southern public higher education that some had envisioned. A decade and a half after HEW had established its Title VI desegregation criteria, and two decades after Judge Pratt's first order affecting higher education, access by blacks to state university systems that operated HBCUs was no greater.

The most ambitious hopes of those who planned the *Adams* litigation in 1972, and of those who developed the HEW criteria in 1977, were that those initiatives would not only desegregate state university systems but also make public higher education more accessible to blacks. Table 2 summarizes the available data for 1972–92, detailing the percentage of black students in the total student populations of four-year public institutions of higher education in states with HBCUs. The overwhelming pattern across the nineteen states is that the percentage of black enrollment in state systems of higher education did not increase during the course of the *Adams* litigation. Rather, black enrollment remained remarkably constant during the twenty-year period following Judge Pratt's first order in *Adams.*

PERHAPS THE poor results in *Adams* heightened the hopes of some civil rights proponents that a decision from the Supreme Court in *Fordice* might accomplish what *Adams* and the HEW criteria had not. Not only had Julius Chambers of the Legal Defense Fund declared *Fordice* to be a landmark civil rights case, but there was also national publicity about the case during the summer of 1991 because of President Bush's

TABLE 2.

Black Students as a Percentage of Total Student Population in Four-Year
Public Institutions of Higher Education in States with HBCUs

State[a]	1972	1976	1980	1982	1984	1986	1992
Alabama	21	24	24	24	21	21	19
Arkansas*	14	15	16	15	15	13	13
Delaware	11	11	11	11	10	11	11
Florida*	10	11	11	10	9	9	8
Georgia*	16	20	20	20	19	17	17
Kentucky	6	7	7	7	7	6	6
Louisiana*	24	24	23	21	22	23	23
Maryland*	11	17	18	18	16	15	15
Mississippi*	25	32	32	32	28	28	26
Missouri	6	7	8	7	8	7	7
North Carolina*	18	20	21	20	18	18	17
Ohio	8	8	9	9	8	7	7
Oklahoma*	5	6	6	6	6	6	6
Pennsylvania*	5	6	7	6	6	6	6
South Carolina	16	23	24	22	20	19	20
Tennessee	13	15	17	16	14	14	13
Texas	8	9	9	9	9	8	9
Virginia*	14	15	16	16	14	13	13
West Virginia	4	5	5	4	4	4	3
Average Percentages							
All 19 states	12	14	15	14	13	13	13
10 *Adams* States	14	15	15	15	15	15	14

Sources: statistics for 1972–1986: American Council on Education, *Fact Book on Higher
Education* (New York: Macmillan, 1990); statistics for 1992: Editors of the Chronicle of
Higher Education, *The Almanac of Higher Education, 1992* (Chicago: University of Chicago
Press, 1992).

Note: Percentages include black student enrollment in *both* black and white four-year public institutions.

a. The original *Adams* states are indicated by asterisks.

unprecedented personal involvement in the case. The plaintiffs' counsel did little to dampen the high expectations regarding the significance of the case. Several days before the Court announced its decision, Alvin Chambliss, awaiting the result in Oxford, Mississippi,
stated that the decision would have "a profound effect across the nation" that would "either make or break black colleges."[71] On the next-

258 ON THE LIMITS OF THE LAW

to-last day of the Court's term in June 1992, the Court handed down its opinion.

The Court's Decision in Fordice

By a surprising eight-to-one margin, the Court ruled that Mississippi had not met its affirmative obligation to dismantle its prior system of segregated higher education. The Court held that merely adopting nondiscriminatory admissions policies was not enough to demonstrate that the state had completely abandoned its prior system:

> If the state perpetuates policies and practices traceable to its prior system that continue to have segregative effects — whether by influencing student enrollment decisions or by fostering segregation in other facets of the university system — and such policies are without sound educational justification and can practicably be eliminated, the State has not satisfied its burden of proving that it has dismantled its prior system. Such policies run afoul of the Equal Protection Clause, even though the state has abolished the legal requirement that whites and blacks be educated separately and has established racially neutral policies not animated by discriminatory purpose.[72]

In applying the above standard to Mississippi's system of higher education, the Court concluded that there were "several surviving aspects of Mississippi's prior dual system which are constitutionally suspect,"[73] and which, on remand, required review. Those aspects were admission standards; program duplication; institutional mission assignments; and the viability of continuing to operate all eight public colleges in the state. These four features of the state system, however, were not an exhaustive "list of the unconstitutional remnants of Mississippi's prior *de jure* system."[74] The Court ruled that in addition to the four policies identified above, "each of the other policies now governing the State's university system that [might be] challenged on remand" must be reviewed to determine whether it met the legal standard advanced by the Court.[75]

There were enthusiastic reactions to the Court's decision from an odd combination of quarters — the Bush administration, civil rights lawyers, the liberal establishment, and leaders in the movement to protect historically black colleges. Kenneth Starr, Bush's solicitor general, praised the decision as "a magnificent victory."[76] There were uniformly favorable comments from such prominent civil rights lawyers as Norman Chachkin of the NAACP Legal Defense Fund, David Tatel, former director of OCR in the Carter administration, and J.

Clay Smith of the Howard University Law School. Tatel believed that *Fordice* was "quite a strong statement reaffirming the principles of *Brown*" and "a very, very good development for improving higher education opportunities for blacks in the South."[77] Elated by the decision, J. Clay Smith commented that it could have been written by the Warren Court, and that it showed that the "spirit of Thurgood Marshall lives on in this Court."[78] William H. Gray, who had recently retired from a powerful seat in Congress to head the United Negro College Fund, hailed *Fordice* as "a victory for America's black colleges, and for America."[79] Carl Rowan and William Raspberry, two African American syndicated journalists, wrote articles extolling the decision,[80] and the Eastern liberal establishment offered its blessing with laudatory editorials in the *New York Times* and the *Washington Post*.[81] Victorious after seventeen years of litigation, Alvin Chambliss, echoing the earlier assessment of Julius Chambers of the LDF, called *Fordice* "the most important [decision] since *Brown v. Board of Education*."[82]

Though I have enormous regard for the prodigious effort that Chambliss made, I am wary about *Fordice* and what it will yield. Supreme Court decisions acclaimed as civil rights landmarks rarely deliver what they promise. If read carefully, the *Fordice* opinion did not even promise much. What is most troubling about the decision is what it did not say. It did not hold that a state may operate HBCUs that, by their traditions, orientation, and culture, are geared to the needs of black students. Indeed, the opinion contains language that could be construed as undermining the very existence of HBCUs. As some nineteen states with public HBCUs proceeded to "desegregate," in the wake of *Fordice,* the Court left disturbingly unresolved the guidelines and principles that should be used to determine whether those states were complying with the Constitution and Title VI. The opinion did not specify, in any way that would provide meaningful guidance to lower courts, OCR, or the states, the remedial measures that states had to initiate or the standards against which to measure the adequacy of proposed remedies. Moreover, since there had been no major Supreme Court decisions on desegregation in higher education in the years after *Brown v. Board,* there were no other cases upon which to rely for answers to those questions.

The Court framed its review of Mississippi's educational policies in *Fordice* almost exclusively in terms of two considerations that are potentially dangerous to HBCUs: first, whether state university policies restrict a student's freedom of choice, and second, whether they have segregative effects. In each of the four educational policies it analyzed—admission standards, mission designations, duplicative programs, and funding for all eight public colleges and universities in Mississippi—the Court focused on the need to maximize free choice and minimize racial segregation.

Admissions Policies. In reviewing the history of the state's admissions policies, the Court emphasized the "discriminatory taint" of Mississippi's 1963 decision that to be admitted to the three white comprehensive institutions students required a minimum score of fifteen on the ACT. It noted that the average ACT score for white students that year was eighteen and the average for black students was seven,[83] and that in addition, there was no minimum score established for admission to the three black institutions. The state had developed the 1963 policies while it was experiencing the initial pressures to end segregation in the state university. In 1976, to deal with the problem of students who had been admitted to some institutions in spite of extremely low ACT scores, the board of trustees of the state university system decided that no student would be admitted to any institution unless he or she had scored at least a nine on the ACT.[84] Institutions already requiring higher admission standards (i.e., the three comprehensive, traditionally white institutions) retained those higher standards. Referring to the 1976 reform, the Supreme Court ruled that this "midpassage justification for perpetuating a policy enacted originally to discriminate against black students does not make the present admissions standards any less constitutionally suspect."[85]

At the time of trial in *Fordice,* Mississippi still admitted students to the traditionally white institutions solely on the basis of ACT scores. Any applicant who scored a fifteen automatically qualified to be admitted to any of the five traditionally white institutions, except for Mississippi University for Women, which required an eighteen for automatic admission, unless the student had a 3.0 high-school average. Students scoring thirteen or fourteen qualified for admission to the three historically black institutions, but with limited exceptions they were precluded from attending any of the five traditionally white institutions. The Court ruled that those standards had a "segregative effect" (2739).* Indeed, in 1985, 72 percent of Mississippi's white high-school seniors scored fifteen or above, whereas less than 30 percent of black high-school seniors attained that score.

In light of this history, the Court found that Mississippi's admis-

---

*In this discussion of *Fordice,* page numbers in the *Fordice* decision are given parenthetically in the text.

sions policies were "constitutionally suspect" because they were "trace-able to the *de jure* system," had originally been adopted for a discrimi-natory purpose, and had continuing "discriminatory effects" (2738, 2739). It is important to appreciate how the Court determined whether there were any present-day discriminatory effects of the state's de jure system because, absent continuing discriminatory effects, the state's practices would not have been constitutionally suspect. The Court measured the present-day discriminatory effects of past admis-sions practices in terms of their impact on student choice and racial segregation on campuses. The admissions policies "restrict[ed] the range of choices of entering students . . . in a way that perpetuates segregation"; and that "segregative effect," the Court ruled, was re-flected in campuses that "remain predominantly identifiable by race" (2739).

Program Duplication. Whereas the Court's decision on duplica-tive programs turned on technical evidentiary issues, the Court ac-cepted the legal standard used by the district court, focusing on whether duplicative programs contributed to the racial identifiabil-ity of institutions and whether eliminating duplication would "de-crease institutional racial identifiability" and "affect student choice" (2741).

Mission Designations and the Maintenance of All Eight Campuses. In examining whether the "mission designations" were constitutionally suspect, the Court proceeded as it had in reviewing admission poli-cies. It noted that the designations had "their antecedents [in] the poli-cies enacted to perpetuate racial separation during the *de jure*" era and that the state's existing policy continued to have "discriminatory effects" (2742). How did the Court measure continuing discrimina-tory effects? It returned to the two measures that it employed through-out the opinion. It found that it was "likely that [the mission designa-tions] interfere with student choice and . . . perpetuate a segregated system" (2742). The Court adopted precisely the same mode of anal-ysis in discussing whether Mississippi should continue funding all eight campuses. It ruled that the existence of eight institutions was traceable to the era of de jure segregation and that to determine whether it was permissible for the state to continue that policy, one needed to determine the policy's current impact on students' freedom of choice and on racial segregation on campuses. Accordingly, the Court directed that "on remand this issue should be carefully explored by . . . determining whether retention of all eight institutions affects student choice and perpetuates the segregated higher education system" (2743).

Problems in Applying the Fordice Decision

It is unclear how the Court's concerns about segregative effects and student choice will affect HBCUs and the future configuration of state systems, because those two considerations can be applied in different ways with different results. For example, it is unclear what policies are likely to produce segregative effects. Enhancing HBCUs may arguably increase segregation by providing an attractive educational option to African American students who, in the absence of enhanced black institutions, might decide to attend white schools. Enhanced HBCUs offering black students both academic excellence and a more "comfortable" environment may keep good black students in black institutions, thereby contributing to segregation. By contrast, however, one could just as plausibly contend that enhancing black institutions by locating attractive academic and professional programs on those campuses makes HBCUs more attractive to whites who have traditionally shunned them, thereby decreasing segregation.

Nor is the requirement of providing students with a "free choice" without its conceptual and practical problems. Defining "free choice" in the context of higher education, and then devising the educational policies that will maximize choice, will be even more troubling than determining policies that minimize racial segregation. Free choice is a slippery concept, and the Court dealt with it sloppily. Justice White, writing for the majority, refers to the idea in six places in the opinion, summarized below:

- Certain policies and practices traceable to the prior system may have a segregative effect "by influencing student enrollment decisions" (2737).
- Even racially neutral policies may "substantially restrict a person's choice of which institution to enter" (2738).
- Mission designations "interfere with student choice and tend to perpetuate the segregated system" (2742).
- A larger rather than a smaller number of institutions from which to choose "makes for different choices" (2742).
- On remand, the district court should inquire "whether retention of all eight institutions itself affects student choice" (2743).
- Because the prior system of segregation under law "impeded the free choice of prospective students, the State in dismantling that

system must take the necessary steps to insure that this choice is now truly free" and "must examine the full range of policies and practices . . . with this duty in mind" (2743).

It is hard to know what to make of such a litany of references to free choice, save that, as part of desegregation in higher education, the Court thinks that it is important to protect student choice. Beyond that, little is clear. Indeed, as the above references document, the Court expressed its concern about the impact that state policies may have on student choice in various ways at different points in the opinion. In the first and fifth references, the Court expressed concern about policies that might "influence" or "affect" a student's choice. In the third and sixth references, it seemed to take a dim view of state policies that might "interfere with" or "impede" free choice. Finally, in the second reference, it implied that it disapproved of policies that "*substantially* restrict" a student's choice (emphasis added). The imprecise language left unclear the standard the Court would apply. Did it intend to prohibit vestiges of the old system that affected or influenced free choice, or did it prohibit only those vestiges that "substantially restrict[ed]" choice?

What is more distressing is that whereas the Court repeated its concern about free choice throughout the opinion, it never defined what that concept meant and how lower courts might apply it. Nor can the meaning of free choice be determined from the Court's prior school desegregation decisions at the elementary and secondary school levels, for the Court itself acknowledged that student choice in higher education has no parallel to choice at the lower grades, where students are typically "assigned" to schools (2736).

How will the Court's concerns about freedom of choice be applied to and affect HBCUs? The relationship between free choice and continuing state support for black institutions depends on the perspective one brings to the question. "Whose 'free choice' are we talking about?" one might ask. From the standpoint of black students, strong black institutions increase choice because they offer those students educational programs and an academic environment geared to their needs. Similarly, one could argue that strong HBCUs offer white students a chance to experience a different environment and, in that sense, widen the range of choice for them as well. More likely, however, state officials and white students are apt to conclude that the existence of "black" institutions restricts the choices of the many whites who are not likely to think that the option of attending a "black" institution increases their range of choices. If three of eight institutions are predominantly black, most whites will probably not consider attending those institutions, and therefore, from their vantage point, the existence of black institutions circumscribes choice. Historically, this has certainly been the perception and experience.

The Court's argument on free choice could be construed to justify closing or eliminating all HBCUs. As noted, the Court maintained that where practices traceable to the previous de jure segregated system continue to impede free choice, the "State, in dismantling that system, must take the necessary steps to insure that this choice now is truly free" and must consider the "full range of policies and practices . . . with this duty in mind" (2743). HBCUs are traceable to de jure segregation and doubtless continue to affect choice by whites and blacks alike. Eliminating HBCUs and leaving only the traditionally white institutions would arguably compel both whites and blacks to make choices that would be freer of racial considerations. Moreover, integrating HBCUs to the point where they are not in any way racially identifiable would also, arguably, increase choice by eliminating the racial identity of the institution as a factor in student decisions. Though the Court may not have intended for states to eliminate HBCUs to protect free choice, by failing to analyze the concept of free choice it left states, lower courts, and OCR the option of advancing such remedies and supporting them by referring to the Court's own language.

The Court also imperiled HBCUs by observing that continuing to operate all eight institutions in Mississippi was "wasteful and irrational" and that "certainly closure of one or more institutions would decrease the discriminatory effects of the present system" (2741–43). In light of those concerns, the Court ruled that, on remand, the closure issue "should be carefully explored by inquiring and determining whether retention of all eight institutions itself affects student choice and perpetuates the segregated higher education system, whether maintenance of each of the universities is educationally justifiable, and whether one or more of them can be practicably closed or merged with other existing institutions" (2741–43). In responding to those considerations, Justice Scalia observed that preserving eight institutions is "perhaps Mississippi's single policy most segregative in effect" (2752).

More fundamentally, the Court's twin objectives of maximizing free choice and minimizing segregative effects are not necessarily reconcilable. Free choice may itself have a segregative effect. For example, though strong HBCUs enhance the range of choice for black students by offering them an attractive option, that greater freedom of choice may perpetuate racially identifiable institutions, thereby increasing racial segregation. In short, the freedom to choose may very well produce choices that funnel blacks to schools with other blacks and whites to schools with whites. Indeed, in a trenchant comment, Justice Scalia observed, "There is nothing unconstitutional about a 'black' school in the sense, not of a school that blacks must attend and that whites cannot, but of a school that, as a consequence of private choice in residence or in school selection, contains, and has long contained, a large black majority" (2752).

What is so bedeviling and worrisome about *Fordice* is that, notwithstanding these and other fertile sources of possible confusion and uncertainty, the Court offered lower courts, states, and OCR virtually no guidance for applying its ruling and resolving these dilemmas. Norman Chachkin of the NAACP Legal Defense Fund said that, in *Fordice,* the Court "clearly and unequivocally rejects the state's argument that they did enough when they just took the signs down that said 'whites' and 'blacks'."[86] He was right—that was clearly what the Court decided. What is not so clear, however, is what else the opinion holds. The only other thing that the Court did "clearly and unequivocally" was to leave enormous discretion in the hands of the lower courts in applying the ruling.

Inevitably, *Fordice* will be applied in different and even inconsistent ways in different states, and all without even a word of guidance or caution from the Court regarding the special value and role of HBCUs. The Court's failure to provide such guidance and caution is disconcerting. The justices had to recognize that it was because *Fordice* involved the fate of HBCUs that it received the attention it did. Yet, the Court did not directly address the issue. Its failure to argue for strengthening HBCUs—or, for that matter, even for protecting or continuing them—is especially troubling since it contrasted with the consistent line of policies developed by HEW in its 1977 desegregation criteria, by the federal courts in the *Adams* litigation, by Congress, and by successive presidents of both parties supporting the preservation and enhancement of those institutions.

THE CONTEXT OF *FORDICE:* PRIOR PRESIDENTIAL AND CONGRESSIONAL POLICIES TO ENHANCE HBCUS

Presidential Actions and Initiatives

The Nixon Administration

In July 1969, the presidents of twenty black colleges, participating in a conference sponsored by the Office of Education, drew up a resolution expressing their dismay at the federal government's failure to do anything about the inadequate support for their institutions or the limited participation of their institutions in federal programs. These problems moved the presidents to unite into the national organization that ultimately became NAFEO. The first act of the new organization was to petition the president of the United States about the plight of the HBCUs.[87]

HEW secretary Finch acknowledged that the federal government had not always been responsive to the needs of the HBCUs and noted that efforts to remedy that situation were under way. In October 1969, the White House convened a meeting of top federal education officials to discuss how their agencies' support for black colleges could be improved.[88] The first federal report on this subject, issued by the Nixon administration, concluded:

> The neglect of these institutions has persisted too long. The administration must redouble its efforts to ensure that equal educational opportunity at the college level becomes a reality for the minority youth of this country. . . . [B]lack colleges, which enroll half of all [black] baccalaureate candidates, must be assisted if they are to provide a rising level of quality education.[89]

In President Nixon's February 1971 message to Congress on expanding opportunities in higher education, there was a section labeled "Special Help to Black Institutions." It stated, "Colleges and universities founded for black Americans are an indispensable national resource."[90]

The president proposed (1) making reforms in student aid programs that would "significantly aid students at black institutions"; (2) directing special efforts to assist black colleges through the National Foundation for Higher Education; and (3) providing additional funds for black colleges in programs administered by the U.S. Office of Education, the National Science Foundation, and the Department of Agriculture.[91] Nixon backed up his words with action. Between 1969 and 1973, federal educational outlays to the HBCUs increased nearly 150 percent, to more than $250 million.[92] More ambitious initiatives followed in succeeding administrations.

The Carter Administration

In December 1976, shortly before leaving office, President Ford created the National Advisory Committee on Black Higher Education and Black Colleges and Universities. The committee, whose membership was to include at least five presidents of HBCUs, was to "examine all approaches to the higher education of black Americans as well as the needs of historically black colleges and universities."[93] Speaking about the role of HBCUs, President Carter commented:

> One of the obvious purposes is to give a superb education to those students in our Nation who otherwise could not afford it. Another one is to preserve the uniqueness of a curriculum and student body commitment that mirror . . . the dreams and aspirations of families of those students who, because of racial prejudice and discrimination, did not have a chance for a good education. . . . [I]n many ways these modern day students of minority groups represent not only themselves but they represent their families and their other ancestors who have been so severely deprived.[94]

Carter was no less cognizant of the need to preserve and assist HBCUs than were his Republican predecessors. The president's statement recognized the singular and indispensable role that HBCUs play in remedying the effects of past discrimination against black Americans.

To meet the obligation of which he spoke, President Carter in January 1979 sent the heads of the executive departments and agencies a memorandum noting that HBCUs "continue to play a unique and important role in providing educational opportunities" and emphasizing that his administration had issued the HEW criteria "to strengthen the historically black public institutions through increased financial support, new and expanded programs, and the elimination of educationally unnecessary program duplication between them and their traditionally white counterparts."[95]

The president's memorandum required his agency heads to (1) review their departments' operations to ensure that the HBCUs had a "fair opportunity" to participate in federal programs; (2) identify areas in which the HBCUs could participate more fully in departmental activities; (3) establish goals and timetables, where appropriate, to increase participation by HBCUs in federal programs; (4) establish methods to consult with the HBCUs regarding their role in the department; and (5) appoint a high-level liaison to oversee these matters. The next year, Carter followed up with a more expansive initiative. In August 1980, he issued Executive Order 12232, the first of three executive orders issued by consecutive presidents that mandated specific, affirmative initiatives by the federal government to enhance the education provided to students at HBCUs.[96]

Carter's executive order required the secretary of education to eliminate the "barriers which may have unfairly resulted in reduced participation in, and reduced benefits from, federally sponsored programs" and to identify the legal authority under which the departments could "provide relief from specific inequities and disadvantages . . . in the agency programs." It required each executive agency to "initiate new efforts" to increase participation by HBCUs in agency programs,[97] and ordered the secretary of education to submit an annual report detailing the levels of participation by HBCUs in the programs of each executive agency and to issue recommendations for improving that performance.

The Reagan Administration

In his first year in office, President Reagan issued an executive order expanding the federal government's measures to enhance HBCUs. Before signing the order, the president announced a $9.6-million increase in Title III funds for the HBCUs, observing that "it should never be forgotten that when educational opportunities were denied elsewhere, these institutions offered hope to black Americans."[98]

Reagan's executive order required each executive department and agency designated by the secretary of education to develop an annual plan to achieve a "significant increase" in the participation of HBCUs in federally sponsored programs.[99] It directed the secretary of education to review the plan of each agency and to develop a comprehensive "Annual Federal Plan for Assistance of Historically Black Colleges" to be submitted to the Cabinet Council on Human Resources. The Reagan executive order broke new ground by requiring the secretary of education to elicit initiatives from the private sector to strengthen the management, financing, and research capabilities of the HBCUs.[100] To coordinate overall planning and to gather statistics from federal agencies, the secretary of education created the Office of White House Initiatives in the Department of Education. Reagan's policies derived from his administration's position that the HBCUs were "a national resource" and from his belief that HBCUs were "unique educational institutions" that held an "unparalleled" place in American history.[101]

The Bush Administration

President Bush met with representatives of the presidents of the HBCUs while president-elect, and within the first one hundred days of his administration signed the most comprehensive, far-reaching executive order dealing with HBCUs in history. Noting that the HBCUs were "a special part of our heritage" and had supported a "noble educational tradition," his executive order was unprecedented in the breadth of the initiatives it required to enhance and improve the HBCUs.[102]

Dealing with institutional finances, planning, and management, and the development of students, faculty, and curriculum, the order required, among others, the following measures: (1) the creation of an advisory board to counsel the secretary of education on the development of an annual plan to increase HBCUs' participation in federal programs and the development of measures to increase the private sector's role in the strengthening of HBCUs; (2) the assignment of the advisory board to "high priority" status within the White House Office of National Service, so that the board could enlist the resources and experience of the private sector to develop matching funds to support increased endowments, task forces for institutions in need of assistance, and programs to develop more effective ways to manage finances, improve information management, strengthen faculties, and improve course offerings; and (3) efforts by the secretary of education to develop alternative sources of faculty talent, particularly in science and technology.

Policy Initiatives by OCR

In enforcing Title VI, OCR, housed initially in the Department of Health, Education, and Welfare and later in the Department of Education, was the governmental agency with the primary legal responsibility for and the greatest experience in desegregating colleges and universities. As noted in chapter 4, between January 1969 and February 1970 OCR notified ten states—Mississippi among them—that they were violating Title VI by operating segregated systems of higher education. OCR requested that the states submit desegregation plans. For example, in December 1969 OCR director Leon Panetta wrote Governor Godwin of Virginia to advise him that "educational institutions which have previously been legally segregated have an affirmative duty to adopt measures to overcome the effects of past segregation," and that it was "not sufficient that an institution maintain a nondiscriminatory admissions policy if the student population continues to reflect the formerly *de jure* racial identification of that institution."[103] Hence, from the beginning of its efforts to enforce Title VI in higher education, the federal government rejected the remedy advanced by Mississippi in *Fordice*. Rather, HEW suggested that states initiate a range of affirmative measures such as statewide plans for interinstitutional cooperation involving faculty exchanges, student exchanges, and the sharing of institutional resources.[104]

In 1973 and 1974, in response to Judge Pratt's initial order in *Adams,* HEW again sent letters to the ten state systems of higher education involved in the litigation. To place the *Fordice* decision in the context of decisions by the other branches, one must stress that HEW's 1973–74 letters required that state desegregation plans ensure that HBCUs not bear the burden of desegregation and that HBCUs receive the resources they needed to overcome past discrimination, to attract both black and white students, and to play a vital role in an integrated system.[105]

By 1978, HEW had considerable experience in desegregation in higher education as a result of its efforts to apply Title VI in that area for nearly a decade. To develop its 1977 criteria, the agency called upon its own experts, those of other agencies, and specialists outside of government. To this day, the HEW criteria remain the most comprehensive and elaborate guidelines for desegregation in higher education ever prepared by the federal government. Part I of the criteria, dealing with the need to strengthen the HBCUs, stressed that when desegregating it was necessary "to guard against the diminution of the higher educational opportunities for black students [and] to take into account the unique importance of traditionally black colleges."[106] The criteria required that desegregation plans include, among other things, the elimination of educationally unnecessary program duplication among black and white institutions in the same areas, in a manner "consistent with the objective of strengthening the traditionally black colleges"; and the giving of "priority consideration" to the placement of any new undergraduate, graduate, or professional degree programs at traditionally black institutions, consistent with their mission.[107]

Congressional Initiatives

In the years preceding the *Fordice* decision, Congress had also been an active policy maker and partner in the developing national consensus to strengthen and preserve HBCUs. In the 1980 amendments to the Higher Education Act and in subsequent authorizations under Title III, Congress set aside $47.5 million for black colleges.[108] Notwithstanding its policy against quotas and affirmative action, the Reagan administration consistently supported that set-aside. In the Higher Education Amendments of 1986, Congress reauthorized and revised the Higher Education Act of 1965 and specifically included a section entitled "Strengthening Historically Black Colleges and Universities." This provision was intended to ensure that black colleges continued to receive Title III monies for purchasing or leasing laboratory equipment, improving classrooms, libraries, and laboratories, maintaining faculty exchange programs, establishing new academic programs in fields where black Americans have been historically underrepresented, and paying for tutoring and counseling of low-income students.[109]

Lest there be any mistake about the motivation for the above measures, the legislation contained language about the specific congressional "findings" that gave rise to and justified them: "This Congress finds that . . . the current state of Black colleges and universities is partly attributable to the discriminatory action of the States and the Federal Government."[110] In making that finding, Congress determined, in effect, that the condition of public HBCUs across the nation is a vestige of the former system of de jure segregation. The holdings of the Supreme Court require eliminating such vestiges where they exist.

THE SUPREME COURT'S *FORDICE* DECISION SEEN IN THE CONTEXT OF PAST EXECUTIVE AND CONGRESSIONAL INITIATIVES

The above review of the policies that the federal government had initiated before the Court decided *Fordice* establishes that there had been a consistent line of national policies advanced by successive presidents, OCR, and Congress recognizing the need to remedy the effects of past discrimination against blacks in higher education and to equalize educational opportunities by enhancing historically black colleges and universities. That national policy reflected an understanding that it was imperative to ensure that desegregation in higher education not affect HBCUs adversely. In deciding the constitutional issues in *Fordice* involving HBCUs, the prior national policies of the other branches, and the historical reasons that caused the federal government to adopt those policies, should have been given great weight by the Court. Instead, they were not even acknowledged.

The experience in elementary and secondary school desegregation suggests that federal courts should weigh seriously the recommendations of professional educators and civil rights enforcement officials in the executive branch, and the national policies reflected in congressional enactments. Recall that in 1965 and 1966, HEW announced desegregation "Guidelines" for elementary and secondary education that were later paralleled by its 1977 "criteria" for desegregation in higher education. The most significant judicial interpretation of the requirements of Title VI and of the Guidelines occurred in the Fifth Circuit's decision in *United States v. Jefferson County Board of Education*.[111] In addressing the legal status of the HEW Guidelines, the Fifth Circuit ruled:

> We hold, again, in determining whether school desegregation plans meet the standards of *Brown* and other decisions of the Supreme Court, that courts in this circuit should give "great weight" to HEW Guidelines. Such deference is consistent with the exercise of traditional judicial powers and functions. HEW Guidelines . . . are prepared in detail by experts in education and school administration, and are intended by Congress and the executive to be part of a coordinated national program. The Guidelines present the best system available for uniform application, and the best aid to the courts in evaluating the validity of a school desegregation plan and the progress made under that plan.[112]

The Eighth Circuit also held that, to ensure national uniformity of standards and to prevent recalcitrance in complying with civil rights requirements, "the courts should endeavor to model their standards after those promulgated by the executive."[113]

Noting that in enforcing Title VI the executive branch had "experts in education and school administration" who have "day-to-day experience with thousands of school systems," Judge Wisdom remarked in *Jefferson* that "judges and school officials can ill afford to turn their backs on the proffer of advice from HEW."[114] In addition, the Fifth Circuit also noted in *Jefferson* the obligation of courts in school desegregation cases to consider the national policies developed by Congress.[115] For similar reasons, in *Fordice* the Court should have given "great weight" to the policies of the federal executive branch under Title VI and to the congressional policies intended to preserve and enhance HBCUs. Yet, the Court did not make a single reference to the HEW criteria, the executive orders, or congressional policies.

In *Fordice,* the Court should have deferred to the policies of its sister branches. Those policies recognized that the education that HBCUs offered black students was inextricably linked to a history of discrimination against blacks in higher education, and that the commitment to enhance HBCUs reflected a national consensus about what it was fair, just, and wise to do for the students served by those institutions. The congressional and executive policies also reflected an appreciation for the singular role that HBCUs had played and continued to play in providing equal educational opportunities for black Americans. The policy consensus about the national government's obligation to nurture HBCUs emerged over more than two decades, under three Republican administrations and one Democratic one. The Court's decision in *Fordice* disregarded that national consensus and the policies aimed at realizing its goals.

What is so disturbing about the *Fordice* decision is that, in the face of an unwavering line of policies from all three branches of government recognizing both the need to enhance HBCUs and the threats that HBCUs faced in the desegregation process, the Court ignored those policy precedents and instead, rendered a decision that conflicted with them. Indeed, in contrast to every other federal governmental institution that had examined the question, the Court's opinion in *Fordice* stood out for failing to acknowledge the unique contributions of HBCUs and for failing to require measures to mitigate the untoward consequences that desegregation might have on them. It is hard to imagine that that silence was inadvertent. The only plausible conclusion is that the justices discussed the issue and decided that they would not address it directly. What they said indirectly, however, offered little comfort to those concerned about the future of the historically black institutions. Though it remains unclear how the lower courts will apply the Court's principal directives about maximizing freedom of choice and minimizing segregation, supporters of HBCUs have little reason to feel comforted, because it can be argued that HBCUs do not advance either goal.

THE IMPLICATIONS OF *FORDICE* FOR HBCUs

The uncertain status of HBCUs after *Fordice* is illustrated by the disagreement between Justices Scalia and Thomas about what the opinion meant for the future of those institutions. In a concurrence, joined by no other member of the Court, Justice Thomas tried to wrest from the majority opinion the conclusion that, whereas it did not require states to maintain HBCUs, it did not forbid them from doing so. That strained reading of the opinion was rebutted by Justice Scalia, who, in a sharply worded lone dissent, concluded that the Court's opinion eliminated "non-integrated options," evinced an "antagonism to unintegrated schooling," and reflected an "insistence, whether explicit or implicit, that [HBCUs] not be permitted to endure." "Predictable impairment" of HBCUs will result, warned Scalia, "for incidentally facilitating—indeed, even tolerating—the continued existence of [HBCUs] is not what the Court's test is about." Rather, said Scalia, "What the Court's test is designed to achieve is the elimination of predominantly black institutions."[116]

The Court's treatment of the question of funding for HBCUs gave credibility to Scalia's contention that the majority opinion, properly understood, was hostile to them. In a significant and subtle passage that needs to be read with care, the Court said:

> If we understand private petitioners to press us to order the upgrading of Jackson State, Alcorn State and Mississippi Valley [all HBCUs] *solely* so that they may be publicly financed, exclusively black enclaves by private choice, we reject that request. The State provides these facilities for all its citizens and it has not met its burden under *Brown* to take affirmative steps to dismantle its prior *de jure* system when it perpetuates a separate but "more equal" one. Whether such an increase in funding is necessary to achieve a full dismantlement under the standards we have outlined, however, is a different question and one that must be addressed on remand.[117]

Note the way the Court framed the issue. It did not say that the petitioners had in fact argued for upgrading the HBCUs so that they could become "exclusively black enclaves." Rather, the Court prefaced its statement by the carefully selected phrase "*If we understand* private petitioners to press us to order the upgrading" (emphasis added). There is no evidence whatsoever that petitioners had urged the Court to order funding to upgrade the HBCUs so that those institutions might be "*exclusively* black enclaves," by private choice or otherwise. Indeed, in dealing with the funding issue in their reply brief, the petitioners raised the very concerns stressed by the Court — the need to maximize free choice and to desegregate. They argued that "existing disparities between the HBIs [historically black institutions] and the HWIs [historically white institutions] impede the HBIs' abilities to attract desegregated student populations,"[118] and that the goal of rectifying historic inequalities in funding "will be to *end* the ugly past, not to continue . . . or perfect . . . it."[119] In light of such statements in the petitioners' brief, how could the Court have "understood" the petitioners to be pressing for greater funding "solely" to establish HBCUs as "exclusively black enclaves"?

It is simply not credible that the Court could have understood the petitioners to be advancing such an argument. The Court's troubling and misleading characterization of the petitioners' objectives misstated their position and the heart of the issue involving HBCUs. Neither the petitioners nor any of the amici who supported them argued that HBCUs must be enhanced "solely" so that they could function "exclusively" as African American enclaves. Indeed, upgrading HBCUs would inevitably mean that whites would find those institutions more attractive and would apply in unprecedented numbers, thereby desegregating them more than ever.

Characterizing the issue as it did enabled the Court to answer an easy question that was never really at issue, and to sidestep the difficult question that was central to the case. The Court had to "reject" the ordering of enhanced funding for HBCUs as "exclusively black enclaves." By casting the funding issue as it did, the Court avoided the question that was at the heart of the case: For reasons of educational policy, may states fund colleges or universities that, while admitting students of all races, take steps to ensure that black students predominate on campus and that the curriculum, academic programs, and environment on campus are oriented to the needs of black students?

Though the Court ruled that increased funding to make HBCUs "exclusively black enclaves" was not permissible, it conceded that whether "an increase in funding is necessary to achieve a full dismantlement . . . is a different question, and one that *must* be addressed on remand."[120] It is unfortunate that the Court raised that critical question and then never discussed the factors that should be considered in answering it on remand. The issue doubtless will be the subject of further controversy and may well have to be raised before the Court again. For the meantime, however, the Court left the district courts in Mississippi and other states to their own devices in determining whether one can desegregate a formerly de jure system of higher education without providing increased funding to correct for the historical underfunding of HBCUs. To leave the lower courts, the states, and OCR without guidance on that question guaranteed uncertainty, inconsistency in the decisions in different states, delay, and of course, further litigation.

No one disputes that all the states that operated de jure segregated systems have historically underfunded HBCUs, and that to some degree, the current limited educational offerings and inferior physical plants at the HBCUs are traceable to, and hence constitute vestiges of, that past practice. Consequently, all the states with public HBCUs will inevitably confront the question of what kind of legal obligation they have to eliminate those vestiges of inequality in the course of dismantling their former de jure systems. That is not a question that lower courts should have to answer by themselves on an ad hoc basis, without guidance from the Supreme Court. Yet, that is precisely the posture in which the Court left them.

The Court's position on enhanced funding suggests that, whereas courts should not direct monies to HBCUs as "black" institutions, courts "must" consider whether "an increase in funding is necessary to achieve a full dismantlement under the standards [the Court] outlined."[121] Hence, though the Court seemed to conclude that greater funding was not warranted to support HBCUs as "black" institutions, it indicated that increased funding might be justified to dismantle the de jure system — that is, presumably, to ensure that there no longer were institutions identifiable by race. Hence, it is arguable that the import of the Court's reasoning is that historically black institutions may be entitled to increased funding only if the objective of the funding is to put them out of business as black institutions.

Ironically, to the degree that states make greater funding available to HBCUs under any rationale, such an action may undermine them as "black" institutions. As noted earlier, "enhancing" HBCUs with better libraries, laboratories, recreational facilities, or other physical plant improvements and placing a broader range of academic programs at those institutions will attract more white students to them, and may cause them to lose their distinctive educational orientation and historic mission. In that scenario, HBCUs run the risk of being transformed into indistinguishable campus cogs in the state university system. In short, truly enhancing HBCUs may inevitably destroy, or at least jeopardize, them as HBCUs. I suspect that this is precisely what the Court had in mind when it identified the need "to achieve a full dismantlement" as the only legitimate justification for increased funding. Yet, that justification also raises unanswered legal and educational policy perplexities.

How does one know or determine when a black institution is or has remained a "black" institution? Does it require a certain racial percentage in the student body or in the faculty? Does it require certain student programs or curricular offerings? Or does one just know it when one sees it, as Justice Stewart once observed about another subject? In sum, whether one wants to preserve and enhance HBCUs or dismantle them, one needs to determine what specific, identifiable factors, other than a historic label, make an institution a historically black college or university. There is little scholarship by educators, and even less analysis by lawyers and judges, addressing that issue. *Fordice* offered an opportunity to raise, if not resolve, some of these issues. Yet, the Court did not in any way advance our understanding of these issues. Indeed, it did not even address them. Rather, the Court's twin focus on "free choice" and "segregative effects" advanced a simplistic, irreconcilable, and unworkable set of criteria for planning the future of HBCUs or restructuring publicly supported southern higher education. Again, recourse to the law actually impeded the development of constructive educational policies.

In addition to generating confusion by its careless use of the concepts of free choice and segregative effects, the Court also doomed any possible clarity that might have emerged from its decision by ruling that otherwise unconstitutional state practices could be legally justified either if they had a "sound educational justification" or if they could not "be practicably eliminated."[122] The Court's initial statement of these justifications appears in its holding, where it ruled that if a state perpetuates policies that can be traced to the de jure system and that continue to have segregative effects, it has not met its burden to dismantle the prior system *unless* it can show that the policies in question have a "sound educational justification" or cannot be "practicably eliminated."[123] In analyzing each of the four policies it found constitutionally suspect, the Court noted that on remand the lower court should consider whether the state could justify continuing the policies because there was a sound educational basis for doing so or because the policy could not practicably be eliminated.[124] What confusion creative lawyers, educational administrators, and judges will effect in construing the rubbery language in those two qualifying phrases. What wide options those ambiguous phrases give anyone attempting to enforce the Court's policy.

What the Court seems to have created in *Fordice* is a kind of rebuttable presumption, at least with respect to the four practices it discussed. It treated those practices as presumptively unconstitutional unless states could rebut that presumption by establishing that the practices could be explained on the basis of either of the two acceptable justifications the Court identified. States will be well positioned to resist change by making such claims, and the Court's weak and confusing opinion will offer little guidance or legal basis for lower courts or OCR officials seeking to reject those claims.

Consider just one example. In 1981, the statewide board of trustees for Mississippi's state university system assigned institutions new mission designations that largely paralleled the educational missions historically given the traditionally white and black institutions during the days of de jure segregation. Indeed, throughout the long litigation in *Fordice,* Mississippi argued that there were compelling reasons, in terms of both educational policy and practicality, for building the future of the system largely along the lines of its prior development. Imagine the practical dislocations and policy complications, for example, associated with transforming a small undergraduate institution into a comprehensive university, or vice versa.

In evaluating the educational policy justification or practicality argument for virtually any questionable practice, a federal judge will have to give considerable deference to the determinations of state educational officials. Moreover, to the degree that a state alleges, as many doubtless will, that lack of money makes certain options "impracticable," it will take a most unusual federal judge to second-guess that evaluation and order the state either to spend money that it says it does not have, or to spend money in ways that conflict with the higher educational priorities the state has established.

In supporting their justifications for continuing certain educational practices, states will also enjoy other important advantages. They will have ready access to "experts" in state educational bureaucracies to help advance justifications for questionable practices and to analyze data, conduct and evaluate studies, and in general, provide the firepower to "outgun" plaintiffs. Finally, as further evidence of the advantage state universities will have over both plaintiffs and OCR in this realm, consider the strong tradition of academic independence in higher education.

The cry of academic freedom will inevitably be heard from states when judges evaluate whether "sound educational policy" justifies a particular practice. Once they get their money from the legislature, state university administrators and boards of trustees are accustomed to developing state universities on the basis of their independent professional educational judgment. The protracted struggle in North Carolina illustrates just how tenaciously university officials and boards will fight to preserve that prerogative. Consequently, whereas we are accustomed to seeing and accepting federal district court judges in the role of powerful educational policy makers in school desegregation at the elementary and secondary school levels, we are not likely to see judges, at any level, playing nearly as powerful and interventionist a role in the desegregation of state university systems.

In distinguishing between desegregation in higher education and its counterpart at the elementary and secondary school levels, consider the difference in the political stakes and in the people involved. At the elementary and secondary school levels, federal judges come up against mayors, local school boards, superintendents of schools, and parents. In desegregation in higher education, by contrast, the governors of states, state departments of education, state university presidents, faculty associations, and powerful alumni are invariably involved and consider themselves to have a vital stake in the process. Because the political visibility and the stakes are of a different order of magnitude in such conflicts, any federal judge will have to proceed with greater caution in those conflicts. As a consequence, when governors, state university presidents, and boards of trustees argue that certain practices should not be changed, either because there is a "sound educational policy" for retaining them or because it would be "impracticable" to eliminate them, it will be difficult for federal judges not to give great weight to those assertions. In such circumstances, the absence of strong and specific directives from the Supreme Court in *Fordice* will hamper the ability and willingness of federal judges to play an active role.

CONCLUSION

Until *Fordice, Adams* was the most far-reaching litigation affecting HBCUs. Both the District of Columbia Circuit and Judge Pratt had expressed concern that desegregation in higher education should not proceed in a way that would harm those institutions. In a major 1975 ruling in *Adams* that is analyzed in chapter 4, the court of appeals declared that desegregation plans must take "into account the special problems of minority students and of black colleges" and recognize that HBCUs "fulfill a crucial need and will continue to play an important role in black higher education."[125] In a subsequent decision in *Adams,* Judge Pratt ruled, "The process of desegregation must not place a greater burden on Black institutions or students' opportunity to receive a quality higher education. The desegregation process should take into account the unequal status of the Black colleges and the real danger that desegregation will diminish higher education opportunities for Blacks."[126] In those two sentences, Judge Pratt expressed the apprehension many felt about the desegregation process in the nineteen states with public HBCUs. Solicitor General Starr reflected that same sentiment when, following the Supreme Court's decision in *Fordice,* he observed, "It certainly would not do for the burden of dismantlement [of segregation] to fall on the shoulders of minority citizens."[127] It certainly would not. Yet, in the majority opinion in *Fordice* there was little more than a scintilla of concern for that issue, and little protection against that eventuality.[128]

In the aftermath of *Fordice,* there was something eerily anticlimactic and disappointing about the decision. It had certainly been a long time in coming. The dispute over desegregation in higher education extended back to the early efforts to enforce Title VI in the 1960s. Nearly two decades of the *Adams* litigation had turned on disputes about what the law required states to do in desegregating state universities. The dispute in *Fordice* itself went back nearly a quarter of a century. Alvin Chambliss, a heroic black lawyer waging war against the state from a tiny, poorly funded legal aid office in a rural part of Mississippi, had battled for nineteen years to bring his case to the nation's highest court. It all seemed historic — so appropriate and propitious an occasion to resolve so much.

And yet, when the Court finally issued its opinion, it seemed to resolve so little and to offer so little instruction and direction about the future. *Fordice* was, at best, inconclusive, leaving much unsettled, undecided, and uncertain. It raised far more questions than it answered. The extensive attention given the case in advance of the Court's decision made that end result all the more disappointing and unsatisfying. One got the sense that for all the publicity, both before and after the case, little of import would change in the short term, and years of further litigation and governmental equivocation were in the offing.

Though the Court only alluded to it in a veiled way, the shadow of *Plessy v. Ferguson* and the "separate but equal" doctrine loomed over the *Fordice* case.[129] Anxiety about racial separation in black-controlled institutions was a crucial, albeit unspoken, consideration in *Fordice*. Uneasiness about legitimating racial separation partially explained the Justice Department's initial position on the funding question, the Court's exaggerated emphasis on whether HBCUs were entitled to increased funding as "exclusively black enclaves," and the widespread attention given the case. The Court should have analyzed, rather than ducked, the racial separation issue. That issue will be a central factor in deciding the future of HBCUs because so many critics will contend, mistakenly, that preserving those schools is tantamount to resurrecting and perfecting the *Plessy* doctrine. To argue that states have a constitutional duty that goes beyond establishing racially neutral admissions policies and encompasses an obligation to enhance HBCUs is not to endorse racial separatism or the doctrine of "separate but equal." It is to require states that have for generations discriminated against blacks in public higher education to begin to take effective measures to provide for equal educational opportunity along the lines commanded by the Court in *Brown v. Board of Education*.

Access to higher education has historically proven to be one of the best ways, not to separate people from mainstream American society but rather, in the best sense of the word, to "integrate" them. Education provides the skills, credentials, and attitudes that people need to function in and contribute to society. The Court itself recognized that salutary social by-product of education in *Brown v. Board of Education*.

We need reminding that the core injury recognized in that decision was not that black children were prevented from going to school with white children or from sitting next to them in "integrated" classrooms, but rather that racial segregation in schools was a method states used to deny blacks access to educational skills that were indispensable to enjoying and succeeding in life. The decision was founded on the constitutional obligation to equalize educational opportunity in public schools in light of the importance of education in contemporary American life and in a democratic political order:

> Today, education is perhaps the most important function of state and local governments. Compulsory school attendance laws and the great expenditures for education both demonstrate our recognition of the importance of education in our democratic society. It is required in the performance of our most basic public responsibilities, even service in the armed forces. It is the very foundation of good citizenship. . . . In these days it is doubtful that any child may be reasonably expected to succeed in life if he is denied the opportunity of an education. Such an opportunity, where the state has undertaken to provide it, is a right which must be made available to all on equal terms.[130]

If anything, the significance of education has increased since the Court wrote those words. As we have moved from an economic system centered on manufacturing and industry to a service, information, and high-technology economy, the need for education, and in particular for higher education, has grown ever greater. Whereas a high-school diploma provided a level of educational achievement that may have been sufficient to qualify most American workers for the labor force in 1954, that is scarcely the case today, especially in light of the demographic and economic transformations that have affected the lives of so many urban blacks.

There can be no disputing that the American educational establishment has failed blacks, and that this failure has been devastating both for blacks and for the nation as a whole. By contrast, the HBCUs are a unique educational success story. For generations, they have been in the forefront of the effort to provide blacks, especially those of limited means, opportunities for a college education. There is much that the successes of those institutions can teach us about how to educate and graduate black students. Inadequately financed, operating under adverse conditions and in hostile environments, educating students who were often poorly prepared and of limited means, the HBCUs have an extraordinary record of accomplishment. Indeed, more than any other educational institutions they have achieved the historic objective of providing large numbers of blacks with a means of economic and political empowerment. Their unique educational contribution and potential, while consistent with the central goals of *Brown,* went without mention in *Fordice.*

The Court grievously misconstrued the import of *Fordice* by concluding that freedom of choice and racial segregation were the central issues in the case. They were not. Equal educational opportunity was the central issue, but as with the countless other examples documented in these pages, the requirements of "the law" blurred our vision, distorted our priorities, and focused our attention on ill-considered and largely irrelevant legal questions and remedies. Though achieving equal educational opportunity was, from the outset, the ultimate goal of school desegregation, as I argued in chapter 3, we lost sight of that goal in the process of desegregating elementary and secondary schools. After *Fordice,* as we proceed to desegregate in higher education, we are in danger of losing sight of that goal yet again. The lodestar for the Court in deciding *Fordice* should have been neither *Plessy, Bazemore,* nor *Green,* but rather *Brown v. Board* itself. Enhancing the HBCUs, to enable them to do better and to do more of what they have done so well for so long, offered one of the most promising avenues for realizing the vision of *Brown.*

8

CONCLUSIONS

[A] certain kind of rights talk in our political discussion is both a symptom of, and a contributing factor to, this disorder in our body politic. Discourse about rights has become the principal language that we use in public settings to discuss weighty questions of right and wrong, but time and again it proves inadequate.

Mary Ann Glendon, *Rights Talk: The Impoverishment of Political Discourse*

WHEN I FIRST STARTED TO write this book, I thought of the enforcement of Title VI in terms of the simplest of concepts, which I labeled "active" and "inactive" enforcement. Active enforcement produced a busy pace of administrative initiatives intended to meet the requirements of the law. Enforcement during the Johnson administration, to my mind, typified active enforcement. Inactive enforcement by contrast, involved a deliberate failure to take steps to effectuate the goals of the law. The Nixon administration record reflected that kind of enforcement. Indeed, it was the contrast between the two administrations and the unusual litigation that each produced that prompted my interest in writing this book. I have since concluded that thinking of the enforcement of Title VI in terms of facile comparisons between those two administrations simplifies complex questions, produces a focus on tangential issues, and blinds us to a basic problem — the way in which the emphasis on "legal rights" in every administration since 1964 transformed the effort to achieve racial equality in educational opportunity.

OCR's Discretion to Choose Enforcement Methods and Priorities

The Choice of Enforcement Programs and Strategies

One of the central issues regarding the enforcement of Title VI is not whether the Office for Civil Rights was "active," but in what way it was active or chose to be active. This speaks to the programs and strategies it developed to achieve compliance with the law. No enforcement agency is ever entirely inactive. Bureaucracies are always doing something, if only to justify themselves to the public and the legislatures that fund them. The more important question is not whether an enforcement agency such as OCR is busily involved in doing things, but whether, given its resources, it is doing the most effective things to protect legal rights.

A high level of frenetic but ineffectual activity may be the most subtle and insidious way for an agency such as OCR to undermine the protection of civil rights. It enables the agency to masquerade as "active" in enforcing rights when, in fact, the way in which it is active, either by deliberate choice or otherwise, produces meager results. Expending great energy and resources in the processing of complaints raises that danger. In 1975, in the *Adams* litigation, Judge Pratt ordered OCR to enforce Title VI by investigating all complaints and resolving them within specified periods of time. Hence, after *Adams,* OCR stepped up the pace of its investigations, and fewer complaints sat for extended periods without attention and action. In that sense, *Adams* produced enforcement activity. Yet, there were limits to what was gained from that activity.

An enforcement strategy focusing on the investigation of complaints is "reactive" in that the agency waits for complainants to bring issues to it, and this skews the agency's agenda and attention in favor of problems raised in complaints. However active and efficient OCR may be in handling complaints — as administration after administration has held — the agency could provide greater protection of rights if it were less "active" vis-à-vis complaints and devoted more energy and resources to other enforcement methods. To the extent that *Adams* compelled the agency to investigate, within an allotted time, each complaint lodged with it, the number of compliance reviews it could initiate decreased. That decrease had important implications. Complaints focus on specific instances of discrimination. Compliance reviews are comprehensive, systemwide investigations of civil rights practices within a school system or specific institution. Historically, compliance reviews have been initiated by OCR on the basis of information it collects that suggests that a pattern of discrimination may exist.

An enforcement strategy emphasizing well-chosen compliance reviews has advantages over one driven by the need to investigate complaints. First, because compliance reviews are investigations of institutional practices, they affect larger numbers of people. Second, because OCR selects the compliance reviews, those reviews may assist individuals who suffer illegal discrimination but who, for lack of information, time, money, or fortitude, would not otherwise bring a complaint. Third, the likelihood of finding a civil rights violation may be greater in compliance reviews than in complaint investigations because reviews may be selected on the basis of information that suggests a high probability of finding a violation and because a wider range of behavior is monitored. How OCR allocates resources between complaint investigation and compliance reviews has an impact on what the agency accomplishes in eliminating or deterring illegal discrimination. In any rational scheme, the trade-offs in allocating resources between the two enforcement methods should be carefully considered. The *Adams* litigation precluded that.

The controversy over OCR's investigation of complaints was a direct product of the agency's discretion under Title VI, a discretion that made potentially contradictory results possible. Depending upon how OCR officials chose to use their discretion, they could either maximize the impact of Title VI or neutralize the provision. On the one hand, by concentrating on enforcement actions that would have the widest impact in uncovering, deterring, and eliminating discrimination, OCR officials could use their discretion to maximize the protection afforded by the statute. On the other hand, by concentrating on insignificant complaints and by selecting compliance reviews likely to produce little lasting effect, those officials could use their discretion to minimize the impact of the provision and the legal protection it afforded. Confronted with these realities, civil rights litigators chose to use litigation to limit the discretion of those enforcing Title VI so that those officials could not enforce the law in ways that minimized its effect. Hence, the litigators sought court orders requiring that each and every complaint be investigated and treated on an equal basis. As I have argued, that obligation imposed its own limits on what OCR could accomplish.

Yet another discretionary choice in the strategies used to enforce Title VI derived from the language of the statute itself. Congress provided that Title VI could be enforced either by terminating federal funds or by "any other means authorized by law." Recall that the latter alternative meant referral of the case to the Justice Department for prosecution, and that in school desegregation cases this proved to be an ineffectual and costly method of enforcement. The Nixon administration used its discretion to adopt an enforcement strategy emphasizing referrals to the Justice Department rather than terminations of funding, precisely because it believed that this strategy would minimize school desegregation. The use of that enforcement method by choice in the Nixon years, or later by statutory constraint under the Eagleton-Biden Amendment, is a far more significant factor than how "active" OCR was in referring cases to the Justice Department and how active the department was in initiating lawsuits in those cases. No matter how many cases OCR referred to the Justice Department and how many lawsuits the department brought, referrals were an ineffectual enforcement method when compared to administrative proceedings holding out the credible threat of termination of funds.

Ideally, for each unit of time or money it expends, OCR should seek to maximize the extent to which discrimination is either eliminated or deterred. The process of deciding how to accomplish that task is complicated by the need to decide how to allocate the agency's resources among the various civil rights concerns over which OCR has responsibility. For each legal right OCR must enforce, there is an organized constituency that may perceive that when the agency commits resources to enforce one civil rights statute, that commitment limits the agency's capacity to enforce other statutes.

The Choice of Enforcement Priorities

If one thinks in terms of the "active" enforcement of a law, one must ask, with respect to what particular problems, and in the context of what overall set of resources and responsibilities, is the enforcement active? *Active* is a relative, not an absolute, term; it has meaning only in context.

An agency's enforcement priorities establish which of the issues within its jurisdiction it decides to emphasize, how it allocates its resources among the problems for which it has responsibility, and under what circumstances it will invoke the penalties it is authorized to impose. Most analysts would probably agree that by initiating hundreds of enforcement proceedings and terminating federal funds in scores of cases, the Johnson administration adopted the most vigorous and effective policy for enforcing Title VI. With those actions, the administration desegregated hundreds of southern school districts that had successfully resisted desegregation in the years following *Brown v. Board*. Viewed in the context of the history of southern race relations and of segregated public education, or in comparison with subsequent administrations, the Johnson administration enforced Title VI in a uniquely active and energetic way.

Yet, the enforcement of Title VI during the Johnson years was limited in scope to the South, to elementary and secondary schools, and to a large extent to non-urban districts with small minority populations. Consequently, Johnson's "active" enforcement of Title VI did not affect most of the major metropolitan centers of the South, where the overwhelming proportion of southern blacks attended public schools, nor did it affect segregated institutions of higher education in the South, or segregated schools in the North. This illustration from the Johnson years highlights the central impact that enforcement priorities can have. The history reviewed in this volume suggests that the following factors have determined OCR's enforcement priorities: (1) the agency's overall legal responsibilities; (2) its resources; (3) the political factors operating on and within it; and (4) the power of the interest groups with a stake in its work.

OCR's Overall Responsibilities

One cannot understand the history of Title VI without appreciating the growth of OCR's responsibilities for enforcing civil rights in areas other than Title VI. OCR's obligations under Title IX of the Education Amendments of 1972, prohibiting discrimination based on gender, and Section 504 of the Rehabilitation Act of 1974, prohibiting discrimination based on mental or physical disability, are especially important. As the agency's responsibilities grew, establishing priorities became more important and more complicated. During the Johnson administration, Title VI was the only civil rights provision that HEW enforced. By the early 1970s, however, racial discrimination was but one of many civil rights concerns that competed for the attention of OCR officials.

Organizational Resources

It takes money and personnel to enforce laws. As there are invariably many more things for a law enforcement agency to do than there are resources with which to do them, all enforcement agencies, in attempting to meet their mandated responsibilities, choose to do some things and not others. OCR was no exception. It had to choose the degree to which various civil rights problems within its jurisdiction would receive resources, close scrutiny, and quick action.

Monitoring all educational institutions across the country to determine whether they discriminate on the basis of race or national origin is an immense administrative task. It is not possible to monitor every "program or activity," to use the statutory phrase, that receives federal funding. Necessarily, only a fraction of a percent of the covered educational programs will ever be monitored by OCR. Hence, OCR must select the programs it will review and the resources it will allocate to the different kinds of discrimination for which it has responsibility.

Competition for resources became an issue in negotiating the settlement orders in June 1976 and again in December 1977, when OCR negotiated with its major constituencies about how it would divide its time and energies. Lawyers participating in those discussions at the behest of the NAACP Legal Defense Fund, the Women's Equity Action League, the Mexican American Legal Defense and Education Fund, and advocacy groups for the disabled focused time and again on the issue of dividing OCR's resources equitably among the different interests of those groups. This, in turn, led to conflict and tension among the groups.

Allocating organizational resources was also an issue for OCR personnel. Many senior career bureaucrats in the unit had begun doing civil rights work in the black civil rights movement. Some of them resented expending substantial agency resources on behalf of middle-class white women.[1] The difficulties in allocating resources and establishing enforcement priorities derived not only from bureaucratic considerations internal to the agency but also from political considerations outside the agency.

Political Factors

Politics has influenced Title VI enforcement priorities from the beginning. The Johnson administration's decision to focus on southern school desegregation and to restrict enforcement in the North grew out of political calculations. Similarly, the Nixon administration emphasized bilingual and bicultural education for Hispanics in order to win political support from that group. In the 1970s, OCR turned its attention away from racial discrimination because of the political perception that enough had been done to redress racial discrimination and because of an emerging political awareness of and concern about discrimination against the disabled and women. Those two "new"

OCR constituencies, along with Hispanic Americans, emulated in the 1970s and the 1980s the political movement of blacks in the 1950s and 1960s.

In the 1970s, the new civil rights constituencies established their legitimacy and credibility as part of an expanded and altered civil rights movement. They formed national interest groups, received foundation money and legal support to press their goals, and became more knowledgeable, vocal, and insistent that government address their problems. By 1980, those groups were competing with blacks for the attention and limited resources of OCR, which by then had legal responsibilities under federal law to protect those groups from discrimination in federally funded programs. Moreover, the problems of black Americans declined as a national political priority in the 1970s and virtually disappeared as a priority in the 1980s. These crosscurrents in our national politics changed priorities within OCR, making it more politic for the agency to enforce antidiscrimination provisions for the new groups, rather than continuing to press on behalf of its original constituency and cause — blacks in segregated schools.

The *Adams* litigation was an effort by the LDF to counteract the altered political and civil rights priorities of OCR and the nation. It was an attempt by the organization, like others before it, to use litigation to compel attention to a problem that the political process was content to neglect. Complicating matters for the *Adams* plaintiffs was the fact that the problem of racial discrimination in the 1970s and 1980s had become more complex and subtle.

Unlike the LDF's earlier landmark civil rights cases, *Adams* was not an attempt to win new legal protections for blacks through pioneering judicial pronouncements that established new substantive rights. That goal, of course, had been the focus of the LDF's historic legal attack against racial discrimination leading up to *Brown v. Board*. *Adams* was different. Its objectives, though no less difficult, were less dramatic and stirring — and perhaps somewhat anticlimactic. In *Adams,* the LDF sought to use litigation to render legal rights already written into our law — rights ostensibly protected by Title VI — meaningful. The goal was to use litigation to limit the extent to which Title VI might be administratively neglected and ineffectively enforced for political reasons. *Adams* was a new kind of civil rights litigation, reflecting the legal and political problems of a new era and generation — problems that arose after *Brown v. Board* and after the great civil rights legislative victories of the 1960s.

The struggle over the enforcement of Title VI reflected the metamorphosis in the civil rights movement during the last quarter century, and the attendant difficulties that this development posed for black Americans. Once the LDF won its initial legal victory in *Adams,* it was inevitable, in the new civil rights environment that had emerged, that lawyers for other rights groups would sue on the basis of that precedent, insisting on similar treatment for their groups. That is the way the law works. Yet, in that development, the LDF became a victim of its own success. As lawyers for other groups followed the LDF's example, those lawyers complicated the situation both for the LDF and for Judge Pratt, and diminished the possibility of future successes by the LDF. Pratt made it evident, as did the District of Columbia circuit court of appeals in its final two decisions in the case, that it was the sprawling and unwieldy expansion of the *Adams* litigation that necessitated its dissolution.

There was a positive side to the expansion of the litigation. As *Adams* mushroomed to include issues of discrimination on the basis of national origin, gender, and disability, LDF lawyers had to search for mutually beneficial strategies with and to cooperate with representatives of other major national civil rights organizations. Hence, *Adams* contributed to increased communication and coordination at least among the lawyers for these various civil rights groups.

However, the emergence of civil rights movements for "new" groups and the involvement of those groups in the *Adams* litigation had negative consequences for blacks. It lumped the grievances of blacks, the discrimination they experienced, and the legal rights intended to protect them together with the problems and rights of other groups, and made the injuries suffered by those groups and the need to remedy their injuries comparable — if not indistinguishable. The result was that black Americans became viewed and treated as one among a number of historically mistreated groups in need of legal protection. In that change, the nation lost a sense for the unparalleled place and virulent force of racial discrimination. We no longer appreciated the unique historical evils and continuing injuries inflicted on the basis of race — that is, the incomparable disadvantage of being born with black skin. The lumping together of the injustices suffered by the various mistreated groups, and of their respective moral and legal claims, made it more tenuous to assert, either in society generally or in the *Adams* litigation, that America's treatment of its black population was a singular historic evil that produced continuing, incomparable harm deserving paramount attention and priority.

The expanded civil rights movement, reflected both in the growth of OCR's jurisdiction and in the burgeoning of the *Adams* litigation, evidenced a profound transformation in the way the nation and its courts thought about the plight of African Americans. Prior to that transformation, to use the term *civil rights,* both in everyday and legal parlance, was to refer to "black" civil rights.[2] When blacks lost that exclusive connection—that monopoly in our language and thinking—they suffered an incalculable loss. Prior to *Adams* and OCR's expansion, blacks were the primary beneficiaries of the twentieth-century struggle for civil rights in the United States, enjoying an unrivaled position as the minority group most in need of and most deserving of governmental remedial efforts.

The expansion of the civil rights movement, fueled by people inspired by the black struggle and hoping to emulate its success, blurred the distinction between blacks and members of other groups claiming that they, like blacks, had been treated unjustly in American society. Moreover, those groups, whether they were women, the disabled, the aged, or more recently, homosexuals, were overwhelmingly white. Hence, the expanded civil rights movement displaced blacks as the primary beneficiaries of civil rights efforts and enabled groups that were predominantly white to compete for the limited benefits provided for historically disadvantaged people.

The proliferating claims of historic mistreatment, and the indictment of American society that was advanced with the claims of each group, also devalued the generic allegation of discrimination and helped produce a countereffect—in popular parlance, a backlash. As the civil rights movement became transformed to include many groups, and as new legal protections for each of those groups emerged, the moral force of their arguments seemed to dissipate, and the causes themselves seemed to lose legitimacy. Replacing the moral power and legitimacy that once marked the black civil rights movement and that produced the Civil Rights Act of 1964, there emerged a bureaucratic, institutionalized "system" to "process" claims of discrimination. The surge of groups seeking what some viewed as "special" treatment on the grounds of historic discrimination produced a backlash not only against those groups but also against their patron in our national politics, the Democratic Party. That backlash remains a central factor in our domestic politics into the 1990s, and has caused the leadership of the Democratic Party to distance itself from the black cause and such national leaders as Jesse Jackson.

Though the transformation of the civil rights movement meant that many groups could lay claim to the benefits to be provided to historically mistreated people, middle-class white women enjoyed a special advantage in that competition.[3] That produced a certain awkwardness in the relationship between lawyers for the LDF and lawyers for women's groups. Recall that WEAL modeled its lawsuit after the case brought by the LDF, and that in the negotiations surrounding critical settlements in *Adams* the greatest tension existed between lawyers for the LDF and lawyers for WEAL. Though lawyers for these two groups did cooperate and attempt to limit friction, it is also true that they were the most committed, competitive, and aggressive lawyers in the negotiations, looking first to win for their own clients.

The issue of priority (that is, the relative preference to be given to the claims of various disadvantaged groups) is a sensitive one. Members of each group have, in fact, experienced prejudice, discrimination, and injury because of their status. As groups that have been historically mistreated, they share a common circumstance that makes them natural allies. Moreover, many on the American Left view it as morally offensive and tactically foolish for those at the bottom of the social order to squabble among themselves about the relative severity of their privation and their respective entitlement to special dispensations. Such squabbling, it is argued, takes attention and pressure away from their proper targets — those at the top of the heap, who enjoy systematic and often unwarranted advantages. Indeed, many on the Left suspect that the Right deliberately tries to fuel animosities among the members of the most powerless groups. For these and other reasons, our society and legal system deny that there are significant distinctions that should be drawn among these groups, their claims, and their entitlements.

It is particularly awkward to distinguish among the claims of various disadvantaged groups in legal proceedings, where so high a value is placed on a formal and principled equality of treatment. For example, though Judge Pratt probably believed that OCR's failure to enforce laws against racial discrimination was more serious and deserving of judicial attention and intervention than were the claims regarding the failure to enforce laws prohibiting gender discrimination, there was no defensible way for him to do anything about that preference or priority. Legally, the groups and their claims required equal treatment and attention.

The Organizational Capacities of Civil Rights Groups

The extent to which a group was organized, persistent, politically knowledgeable, and well connected influenced the priority OCR assigned to its concerns. The better informed a group was about OCR's enforcement actions, and the more it demonstrated its knowledge to the agency, the less possible it was for OCR to ignore it. A group's capacity to take legal action was especially important in determining the agency's responsiveness. Federal agencies are not immune to the fear of lawsuits — especially where legal actions can embarrass them.

The LDF's access to outstanding attorneys, both in-house and at Joseph Rauh's law firm, forced OCR to respond to issues that the LDF raised. OCR officials preferred to avoid legal action initiated by LDF attorneys. Hence, those attorneys calculatingly threatened such action from time to time and had to make good on such threats periodically to maintain their credibility and power. To a similar but lesser degree, this was also true of the lawyers representing WEAL.

In the 1970s and 1980s, because of *Adams,* OCR had to deal with civil rights groups in a much different way than in the 1960s. During the Johnson years, civil rights groups did little monitoring of the enforcement of Title VI. In the struggles over elementary and secondary school desegregation in the South, HEW essentially determined its own agenda and strategy, engaging in little communication with the LDF or other civil rights groups. By contrast, because of the *Adams* litigation, the LDF was instrumental during the 1970s in pressing OCR to proceed with desegregation in higher education, in negotiating with OCR about the standards governing that desegregation, and in influencing OCR's enforcement strategies and priorities. Indeed, as a result of *Adams,* virtually all of the constituencies with a stake in OCR's enforcement programs had institutionalized a role, a place, and power for themselves vis-à-vis the agency. They became "insiders" in a way they never had been before.

The *Adams* litigation won civil rights lobbyists access to information about how OCR worked and what it did. That access assured them a close, detailed view of the agency's enforcement actions and plans and made them, if not partners in the enforcement process, at least well-informed critics who could use the information they received to enhance their bargaining power. OCR officials were conscious that these clientele groups could peer over their shoulders, so to speak, to assess and second-guess the agency's work. Consequently, under *Adams* there was more occasion than ever for informal contact and negotiation between civil rights lobbyists and OCR officials. However, though *Adams* brought the civil rights groups greater access to the agency and greater ability to monitor its actions, civil rights organizations did not "capture" the agency politically in the classic sense in which some interest groups control the policies of the regulatory agencies most important to them. Rather, the gains won by the groups through litigation were largely procedural in character, transforming the way in which OCR processed complaints of discrimination.

Control over the substance of OCR's policies on Title VI, however, eluded the civil rights groups working on behalf of blacks and others. What Title VI required of funding recipients — how it defined illegal racial discrimination, and what remedies it authorized for that discrimination — remained remarkably tangential to most of the legal battles chronicled in these pages. Of course, those substantive questions are the toughest and most critical ones to answer, which ultimately explains the limited attention they received.

The Commitment to the Termination Sanction

One cannot understand the history of the enforcement of Title VI without acknowledging the special character of the sanction the statute imposes. The termination of federal funds is a most difficult and awkward sanction to invoke. It has been used in no more than a handful of cases in the last two decades, and there is little prospect of seeing a substantially different record any time soon. Indeed, Julius Chambers, former general counsel of the LDF, declared that there "has been a bipartisan anathema to employing even the threat of fund termination." Chambers thought that this was a grave problem, because "it is only the willingness to use the stick of Title VI that makes the carrot — voluntary compliance — effective."[4] Leon Panetta confirmed the importance of having a credible sanction in enforcing Title VI when he observed that the "evidence is clear that without the leverage of funding termination, Title VI and the other civil rights statutes based on Title VI — are meaningless."[5]

Only for a brief and atypical period during the Johnson era was fund termination used with any regularity to combat racial discrimination in schools. Today, terminating funds to any school district or educational institution would jeopardize Title VI itself, as many in Congress would probably amend the statute if its penalty were actually invoked. The failure to use the sanction for so long ensures that any attempt to use it in the future would be characterized as a striking departure from standard enforcement practice. Joseph Califano, who had witnessed many terminations as a presidential assistant in the Johnson administration, announced early in his tenure as Carter's HEW secretary that he would not hesitate to terminate funds. Indeed, when he entered office there were five termination orders on his desk, compliments of the outgoing Ford administration, just as there had been termination orders awaiting Nixon's first HEW secretary, Robert Finch, primed by the outgoing Johnson administration. Califano, like Finch before him, never signed those orders.

National politics and attitudes on racial justice have evolved to make termination viable, if at all, only in the face of the most egregious and flagrant discrimination by an educational institution. Absent shocking or blatantly racist behavior, recipients of federal educational largesse can be assured that, whatever else might happen if they are accused of discriminating, the federal funds will keep rolling in. There is a broad political consensus that the racial inequalities that pervade our nation's "desegregated" educational system are not the result of racial discrimination, or that if they are, the wrongs do not warrant the disruptions that would be occasioned by interrupting the flow of federal dollars. Stated otherwise, there is an insufficient political base to support the termination of funding as a penalty for the educational inequalities that remain. No one states the case so boldly, nor has a deliberate, calculated, and explicit decision along those lines been made by any administration. Nonetheless, that is the underlying and determinative political context in which OCR must enforce Title VI. The authority to terminate funding was the heart of that historic civil rights provision. It is a power that has fallen into disuse because Title VI itself is a measure that the political order would rather forget and ignore. And for the most part, both Democratic and Republican administrations alike have done exactly that.

Clear Policy Goals and Compliance Standards

From the very inception of Title VI, it was unclear what compliance with the statute required. The statute did not define discrimination based on race or national origin—it merely outlawed it. Nor did the legislative history provide a workable definition. Yet, such a definition of discrimination is a necessary prerequisite to any enforcement policy. The need to define discrimination speaks to the need for "explicit, certain and definite" guidelines for Title VI.[6] Leon Panetta, who knew firsthand of the political pitfalls in enforcing Title VI, explained the value of clear enforcement standards:

> Strong enforcement demands that there be clarity in the law, not only a commitment to the law, but certainty and clarity in the law. It is tough enough to enforce civil rights laws under the best of circumstances. . . . It is always an emotional issue; it is always a controver-

sial issue; it always involves a very tough laying out of the evidence to make the case; it involves solutions that are never easy. . . .

All of those factors make it tough enough to deal with the enforcement of civil rights laws. If you add to that confusion in the law, it becomes virtually impossible.[7]

Though it is hard to argue with Panetta's observations, two difficulties militate against the establishment of clear standards for measuring compliance with Title VI in educational institutions. The first is political, the second intellectual. Together, the political and intellectual difficulties have proven to be so formidable that they have produced legal standards that fail to address central issues in the fight for equal educational opportunity.

Clear Standards: The Political Limitations. In combating racial discrimination in schools under Title VI, the political context is not conducive to developing clear and strong enforcement standards. Developing clear standards that define racial discrimination and that measure a recipient's compliance with Title VI poses political risks for both judges and federal bureaucrats. Race has been the most enduring, volatile, and intractable domestic issue in all of our history. Americans feel vulnerable and defensive about the issue. In our nation's treatment of black Americans, more than in any other facet of our history, our behavior belies our stated ideals. The psychological and historical legacy of American racism, for white and black alike, makes candid, clear-thinking analysis and straightforward action difficult to achieve.

In a society rooted for centuries in slavery and racial inequality, and still seething with racial tension, officials charged with establishing policies to define and punish racial discrimination carry an unenviable political burden. It is tempting for such officials to ease that burden by pronouncing high-sounding, vaguely worded standards to define illegal discrimination. The political problems of defining unlawful discrimination under Title VI are exacerbated by the severe political repercussions associated with its sanction — the termination of federal funds. Given the sensitivity of the subject matter and the severity of the sanction, bureaucrats and judges alike are disinclined to develop forthright, precise, and unequivocal statements defining unlawful discrimination.

Policies that offer equivocation, delay, ambiguity, and even obscurity offer political advantages. They provide enforcement officials with the flexibility to apply the rules about discrimination so as to minimize the political consequences such rules may bring down upon them and their superiors. The most creative resolution of this political dilemma occurred during the Johnson administration, when HEW bureaucrats and judges acted to reinforce and legitimate each other's decisions. By cooperating in evolving enforcement standards for southern school desegregation, federal judges and HEW officials succeeded in deflecting much of the political criticism triggered by those standards. That creative synergism lasted for a brief period during the middle and late 1960s. It was possible only because a national political consensus had emerged that supported a clear standard: legally mandated segregation in southern schools would no longer be countenanced. Since that time, on no other issue involving racial discrimination in educational institutions has a comparable national consensus existed.

Though enforcement officials are loath to develop specific and comprehensive standards defining discrimination, educational institutions — ironically — have occasionally preferred precise directives as to what the law requires. This was true in the Johnson years, when some moderate southern school districts wanted to know what they had to do to comply with the law and thereby retain federal funds. More important, if moderate southern leaders wanted to end racial discrimination in schools but faced local opposition in doing so, they could use HEW's unequivocal enforcement requirements as a shield against local political criticism. They could tell local critics that the federal government required specific actions, that there was no room to sidestep those requirements, and that, in essence, the school district had no choice but to comply if it wanted Washington's dollars.

Specific and clear legal requirements also enabled OCR officials to defend themselves against criticism by the civil rights lobby. For instance, during the Carter administration OCR officials often explained to civil rights lobbyists that the Eagleton-Biden Amendment limited their authority to require busing as a condition for receiving federal funds. They insisted that, as much as they might have liked to move more aggressively to enforce Title VI, they were precluded from doing so by the strictures of the amendment. Yet, had that congressional obstacle disappeared, OCR's requirements on busing would probably not have changed. No president would long tolerate OCR's ordering busing as a condition for the receipt of federal funds. However, the Eagleton-Biden Amendment was a shield enabling OCR enforcers to insist that the law prevented them from even considering the option.

In sum, those subject to a politically controversial civil rights law may find it easier to comply with the law when they can contend that, although they might personally prefer to do otherwise, they have no choice but to adhere to the requirements of "the law." Similarly, those enforcing such a law often characterize their demands as the direct outgrowth of specific and authoritative legal requirements over which they, too, have no control. By maintaining that their decisions derive not from personal preferences but from the clear and binding commands of the law, both those enforcing the law and those complying with it shield themselves against political attack.

Whereas the executive and judicial branches cooperated and shared the political burden in developing school desegregation standards during the Johnson administration, such cooperation did not continue into the Nixon era. During that period, the standards defining racial discrimination came almost entirely from the Supreme Court. Civil rights groups and career bureaucrats in OCR who were committed to equality for blacks used the decisions of the Court in *Alexander, Swann, Keyes,* and *Green* as leverage to compel the agency to enforce Title VI in an increasingly hostile national political climate and in a presidential administration disinclined to enforce the provision. In the Supreme Court's decision in *Fordice,* we also saw the opposite of what occurred during the Johnson period. Rather than support and reinforce the standards that Congress and the executive branch had developed for dealing with historically black colleges and universities, the Court disregarded the policies of other branches and advanced its own standards.

The political problems associated with developing clear standards for Title VI are especially thorny in desegregation in higher education. Considerable uncertainty remains about how courts will determine when a state's funding of historically black colleges or its designated educational missions for them constitute a violation of Title VI. In addition, where a court determines that unlawful racial segregation exists on a campus, there may be much uncertainty about the standards to use in determining the precise level of racial integration required as a remedy.

In all but the most blatant violations of Title VI, therefore, there is inescapable discretion in determining both whether a violation exists, and which of a range of possible remedial actions meets the legal requirements of the provision. Such discretion is not conducive to strong enforcement, because the more discretion bureaucrats have, the more likely it is that political considerations will be introduced by OCR, educational institutions, congressional representatives, the White House, interest groups, or some combination of the above. In these discretionary and politicized contexts, the preferences of racial minorities are compromised because discretionary administrative choices almost always come down on the side of those with greater political power.

The HEW Guidelines in the 1960s were effective, in part, because they required remedial measures that were quantifiable. Similarly, the time frames in the *Adams* case were workable and enforceable because they, too, were quantifiable. Quantifiable standards are easier to enforce because there is little or no discretion in determining whether or not their requirements have been met. A "politicized" enforcement decision is, therefore, less likely to result. Because of the politically charged character of the legal rights protected by Title VI, and because it is difficult to define racial discrimination in the first place, in situations where quantifiable standards are not readily applicable the bench and the bureaucracy alike are apt to produce flexible and ambiguous standards that resolve little and that often do not address central issues.

Clear Standards: The Intellectual Dilemmas. What practices and behaviors should be defined as constituting illegal discrimination in educational institutions under Title VI? What are the "legal rights" protected by Title VI in schools receiving federal aid? These questions raise formidable intellectual and philosophical dilemmas, and liberals have been afraid to acknowledge that. They fear that admitting these difficulties would embolden conservative critics and undermine civil rights protections. Though that fear is understandable, it reflects an unacceptable failure of nerve, will, and intellect. Dilemmas do exist in defining rights and remedying racial discrimination in schools, and those dilemmas do raise legitimate, vexing problems — problems that compound the political quandaries analyzed in the preceding section and that highlight the limitations of a strategy that seeks to achieve equal educational opportunity by relying on "legal rights."

Devising standards for Title VI became much more difficult once de jure segregation in elementary and secondary schools in the South ended. There were advantages to applying Title VI against the "old" South. Because de jure discrimination was explicitly written into law, it was there for all to see and could be attacked with compelling argumentation buttressed by easily marshalled evidence. Moreover, as noted, by the mid-1960s a national consensus had developed demanding an end to that kind of segregation. In the 1970s and 1980s, by contrast, racial discrimination occurred in educational institutions and elsewhere in a less formal and explicit way. Accordingly, how one measured and remedied that discrimination became much less self-evident. Indeed, it became quite complicated.

The racial discrimination in schools today, even where discrimination is pervasive and its effects are obvious, is more subtle and sophisticated in its origins, structure, and operation than the discrimination fought in the 1960s and early 1970s. Consequently, the legal rights and remedies used to combat that discrimination are often perceived as intellectually, politically, and legally less defensible. For instance, the standards for determining what constitutes illegal de facto segregation in the North are much less clear than the criteria for identifying de jure segregation in the South. The evidentiary burden is much greater and more complex, both for the lawyers who bring the cases and the judges who decide them.

Attorneys and judges may have to examine the minutes of meetings of school boards, statements by board members or school administrators, the selection of sites for public housing, and the historical pattern of school construction, attendance zones, and residential segregation. They must then make inferences about the link between those factors and segregation in schools. Moreover, such "second generation" problems as racially discriminatory disciplinary practices, disproportionate assignment of minorities to special education and vocational education classes, racially biased competency testing, and other subtle forms of discrimination within the school and classroom are even less amenable to redress through the application of ideas about legal rights. Even more difficult problems arise in trying to develop ways of identifying and measuring the "discrimination" that occurs when teachers are uncomfortable with black students, view them as unable to learn, and expect them to fail and treat them accordingly.[8] How does one deal with that kind of insidious problem occurring one-on-one inside classrooms? The answer is that no system of legal rights and remedies can deal with these issues in a meaningful way, and that thinking of these problems as involving violations of "legal rights" does not take us very far in either understanding or resolving them. The intellectual problems of articulating standards of legal rights and remedies in desegregation in higher education are no less vexing.

Part of the predicament in higher education, both for Judge Pratt and for OCR, involved the issue analyzed in the preceding section of this chapter. The subject matter was so politically charged that it became politically unrewarding, if not dangerous, to develop clear, straightforward, easy-to-understand enforcement standards about legal rights and remedies. However, there were also bona fide intellectual obstacles to progress: In states where blacks had been historically excluded from the mainstream state university and consigned to separate black colleges, exactly what legal rights did they have under Title VI and the Fourteenth Amendment? Was there a legal right protecting the continued existence of black institutions, or ensuring that blacks could attend, or be given preference in admission to, the traditionally white institutions? Did the states have an obligation to compensate for past discrimination against black individuals by enhancing black institutions? How did desegregation in higher education relate to the goals in and the holding of *Brown v. Board of Education?*

In truth, there wasn't much clarity about what the law required, what the ultimate objective of desegregation in higher education was, and how one measured when a state university system, once segregated by law, had met its legal obligations in the post-*Brown* era. The Supreme Court's decision in *Fordice* did little to change that uncertainty. Quantitative standards based on the need to alter the racial composition of student bodies, while perhaps one element of a plan, address only part of the problem. In recognizing that desegregation in higher education raised a tangle of legal, educational, and philosophical problems about the "legal rights" to be protected, I do not mean to suggest that the task was impossible or ought not to have been attempted. Rather, I mean only to insist that in this area there are bedeviling uncertainties about what the appropriate legal rights should be.

The issue of racial discrimination at the elementary and secondary school level has centered on what I call racial body counts. That concern focuses on the disproportion between the racial breakdown of a school's student body and the racial breakdown of students across the school district. *Swann* established that criterion. Although the Court ruled that "[t]he constitutional command to desegregate schools does not mean that every school in every community must always reflect the racial composition of the school system as a whole," racial ratios were "a useful starting point in shaping a remedy to correct past constitutional violations." Conceiving of racial discrimination as being primarily reflected in the racial composition of schools, the Court ruled that "the need for remedial criteria of sufficient specificity . . . warrants a presumption against schools that are substantially disproportionate in their racial composition."[9] Consequently, moving students from one school to another to rectify such racial disproportions has a long tradition in desegregation at the elementary and secondary school levels and eventually became the primary criterion by which the federal government measured racial discrimination in schools.

It is certainly legitimate to consider racial segregation when measuring illegal discrimination in public schools. Yet racial separation in schools is only one manifestation of racial discrimination, albeit an important one. Focusing on racial body counts to measure and remedy discrimination may well conceal other kinds of racial discrimination, such as the subtle and insidious inequalities produced by the "second generation" problems of racial discrimination alluded to earlier. Ultimately, a law such as Title VI must address not merely the physical intermingling of the races but also the comparability of the public educational services provided to the two races. In other words, the quality and character of the public education provided to black and white children ought to be the central concern of those charged with achieving what *Brown v. Board* mandated — equal educational opportunity. Yet it never has been.

Given that federal funds underwrite public school systems across the nation, in order to enforce Title VI one must ask, how does the education delivered to black children compare with the education delivered to white children throughout our federally subsidized public educational establishment? To address that issue, it is necessary to answer two prior questions. First, what are the goals of public education in elementary and secondary schools? And second, how can the federal government measure the relative degree to which those goals have been achieved in any specific context for both white and black school populations? In short, before one can determine whether our school systems are discriminating on the basis of race, it is necessary to establish the purpose of their service and the way in which one could measure and compare the quality of the service provided to white and black students. The most conventional way of "measuring" the quality of the education a child receives is to use standardized achievement tests to assess the skills the student has mastered, an approach full of pitfalls because using such tests to evaluate educational achievement has itself come under attack as racially discriminatory. However, even if one were to accept performance on such tests as a valid indicator of educational attainment by black and white children, other problems remain.

The single best predictor of academic performance in school and on standardized tests is the socioeconomic status of a child's family. Therefore, even if school systems provided equal educational services to all black and white children, we would still see marked racial distinctions in educational achievement because of the generally lower socioeconomic status of black families. The great difficulty, of course, is that to achieve nondiscriminatory results in conventional educational achievement and to equalize educational opportunities, disproportionately greater attention and resources need to be given to children — white as well as black — of low socioeconomic origins.* In other words, to achieve greater equality in academic achievement and educational opportunity, we apparently need to make unequal efforts in providing educational services to different social and economic classes.[10] In light of that reality, the questions we face in devising federal civil rights policies to achieve those goals become treacherously difficult — both at the philosophical and pragmatic levels.

What are the formulas, standards, or criteria by which the federal government should insist that local school systems redistribute public educational resources to "correct" for the discriminatory educational results and opportunities produced by socioeconomic inequalities among the families of public school children? I suspect that most of us would rather not deal with that question. So, too, has it been with the courts and OCR. The dilemmas associated with defining and measuring "discrimination" in education explain, in part, why both courts and OCR have preferred to focus on standards and goals involving racial body counts. Such standards are, if nothing else, reducible to statistical measurement. Quite predictably, the bench and the bureaucracy prefer to resolve the dilemma in this manner. Perhaps one cannot blame them. But the distortion and confusion that this simple fix has produced in our definitions of and remedies for racial discrimination and our ideas about the legal rights of blacks in educational institutions have left a dubious legacy.

Part of the problem is that we are too predisposed to analyze how the educational system serves or disserves blacks by examining the issues through the lens of the law. That predisposition causes us to define and analyze the issues in terms of narrow legal questions focusing on legal rights. Title VI is a good example of that predisposition. It asks, does the school or school district receiving federal funds engage in racial discrimination? The operative legal right is the right to attend an institution that does not "discriminate." To pose the problem in those terms limits our understanding of how and why schools fail black children, and of what can and should be done about that.

---

*Of course, precisely the opposite of that occurs in suburban public schools and elite private schools, where better services are provided to the children of wealthy families, thereby increasing the advantage those children already enjoy.

The initial and critical error is trying to conceive of the underlying problem in terms of a legal right — in terms of a concept such as "racial discrimination." Because Title VI, along with the rest of the 1964 Civil Rights Act, was a dramatic legal reform, its meaning and effect, not surprisingly, have been determined by lawyers, judges, and litigation. Enacting the provision, defining its thrust in terms of racial discrimination, and then litigating about its meaning and enforcement presume a confidence in the capacity of the legal system to identify the problems and remedy the plight of blacks in schools.

"Racial discrimination" is too limited and brittle a concept through which to understand why and how schools fail black children, and litigation is too clumsy and confining a process through which to understand and remedy that problem. In sum, civil rights laws, law enforcement, legal rights, and litigation may be ill suited for the task of restructuring our educational system so that it functions more effectively and fairly for African Americans.

On matters of race and education we have routinely come to rely on laws, law enforcement, and litigation to resolve problems perhaps better dealt with by other means. Indeed, in the nearly three decades since Congress enacted Title VI, legal reforms and litigation have become increasingly futile, irrelevant, and symbolic surrogates for real solutions to our racial problems — in schools and elsewhere. Yet, we persist in treating so many educational issues affecting black students as legal questions.

I have described dilemmas in measuring racial discrimination in schools and have emphasized the limits of legal reforms because I believe that we need to recognize that simple, quantitative, easily applied, and compellingly persuasive legal standards for measuring discrimination, under Title VI or the Constitution, rarely exist. One of the curses of American racism is that it is by no means clear how, even in an ideal world, we ought to proceed to eradicate it from our national life. The dilemmas confronted in defining and applying the legal rights protected by Title VI illustrate that point.

POLITICAL FACTORS IN TITLE VI ENFORCEMENT

Administrative Enforcement of Title VI

Although there may be disagreement about the standards for measuring illegal discrimination in schools, there is little uncertainty about the functional advantages of fighting such discrimination by administrative action rather than litigation. A federal agency such as the Office for Civil Rights has capacities that are better suited than those of federal courts to the task of combating racial discrimination in American schools. The large number of institutions to be monitored, the voluminous information about recipients that has to be collected and analyzed, the need for systematic monitoring of recipients, the national standards to be developed and enforced — all of these characteristics of the tasks to be performed highlight the functional advantages of trying to accomplish the job through the actions of a federal agency.

Most of the career bureaucrats in OCR are committed to governmental efforts to improve the lot of African Americans. There is some camaraderie between OCR career personnel and civil rights activists. Both appreciate the political weakness from which they operate and the extent to which they need each other's support. Vigorous enforcement of a powerful and controversial civil rights provision such as Title VI is a political liability to any presidential administration. Those arguing for strong enforcement, both within government and outside it, do not argue from a position of political strength. By cooperating with one another they can bolster their weak positions. To the extent that OCR personnel received encouragement and support from civil rights lawyers at critical junctures, that support buoyed the spirits and sustained the efforts of many career employees within the civil rights unit. This was especially true during the Nixon period. Even though civil rights groups criticized the Nixon administration's policies, they recognized that many line personnel in OCR opposed those policies and were themselves exasperated by them.

Notwithstanding such cooperation, the relationship between career civil rights officials and outside activists is typically adversarial. Career personnel in OCR insist that they are committed to civil rights enforcement. Activists outside the agency, however, are as a matter of course critical of their work. The civil servants do work within a constraining political environment. They must walk a tightrope reconciling — or at least attempting to reconcile — divergent demands. They must enforce Title VI in a way that pleases the White House, minimizes battles with members of Congress, and satisfies political appointees in the Office of the Secretary. In addition, OCR officials face the competing claims of the numerous civil rights groups that press the agency and vie for its resources and attention. These political limitations make it frustrating for civil rights activists to work in OCR. One gets the sense that career people at OCR would like to say to civil rights advocates on the outside, "We, too, believe in civil rights or we wouldn't be here. We, too, want effective enforcement, but things are not as easy or as simple as you folks on the outside would believe. We simply can't do what you insist we do. Give us more time. Be patient. Trust us."

The President, Congress, and the Enforcement of Title VI

More than any other person, the president sets the nation's agenda, establishing the priorities of the executive branch and determining the importance attached to civil rights enforcement. Presidents who have wanted to control the overall direction of Title VI enforcement have been able to do so. However, an administration's political calculations about Title VI operate against an important backdrop. Racial issues are especially sensitive political matters for any president; and since *Brown v. Board,* racial discrimination in educational institutions has consistently been at the core of America's racial controversies. The volatility and durability of that issue has meant that any president must be acutely conscious of the political ramifications of his Title VI policies. In addition, Title VI threatens, at least theoretically, that federal funds may be withheld, and presidents, like other politicians, win friends and elections by disbursing monies, not withholding them. These responsibilities and powers make OCR one of a handful of agencies whose work is always politically sensitive.

Congress has influenced the enforcement of Title VI most significantly by passing legislation limiting the desegregation remedies that OCR could require as a condition for receiving federal funds. The most powerful congressional restriction on OCR's enforcement of Title VI has been the Eagleton-Biden Amendment prohibiting OCR from requiring busing beyond the school nearest a student's home. This amendment crippled OCR in dealing with student assignment problems in cities because typically, where there are segregated schools in cities, the only effective means to achieve integration is by busing. Because of the prohibition in the Eagleton-Biden Amendment, when OCR finds such violations its only option is to refer the case to the Justice Department for prosecution of the school district in federal court. As noted, there are no limits as to how long the Justice Department may take in deciding what enforcement action to initiate, if any, after receiving a referral from OCR. The litigation approach that Eagleton-Biden compelled was ironic because Title VI was passed out of recognition that desegregating schools through litigation had proven impractical and that administrative enforcement of school desegregation would be more effective.

Not surprisingly, civil rights lawyers tried to use litigation to counteract the Eagleton-Biden Amendment. In a decision upholding the constitutionality of the statute, the U.S. Circuit Court of Appeals for the District of Columbia held that the law was not unconstitutional because, though it precluded OCR from enforcing statutory and constitutional rights, it left open the opportunity to enforce those rights through referral to the Justice Department.[11] Attorneys active in Title VI litigation believed that they might be able to demonstrate that, in practice, referrals by OCR to the Justice Department were ineffectual because of the department's unwillingness to act promptly and vigorously on those referrals. They speculated on how, if they were armed with documentation to that effect, they might be able to obtain a court order either declaring the Eagleton-Biden Amendment unconstitutional as applied, or ordering the Justice Department to litigate specific Title VI cases referred to it. Though they never attempted to get such an order, their discussions about trying to do so illustrate the persistent efforts to explore how litigation could be used, even in the most extreme cases, to control the discretion of those enforcing Title VI.

The Courts and the Enforcement of Title VI

In each presidential administration since the passage of Title VI, the courts have shaped the enforcement of the statute. During the Johnson years, federal courts legitimated HEW's desegregation Guidelines and pushed beyond them in faculty desegregation and freedom of choice. Those judicial victories, in turn, emboldened HEW to advance even more demanding Title VI standards. During the Nixon administration, Supreme Court decisions in *Alexander, Swann, Keyes,* and *Milliken* set the basic constitutional doctrine under which HEW could proceed. In the Carter years, the *Dayton* and *Columbus* cases offered new guides for school desegregation,[12] and during the Reagan era *Grove City College* limited the scope of Title VI and other civil rights laws.

Beyond the constitutional litigation, the most enduring legal challenge to the enforcement of Title VI came, of course, in the *Adams* litigation. That case ushered in a new era and a new relationship between OCR and the courts. Consider the different role played by courts with respect to standards for Title VI in the Johnson and Carter administrations. During the Johnson years, the courts were deeply involved in developing substantive standards to be applied by HEW. In the Carter and Reagan eras, both the civil rights plaintiffs and the federal judges in *Adams* scrupulously avoided involving the courts in the development of substantive standards for Title VI. To be sure, *Adams* did have a sprawling and enormous effect—especially on the management of OCR.

In *Adams,* civil rights lawyers tried to use litigation to insulate Title VI from politically inspired efforts to negate the provision. The litigators were imaginative and relentless. As advocates, they were indefatigable. The litigation they mounted was historic, surviving over the course of some twenty years. Yet, at best, the results were mixed—successful in minor respects, but disappointing in major ways.

Virtually all of the litigation in *Adams* was procedural in nature. The closest that a decision came to even the remotest consideration of substantive standards was in the portion of the litigation dealing with higher education, and there the involvement in substantive standards was indirect. Rather than developing desegregation standards himself, Judge Pratt ordered HEW to do so. This shift—from substantive judicial guidance in the enforcement of Title VI in the 1960s, to an almost exclusively procedural intervention in the 1970s and 1980s—constituted a significant change in the way courts influenced those enforcing Title VI. Among other things, it placed upon OCR alone the political burden of developing Title VI standards in the volatile area of desegregation in higher education.

Bureaucratic and presidential politics guarantee that, left to its own devices and barring extraordinary circumstances, no federal agency will advance and enforce firm standards combating racial discrimination in schools. Federal courts must be enlisted to prod OCR to enforce Title VI. Yet, civil rights lawyers did not ask Judge Pratt to intervene substantively, for they believed, quite rightly, that he was loath to dictate substantive standards to OCR defining what Title VI required. Rather, the *Adams* litigation concentrated almost exclusively on procedural protections and reform. Not surprisingly, therefore, its primary impact was to produce a better-organized, more efficiently administered agency.[13] Judicial insistence on procedural regularity is doubtless important, and to the degree that *Adams* achieved greater procedural fairness in civil rights enforcement, that should not be minimized. After *Adams,* it was easier, for instance, for OCR itself and others to know exactly what the agency was doing, and where, when, and to whom it was being done.

Though the U.S. Commission on Civil Rights called *Adams* "a milestone in desegregation law," and the *Washington Post* observed that it was "a case study on how a lawsuit can drive the federal government," the end result of the reforms produced by the litigation is disappointing.[14] The litigation achieved a managerial and procedural regularity that enshrined a substantive inequality. That was an insidious result — insidious because the legal "victories" misdirected attention from the central problems of educational inequality in American life and offered instead an illusory sense of progress in the struggle against that inequality.

The injustice that black children experience in the federal government's subsidization of the nation's educational system is hardly a procedural injustice. It is substantive. It speaks to the role that public educational institutions, among others, play in failing to meet the needs of the African American community, thereby keeping that community in an inferior and disadvantaged condition. It is the gross inadequacy in the substance, quality, character, and end results of the public education provided to the mass of black children that constitutes the central injustice to which they are subjected. The public educational system in this country, underwritten by prodigious amounts of federal funding, fails black people by any conventional measure one might use. That failure is the profound *substantive* injustice that exists and is the "discrimination"— if one must use that word — on which OCR officials and civil rights lawyers ought to focus their efforts.

I am not suggesting that it would be easy or inexpensive to rectify the inequalities that exist in our educational system or that, even if we had the will, commitment, and resources to do so, we would necessarily know how best to achieve that goal. The problems confronted in educating large numbers of poor African American children, especially in our nation's cities, pose challenges of the first magnitude. Yet, it must be conceded that we are failing, that little has been done effectively at the national level to address the issue, and that despite ceaseless legal initiatives of heroic proportions by dedicated and resourceful people, the courts and civil rights lawyers have been largely helpless to rectify the situation.

I RESPECT and admire the lawyers who brought the litigation I have analyzed. To a person, they strike me as creative and committed men and women motivated by the loftiest of goals. Yet, I cannot help but wonder whether twenty years of litigation in *Adams* and thousands of hours spent by organizational officials, private and government lawyers, and federal judges provided a return commensurate with the resources expended. Nor can we look to civil rights lawyers to answer that question, for as Derrick Bell has commented, "it's difficult for any civil rights lawyer . . . to be objective about the worth of litigation in bringing about racial reform."[15]

Civil rights lawyers do what they know how to do — they litigate.

That ability gives them a place and power in a social movement and a way to serve that movement. Thurgood Marshall is an American hero because of what he was able to do through the courageous, persistent, and creative use of his skills as a civil rights lawyer. Marshall's tradition is a rich one, with much allure for those who followed him. There is a kind of "high" that one gets in engaging in civil rights litigation — in using one's professional skills tenaciously, combatively, and masterfully in pursuit of the highest and most laudable goals. Civil rights lawyers do not merely have a job — they have a calling. For the American liberal community since *Brown v. Board,* the civil rights lawyer has been the contemporary manifestation of the medieval knight-errant, wandering the land in the service of a noble cause, confronting historic challenges to advance lofty goals, exhibiting professional skills and commitment in a kind of combat, and doing good by vanquishing evil. As commendable a role as this may be, however, objective evaluation of the civil rights litigation involving Title VI suggests the need to reconsider the liberal love affair with civil rights laws and litigation.

The history of Title VI should caution us about the limits of law and litigation. Those involved in the sprawling litigation over Title VI were engaged in a political battle to control the fate of a powerful civil rights provision. The litigation was long-lived, the combatants tireless, and the judiciary's involvement extensive. However, in retrospect the litigation offered few options for remedying educational inequality and limited our thinking about what should be done to make schools better serve African Americans. The irony is that the "success" of civil rights legislation and litigation is used as evidence that there is less need for continuing efforts to redress racial injustices, and even more insidiously, as evidence that the continuing plight of blacks derives primarily from their own failings. By offering the appearance, symbolism, and rhetoric of equality, the most important contemporary function of a civil rights protection such as Title VI is to legitimate and further entrench the inequality in educational opportunity that exists. That inequality, of course, perpetuates the subordination of black Americans. My reservations about using Title VI litigation to attack educational inequalities are only reinforced when one examines the other legal track for remedying educational inequalities for blacks — constitutional litigation to enforce the protections in the Fourteenth Amendment.

As I noted in chapter 1, the struggle in the twentieth century to combat racial discrimination in schools grew out of deliberate attempts by whites to limit the educational opportunities provided to blacks. Hence, in its origins, the constitutional assault on racial discrimination in schools in this century concentrated on the inadequate quality of education provided to African Americans. That legal battle was part of a larger political struggle, dating back to the end of the eighteenth century, to provide greater educational opportunities to African Americans. Both the courts and civil rights litigators lost sight of the focus on educational opportunity and quality in enforcing the two greatest legal victories in that struggle — that is, *Brown v. Board* and Title VI. Instead, in working to implement those legal landmarks, both courts and litigators assumed that merely eliminating the barriers that segregated students in schools would equalize educational opportunity. That proved to be a simpleminded and fatally flawed assumption.

The first formal efforts to educate blacks began with antislavery societies during the Revolutionary period. By the end of the eighteenth century, through churches and mutual aid organizations, free blacks operated their own schools in some cities.[16] In the South, of course, it was a crime to teach a slave to read or write. Educated slaves, whites correctly assumed, would be dangerous slaves. After the Civil War, however, blacks fought in every southern state to establish public schools. During its brief existence, the ill-fated Freedman's Bureau, for example, founded more than four thousand schools.[17] Yet, when southern states instituted public education, they offered only circumscribed educational opportunities for blacks — opportunities intended to provide blacks with limited skills appropriate to the limited roles to which whites consigned them. By 1910 only one of every twelve blacks of high-school age in the South was enrolled in school.[18]

The most profound struggle over the education of blacks involved the efforts of black educators, in publicly supported black colleges, to offer a bona fide collegiate education. That struggle pitted black educators against state legislatures intent on keeping the black colleges little more than vocational schools or glorified high schools. Hence, the legal attack against discrimination in educational institutions in the twentieth century is best understood as a continuation of the enduring, historic struggle by blacks to fight against inferior educational systems that limited their economic horizons, political power, and life opportunities. Stated otherwise, blacks' centuries-old struggle for access to education was a crusade for black access to the power and privileges that came with education. It was not, at least not until the late 1960s, a struggle about desegregating schools.

Unequal treatment in schools was qualitatively different from unequal treatment or segregation in transportation, movie theaters, restaurants, restrooms, and other public facilities. Denying blacks access to education was more pivotal in perpetuating their subordination. In light of these considerations, it is not surprising that the early legal attacks in this century on discrimination in schools focused on the quality of the educational opportunities provided to blacks. It is crucial to understand how those legal initiatives in the first half of this century differed from the initiatives since *Brown v. Board* and under Title VI.

In *Brown v. Board* and the major cases that preceded it, equal opportunity for an education was the objective that blacks sought and that the Supreme Court required. The Court recognized that equal access to educational opportunities, irrespective of race, was important because of the contribution that public education made to the collective life of the nation and because of its impact on the life opportunities of individuals. Therefore, *Brown v. Board* and the pre-*Brown* cases stressed not segregation, but the injury resulting from being denied an opportunity to receive an equal education. To document that point, the pre-*Brown* cases, dealing exclusively with higher education, are discussed briefly below.

In 1938, in *State of Missouri ex rel. Gaines v. Canada,*[19] Missouri refused to admit Gaines, a black man, to its state law school, arguing that it had fulfilled its constitutional obligation by arranging for Gaines to attend law school out-of-state. Rejecting that argument, the Supreme Court characterized attendance at law school as an educational opportunity and ruled that the state violated the constitutional requirement of equal protection when blacks had to travel out-of-state to enjoy an educational opportunity provided to whites in-state.[20] In 1948, when Oklahoma denied a black person admission to its state law school solely on account of race, the Court rejected Oklahoma's action and again couched its ruling in terms of equal access to public education.[21] Two years later, in *Sweatt v. Painter* and *McLaurin v. Oklahoma,*[22] the Court continued its emphasis on equality of educational services and opportunities. In the former case, the Court ruled that Texas had denied Sweatt a "legal education equivalent to that offered . . . to students of other races" because the University of Texas Law School for whites surpassed the newly created law school for blacks, as measured by the size and quality of the faculty, the size of the library, the experience of administrators, the influence of alumni, the variety of course offerings, and the school's standing and prestige.[23]

That segregation denied blacks educational and professional opportunities was even more central in *McLaurin,* where the University of Oklahoma admitted McLaurin to its doctoral program in education but compelled him to sit apart at a designated desk in the library and in an anteroom outside the classroom, and to eat in the cafeteria at a different time from the other students.[24] Striking these requirements, the Court held that they "handicapped" McLaurin by "impair[ing] and inhibit[ing] his ability to study, to engage in discussions and exchange views with other students, and, in general, to learn his profession."[25]

The underlying constitutional injury recognized in *McLaurin* and *Sweatt* was not the state's attempt to "segregate" the black men who brought those cases. Rather, it was that through segregation the state ensured that their educational opportunities would be diminished and thus unequal to those provided to whites. The wrong was the effect that racial segregation had on the plaintiffs' educational experiences. The injury was what racial segregation produced, and not the segregation itself. Segregation was a method, only one among many, used by states to achieve an unlawful end—the denial of equal educational opportunities because of race. Inadequate funding for black schools, for example, was another method used to accomplish that same goal.

Building on its reasoning in *Sweatt* and *McLaurin,* the Court expressly founded its decision in *Brown v. Board* on the constitutional right to equal educational opportunity. In no less than five places in that opinion, the Court referred to the concept of equalizing educational opportunity. First, it stated that *Sweatt* stood for the proposition that "segregated law schools for Negroes could not provide them *equal educational opportunities.*"[26] Second, it declared that segregation at the elementary and secondary school levels had an adverse effect on *"educational opportunities."*[27] Third, the Court approvingly cited the finding by the district court in the Delaware case, one of five consolidated for review in *Brown v. Board,* that "state-imposed segregation . . . results in Negro children, as a class, receiving *educational opportunities* which are substantially inferior to those available to white children."[28]

In its fourth reference to equal educational opportunity, the Court stated that the central constitutional question in the entire case turned on that very concept:

We come then to the question presented: Does the segregation of children in public schools solely on the basis of race, even though the physical facilities and other "tangible" factors may be equal, deprive the children of the minority group of equal educational opportunities? We believe it does.[29]

It was no accident that the Court's most historic attack on racial discrimination targeted unequal treatment in schools. In its fifth and final reference to educational opportunity, noted previously in chapter 7, on *Fordice,* the Court explained why racial discrimination in schools was so unacceptable:

Today, education is perhaps the most important function of state and local governments. . . . *[I]t is doubtful that any child may reasonably be expected to succeed in life if he is denied the opportunity of an education. Such an opportunity, where the state has undertaken to provide it, is a right which must be made available to all on equal terms.*[30]

Relying on its rulings in *Gaines, McLaurin,* and *Sweatt, Brown v. Board* established the state's constitutional obligation to equalize educational opportunities between blacks and whites. Moreover, the Court's reasons for recognizing that obligation were scarcely insignificant, as the Court made it unmistakable that in its view, education provided a critical foundation for black and white children alike, profoundly affecting a child's sense of self and life opportunities. In *Brown v. Board,* the Court confirmed what those who had deliberately denied educational opportunities to African Americans had known for generations: Education is a powerful weapon. Armed with that weapon, educated people have a far better chance to carve out successful lives and to provide for and protect themselves and their families. That is what makes a good education so potent and so potentially dangerous. That is why some would deliberately deny it to others.

Insisting that the state must equalize opportunities for its citizens is a powerful theme in American political history, dating at least to the ideology that animated the Jacksonian reforms in the 1820s and 1830s and later spawned the crusade for free, tax-supported public education. Yet, *Brown v. Board* added a new dimension to the struggle for equal educational opportunity for blacks. Until that decision, in both the North and the South, education for blacks and whites, with rare exceptions, was segregated. In *Brown v. Board,* the Court declared, for the first time, that segregation itself was an evil — indeed, that separate educational facilities were "inherently unequal."[31]

Hence, under the reasoning in *Brown v. Board,* if equal educational opportunity was to be achieved, segregation had to end. This new proposition changed the course and direction of future legal action, both in constitutional litigation and in the enforcement of Title VI. It produced a new word, *desegregation,* a word not used in the pre-*Brown* cases. It also produced a legal and political controversy about the measures that school systems had to take to "desegregate" and thereby comply with *Brown.* [32] In the face of the difficulties associated with implementing *Brown,* the courts, civil rights lawyers, and those enforcing Title VI searched for objective and easy-to-measure standards for overcoming southern resistance and evaluating progress in doing so. In that struggle, HEW's Title VI Guidelines were of historic significance.

The Guidelines advanced a new understanding of how to measure success in realizing the aims of *Brown v. Board.* Building on the rationale and objectives in the Guidelines, subsequent Supreme Court cases imposed an affirmative obligation upon school districts to integrate schools. The phrase "educational opportunity" does not appear in *Green, Alexander,* or *Swann,* nor, for that matter, do the opinions reflect any concern for the quality or character of the education provided to black children, other than ensuring that the districts put them in schools with whites.

The HEW Guidelines, and the judicial validation of the approach they employed, instituted a profound policy transformation. In the Guidelines, and especially in the *Green* decision, the federal government sought to realize the goal of equalizing educational opportunity by playing a racial numbers game — a game whose basic object was distributing black and white students randomly throughout the school buildings of a system. After the Guidelines and the cases confirming their approach, there was no longer much concern in the legal process for the quality or character of the education provided to blacks — for the value of the education imparted to them, as measured by enhanced life opportunities or contributions to the nation. Instead, the focus was on the need to mix students in the schools on the basis of their skin color.

Realizing the vision of *Brown v. Board* became defined, almost exclusively, as the achievement of integrated student bodies in schools (what critics pejoratively called "racial balancing"), and the elimination of the administrative structures that, before *Brown,* had kept students segregated. Achieving the appropriate black-to-white student ratio became the ultimate — and really the *only* — objective under the Constitution and Title VI. Equal educational opportunity for black children — a meaningful chance to obtain the skills, training, and preparation that schools supposedly offered — was no longer the objective or the legal right to be realized, and was seldom even discussed. The struggle to enforce Title VI had transformed the objective of the long battle to provide black Americans access to education and the opportunities and power it brought. The ultimate bankruptcy of this momentous policy shift was evident in 1974 in *Milliken v. Bradley*.[33]

Milliken, the death knell for urban desegregation, legitimated the racial divide between city and suburb discussed earlier in this book. By 1974, a majority of the nation's black children attended schools in the large urban systems, where there were fewer and fewer white children.[34] *Milliken* meant that even the limited goal that had evolved as the hallmark of *Brown v. Board* — the balancing of the races in schools — would not be achieved in America's great metropolitan areas. If the command of *Brown v. Board* had been transformed to require racial body counts so that school systems sprinkled black and white students throughout school districts, after *Milliken* that sprinkling would not extend beyond the city's boundaries but would be limited to the city proper, with the bodies to be drawn only from the city. *Milliken* blessed the suburbs and their schools with the constitutional protection they needed to continue to function as safe havens from the people and problems of cities. Suburban school districts could continue to operate, insulated from the poorer and blacker central city systems they surrounded. More than ever, after *Milliken*, the suburbs took on the function and character of walled-off, white middle-class citadels.

The history of the constitutional litigation seeking to enforce *Brown v. Board* and the history of the litigation seeking to enforce Title VI are strikingly comparable. In each case, the litigation became misdirected, losing sight of the educational objectives that were its original goal. In the litigation over Title VI, there was little attempt to understand how and why educational institutions, at all levels, underwritten by federal dollars, failed to educate blacks in such large numbers and with such depressing and predictable regularity. Instead, that litigation focused on ensuring that a routinized set of procedures existed for investigating complaints of racial discrimination. In the constitutional litigation, the Court decided to measure success in the fight against racial discrimination by counting the distribution of children by race throughout a school system, rather than by evaluating the skills, services, and training that schools provided to black children.

School desegregation litigation under the Constitution and the effort to enforce Title VI were part of a struggle to use legal reform and rights to alter the power relationship between blacks and whites by achieving greater racial fairness in access to education and to the life opportunities that education provides. Unable to provide much more than marginal changes in that access, the law, perhaps inevitably, retreated into a formalism of rights, in which both the jurisprudence and the legal rights were empty of much real meaning.

After the passage of Title VI, it was only in the litigation over desegregation in higher education that educational issues remained — for a time — the focus of attention. Therein, of course, lay the promise and hope of that litigation. However, when the Court had a chance in *Fordice* to address the issues of unequal access to public higher education and of the future role of historically black colleges, it failed conspicuously to do so. Instead, it issued an opinion focused not on educational issues but on "free choice" and racial desegregation — an approach that paralleled the limited range of its concerns in desegregation in elementary and secondary schools.

The history of the efforts to use litigation to achieve equal educational opportunity teaches that when a social problem is addressed through litigation, lawyers and judges redefine the terms of debate about the problem, and nonlawyers lose control over the resulting public discourse. Those outside the legal system lose the power to frame the questions asked about the problem and to provide the analytical framework for understanding and remedying it. In that way, litigation can deflect attention away from the root causes and problems that prompted the litigation and motivated the resort to the law in the first place.

In first denying blacks access to education altogether and later providing them with inferior education, the nation circumscribed their place in society and their contributions to it. Historically, those educational policies enabled whites to control blacks and to limit their ability to compete with whites in the labor force. Restructuring American schools so that educational achievement and opportunity no longer correlated with race was never likely to be achieved easily, quickly, or cheaply. It required nothing short of a social revolution. Indeed, the Court was correct in *Brown v. Board* when it concluded that educational opportunity and achievement are the key to the good life in America — the critical ingredient for success in the job market, access to the professions, and full participation as a citizen. No court, whatever its personnel, level of commitment, or politics, could have accomplished that goal alone. The effort to achieve that magnitude of change, primarily through legal reform, was doomed from the outset. And so the Court and those enforcing Title VI settled for what they could get. They dismantled the system of legally enforced racial separation in southern schools and eliminated the most egregious manifestations of segregation that prevailed within the legal boundaries of northern cities. In achieving those more limited objectives, they altered the historic aims of the movement for racial equity in the American educational system.

The Overarching Political Context

Commitment to the goals of Title VI, whether on the part of bureaucrats, political appointees, congressional representatives, or presidents, does not occur in a social or political vacuum. It is an outgrowth of the national mood on racial questions and black-white relations. Though presidents, more than anyone else, set the tone and character of enforcement policies, they, too, are captives of the national political premises and preferences prevailing on issues of race. Similarly, the way in which OCR enforces Title VI necessarily reflects society's commitment to eradicating racial inequality in educational opportunity. Suffice it to say, if the Supreme Court, as Mr. Dooley observed, follows the election returns and hence the national mood, so, too, do those who enforce civil rights laws such as Title VI. There is ample discretion for those individuals, even after two decades of *Adams* litigation, to mold the agency's substantive decisions so that they reflect, or at least do not conflict with, the national political consensus on the question of racial inequality in schools.

I recall vividly the comments made by a senior administrator in OCR after I had turned my recorder off, thanked him for the interview, and started to exit his office. We were chatting about the differences between the Nixon and Carter administrations' enforcement of Title VI, and he explained that although he saw obvious differences in rhetoric, the enforcement record, in his view, was only marginally dissimilar. "The bottom line," he offered, "is that whites had gone about as far as they were going to go on racial questions." By the early 1980s, the dominant white society, he correctly intimated, had reached the limits of its willingness to attend to the problems of race in America. White America had grown unresponsive to the call for further reforms—reforms that many whites increasingly perceived, especially in the bitter disputes over affirmative action, might adversely impact their own educational and life opportunities.

It is this prior condition and political context, more than any other factor, that has determined the fate of Title VI and explains why its enforcement has languished and why civil rights lawyers have tried to resuscitate it through litigation. They have striven tirelessly but unsuccessfully to free Title VI from the political forces and constraints that have shackled it. Their failure is not surprising. Only a substantially altered national political climate and consensus could rescue the provision from the fate it has suffered.

Many analysts would contend that notwithstanding the political dangers, a president from the far left wing of the Democratic Party would choose to enforce Title VI so differently that impressive results would be achieved. In that view, the enforcement of Title VI would be markedly different in, let us say, the administration of a Pat Buchanan or of a Pat Robertson than it would be in the administration of a Ted Kennedy or a Jerry Brown. True enough, there would be differences. Yet, I maintain that the differences both in how the statute would be enforced and in its actual impact would be marginal. The analysis in this volume suggests that the range of options that can be considered and pursued by any American president in enforcing Title VI is narrow.

The striking thing about the historical record on Title VI is not how much administrations have differed from one another, but rather, how alike they have been and will likely continue to be. A fundamental insight is achieved by recognizing the limited degree to which either major political party, or any president of either party, might actually employ Title VI to ameliorate the conditions that afflict the mass of black students in the nation's educational system.

This analysis suggests that Title VI has become unenforceable for Republican and Democratic presidents alike. That means that the most important way in which political leaders influence the enforcement of Title VI is not by what they do, but by what they do not do, or believe that they dare not do. They dare not decide to discontinue using federal funds to underwrite the operation of largely separate and grossly unequal educational systems for the vast majority of white and black children. They dare not terminate funds in a serious and aggressive national effort to end racial inequality in educational opportunity.

CONCLUSION

Title VI was an unusual civil rights measure, in large part because it was a weapon of substantial potential power. The prohibition of discrimination, the federal subsidization of education at all levels, the dependence of educational institutions on those monies, the authority to terminate funding, and the capacity to monitor compliance nationally through a federal agency all endowed Title VI with immense power, at least theoretically, to fight racial inequality in educational services. What is so distressing is that so small a fraction of that potential has been realized or appears to be realizable within the prevailing currents of American politics. In some ways, the potential of Title VI and the severity of its sanction determined its destiny. Its potential power explains both the protracted struggle that has surrounded its enforcement and the ultimate emasculation that has been its fate.

To the extent that one can escape from the inequalities of American life, as many white ethnics have learned, it is through a public educational system that, when it works, provides upward mobility for children of the poor and the working class. Title VI, if interpreted broadly and enforced creatively with an eye toward achieving far-reaching change, held out the prospect that the education offered to blacks could provide that mobility with greater frequency than it had in the past. In turn, that held out the possibility, however slim, of transforming our social structure so that blacks would not be so statistically overrepresented in the American underclass. More equal and effective educational services to blacks — however measured — would go some distance toward making poverty a more randomly occurring social phenomenon — that is, a social phenomenon less statistically related to race. In spirit, the civil rights movement of the 1960s and the *Brown v. Board* decision itself envisioned precisely such a social revolution. Seen in this perspective, the history chronicled in these pages is simple to understand.

What is most notable about Title VI is that because its political potential, at least in theory, was so considerable, the heart of its legal requirements and powers became unenforceable. In other words, as a civil rights statute, Title VI was too threatening, both politically and socially. That understanding of the provision helps explain much of its history. The weakness of the political base supporting the enforcement of the legal right in Title VI is directly related to the need, in the first place, to resort to the law to establish the right and then to the need to litigate relentlessly about its implementation. Civil rights legislation and litigation is the refuge of the powerless. In America civil rights legislation and litigation constitute efforts to compel the society to do what it lacks the political will to do. And that prior context, of course, poses a grand dilemma, for it shackles those efforts and often foredooms them to failure. It is imperative that we understand that and adjust our future strategies accordingly.

Were I philosopher-king, I would have little difficulty determining that it was sensible and wise, indeed imperative, to spend many more public dollars per capita on educating poor children, both black and white, than on educating middle-class children. Yet what we spend on educating children, white or black, and how good a job we do in educating them, are fundamentally not questions of legal rights. They are issues of public philosophy and public policy, perhaps even public morality, not readily reducible to or controllable by litigation or notions of legal rights. They reflect our values as a society — our collective sense of what it is wise, humane, and proper to do.

The history of Title VI suggests that in dealing with questions of educational equality and opportunity, we rely excessively on legal rights and litigation, and depend on litigation, in particular, where we cannot sustain the political will to address problems. Yet, litigation has not proven to be an effective substitute for political nerve and will. It cannot replace sustained, well-conceived, and well-financed social policies intelligently constructed to ameliorate complex problems. The history of the efforts to achieve equal educational opportunity through civil rights legislation and litigation suggests that the focus on winning legal rights became a substitute for, or at least dissipated the energy available for, a struggle to establish enduring, comprehensive, and effective educational policies geared to the needs of African Americans. When we use litigation as a surrogate for political action and social policy, we pay a price. The litigation process itself seems to alter how we define problems and what we do about them. It redirects the focus of reform and saps energy and attention from other initiatives. It seduces us — too often producing illusory and largely symbolic gains.

The failure of Title VI and of the litigation intended to effectuate its provisions has implications beyond the specific legal and political battles analyzed in this volume. The history chronicled in these pages ultimately reflects the failure of the liberal legal reform movement to acknowledge its limitations, reconsider its assumptions and strategies, and realize its vision. We are all the lesser for it.

A PERSONAL EPILOGUE

> The great tragedy — but possibly the great salvation, too —
> of the Negro and white in America is that neither one can
> be free of the other.
> > Kenneth B. Clark, *The Dark Ghetto*, 1964

> However large the number of individual white men who do
> and will identify themselves completely with the Negro
> cause, the white race in America will not admit the Negro
> to equal rights if it is not forced to do so. Upon that point
> one may speak with a dogmatism which all history justifies.
> > Reinhold Niebuhr, *Moral Man and Immoral Society*

TITLE VI GREW OUT OF the civil rights struggles of the 1960s. It addressed what has emerged as the most central, most debated, and most enduring component of that struggle: racial discrimination in educational institutions. With the passage of the 1964 Civil Rights Act, the 1965 Voting Rights Act, and the 1968 Fair Housing Act, the United States set out to use legal reform, centered on the creation of "legal rights," as the primary instrument for remedying racial injustices. Not for a century, not since the post–Civil War period, had legal reforms been so calculatingly used to deal with the problem of race. The federal civil rights measures of the 1960s mark a watershed in American law and politics.

I came of political age during that period and was inspired by the noble things that it seemed possible to accomplish through civil rights laws and litigation. For me, as for many others of my generation, civil rights laws and litigation offered redemption from an ignoble past. They offered hope and a way to struggle in an honorable, uplifting cause against a great evil. There seemed to be an implicit faith that through the creative use of law and litigation we could recapture the promise of America and redeem her from the most deplorable injustice committed in her name. Title VI was a product of that implicit

322

faith. It was a prototypical attempt to use what has been referred to as "neutral principles of law" to combat racism in American life.[1] The neutral principle in question was that tax monies taken from everyone should not be used to support programs that benefited only some.

In the 1960s, many liberals believed that neutral principles written into our law, mandating a formalistic equality of treatment between the races, could be a powerful weapon against racial inequality. Four decades after *Brown v. Board,* after both Title VI and the Constitution have been used to fight racial inequality in schools, a kind of empty legal formalism reigns. This formalism presumes that, as a legal matter, systematic and deliberate racial inequality in public education no longer exists. The official racial "equality" said to exist is legitimated by and is a product of the law. Ironically, the efforts to attack the educational problems of blacks through legal initiatives have produced legal doctrines that rationalize the pervasive inequalities in our educational system. As the quote from Derrick Bell at the beginning of this book suggests, those struggling through the law to restructure American education for African Americans have unwittingly helped to create the legal edifices that sustain the cruel inequalities that prevail.

Analyzing racial issues in terms of legal rights is so pervasive in American culture that one cannot study race as a contemporary issue in the United States without concentrating on legal initiatives. The reasons for that heavy reliance on law are little appreciated. By resorting to law we reject violence, channel racial protest into acceptable behavior and a safe forum, and pacify the yearning of black and white elites who want to believe, or foster the belief, that we are progressing in resolving racial conflict.

Historically, whites have hoped that civil rights laws and litigation will buy racial peace. David Garrow's description of Lyndon Johnson's actions after the signing of the 1964 Civil Rights Act is a fitting reminder of that motivation. Garrow notes that Johnson met privately with Martin Luther King Jr., Roy Wilkins, Whitney Young, and other black leaders following the public signing ceremony. At that meeting the president admonished the assembled civil rights leaders, according to Garrow, that there had to be "an understanding . . . that the rights Negroes possessed could now be secured by law, making demonstrations unnecessary and possibly even self-defeating."[2]

One cannot understand the close link between race and law without appreciating the link between race and violence. Where we have been able to establish a precarious peace between the races, that peace has always veiled an underlying fear of violence that cuts both ways. Blacks fear violence by whites because whites outnumber them, hold greater power, and have demonstrated a willingness to use that power in brutal ways. That breeds in blacks an almost paranoid, usually unspoken, but understandable fear of what whites may do with their power, if provoked. Whites fear blacks, in turn, not only because so much contemporary violent crime is statistically linked to blacks but also, more importantly, because any group that presides over the systematic mistreatment and abuse of another must fear reprisal and revenge by the subjugated group. It is black rebellion that whites fear — rebellion at the individual or collective level. Indeed, as the second chapter of this volume documented, the very passage of the 1964 act was driven, in significant measure, by white fear of black violence and rebellion.

This is also why Malcolm X remains so powerful a figure for whites and blacks alike. He was an articulate, intelligent, angry black man unafraid to discuss and display his anger. For blacks, his rebelliousness was a heroic trait; for whites, a threatening one. By contrast, a commitment to fighting racial injustice through the law offers whites and blacks a moderate, establishmentarian option that eschews anger and violence and that evinces a commitment to the institution that, more than any other, personifies and protects established authority. The law is an appealing way to deal with our society's racial problems because the methods and processes of the law diffuse the social disruptions threatened by black-white tensions. In other words, a commitment to civil rights legislation and litigation represents an attempt to contain the explosive and potentially violent character of racial conflict in the United States.

Law stands for everything that race relations in the United States are not. The legal process is presumed to reject the visceral and irrational. It is dedicated to resolving disputes peaceably and objectively, through the presentation and evaluation of reliable factual information. The resort to law transmogrifies our not-so-concealed apprehensions into rational, manageable, definable questions concerning race, about which there can be polite, boring, and intellectual — but most importantly, orderly and peaceful — deliberations.

The critical role of black civil rights lawyers in this process is little appreciated. Those lawyers enjoy a unique status in both the black and white communities. Within the black community, they are venerated because they challenge the dominant white society and advocate the cause of their people. However, they do so by using the white man's tools and rules. For that reason, within the white community they are virtually the only black role models who may be aggressive and assertive vis-à-vis whites and yet still not frighten white people. Black lawyers are just too much of the establishment for the establishment to worry much about them. Derrick Bell has noted that, for blacks, racism in this country produces "a rage we dare not show to others or admit to ourselves."[3] For black civil rights lawyers, I suspect, litigation provides a socially acceptable and lawful way of channeling that rage.

At the outset of this book, I argued that one could not understand the struggle over the enforcement of Title VI without appreciating that the provision dealt with the subject of race and that the history of its enforcement reflected much about race as an issue in the United States. In making that point, I am not arguing that the collective status of black America is a product of the enforcement of Title VI or of the litigation that focused on that provision. Obviously, it is not. However, the history of Title VI does offer a lens through which to view and try to understand the course of race relations since the landmark legal reforms of the 1950s and 1960s. That history suggests that once America ended de jure school segregation in the South, it settled for a kind of stasis in its efforts to eradicate racial inequality from our educational system. It is true that the changes wrought by the legal reforms of the civil rights revolution have had positive effects. For example, a token number of blacks who possess middle-class skills and attitudes have benefited in seeking jobs and gaining admission to colleges and universities. For that minority of the black minority, things have indisputably improved since 1964.

As for the mass of America's black population, however, white America manifests little interest in alleviating their condition, either in schools or in any other facet of life. Most whites have a sense for the privations and dangers that prevail among the black underclass — enough so, at least, to want to distance themselves from those people and their neighborhoods. And that is my point. There is a belief in white America that whites can insulate themselves from the problems of blacks by establishing residence at a safe physical distance from the inner city and by depending more and more on police and law enforcement to contain the violence and illegality that inner-city life breeds.

Whites evince a combination of contempt for and fear of blacks. I say contempt because of the callous disregard that characterizes America's continued acceptance of the lot of black America. Be it education, income, health care, employment, housing, life expectancy — by whatever standard one measures quality of life — more than a quarter century after the civil rights "revolution," the mass of black citizens remain disproportionately excluded from the "good life" in America.

I say fear because whites do fear blacks. That is not surprising. If people are treated contemptuously long enough, they come to hate, and that, in turn, leads those who have acted contemptuously to have cause to fear those people. Historically, white fear of blacks produced the violence and intimidation directed at blacks and intended to control them. Today, whites' fear of and anxiety about blacks has produced the great distance, physical and psychological, that white America puts between itself and most of its black citizenry. In the future, white fear will continue to determine what America does for and to blacks. In 1964, white fear galvanized support for the Civil Rights Act. The mood among whites three decades later is more difficult to ascertain and understand. While reluctant to talk about it, most whites are increasingly anxious about the condition of black America. Yet, they have turned inward, and in increasing numbers are concluding that there is no public, governmental solution to the problem, only a private one. That private solution, for increasing numbers of whites, is to distance themselves and their families from the unseemly and unsafe racial edge that is all but palpable.

White middle-class America defends and protects itself by insulating itself. As best we can, we ignore the condition and suffering of black Americans, while simultaneously fearing, like a contagion, the spread of the social ills produced by that suffering. Our strategy is to escape, or at least to think that we can. Some of us retreat to comfortable suburbs with pleasing amenities and, by the way, fine schools. Others find refuge in urban high-rise apartment buildings with doormen and sophisticated security systems, or in quiet, urban residential neighborhoods in private homes equipped with burglar alarms. White middle-class people with children who elect to remain in cities shun the public school system, choosing either to flee to the suburbs when their children come of school age or to opt for the "safe" confines of urban private or parochial schools.

There is no mistaking what we do, and no mistaking its link to race. We shut ourselves off physically, psychologically, and emotionally from blacks. It is denial. We try to deny that they exist, yet we know full well that they are there and will not go away. Though we are loath to acknowledge it, most whites resent and blame blacks for making us feel as we do about them — uncertain, insecure, and apprehensive.

In acting as we do, we perpetuate a tragedy for white and black alike and court future disaster. Of future disasters, there should be little doubt. One does not need graduate training in sociology to predict the escalating violence that our neglect and denial will yield.

Yet the damage that occurs as a result of crime or even urban riots is only one kind of violence. True, riots produce dramatic destruction that rivets our attention, if only momentarily. However, the violence of contemporary urban crime and lawlessness is ultimately a reflection and by-product of insidious, institutionalized conditions that ruin lives as brutally as does physical assault. Consider the violence of a social system that produces masses of uneducated, unskilled youths with little chance of getting decent employment now or in the foreseeable future, and with little prospect that their situation will change appreciably over the course of their lives. Consider the violence done by an educational system that typically does little more than warehouse poor black children until they are older adolescents — alienated and disengaged, with little to do but roam city streets. Consider the violence done by a welfare system that perpetuates poverty across generations, or the violence bred by drugs, joblessness, hopelessness, and self-hate — a violence that permeates inner-city neighborhoods and that each day touches the lives of millions of black children. Can whites truly divorce and shield themselves and their loved ones from the effects of this powder keg? Can it be in the self-interest of whites to preside over a power structure that permits, perpetuates, and institutionalizes such conditions? Are we too short-sighted to recognize that neither blacks nor whites are served by the social conditions that prevail?

The 1990s differ from the period preceding the passage of the 1964 Civil Rights Act in that today there is no urgent sense of the need to address our racial predicament. In 1964, at least, there was a recognition among whites of diverse political persuasions that trying to do something significant about the condition of black Americans was imperative. Whites acted then because, along with their fear, they felt the righteousness of the black cause. Now whites feel, at best, indifferent to that cause, and at worst, hostile to it.

White, middle-class America, increasingly beset by its own economic discomfort, has written off the majority of black Americans. So, too, not surprisingly, have the politicians of the white middle class of both political parties. That is the crucial difference between 1964 and 1994. The only sense of urgency that white Americans feel today is the sense that the black underclass needs to be kept physically at bay and geographically contained. Our failure to attend to our racial problems will require an increasing reliance on police and prisons to control a growing, alienated, and angry black America. That approach, of course, will generate further resentment in that community and, in turn, greater white apprehension and dependence on that very tactic. In 1995, we are in the middle of that downward spiral.

White America will move beyond the reliance on superficial legal measures only when it appreciates that it is in its own self-interest to do so. I fear that we have become too calloused or frightened, or both, to recognize that our own self-interest is, indeed, at stake. Perhaps we have shut ourselves off for so long that we are too numbed or paralyzed to act. Perhaps we have lived too unfairly for too long, or are simply too afraid to confront the demon of race. The divisions, apprehensions, and animosities between white and black cut so deep and are so ingrained in our culture that they may well be ineradicable. Whatever our station or personal history, blacks and whites alike, if we are honest with ourselves, will acknowledge that we fear and distrust one another. That, in turn, has made honest communication between the races about our mutual predicament nearly impossible. Instead, silence and suspicion reign. We are cursed by our historical relationship.

To overcome our history, those concerned about the future must cast their appeal for action to the enlightened self-interest of whites. Arguments founded on ethical considerations, however morally compelling they may be, will not prevail. Thus, we cannot rely on what Lincoln, in his first inaugural speech, called the "better angels of our nature." If it is to succeed, the case for a dramatic, costly, and sustained drive to transform the condition of black Americans must be made on the basis of white self-interest. That drive must be founded on the premise eloquently advanced by Justice Harlan a century ago in his dissent in *Plessy v. Ferguson,* when he declared that the fates of the two races are "indissolubly linked." I have always been moved by the wisdom of that observation.

As much as we might wish otherwise, we cannot divorce ourselves from one another. Black and white alike are here to stay, and the financial and social costs of our continued failure to "integrate" blacks into American society, in every sense of that word, threatens our security just as gravely as would a military threat. Ultimately, none of us — not a single one — will be able to shield ourselves or our loved ones from the physical dangers and burgeoning financial costs caused by our failure to provide so many black people a chance to lead a decent life. In an ironic twist, we will be compelled to treat our brothers and sisters as if they were such, not because we want to, but because our mutual predicament will compel us to. It would be wise to perceive that need, and to act on it, sooner rather than later.

I am not naïve. I recognize that eradicating the insidious and ravaging effects of racism will require a prodigious effort. Yet, we have somehow managed to bear enormous burdens when we perceive a grave risk to our collective well-being. For nearly half a century, we steeled ourselves at a staggering cost to struggle in a "war" against communism. We did so because we believed that communism threatened our security and survival. The dominant white society must be made to recognize that the stakes are no less portentous in the struggle over race. Somehow, blacks and whites together—for it can only be done together—must summon the wisdom, courage, and good sense to link arms anew and to create a political movement to sustain the national commitment required. We must commence and persevere in an unrelenting drive at all levels of government to spare ourselves and our children the scourge of violence, fear, hatred, and social chaos that will assuredly ensue if we fail to come to terms with one another. I am not certain that we can succeed in that effort. I am certain, however, that it will be disastrous for both races if we fail to make the attempt. There is no choice. Like it or not, and many of both races will not like it, our destinies are, indeed, "indissolubly linked."

Appendix A

TITLE VI OF THE 1964 CIVIL RIGHTS ACT, PUBLIC LAW 88-352, 2 JULY 1964

TITLE VI – NONDISCRIMINATION IN FEDERALLY ASSISTED PROGRAMS

SEC. 601. No person in the United States shall, on the ground of race, color, or national origin, be excluded from participation in, be denied the benefits of, or be subjected to discrimination under any program or activity receiving Federal financial assistance.

SEC. 602. Each Federal department and agency which is empowered to extend Federal financial assistance to any program or activity, by way of grant, loan, or contract other than a contract of insurance or guaranty, is authorized and directed to effectuate the provisions of section 601 with respect to such program or activity by issuing rules, regulations, or orders of general applicability which shall be consistent with the achievement of the objectives of the statute authorizing the financial assistance in connection with which the action is taken. No such rule, regulation, or order shall become effective unless and until approved by the President. Compliance with any requirement adopted pursuant to this section may be effected (1) by the termination of or refusal to grant or to continue assistance under such program or activity to any recipient as to whom there has been an express finding on the record, after opportunity for hearing, of a failure to comply with such requirement, but such termination or refusal shall be limited to the particular political entity, or part thereof, or other recipient as to whom such a finding has been made and, shall be limited in its effect to the particular program, or part thereof, in which such noncompliance has been so found, or (2) by any other means authorized by law: *Provided, however,* that no such action shall be taken until the department or agency concerned has advised the appropriate person or persons of the failure to comply with the requirement and has determined that compliance cannot be secured by voluntary means. In the case of any action terminating, or refusing to grant or continue, assistance because of failure to comply with a requirement imposed pursuant to this section, the head of the Federal department or agency shall file with the committees of the House and Senate having legislative jurisdiction over the program or activity involved a full written report of the circumstances and the grounds for such action. No action shall become effective until thirty days have elapsed after the filing of such report.

SEC. 603. Any department or agency action taken pursuant to section 602 shall be subject to such judicial review as may otherwise be provided by law for similar action taken by such department or agency on other grounds. In the case of action, not otherwise subject to judicial review, terminating or refusing to grant or to continue financial assistance upon a finding of failure to comply with any requirement imposed pursuant to section 602, any person aggrieved (including any State or political subdivision thereof and any agency of either) may obtain judicial review of such action in accordance with section 10 of the Administrative Procedure Act, and such action shall not be deemed committed to unreviewable agency discretion within the meaning of that section.

SEC. 604. Nothing contained in this title shall be construed to authorize action under this title by any department or agency with respect to any employment practice of any employer, employment agency, or labor organization except where a primary objective of the Federal financial assistance is to provide employment.

SEC. 605. Nothing in this title shall add to or detract from any existing authority with respect to any program or activity under which Federal financial assistance is extended by way of a contract of insurance or guaranty.

Appendix B

THE EVOLUTION OF THE LANGUAGE OF TITLE VI IN THE LEGISLATIVE PROCESS

AN OVERVIEW OF THE LEGISLATIVE HISTORY

There were five versions of Title VI that existed before the Senate and House finally agreed on the sixth version on 30 June 1964. In June 1963, the Kennedy administration introduced the Civil Rights Act of 1963 (H.R. 7152 and S. 1731) into both houses of Congress. The Senate version of the bill, along with the Senate hearings on the bill, was aborted in August 1963, as noted in chapter 2, above. The House version survived, and Subcommittee Number 5 of the House Judiciary Committee held hearings during the summer of 1963. The subcommittee reported out a version of Title VI in October 1963, and then the full Judiciary Committee reported out a different version in November 1963. Title VI, along with the rest of the Civil Rights Bill, was considered by the whole House in January 1964. The House passed a version of the bill, including a new, slightly revised version of Title VI, on 10 February 1964. The bill went to the Senate for its deliberations, and the Senate passed it in June 1964, making some modifications in the version that had passed the House. The bill then went back to the House, which quickly passed it on 30 June 1964, as House Resolution 789, which included no changes in Title VI. The bill was signed into law on 4 July 1964.

The following material documents the changes in Title VI, from the Kennedy administration's proposal in June 1963 to enactment into law in July 1964. In the versions that follow I have inserted bracketed, italicized footnotes highlighting the major changes made at each stage of the legislative process. My comments are indicated by brackets and italics, deletions are indicated by a line through the deleted material, and additions to a previously existing section are indicated by braces around the added material. When a section has not changed from the previous version, its text is omitted. In analyzing the first paragraph of the version of Title VI that emerged from the House Judiciary Subcommittee (version 2), since that paragraph drastically revised the language in the administration's bill, I concluded that indicating additions and deletions would be too cumbersome. Consequently, I simply reprinted, in an unmarked fashion, the entire new paragraph as rewritten by the subcommittee.

The sources of the versions are as follows: version 1 is from *Message from the President of the United States Pertaining to Civil Rights*, 88th Cong., 1st sess., 1963, H. Doc. 124, serial 12567, p. 24; version 2 is from *Civil Rights Act of 1963*, 88th Cong., 1st sess., H.R. 7152, 2 Oct. 1963; version 3 is from *Civil Rights Act of 1963*, 88th Cong., 1st sess., 1963, H. Rept. 914, serial 12544, p. 8; version 4 is from *Civil Rights Act of 1964*, 88th Cong., 2d sess., 10 Feb. 1963, H.R. 7152; and version 5 is from *Civil Rights Act of 1964*, 88th Cong., 2d sess., 19 June 1964, H.R. 7152.

Version 1: The Initial Kennedy Administration Proposal for Title VI—H.R. 7152, 19 June 1963

Section 601. Notwithstanding any provision to the contrary in any law of the United States providing or authorizing direct or indirect financial assistance for or in connection with any program or activity by way of grant, contract, loan, insurance, guaranty, or otherwise, no such law shall be interpreted as requiring that such financial assitance shall be furnished in circumstances under which individuals participating in or benefiting from the program or activity are discriminated against on the ground of race, color, religion, or national origin or are denied participation or benefits therein on the ground of race, color, religion, or national origin. All contracts made in connection with any such program or activity shall contain conditions as the President may prescribe for the purpose of assuring that there shall be no discrimination in employment by any contractor or subcontractor on the ground of race, color, religion or national origin. *[1]*

Version 2: House Judiciary Subcommittee Version of Title VI, 2 October 1963

Section 701. *[Previously numbered 601.]* Notwithstanding any inconsistent provision of any other law, no person in the United States shall, on the ground of race, color, or national origin, be excluded from participation in, be denied the benefits of, or be subjected to discrimination under any program or activity receiving federal financial assistance. *[2]*

[1. *This provision did not require the administration to terminate financial assistance where the beneficiaries or participants of a program experienced discrimination, nor did it confer a right to be free of such discrimination. It did not explicitly authorize the withholding of financial assistance. It merely provided that no law providing federal financial assistance could be construed to require that funds be disbursed where there was discrimination based on race, color, religion, or national origin. Note that Congress subsequently dropped the "religion" provision.]*

[2. *This is the first time that an outright prohibition on discrimination based on race, color, or national ori-*

Section 702. *[Added section.]* Each federal department and agency which is empowered to extend federal financial assistance to any program or activity, by way of grant, contract, loan, insurance, guaranty, or otherwise, shall take action to effectuate the provisions of Section 701 with respect to such program or activity. *[3]* Such action may be taken by or pursuant to rule, regulation, or order of general applicability and shall be consistent with achievement of the objectives of the statute authorizing the financial assistance in connection with which the action is taken. *[4]* Compliance with any requirement adopted pursuant to this section may be effected (1) by suit under section 703 of this title, (2) by the termination of or refusal to grant or to continue assistance upon an express finding that there has been a failure to comply with such requirement, or (3) by any other means authorized by law: *[5]* PROVIDED, HOWEVER, that no such action shall be taken until the department or agency concerned has advised the appropriate person or persons of the failure to comply with the requirement and has determined that compliance cannot be secured by voluntary means. *[6]*

Section 703. *[Added section—Authorization for civil action.]* Any requirement adopted pursuant to section 702, whether by rule, regulation, order, agreement, or otherwise, shall be enforceable in the district courts of the United States by means of a civil action or other proper proceeding, including an application for a permanent or temporary injunction, restraining order, or other order, brought by or on behalf of the United States or any agency or officer thereof expressly authorized to bring suits by Act of Congress. *[7]*

---

gin was proposed, creating a right to participate in and enjoy the benefits of programs receiving federal financial assistance irrespective of one's race, color, or national origin. Note that the bar on discrimination based on religion is dropped in this version.]

[3. This sentence imposes an affirmative obligation on each federal agency or department to act in an unspecified way to realize the right established in section 701.

[4. Action to enforce the title could be taken under an agency rule, regulation, or order of general applicability so long as that action was consistent with the obligations of the statue through which the funds were provided.]

[5. This sentence contained the first explicit acknowledgment that the government could seek compliance with the title by terminating federal financial assistance. Note, however, that this version of the title provides two other alternative methods by which to achieve compliance—a lawsuit under a specific provision in the title, and other actions "authorized by law."]

[6. Before an agency took enforcement actions, it first had to "determine" that it could not achieve compliance voluntarily without resorting to those enforcement actions. The provision does not say how an agency is to make that determination. This change was ultimately written into the law.]

[7. This authorizes the United States to enforce agency requirements in federal courts on behalf of the appropriate federal agency. The language preceding the words "proper proceeding" fails to specify whether this section contemplated a private right of action by individuals to remedy violations of agency requirements. This section was deleted by the full Judiciary Committee.]

Section 704. *[Added section—Judicial review.]* Any department or agency action taken pursuant to section 702 shall be subject to such judicial review as may otherwise be provided by law for similar action taken by such department or agency on other grounds. *[8]* In the case of action, not otherwise subject to judicial review, terminating or refusing to grant or to continue financial assistance upon a finding of failure to comply with any requirement imposed pursuant to section 702, any person aggrieved (including any State or political subdivision thereof and any agency of either) may obtain judicial review of such action in accordance with section 10 of the Administrative Procedure Act, and such action shall not be deemed committed to unreviewable agency discretion within the meaning of that section. *[9]*

Version 3: The Full Judiciary Committee's Version of Title VI, 20 November 1963

Section 601. *[Previously numbered 701. Language remains the same.]*

Section 602. *[Previously numbered 702.]* Each federal department and agency which is empowered to extend federal financial assistance to any program or activity, by way of grant, contract, {or} loan, ~~insurance, guaranty, or otherwise,~~ *[10]* shall take action to effectuate the provisions of section 601 with respect to such program or activity. Such action may be taken by or pursuant to rule, regulation, or order of general applicability and shall be consistent with achievement of the objectives of the statute authorizing the financial assistance in connection with which the action is taken. Compliance with any requirement adopted pursuant to this section may be effected ~~(1) by suit under section 703 of this title,~~ *[11]* (2) {(1)} by the termination of or refusal to grant or to continue assistance {under such program or activity to any recipient as to whom there has been} ~~upon~~ an express finding ~~that there has been~~ {of} a failure to comply with such requirement, or ~~(3)~~ {(2)} by any other means authorized by law: Provided, however, That no such action shall be taken until the department or agency concerned has advised the appropriate person or persons of the fail-

---

[8. Agency actions to enforce the requirements of Title VI are subject to judicial review. This change was ultimately written into the law.

[9. Note the significant transformation of the Title VI provision by the House subcommittee. A fairly innocuous one-paragraph provision consisting of approximately 140 words became a more powerful, complicated provision consisting of four paragraphs, three times the length of the administration measure and potentially much more far-reaching.]

[10. Reference to contracts of insurance or guaranty is omitted from the language in this version.]

[11. This language is omitted because the full Judiciary Committee removed what was Section 703 in the subcommittee version of Title VI—the section authorizing civil actions in federal district courts to enforce the requirements of the provision.

ure to comply with the requirement and has determined that compliance cannot be secured by voluntary means.

Section 603. *[Previously numbered 704. Language remains the same.]*

VERSION 4: TITLE VI AS PASSED BY THE HOUSE OF REPRESENTATIVES, 10 FEBRUARY 1964

Section 601. *[Remains the same.]*

Section 602. Each Federal department and agency which is empowered to extend Federal financial assistance to any program or activity, by way of grant, ~~contract, or~~ loan, {or contract other than a contract of insurance or guaranty,} shall take action to effectuate the provisions of section 601 with respect to such program or activity. *[12]* Such action may be taken by or pursuant to rule, regulation, or order of general applicability and shall be consistent with achievement of the objectives of the statute authorizing the financial assistance in connection with which the action is taken. {No such rule, regulation or order shall become effective unless and until approved by the President.} *[13]* {After a hearing,} compliance with any requirement adopted pursuant to this section may be effected (1) by the termination of or refusal to grant or to continue assistance under such program or activity to any recipient as to whom there has been an express finding of a failure to comply with such requirement, or (2) by any other means authorized by law: Provided, however, That no such action shall be taken until the department or agency concerned has advised the appropriate person or persons of the failure to comply with the requirement and has determined that compliance cannot be secured by voluntary means. {In the case of any action terminating, or refusing to grant or continue, assistance because of failure to comply with a requirement imposed pursuant to this section, the head of the Federal department or agency shall file with the Committees of the House and Senate having legislative jurisdiction over the program or activity involved a full written report of the circumstances and the grounds for such action.} *[14]* {No such action shall become effective until thirty days have elapsed after the filing of such report.} *[15]*

[12. Contracts of insurance or guaranty are explicitly excluded from coverage in this version.]

[13. Note the intention to hold the president accountable for rules and regulations promulgated under Title VI.]

[14. Where enforcement action leads to the termination of funds, the version of Title VI passed by the full House requires the agency terminating funds to advise the appropriate congressional committee of that and to justify the termination to the committee. Congress enacted this change into the law.]

[15. Note the intention to provide for additional time after the agency files its report, during which settlement discussions might occur. Congress enacted this change into law.]

Section 603. *[Remains the same.]*

VERSION 5: TITLE VI AS PASSED BY THE SENATE, 19 JUNE 1964

Section 601. ~~Notwithstanding any inconsistent provision of any other law,~~ No person in the United States shall, on the ground of race, color, or national origin, be excluded from participation in, be denied the benefits of, or be subjected to discrimination under any program or activity receiving Federal financial assistance.

Section 602. Each Federal department and agency which is empowerd to extend Federal financial assistance to any program or activity, by way of grant, loan, or contract other than a contract of insurance or guaranty, {is authorized and directed} ~~shall take action~~ to effectuate the provisions of section 601 with respect to such program or activity ~~Such action may be taken by or pursuant to rule~~ {by issuing rules,} regulation{s}, or order{s} of general applicability ~~and~~ {which} shall be consistent with achievement of the objectives of the statute authorizing the financial assistance in connection with which the action is taken. *[16]* No such rule, regulation or order shall become effective unless and until approved by the President. ~~After a hearing,~~ Compliance with any requirement adoped pursuant to this section may be effected (1) by the termination of or refusal to grant or to continue assistance under such program or activity to any recipient as to whom there has been an express finding {on the record, after opportunity for a hearing,} *[17]* of a failure to comply with such requirement, {but such termination or refusal shall be limited to the particular political entity, or part thereof, or other recipient as to whom such a finding has been made and, shall be limited in its effect to the particular program, or part thereof, in which such noncompliance has been so found,} *[18]* or (2) by any other means authorized by law: Provided, however, That no such action shall be taken until the department or agency concerned has advised the appropriate person or persons of the failure to comply with the requirement and has determined that compliance cannot be secured by voluntary means. In the case of any action terminating, or refusing to grant or continue, assistance because of failure to comply with a requirement imposed pursuant to this section, the head of the Federal

[16. The change in the language in this sentence mandates that each federal department or agency effectuate the purposes of the title by issuing rules or regulations. The version passed by the full House of Representatives provided that, to effectuate provisions of Title VI, agencies "may" issue appropriate rules and regulations.]

[17. Note the procedural requirement that these be an "express finding on the record."]

[18. Note the limit on the scope of the funding that may be terminated for a violation of Title VI.]

department or agency shall file with the committees of the House and Senate having legislative jurisdiction over the program or activity involved a full written report of the circumstances and the grounds for such action. No such action shall become effective until thirty days have elapsed after the filing of such report.

Section 603. *[Remains the same.]*

Section 604. *[Added section—Employment.]* Nothing contained in this title shall be construed to authorize action under this title by any department or agency with respect to any employment practice of any employer, employment agency, or labor organization except where a primary objective of the Federal financial assistance is to provide employment. *[19]*

Section 605. *[Added section— Contracts of insurance or guaranty.]* Nothing in this title shall add to or detract from any existing authority with respect to any program or activity under which Federal financial assistance is extended by way of a contract of insurance or guaranty. *[20]*

VERSION 6: PUBLIC LAW VERSION OF TITLE VI PASSED BY THE HOUSE, 30 JUNE 1964

Section 601. *[Remains the same.]*

Section 602. *[Remains the same.]*

Section 603. *[Remains the same.]*

Section 604. *[Remains the same.]*

Section 605. *[Remains the same.]*

[19. Note the intent to exclude employment practices from coverage under Title VI.]
[20. This section was added to Title VI as part of the Mansfield-Dirksen Amendment on 17 June 1964. It was championed by Senator Long of Louisiana. Note the desire to ensure that Title VI would not affect any existing authority under contracts of insurance or guarantee.]

NOTES

ABBREVIATIONS FOR LEGAL SOURCES

C.F.R.	*Code of Federal Regulations*
F. Supp.	*Federal Supplement*
F.2d	*Federal Reporter*
Fed. Reg.	*Federal Register*
S.Ct.	*Supreme Court Reporter*
Stat.	*Statutes at Large*
U.S.	*U.S. Reports*
U.S.C.	*United States Code*
U.S.C.A.	*United States Code Annotated*
U.S.C.C.A.N.	*United States Code Congressional and Administrative News*

Chapter 1—RACE, LITIGATION, AND THE LEGAL RIGHTS FIXATION

1. David Garrow, *Bearing the Cross: Martin Luther King, Jr., and the Southern Leadership Conference. A Personal Portrait* (New York: William Morrow, 1986), 338; Kermit Hall, *The Magic Mirror* (New York: Oxford University Press, 1989), 324.

2. *Congressional Record*, 88th Cong., 2d sess., 30 Mar. 1964, 6544.

3. Whereas the ban on discrimination in Title VI has been enforced most conspicuously vis-à-vis educational institutions, the prohibition applies wherever federal monies flow. Consequently, all federal agencies dispensing monies have an obligation to enforce the provision. Although the efforts by the Department of Housing and Urban Development and the Department of Labor to enforce Title VI have occasionally given rise to controversy, it is in the realm of federally funded programs for education that Title VI has had by far its greatest impact.

4. Some of the most provocative observations on this general subject have been advanced by Kenneth Tollett. In this regard, see Kenneth Tollett, "Black Colleges as Instruments of Affirmative Action," occasional paper, Institute for the Study of Educational Policy, Howard University, 1982, 19–29; idem, "The Right to Education," occasional paper, Institute for the Study of Educational Policy, Howard University, 1983, 55–56; and idem,

"The Faculty and the Government," in *Education and the States,* ed. John Hughes (Washington, D.C.: American Council on Education, 1975), 226–27.

5. White House Task Force on Civil Rights, *To Fulfill These Rights* (Washington, D.C.: Government Printing Office, 1966), 63.

6. Gerald Rosenberg, *The Hollow Hope* (Chicago: University of Chicago Press, 1992); and Donald Horowitz, *The Courts and Social Policy* (Washington, D.C.: Brookings Institution, 1977), are among the best of this genre. For a brilliant treatment of the adverse consequences resulting from the excessive resort to legal rights to resolve public policy problems, see Mary Ann Glendon, *Rights Talk: The Impoverishment of Political Discourse* (New York: Free Press, 1993).

7. Title VI falls into the category of what R. Shep Melnick has called "programmatic rights"—rights that "are the joint creation of the courts, Congress, and federal administrators." R. Shep Melnick, "The Courts, Congress, and Programmatic Rights," in *Remaking American Politics,* ed. Sidney Milkis and Richard Harris (New York: Westview, 1989), 189.

8. Patricia Williams, "Alchemical Notes: Reconstructing Ideals from Deconstructed Rights," in *A Less than Perfect Union,* ed. Jules Cobel (New York: Monthly Review Press, 1988), 64.

9. *The Guide to American Law* (St. Paul, Minn.: West Publishing, 1984), 9:45.

10. Willie Lee Rose, *Rehearsal for Reconstruction* (New York: Oxford University Press, 1964), 86.

11. Leon Litwack, *Been in the Storm So Long* (New York: Alfred A. Knopf, 1979), 5.

12. Rose, *Rehearsal for Reconstruction,* 86.

13. Litwack, *Been in the Storm,* 5.

14. Ibid., 3.

15. James Anderson, *The Education of Blacks in the South, 1860–1935* (Chapel Hill: University of North Carolina Press, 1988), 23.

16. Ibid., 3.

17. Mark Tushnet, *The NAACP's Legal Strategy against Segregated Education* (Chapel Hill: University of North Carolina Press, 1987), 34.

18. The analysis of the transformations in urban America during 1940–80 that appears in this paragraph and the six that follow was originally prepared by Scott Henderson in a readings seminar he did with the author during the 1992–93 academic year. In its language and analysis, the material in those paragraphs draws extensively on Henderson's work.

19. Nicholas Lemann, *The Promised Land: The Great Black Migration and How It Changed America* (New York: Alfred A. Knopf, 1991), 6. General works on African-American migrations, especially those before 1950, include Neil Fligstein, *Going North: Migration of Blacks and Whites from the South, 1900–1950*

(New York: Academic Press, 1981); Florette Henri, *Black Migration: Movement North, 1890-1920* (New York: Anchor Books, 1975); George Groh, *The Black Migration: The Journey to Urban America* (New York: Weybright & Talley, 1972).

20. John Morton Blum, *Politics and American Culture during World War II* (New York: Harcourt Brace Jovanovich, 1976), 200; Richard Polenberg, *One Nation Divisible: Class, Race, and Ethnicity in the United States since 1938* (New York: Viking Press, 1980), 54, 72-73.

21. Lemann, *Promised Land,* 6.

22. Landon Y. Jones, *Great Expectations: America and the Baby Boom Generation* (New York: Coward, McCann & Geoghegan, 1980), 38-39.

23. Kenneth Jackson, *Crabgrass Frontier: The Suburbanization of the United States* (New York: Oxford University Press, 1985), 213.

24. Barry Bluestone and Bennett Harrison, *The Deindustrialization of America: Plant Closings, Community Abandonment, and the Dismantling of Basic Industry* (New York: Basic Books, 1982), 12, 16, 75, 80, 118, 139, 152.

25. Dorothy S. Strickland and Carol Ascher, "Low-Income African American Children and Public Schooling," in *Handbook of Research on Curriculum,* ed. Philip W. Jackson (New York: Macmillan, 1992), 609-23.

26. For an excellent analysis arguing that school desegregation has involved "ritualized conflict" that has served the status quo, see Daniel J. Monti, *A Semblance of Justice: St. Louis School Desegregation and Order in Urban America* (Columbia: University of Maryland Press, 1985).

27. In this regard, see U.S. Bureau of the Census, *School Enrollment—Social and Economic Characteristics of Students: October 1991,* Current Population Reports, ser. P-20, no. 469 (Washington, D.C.: Government Printing Office, 1993), table 5.

28. Derrick Bell, *And We Are Not Saved: The Elusive Quest for Racial Justice* (New York: Basic Books, 1987), 5.

Chapter 2—THE KENNEDY LEGACY AND LEGISLATIVE HISTORY

1. Richard C. Flemming, "The Federal Executive and Civil Rights," *Daedalus* 94 (1965): 942. See also the statistics presented in House Committee on the Judiciary, *Civil Rights, Part 3: Hearings before Subcommittee No. 5 of the Committee on the Judiciary,* 88th Cong., 1st sess., 17-19, 24-26, 31 July, 1, 2 Aug. 1963, ser. 4, pt. 3, pp. 2587-95. (Hereafter these hearings are cited as *Subcommittee No. 5.*)

2. Murray and the statement from the Notre Dame meeting are both cited in *Subcommittee No. 5,* pt. 3, pp. 2553, 2566.

3. As cited in ibid., pt. 3, p. 1197.

4. *The Public Papers of the Presidents of the United States: John F. Kennedy, 1963*

(Washington, D.C.: Government Printing Office, 1964), 483. See also Alan Wolk, *The Presidency and Black Civil Rights: Eisenhower to Nixon* (Rutherford, N.J.: Fairleigh Dickinson University Press, 1971), 235.

5. Arthur M. Schlesinger, *A Thousand Days: John F. Kennedy in the White House* (Boston: Houghton-Mifflin, 1965), 966; Hanes Walton Jr., *When the Marching Stopped* (Albany: State University of New York Press, 1988), 183; Gary Orfield, *The Reconstruction of Southern Education* (New York: John Wiley & Sons, 1969), 36, 46.

6. Orfield, *Reconstruction*, 34.

7. *New York Times*, 13 June 1963, 32.

8. Beryl Radin, *Implementation, Change, and the Federal Bureaucracy: School Desegregation Policy in HEW, 1964–68* (New York: Teachers College, 1977), 36.

9. Bullock and Rodgers concluded that Congress had passed the 1964 act "in reaction to mounting demonstrations and sporadic violence." Harrell Rodgers and Charles Bullock, *Law and Social Change: Civil Rights Laws and Their Consequences* (New York: McGraw-Hill, 1972), 212.

10. *Subcommittee No. 5*, pt. 3, p. 2562.

11. Quoted from *Public Papers: John F. Kennedy, 1963*, 469, 470.

12. Ibid., 484.

13. *U.S. News and World Report*, 29 July 1963, 60; Arthur Schlesinger, *Robert Kennedy and His Times* (Boston: Houghton Mifflin, 1978), 346–47.

14. *New York Times*, 16 Sept. 1963, 1.

15. *New York Times*, 16 Sept. 1963, 26.

16. *Subcommittee No. 5*, pt. 1, p. 1323.

17. Ibid., pt. 2, p. 1202.

18. *Congressional Record*, 88th Cong., 2d sess., 10 Apr. 1964, 7512.

19. Ibid.

20. As cited in Irving Bernstein, *Promises Kept: John F. Kennedy's New Frontier* (New York: Oxford University Press, 1991), 103.

21. Rivers, Maslow, and Dorn were quoted in *Subcommittee No. 5*, pt. 3, pp. 1819, 1590, 1363.

22. James R. Dunn, "Title VI, the Guidelines, and School Desegregation in the South," *Virginia Law Review* 53 (1967): 51.

23. *Oklahoma v. U.S. Civil Service Commission*, 330 U.S. 143, 67 S.Ct. 552 (1947).

24. As cited in *The Public Papers of the Presidents of the United States: Dwight D. Eisenhower, 1953* (Washington, D.C.: Government Printing Office, 1960), 1:108.

25. Orfield, *Reconstruction*, 24.

26. *Congressional Record*, 88th Cong., 2d sess., 7 Apr. 1965, 6835. Powell is reported to have introduced such an amendment on more than one hundred occasions. Raymond J. Celada, Congressional Research Service, *Nondiscrimination in Federally Assisted Programs: Legislative History and Analysis of Title VI*

of the Civil Rights Act of 1964 (Washington, D.C.: Government Printing Office, 1965), 6. Such measures were often opposed not only by conservative Republicans and southern Democrats but also by liberals of both parties who argued that, though they favored the principle of nondiscrimination, they feared that attaching a nondiscrimination provision to an aid bill would result in protracted debate, or even a filibuster, would jeopardize the entire aid package, and thus would result in no aid at all to those in greatest need. In 1956 and 1957, Powell's integration riders led to disputes that, in fact, did kill efforts to provide federal aid for school construction. *New York Times*, 7 Jan. 1958, 23.

27. *Cooper v. Aaron*, 358 U.S. 4, 78 S.Ct. 1403 (1958), emphasis added.

28. Reed Sarratt, *The Ordeal of Desegregation* (New York: Harper & Row, 1966), 63. The 1961 recommendation appeared in *Report of the United States Commission on Civil Rights* (Washington, D.C.: Government Printing Office, 1961), 181.

29. *Congressional Quarterly*, 9 Apr. 1965, 621.

30. Comment, "Title VI of the Civil Rights Act of 1964 — Implementation and Impact," *George Washington Law Review* 36 (1968): 828 n. 22.

31. *Subcommittee No. 5*, pt. 3, p. 2091.

32. Radin, *Implementation*, 6–7. In 1963, the federal government sponsored more than 190 different programs affecting education. Celada, *Nondiscrimination*, 3.

33. *Congressional Record*, 88th Cong., 2d sess., 7 Apr. 1964, 7065.

34. Radin, *Implementation*, 56; see also Orfield, *Reconstruction*, 29–30.

35. *Congressional Record*, 88th Cong., 2d sess., 7 Apr. 1964, 7065.

36. Orfield, *Reconstruction*, 29–30.

37. These prohibitions were contained, respectively, in Executive Order 11063, 3 C.F.R. § 652 (1962); Executive Order 11063, 3 C.F.R. § 302(a)-(c) (1962); and Executive Order 10925, 3 C.F.R. § 301(1) (1961). For information on the executive orders, see Comment, "Title VI," *George Washington Law Review* 36 (1967): 827 n. 11. Some actions had been taken through departmental regulations that prohibited discrimination in particular programs, such as Manpower Development Training activities, teacher-training institutes, mental health and mental retardation projects, apprenticeship programs, and employment in state agencies administering certain federal programs. U.S. Commission on Civil Rights, *Civil Rights under Federal Programs — An Analysis of Title VI, the Civil Rights Act of 1964* (Washington, D.C.: Government Printing Office, 1965), 5. Several departments of the federal government voluntarily initiated a policy of nondiscrimination in certain aspects of their work. The Department of the Interior determined that federal land that it sold to states and localities could be purchased only on the condition that the land remain open to public recreation without discrimination. The

Federal Home Loan Bank Board in 1961 established a policy that member banks could not discriminate in making loans. Finally, the Rural Electrification Administration conditioned its loan contracts on a commitment that the borrower pursue a nondiscriminatory employment policy. *Subcommittee No. 5*, pt. 3, p. 2093.

38. See Executive Order 10479, 18 C.F.R. § 4899 (1953); as amended by Executive Order 10482, 18 C.F.R. § 4944 (1953); and Executive Order 9981, 3 C.F.R. § 722 (1948).

39. *Subcommittee No. 5*, pt. 3, p. 2615. At the time, for example, Mississippi received federal grants in aid amounting to twice the tax revenue produced in the state. In this regard, see also *Public Papers: John F. Kennedy, 1963*, 334.

40. Orfield, *Reconstruction*, 32.

41. Harold W. Chase and Allen H. Lerman, eds., *Kennedy and the Press* (New York: Thomas Y. Crowell, 1965), 428.

42. Theodore C. Sorensen, *Kennedy* (New York: Harper & Row, 1965), 497.

43. *Subcommittee No. 5*, pt. 3, p. 2117.

44. *Public Papers: John F. Kennedy, 1963*, 492.

45. See the comments of Attorney General Kennedy and Secretary of Labor Wirtz in *Subcommittee No. 5*, pt. 2, p. 1381; and pt. 1, p. 1491, respectively. HEW had unilaterally imposed nondiscrimination requirements in eight programs. See *Subcommittee No. 5*, pt. 2, pp. 1540-41, for a listing and description of the programs. Five federal departments imposed requirements of nondiscrimination for funds provided through specific programs they administered. See *Subcommittee No. 5*, pt. 3, p. 2107.

46. House Committee on Education and Labor, *Integration in Public Education Programs: Hearing before the Subcommittee on Integration in Federally Assisted Public Education Programs of the Committee on Education and Labor*, 87th Cong., 2d sess., 27 Feb. 1962, 58.

47. In this regard, see the comments of John Roche, president of Americans for Democratic Action, in *Subcommittee No. 5*, pt. 2, p. 1244; Roy Wilkins, executive director of the NAACP, in pt. 3, pp. 2172-73; John J. Pemberton, executive director of the American Civil Liberties Union, in pt. 3, p. 2122; Sidney Zagri, legislative counsel for the International Brotherhood of Teamsters, in pt. 3, p. 2093; and Joseph Rauh, vice-chairman of Americans for Democratic Action, in pt. 3, p. 1861.

48. *Public Papers: John F. Kennedy, 1963*, 492.

49. *Civil Rights Act of 1963*, 88th Cong., 1st sess., H.R. 7152.

50. Celada, *Nondiscrimination*, 10. For a summary of the changes that the subcommittee made in the language of the administration's bill, see Comment, "Title VI," 832-34; and House Report No. 914, 88th Cong., 115.

51. Celada, *Nondiscrimination,* 12.

52. In this regard, see Norbert A. Schlei, oral history interview by John Stewart, 20-21 Feb. 1968, 43-44, 53, John F. Kennedy Library, Boston, Mass.; Hugh Graham Davis, *The Civil Rights Era: Origins and Development of National Policy, 1960-1972* (New York: Oxford University Press, 1990), 82; and Schlesinger, *Robert Kennedy,* 347.

53. Robert D. Loevy, *To End All Segregation: The Politics of the Passage of the Civil Rights Act of 1964* (Lanham, Md.: University Press of America, 1990), 70-71.

54. Ibid., 43-44.

55. *Congressional Record,* 88th Cong., 2d sess., 7 Apr. 1964, 7065; see also *Cannon v. University of Chicago,* 441 U.S. 714-16 nn. 50-51, 99 S.Ct. 1967 nn. 50-51 (1979).

56. Senate Committee on the Judiciary, *Civil Rights—The President's Program, 1963: Hearings before the Senate Committee on the Judiciary,* 88th Cong., 1st sess., 23 Aug. 1963, 350, 351.

57. See *Cannon,* 441 U.S. 714, 99 S.Ct. 1967; and *Congressional Record,* 88th Cong., 2d sess., 7 Apr. 1964, 7065.

58. Senate Committee, *Civil Rights—The President's Program, 1963,* 333.

59. Ibid., 334.

60. Debate on the act produced the lengthiest filibuster since the adoption of the cloture rule in 1917 by the U.S. Senate. *New York Times,* 11 June 1964, 1. The action to end debate marked the first time ever that the Senate voted cloture on a civil rights measure. *Washington Post,* 11 June 1964, 1. It was only the sixth time in history that the Senate successfully voted cloture.

61. Radin, *Implementation,* 56.

62. Orfield, *Reconstruction,* 35; Nicholas Katzenbach, oral history interview by Anthony Lewis, 16 Nov. 1964, 130, John F. Kennedy Library.

63. Radin contends that the provision was originally included in the proposed legislation as a bargaining chip to be dropped during the legislative negotiations that the administration anticipated. Radin, *Implementation,* 56.

64. Comment, "Title VI," 843-44.

65. *Subcommittee No. 5,* pt. 2, pp. 1536-39.

66. Testimony of HEW Secretary Anthony Celebrezze, in ibid., pt. 2, p. 1531.

67. As cited in Comment, "Title VI," 843 n. 5.

68. 42 U.S.C.A. § 2000d-1 (1964), emphasis added.

69. For example, see the testimony of Sidney Zagri, legislative counsel, International Brotherhood of Teamsters, in *Subcommittee No. 5,* pt. 3, p. 2093.

70. *Subcommittee No. 5,* pt. 3, pp. 2161, 2229.

71. See, e.g., Congressman McCulloch's comments in ibid., pt. 2, pp. 1465, 1520. Others voiced similar reservations; see, e.g., ibid., pt. 2, pp. 1519-20, 1748, 1983.

72. *Subcommittee No. 5*, pt. 2, p. 1583.

73. *New York Times*, 26 Apr. 1964, 1.

74. *Subcommittee No. 5*, pt. 3, p. 2520.

75. In this regard see the comments of Congressmen Watson and Mathias, in ibid., pt. 3, p. 1522.

76. Ibid., pt. 3, p. 1465.

77. Ibid., pt. 2, pp. 1520–21.

78. Ibid., pt. 2, pp. 1522.

79. See House, *Civil Rights Act of 1963*, 88th Cong., 1st sess., 1963, H. Rept. 914, serial 12544, reproduced in app. B of this volume; and Comment, "Title VI," 833–34.

80. 42 U.S.C.A. § 2000c-6 (1964).

81. *Congressional Record*, 88th Cong., 2d sess., 7 Apr. 1964, 7060.

82. See *United States Code Congressional and Administrative News*, 88th Cong., 2d sess., 1964, 2393.

83. *Congressional Record*, 88th Cong., 2d sess., 7 Apr. 1964, 7061, 7063.

84. *Congressional Record*, 88th Cong., 2d sess., 7 Feb. 1964, 2499.

85. See Lindsay's remarks on this subject at *Congressional Record*, 88th Cong., 2d sess., 7 Feb. 1964, 2499–2500.

86. 42 U.S.C.A. § 2000d-1 (1964).

87. *Congressional Record*, 88th Cong., 2d sess., 30 Mar. 1964, 6544.

88. 42 U.S.C.A. § 2000d-1 (1964).

89. *Congressional Record*, 88th Cong., 2d sess., 7 Feb. 1964, 2505–6.

90. See the comments of Senator Pastore on this point in *Congressional Record*, 88th Cong., 2d sess., 7 Apr. 1964, 6837–44.

91. *Congressional Record*, 88th Cong., 2d sess., 4 June 1964, 12714–15. Senator Pastore also emphasized that "Title VI is not a device to terminate all Federal aid to a State or community because there has been discrimination in one specific program," and added that "only the program in which discrimination has been practiced" would be affected by Title VI. *Congressional Record*, 88th Cong., 2d sess., 7 Apr. 1964, 7059.

92. *Congressional Record*, 88th Cong., 2d sess., 7 Apr. 1964, 7059.

93. In this regard, see *Subcommittee No. 5*, pt. 2, pp. 1748, 1788, 1890–91, 2404–6; and *Congressional Record*, 88th Cong., 2d sess., Mar. 18, 1964, 5605.

94. *Subcommittee No. 5*, pt. 3, p. 2406.

95. Senator Pastore half-jokingly observed, "If any unfairness existed, one can imagine what the repercussions would be on the floor of the Senate within those 30 days. Talk about a Filibuster—it would be a Roman holiday." *Congressional Record*, 88th Cong., 2d sess., 7 Apr. 1964, 7059.

96. This enumeration is drawn from *Congressional Record*, 88th Cong., 2d sess., 7 Apr. 1964, 6846–47.

Chapter 3—The Johnson Years: Implementing
and Redefining the Right to Equal
Educational Opportunity

1. *Brown et al. v. Board of Education of Topeka et al.* 347 U.S. 493, 74 S.Ct. 691 (1954).

2. *United States v. Jefferson County Board of Education,* 380 F.2d 385 (5th Cir. 1967) *(en banc).*

3. *Green v. County School Board of New Kent County, Virginia,* 391 U.S. 430 (1968).

4. Comment, "School Desegregation and the Office of Education Guidelines," *Georgetown Law Journal* 55 (1966): 327.

5. U.S. Commission on Civil Rights, *Survey of School Desegregation in the Southern and Border States, 1965-1966* (Washington, D.C.: Government Printing Office, 1966), 1.

6. Ibid., app. B, n. 3.

7. *New York Times,* 30 Apr. 1965, 1.

8. As cited in Louis H. Pollak, "Ten Years after the Decision," *Federal Bar Journal* 24 (1964): 123.

9. *Watson v. City of Memphis,* 373 U.S. 526, 530, 83 S.Ct. 1317, 1322 (1963); *Griffin v. County School Board of Prince Edward County,* 377 U.S. 229, 84 S.Ct. 1232 (1964).

10. Gary Orfield, *The Reconstruction of Southern Education* (New York: John Wiley & Sons, 1969), 79.

11. One analyst has contended that political considerations surrounding the 1964 presidential election caused Johnson to postpone the issuance of regulations until after the election. See Beryl Radin, *Implementation, Change, and the Federal Bureaucracy: School Desegregation Policy in HEW, 1964-68* (New York: Teachers' College, 1977), 77.

12. *Saturday Review,* 20 Mar. 1965, 60.

13. Indeed, the U.S. Commission on Civil Rights complained in its February 1966 report that, for purposes of demonstrating compliance with Title VI, the Office of Education had accepted promises to comply with court orders whose terms fell "far below standards required by that office for school districts desegregating under voluntary plans." U.S. Commission on Civil Rights, *Report of the U.S. Commission on Civil Rights, February 1966* (Washington, D.C.: Government Printing Office, 1966), 85.

14. *New York Times,* 7 Mar. 1965, 30.

15. As part of the requirements of Title VI, Education Commissioner Francis Keppel announced that desegregation plans from southern school districts had to be received by his office by 30 June 1965, because that was the deadline for allocating available federal funds. *New York Times,* 30 Apr. 1965,

21. Hundreds of school officials came to Washington to complain to or negotiate with the Office of Education. During one week near that deadline, the Office of Education received fourteen hundred desegregation plans from districts in southern and border states. *New York Times,* 11 July 1965, 47.

Lawyers for the Office of Education reviewed the desegregation plans to determine if they conformed to the Guidelines. By Labor Day, however, the agency had still not approved plans submitted by 636 school districts. *Singleton v. Jackson Municipal School District,* 348 F.2d 731 (5th Cir. 1964).

16. *New York Times,* 7 Mar. 1965, 1.

17. See Orfield, *Reconstruction,* 78, 100, 148; Radin, *Implementation,* 104; *New York Times,* 9 May 1965, 40. The April 1965 Guidelines were officially entitled "General Statement of Policies under Title VI of Civil Rights Act of 1964 respecting Desegregation of Elementary and Secondary Schools."

18. 42 U.S.C. § 2000d-5, Supp. II, 1965–66.

19. *Congressional Record,* 89th Cong., 2d sess., 20 Oct. 1966, 28215.

20. Alexander Bickel, "Forcing Desegregation through Title VI," *New Republic,* 9 Apr. 1966, 8–9; U.S. Commission on Civil Rights, *Survey, 1965–66,* 2.

21. White House memorandum, 23 Apr. 1965, in *Civil Rights during the Johnson Administration, 1963–1969* (Frederick, Md.: University Publications of America, 1984), pt. 1, pp. 0411 and 0413.

22. *New York Times,* 11 July 1965, sec. 3, p. 47.

23. Orfield, *Reconstruction,* 120.

24. U.S. Commission on Civil Rights, *Survey, 1965–66,* 29.

25. *New York Times,* 3 Mar. 1965, 26.

26. *New York Times,* 14 Mar. 1966, 25.

27. See *United States v. Jefferson County Board of Education,* 372 F.2d 859 (5th Cir. 1966).

28. As cited in ibid.

29. U.S. Commission on Civil Rights, *Survey, 1965–66,* 46.

30. *Lee v. Macon County Board of Education,* 267 F. Supp. 467 (M.D. Ala. 1967).

31. *Jefferson,* 372 F.2d 859 n. 50.

32. *Saturday Review,* 20 Mar. 1965, 60.

33. Comments, "School Desegregation and the Office of Education Guidelines," *Duquesne Law Review* 6 (1967–68): 382.

34. *Congressional Record,* 89th Cong., 2d sess., 6 Oct. 1966, 25578; Robert G. Sherrill, "Guidelines and Frustration," *Nation,* 16 Jan. 1967, 70; U.S. Commission on Civil Rights, *Survey, 1965–66,* 26.

35. This provision was ultimately changed during the Carter administration when, by executive order, the authority to review rules, regulations, and orders of general applicability under Title VI was delegated to the attorney general in Executive Order 12250, 45 *Fed. Reg.* 72995 (1980).

36. Radin, *Implementation*, 105. See also Notes and Comments, "The Courts, HEW, and Southern School Desegregation," *Yale Law Journal* 77 (Dec. 1967): 363. HEW secretary Celebrezze apparently decided that HEW and not the president should bear the political brunt of the Guidelines, and hence the Guidelines were not issued as regulations approved by the president. White House memorandum, 23 Apr. 1965, in *Civil Rights during the Johnson Administration, 1963–69*, pt. 1, p. 0411.

37. Indeed, the Office of Education never did bring itself to decide formally whether to issue the 1965 Guidelines. In this regard, see Radin, *Implementation*, 104–7; and Alan Wolk, *The Presidency and Black Civil Rights: Eisenhower to Nixon* (Rutherford, N.J.: Fairleigh Dickinson University Press, 1971), 115.

38. *Singleton*, 348 F.2d 729.

39. *Evers v. Jackson Municipal Separate School District*, 324 F.2d 408 (5th Cir. 1964).

40. *Singleton*, 348 F.2d 729–30.

41. Ibid.

42. *Price v. Denison Independent School District*, 348 F.2d 1010 (5th Cir. 1965). The Eighth Circuit also indicated that it placed great reliance on the HEW Guidelines. It ruled that the Guidelines "must be heavily relied upon," and that the "courts should endeavor to model their standards after those promulgated by the executive." *Kemp v. Beasley*, 352 F.2d 18–19 (8th Cir. 1965). In another case, the Eighth Circuit found that the Guidelines "are entitled to serious judicial deference." *Smith v. Board of Education of Morrilton*, 365 F.2d 770 (8th Cir. 1966).

43. Price, 348 F.2d 1013.

44. *Singleton v. Jackson Municipal Separate School District*, 348 F.2d 869 (5th Cir. 1966).

45. *New York Times*, 23 Aug. 1965, 19.

46. Francis Keppel to Joseph Califano, memorandum, 16 Aug. 1965, in *Civil Rights during the Johnson Administration, 1963–69*, pt. 1, p. 0416.

47. *New York Times*, 14 Sept. 1965, 30.

48. Harold Howe II to Douglas Cater, memorandum, 19 Jan. 1966, in *Civil Rights during the Johnson Administration, 1963–1969*, pt. 1, reel 8, p. 0572; Cater to F. Peter Libassi, memorandum, 21 Jan. 1966, in *Civil Rights during the Johnson Administration, 1963–1969*, reel 13, p. 0377.

49. As cited in Wolk, *Presidency*, 119.

50. 45 C.F.R. § 181.54, amending 45 C.F.R. § 181.5 (Supp. 1966).

51. See F. Peter Libassi to Lee White and Douglas Cater, memorandum, 4 Feb. 1966, in *Civil Rights during the Johnson Administration*, 1963–1969, reel 13, p. 0381.

52. 45 C.F.R. § 181.54, amending 45 C.F.R. § 181.5 (Supp. 1966).

53. 45 C.F.R. § 181.13(b)-(d), amending 45 C.F.R. §181.5(b)(1) (Supp. 1966).

54. Sherrill, "Guidelines," 70, 69, emphasis in the original.

55. *New York Times,* 30 Sept. 1966, 26.

56. Orfield, *Reconstruction,* 147.

57. *New York Times,* 12 Apr. 1966, 18.

58. Orfield, *Reconstruction,* 277.

59. *New York Times,* 14 Mar. 1966, 25.

60. *New York Times,* 12 Apr. 1966, 18. See also the comments of Congressman Whittener in *Congressional Record,* 89th Cong., 2d sess., 6 Aug. 1966, 18703.

61. Orfield, *Reconstruction,* 246.

62. *Washington Post,* 1 Jan. 1967, A5.

63. *Congressional Record,* 89th Cong., 2d sess., 9 Aug. 1966, 18701.

64. *Congressional Record,* 89th Cong., 2d sess., 9 Aug. 1966, 18704.

65. *Congressional Record,* 89th Cong., 2d sess., 9 Aug. 1966, 18709.

66. *Congressional Record,* 89th Cong., 2d sess., 9 Aug. 1966, 18717. For the Senate debate on Title VI that focused on this distinction, see ibid., 88th Cong., 2d sess., 4 June 1964, 12715, 12717.

67. *Congressional Record,* 89th Cong., 2d sess., 9 Aug. 1966, 18711.

68. For these remarks, see *Congressional Record,* 89th Cong., 2d sess., 9 Aug. 1966, 18711, 18720, 18716, 18721, 18706, 18717.

69. *Congressional Record,* 89th Cong., 2d sess., 9 Aug. 1966, 18717.

70. *Congressional Record,* 89th Cong., 2d sess., 9 Aug. 1966, 25574.

71. *Congressional Record,* 89th Cong., 2d sess., 9 Aug. 1966, 18718, 18719, 18720.

72. *New York Times,* 12 May 1967, 39. For the House debate, see *Congressional Record,* 89th Cong. 2d sess., 20 Oct. 1966, 28207-15.

73. *New York Times,* 30 Sept. 1966, 1.

74. *Jefferson,* 372 F.2d 836, 853.

75. Ibid., 847.

76. *Jefferson,* 372 F.2d 836, 896-902.

77. *Jefferson,* 380 F.2d 385 (5th Cir. 1967).

78. Case Comments, *Harvard Law Review* 81 (1967): 77. The strong endorsement of the HEW Guidelines by the *Jefferson* court was all the more unusual because the court raised the issue *sua sponte* in its request for supplemental briefs. In this regard, see *Jefferson,* 372 F.2d 848 n. 13; and *Jefferson,* 380 F.2d 401, 413.

79. Kenneth B. Clark, *Dark Ghetto* (New York: Harper & Row, 1965), 111, 117.

80. Charles E. Silberman, *Crisis in Black and White* (New York: Vintage Books, 1964), 302, 304.

81. *Davis v. Board of School Commissioners,* 364 F.2d 898 (5th Cir. 1966).

82. In this regard, see Case Comments, *Harvard Law Review* 81 (1967):

477; and Jack Peltason, *Fifty-eight Lonely Men* (New York: Harcourt, World, & Brace, 1961).

83. Case Comments, *Harvard Law Review* 81 (1967): 477.

84. *Jefferson*, 372 F.2d 856, 852.

85. Ibid., 854; Radin advances a different view of the character and capacities of the judicial process. She examines the administrative and the judicial process and concludes that there are certain advantages to the latter in desegregation cases. "The court system provided an opportunity for both parties involved to present a case, describing the local conditions as they perceived them. The information presented about the case (and the remedy that was eventually struck to change conditions) was tailored for a specific district. And if a Black parent or officials from a school district felt that satisfactory treatment was not accorded during initial hearing, the appeal process provided an opportunity for higher level federal courts to review the case." Radin, *Implementation*, 100.

86. See Peltason, *Fifty-eight Men*, 251, for a similar view.

87. *Jefferson*, 372 F.2d 860, 854, 855.

88. Ibid., 854.

89. *Jefferson*, 380 F.2d 401, 412.

90. *Jefferson*, 372 F.2d 848 n. 13.

91. See Michael W. Giles and Thomas G. Walker, "Judicial Policy-Making and Southern School Desegregation," *Journal of Politics* 37 (1975): 918–19.

92. *Jefferson*, 372 F.2d 860–61.

93. *Singleton*, 348 F.2d 731; and *Jefferson*, 372 F.2d 859. For a similar point noted in an Eighth Circuit case, see *Kemp*, 352 F.2d 14.

94. *Singleton*, 348 F.2d 731.

95. *Price*, 348 F.2d 1013–14.

96. *Jefferson*, 372 F.2d 855, 896.

97. See Radin, *Implementation*, 57–61; and Orfield, *Reconstruction*, 78.

98. White House Task Force on Civil Rights, *To Fulfill These Rights* (Washington, D.C.: Government Printing Office, 1966), 63.

99. F. Peter Libassi to Joseph Califano, Douglas Cater, and Nicholas deB. Katzenbach, memorandum, 1 Aug. 1966, in *Civil Rights during the Johnson Administration*, 1963–69, pt. 1, p. 0711.

100. Sherrill, "Guidelines," 70, 73.

101. *Price*, 348 F.2d 1014.

102. *Jefferson*, 372 F.2d 884.

103. In this regard, see *Cooper v. Aaron*, 358 U.S. 7, 78 S.Ct. 1404 (1957); *Watson*, 373 U.S. 530, 83 S.Ct. 1317; *Griffin*, 377 U.S. 229, 84 S.Ct. 1232.

104. *Singleton*, 348 F.2d 731.

105. *Jefferson*, 372 F.2d 856, 852; emphasis added.

106. Ibid., 848, 859–60, 856.

107. Case Comments, *Harvard Law Review* 81 (1967): 478.

108. *Jefferson,* 372 F.2d 910. Judge Wisdom did note that in any school desegregation case the basic issue involved constitutional rights, and not rights under Title VI. Consequently, he acknowledged that though the court gave great deference to the HEW Guidelines, that deference did not preclude challenges to those Guidelines by any party. To emphasize that point, he cited three cases in which courts had found desegregation plans approved by HEW to be inadequate to protect the constitutional rights of black schoolchildren. *Jefferson,* 372 F.2d 895.

109. Orfield, *Reconstruction,* 73; see also 116, 134, 142, for comments indicating the administration's fear of reversals to its policies in southern federal courts.

110. Ibid., 74–75.

111. Wolk, *Presidency,* 116; House Committee on Appropriations, *Departments of Labor and Health, Education, and Welfare Appropriations for 1968: Hearing before the Subcommittee on Departments of Labor and Health, Education, and Welfare and Related Agencies Appropriations of the Committee of Appropriations,* 90th Cong., 1st sess., 1–3, 9, 10, 13, 22 Mar. 1967, pt. 2, p. 101.

112. Orfield, *Reconstruction,* 145.

113. As cited in Wolk, *Presidency,* 121.

114. Ibid.

115. *Singleton,* 348 F.2d 869, emphasis in original.

116. *Jefferson,* 372 F.2d 895, footnote omitted from quotation.

117. Notes and Comments, "The Courts," 328–29.

118. *Kemp,* 352 F.2d 19.

119. *Clark v. Board of Education of Little Rock School District,* 374 F.2d 569 (8th Cir. 1967).

120. *Kemp,* 351 F.2d 19.

121. In this regard see *Jefferson,* 372 F.2d 845 n. 3. In the seven cases from Alabama and Louisiana consolidated in *Jefferson,* the desegregation of schools did not begin until 1965. In both states the overall percentage of black schoolchildren attending desegregated schools was less than 1 percent.

122. For statistical information on the slow rate of progress toward desegregation in the Deep South, see *Jefferson,* 372 F.2d, app. B, 903.

123. *Smith,* 365 F.2d 770, 784.

124. Radin, *Implementation,* 117, 118.

125. *Alabama NAACP State Conference of Branches et al. v. Wallace,* 269 F. Supp. 349 (M.D. Ala. 1967).

126. *Lee,* 267 F. Supp. 458.

127. *Lee v. Macon County Board of Elections,* 270 F. Supp. 864–65 (M.D. Ala. 1967).

128. Ibid., 863.

129. Ibid., 866.

130. *Alabama NAACP,* 269 F. Supp. 352.

131. "Summary of the File concerning Accomplishments in Civil Rights in 1965," undated memorandum, in *Civil Rights during the Johnson Administration, 1963–69,* reel 8, p. 0574.

132. Giles and Walker, "Judicial Policy-Making," 923.

133. As cited in Wolk, *Presidency,* 145.

134. Radin, *Implementation,* 47.

135. Wolk, *Presidency,* 122.

136. In this regard, see Radin, *Implementation,* 105–6.

137. Wolk, *Presidency,* 117.

138. In this regard, see Orfield, *Reconstruction,* 64.

139. *New York Times,* 31 Dec. 1966, 1.

140. *Washington Post,* 31 Dec. 1966, A17.

141. *Washington Post,* 1 Jan. 1967, A5.

142. *New York Times,* 1 Jan. 1967, 43.

143. Peltason, *Fifty-eight Men,* 77–81.

144. Notes and Comments, "The Courts," 328–29.

145. See Orfield, *Reconstruction,* 109–11.

146. *New York Times,* 1 Jan. 1967, 43.

147. White House Task Force, *To Fulfill These Rights,* 63.

148. Notes and Comments, "The Courts," 360.

149. Ibid., 356.

150. *International Encyclopedia of the Social Sciences* (New York: Cromwell, Collier, & Macmillan, 1968), 9:244, emphasis added.

151. *Jefferson,* 372 F.2d 884, emphasis in original.

152. *Jefferson,* 380 F.2d 389.

153. *Briggs v. Elliot,* 132 F. Supp. 776 (E.D. S.C. 1955). The *en banc* court in *Jefferson* notes at 380 F.2d 389 n. 2 that the distinction between integration and desegregation was first expressed in the *Briggs* case.

154. *Briggs,* 132 F. Supp. 777.

155. The Eighth Circuit rejected the *Briggs* approach in *Kemp,* 352 F.2d 14, 21; and in *Kelley v. Altheimer,* 378 F.2d 488 (8th Cir. 1967); as did the Tenth Circuit in *Board of Education of Oklahoma City Public Schools et al. v. Dowell et al.,* 375 F.2d 158 (10th Cir. 1967); and as did the Third Circuit in *Evans v. Ennis,* 281 F.2d 385 (3d Cir. 1960), *cert. denied* 364 U.S. 802, 82 S.Ct. 22 (1961).

156. *Jefferson,* 380 F.2d 389.

157. *Green,* 391 U.S. 442. Gerald Gunther, a noted constitutional law scholar, linked the Supreme Court's conceptual approach in *Green* to the Fifth Circuit's decisions in *Jefferson.* Writing of the Court's ruling in *Green,* he observed, "The increasing emphasis on affirmative obligations to overcome

past de jure segregation, on results rather than process, had come somewhat earlier in lower federal courts and in HEW guidelines issued under the 1964 Civil Rights Act. See, e.g., the extensive discussion of the "duty to desegregate–duty to integrate distinction" in *United States v. Jefferson County Board of Education.*" Gerald Gunther, *Constitutional Law: Cases and Materials,* 11th ed. (Mineola, N.Y.: Foundation Press, 1991), 730 n. 4. In a similar vein, Harvard Law School's Laurence Tribe also acknowledged the direct connection between *Green* and the Guidelines. He noted that the *Green* decision, "requiring not only cessation of discriminatory activities, but actual disestablishment of a dual system, in effect supported the HEW guidelines . . . upheld somewhat earlier in lower courts." Laurence Tribe, *American Constitutional Law,* 2d ed. (Mineola, N.Y.: Foundation Press, 1988), 1409 n. 23.

158. For early lower-court cases dealing with this issue, see *Taylor v. Board of Education,* 191 F. Supp. 181 (S.D. N.Y.), *aff'd,* 294 F.2d 36 (2d Cir.), *cert. denied,* 368 U.S. 940, 82 S.Ct. 382 (1961); and *Dowell v. School Board of Oklahoma,* 244 F. Supp. 981 (W.D. Okla. 1965).

159. Gerald Gunther, *Constitutional Law,* 12th ed. (Mineola, N.Y.: Foundation Press, 1975), 729.

160. Gunther, *Constitutional Law,* 730.

161. *Green,* 391 U.S. 438, 439, 88 S.Ct. 1694, 1695.

162. For cases making this point, applying the principles of *Green,* see *Raney v. Board of Education of Gould School District,* 391 U.S. 444, 88 S.Ct. 1697 (1968); and *Monroe v. Board of Commissioners of City of Jackson,* 391 U.S. 452, 88 S. Ct. 1700 (1968).

163. 33 *Fed. Reg.* 4956 (1968); see also *Washington Post,* 20 June 1969, A2.

Chapter 4 – The Nixon-Ford Years: Litigating against the Political Backlash

1. Frederic T. Spindel, "Constitutional Law — Notes," *Texas Law Review* 46 (1967): 268–69 n. 13.

2. U.S. Commission on Civil Rights, *Southern School Desegregation, 1966–67* (Washington, D.C.: Government Printing Office, 1967), 6–7, 10. The figure provided by the Office of Education for 1965–66 was 7.5 percent (U.S. Commission on Civil Rights, *Southern School Desegregation,* 10); see also *Congressional Record,* 89th Cong., 2d sess., 6 Oct. 1966, 25578.

3. Bullock and Rodgers argue that inasmuch as federal funds disproportionately benefited black children, many districts found the loss of federal monies to be an "acceptable price to pay" for maintaining segregation. Charles Bullock and Harrell Rodgers, "Coercion to Compliance: Southern School Districts and School Desegregation Guidelines," *Journal of Politics* 38 (1976): 994.

4. Rowland Evans and Robert Novak, *Nixon in the White House* (New York: Random House, 1971), 141.

5. *New York Times,* 9 Feb. 1968, 20.

6. Gary Orfield, *Must We Bus?* (Washington, D.C.: Brookings Institution, 1978), 242.

7. Evans and Novak, *Nixon,* 139.

8. As cited in ibid., 139–40; see also p. 141 for additional comments by Nixon on freedom-of-choice plans.

9. As cited in Evans and Novak, *Nixon,* 140–41. In this regard see also Orfield, *Bus,* 282.

10. U.S. Department of Health, Education, and Welfare, *Title VI of the Civil Rights Act of 1964 — Ten Years Later, An Anniversary Progress Report* (Washington, D.C.: Government Printing Office, 1974), 2; *New York Times,* 8 July 1969, 20.

11. Evans and Novak, *Nixon,* 138.

12. As cited in Allan Wolk, *The Presidency and Black Civil Rights: Eisenhower to Nixon* (Rutherford, N.J.: Fairleigh Dickinson University Press, 1971), 149–50.

13. *U.S. News and World Report,* 10 Mar. 1969, 38–46.

14. *Washington Post,* 16 Mar. 1969, A1.

15. 42 U.S.C. § 2000d-1.

16. David Kirp, *Just Schools* (Berkeley and Los Angeles: University of California Press, 1982), 35; see also Orfield, *Bus,* 285–86.

17. *Washington Post,* 27 July 1969, A1.

18. Ibid.

19. Ibid.

20. *Washington Post,* 13 Sept. 1969, A1.

21. Harrell Rodgers and Charles Bullock, *Law and Social Change: Civil Rights Laws and Their Consequences* (New York: McGraw-Hill, 1972), 99.

22. As cited in Bullock and Rodgers, *Law,* 90; see also Orfield, *Bus,* 325–27; and Gary J. Greenberg, "Revolt at Justice," *University of Chicago Magazine,* Mar.–Apr. 1970, 24.

23. As quoted in Stephen E. Ambrose, *Nixon* (New York: Simon & Schuster, 1987), 331.

24. *Washington Post,* 29 June 1969, A1.

25. As cited in Wolk, *Presidency,* 152.

26. As cited in Bullock and Rodgers, *Law,* 91.

27. *National Journal,* 28 Feb. 1970, 435.

28. As cited in Tom Wicker, *One of Us: Richard Nixon and the American Dream* (New York: Random House, 1991), 501.

29. *National Journal,* 7 Mar. 1970, 487.

30. *New York Times,* 4 Mar. 1970, 29.

31. As cited in Ambrose, *Nixon*, 332.

32. Ibid.

33. As cited in Wicker, *One of Us*, 488, emphasis in original.

34. Ambrose, *Nixon*, 365, 407.

35. *Alexander v. Holmes*, 396 U.S. 1218, 90 S.Ct. 14, *per curiam* (1969), emphasis added.

36. *The Public Papers of the Presidents of the United States: Richard Nixon, 1970* (Washington, D.C.: Government Printing Office, 1971), 1:750.

37. Richard Nixon, *Memoirs of Richard Nixon* (New York: Grossett & Dunlap, 1978), 440.

38. As cited in Wicker, *One of Us*, 494.

39. As noted in *Swann v. Charlotte-Mecklenburg Board of Education*, 402 U.S. 15 n. 5., 91 S.Ct. 1275 n. 5 (1971).

40. *Swann*, 402 U.S. 15, 16, 25, 91 S.Ct. 1275, 1276, 1280.

41. *Swann*, 402 U.S. 26, 91 S.Ct. 1281.

42. *Swann*, 402 U.S. 28, 91 S.Ct. 1282.

43. *Bradley v. Milliken*, 484 F.2d 245 (6th Cir. 1973).

44. Ibid., 814–15 (Marshall, J., dissenting).

45. Laurence H. Tribe, *American Constitutional Law*, 2d ed. (New York: Foundation Press, 1988), 1495.

46. The *Adams* litigation produced numerous decisions by the U.S. District Court for the District of Columbia and the U.S. Court of Appeals for the District of Columbia. As the secretaries of the Department of Health, Education, and Welfare, and later the Department of Education, changed, the named defendant in the case changed. Occasionally, a written opinion in *Adams* was reported under the name of the Women's Equity Action League, a party whose separate lawsuit became joined with the *Adams* litigation. The following is a complete list of the written opinions issued in the *Adams* litigation: *Adams v. Richardson*, 358 F. Supp. 97 (D.D.C. 1973); *Adams v. Richardson*, 480 F.2d 1163, (1973) *(en banc); Adams v. Weinberger*, 391 F. Supp. 265 (D.D.C. 1975); *Adams v. Califano*, 430 F. Supp. 119 (D.D.C. 1978); *Adams v. Bell*, 711 F.2d 164, (D.C. Cir. 1983) *(en banc); Women's Equity Action League v. Bell*, 743 F.2d 43 (D.C. Cir. 1984); *Adams v. Bennett*, 675 F. Supp. 668 (D.D.C. 1987); *Women's Equity Action League v. Cavazos*, 879 F.2d 880 (D.C. Cir. 1989); *Women's Equity Action League v. Cavazos*, 906 F.2d 742 (D.C. Cir. 1990).

47. *Washington Post*, 5 Sept. 1992, A1.

48. *New York Times*, 5 Sept. 1992, 28.

49. Ibid.

50. Plaintiffs' Complaint for Declaratory and Other Relief, 5, *Adams*. All of the written documents cited from the *Adams* case were obtained by reviewing the materials on file at the federal district court for the District of Columbia or by obtaining copies of the documents from the lawyers involved

in the *Adams* litigation. The author is particularly indebted to Elliot Lichtman for providing access to his litigation files on the case.

51. As noted in *Women's Equity Action League v. Cavazos,* 879 F.2d 881.

52. Plaintiffs' Reply to Defendants' Objections to Proposed Decree, 2, *Adams.*

53. *New York Times,* 20 Oct. 1970, 32.

54. Defendants' Objections to Plaintiffs' Proposed Decree, 4 Jan. 1973, 3, *Adams.*

55. *Adams v. Richardson,* 356 F. Supp. 97.

56. Ibid., 94.

57. Ibid., 97.

58. Ibid., 96.

59. *New York Times,* 17 Nov. 1972, 24.

60. *Adams v. Richardson,* 480 F.2d 1163 n. 4, 1164, 1165.

61. Ibid., 1164.

62. Ibid., 1165.

63. Ibid., 1165.

64. Ibid., 1163; emphasis added.

65. *Women's Equity Action League v. Weinberger,* U.S. District Court for the District of Columbia, C.A. no. 74–1720.

66. *Adams v. Weinberger,* 391 F. Supp. 265.

67. That requirement was contained in 45 C.F.R. § 80.7(c).

68. *Adams v. Weinberger,* 391 F. Supp. 271.

69. "Administration and Enforcement of Civil Rights Laws and Authorities," 40 *Fed. Reg.* 24148–49 (1975).

70. Ibid.

71. 45 C.F.R. § 81.5.

72. Cynthia G. Brown, "Twenty Years On: Equity in Education and Civil Rights Enforcement" (1986), 14.

73. Affidavit of Martin Gerry, 6 Feb. 1976, 16, *Adams v. Weinberger.*

74. Complaint, 8–9, *Adams and Martinez v. Mathews.*

75. Complaint for Temporary Restraining Order, Preliminary Injunction and Declaratory Judgment Civil Action, 2, *Adams v. Weinberger.*

76. Affidavit of Martin Gerry, 12–13, 23.

77. Affidavit of Peter Holmes, sworn to on 3 June 1975, 28–29, *Adams v. Weinberger.*

78. Martin Gerry, press conference, 15 June 1976, 27, 37, OCR Office of Public Affairs, Washington, D.C.

79. Ibid., 5.

80. *Adams v. Mathews,* U.S. District Court for the District of Columbia, transcript of the proceedings, 14 June 1976, 28.

81. *Washington Post,* 18 May 1969, A1.

82. As cited in Q. Whitefield Ayers, "Desegregating or Debilitating Higher Education," *The Public Interest*, no. 69 (fall 1982): 101–2.

83. North Carolina's Motion for Preliminary Injunction, with attached Affidavit of Raymond Danson, 13 Apr. 1979, 1, *North Carolina v. United States*. (This document was obtained from the Office of Public Affairs of the Office for Civil Rights, Washington, D.C.)

84. The tenth state, Louisiana, declined to submit a plan, and its file was referred to the Justice Department, which brought a desegregation suit against the state.

85. Peter Holmes to the Hon. William Waller, 18 Apr. 1974, 1.

86. "Office of Civil Rights Response to Mississippi's 'Plan of Compliance to Title VI of the Civil Rights Act of 1964 — February 1974,'" 2–4.

87. The items outlined above are drawn from ibid., passim.

88. See Reply Memorandum in Support of Plaintiffs' Motion for Further Relief, 26 Nov. 1975, 4–6, 9–11, *Adams*.

89. Ibid., 1.

90. Defendants' Reply Brief in Opposition to Plaintiffs' Motion for Further Relief, 3, *Adams*.

91. Ibid.

92. *Adams v. Richardson*, 480 F.2d 1164.

93. Transcript of proceedings, 23, *Adams*.

94. *Chronicle of Higher Education*, 22 Dec. 1974, A1.

95. Gerry to Mandel, 15 Sept. 1975, 1, OCR Office of Public Affairs.

96. *Mandel v. U.S. Dept. of Health, Education and Welfare*, 411 F. Supp. 542 (D.-Md. 1976).

97. Ibid., 556–59, 564.

98. Ibid., 558.

99. *Adams v. Richardson*, 480 F.2d 1164.

100. *Brown v. Weinberger*, 417 F. Supp. 1215 (D.D.C. 1975).

101. U.S. Department of Health, Education, and Welfare, *Title VI — Ten Years Later*, 2.

102. Marc Gallanter, "Why the 'Haves' Come Out Ahead: Speculations on the Limits of Legal Chance," *Law and Society Review* 9 (1974–75): 164.

103. *Chronicle of Higher Education*, 23 Feb. 1976, A10.

Chapter 5 — Carter: Litigation and the New Civil Rights Priorities

1. As cited in Gary Orfield, *Must We Bus?* (Washington, D.C.: Brookings Institution, 1976), 275.

2. Ibid.

3. *Title VI Forum* 3 (fall 1977): 1, emphasis in original.

4. *New York Times,* 22 July 1977, 22.

5. *Title VI Forum* 3 (winter 1977): 8.

6. On the other side of the ledger, black civil rights leaders opposed the choice of Griffin Bell as attorney general. See Orfield, *Bus,* 354–55.

7. *New York Times,* 27 Jan. 1977, 19.

8. The last school system to have its funds terminated for Title VI violations, up to that point, was Ferndale, Michigan, in June 1972.

9. *Washington Post,* 18 Feb. 1977, A12.

10. That lengthy delay did not violate the time frames in *Adams* because the time frames applied only until administrative proceedings to enforce Title VI began, or OCR referred a matter to the Justice Department.

11. *Washington Post,* 13 May 1977, A13.

12. Points and Authorities in Support of Defendant's Motion to Consolidate Actions, for Leave for Consolidated Order, and for Enlargement of Time, June 1977, 2, *Adams v. Califano.* OCR had new responsibilities to enforce the Age Discrimination Act of 1975. 42 U.S.C. § 601 *et seq.* Section 303 of the act prohibited discrimination on the basis of age in programs receiving federal financial assistance. OCR was also given authority to enforce sections of the Indian Self-Determination and Education Assistance Act, which required preferences for Indian organizations in the award of contracts or grants under the act and preferences for training and employment of Indians in connection with contracts under the act. 25 U.S.C. § 450(b).

13. Points and Authority in Support of Defendant's Motions to Consolidate Actions, 14, *Adams.*

14. *Washington Post,* 6 June 1977, A5.

15. Points and Authorities in Support of Motion for Interim Relief and for Expedited Scheduling of Any Oral Argument, 27 Sept. 1977, 3, *Adams.*

16. Affidavit of David Tatel, 6 June 1977, 4, *Adams.*

17. Ibid.

18. Affidavit of David Tatel, 20 Sept. 1977, 21–23, *Adams.*

19. Points and Authorities in Support of Motion for Entry of Consolidated Order Modifying Order of June 14, 1976, 4, *Adams.*

20. Califano was one of the few government officials who declined to be interviewed for this book.

21. *Chronicle of Higher Education,* 17 Oct. 1977, 12.

22. Order, 25 Oct. 1977, 2, *Adams.*

23. Supplemental Memorandum of Section 504 Plaintiffs in Support of Application for Leave to Intervene and in Opposition to Defendants' Motion to Modify Order of June 14, 1976, by Entry of Proposed Consolidated Order, 23 Sept. 1977, 3, *Adams.*

24. Statement of Joseph Califano Jr., 29 Dec. 1977, 3, obtained at Office of Public Affairs, Office for Civil Rights, Washington, D.C.

25. *Washington Star*, 30 Dec. 1977, 4. Civil rights lawyers, by contrast, argued that the initiatives that OCR had taken in compliance reviews had been prompted by *Adams, Brown,* and other lawsuits. Cindy Brown to the Ad Hoc Civil Rights Coalition, memorandum re: OCR self-initiated reviews in elementary and secondary education under Title VI, 25 May 1976, 1. (A copy of this memorandum was provided to me by Cindy Brown.)

26. *Chronicle of Higher Education*, 9 Jan. 1978, 3.

27. Cynthia G. Brown, "Twenty Years On: Equity in Education and Civil Rights Enforcement" (1986), chap. 3, p. 22.

28. *Chronicle of Higher Education*, 11 Apr. 1977, 4.

29. *Washington Post*, 1 Apr. 1977, A2.

30. 42 *Fed. Reg.* 40927–33 (1977).

31. 43 *Fed. Reg.* 7051 (1978).

32. 20 U.S.C. § 1714(a) (1974).

33. The language was as follows: "[T]he provisions of this chapter are not intended to modify or diminish the authority of the courts of the United States to enforce fully the Fifth and Fourteenth Amendments to the Constitution of the United States." 20 U.S.C. § 1702(b) (1974).

34. Public Law 95–205, 91 Stat. 1460 (1977).

35. See the comments of Senators Eagleton and Biden, in *Congressional Record—Senate*, 95th Cong., 1st sess., 28 June 1977, 10898, 10915–17; and of Congressmen Obey, Blanchard, and Edwards in *Congressional Record—House*, 95th Cong., 1st sess., 28 June 1977, 6047–52.

36. *Congressional Record—Senate*, 95th Cong., 1st sess., 28 June 1977, 10917.

37. *Congressional Record—Senate*, 95th Cong., 1st sess., 28 June 1978, 10915–16.

38. *Congressional Record—Senate*, 95th Cong., 1st sess., 28 June 1978, 10907.

39. When Congress passed the measure, there were only seventeen school districts in the nation in which HEW had determined that busing was required for the districts to comply with Title VI.

40. Justice Department Brief, *Brown v. Califano*, 28, 28 Feb. 1978.

41. *The Public Papers of the Presidents of the United States: Jimmy Carter, 1977* (Washington, D.C.: Government Printing Office, 1979), 2:2088.

42. *Brown v. Califano*, 455 F. Supp. 837 (D.D.C. 1978).

43. *Brown v. Califano*, 627 F.2d 1221 (D.C. Cir. 1980).

44. *Adams v. Califano*, 430 F. Supp. 119 (D.D.C. 1977).

45. Ibid., 120.

46. Ibid.; footnotes are omitted.

47. 43 *Fed. Reg.* 6658, 6660 (1978).

48. 43 *Fed. Reg.* 6659 (1978).

49. Ibid.

50. Ibid.

51. *Baltimore Sun*, 6 July 1977, 3.

52. *New York Times,* 6 July 1978, 14.

53. *Chronicle of Higher Education,* 11 July 1977, 4.

54. *Washington Post,* 7 July 1977, A4.

55. *Atlanta Constitution,* 14 July 1977, 1.

56. *HEW News,* 2 Feb. 1978, 1.

57. *Washington Post,* 14 Feb. 1978, A12.

58. *Public Papers: Jimmy Carter, 1977,* 1:310.

59. In fiscal year 1978, North Carolina received $88 million in federal aid, of which $55 million came from HEW. Affidavit of Raymond Dawson, 1, *North Carolina v. HEW* (E.D. N.C.) (Civ. Action no. 79–217-CIV-5).

60. Joseph A. Califano Jr., press conference, 22 Mar. 1978, 6–7. (I obtained a copy of this document from the OCR's Office of Public Affairs.)

61. As cited in Motion for Preliminary Injunction, 2, *North Carolina v. HEW.*

62. *HEW News,* 22 Mar. 1978, 1.

63. *Washington Post,* 25 Mar. 1978, A6.

64. *Raleigh News and Observer,* 15 Aug. 1978, 3.

65. *Raleigh News and Observer,* 12 Nov. 1978, 2.

66. *Detroit News,* 23 Dec. 1978, 6.

67. *New York Times,* 15 Apr. 1979, 18E.

68. *Chronicle of Higher Education,* 25 July 1978, 15.

69. *New York Times,* 6 Sept. 1976, A29.

70. *Chronicle of Higher Education,* 1 May 1978, 4.

71. *Adams Report,* May 1978, 2. The *Adams Report* was a newsletter, published with a Ford Foundation grant, that evaluated the impact of the *Adams* litigation on historically black colleges and universities. I am indebted to Professor Leonard Haines III for making the reports available to me.

72. Ibid.

73. *Geier v. Blanton,* 427 F. Supp. 644 (M.D. Tenn. 1977).

74. *Chronicle of Higher Education,* 4 Apr. 1977, 5.

75. *Chronicle of Higher Education,* 25 July 1978, 15.

76. In Maryland, for instance, the desegregation plan submitted by the state and accepted by HEW established a goal of 14-percent to 18-percent minority enrollment in the state's professional schools by 1980.

77. *Bakke v. Regents of University of California,* 438 U.S. 265, 98 S.Ct. 2733 (1977).

78. *New York Times,* 9 Aug. 1978, 14.

79. *U.S. News and World Report,* 14 Mar. 1978, 6.

80. *New York Times,* 2 Dec. 1979, 1.

81. *Washington Post,* 18 July 1978, A2.

82. William J. Wilson, *The Declining Significance of Race: Blacks and Changing American Institutions* (Chicago: University of Chicago Press, 1978).

83. 44 *Fed. Reg.* 5204 (1979).

84. Leonard Levy, Kenneth Karst, and Dennis Mahoney, *Civil Rights and Equality* (New York: Macmillan, 1988), 228.

Chapter 6—Reagan: The Irrelevant Formalism of the Legal Battles

1. House Committee on the Judiciary, *Department of Justice Authorization for Fiscal Year 1983: Hearing before the Committee on the Judiciary,* 97th Cong., 2d sess., 23 Feb. 1982, 92.

2. *New York Times,* 12 Feb. 1982, 20.

3. *New York Times,* 14 Dec. 1981, 21.

4. House Committee, *Department of Justice Authorization for Fiscal Year 1983,* 92; *National Journal,* 27 Mar. 1982, 536.

5. *National Journal,* 27 Mar. 1982, 539.

6. House Committee on the Judiciary, *Authorization Request for the Civil Rights Division of the Department of Justice: Hearing before the Subcommittee on Civil and Constitutional Rights of the Committee on the Judiciary,* 97th Cong., 2d sess., 4 Mar. 1982, 7.

7. House Committee on Education and Labor and the Judiciary, *Hearings on Higher Education Civil Rights Enforcement: Joint Hearings before the Subcommittee on Postsecondary Education of the Committee on Education and Labor and the Subcommittee on Civil and Constitutional Rights of the Committee on the Judiciary,* 98th Cong., 1st sess., 18 May 1983, 290.

8. Senate Committee on the Judiciary, *Nomination of William Bradford Reynolds to Be Associate Attorney General of the United States: Hearing before the Committee on the Judiciary,* 99th Cong., 1st sess., 5 June 1985, 181.

9. *New York Times,* 22 Mar. 1983, A23; *National Journal,* 28 May 1983, 1122.

10. *Boston Globe,* 27 Mar. 1981.

11. House Committee on Education and Labor, *Guaranteed Student Loan and Civil Rights Enforcement: Hearing before the Subcommittee on Postsecondary Education of the Committee on Education and Labor,* 97th Cong., 2d sess., 12 May 1982, 3.

12. Senate Committee, *Nomination of William Bradford Reynolds,* 181, 180.

13. House Committee, *Hearings on Higher Education Civil Rights Enforcement,* 301.

14. *New York Times,* 8 Sept. 1982, A18, and 12 Sept. 1982, A1. These individuals were members of fifty state advisory committees established by the U.S. Commission on Civil Rights.

15. *New York Times,* 8 Sept. 1982, A18.

16. *National Journal,* 27 Mar. 1982, 536.

17. Joel L. Selig, "The Reagan Justice Department and Civil Rights: What Went Wrong," *University of Illinois Law Review* 4 (1985): 787.

18. *New York Times,* 9 July 1984, A10.

19. *New York Times,* 14 Apr. 1981, A35.

20. See Public Law 96–88, 93 Stat. 668 (1979).

21. *New York Times,* 10 Mar. 1981, B8.

22. House Committee on the Judiciary, *Civil Rights Enforcement in the Department of Education: Hearing before the Subcommittee on Civil and Constitutional Rights of the Committee on the Judiciary,* 97th Cong., 2d sess., 30 Sept. 1982, 9.

23. Ibid.

24. *Washington Post,* 15 Jan. 1982, A13.

25. *National Journal,* 27 Mar. 1982, 537.

26. House Committee, *Hearings on Higher Education Civil Rights Enforcement,* 190, 289.

27. *New York Times,* 15 Dec. 1981, 22.

28. Ibid.; see also *Washington Post,* 8 Jan. 1982, A21.

29. *North Haven Board of Education v. Bell,* 456 U.S. 538, 102 S.Ct. 1926 (1982).

30. House Committee, *Hearings on Higher Education Civil Rights Enforcement,* 266.

31. E.g., see Statement of the U.S. Commission on Civil Rights, "Civil Rights Enforcement in Education," 14 June 1983, 5, obtained by the author through a request under the Freedom of Information Act.

32. *University of Richmond v. Bell,* 543 F. Supp. 321 (E.D. Va. 1982).

33. Ibid., 333; emphasis added.

34. House Committee, *Hearings on Higher Education Civil Rights Enforcement,* 267. See also *National Law Journal,* 18 July 1983, 30.

35. *Grove City College v. Bell,* 687 F.2d 700 (3d Cir. 1982).

36. *Hillsdale v. Department of Health, Education, and Welfare,* 696 F.2d 430 (6th Cir. 1982).

37. Brief for Respondent, 15–16, *Grove City College v. Bell,* 465 U.S. 555, 104 S.Ct. 1211 (1984).

38. *Washington Post,* 8 Mar. 1984, A22.

39. *Washington Post,* 9 Aug. 1983, A2.

40. *Grove City College,* 465 U.S. 574, 104 S.Ct. 1221 (1984).

41. Senate Committee on Labor and Human Resources, *The Civil Rights Restoration Act of 1987: Report Together with Minority Views (to Accompany S. 557),* 100th Cong., 1st sess., 5 June 1987, 11.

42. *New York Times,* 3 June 1984, A21.

43. House Committee on the Judiciary, *Discrimination in Federally Funded Programs: The Impact of the Grove City Decision. Oversight Hearing before the Subcommittee on Civil and Constitutional Rights of the Committee on the Judiciary,* 99th Cong., 2d sess., 7 Aug. 1986, 171, emphasis added. See also House Committee on Education and Labor, *A Report on the Investigation of the Civil Rights Enforcement*

Activities of the Office for Civil Rights, U.S. Department of Education, 100th Cong., 2d sess., Dec. 1988, 23.

44. House Committee on Governmental Operations, *Investigation of Civil Rights Enforcement by the Department of Education: Hearing before a Subcommittee of the Committee on Governmental Operations,* 99th Cong., 1st sess., 18 July, 11 Sept. 1985, 378.

45. House Committee, *Report on Enforcement Activities of the Office for Civil Rights,* 23, 24.

46. House Committee on Education and Labor, *Civil Rights Act of 1984: Joint Hearings before the Committee on Education and Labor and the Subcommittee on Civil and Constitutional Rights of the Committee on the Judiciary,* 98th Cong., 2d sess., 9 May 1984, 25.

47. Ibid., 75.

48. House Committee, *Discrimination in Federally Funded Programs,* 13.

49. *United States v. State of Alabama,* 828 F.2d 1532, 1551 (11th Cir. 1987).

50. *New York Times,* 3 Mar. 1988, A20.

51. House Committee on Education and Labor, *Civil Rights Restoration Act of 1985: Joint Hearings before the Committee on Education and Labor, and the Subcommittee on Civil and Constitutional Rights of the Committee on the Judiciary,* 99th Cong., 1st sess., 7 Mar. 1985, 231.

52. Public Law 100–259, § 908(1)(A–B), 102 Stat. 28 (1988).

53. Ibid., § 908(2)(A).

54. *New York Times,* 29 Jan. 1988, A1.

55. *Washington Post,* 3 Mar. 1988, A4.

56. *New York Times,* 29 Jan. 1988, A36.

57. *Washington Post,* 23 Mar. 1988, A1.

58. Ibid.

59. *New York Times,* 23 Mar. 1988, A1.

60. *New York Times,* 23 Mar. 1988, A6.

61. *The Public Papers of the Presidents of the United States: Ronald Reagan, 1988* (Washington, D.C.: Government Printing Office, 1989), 1:345–46.

62. *Public Papers: Ronald Reagan, 1988,* 345–46.

63. *Washington Post,* 23 Mar. 1988, A1.

64. House Committee, *Investigation of Civil Rights Enforcement by the Department of Education,* 115, 113.

65. House Committee on Appropriations, *Departments of Labor, Health and Human Services, Education, and Related Agencies Appropriations for 1986: Hearing before the Subcommittee on the Departments of Labor, Health and Human Services, Education, and Related Agencies of the Committee on Appropriations,* 99th Cong., 1st sess., 30 Apr. 1985, 1483, 1491.

66. House Committee on Appropriations, *Departments of Labor, Health and Human Services, Education, and Related Appropriations for 1988, Part 6: Hearings*

before the Subcommittee on the Departments of Labor, Health and Human Services, Education, and Related Agencies of the Committee on Appropriations, 101st Cong., 1st sess., 2 Mar. 1987, 1632–33.

67. House Committee on Government Operations, *Investigation of Civil Rights Enforcement by the Office for Civil Rights at the Department of Education: Twenty-fourth Report by the Subcommittee on Intergovernmental Relations and Human Resources,* 99th Cong., 1st sess., 30 Dec. 1985, 90.

68. House Committee, *Report on Enforcement Activities of the Office for Civil Rights,* 103, 102, 100.

69. Ibid., 3.

70. In this regard, see Senate Committee on Appropriations, *Departments of Labor, Health and Human Services, Education, and Related Agencies Appropriations for Fiscal Year 1983: Hearing before the Subcommittee on Labor, HHS, and Educational Appropriations of the Committee on Appropriations,* 97th Cong., 2d sess., 17 Mar. 1982, pt. 4, 148; and House Committee on Appropriations, *Departments of Labor, Health and Human Services, Education, and Related Agencies Appropriations for 1987: Hearing before the Subcommittee on the Departments of Labor, Health and Human Services, Education, and Related Agencies of the Committee on Appropriations,* 99th Cong., 2d sess., 14 Apr. 1986, 990, 993.

71. House Committee, *Report on Enforcement Activities of the Office for Civil Rights,* 148.

72. Ibid., 130.

73. House Committee, *Report on Enforcement Activities of the Office for Civil Rights,* 3.

74. House Committee, *Investigation of Civil Rights Enforcement by the Department of Education,* 139.

75. *Washington Post,* 2 Jan. 1986, A5.

76. House Committee, *Report on Enforcement Activities of the Office for Civil Rights,* 12.

77. Ibid., 96.

78. House Committee on Appropriations, *Departments of Labor, Health and Human Services, Education, and Related Agencies Appropriations for 1985: Hearing before the Subcommittee on the Departments of Labor, Health and Human Services, Education, and Related Agencies of the Committee on Appropriations,* 98th Cong., 2d sess., 29 Mar. 1984, 1404.

79. Ibid.

80. House Committee, *Report on Enforcement Activities of the Office for Civil Rights,* 44–45.

81. Ibid., 80–81.

82. House Committee, *Investigation of Civil Rights Enforcement by the Office for Civil Rights at the Department of Education,* 3.

83. House Committee, *Hearings on Higher Education Civil Rights Enforcement*, 387.

84. House Committee, *Report on Enforcement Activities of the Office for Civil Rights*, 42.

85. House Committee, *Investigation of Civil Rights Enforcement by the Office for Civil Rights at the Department of Education*, 32–33.

86. House Committee, *Hearings on Higher Education Civil Rights Enforcement*, 287.

87. House Committee, *Investigation of Civil Rights Enforcement by the Department of Education*, 143.

88. *Adams v. Bell*, 711 F.2d 179 (D.C. Cir. 1983).

89. Ibid., 178; emphasis added.

90. *New York Times*, 16 July 1981, A18.

91. *Adams v. Bell*, 711 F.2d 164.

92. *Washington Post*, 21 June 1981, A11.

93. House Committee, *Hearings on Higher Education Civil Rights Enforcement*, 43.

94. *Washington Post*, 1 Feb. 1984, A18.

95. As cited in *Adams v. Bell*, 711 F.2d 174 (Wright, S., dissenting).

96. As cited in ibid., 164 n. 24.

97. Ibid., emphasis added.

98. House Committee, *Report on Enforcement Activities of the Office for Civil Rights*, 19.

99. Ibid., 32, 33.

100. House Committee on the Judiciary, *Civil Rights Enforcement in the Department of Education: Hearing before the Subcommittee on Civil and Constitutional Rights of the Committee on the Judiciary*, 97th Cong., 2d sess., 30 Sept. 1982, 14.

101. Ibid., 13.

102. Ibid., 19.

103. Ibid., 22.

104. Senate Committee, *Departments of Labor, Health and Human Services, Education, and Related Agencies, Appropriations for Fiscal Year 1983*, pt. 4f, p. 1127.

105. House Committee, *Hearings on Higher Education Civil Rights Enforcement*, 181; Office for Civil Rights, *Third Annual Report: Fiscal Year 1983* (Department of Education, *1983*), 60.

106. As cited in Robert Plotkin, "Reagan Civil Rights: The First Twenty Months—A Report by the Washington Council of Lawyers," *Human Rights Annual* 1 (1983): 61.

107. Ibid., 33.

108. *Women's Equity Action League v. Bell*, 743 F.2d 43 (D.C. Cir. 1984).

109. Ibid. The administration advanced very similar arguments before the House Subcommittee on Intergovernmental Relations and Human Re-

sources when that subcommittee held hearings in July and September 1985. At those hearings, the assistant secretary for civil rights, Harry Singleton, argued that though the various *Adams* orders were useful for a limited time and purpose, they had come to have a disproportionate influence on OCR and its allocation of resources. He noted, for example, that the orders required investigating individual complaints rather than "planning and conducting more efficient large scale compliance reviews." House Committee, *Investigation of Civil Rights Enforcement by the Department of Education,* 112. Singleton explained:

> *Adams* . . . has mushroomed and . . . has become an unnecessary interference by the judiciary into the affairs of the executive. . . .
>
> Could you imagine . . . the courts telling this subcommittee . . . how long it had to take to work up an investigation, how long it had to take to hold hearings and when it had to report out a bill to committee — to the full committee. When the full committee had to report that bill out to the floor and then how much time the House would have to deliberate and then report that bill out? (House Committee, *Investigation of Civil Rights Enforcement by the Department of Education,* 112)

Singleton's analogy falls apart upon reflection. Congressional committees do not have a legal obligation to act to do anything. Title VI, by contrast, imposes legally binding obligations on all agencies disbursing federal monies.

110. Brief for Appellants, *Women's Equity Action League v. Bell,* 49.

111. Ibid., 16.

112. *Women's Equity Action League v. Bell,* 743 F.2d 43 (D.C. Cir. 1984).

113. *Allen v. Wright,* 468 U.S. 737, 104 S.Ct. 3315 (1983).

114. *Women's Equity Action League v. Bell,* 743 F.2d 43–44, emphasis in the circuit court opinion; citations are omitted.

115. Ibid.

116. *Adams v. Bennett,* 675 F. Supp. 668, 674 (D.D.C. 1987).

117. Ibid., 677.

118. *Washington Post,* 15 Dec. 1987, A9.

119. *Women's Equity Action League v. Cavazos,* 879 F.2d 880 (D.C. Cir. 1989).

120. Ibid., 885–86.

121. Ibid., 886, 887.

122. Ibid., 887.

123. Ibid., 887.

124. Ibid., 887 n. 5.

125. The government analyzed the *Cannon* case extensively in its 1983 briefs, discussing it on pages 30, 38, 43, 50, 62, 65, 66, and 67 of its initial brief and on pages 11, 14, and 15 of its reply brief. It discussed the *Council of the Blind* case on pages 42, 43, and 61 of its initial brief, *Vermont Yankee* on pages

29, 48, and 56 of its initial brief and page 10 of its reply brief, and the *Gorsuch* case on pages 8, 9, 10, and 12 of its reply brief.

126. *Women's Equity Action League v. Cavazos,* 906 F.2d 742 (D.C. Cir. 1990).

127. Ibid., 747, 748–49.

128. Ibid., 749, referring to language in *Brown v. Califano,* 627 F.2d 1233 n. 73 (D.C. Cir. 1980).

129. Ibid., 749 n. 9, 749.

130. Ibid., 744.

131. Ibid., 745, 746.

132. Ibid., 749 n. 9.

133. Ibid., 744.

134. For a discussion of these points, see House Committee, *Investigation of Civil Rights Enforcement by the Department of Education,* 20–21.

135. Plaintiffs' Reply Brief in Support of Renewal Motion for Further Relief Concerning State Systems of Higher Education, 23 Feb. 1983, 3, 4, *Adams v. Bell.*

136. Ibid., 11.

137. House Committee, *Civil Rights Enforcement by the Department of Education,* 2.

138. As cited in House Committee, *Report on Enforcement Activities of the Office for Civil Rights,* 267.

139. Ibid., 271.

140. House Committee on Government Operations, *Civil Rights Enforcement by the Department of Education: Hearing before a Subcommittee of the Committee on Government Operations,* 100th Cong., 1st sess., 23 Apr. 1987, 265–66.

141. *Washington Post,* 7 Aug. 1987, A6.

142. House Committee, *Civil Rights Enforcement by the Department of Education,* 14, 15.

143. Ibid., 19.

144. Ibid., 14–15.

145. House Committee, *Report on Enforcement Activities of the Office for Civil Rights,* 333.

146. *Washington Post,* 11 Feb. 1988, A3.

147. House Committee, *Report on Enforcement Activities of the Office for Civil Rights,* 333–34.

148. House Committee, *Civil Rights Enforcement by the Department of Education,* 28.

149. Ibid., 293–94.

150. *Washington Post,* 11 Feb. 1988, A3.

151. *New York Times,* 11 Feb. 1988, 1.

152. Ibid.

Chapter 7–*FORDICE:* The Disappointing Legacy of the Rights Strategy

1. *Green v. County School Board of New Kent County, Virginia,* 391 U.S. 440, 88 S.Ct. 1696 (1968).

2. *Alabama State Teachers Association v. Alabama Public School and College Authority,* 289 F. Supp. 784 (M.D. Ala. 1968), *aff'd per curiam,* 393 U.S. 400, 89 S.Ct. 681 (1969); *Norris v. State Council of Higher Education for Virginia,* 327 F. Supp. 1368 (E.D. Va.), *aff'd* 404 U.S. 907, 92 S.Ct. 227 (1971); *Bazemore v. Friday,* 478 U.S. 390, 106 S.Ct. 3000 (1986).

3. *Alabama State Teachers Association,* 289 F. Supp. 788.

4. *Norris,* 327 F. Supp. 1373.

5. *Bazemore,* 478 U.S. 407, 106 S.Ct. 3012.

6. *Bazemore,* 478 U.S. 407, 106 S.Ct. 3012.

7. Ibid.

8. *Bazemore,* 478 U.S. 408, 106 S.Ct. 3013.

9. Ibid.

10. *Ayers v. Allain,* 674 F. Supp. 1530 (N.D. Miss. 1987).

11. Plaintiffs' Brief before the United States Supreme Court, July 1991, 56 n. 101, *Ayers v. Mabus.* For the details of OCR's findings as to Mississippi's violations of Title VI, see Motion for Leave to File and Brief of the NAACP Legal Defense and Educational Fund, Inc., as *Amicus Curiae* in Support of Petitions for Writs of *Certiorari* to the United States Court of Appeals for the Fifth Circuit, July 1991, 17–20, *Ayers v. Mabus.* All of the written documents cited in connection with *Ayers v. Mabus,* subsequently styled as *United States v. Fordice,* were obtained from lawyers involved in the litigation.

12. Ibid., 62 n. 109.

13. *Ayers v. Allain,* 674 F. Supp. 1530.

14. When a funding agency makes a referral, the attorney general has the authority to sue on behalf of the United States to enforce the statutory requirements and contractual assurances of nondiscrimination made by institutions of higher education receiving federal funds. 42 U.S.C. § 2000d-1.

15. *Ayers v. Allain,* 674 F. Supp. 1525.

16. *Ayers v. Allain,* 893 F.2d 735 (5th Cir. 1990) *(en banc).*

17. *Chronicle of Higher Education,* 25 Sept. 1991, A32.

18. *Ayers v. Allain,* 893 F.2d 752.

19. *Black Issues in Higher Education,* 5 Dec. 1991, 34.

20. To accommodate especially talented but high-risk students who scored between nine and fourteen on the ACT, the TWIs enrolled fifty such students per year, or a number not to exceed 5 percent of the freshman class during the previous year, whichever was greater. *Ayers v. Allain,* 674 F. Supp. 1534.

21. The material in this paragraph is drawn from *Ayers v. Allain,* 893 F.2d 736–38.

22. The material in this paragraph is drawn from ibid., 738.

23. The material in this paragraph is drawn from ibid., 738–39.

24. The material in this paragraph is drawn from ibid., 741–42.

25. *Ayers v. Allain,* 674 F. Supp. 1525–26.

26. *New York Times,* 16 Apr. 1991, A1.

27. *New York Times,* 29 May 1991, A1.

28. *Washington Post,* 25 Aug. 1991, C6.

29. See *Chronicle of Higher Education,* 24 Apr. 1991, A1, 10 July 1991, A1, and 25 Sept. 1991, A1; Stephen C. Halpern, "Still Separate, Still Unequal," *National Law Journal,* 9 Dec. 1991, 13–14.

30. *Black Issues in Higher Education,* 24 Oct. 1991, 16.

31. American Council on Education, Education Commission of the States, *One-third of a Nation: A Report of the Commission on Minority Participation in Education and American Life* (Washington, D.C.: American Council on Education, Education Commission of the States, 1988), 16.

32. Senate Committee on the Budget, *Historically Black Colleges and Universities of Higher Education, 1989: Hearing before the Committee on the Budget,* 101st Cong., 1st sess., 13 Nov. 1989, 80.

33. *Chronicle of Higher Education,* 16 Oct. 1991, A60.

34. *Black Issues in Higher Education,* 24 Oct. 1991, 28.

35. *Chronicle of Higher Education,* 16 Oct. 1991, A60.

36. Albert Baxter, "The Affirmative Duty to Desegregate Institutions of Higher Education: Defining the Role of the Traditionally Black College," *Journal of Law and Education* 11 (1982): 39.

37. Brief of the United States in Opposition to the Petition of Mississippi for an *En Banc* Rehearing before the Fifth Circuit, 14, *Ayers v. Allain.*

38. Brief of the United States on Appeal from the U.S. District Court, 14, *Ayers v. Allain.*

39. Ibid., 14.

40. Brief of the United States, on Writ of Certiorari to the United States Court of Appeals for the Fifth Circuit, July 1991, 23, *U.S. v. Fordice.*

41. Ibid., 32–33.

42. Elias Blake to Dr. William Harvey, chair, HBCU Joint Committee, memorandum, 10 July 1991, 12. (This document was made available to me by its author.)

43. *Chronicle of Higher Education,* 10 July 1991, 1.

44. *Chronicle of Higher Education,* 16 Oct. 1991, A41.

45. *Chronicle of Higher Education,* 10 July 1991, 1.

46. *Washington Times,* 10 July 1991, A3.

47. *Black Issues in Higher Education,* 24 Sept. 1991, 25.

48. *Washington Times*, 10 July 1991, A3; *Chronicle of Higher Education*, 10 July 1991, A22.

49. *Washington Post*, 25 Aug. 1991, C6.

50. *Black Issues in Higher Education*, 26 Sept. 1991, 12.

51. *New York Times*, 22 Oct. 1991, B6.

52. *Black Issues in Higher Education*, 26 Sept. 1991, 24.

53. *Chronicle of Higher Education*, 16 Oct. 1991, A41.

54. *Washington Post*, 7 Oct. 1991, A9. J. Clay Smith stated that he hoped "to get the DOJ [Department of Justice] to conform its position to that of the Executive Branch." J. Clay Smith, "Black Colleges at the Crossroads: The Future of Black Colleges Is Today," handout at oral argument of *Fordice* case, 3. (This document was made available to me by its author.)

55. *New York Times*, 22 Oct. 1991, B6.

56. Ibid.

57. Reply Brief of the United States, On Writ of Certiorari to the U.S. Court of Appeals for the Fifth Circuit, October 1991, 16, *United States v. Fordice*.

58. Ibid.

59. Smith, "Black Colleges at the Crossroads," 3.

60. *Chronicle of Higher Education*, 16 Oct. 1991, A41.

61. *New York Times*, 22 Oct. 1991, B6.

62. *Chronicle of Higher Education*, 16 Oct. 1991, A41.

63. *Chronicle of Higher Education*, 16 Oct. 1991, A60.

64. Ibid.

65. *Black Issues in Higher Education*, 26 Sept. 1991, 24.

66. *Chronicle of Higher Education*, 25 Sept. 1991, A32.

67. *New York Times*, 29 May 1991, A21.

68. Ibid.

69. This description of the "dry run" moot court is based on my personal recollections.

70. Derrick Bell, *And We Are Not Saved: The Elusive Quest for Racial Justice* (New York: Basic Books, 1987), 107.

71. *Atlanta Journal and Constitution*, 22 June 1992, C3.

72. *United States v. Fordice*, 112 S.Ct. 2737 (1992).

73. Ibid., 2738.

74. Ibid.

75. Ibid.

76. *Washington Post*, 27 June 1992, A11.

77. *Los Angeles Times*, 28 June 1992, A1; *Washington Post*, 27 June 1992, A10.

78. *New York Times*, 27 June 1992, A11.

79. *New York Times*, 27 June 1992, A10.

80. *Buffalo News*, 2 July 1992, B3; *Washington Post*, 29 June 1992, A19.

81. *New York Times,* 2 July 1992, A23; *Washington Post,* 28 June 1992, C6.

82. *Chronicle of Higher Education,* 8 July 1992, A16.

83. *Fordice,* 112 S.Ct. 2738.

84. *Ayers v. Allain,* 674 F. Supp. 1532.

85. *Fordice,* 112 S.Ct. 2738.

86. *New York Times,* 27 June 1992, A10.

87. Federal Interagency Committee on Education, *Federal Agencies and Black Colleges, Fiscal Years 1972 and 1973* (Washington, D.C.: Government Printing Office, 1974), 1.

88. Federal Interagency Committee, *Federal Agencies, 1972 and 1973,* 1.

89. Federal Interagency Committee on Education, *Federal Agencies and Black Colleges, Fiscal Year 1969* (Washington, D.C.: Government Printing Office, 1970), 6–7.

90. *Weekly Compilation of Presidential Documents* 7 (no. 9, 1 Mar. 1971): 282–83.

91. *Weekly Compilation of Presidential Documents,* 7 (no. 9, 1 Mar. 1971): 283.

92. Federal Interagency Committee, *Federal Agencies, 1972 and 1973,* 3.

93. 42 *Fed. Reg.* 31496 (1977).

94. *The Public Papers of the Presidents of the United States: Jimmy Carter, 1977* (Washington, D.C.: Government Printing Office, 1978), 1:2003–4.

95. Ibid., 3:49.

96. Ibid., 4:1518–19.

97. Ibid., 1518.

98. *The Public Papers of the Presidents of the United States: Ronald Reagan, 1981* (Washington, D.C.: Government Printing Office, 1982), 1:795.

99. Ibid., 794, § 1.

100. Ibid., § 6.

101. White House Initiative on Historically Black Colleges and Universities, *Annual Performance Report on Executive Agency Actions to Assist Historically Black Colleges and Universities for the Fiscal Year 1984* (Washington, D.C.: Government Printing Office, 1985), 60; *Public Papers: Ronald Reagan, 1981,* 2:795; White House Initiative, *Annual Performance Report,* 62.

102. *Weekly Compilation of Presidential Documents* 25 (no. 17, 28 Apr. 1989): 632–33, 634–36.

103. As cited in John B. Williams III., ed., *Desegregating America's Colleges and Universities* (New York: Teachers' College Press, 1988), 6, emphasis added.

104. Ibid., 7.

105. Arline Pacht, "The *Adams* Case: An HEW Perspective," *Howard Law Journal* 22 (1979): 436 n. 35.

106. 43 *Fed. Reg.* 6662, § II (1978).

107. 43 *Fed. Reg.* § IID, ID (1978).

108. Senate Committee on Labor and Human Resources, *Higher Educa-*

tion Amendments of 1986: Report of the Committee on Labor and Human Resources to Accompany S. 1965, 99th Cong. 2d sess., 13 May 1986, 22.

109. 20 U.S.C. § 1060 (1988).

110. 20 U.S.C. § 1060(3) (Supp. 1988).

111. *United States v. Jefferson County Board of Education*, 372 F.2d 836 (5th Cir. 1966), *aff'd* 380 F.2d 385 (1967) *(en banc)*.

112. *Jefferson*, 372 F.2d 847.

113. *Kemp v. Beasley*, 352 F.2d 19 (8th Cir. 1965).

114. *Jefferson*, 372 F.2d 890.

115. Ibid., 850.

116. *Fordice*, 112 S.Ct. 2751, 2752.

117. Ibid., 2743; emphasis in the original.

118. Reply Brief of the Private Petitioners, 19, *United States v. Fordice.*

119. Ibid., 19 n. 39, citations omitted, emphasis in original.

120. *Fordice*, 112 S.Ct. 2743, emphasis added.

121. Ibid., 2743.

122. Ibid., 2737.

123. Ibid., 2737.

124. On entrance requirements, see ibid., 2738; on duplication, see p. 2740; on mission designations, see p. 2741; and on maintaining all eight institutions, see p. 2742.

125. *Adams v. Richardson*, 480 F.2d 1165 (D.C. Cir. 1973) *(en banc)*.

126. *Adams v. Califano*, 430 F. Supp. 120 (D.D.C. 1973).

127. *Wall Street Journal*, 29 June 1992, A10.

128. In a footnote in *Fordice*, following its observation that "certainly closure of one or more institutions would decrease the discriminatory effects of the present system," the Court did refer, without further comment, to a 1973 letter from HEW to the board of trustees observing that closure of a black institution "would create a presumption that a greater burden is being placed upon the black students and faculty in Mississippi." *Fordice*, 112 S.Ct. 2743 n. 11. The Court neither endorsed nor rejected the idea in the HEW letter.

129. William F. Winter, Mississippi's governor from 1980 to 1984, declared, for example, that "in a pluralistic society, the primary commitment to racially separate institutions is counterproductive." *Chronicle of Higher Education*, 25 Sept. 1991, A32.

130. *Brown et al. v. Board of Education of Topeka et al.*, 347 U.S. 493, 74 S.Ct. 691 (1954).

Chapter 8 – Conclusions

1. Tensions between the abolitionist and suffragist movements in the nineteenth and early twentieth centuries paralleled the modern-day tensions between the black civil rights and women's movements. On the difficulties in the earlier period, see Israel Kugler, "The Trade Union Career of Susan B. Anthony," *Labor History* 2 (winter 1961): 90–91.

2. I am indebted to my colleagues Henry Taylor and Stefan Fleischer for first bringing this and related points to my attention.

3. In this regard, see Paula Giddings, *When and Where I Enter* (New York: William Morrow, 1984), 308–9; and Toni Morrison, "What the Black Woman Thinks about Women's Lib," *New York Times Magazine*, 22 Aug. 1971, 14.

4. As cited in House Committee on Government Operations, *Failure and Fraud in Civil Rights Enforcement by the Department of Education: Twenty-second Report*, 100th Cong., 1st sess., 2 Oct. 1987, 6.

5. House Committee on Education and Labor, *Civil Rights Act of 1984: Joint Hearings before the Committee on Education and Labor and the Subcommittee on Civil and Constitutional Rights of the Committee on the Judiciary on H.R. 5490*, 98th Cong., 2d sess., 9 May 1984, 26.

6. The language is drawn from *Alabama NAACP State Conference of Branches et al. v. Wallace*, 269 F. Supp. 352 (M.D. Ala. 1967).

7. House Committee, *Civil Rights Act of 1984*, 24.

8. Nationwide, for example, black children are three times as likely as white children to be assigned to classes for the mentally retarded, and only half as likely to be placed in programs for the "gifted." Jonathan Kozol, *Savage Inequalities* (New York: Harper Collins, 1991), 119.

9. *Swann v. Charlotte-Mecklenburg Board of Education*, 402 U.S. 25, 26 (1971).

10. Jonathan Kozol stated the issue this way: "Equity, after all, does not simply mean equal funding. Equal funding for unequal needs is not equality." Kozol, *Savage Inequalities*, 54.

11. *Brown v. Califano*, 627 F.2d 1233 (D.C. Cir. 1980).

12. *Dayton Board of Education v. Brinkman*, 443 U.S. 526, 99 S.Ct. 2971 (1979); *Columbus Board of Education v. Penick*, 443 U.S. 449, 99 S.Ct. 2941 (1979).

13. Where civil rights lawyers won an occasional substantive victory, as one might argue that they did in HEW's higher-education desegregation criteria, it resulted not from prevailing in court but from extensive informal negotiations between OCR and LDF officials. And, as was true with the criteria, those substantive gains often proved impossible to enforce.

14. U.S. Commission on Civil Rights, *Black/White Colleges: Dismantling the Dual System of Higher Education*, Clearinghouse Publication 66, ERIC

ED206299 (April 1981), 66; *Washington Post*, 24 May 1982, A4. A *Washington Post* reporter, writing of the *Adams* litigation, quipped that if the case were a Broadway production, it would have won a Tony Award for the longest-running play in American stage history. *Washington Post*, 8 Mar. 1985, A21.

15. Derrick Bell, *And We Are Not Saved: The Elusive Quest for Racial Justice* (New York: Basic Books, 1987), 59.

16. August Meier and Elliot Rudwick, *From Plantation to Ghetto*, 3d ed. (New York: Hill & Wang, 1990), 109–10.

17. Ibid., 438.

18. Ibid., 601.

19. *State of Missouri ex rel. Gaines v. Canada*, 305 U.S. 337, 59 S.Ct. 232 (1938).

20. *Gaines*, 305 U.S. 349, 59 S.Ct. 236.

21. *Sipuel v. Board of Regents*, 332 U.S. 631, 68 S.Ct. 299 (1948).

22. *Sweatt v. Painter*, 339 U.S. 629, 70 S.Ct. 848 (1950); *McLaurin v. Oklahoma*, 339 U.S. 637, 70 S.Ct. 851 (1950).

23. *Sweatt*, 339 U.S. 633–34, 70 S.Ct. 849–50.

24. *McLaurin*, 339 U.S. 640, 70 S.Ct. 853.

25. *McLaurin*, 339 U.S. 641, 70 S.Ct. 853.

26. *Brown et al. v. Board of Education of Topeka et al.* 347 U.S. 493, 74 S.Ct. 691 (1954), emphasis added.

27. *Brown v. Board*, 347 U.S. 494, 74 S.Ct. 691, emphasis added.

28. *Brown v. Board*, 347 U.S. 494–95, 74 S.Ct. 691–92, emphasis added.

29. *Brown v. Board*, 347 U.S. 493, 74 S.Ct. 691.

30. Ibid., emphasis added.

31. Ibid.

32. Robert L. Carter, one of the chief strategists for the NAACP Legal Defense Fund in *Brown v. Board*, declared, "[T]he basic postulate of our strategy was that the elimination of enforced segregated education would necessarily result in equal education. And as I read *Brown I*, the United States Supreme Court was clearly of the same view." Robert L. Carter, "A Reassessment of *Brown v. Board*," in *Shades of Brown*, ed. Derrick Bell (New York: Teachers College Press, 1980), 45.

33. *Milliken v. Bradley*, 418 U.S. 717, 94 S.Ct. 312 (1974).

34. By 1991, more than four million black children, nearly 60 percent of the nation's total, attended public schools in central cities.

A Personal Epilogue

1. See Herbert Wechsler, "Toward Neutral Principles of Constitutional Law," *Harvard Law Review* 73 (1959): 32–34.

2. David Garrow, *Bearing the Cross: Martin Luther King, Jr., and the Southern*

Christian Leadership Conference. A Personal Portrait (New York: William Morrow, 1986), 338–39.

    3. Derrick Bell, *Faces at the Bottom of the Well* (New York: Basic Books, 1992), 6.

INDEX

Numbers in parentheses following references to endnotes refer to the text pages on which the note references appear.

Library of Congress Cataloging-in-Publication Data

Halpern, Stephen C.
    On the limits of the law : the ironic legacy of Title VI of the 1964 Civil Rights
Act / Stephen C. Halpern.
      p.   cm.
    Includes bibliographical references and index.
    ISBN 0-8018-4896-2. — ISBN 0-8018-4897-0 (pbk. : acid-free paper)
    1. Civil rights — United States.   2. Race discrimination — Law and legislation
— United States.   3. Economic assistance, Domestic — Law and legislation —
United States.   I. title.
KF4755.H35 1995
342.73'085 — dc20
[347.30285]   94-28375
                                                    CIP

STOLEN APPLES

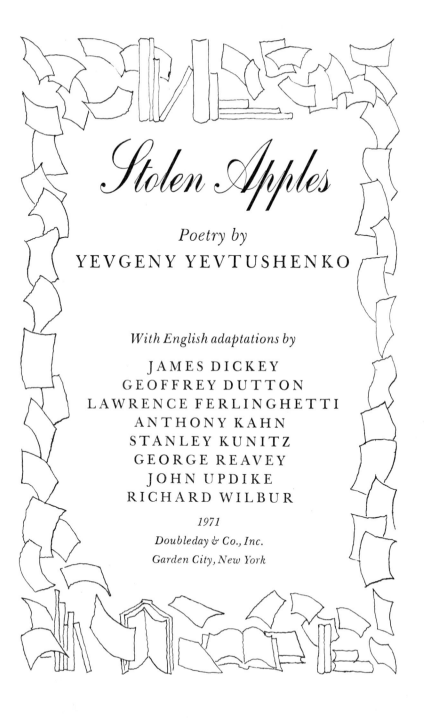

Stolen Apples

Poetry by

YEVGENY YEVTUSHENKO

With English adaptations by

JAMES DICKEY
GEOFFREY DUTTON
LAWRENCE FERLINGHETTI
ANTHONY KAHN
STANLEY KUNITZ
GEORGE REAVEY
JOHN UPDIKE
RICHARD WILBUR

1971

Doubleday & Co., Inc.
Garden City, New York

Some of these poems and text previously appeared in the following publications: "Rhythms of Rome," *Saturday Review,* Copyright © 1967 by George Reavey; "In a Steelworker's Home," "Monologue of a Broadway Actress," "Cemetery of Whales," "New York Elegy," "Monologue of an American Poet," "Monologue of a Polar Fox on an Alaskan Fur Farm," "Smog," *Holiday,* Copyright © 1968 by The Curtis Publishing Company; "The Restaurant for Two," "A Ballad About Nuggets," *Life,* Copyright © 1967 by Time Inc.; "Flowers & Bullets" and "Freedom to Kill," in the book *Flowers and Bullets & Freedom to Kill,* Copyright © 1970 by City Lights Books; "Being Famous Isn't Pretty," *Harper's;* "The Snow Will Begin Again," "I Fell Out of Love With You," "The Old House," "Black and White," "The Torments of Conscience," "In Jest," "The Stage" in the book *New Poems,* published by Sun Books Pty Ltd.

DRAWINGS BY RAYMOND DAVIDSON

Library of Congress Catalog Card Number 77–157640
Translations Copyright © 1971 by Doubleday & Company, Inc.
All Rights Reserved
Printed in the United States of America

9 8 7 6 5

Poetry gives off smoke
but it doesn't die out.
It acts kind of crazy, flutteringly,
when it chooses us.

VI

CONTENTS

CONTENTS

VIII

III. МУКИ СОВЕСТИ

IV. ПРОЦЕССИЯ С МАДОННОЙ

III. THE TORMENTS OF CONSCIENCE

V. PROCESSION WITH THE MADONNA

V. КЛАДБИЩЕ КИТОВ

V. CEMETERY OF WHALES

APPENDIX OF THE RUSSIAN ORIGINAL TEXTS

BEING FAMOUS ISN'T PRETTY

In taking this line from Pasternak as the title for my foreword, I've acted without arrogance or self-disparagement, a thing far worse than pride. Let me assure my readers of that. Not that in my poetic adolescence I didn't dream of fame. I did. Nor will I say that now when I write poetry or even this foreword I'm indifferent to the opinion of my readers. That would also be a lie. But fame is a far from charming mistress. She demands endless gifts and tokens of affection; she gets hysterical, jealous; she makes me quarrel with my friends, kills my concentration, drags me off on senseless visits, threatens me with abandonment. Many envy me such a spectacular prize. If they lived with her a while they'd change their minds. But then, jealousy never admits to being itself. It hides behind its own suspicions: "What crooked route led that fellow to glory? After all, we're honest and yet, unknown."

And so, legends of suspicion arise with the myths of praise. And when you've heard enough of them about yourself, you're bound to lose your bearings and wonder fearfully who you really are. If you live under the magnifying glass of public curiosity, just as your every honest act seems heroic to some, so your every weakness seems criminal to others. Even your honest acts come into question. Of course, where there's smoke there's fire, but the smoke of a myth can sometimes obscure the nature of the fire. Fame is the Medusa's head, horrid and hissing with the snakes of gossip. To look in her face is to turn to stone, even if they call the stone a monument. You need the trusty shield of Perseus to see a safe reflection of your fame. At the start of his journey an artist must struggle for fame; once it's been won, he must learn how to struggle with it.

When I read certain articles about myself in the West I wonder who in the hell this damned "Y.Y." can be. A movie star, tanned by photographers' flashbulbs? A matador, teasing his red cape in the bull's snout of the age? A tightrope walker, toeing the slack wire between East and West? Or, as one of England's ex-angry-young-men Kingsley Amis hinted, an unofficial diplomat, performing certain secret missions for the Kremlin? A rebellious Stenka Razin,* as a laureate of the Goncourt Prize, Armand Lanoux, once wrote? Or maybe a nice, inquisitive traveler, as the magazine *America,* distributed in the USSR, once had it, asking everyone to call him "just Zhenya." A Soviet Beatle? An export item, perhaps, like vodka or black caviar? A conformist masquerading as a champion of liberalization? A radical in moderate's clothing? Or are all these mere ingredients blended in the shaker of the age into a strange cocktail called Yevtushenko?

On the one hand, he's in the fight against anti-Semitism, bureaucratism, etc. You'd like to take the lanky Russian in your arms and whisper to him confidentially, "We're with you in your selfless struggle." On the other hand, he doesn't much care for Western society. In fact, he harshly indicts it for the war in Vietnam, the murders of Martin Luther King and the Kennedys, for bigotry, hypocrisy, and corruption. You get suspicious: If this Russian is really on the side of truth, an honest man in a totalitarian society, what's he doing out of jail? Why does he go abroad from time to time, and then unaccompanied by commissars? Isn't he perhaps a commissar himself?

An aerial diver in a suit, his luggage bulging with hidden microfilms, even went so far as to say that, according to information at his disposal, one out of every two Soviet writers abroad was an agent of the Secret Police, that if one of them traveled alone he was an agent for sure, and that someday Yevtushenko would have to render

* Razin was a leader of a Cossack and peasant rebellion on Russia's southeastern frontier in the late 1660s. He was captured by Cossacks loyal to Moscow and, in 1671, tortured and executed in the capital. [A.K.]

an account of the reports he wrote on returning home. In his haste he apparently forgot that somewhat earlier in his fascinating confession he admitted informing on that same Yevtushenko as a leader of an intelligentsia underground center. Amazing, isn't it, this charming little contradiction?

But the most amazing thing of all happened in 1967 in Santiago de Chile. There, on the day of my reading, two groups of young people organized demonstrations against me on two different squares. On one, the solemn "ultra-leftists" burned me in effigy as an American spy. On the other the "ultra-rightists" burned me as a Red spy. To be honest, I was pleasantly surprised to find these charming youths rating my services as high as those of some latter-day Mata Hari.

When in 1968 English students supported me as a candidate for the position of Oxford's Professor of Poetry, God! how the afore-mentioned Amis & Company put me to the knife, calling me a wily propagandist, an official mouthpiece of the Soviet government, and on and on. Again, I was pleasantly surprised that my social standing in the USSR seemed so strong. And after all the noise about me as a political agent extraordinaire, there suddenly came the quiet voices of Arthur Miller and William Styron, both of them *obliged to announce that, in their opinion, I was an honest man.* And the voice of my translator, Robin Milner Holland, *compelled to explain that I was a poet,* and not something else.

Even in his own country people not too familiar with this strange fellow, this Yevtushenko, can be found. For the radicals I'm too moderate, for the liberals too radical, for perfervid dogmatists, almost the devil himself. In a lamentably much discussed novel, one writer, depicting a traitor to the Motherland, a fascist collaborator hiding from retribution, even went so far as to put some of my verses on his lips. One poet in his time accused me of being unpatriotic. "What kind of Russian are you," he said, "when you've forgotten your own people?" They've called me a "singer of dirty bedsheets," a "poet of the mod set," and more. To lovers of the philosophical lyric I seem too simplistic, to lovers of the intimate lyric, too rational—a pamphleteer. And to others who interpret poetry only politically, too ambivalent.

Lovers of political poetry, incidentally, are themselves rather sharply split in two. The first group applauds all my lines that condemn Western society and praise the Motherland. "There, that's the way he should always write." But let one line about our ills drop from my pen and they're at me: "There he is, messing around in the wrong country again." They're a suspicious group. Even in my poems about other countries they detect hints directed at our own, and in poems about the pre-Revolutionary past, dangerous allusions to the present.

The second group is the opposite of the first. They take offense at political poems dealing, say, with Vietnam, or the glories of the Motherland, seeing in them no sincere movement of the soul but a political maneuver to gain the favor of those in power. Just as the first group, deaf to their neighbor's groan behind the wall, listens only to the bombs in Vietnam, so the second thinks the problems of the world are nothing next to their aching corns. The second group wants only negative poems on domestic problems. Somehow they find it morally questionable to speak of the corruption of the Western world when in the Soviet Union the price of cognac is on the rise, the meat supply uncertain, and the stores, in general, unjust.

When, then, you ask, is Yevtushenko sincere? When writing of Vietnam or Babi Yar? There isn't much profit in defending yourself, but, alas, I must.

It's easy to forget the simple fact that a man can speak sincerely of both Vietnam and Babi Yar, and in both a major and a minor key. Art in general is higher than questions of "for" or "against" alone. Art is a rainbow broad enough even for black. But a rainbow stretched across two shores casts all its colors equally on each. It doesn't leave one side in bright light and the other in the dark.

Injustice is as widely traveled as justice, and a scoundrel with an American passport is no better than a louse with a Soviet one. As Mayakovsky once said, "The widest choice of scoundrels roams through our land and about."

I know, of course, that this one world is really two, even, as they say, three, and tomorrow, maybe four. Still, I think our old, good woman Earth, though torn by political conflict, is the only world we have and we're all her tenants depending in one way or another on each other. A little-known Russian poet, Stefanovich, put it this way:

> All of us share one lot.
> Just sprain your ankle
> And instantly in Addis Ababa
> Someone shrieks in pain.

And so, I write poems about Vietnam and Babi Yar and Kent University student Allison Krause and a Siberian concrete-pourer, Nyushka, and a general in the army of freedom, Pancho Villa, and my own mother, who lost her voice singing concerts in snowstorms on the front lines, and a Chilean prostitute who hung a portrait of Leo Tolstoy in her closet and Sicilian women in black and young girls in white and my own beloved and my son and myself. I want to be a mail boat for everyone divided by the ice of estrangement, a craft before the coming of large navigation, moving through the drifting ice with letters and parcels.

Still, sometimes I deeply resent being discussed as a political personality and not as a poet, and having my poetry examined on the whole from one political standpoint or another. Of course, Heinrich Boll was right when he said that everything published was already committed. Every writer is committed by his conscience and his talent, even if he declares himself "above the fray."

> It's a disgrace to be free of your age.
> A hundred times more shameful than to be its slave.

I don't want to be free from the struggle for freedom. But I do want to be free to determine the forms it will take. Although I once had the indiscretion to say that a poet in Russia is more than a poet, I've never pretended to be a political prophet. In politics I'm undoubtedly a dilettante, even though my loathing for professional politicking prompts me to think it will be a great day for mankind when its politics are in the hands of amateurs rather than professionals.

Compared to the refined, cold master Salieri, who "verified his harmonies with algebra," Mozart must have seemed a dilettante. But it was Mozart, and not Salieri, who advanced the development of the world's music. History flows to the laws of music, and the Mozarts of the world are her masters. Blok's rallying call "Listen to the music of the Revolution!" is eternal, for revolution is protean and, despite what pessimists may say, the revolution in human consciousness will never end.

You can wave art aside as a weapon in that revolution if you want; it's true, for all the beauty art creates, mankind wallows every day in the filth of its inhumanity. But I'm bold enough to believe that if there is anything exalted in man, if the revolution in consciousness still goes on, by that much is mankind indebted to art.

In the long run I don't much care who picks me to pieces or how, or who puts me in what category. I know that I'm one of the workmen of art, that I toil in her hot, unhealthy shop, poetry, and that this is the meaning of my life. Politically untutored and forever concerned with those little things that so enrich our suffering lives with beauty, I've never formulated any new political concepts. I've only reminded people of the commonplaces of good and evil, justice and injustice. The myths about me spring, of course, not from my "renown" alone, but from my attempts to speak in the same language of justice and injustice, addressing two shores divided by conflict but, like mankind itself, at one in their meaning and destiny.

It does sound suspicious. I'm sometimes guilty of trying to grasp the ungraspable and, as a wise man once said, "When you try to embrace all mankind, you sometimes forget your wife." My strength perhaps, but also my failing, is a greediness for life. My fear of not expressing myself on some topic makes me express myself at times too superficially. Leaping like a seismograph to the quivers of Earth's core, I'm often deaf to the silence. In general, we the poets of the atomic age too often substitute nervousness for spirituality.

I may have won the ear of many nations, but it's a mixed blessing. Readers are too despotic. Once in love with a poet for something, they expect it to appear again and again, forever. They interpret any change in a poet's character, and consequently in his poetry, not as a normal development but as a retreat from principle. There aren't even two readers alike in the world, and if they number in the hundred thousands how can you please them all? You shouldn't try. A writer who has won the public's interest is misguided if he thinks he'll be free in the end; he'll soon feel its spur and bridle on his flesh.

Not long ago a young teacher from Saratov came to me with this reproach. "All you do now is analyze and analyze," she said, "but you can't uplift the masses with analysis alone. They rally to calls and appeals."

When you're young it's easy enough to streak appeals across the sky like rockets. But as you get older you feel increasingly responsible for those traveling the road your rocket lights. What if you've led them wrong? You grow wary of making reckless appeals, and a sense of responsibility must be tempered above all with analysis and reflection. Relentless analysis alone, not childish shouting, embodies the true appeals.

Once someone lovingly retyped all eight volumes of my collected works as a birthday present. Full of anticipation and delight I lay down on the sofa to read. I was instantly aghast. The lines seemed so naïve and precocious, sometimes criminally so, and congested with slogans. It was too late to do anything. "The word's no sparrow; once it goes, it won't fly back." Since that time my relationship with paper has undergone considerable change. I've begun to fear her, although certainly not enough.

Before judging his age a writer must find the courage to judge himself. Pushkin was strong enough not only to write poems for the overthrow of autocracy but to say of himself, "And reading my own life with loathing, I tremble and curse." You musn't be misled by the sins your myth ascribes but look soberly through to the real failings beneath.

Clearly many of my poems have not withstood the test of time, but I secretly believe something of me will survive my stay on Earth. Something at least of my fits of spirit, I hope, even if screened by smoke, may influence the feelings of my descendants, restored to each other at last from the ice of estrangement. That done, it little matters if, hearing the velvety whistles of magnificent ships to come, they don't recall the hoarse voice of the mail boat.

No one can foretell the outcome of our lives. What then must we do?

> Live, and by the smallest measure
> Never step back from oneself,
> But be alive, fully alive,
> Alive and only, to the end.

B. PASTERNAK

Yevgeny Yevtushenko

Translated by Anthony Kahn

A TRANSLATOR'S PREFACE

No translator is at heart either a traitor or a tailor. In approaching the work of another man his function is neither to stick a knife in the other man's throat nor to dress him up in the fashion of the times. No voice can really speak for another, only to, and in the process the truth at stake and the measure of success is the honesty of the interchange. Something—or someone—deeply felt, as Yevtushenko was by all of us who worked with him, comes in at the heart and goes out the same way, as little like an echo as two people saying, "I love you," to one another.

A person seeking the "real" Yevtushenko will never find him anyway, only an image shaped by one's own feeling for the world and the truth—the main concerns of Yevtushenko's poetry—changing, as it must for Yevtushenko himself, from one moment to the next. A poem, a "translation," an "adaptation," though more concrete, is itself merely a record of impressions felt, analyzed, integrated into a point of view.

Yevtushenko asked each of the poets involved in this project to assume the most demanding freedom: to translate only poems he liked; and to be fully himself in his work. For some of us that meant working on an intimate lyric, for others a narrative as fluid and far-flung as the Pechora. For everyone it meant riding the impulse the original voice set off, as long and in such a way as he wished. The result—these English adaptations—are interchanges between one poet and another.

At times translating Yevtushenko meant yielding, as it did for John Updike, to the public energy of the man and letting its curve "carry him into English combinations like nothing in our poetry since Whitman." For Geoffrey Dutton it often meant "listening to the ghosts" in Yevtushenko's verse, the voices that fed his own—Spanish, Armenian, German, Kirghiz, English, and Tajik—and feeling, through the music, the man's sharp hunger for the truth of his own experience. Richard Wilbur responded to the shock of a fresh voice speaking through traditional poetic forms, to the daring of the man, to the intimacy of his love for the world, to his public display of the most private moments. Dickey's Yevtushenko leapt from the page "ebullient, rapid-fire, devil-take-the-hindmost-missing-nothing," flashing on the world with intense, unbounded imagination, hoisting the "hell-with-it" to a power that transformed it into the deepest possible involvement with life-at-flow. Stanley Kunitz found joy in discovering "the other Yevtushenko, the one with the north-country child in him, the lyric one with his sense of roots and natural affections." Each poet in his own way returning to his Yevtushenko the life-enhancing quality the man evoked. Each poet answering poetry with poetry and responding as one can only to a contemporary whose voice still strikes the ear and whose eyes still cut across the table, as they did for Ferlinghetti, where the glasses are unclouded and the vodka in them clear.

Each of us has met Yevtushenko in person and in print, and each of us has honestly tried to honor the request of our Russian friend who wrote to us:

> Doubleday and Company is to publish a volume of my verse in English translation. I have compiled the collection myself. The publication of this book is, for me, a matter of principle.
>
> I would hope my poetry could be translated by some of the very best poets writing in English today, and so I turn to you with a request for your help. You are, I know, a busy man, but really and truly, if we the poets of this world won't lend one another a hand, what then will befall the rest of mankind? In return for your help I give my solemn word to "take revenge" and translate several of your own poems which you might choose for me. I grant you, of course, full freedom in your work, for I know well from my own experience that only a free and unrestricted translation can in any way claim to be poetry.

Yours,

YEVGENY YEVTUSHENKO

Anthony Kahn
Cambridge, Massachusetts
1971

STOLEN APPLES

I

Pitching
and Rolling

THE HUT

And once again a fisherman's hut
opening to me late in the night,
suddenly as much a part of me
as the one along whose floor I used to crawl.

Quietly I lay down in the corner
as if it were my old lost place:—
that shaky, chinky floor,
whose every crack and knot I knew.

And I was home again, painfully at home,
amid the smells of fish and tobacco,
children, kittens, borscht,
fumes rising, purifying.

Already the room rocked with the fisherman's snores;
the children already had climbed into their bunks,
their teeth nibbling
on steamy pancakes.

Nobody but the housewife stirred,
washing, scrubbing.
A poker, a broom, a needle—
there must always be something in her hands.

4

Outside a storm was brewing on the Pechora:*
you could hear the river seethe.
"She's kicking up her heels," she said,
as if speaking of a coffee-colored cow.

A puff, blowing out the smoky lamp,
left the room to its own darkness.
I could hear the slap-slosh sound
of her laundry chores in the kitchen.

An old clock creaked in the night,
dragging the weight of history.
From the freshly laid kindling
a white fire broke and crackled.

And, full of wonder and fear,
untamed, from the shadows,
eight children's eyes gleamed
like eight sprays from your waters, Pechora.

They leaned out over their bunks
from an impossibly distant distance,
four little selves (myself)
watching a grown-up, me.

* Pechora: a Russian river over 1100 miles long, flowing south from Archangel, then west and north, widening steadily until it swings again north to its delta and the Pechora Sea. It is frozen from about November to April, when the thaw brings severe ice jams and flooding. [A.K.]

A silent prayer crossed my lips,
as I lay still, pretending to sleep.
And the kitchen noises stopped:
I heard the door squeak open.

And in this depth of solitude,
through the veil of this slumber,
I felt the touch of something
remembered from my childhood.

A sheepskin coat—that's what it was—
thrown on me snugly, shaggily, warmly;
and a moment later, from the kitchen tub,
the slapping of the clothes again.

I could almost see those hands dancing
through diapers, bedsheets, dungarees,
to the music of all our passions,
to the roar of world events.

Certainly more than one pretentious nonentity
had wormed his rotten way into eternity,
but only this recurring slap-slosh
struck me, in essence, as eternal.

6

And a teeming sense of fate
overwhelmed me,
like the exhalation of a hut
where life lies heavy on millions of women,

and where—who knows when?—
after the mastery has been won,
a million little selves (myself)
will watch a grown-up, me.

1964

TRANSLATED BY STANLEY KUNITZ

WITH ANTHONY KAHN

WOUNDED BIRD

to A. Voznesensky

Here to these wild stretches of the north
where the world first quacked and spawned,
I flew, a wounded bird, a drake,
and settled down on the Pechora.

From my covert by the woods
all my nerve-ends tingled
at the smell of ice-floes and seals,
the majesty, the vibrant breath, of ocean.

The sea was what I breathed,
it was sorrow I exhaled;
and the scattered buckshot in my blood
I gave as keepsake for Pechora,

my gift of leaden pellets
to the cold river bed. And trembled
and rose again and flapped my wings,
beating the air with a sudden power.

The winds rocked me gently,
adrift over mosses and bushes;
muskrats showed me the way, puffing down trails
behind their wet whiskers.

8

Through corridors of unplowed lands,
past flowering brakes and stands of hazelnut
tender-eyed deer bore me
on the velvet buds of their antlers.

Then the tussocks received me,
the tundra said, "Taste me,"
proffering its Iceland moss,
its cranberries sweetened through the winter.

And I—tuned to the clang of bolts and breechblocks—
knew that my life was precious,
only because you, shining, touched me,
caressed me, Pechora.

Sometime again, a mighty drake,
unrecognized by you, Pechora,
I'll fly over the north country,
flashing the brocade fan of my feathers.

And you will scan the arc of sky,
lost in the plumage and the flight,
forgetting that the gift was yours,
the saving gift, Pechora;

and how one spring you harbored me,
when unremittingly
that plumage spilled its tears of blood
into your light blue hem, Pechora.

1963

TRANSLATED BY STANLEY KUNITZ
WITH ANTHONY KAHN

MATING FLIGHT OF THE WOODCOCK

Shoulder your gun, be steady, sight.
With bill outstretched, needle-sharp,
the woodcock plunges out of the moon
straight toward you, darkening the moon.

He pitches, whistling on the wing,
down through the evening air. Tell me,
why is he drawn to you, as on a string,
why is your muzzle guided by a string?

Joy is the music of his fall.
Trembling, you hug your weapon tight.
Hunter, he is your unarmed double.
You are his doomed and wingless double.

Can you atone for winglessness
with a blast of wings? Squeeze out your shot:
but that's yourself in careless flight,
yourself you're shooting down in flight.

TRANSLATED BY STANLEY KUNITZ
WITH ANTHONY KAHN

GLASHA, BRIDE OF THE SEA

A Tale of the North Country

She knows the river, net and hook,
and hunts it deep as any.
Love opens her a petaled look:
"I couldn't care a penny!
You're better dead."
She shakes her head:
her angry earrings dance.
She walks in scarf and sarafans
she spins from Northern Light!
No other finger trains her hair
or teaches tress to toss and play,
no other ribbon winds her braid
but the river's wave!
She moves along the shore
and mends her nets. She beams
a leaping look beneath her brow
like salmons scale a stream!
I stood enchanted at the root
and dared a timid dream of fruit.

But tongues did roll in pub and spire
and toss about her name
and bandy it in crew and choir
and gossip she was tamed.
O!
    "Who bends the wind? Who drowns the rain?"
Mad I walked.
                "It's all a joke!"
The townsmen puffed their pipes and spoke
me silent smoke.
"Who rings her finger? Who braids her hair?"
I faced northwest
and asked the air.

Suddenly up by my side
pops a tramp,
sprouted like a tundra toadstool
in the damp.
"Give a drink and get an answer
by and by," says he.
"I'll shed a secret on your saucer
like a sprig of tea." So,
he drains a glass and drains another
and when my money's dry,
"The icy ocean is her lover,"
he winks.
"And she's his bride."

I stood up fierce, my stormy fists
raged to pound his frame,
"They make a plaything of my pain
for fowl and fish to see,
the deep pike cackles in the river,
the high loon howls at me!"

Glasha busies at her boat,
tarring back and side,
and shows the sun her mended sail
stitched to leak no light.
I speak my heart:

     "Above the wave
the fish leaps and the dipping drake
skims a hungry beak.
For your velvet look I'd lay
the tundra at your feet
and lullaby your tattered coat
to sleep in ermine sheets
and track the fishes' mating steps
from ocean dance to spawning pool
and catch a salmon in my net
rich with roe of pearls,
and trap you dreams you never dared
and what you wished of wildest fruit
to slake the travels of your boots
through salty sea and scale.
You tricked my lip upon your hook
and lure of flashing teeth,

and now I'm bluffed of coin and keep
and townsmen tell me, drunk and brief,
you're promised to the sea!"

Answers Glasha,
                    "I'm his bride.
Look at the river. Restless water
runs beneath the wave
and hastens to the greyer fathoms
where my lover waits. Today
I'll lift an oar and lure a breeze
to sail me, unannounced, to sea.
I'll drop beneath the cloudy night
and hug the thunder of his breast
till all is dark forgetfulness
and dreams of things that come and go
upon the sighing of a pillow
made of porpoises at rest.
I'll ask my age, I'll hear him say
that all my turns about the sun
were seventeen salmon in a wave
and seventeen fishscales on a blade.
In rolling thunder
and chilly light
he'll rumble me his answers
and speak to me of life.
Lad, your words won't win a wife
for all they'll ever say of life
when I have heard the sea!"

Her ship gained snowy sail at that,
cupped a breeze,
and drew her on a sharp tack
to the sea.
I whispered words I soon forgot
and turned with empty eyes from what
I might have had of life, but for the sea.
And felt the fact drop like a hook
that caught and drew a moan from me,
"What will I ever say of life
to ears that heard the sea?"

TRANSLATED BY ANTHONY KAHN

BALLAD ABOUT FALSE BEACONS

*. . . and those far, elusive lights plunged the souls of seamen into
darkness, offering them false hope . . .*

From an ancient pilot's manual

We've been bewitched by countless lies,
by azure images of ice,
by false promises of open sky and sea,
and rescued by a God we don't believe.
Like coppers rattling from a beggar's plate
guiding lights have fallen on our days
and burned and died.
                   We've pressed our ship
a pilgrimage of nights toward such lights
as, always elusive, lured and tricked
the keel upon the rocks and ripped
the helmhold from the hand and lashed
the beggared palm to scraps.
Ice tightens at the bow and breath.
To dock, to drop the anchor to its rest,
to drift (a dream!) on waters quieted
and calmed. We can't. We're after a mirage.
(The whiskered walrus brays; the salt sea thaws.
Again, we're off!)
Raised on powdered milk, we'll have no faith
in beacons any longer, nor mistake
real for fake, or waking for a dream.
Beacons can't be trusted. Trust instead

the will of your own hand and head.
Again the captain waves his glass,
sights a beacon, turns and cries
"Helmsman! There's a beacon. Are you blind?"
But Helmsman, with the truer eye
thinks mutiny and grumbles,

"A mirage."

1964

TRANSLATED BY ANTHONY KAHN

PITCHING AND ROLLING

Here we go! We're RE-E-ELING!
            The glass-framed instructions
                       rip off their nails.—
A Spidola record player bashes you in the head
                    with Doris Day.—
Borscht, lazing in the galley,
              takes off straight up, splashing
                       madly—
A bay leaf from the borscht,
               stuck to the ceiling, steams.
Reel on! buddy!
       Sure; you'd like to catch hold of a bush or some grass
                      with your hands!
The cabin boy staggers.
              The helmsman staggers.
                    The boatswain staggers.
                      I'm staggering—
The waves like wolfhounds—
        You're just the same, Twentieth Century,
right-left
       left-right
           up-down
              down-up—

Reeling!
　　　　All instructions shatter—
　　　　　　　　　　all the portraits smash to hell!
Faces are death　　white drawn　　wasted
　　　　　　　　　　　　under the stern, a
　　　　　　　　　　　　　　rat-like
　　　　　　　　　　　　screech
And all over the place it's dense with kasha
　　　　　　　　　　with downwind screams
nothing but pitching and rolling, staggering, curving
with the taste of sick stomach in your mouth.
　　Reeling!
　　　　　　A barrel jumps down the deck
throwing itself at people.
Hey, old buddies, we're in for it now
　　　　　　　　　　but keep it cool anyway.
Crawl out of your cabins, otherwise
　　　　　　　　　　it's *kaput* for us all.
Reeling . . .
　　　　　　But the eyes of the harpooner
　　　　　　　　　　a ringtailed roarer
are strained, and his forelock's standing straight up.
He makes a soundless sign to the sailors
　　　　　　　　　　and steals sideways
with a rope
　　　　　to the flipped out barrel
and pitches himself like a cat
　　　　　　　　　splitting open the crowd,
For he knows, you bastard pitch and roll, things can get rough—
He's learned by heart, right through his skin, his red head,

He's had it beat down through his skull:
Either you jump on the barrel
        or it'll jump all over you!
We're reeling!
            But the barrel's still, it's no longer running
                      wild . . .
We're reeling!
            Clear weather won't run off from us . . .
Reeling!
          We may be seasick, darkness in front of our eyes—
But we'll out-reel you
               bad trip

                    anyway . . .

TRANSLATED BY JAMES DICKEY
WITH ANTHONY KAHN

II

Doing the Twist on Nails

THE INCENDIARY

You are completely free of affectation:
silent you sit, watchfully tense,
just as silence itself pretends to nothing
on a starless night in a fire-gutted city.

Consider that city—it is your past,
wherein you scarcely ever managed to laugh,
now raging through the streets, now sunk in self,
between your insurrections and your calms.

You wanted life and gave it all your strength,
but, sullenly spurning everything alive,
this slum of a city suffocated you
with the dreary weight of its architecture.

In it every house was shuttered tight,
in it shrewdness and cynicism ruled,
it never hid its poverty of spirit,
its hate for anyone who wasn't broken.

And so one night you burned it down
and ran for cover, frightened by the flames,
till chance produced me in your way, the one
you stumbled on when you were fugitive.

I took you in my arms, I felt you tremble,
as quietly your body clung to mine,
not knowing me or caring, but yet,
like an animal, grateful for my pity.

Together then we sallied . . . where did we go?
Wherever our eyes, in their folly, took us.
But intermittently you had to turn
to watch your past ominously burning.

It burned beyond control, till it was ashes.
And I remain tormented to this day
that you are drawn, as though enchanted,
back to that place where still the embers glow.

You're here with me, and yet not here.
In fact you have abandoned me. You glide
through the smoldering wreckage of the past,
holding aloft a bluish light in your hand.

What pulls you back? It's empty and gray there!
Oh the mysterious power of the past!
You never could learn to love it as it was,
but yet you fell madly in love with its ruins.

Ashes and embers must be magnets too.
How can we tell what potencies they hold?
Over what's left where once she set her fire
the incendiary cries like a little child.

TRANSLATED BY STANLEY KUNITZ
WITH ANTHONY KAHN

□ □ □

Damp white imprints dog the feet;
snowbound trolley, snowbound street.
Her tip of glove to lip and cheek,
"Goodby." Go.
Deathly, into soaring snow
and stillness, as expected, go.
A turn:
          the plunge to the metro.
A blare of lights. A melting hat.
I stand, am spun in drafts, see black
take the tunnel, train, and track,
sit and wait as others sat,
touch cold marble, chill my hand
and, heavy-hearted, understand
that nothing ever really happened,
ever would, ever can.

1956

TRANSLATED BY ANTHONY KAHN

MASHA

A girl goes along the seashore
blushing and shy
a tide rising in her
a woman rising in her

She takes off her shoes by the sea
and steps into it as into music
And she understands everything
though she doesn't understand a thing

Reason and rashness mixed—
A keen glance through us
and then again withdrawn—
All this is Masha—
a serious wide-eyed being

And the roof of my mouth goes dry
when her slender boyish legs
heedless of some grown-up's opinion
bear her helplessly to me

And on the wet sand by an old boat
with growing confidence I kiss
all that Masha's arms are—from elbow
to the rose petals of her nails

I put on my snorkel gear
and Masha swims somewhere above me
I search for Masha through the glass
as if drunk among the crabs and flowers

And I see in the bright green gloaming
in a bank of clouds above the underwater ridge
her legs like white stalks
fluttering submerged

And I swim and swim in the underwater thickets
and I swim, my fins thatching the water,
and I'm unhappy because I'm happy
and then happy because I'm unhappy

What can I say? Tell Mother not to worry
Masha I'll do you no harm
Masha I ask so little of you
and yet so much—just that you exist—

In meditations on death and eternity
gripped by hope and melancholy
I look through your slender little heart
as through a transparent pebble in the sea

1958

TRANSLATED BY LAWRENCE FERLINGHETTI
WITH ANTHONY KAHN

LET'S NOT . . .

Let's not . . .

        Everything's ghostly—

                the blank windows watching,
the snow reddening behind the stoplights of the cars.
Let's not . . .

        Everything's ghostly, lost in mist,
like a garden in March emptied of men and women,

                        paraded by
                          shadows.

Let's not . . .

        I stand by a tree,

                not speaking, undeceiving,
facing

        the double glare of the headlights,
and with a quiet hand touch

                but do not break
the tender icicle imprisoning a twig.
Let's not . . .

        I see you in the sleepy, reeling trolley
with spectral Moscow rocking in the window,
your cheek propped on a child's wool mitten,
thinking of me with a woman's rancor.

Let's not . . .

        You'll be a woman soon enough, subtle and worn,
hungry for praise, for the balm of a caress;
it will be March again,

            a callow boy will whisper in your ear,
your head will whirl inconsolably.
Let's not . . .

        For both your sakes,
don't stroll with him down the slippery paths,
don't place

      your insubordinate hands
upon his shoulders,

          even as I do not place them today.
Let's not . . .

        Oh disbelieve, like me, in the ghostly city.
Be spared

     from waking in the wasteland,

              terrified.

Say: "Let's not . . ."

         bending your head,
as I this moment

       say

      "Let's not . . ."

           to you . . .

1960

TRANSLATED BY STANLEY KUNITZ
WITH ANTHONY KAHN

ASSIGNATION

No, no! Believe me!

                          I've come to the wrong place!

I've made a god-awful mistake! Even the glass

In my hand's an accident

                         and so's the gauze glance

Of the woman who runs the joint.

                             "Let's dance, huh?

You're pale . . .

                Didn't get enough sleep?"

And I feel like there's no place

To hide, but say, anyway, in a rush

"I'll go get dressed . . .

                    No, no . . . it's just

That I ended up out of bounds . . ."

And later, trailing me as I leave:

                     "This is where booze gets

                             you . . .

What do you mean, 'not here'? *Right* here! Right here every time!

You bug everybody, and you're so satisfied

With yourself about it. Zhenichka,

You've got a problem."

I shove the frost of my hands
Down my pockets, and the streets around are snow,
Deep snow. I dive into a cab. Buddy, kick this thing! Behind
the Falcon
There's a room. They're supposed to be waiting for me there.
She opens the door
but what the hell's wrong with her?
Why the crazy look?
"It's almost five o'clock.
You sure you couldn't have come a little later?
Well, forget it. Come on in. Where else could you go now?"
Shall I explode
with a laugh
or maybe with tears?
I tell you I was scribbling doggerel
but I got lost someplace.
I hide from the eyes. Wavering I move backwards:
"No, no! Believe me! I've come to the wrong place!"
Once again the night
once again snow
and somebody's insolent song
and somebody's clean, pure laughter.
I could do with a cigarette.
In the blizzard Pushkin's demons flash past
And their contemptuous, bucktoothed grin
Scares me to death.

And the kiosks

And the drugstores

and the social security offices

Scare me just as much . . .

No, no! Believe me! I've ended up

In the wrong place again . . .

It's *horrible* to live

And even more horrible

not to live . . .

Ach, this being home-
less

Like the Wandering Jew . . . Lord! Now I've gotten myself
Into the wrong century

wrong epoch

geologic era

wrong
number

The wrong place again

I'm wrong

I've got it wrong . . .

I go, slouching my shoulders like I'd do
if I'd lost some bet,

and Ah, I know it . . . everybody knows
it . . .

I can't pay off.

TRANSLATED BY JAMES DICKEY
WITH ANTHONY KAHN

THE SNOW WILL BEGIN AGAIN

The snow will begin again, falling, falling,
and in its canvas I will read
the image of my youth again, calling
me wherever it may lead.

And it will lead me by the hand to the mystery
of someone's shadow, the tap of feet,
drawing me into the old, old conspiracy
of the lights, the trees, the blizzard in the street.

And those Moscow streets, the Mokhovayas,
the Stretenka, it will seem to me,
it will seem to me I still have not been young yet
but am touching the possibility.

And the vortex of night will start whirling, whirling,
and I will be funneled into wrong,
and my youth I have been following will be curtained
off by snow, nothing will belong.

But suddenly under the impartial sunstream
all her make-up is there to see,
like a gypsy bitch who has rubbed her orgasm against me
my youth will clear off and abandon me.

I will start over again, and change my life's pattern,
will put my naïveté to shame,
and gloomily will hold out my neck and attach
myself, like a stray dog, to a chain.

But the snow will begin again, falling, falling,
everything turning round like a spindle,
and my youth like a gypsy girl will be calling
again to me outside my window.

And the snow will begin again, falling, falling,
and I will gnaw my way through the chain,
and my life like a snowball will be rolling
towards a girl's fur boots again.

TRANSLATED BY GEOFFREY DUTTON
WITH IGOR MEZHAKOFF-KORIAKIN

I FELL OUT OF LOVE WITH YOU

I fell out of love with you—what a banal denouement,
just as banal as life, just as banal as death is.
Let me snap the string of this intolerable love-song,
smash the guitar in two—why force a comedy!

Only the pup, shaggy little monster, cannot understand
why you and I make complex every simple thing.
As soon as I let him in, he runs to your door and scratches,
but he scratches at my door every time you let him in.

Really, you could go mad, dashing about like this.
Sentimental dog, I know you're immature,
but I refuse to become a sentimentalist.
To drag out the last act is to prolong the torture.

To be sentimental is not a weakness but a crime—
when you soften again, again promise reconciliation,
and groaning attempt to stage a show, yet another time,
under the insipid name of "Love's Salvation."

You should start saving love right at the beginning
from those passionate "Forevers!", those childish "Nevers!"
"Do not make promises!"—the trains were bellowing.
"Do not make promises!"—mumbled the telephone wires.

Half-cracked branches of trees and the smoke-smudged sky
were warning us, so ignorant in our conceit,
that optimism is merely untaught simplicity,
that hopes are always safer when they are not too great.

It is kinder to stay quite sober and soberly weigh the worth
of the links before putting them on—that's the creed of the chain,
not to promise heaven but at least to give the earth,
not to promise until death do part but at least give life again.

When you are in love it is kinder not to keep on saying "I love you."
How hard it is later, from the same mouth, to hear it destroyed
in words that are void of truth, in sneers, gibes that mock you,
making the world we had thought perfect seem false and void.

It is better not to promise. Love is something one can't realize,
why then lead someone into deceit as to the altar?
Of course the vision is wonderful, until it flies.
It is kinder not to love when you know love has no future.

Our poor dog keeps on whining, enough to drive us to madness,
with his paws scratching now on your door, now on my door.
I no longer love you; for that I do not ask forgiveness.
I did love you; that is what I ask forgiveness for.

TRANSLATED BY GEOFFREY DUTTON
WITH IGOR MEZHAKOFF-KORIAKIN

□ □ □

In aircraft, the newest, inexorable models,
I was zooming up like passion,
Flying from hope to hope,
Killing this one, then that one.

But hope was in the middle,
Beyond this flinging and the take-off markers,
Like a seal on a chip of ice
With its sad muzzle lifted.

I pressed my lip to my lip
On the bitter sweetness of flight
Candy, but got scared quick, bursting with a double-love
Like an empty aerogram.

Tenderness called me like the void
Into the rustling of fallen-off clothes,
But the touch of any hope plunged me
Again into hopelessness.

I sped back and forth in a sick panic,
With a hard-hit mask of a face,
With a mind split two ways,
Both ways false.

Look: once through the whirling of the earth
I saw from a taxi window
That a center-split pine
Moaned by the road like a lyre.

So you see it wasn't *that* crazy
That, a flying Wandering Jew, I
Involved the sky—right?—I said
The sky, in my private life.

And the straight routes of the flights slice through
The downpours, now here, now there—you almost want to cut them,
Like the strings of a groaning lyre
Between two hopeless hopes.

TRANSLATED BY JAMES DICKEY
WITH ANTHONY KAHN

DOING THE TWIST ON NAILS

When you throw your dancing shoes out, back over your shoulder,
And lose yourself, you find yourself twisting on the stage,
                                        dancing,
                                        dancing,
                                                dancing—
let that pink boy whip you around—I can tell you:
Life doesn't dance this way—
                That way dances death.
Thighs
            shoulders
                        breasts:
                                    they're all in it!
Inside you, dead drunk,
                        wheezes of air are dancing
Somebody else's ring
                        dances on your hand,
And your face by itself
                        doesn't dance at all
Flying, lifelessly, above all the body's life
Like a mask taken off your dead head.
And this stage—
                is only one part of that cross
On which they once
                crucified Jesus;

The nails shot through to the other side, and you began
To dance on them,

        sticking out.

             And you dance

On the nails

       nails

On scandals red as rust

         on the thorn-points of tears: Listen,
Because I once loved you, tiresomely, gloomily,
I also hammered the crooks of my nails

            into this stage.

Ah, bestial, beastly music,

        do you keep on getting stronger?

No one can see the blood

        ooze from your foot-soles—

To wash the steps with clean water,
I'd rather you'd do it, Mary Magdalene,

          not Jesus.

I'll wash all their days, their yesterdays, not like a brother would
For a sister,

       but like a sister for a sister.

I'll kneel down and pick up your feet
And hold them quietly, and with kisses try to do something
About their wounds.

TRANSLATED BY JAMES DICKEY
WITH ANTHONY KAHN

THE INEXPRESSIBLE

I want what's inexpressible!
Impudent, I play with fire without a queen

My queen-reason is under the knight's hooves
What joy to lose to the fire!

What flaming in the uncombed night
From slender you, as from a candle!

How you've fired-up
The idea of sin!

I writhe but the cry of my flesh is bliss
The heretic is already freed by the fire

Gul'ripshi
New York Paris Madrid in flames
And someone dear to me burns in them

But if from the heretic's fire
The flame leaps to some poor bastard's roof

All the heretic burns for
Shall be forever damned to hell

For truth, when you burn down the scene
of someone nearby,
Is no longer truth but a lie.

TRANSLATED BY LAWRENCE FERLINGHETTI

WITH ANTHONY KAHN

□ □ □

Light died in the hall . . . Yet while, upon the boards,
Darkness arose and played the only role,
There poured through all my veins, in icy chords,
The chill of an inaudible chorale.

I knew that there, prepared for the prologue, seen
By none, perhaps, but the wide eye of God,
Like a sliver of the darkness, like a lean
Shade among shadows, slim and alive, you stood.

I had not God's high vision, yet within,
Like the voice of God, I felt the music rise,
And I saw, not with my sight but with my skin,
As with a thousand small, concerted eyes,

And there, in the dark, in the intermittencies
Of someone's breathing, the dense transparencies
Of the incorporeal shadows, I discovered
With a wild guess, and could in rapture tell
That point, apart from paradise or hell,
Where, waiting for its flame, a candle hovered.

And you were kindled, and the light re-uttered,
And the chaos of strange blackness was no more,
And only a little golden forelock fluttered
Before me, like a wind-whipped tongue of fire.

TRANSLATED BY RICHARD WILBUR

WITH ANTHONY KAHN

STOLEN APPLES

Fences careened in the storm;
we stole through the bitter shadows
like thieving children warmed
by shirtfuls of stolen apples.

The apples wanted to spill;
to bite them was scandalous.
But we loved one another
and that fact redeemed us.

Secluding the criminal twins
in a cosmos of dirty waves,
the snug cottage whispered,
"Be brave and love . . . be brave . . ."

The cottage's owner, an ex-
soccer hero, from his photo
dim on the glimmering mantel,
urged, "Be bold . . . plunge through . . ."

So, pivoting and twisting,
we burst through the penalty zone,
slipped past the last defender,
and billowed the nets of the goal!

Rest period. Above us, dust
flickered; we seemed to dream,
small soccer shoes vibrated
on an invisible field.

"Play," each mote insisted,
"Play, but play earnestly.
The earth's heavy globe is a speck
Like us, essentially."

We played again; we kicked.
The game perhaps was stupid
but we did love one another
and that felt splendid.

Drugged by its roaring, the sea
mumbled of something profound
but then a golden fish, your bang,
splashed upon your brow,

and I was unconcerned to know
that once on the storm's other side,
for all my bravura folly,
I'd sink back with the tide.

Let slander pursue me;
love isn't for the feeble.
The odor of love is the scent
not of bought but of stolen apples.

What matters the watchman's shout
when, wrapped in the sea's far hiss,
I can cushion my head between
two salty apples I've filched.

TRANSLATED BY JOHN UPDIKE
WITH ANTHONY KAHN

□ □ □

I dreamed I already loved you.
I dreamed I already killed you.

But you rose again; another form, but you,
A girl on the little ball of the earth,
Naïve simplicity, curve-necked
On that early canvas of Picasso,
And prayed to me with your ribs
"Love me," as though you said, "Don't push me off."

I'm that played-out, grown-up acrobat,
Hunch-backed with senseless muscles,
Who knows that advice is a lie,
That sooner or later there's falling.

I'm too scared to say I love you
Because I'd be saying I'll kill you.

For in the depths of a face I can see through
I see the faces—can't count them—
Which, right on the spot, or maybe
Not right away, I tortured to death.

You're pale from the mortal balance. You say
"I know everything; I was all of them.
I know you've already loved me.
I know you've already killed me.
But I won't spin the globe backwards
We're on: Love again, and then kill again."

Lord, you're young. Stop your globe.
I'm tired of killing. I'm not a damn thing but old.

You move the earth beneath your little feet,
You fall, "Love me."
It's only in those eyes—so similar, you say
"This time don't kill me."

TRANSLATED BY JAMES DICKEY
WITH ANTHONY KAHN

THE OLD HOUSE

The old house was swaying, composing a chorale with its creaking,
and the creaking of the chorale was a funeral service sung for us.
This house of many creaks could sense that secretly
you and I were slowly mingling with its dust.

"Do not die yet"—the words were in the neighing from the meadows,
in the long howl of the dogs, the incantation of the pines,
but side by side, each to the other, we were dying already,
and that is the same as is generally known as dying.

And yet what a yearning to live! The woodpecker tapping the
                                                    pine-log,
a tame hedge-hog running about in the mushrooms near the house,
and the night floating like a shaggy-coated, wet, black dog,
holding a star like a water lily in its mouth.

Through the window the darkness was breathing the scent of wet
                                                    raspberries,
and behind my back—my back had eyes that never missed!—
my beloved was sleeping with Platonov's *Fro*,* worn out with worries,
as peacefully as with a newly discovered sister.

* A novel by the modern Russian writer Platonov (1899–1951). His story,
Fro (first published in 1936), depicts a woman in love.

I lay thinking of the dull imperfection of marriages,
of the dishonorableness of us all—traitors, dissemblers.
For I loved you as much as forty thousand brother-warriors,
and was destroying you as if they all were enemies.

What good thing then has all my fiery declaiming stirred,
if, scattering myself from the stage, making the clichés roll,
I wanted to give happiness to the whole world
and found I could not give it to one living soul?

Yes, you're a different person now. The tightening of your eyelids
is angry and merciless. Bitter your ridicule of other people.
And yet, who but we ourselves make those we love
into such creatures, loving them is beyond our power?

Yes, we were dying. But there was something that would not let me
be completely convinced that you and I did not exist.
Love still existed there. Love could still draw breath
and mist the mirror held in front of her weak lips.

Swaying and creaking amongst the nettles the old house survived,
volunteering to lend us its endurance.
We were dying in it, but we were still alive.
We loved each other, this was the proof of our existence.

Some time in the future—God do not let me, do not let me!
when I will fall out of love with you, and really die,
my flesh will stir in the darkness and secretly laugh at me:
"You're alive!"—it will whisper in the deceptive fever of the night.

But in the drive of passion, wiser, though sadly mortified,
suddenly I will understand that the voice of the flesh tells lies,
and I will say to myself: "I fell out of love. I died.
But once upon a time I loved and was alive."

TRANSLATED BY GEOFFREY DUTTON
WITH IGOR MEZHAKOFF-KORIAKIN

INCANTATION

Think of me on spring nights
and think of me on summer nights,
think of me on autumn nights
and think of me on winter nights.
Though I'm not there, but somewhere gone,
far from your side, as if abroad,
stretch yourself on the long cool sheet,
float on your back, as in the sea,
surrendering to the soft slow wave,
with me, as with the sea, utterly alone.

I want nothing on your mind all day.
Let the day turn everything upside down,
besmudge with smoke and flood with wine,
distract you till I fade from view.
All right, think of anything by day,
but in the night—only of me alone.

Over the locomotive whistles, over
the wind, ripping the clouds to shreds,
listen to me, for pity's sake:
show me again, in the narrow room,
your eyes half-shut with ecstasy and pain,
your palms pressing your temples till they ache.

I beseech you—in the stillest stillness,
or when the rain patters on your roof,
or the snow sparks on your windowpanes,
and you lie between sleep and waking—
think of me on spring nights
and think of me on summer nights,
think of me on autumn nights
and think of me on winter nights.

1960

TRANSLATED BY STANLEY KUNITZ
WITH ANTHONY KAHN

BLACK AND WHITE

To Lannie MacNulty

I

Senegal,
I dive to the very dregs of the pubs
                        safe from toadies and narks,
with black circles
round my eyes
        after crazy nights of crashing around in the dark.
I spit
on all those hypocrites splashing on the surface—
                        those and these,
and I swim
amongst the underwater plants,
        the violet-shimmering bodies.
Wailing,
two mulatto girls shake on the stage
        and under them the earth thrashes.
Their gaze
is greedy as sea anemones
        inside the tentacles of their eyelashes.
But, caught through
the smoke-fumes scarce swaying
        I am drawn across years and hours

by your two
brown eyes,
      like two truthful underwater flowers.
We are bound
together, children of fated, Shakespearean feuding and
                                      hating,
the White House
the Grey House*
we've forced our way through your nets
                  to our very own meeting.
We're on the run,
they're after us,
      with bloodhounds, sirens, bedlam's blare.
We have flung
ourselves at the feet of our one true mother—
                         eternity, stroking our hair.
Lannie—
      you've landed
beside me like a doe
         who has jumped over seas, rockets and
                                    destroyers.

Where is the banned
border zone between us?
                  Only my skin and yours.
So try
to jump over even this border
      and give me your open lips to drink right down.

---

* Yevtushenko's note: "The Grey House" is what the progressive youth of
South Africa call their Parliament House.

If we two lie
skin pressed into skin
        we will make ourselves one.
O night,
      scream!
Drunken mobs are exploding inside you
        like an atomic nightmare.
Knives gleam
and flicker like maddened fish
        over the seaweed of hair.
Scraped back,
chairs take off into the air,
        brass knuckles scrunch into guts.
Like maniacs
whites stab blacks,
        blacks whites,
          and the yellow hack them all to bits.
Over bellowing cattle
and above the brawling,
        as if icy Biblical clouds rang,
hail rattling,
the cocktail shaker dances
        in the barman's tenacious passionless hands.
The switch-blade twists
through ribs, the cosh smashes home
        while the barman stands above the crunch of
            bones and claws—

God exists!—
the barman whips up our souls
           into a cocktail ordered
                      centuries before.
Over thieves
over beasts
        I cautiously take hold of your white hand.
We have each other.
"Aren't you frightened?" I ask with my eyes,
        and your eyes answer: "No, I'm not frightened."
What do I care
for the malice of all the world's bandits,
                  or its coming doom,
if through the glare
        of this horrible brawl

                a face
                  is coming to me?
What is the cause
of this brawl?
        Why should we care!
                And maybe, all these knives
draw us
together
     to press one to the other
              in this maelstrom of nights.
What is love?
It is you, and it is I
        over the brass-knuckles, the shots,
                the assaults on existence.

What is love?
It is the eternal OVER
   the throat-cutting of races, prejudices,

          systems.

What is love?
It is the eternal OUTSIDE.
It's outside all fights, all sorts of brawls,
   it's the union of Juliet and Romeo.
What is love?
"Aren't you frightened?"—the question with the eyes,
   and the eyes' answer "No."

II

I came to see you off
   with my two dark helpless hands—
not laden with flowers.
My Irish girl, farewell for ever . . .
     But maybe?
      Do you understand . . . ?
Goodbye, until we meet again . . .
Your name remains safe with me
    to my last hour,
sacred,
  Lannie.
If only we could see each other in this world
     at least once more . . .

Goodbye, until we meet again!
"Ladies and gentlemen,
             the aircraft for Paris
                        ready for departure!"
On a conveyor belt
suitcases swim
        as if along a grey river to nowhere,
into the Caravelle.
We hold each other tight
        lost like savages
in the hullabaloo
        of speculators in
                hashish,
                  ideas,
                      prostitutes,
                          and
even us two.
We are powerless, you and I,
        and maybe we are just infantile,
and spineless?
There are handcuffs on my hands
        and shackles on my ankles,
the only difference—
        they don't clank.
I'm giving you away
        and you are giving me away—
             whoever may win
we are running away.

The handcuffs on your hands
                        show through
                            your white skin
cutting their way.
We are prisoners of our age,
            prisoners of our governments and of our race.
Everywhere
        there are fetters.
Of real freedom, for you or for us,
                        there is no trace.
Only
        a few minutes,
then the python,
            having set free his collapsing victim,
claps on
        his coils again.
What is love?
            Only a minute of freedom.
                        Then
a relapse
        to worse pain.
People do not have rights
                    beyond the ancient right to suffer,
but even in this
the coils of our era
            do not offer
us this
        mean choice.

This age has squeezed our souls,

   and, teasing us with illusions of freedom,
breaks them brutally.
If he who is trapped in the coils

     can't have aeons of freedom,
then take

  a minute!
And afterwards—

   you can hang me,

     skin me by slow degrees,—
just as you need!
But first give me the right

    to suffer as I please,
just as I please!
Let us suffer once more

   if once more I can have what you can give—
then farewell, again!
We think—does that mean we live?

   No, we suffer, that means we live,
to share hell again!

TRANSLATED BY GEOFFREY DUTTON

WITH IGOR MEZHAKOFF-KORIAKIN

III

The Torments of Conscience

COWS

Stockinged in the river's slime,
the cattle coming slow.
This I remember. Precisely, though,
I can't say when.

Cow coats dimmed the earth and drew
a low hem on the hill.
The year was maybe forty-one,
or forty-two.

Burdocked hides, dusty brains
limping through a dream of grain.
Quiet schoolboys led the lean
beef to the train.

Weary too, I walked in back
to close the ranks, my horsetroop hat
a dome bleached white but for the black
memory of a star.

Ah cows, ah cows,
you dipped your pale horns down
into the meadows
like crowns,

and softly spoke and sadly rubbed
the shrubs against your hips
or lifted heads whose silent lips
spilled flowers.

Uneasily the calloused hands
marked by sledge and vein
stripped the throats of string and bell,
led the cattle to the train.

And coat to coat they drank and sang
until a far light spoke.
The cars began to creak and move
in steam and smoke.

White broke upon the darkened door:
a frightened calf with human eyes,
a child's face, and at his side,
the butcher.

Pressed to the cloth, bewildered eyes
that thought the speeding grass and wood
had fled their roots, bewildered eyes
but, like Yesenin's,* blue.

1960

TRANSLATED BY ANTHONY KAHN

* Sergei Yesenin (1895–1925). Peasant-born and, as he described himself, "the last poet of wooden Russia," he welcomed the Revolution as a spiritual event sure to inaugurate the peasant millennium. In the early 1920s he led a Bohemian life in the capital, drank heavily, married and divorced Isadora Duncan, grew disenchanted with himself and the Revolution, and committed suicide in Leningrad.

□ □ □

But only the divine word . . .
                    Pushkin

Poetry gives off smoke
but it doesn't die out.
It acts kind of crazy, flutteringly,
when it chooses us.
                    This fellow's no fool,
sucking tranquillizers,
toting in a little briefcase
a boiled beet-root.
                    Right now he'd like a mousse
or baba au rhum,
                    but the Muse—
                              some kind of Muse!—
grabs him
          by the scruff of the neck!
Thoughts drill a hole in his forehead,
and he's mislaid the spoon—
and he's a giant! Socrates, for the Lord's sake . . .
in an Oblomov dust-jacket. O.K. . . .
he's no Apollo—
                    he's puny and ugly,
skinny: he's like a golden mushroom,
unsteady . . .
          transparent.

But suddenly some sort of whistling
is in his ears, and then . . .

                                            a period!

And like a slugger's hook

                                    across the chops of the ages,

a line!

                And there

                              an insane little bird

falls off its feet,

                        a crazy rag-picker,

                                        drunk,

a kind of society clown. But something gives her the word
and—

        like branches in winter,
God rings from within, and her eyelids turn
to marble.

                And here's a bum

                            a shaman,

really—

        from among the lunatics!
Pour him champagne,

                      bring him

women, not rum cakes!

                          Suddenly an order from within
will come through sternly, and he's the instant
voice of the people, damned near
Savonarola!

Poetry acts kind of strange, it flutters
when it chooses us.
And it has no mercy, either,
afterwards. It stamps "Pure Souls"
on us . . . but who's the judge?
                              Yes,
for the horse-blinkered multitudes we're "decadents,"
but for our*selves,* we ourselves are . . . are . . .
well, yes! Redemption!

TRANSLATED BY JAMES DICKEY

WITH ANTHONY KAHN

IN THE WAX MUSEUM AT HAMBURG

Full of blocky majesty,
arrogant, dock-tailed,
German princes glower
at the Russian communist.

             All the presidents,
chancellors
        in their different kinds of gut-
meanness look darkly out
              each his own kind,
his caste, and all their crooked
vulgarity is in that.
           These are the wounders
of life. They warped it,
            suffocated it, and so
they're immortalized here—
          or, no,
they're waxed.
        In the midst of these grown fat
these greasy fools, and emaciated, malicious monsters
how did you fall,
        Schiller?
How about you,
      Mozart?

You should have landed

                in luminous meadows;
Should have come down among

                    deep-woods flowers.
But you're here—

          my old buddies,
Enemies—

        the whole damned lot. The enemies' looks are trying
To kill me, but it's not so bad,
This not being liked

              by Bismarck, and surely not
By Hitler.

        I keep looking, and gradually I see,
Among them like fatal ghosts,

                  the shaped, candle-stick figures
Of enemies

        still living. Yes. Still living.
There's one

        premier,
There's another one, and *he's*
No shining example

        and he's not either.
But maybe they *are*

        examples: yes,
but of the mean, the cruel,
the phony . . .
I'd like to get them here *themselves,*
Into the wax museum

            by the scruff of the neck,
By the seat of the britches!

It'd be great

To arrange 'em according to their crimes—

And let 'em be buried in wax

as ugly as *they* are!

I tell you, the wax museum is wild

For more bums and bastards!

Me,

I'm sick and tired of 'em! Sons-of-bitches

Have been lying to us too damned long!

It's time to drown 'em alive—

Right! In wax!

Let wax plaster their mouths

Shut, let it stop their hands

where they are

and let them stand

Still

still

very still

And dead

like good little children

very still

very

Obedient.

Right here and now I'm coming out with my

program

For revolution! I call on

EVERYONE! Drag 'em from their platform,

And while you're doing it, laugh and whistle

As loud as you can!

Go *get* 'em,

People! Let's have a little more

Pure rage!

It's time to pull down all this trash
From their easy chairs
                         like pulling nails and being crazy
About pulling nails!
                      It's time, under hot bright lights,
To drag down out of their balconies
This collection of stupid faces
Like carp from scummy green pools.
It's time, it's really time at last
To get rid of junk like this!
                              Into the wax museum
Of liars
         with these priests of a lousy temple!
People!
        SAY IT!
                 Don't clam up!
                                  Into the wax museum
With all heads of state
Who're headless!
                 And if somebody lies, even
if he does it in a new way,
                            then
Stuff his gullet with wax!
                           Into the wax museum!
There's still a lot of bullshit around,
And plenty of liars . . . Hey,
BEES! Get off your ass!
Wax, little brothers! We need it!

TRANSLATED BY JAMES DICKEY
WITH ANTHONY KAHN

THE DEPTH

to V. Sokolov

The bellow of a steamer in the morning
woke the coniferous distances,
and we stood on deck,
spellbound by the Angara,
gazing straight to the river-floor,
where the painted rocks gleamed
through a bright green dimension.
We could not trust our eyes.
It seemed, at times, in our passage
that we could reach over the side
and with our fingertips touch bottom;
for depth could not be gauged
in that transparency of water.
Of course I know that danger lurks
in the unturbidity of the wave,
and that the clearest purling stream
may be the shallowest.
But deepness isn't all.
I wouldn't give a tinker's dam
for a stupid stagnant pond
where the eye sees nothing plain.

Let me be like the flow of a river
obliquely struck by sunset glow,
as deep as measureless,
with each
      small pebble
           shining through!

1952

TRANSLATED BY STANLEY KUNITZ
WITH ANTHONY KAHN

THE TORMENTS OF CONSCIENCE

to D. Shostakovich

We live, dying is not our business,
shame is another lost episode,
but like an unseen madonna, conscience
is standing at every crossroad.

And her children and her grandchildren,
the torments of conscience—strange torments—
with vagrant's crutch and bag are wandering
a world which is everywhere dishonest.

From one gate once more to the next gate,
once again from doorstep to doorstep,
chanting like the old Russian beggars,
they travel with God for their heart's help.

Surely it was they who always haunted
the serfs, tapping with one finger
secretly on their windows, and who pounded
with their fists in the palaces of the Tsars?

Surely they hurried off dead Pushkin
on a sledge in the snow from a black sky,
it was they who drove Dostoievsky to prison,
it was they who whispered to Tolstoy: "Fly!"

The executioners understood it thus:
"He who torments himself is a troublemaker.
Torments of conscience—this is dangerous!
Conscience itself must be liquidated!"

But like the clanging of an alarm bell
rattling their houses at night time,
torments of conscience—terrible—
frightened the executioners with their crimes.

For even the guardians of injustice,
who abandoned all honor long ago,
may no longer know the meaning of conscience,
but the torments of conscience they do know.

And if in this wide world where no one,
no one is guiltless, someone has heard
within himself the cry "What have I done?"
then something can be done with this world.

I do not believe in the prophets construing
the coming of the Second or the Thousandth Rome,
I believe in the words "What are you doing?"
in "What are *we* doing?" bitterly spoken.

And on the slippery edge of lost faith
I am kissing your dark hands,
for you alone are my last faith,
torments of conscience—fierce torments!

1966

TRANSLATED BY GEOFFREY DUTTON
WITH IGOR MEZHAKOFF-KORIAKIN

IN MEMORY OF AKHMATOVA

I

Two ages ours—and gone. How could we weep?
The very thought was dry. Alive,
she was beyond belief.
How could she die?

Gone like a nightsong, feathers
dipped through garden air
to a dim branch, as if forever
gone to Petersburg from Leningrad.

The parted times, the scattered days
regroup within her hazy light.
If Pushkin is our sun, surely she
is our White Night.

Beyond the give and take of breath,
the struggle in the mind of death
and immortality, between
the future and the past, she lies.

The past streamed softly by her grave:
proud grey ladies, lifting faces
shocked in silver, wearing bonnets
of another age.

Yes, time had dimmed that beauty, prized
highly by a Russia that had been,
but, lamps of kindliness, their eyes
still danced against the wind.

And, shoulders still too weak for worlds,
the future comes with molten eyes:
schoolboys, with their hands in fists,
pressing notebooks tight.

And schoolgirls, bearing in their satchels,
surely notes and diaries,
all of them in this alike:
blissful, Russian, and naïve.

And oh, world-wide decay, pass on and never
cut this tie of times—we need its aid.
For, certainly, two Russians cannot ever
exist or two Akhmatovas be made.

II

In another grave, not far away,
like a folk song by the Bible's side
a woman near Akhmatova in age
lay simply dressed, in white.

She lay as if awaiting a marriage
with nothing left to darn or wipe or sweep:
a peasant, said her face, her hands, her carriage,
a domestic, it would seem.

To be no more—how heavenly a state.
The people of the house were kind enough,
and like a child before a holiday
they washed and neatly dressed her up.

True, they didn't smother her with lilies,
but the coffin fit, and, oh,
such fancy slippers on her, new ones nearly
with the repairman's stamp still on the soles.

And there she lay, absolvingly serene,
her dry hands folded on her breast,
reverentially, it seemed,
as if they had a candle there to press.

Alive, those hands, (so skilled at this) had scurried
(writing, true, mere turns and twists)
dark and stern and strong as bronze
and never known a kiss.

Then I thought: perhaps, just suppose
two different Russias do exist:
a Russia of the hands and of the soul,
two different lands that never mixed.

No one ever mourned that woman. Night
dropped upon her with no dawn to come.
And above her, high, aloofly white
Akhmatova's patrician profile hung.

Akhmatova, above mere honor
reposed in state: disdainful, droll.
Acknowledging the high rank placed upon her
above the low impostures of the soul.

Aristocrat! Fair denizen, conveyed
on roadways ringing to the prancing trotters.
Yet her hands, afloat on a bouquet
seemed to rock and, rocking, seemed betrayed.

They labored to their limit, but at times
they reached beyond their strength, and then,
so light in Pushkin's hold, the pen
with sudden weight would grin and break her fingers.

Done with the swift chill of Aix wine
and kisses caught in Petersburg and Nice,
these fingers met upon her breast, resigned
and fragrant with a peasant girl's fatigue.

Without a staff, without a crown a queen
among the tarnished gifts of state and man,
she lay absolvingly serene,
like the woman dressed in secondhand.

And in that other grave the woman lay
who never looked on Nice, and on her brow
appeared Akhmatova's stern grace.
And between them there was no frontier.

TRANSLATED BY ANTHONY KAHN

IN JEST

Goodbye, fame! Put someone else in my niche.
I'd swap a seat in the President's jeep
for a warm corner in a ditch
where I could go soundly off to sleep.
Oh, how I would unload my fears,
pour all my deadly, dreary pride
into the burdocks' hairy ears
as I lay fidgeting on my side.
And I would wake up, with unshaven chin,
amongst the bugs and little insects.
Oh how marvelously unknown!—
someone fit to dance gypsy steps.
Far off, people would grasp for power,
hang by their nails from the top of the tower,
but none of this would send me sour,
in a ditch I would be lower.
And there, embracing a mangy dog,
I would lie down and make my berth
in the friendly dust, holding dialogue
on the highest level—of the earth.
Alongside, the bare feet of a girl
would float innocently by,
and pale blades of grass would twirl
down from the haycarts between me and the sky.

On a bench a smoker would toss out
a cigarette pack, squashed and empty,
and from the label the twisted mouth
of Blok would sadly smile at me.

TRANSLATED BY GEOFFREY DUTTON
WITH IGOR MEZHAKOFF-KORIAKIN

THE STAGE

The curse upon me,

             the waste of my soul in rage,

is the stage . . .

I was young.

          Wanted to climb a pedestal,

wanted the showers of applause and flowers

when I came forward

            and stood, feeling laughable,

on the talcum powder left from the ballet shoes.

As yet I had absolutely nothing to say,

there was only this ringing inside me,

              in my throat,

but something was trying so powerfully to come out

that no stage fright could frighten it away.

And as my breaking voice began to cry,

time, breaking itself, began to shout

and I was that moment of time,

             and it was I.

And on the stage

        in the fiery line of the footlights

it was as if all those things still unexpressed,

hiding their tiny glow within the darkness,

were suddenly in me and I was one great light.

The mystique of the stage was set in motion
and fame stood separate beside us, as the third.
As in the Bible,

                in the beginning was the word,
and then—well then,

                    in the word was the explosion.
You fools—

            of course I'm no great actor!
My bones had no strength in them yet, I know,
but on my face, hacking

               away the pimples,
the features of Mayakovsky began to glow.
And the golden head of Sergey Yesenin,
of all poets the most reckless, the craziest,
with the scent of the wide wheatfields of his origin,
rose above my head, and I was possessed.
My teachers,

            I have not disgraced you, I swear,
and secretly I have given my laurels back to you.
The whole world was applauding us together,
Paris and Melbourne,

              and London,

                   and Hamburg.
But what have you done to me,

                O stage—
is your hunger assuaged?
My verse did not soften

            or disintegrate,
but became cruder and cruder

             in style and theme.

Stage,

     you gave me the light in which to scintillate
but took away the soft shadow and the subtle gleam.
I was turning purple from the intolerable strain.
I was painting great placards,

                      rationalizing slyly
that a watercolor can hardly be seen
in a large hall,

          especially from the gallery.
I began to cherish not quietness—

                  but thunder,
and when you do this it is easy to go wrong.
I could throw the bright colors around,

                make people wonder,
but forgot the intimate shades are just as strong.

And then there was something even more terrible:
when the audience were slipping into their coats
bits of me were scattered amongst thousands of people,
and I was leaving the hall myself,

             becoming remote.
And my double,

        pock-marked with perspiration,
would sit in the make-up room,

           a finished magician,
thousand-faced

     with all the accumulation
of other faces inside him,

        beyond recognition.

O stage—

        why pay such a horrible wage?
"Goodbye, stage . . ."—

                I will whisper quietly,
although I have forgotten the art of whispering.
I will abandon noise and listen for a rustling,
leaning on the slender shoulder of a birch tree.
But, demanding my help, as the moment before the storm
demands the coming explosion

               and the scatter of birds,
everything unexpressed in distant fields and farms
tightens in my throat

          and fuses into words.

The degradation of the living and the dead,
in this world

        still so far from paradise,
still demands my help,

         dragging the shreds
of my voice from the chords I vulgarized.
I am not jealous, other poets are my friends.
I don't need anything—I'll give away all my reserves,
my throat,

      yes, even my voice that so often offends,
in order that you may have what you deserve!
Of course, it will be quite obvious to posterity
That I—

    alas!—

      represent no ideal,

and yet

      whether crudely, or with some dexterity,
from the stage I did awaken some kind feelings.
And I will mutter hoarsely,

                when there is left
not even a whisper of my voice's pride:
"O stage,

      I was what I was, only myself,
and whether I lived as I should have—

                let God decide."
And I will leave the stage for darkness with some courage,
O stage . . .

TRANSLATED BY GEOFFREY DUTTON

WITH IGOR MEZHAKOFF-KORIAKIN

IDOL

Down in the pine needles
in the snowstorm-stogged ravine
an Evenki idol stands
fixing his eyes on the *taiga*.

Aggressively squinting,
he watched until the time came
when Evenki women started
hauling presents to him.

They brought him mukluks and parkas,
they brought him honey and fur,
figuring that he'd pray
but mainly think for them all.

In the dark assurance
that he'd understand,
they'd smear his mouth
with warm deer blood.

But what could he do, the phony
little god,
with his fierce, wooden
whittled-down soul?

Now he's looking through the branches,
abandoned and dead.
No one believes in him;
no one prays to him.

Did I just dream this up? At night
in his ravine, far off yonder,
he sets his eyes
on fire, overgrown with moss,

And listening to the snowstorm
blast down, licks
his lips. Lord, I know it.
He wants blood.

TRANSLATED BY JAMES DICKEY
WITH ANTHONY KAHN

OLD BOOKKEEPER

I don't have any pain. None at all.
Really, I don't estimate anything
unnecessary. Cramming a pillow under the seat
of my pants, I sit down in black oversleeves.

Here the same signatures and stamps
are. On the table papers rustle,
rustle, tired out, and so sadly
rustle, saying I'll be sixty. Soon.

Ah, the Chief—he's young! Powerful!
Today like always, shaved just so . . .
Fiddling with rosaries made out of
paper clips, talking to me about football.

Ah, the Chief! . . . he's clean *enough,*
and not so *much* of a son-of-a-bitch,
but I can see everything he's trying to hide
under that slick shine, his face.

Ah, the Chief—How easy he is
on himself! He wears those signet rings!
Only he don't walk so straight
in his beautiful new suede shoes!

I'll leave this little office. I'll smile,
not knowing why, at spring,
and get on the train that goes out
to Mytischchi, and everywhere farther away.

I'll get off where four ugly women
Live by the river. They're old, too.
One of them's gotten so tired that
any day I'll ask her to marry me.

And when I go back to my closet
in stillness that reminds me of "Prima,"
from the big wormy chest of drawers
I'll take out one snapshot.

There, hands propped on clumsy hipbones,
looking straight into History
at its worst, I stand, a civil guardsman,
not young, in the great year '41.

I'll hear the rumble of planes,
shots and wild songs in the wind,
and my lips will whisper something,
but I can't make it out, myself.

1958

TRANSLATED BY JAMES DICKEY

WITH ANTHONY KAHN

SECRET MYSTERIES

Adolescent mysteries melt away
like mist upon the shore
The Tonyas and Tanyas were all mysteries
even with cold sores on their legs

Stars and animals were mysteries
Mushrooms under aspen trees
and doors creaking mysteriously—
only in childhood do doors creak that way

The world's riddles rose up
like balloons from the mouth
of some seductive fakir
full of crafty schemes

Enchanted snowflakes
fell in fields and woods
Enchanted laughter
danced in young girls' eyes

Mysteriously we whispered something
on the mysterious ice of a skating rink
mystery touching mystery
hand touching hand

Unexpectedly maturity caught up with us
His dress coat worn to holes
the fakir went on tour
in someone else's childhood

We grown-ups forgotten
Ah, fakir, you're a faker!
So unmysterious it hurts
snow falls on our shoulders

Where are you, bewitched balloons?
There's no mystery to our mourning
Others are unmysterious to us
and we're unmysterious to them

And if some hand by chance
caress us lightly
it still is only a hand and not a mystery
a hand, understand, only a hand

Oh give me a mystery, some simple mystery
a secret mystery—silence and timidity—
a fragile mystery, a barefoot mystery—
just one sweet secret mystery!

1960

TRANSLATED BY LAWRENCE FERLINGHETTI
WITH ANTHONY KAHN

□ □ □

A girl was playing the accordion;
the tide of wine was in her head,
and garlic made the blunt end glisten
on a loaf of bread.

It took no breach of blood or brass
to raise a banquet in a shack.
Geologists in arms we were
who caught her song and sang it back.

I knew a girl who knew the land;
I sat beneath her steady chair
and heard her unfamiliar hand
ride my rustling hair.

I sort of drank, I sort of didn't,
and mined the levels of my pain;
I sort of wasn't her beloved
and her beloved all the same.

The other girl did push and pull
a sigh of seas and distant shores
and sang it to the lap of rubber
boots that rubbed her legs and sores.

She sang of lonely, burning days,
an ache at heart, an ash of grief,
of limitless and faraway
fences, fires, trees.

The girl sang on and always on;
her sister, schooled in dust and stone,
wept until the quiet dawn
the tears of old, forgotten bones.

1955

TRANSLATED BY ANTHONY KAHN

THE MARK OF CAIN

In Memoriam R. Kennedy

The poor pilgrims dragged themselves wearily
along to Mecca through gray Syria,
huddled
     and doubled up
the pilgrims stumbled along—
away from delusion and ferment
to repent,
       repent,
          repent . . .
And I was standing like an impenitent sinner
On the summit of the mountain
where once upon a time
                (don't stir!)
Abel was killed by Cain.
And—of all communiques of blood
      the most unforgettable—
the elemental voice was heard:
"Cain,
     where is your brother Abel?"
But once again the Pharisees,
the fascists
      with their vile-sweet voices:

"Why do you worry about visions that are fake?
Yes,

    with Abel maybe we should have held back.
Admittedly, there was a little mistake,
But generally speaking we were on the right track . . ."
And I was standing on the summit
between those ahead and the hosts behind,
above a world

              where people could commit
every corruption of their own kind.
There was no lightning

                and no thunder,
but the stones were crying with mouths opened wide:
"The corruption of the soul may be bloodless
but it is also fratricide!"
And I imagined a gloomy, dead
brick orphanage,

            where as with henbane
the children of Abel are spoonfed
with lies by the children of Cain.
And in the faces of Abel's children,
doing what they know that they must do,
which is always to stay silent,
the red mark of Cain shows through . . .

And I, no one's murderer,
was standing

         on the sticky summit,
but my conscience murmured
like the Bible:

"You won't be able to quit!
You're corrupting your spirit with lies,
and your spirit is crumbling,

                  cracking inside.
And to kill yourself

            —you cannot disguise
that that is also fratricide!
And how many women, you twister,
lie like crucifixions along your way—
but women, they are your sisters,
worth more than brothers can repay.
And the Hussars' toasts 'To the Ladies,'
what are they worth?

          Bravado,

              snide.
To kill love—

          you cannot evade it,
that is also fratricide.
And someone's gray

            brown eyes
staring at you with disdain,
on your forehead cicatrize
you with the eternal mark of Cain . . ."
I shuddered:

          —Quiet, O conscience.
You know this is not comparable,
it is like comparing a children's circus
with a bloody Roman shambles . . .
But the shadow of bony Cain
jutted out from the rocks near at hand,

and the blood of the brother he had slain
was endlessly dripping from my hand.
"Look—

      my bloody hands shake.
As a child it was fun to improvise,
out of curiosity to break
the velvet wings of butterflies.
Everything begins with the butterflies
and then—

      fratricide!
What will you say

        to the eternal skies
and the court of stars

         when you cannot turn back—
To say I am sinless would be telling lies,
but generally speaking I'm on the right track!
You know, all those whom you hate
set this up as the true state,
while the cigarettes take on
the smell of burning flesh, the Winstons

         and the Kents,
and the bullet

      which passed through John
kills Robert Kennedy.
And the bombs charge the earth, turn
brown villages blood-red, fire-black.
Admittedly they fall on children,
but generally speaking they're on the right track . . .
Everything begins with the butterflies,
later it comes round to bombs . . .

No amount of washing purifies—
the blood on your hands will be your doom.
The only murder which is fit—
is to kill
      the Cain inside!"
And I losing my footing on the sticky summit
face to face with the infinite
tore the flesh open in my side
and the strangled
           embryo Cain
                died.
I was strangling everything mean and evil,
all that later you would despise,
but it was far too late to heal
the broken wings of the butterflies.
And the wind, blood-soaked, invisible,
lashed at me from the fury of space
as if the pages of the Bible
were lashing
      me
        on my face.

Damascus-Moscow
1967–1968

TRANSLATED BY GEOFFREY DUTTON
WITH IGOR MEZHAKOFF-KORIAKIN

KAMIKAZE

And I shudder
             and come to my senses—Look!
His elbows dug into the green table,
a former kamikaze pilot—a dead man, Japanese,
truly—is talking about Raskolnikov.
At a "Symposium on the Novel," he's forty-five,
an old man. He's like
polite sobbing . . .
              he's like a scream
strangled by a necktie. And through us
and somewhere past us,
through Shimonoze flak and the shade of Lazo,
like the yellow shine of Hiroshima,
reeling,
        his face flies past.
But in his throat you can't tell
whether it's a lump of tears
or a cough-lump, or what.
                The Emperor wanted him to grow
                           up
humble, his death already assigned . . .
                a kamikaze.

Sure, it's great to swim along
hands and bouquets, to be slapped on the back by the military
there, at the parade. Sure,
it's fine to be a "hero of the people." But hero
in the name of *what?*
      With a few buddies,
this one shucked off his hero-status
and said he'd just as soon stay
alive.
  That took more guts than exploding
for a god-damned lie!
       I'm supposed to be hell-for-leather
myself,
   but what of my life and death, really?
What *do* I think, sinful and mortal,
among sinful, mortal people?
        We're all assigned our deaths . . .
We're kamikazes. The "divine wind" . . .
the wind of death whistles in our ears:
every footfall on this bomb-cratered planet
is a step toward death.
      So what if I get busted-up and crushed
but not because a dictator says so? I'll pull the control column
up by the roots
     firewall the throttle
on collision course, and go out
like the last battering ram.

But sons, daughters,
descendants,

      though my body sifts down in ashes, I'd like,
from the scraps of my plane, something good to explode
through to you.

      How strange it is, though,
to seem to yourself always dying

           in the sky for not
anything! To turn out to be lied-to
And still living in the face of your death-
assignment, and to be evil
as well! Yes, a living evil
long since supposed to be gone!

TRANSLATED BY JAMES DICKEY

WITH ANTHONY KAHN

AN ATTEMPT AT BLASPHEMY

Turning to the eternal magnet
in the pitch-dark night of my soul
I whisper my only prayer:
"O Lord, forgive me, help me."

And the Lord forgives and helps,
however helplessly he shrugs
at man's prolonged ingratitude
for his many mercies.

Clearly his people frighten God.
Call him by any name you choose—
Jehovah, Buddha, Allah—
he's one, and tired of being God.

If he could dematerialize,
or shrink in scale to a pocket idol,
he'd gladly slip away and hide
from our slobber in a private corner.

But it's not right for him to hide,
or stoop, like an African slave.
God also wants to believe in god,
but there's no god in the world for God.

And when, neglectful of our obligations,
we stick him with rotten little petitions,
to whom shall he address his prayer,
"O Lord, forgive me, help me"?

TRANSLATED BY STANLEY KUNITZ
WITH ANTHONY KAHN

AT THE MILITARY REGISTRATION AND ENLISTMENT CENTER

To the low cradle-song of the rails,
like a bone-tired oiler of expresses,
Zima Station slept on and on.
And the steeple on the District Soviet slept,
and a drunk slept in the cunette
and the watchman by the Grain Storage Center.

Like a Zima man, no Muscovite,
I walked and walked, breathing the smoke from my tobacco,
through the rustle of leaves and through somebody's dreams.
The rain touched the snare of the tin roofs . . .
And suddenly I heard a woman:
"Ah, if only there wasn't a war."

The moon slipped through piles of straw,
through little porches, shutters, slatted fences,
and, stopped right in my latest tracks,
sensing something of the future, I saw—
beheld, maybe—like a sad shade of the night,
a woman: one.

She was listening to something hidden in everything
that was dozing off. Her age; well, she was getting on
with it: fifty, at least; maybe more.
She was running along the handrails
with her palm, in a special way, a widow's way,
under the weathered-out signboard on the building:
"The Zima Military Registration and Enlistment Office."
Most likely she was coming from work
when something overran her, pushed her like a wave
to those handrails . . . in her the war came back
to life:
      a war without flags, without bands,
a war that had taken her breadwinner.
                              And here,
leaning on the handrails
—the same ones, the same as before—
she sent a prayer down the tracks after her husband,
and then walked on, heavy with child
and with a right hand whose strength had gone
touched you, handrails, again, and in her left
like death, she held
a Notice: the Notice of all
Notices.
      Ah, if only there wasn't a war!
(His hands held an accordion)
      If only there wasn't . . .
(and a spoon stuck in his right boot)
      . . . a war, if only there wasn't . . .
(a crumb of tobacco on his lip)
      . . . a war . . .

(He was loud when he was drunk a little,—
"Now don't you worry about Leshka!
Not a damn thing's going to happen."—
but in his eyes, a deep pain,
looking out.)
Ah, if only there wasn't a war!

TRANSLATED BY JAMES DICKEY
WITH ANTHONY KAHN

HURRY IS THE CURSE OF OUR CENTURY

Hurry is the curse of our century
and man, mopping the sweat from his forehead,
zigzags through life like a pawn in a fury
of being trapped on the board with his time expired.

Hurriedly we drink, hurriedly we love,
our souls eroding go to waste.
Hurriedly we push and shove
and later we repent, at haste.

But at least once, whether your home
in the world is sleeping or boiling with untruths,
stop, like a horse smothered in foam
sensing the abyss before its hooves.

For God's sake stop, even half way,
trust Heaven, as you would your fate,
think—even if you do not pray
to God—at least of your own state.

When the collapsing leaves flutter,
when the locomotive gives its hoarse cry,
know this: the tired runner is pitiful,
the one who has stopped stands high.

Sweep off the dust of vanity of vanities,
at last remember eternity,
and holy indecision will freeze
your feet to immobility.

There is strength in indecision
when you hesitate to follow
the path leading to perdition
at the end of which false beacons glow.

As you trample on people's faces like leaves,
stop! Like Vij,* you are blind.
Don't forego this last reprieve
by rushing on with a mad wind.

When you stride so confidently towards your goal
over bodies as though they were steps,
stop—you who have forgotten God—
you are really stepping on yourself!

When spite is shoving you forward,
making your own soul a hypocrite,
towards the disgrace of a shot or a word—
don't hurry, don't do it!

---

* Vij is a blind monster-gnome of Ukrainian folklore whose eyelids touch
the ground; if his eyes are opened nothing can be hidden from them. "Vij"
is also the title of Gogol's romantic story with a Ukrainian setting of witch-
craft.

Stop, O people of the Earth as you run
so blindly to the next assault!
Bullet, freeze as you fly from the gun,
and you, bomb in mid-air, halt!

O man, whose very name is sacred,
lifting the prayer of your eyes like a periscope
over disintegration and hatred,
for God's sake stop, for God's sake stop!

1968

TRANSLATED BY GEOFFREY DUTTON
WITH IGOR MEZHAKOFF-KORIAKIN

IV

Procession
with the Madonna

THE CONFESSIONAL

The little window of the confessional . . .
approaching it, in the religious shade
the threadbare face of a ravaged woman,
flickering with hope.

A child of the purlieus of Naples
waits her turn at the side,
an open Bible
on her telltale belly.

Without rifle or service cap
a soldier comes to be judged,
the skin of his back twitching
under the coarse uniform.

Housewives lug from the washtubs
and gamblers from the races
the sins of their imagination
along with their real sins.

Is there no confessional for me?
To whom shall I go, quelling my fears,
with the sinful dust, the foreign dust,
on my errant feet?

Enough of idleness and sloth!
What's the address? I'll find the way.
But people are crawling in my path,
begging to confess to me.

How can the confessor teach
those who are lost and sick at heart,
when he himself, among the sinners,
is worst, and most forsaken?

It is only a game we play
with other people's sins.
Besides, everyone knows
that everyone lies confessing.

And the priest lies too,
wanting to be good to them;
for the cozy fib, the double fib,
coddles and does not burn.

But I have no right to have faith in faith,
however I smash my brains on the stones,
when, almost like a truth to a truth,
a lie confesses to a lie.

Naples-Moscow

TRANSLATED BY STANLEY KUNITZ
WITH ANTHONY KAHN

THE HEAT IN ROME

Monks,

       all soutanes left to the devil,
Dive into those Roman fountains!

                 All right,
Signor premier-ministro,
Into the Po with you! Right down,
Presto-presto! *You!* Get on down
Under it!

       And like burros

            and like mules
To the water, ambassadors!

           To the water, ambassadors' wives!
Millionaire,

       holler in sheer confusion,
"Mister, can you spare me some shade?"

              Get together for once—

                big shots

With the simple people!

        O you common sweat!
*Every*thing's sweat-soaked—

        feelings too.
Newspapers are sticky underwear:

The Madonna cries . . .

                  A miracle!

                          Miracle!

But don't you believe it—

                    sweat's pouring off her.

Over forty Centigrade . . .

                        the thermometer explodes;

Mercury dances dead-drunk in the dust

Like little world-globes

That the countries have all slipped off.

Everything melts to pieces, ravels—

Everything's gotten so soft—

                    even the State.

Gouge off

        the temple-marble

And munch it like chewing gum.

                    And the bronze-coated kings,

heroes,

      gods

          are as miserable as

They'll ever be, as if made of plasticine:

Poke 'em with your finger;

                they'll fall down.

On the Piazza dell' Indipendenza

I drown, more helpless than a baby,

                up to my chest

In melted asphalt.

        Hey! Anybody!

              ANYbody!

No, damn it—

   Nobody answers.

       Living independently . . . ?

You could call it
Drowning independently!

      And over it all

A bare-ass poet drones out

       prophetic lines:

"The cows in the pastures've all rotted,
The Milky Way has curdled in the sky,
Peoples and vegetables give off all
Kinds of stinks! Awful currents of air!
SALVATION! It's in peeling off! A mass striptease!
Friends!

   Romans!

     Don't turn yourselves into corpses!

Don't be afraid of beauty! It's *virginal!*
Only cop-outs wear clothes!

       Rip off your jockey shorts! Your
          panties!"

Ladies gasp, "I've *got* to have it! OZONE! Some *Ozone,* for God's
           sake!"

They've announced,

     giving wings to the tailors,

that the fashionable thing to wear *this* season
Is the dress of the naked king.

      "Ha HA! All History tells you

It's been the *real* fashion

     for *thousands* of years!"

"O dear deputy of ours, you never take one step

                               into the villages,

but the villages have gotten gut-poor . . .

Where is everything you promised?"

"*I* promised?

                Ah yes! Ah yes indeed!—

I forgot . . . but you'll forgive me! It's just this *heat!*"

"Why're you so limp, Baby?

                         Can we straighten you out with

                                      wine?

Let's lie in the ice-box . . .

                   maybe things'll work out in

                          there . . ."

Deputies before their constituents

                        impotents before their wives

Killers before prosecutors

                 lawyers before killers

All justify themselves, good-naturedly as anything:

"There's no *air!* It's stuffy!

                     Stuffy, and hot from lies. Russia!

Lend us some of that damned

Snow!" But rumors're all over—pure gibberish!—that there's no

                                      snow

In Russia!

              And new rumors

Are flying

             circling Rome

That there are no icebergs

At the Poles

             that books are turning green

With mold in the libraries

                  that in the museums the colors are

                        dripping

From the pictures.

           And the weakening City of Night doesn't

                        sleep.

You've got to decide something

Right *now!* Make up your mind, even if those who never drew

                        breath

Say, "There's no air to breathe."

               Lord! From the skin of the

                    world—

Dirty grease!

        If only somebody could *ventilate*

The earth! All planes

          missiles

              destroyers

All submachine guns

        rifles

            and, with 'em,

The false coin of the orator's tongue

             the bronze brows of heads

Of state who've lost out . . . melt 'em! MELT 'em!

                Melt 'em

To make fans!

     Fans! Ah, fans!

Fans.

    Maybe it'd help *some* . . .

TRANSLATED BY JAMES DICKEY

WITH ANTHONY KAHN

RHYTHMS OF ROME

Get up!
Rome-the-giant-alarm-clock shrills by your head.
Whip up with a shaving brush the hissing foam.
And go out towards Rome!
Give yourself up to the dawn thud of shoes, hammers,
and the cries
of milkmaids, news vendors, bakers, green-grocers.
The nuns
with their starched white wings crackling trip in Indian file.
The coppers
in their clay mugs clatter appealing to passersby.
The prostitutes,
after their morning medical, go straight to pray in church.
In a café
the pot-bellied discuss the best cure for constipation.
Gypsy girls
jingle their coin-necklaces near an exhibit of "Super-Pop-Art."
Ministers
speed by in Mercedes. Their hands are calloused from playing
cards.
Hands
calloused from work drift on, expecting nothing.
Lemons
and men, in Italy, cost cheaper than anything else.

Where are
you hurrying, all of you people? Where are you crawling,
the boa constrictors
of the fire pumps, where water swirls strongly like sinews?
To Rome—all of you,
as though to a church for absolution,
and to a market-place,
where they may buy or sell you, perhaps.
I'd snatch
at what Rome has to offer, so as not to perish later in life.
I'd steal
a bit of its rhythm, but no! there's no snatching or stealing it.

There are many Romes,
but as a physical entity Rome hardly exists.
There are many rhythms—
no common rhythm, and that's the secret of its streets.
But I'll become
a bone-and rag man crying the torn tatters of Rome.
I shall swell
like a sponge sucking Rome into my pores.
Till night
I shall eavesdrop, and then sleep not a wink through the night,
an informant
to all mankind about you, Rome, and about myself.
Inside my shirt
I shall hide all that your alleys will shout,
will weep,
whisper, whistle, clang, and murmur.
Let my pursuit

of Rome, through Rome, break and fracture my bones—
like a tape
I shall eagerly wind Rome around me . . .

"Fire! Fire!
    Signora Silvia's aflame!"
"But no,
    you fool,
        it's her apartment . . ."
"Search in the wardrobe—
    you'll find personal linen
and that colander—
    chuck them out of the window!
Throw down the divan
    and the lid of the toilet bowl!
. . . and all's in a heap,
    might as well bang your head on a
        wall . . .
Stop,
    you blockhead.
        Where's our vase?
And where's
    the album,
        the family album? . . ."
"Shut up,
    wife,
        squealing won't help . . ."
". . . Why did I ever get married
        after sinning?"
"Here,
    take this rope,
        and lower the TV set . . ."

"The damn thing is being lowered at last!"
"Don't cry,
    these are just
        saucepans and cans.
Come to,
    wife,
        look—you're all covered with
            down . . ."
"Let go,
    don't push.
        Wait, where's the Madonna?
The Madonna's
        burning!
            They left her upstairs!"
"Good grief,
    what a calamity.
        Did you hear that, my son?"
"Now they'll be locked out of paradise, neighbor.
It's eternal damnation—for Signora Silvia . . .
No Madonna . . .
They forgot her . . . Ai-ai-ai!"

"Who wants the Duce, who wants the Duce!
A fine portrait that!
Come, people,
    flock together,
        crowd round—
no better man in all the world!
The painter's brush—
            admittedly!—
is not that of a Matisse,
but there was a time when the Duce

used to please you *multissimo.*
Drift up,
 flea market,
and do your smart trading.
Among so many odd bird-and-fish,
this little bird is quite unique!
This day there are
no open bidders for the Duce,
but enough concealed ones:
I can tell them by their eyes.
It would serve them better to be bolder,
for the Duce is already cracking.
Who wants the Duce, who wants the Duce?
No one needs the Duce?"

"Come over here, Signore—we sell letters here.
Real letters—do you see the postmarks?
We request you not to remove the stamps—
 you can read the letters, don't hurry . . .
There are enough letters for all—piles of them.
Here is the eighteenth century, if you please:
 'I shall wait for you eternally.'
Here, if you please, is the nineteenth:
 'I shall wait for you a hundred years.'
And here's the twentieth, Signore:
 'Why do you keep twisting and turning?
I've already spent two evenings with you, and nothing doing.'
Here's a World War I letter,
 and one of World War II . . .
(Unfortunately, time has not restored the censor's deletions . . .)
And if there's a World War III, Signore, I imagine,
as you do, we'll be left with no letters at all.

Signore, I believe letters to be the most precious of relics,
but they are sold cheap, and I, old man, buy them.
Letters are the odd pages of a great book, perhaps,
but there's no glue to paste them all together."
"Don't you find it strange, Signor, to trade in letters?"
"Strange? What's strange about it?

Aha, you must be a poet, I guess . . .
And don't you find it strange to trade in songs?
The world's full of strange things,

but nothing is really strange . . ."

"Mama Roma, mama Roma,
don't you have a conscience?
My husband's as thin as a spaghetti,
a spaghetti without any sauce.
Conscience does not prick me—
all that pricks is my frisky blood.
Government,

give us

divorce laws,
or—

I shall emigrate!"

"Signor doctor, please explain what sort of animal I am?"
"I don't understand your question, Signora."
"What's there not to understand, Signor doctor!
Soon as I rise I start darning, ironing, cooking
breakfast for my husband and children—

just like a squirrel in a treadmill.
I don't have time to eat—I'm famished as a wolf.
I go to the factory and do the donkey work.
I return by bus and hiss spite like an old goose.

I go shopping and stagger back as loaded as a camel.
Back home, I launder again, sweep up and cook, work like a
horse.
Dog-weary, I fall into bed.
My husband comes in drunk, plunks down,
    and says: 'Make room, you old cow.'
What sort of an animal am I, Signor doctor, tell me that?"

"I'm at the end of my confession,
Padre.
I've no thick hair left, wisps are all
I have.
You taught us, Father, not to sin
but think.
Foolish me, I've tried, Padre, to live
like that.
As if it were a dream, I remember nothing.
In vain
I lived so righteously, it gives me
the creeps.
I'd like to sin before I die, but it's
too late.
I only remember the sins of very long
ago.
I have no need of anything now—being
a grandma.
It's a long way to the schooldays when I
wore a bow.
Come nearer, grandchildren, I've something
to tell you.
Like a small cross, in your hands I shall
place the truth.

My little ones, of necessary sins be not
afraid;
have fear, instead, of those tedious
coffins.
Run further away from a faith that is
empty
into sins, as into dense forest, a willow-branch
forest.
Quietly, there, grandchildren, amid moaning,
you'll hear:
your one joy before dying is to remember
your sins . . ."

"Lucky lottery tickets,
      tickets,
            tickets!
They'll give you motorbikes,
      Fiats,
            sideboards.
Don't believe in politics,
      or in fool-cybernetics,
believe only in lottery tickets,
      lucky tickets . . .
You wear birettas now,
      but tomorrow you'll be mere skeletons.
Snap up the tickets,
      the lucky tickets!"
"If failure's turned you bald,
      then don't be such dullards, Signori,
buy a policeman out-of-the-ordinary,
      a rubber one.

Pummel him,
    spit on him,
        kick him,
            shove him,
and when you teach him a thing or two,
then you'll get at least partial relief
    from the damnable life you lead . . ."
"And tell me, please
    won't you also have
ministers all made
    of rubber?"
"I won't even promise them.
I regret, Signor—
    they're all sold out."

"Hands off,
    hands off
        Vietnam!
Let's stop laundering now, daughter,
I'm a mother, that's certain.
Why are they bombing
those children—
    the little Vietnamese?
If they're not all childless,
then the papers must be lying."

"I don't give a damn for Vietnam!
I'm all for a quiet life.
All
    I need is a new patch
on my trousers!"

"Signor sergeant,
  Signor sergeant,
off the Piazza di Spagna
I was trying to buy a sideboard
and a secretary for the bedroom.
And suddenly in a gallery window I saw a bed,
and on the bed a girl,
wearing not a stitch as the day she was born,
puffing insolently on a cigarette.
And beside the girl lay
a pair of soiled panties,
and, in addition,
  Signor sergeant,
they were empty . . .
  those things.
And over this disgraceful show
was written:
  'Sculpture.'
Signor sergeant,
  save Rome
and Roman culture!"
"To save Rome, Signora, is complicated . . .
What's to be done . . .
  The younger generation . . .
One can't make out these days
what you can do or can't . . ."

"Striptease, in reverse,
  is the latest thing with us."
"What sort of thing is that?"
  "This is the way it works:

Out comes a floozy—
    wearing only pasties,
and then she starts dressing,
    and that's where the kick comes in."
"An old trick . . .
    all crawl out naked
        on the stage of life,
and then clothe themselves
    in words,
        words,
            words,
but, all the same, behind the words
    they see each other naked.
Striptease, in reverse—such is *la vita* . . ."

"Signor, it's none of my business, of course, but as the bar proprietor,
    I'd like to warn you about that woman, who has just sat down at
    your table. She is—if you'll excuse me, a man . . ."
"You're joking!"
"It's no joke. It's true to life, I regret, Signor. Observe the hands and
    legs—they are rather large and muscular. A special cream has
    been used to remove the facial hair. The long hair is either a wig
    or naturally grown. You may have been deluded by the rounded
    forms of the breasts? That is the result of paraffin injections.
    Painful, but effective. Signor, you are still very young and
    evidently inexperienced. Therefore I considered it my duty to
    warn you somewhat tactlessly . . ."
"You mean this woman is a man?"
"A man, Signor . . ."
"The devil! Incidentally, call me Signora, not Signor. For many days
    now I have been trying to find at least one genuine woman . . .
    But I've had no luck . . ."

"Signori!

In the name and at the instigation of the presidium of the Pederast
Club allow me to propose the first toast to women. Let this
toast be no surprise to you, Signori. For all their physical and
moral deficiencies women are indispensable; they give birth to us,
pederasts. So—here's to women!"

"Tell me, my friend, why should we write verses
amid this terrible disintegration? I don't know.
Though harshly you may try to make this world ashamed,
it refuses to be shamed. Like the flag, shame's been betrayed.

"Salvation lies in feeling ashamed, but that's forgotten,
and at times I have the urge to cry:
'O where, mankind, is your sense of shame—
which is your one and only powerful lever?'

"Shamelessness reigns about us in the night,
while feelings are diminished and maimed—
only the veined noses of the drunkards
blush red with shame for all mankind . . .

"Stop now, stop . . . Your bitter monologue
is verse already . . . It's worth writing verse then.
And if you're reluctant, God will compel you—
the God that groans in us, imperfect ones.

"Yes, shame's forgotten or, rather, it's quiescent,
but why break your heart on that account.
You still feel shame! Why have the others lost
their innate capacity for shame?

"Inactively to watch corruption
is no better than to be openly corrupt,
and, damning corruption from on high,
we ourselves become part of the corruption.

"And doesn't it seem to you, my friend,
that, because we've lost our sight through fear,
we find ourselves in a vicious circle,
unable to see the world beyond the line enclosing us?

"But there are different circles. There are
at this moment, too—intact, as of old—
love, hope, goodness, and honor,
all walking through Rome, unseen.

"They pass in the shade, and thus they see us, too.
They walk along. Like specters we are chased.
And it is they, perhaps, who are right
and eternal, just as this city is eternal.

"My love, we've been forgotten here.
From the park all the people have gone home,
and, leaving the ferris wheel,
the others have wandered off elsewhere.

"The operator was evidently well-meaning—
he did not drop us down to earth.
The great wheel has stopped.
We've been forgotten . . . That's very good!

"Below us lies our poor, proud Rome,
our beloved Rome, our accursed Rome.
It's not aware that we are hovering
in our cabin in the air above.

"Below us the lie-mongering politicians,
the ministers, the trollops, kings,
high personages, the police, the armed forces—
how utterly tedious all this is!

"Someone needs us there below,
and we have to do something about it.
So let's be thankful they've forgotten us
for a while up here in the sky.

"Give that cabin of ours a push
and put your lips to mine,
or I myself will push our cabin
and put my lips to thine."

Stop, war, stop, war . . .
Yes, like Rome, life is terrifying,
but, like Rome, there's only one life . . .
Stop, war, stop, war . . .

1965

TRANSLATED BY GEORGE REAVEY

PROCESSION WITH THE MADONNA

to Ludovico Corrao

I

In the small, untroubled town of Taormina
A grave procession passed with its Madonna.
Smoke from the candles rose and came to nothing,
As frail as any moment's brief enigma.

There in the forefront, all attired in white,
The young girls walked, holding their candles tightly.
Flushed with a timid rapture, on they came,
Full of themselves and of the world's delight.

And the girls stared at the candles in their hands,
And in those flames, unstable in the wind,
They saw stupendous meetings, deep communions,
And heard endearments past all understanding.

Oh, it was right that the young girls should be hopeful.
The hour of their deception was not ripe.
But there behind them, like their fates impending,
The women marched along with weary step.

Attired in black, the women marched along,
And they too held their candles tightly, strongly,

Heavily shuffling, grave and undeceived,
And full of an accustomed sense of wrong.

And the women stared at the candles in their hands,
And in those flames, unstable in the wind,
They saw the scrawny shoulders of their children
And heard the vacant speeches of their husbands.

Thus, street by street, they all went on together,
Declaring that the Madonna was their mother,
And bearing the Madonna like some strange
Victim who stands erect upon her stretcher.

The Madonna's heart, or so it appeared, was pained
Both for the girls and for the women behind them;
And yet—or so it appeared—she had decreed
That life go on like this, world without end.

I walked beside the Madonna, and my glance
Found in the candles no glad radiance,
No weary sorrow, but a muddled vision
Full of sweet hope and bitterness at once.

And so I live—still dreaming, still unmarried,
And yet already doomed forevermore—
Somewhere between the girls in their white dresses
And the grey women in their black attire.

Sicily

TRANSLATED BY RICHARD WILBUR
WITH ANTHONY KAHN

NEAR THE FORGOTTEN ROMAN ROAD

Near the forgotten Roman Road
not far away from Damascus,
the contours of the mountainsides erode
deathly as the Emperors' death masks.

Warming their scales, their heads withdrawn
into their coils, secret and obsessed,
fat snakes are basking in the sun—
just gone from Cleopatra's breast.

The road carried rubies and pearls
and swords of damascene, most rare
of steels, and the squirming slave girls
used to sweep it with their hair.

Pocked with the ulcers of Venus
their coats of mail never showed,
with faces like coins the legionaries
marched along the dead-straight road.

Not yet broken up for junk,
the swaying chariots leaned over
like the curved combs bent
through the Empress's coiffure.

The flagstones of the road were packed
tight by slaves bent with the load,
like their petrified backs
driven down into the road.

Quite exhausted by this fiery land
and the effort of thinking, a soft patrician,
a cup of lemon juice by his hand,
anointed himself with Etruscan lotion:

"Even if only the skulls and ribs
of this rabble are left under the sky,
we at least will not die like pigs
and the road itself will never die . . ."

And the Arab laborer obediently
cracking stones, yet a crafty slave,
a perfidious slave, was thinking obstinately
with every blow his sledgehammer gave:

"Flesh and blood you glorify,
but you have forgotten God.
All right then, even you will die,
all right then, so will the road . . ."

The roots of the empire were rotting in filth.
It was tatty with decrepitude
like an old patchwork quilt
sewn together with threads of blood.

They used the tortures they understood
and subtler pressures on the head,
they tried to mend it all with blood,
but there is no weaker thread.

Roman hypocrisy is naked
since the arrogant toga fell,
and the great empire is quite dead
and the road is dead as well.

They tried the forger's falsehood
that repeats, it has nothing to do with the road,
the road is not guilty of the blood,
the stones do not know why it flowed.

But the wild weeds have many times
well and truly settled the score.
The road which gave birth to crimes
is criminal itself for evermore.

And let all roads that run to hangmen
and all roads that run to tyrants' misdeeds
be rewarded by the highest payment,
which is the highest growth of weeds!

And these were my thoughts beside that road
now closed to soldier and chariot,
beside the road which forgot God
and which, for that reason, God forgot.

Damascus-Moscow
1967–1968

TRANSLATED BY GEOFFREY DUTTON

WITH IGOR MEZHAKOFF-KORIAKIN

V

Cemetery

of Whales

IN A STEELWORKER'S HOME

I love America,
   the America who swam
the Maytime Elbe
   holding aloft whiskey
with a tired right arm,
   paddling with the left;
yes, and Russia swam to meet her in
the Maytime Elbe,
   holding aloft vodka
with a tired left arm,
   paddling with the right,
and vodka and whiskey—
   neat!—without translation
understood
   each other perfectly,
     goddammit,
on the waters where victories met!

I love America,
   the America who now
sits with me in the prefab ranch-house
of a steelworker.

On the worker's arms
blue veins bulge and fork,
like secret tributaries of our Elbe.
There are no governments between us now.
Our invisible government
    has been chosen by us wordlessly—
those same tired soldiers,
    boys from Irkutsk and Kentucky,
who invisibly swim to each other
    until today on the Maytime Elbe.

Murmuring, murmuring,
invisible waves surge
across the plain fraternal table,
and wineglasses of cheap Chianti,
cradled by us on these waves,
redden like guiding buoys.
We talk
    as if we were swimming
to embrace each other like brothers,
    BUT
for twenty years they have polluted the Elbe.
They've dumped so much sewage in her—
the backwaters of falsehood,
    our era's super-cesspools:
Newspapers soaked in poison,
    dregs of inflammatory speeches,
the spit of scoundrels,
    Kleenexes soggy with snot,
and greasy sweat fastidiously wiped

from the hypocrite faces of long-winded orators.
Beneath the surface of our Elbe are hiding
moss-covered mines of distrust
and sleek new submarines
pregnant with torpedoes,
offspring of a marriage of fear
   and science.

Oh, when
   will we understand each other
as vodka and whiskey—
   straight!—without translation
understood
   each other perfectly,
     goddammit,
on the waters where victory met victory!
Really, do we need a new Hitler
to unite us
   again?
A price
   like maybe
     much too high . . .
Russia and America,
   your path
to each other is tortuous,
   but I believe,
     do believe
that through all the refuse and the mossy mines,
   we will swim to one another,
     we will swim,

we will embrace
  as in the Maytime of '45,
and this time,
  I dare believe,
    for keeps!
True, there are oceans of malice between us.
True, the Great Ocean, the Pacific, is between us.
But we will swim it;
  no ocean so great
it cannot become an Elbe!

I love America,
  the America who now,
snuggled in her crib, wiggles her delicate toes;
her slender feet shine for us, the disenchanted,
like candles radiating hope.
What is her name—
  Jan?
    Or, perhaps, Lara?
Her eyes
  are huge
    and blue,
two trusting drops
of that same Elbe,
  our common Elbe
we must not betray.
Russia and America,
  swim closer!

TRANSLATED BY JOHN UPDIKE

WITH ALBERT C. TODD

MONOLOGUE OF A BROADWAY ACTRESS

Said an actress from Broadway
  time had pillaged like Troy:
"There are simply no more roles.
No role
  to extract from me all my tears,
no role
  to turn me inside out.
From this life, really,
  one must flee to the desert.
There are simply no roles any more!
Broadway blazes
like a hot computer
but, believe me, there's no role—
  not one role
amidst hundreds of parts.
Honestly, we are *drowning* in rolelessness . . .
  Where are the great writers! Where?

The poor classics have broken out in sweat,
 like a team of tumblers whose act is too long,
but what do they know
 about Hiroshima,
about the murder of the Six Million,
 about all our pain?!
Is it really *all* so inexpressible?
Not one role!
It's like being without a compass.
You know how dreadful the world is
when it builds up inside you,
 builds up and builds up,
and there's absolutely no way out for it.
Oh yes,
 there are road companies.
For that matter,
 there are TV serials.
But the *roles* have been removed.
They put you off with bit parts.
I drink. Oh I know it's weak of me,
but what can you *do,* when there are no more people,
no more roles?
Somewhere a worker is drinking,
 from a glass opaque with greasy fingerprints.
He has no role!
And a farmer is drinking,
 bellowing like a mule because he's impotent:
he has no role!

A sixteen-year old *child*
  is stabbed with a switchblade by his friends
    because they have *nothing* better to *do* . . .
There are no roles!
Without *some* sort of role, life
  is simply slow rot.
In the womb, we are all geniuses.
But potential geniuses become idiots
without a role to play.
Without demanding anyone's blood,
I
  do demand
    a *role!*"

1967

TRANSLATED BY JOHN UPDIKE
WITH ALBERT C. TODD

ON THE QUESTION OF FREEDOM

Dachau's ashes burn my feet
The asphalt smokes under me
Warheads & bayonets stuck
under my nails

I'll stroke a stray strand of my beloved's hair
And I myself shall smoke
crucified Christ-like on wings of bombers
flying through this night to kill Christ's kids

My skin trembles with explosions
as if it were Vietnam
and breaking my back and ribs
the Berlin Wall runs through me

You talk to me of freedom? Empty question
under umbrellas of bombs in the sky
It's a disgrace to be free of your own age
A hundred times more shameful than to be its slave

Yes I'm enslaved to Tashkent women
and to Dallas bullets and Peking slogans
and Vietnam widows and Russian women
with picks beside the tracks and kerchiefs over their eyes

Yes I'm not free of Pushkin and Blok
Not free of the State of Maryland and Zima Station
Not free of the Devil and God
Not free of earth's beauty and its shit

Yes I'm enslaved to a thirst for taking a wet-mop
to the heads of all the bickerers & butchers of the world
Yes I'm enslaved to the honor of busting the mugs
of all the bastards on earth

And maybe I'll be loved by the people for this
For spending my life
(not without precedent in this iron age)
glorifying unfreedom from
the true struggle for freedom

TRANSLATED BY LAWRENCE FERLINGHETTI
WITH ANTHONY KAHN

THE RESTAURANT FOR TWO

Honolulu,
you loll dreamily on your back in a silver-black nowhere.
        The breeze moves moons
Across the waves and along your mermaidenly thighs.
        ubiquitous scintillation.
Like a savage, you adore glinting trinkets in shopwindows.
        Like brooches
great ships ride pinned in your watery hair.
        In heedless brown hands
you shuffle Yanks, Japs, and cards from Down Under.
        You dance,
and tiny gilded fish tinkle in your heels.
        A Scots laird
in a multicolored kilt reels with you, drooling,
        and lubriciously
slips his hand under somebody's skirt, not his own.
        But a modest hut,
a "Restaurant à deux," on its pilings of palm
        like a gnome on stilts
has attained to the stars, a unique toy temple.
        No aërial
tops its conical cap of green leaves.

Within, the walls
are woven of bamboo and mystery, and what takes place
        is *hush-hush.*
A "boy," Malayan, smirking, fetches up the stairway
        baked shark's fin
steeped in pineapple, golden through and through.
        Two places set.
Two candles. Two conspirators. Two fugitives.
        Into each other's eyes
as if into cathedrals they have fled the world's bedlam.
        It's shaky in here,
it's rickety as a Chinese lantern. Maybe it's wicked.
        It's false, sure.
That is to say, it's substanceless—and still, so pleasant!
        The samba's throb,
the stars' murmuring, the thunder from the breakwater—
        all for these two.
Gladly I would beat it to that Restaurant à deux.
        I would crush
my glass of flat champagne and shout to the sourpussed mob:
        "I am dying,
you bore me so. I yearn for the Restaurant à deux."
        Oh no, you say?
One must do this, do that, but never, never the other?
        I am fed up.
I am tired to death. I want *in* to the Restaurant à deux.
        Reconsider?
Struggle on, be committed? Oh, I gave it a whack—so what?
        That little hut
has shown me the answer, the exit, the Restaurant à deux.

Let them judge me!
I'm off! And yet, running away . . . is cowardly stuff.
WHAT WOULD HAPPEN
IF EVERYBODY WERE TO HIDE IN A RESTAURANT À DEUX?!
That's no way out,
in an epoch of open wounds—to seek shelter from ennui
in a gnome-home,
in the tresses and lips of another, in her knees and brow.
A demon's whisper
impels us to flee; we cannot comprehend
that after flight
it is even worse than before to be a galley-slave.
. . . Amid the stars,
they sit as in a dainty boat, having had their fun, at peace,
two fugitives:
while below them, life with its dogs like a sheriff waits.
The Malayan
daydreams at the foot of the sacrosanct stairway
and scornfully
entertains a stir of pity for innocence so hollow.
He observes
a half-hour remains to closing time (then, scram!)
and switches on
the birdsong tape-recorded to lend the illusion of paradise.

1967

TRANSLATED BY JOHN UPDIKE
WITH EDWARD KEENAN

A BALLAD ABOUT NUGGETS

Night. The town of Fairbanks sleeps,
                          exhausted. But invisible
squeakings walk the snowy streets
                      cloaked in hides and wool.
Wearing the face of an adolescent
                    and a painted caribou parka,
an Eskimo strip-tease *artiste*
                hurries to work in a bar.
Drunken fliers from the air base,
                  aching for a shack-up,
ruttish louts, brave buddies,
              throw snowballs at her back.
But she in darkness carries
            her frozen breath
through the leers like a pure
              white rose in her teeth.
In out of the cold
         as hoary as owls,
in through the saloon doors
            come clamorous clouds
with people inside them!—
           a miner, a hunter, a trapper.
They all toss their caps
         on the walrus-tusk hatrack.

Who comes from where?

                    What nation? Who cares!

Among these Alaskans

              I'm one of the bears;

for us holy vodka

          will answer all prayers.

Pal Bob, fellow sourdough, have a drink,

                      down the hatch.

Your big mitts have hugged me,

                your stiff whiskers scratch.

Your grin gleams with gold.

               You look worn out, man.

"Listen, Rooshian, I've been prospecting

                  all my life, understand?

No ruddier bastard than me swung a pick.

                  Now I'm trash.

My bald head's a runway

           for mosquitoes and gnats.

Now I'm set to cash in,

         to add it up proper:

a mouthful of gold

         and a fistful of copper.

Ah, when I buried my old lady, Viv,

I recall how the sled-dogs gave

a howl at the edge of the hole,

           at the edge of her grave.

Viv was a knockout once, just like

          those Playgirls you unfold.

Her body white as quartz all over,

          with little flecks of gold.

I had a good eye then, as young as you,

                    as lucky and game.

I said to her: 'I've staked you out.

                  Viv, you're my claim.'

I tortured her for forty years.

              I was crazy,

Lifelong crazy, to find my strike,

              to find nuggets.

She didn't ask for fancy clothes

            but, shyly,

for a son. She dreamt of a son like me,

              and I, of nuggets.

I drank. Like yellow fish

          alive in a muddy sea,

they came at me, teased me,

          nuggets.

So I closed up shop,

        a bankrupt boss.

My pick and shovel

        made Viv a cross.

I ain't forgot how I dragged that box

            on the hard-froze earth.

I never dug up my nugget,

        I buried her."

Bob counts the coppers in his paw.

            He is drunk, disconsolate.

"Without gold, I . . . 'Scuse me, Rooshian,

           lend me a stake."

Having forgotten his cap,

        he shakily seeks the way out

and jabs the swinging doors

and plunges into his cloud.

Then I too wander in the dark,

a child of the saloon.

Nothingness pulls on my pockets

as I walk along.

I still haven't shut up shop,

I'm too timid;

but perhaps my nugget

is already buried.

Boyfaced beside me,

a silent companion,

the Eskimo stripper,

exhausted, hurries home.

Zero. Icicles

beard my chin,

and birds frozen in flight fall

like nuggets, with a clink.

1967

TRANSLATED BY JOHN UPDIKE

WITH EDWARD KEENAN

CEMETERY OF WHALES

A cemetery of whales:
  in a snowy graveyard
instead of crosses
  their own bones stand.
They couldn't be gnawed by teeth;
  teeth are too soft.
They couldn't be used for soup;
  pots are too shallow.
The straining wind bends them,
  but they keep their position,
rooted in ice,
  arching like black rainbows.
Thirsty for a snort,
  an Eskimo hunchback,
shaped like a question mark,
  huddles in them as in parentheses.
Who playfully clicked a camera?
  Restrain your photophilia.
Let's leave the whales in peace,
  if only after death.

They lived, these whales,
  without offense to people,
in infantile simplicity,
  reveling in their own fountains,
while the crimson ball of the sun
  danced in a torrent of rays . . .
Thar she blows!
  Come on, lads, let's get 'em!
Where can we hide?
  But you're broader than space!
The world doesn't hold enough water
  for you to dive under.
You think you're God?
  A risky bit of impudence.
One harpoon, smack in the flank,
  rewards enormity.
Enormity commands everyone
  to hunt for it.
Whoever is big is stupid.
  Who's smaller is wiser.
Sardines, like vermicelli,
  are an impossible target,
lost in the generic—
  but greatness is helpless.
On board, binoculars tremble
  as the crew takes aim;
streaming harpoon in his side,
  huge Tolstoy runs from the Kodak.

A baby whale, not full-fledged,
   though evaluated as a whale,
Esenin flutters and kicks,
   hoisted high on a harpoon shaft.
The title of Whale is a bloody dignity.
   Greatness kills greatness.
Mayakovsky himself
   pounds in the lance.
The shallows are also a menace:
   dashed on the shoals by the chase,
Gorky hawks and disgorges
   fragments of steel and hickory.
Without even moaning,
   gliding along the path of blood,
Pasternak with a snatch of lime
   sinks into Lethe.
Hemingway is silent;
   but from his grave a threatening shaft
shoots out of the grass,
   growing up from the coffin.
And hidden behind the mob,
   murder in his eye,
the Dallas whaler
   with a telescopic sight.
A big drive is on;
   we cherish their names posthumously.
Your law is more honest,
   cruel Alaska.

In the cemetery of whales
  by the hummocks of ice
there are no sanctimonious flowers:
  the Eskimos have tact.
Hey, Eskimo hunchback,
  white men have a funny custom:
after planting the harpoon,
  they weep over the corpse.
Murderers mourn like maidens,
  and tearfully suck tranquilizers,
and parade in crêpe,
  and stand honor guard.
The professional hunters,
  who would look out of place,
send wreaths to the whales
  from the State Bureau of Harpoonery.
But the flowers are twisted together
  with steel cables and barbs.
Enough of such goodness!
  Let me live among Eskimos!

1967

TRANSLATED BY JOHN UPDIKE
WITH ALBERT C. TODD

NEW YORK ELEGY

At night, in New York's Central Park,
chilled to the bone and belonging to no one,
I talked quietly with America:
both of us were weary of speeches.

I talked with my footsteps—
unlike words, they do not lie—
and I was answered with circles
dead leaves uttered, falling onto a pond.

Snow was falling, sliding embarrassed
past bars where noisiness never ceases,
settling tinted on the swollen neon veins
on the city's sleepless brow,
on the incessant smile of a candidate
who was trying, not without difficulty, to get in
somewhere, I don't remember just where,
and to the snow it didn't matter where.

But in the Park it fell undisturbed:
the snowflakes descended cautiously
onto the softly sinking leaves,
soggy multicolored floats;

onto a pink and tremulous balloon
childishly fastened with chewing gum
to the trunk of an evergreen
and sleepily rubbing its cheek against the sky;
onto someone's forgotten glove,
onto the zoo, which had shown its guests out,
onto the bench with its wistful legend:
PLACE FOR LOST CHILDREN.

Dogs licked the snow in a puzzled way,
and squirrels with eyes like lost beads
flickered between cast-iron baskets,
amidst trees lost in the woods of themselves.
Great juttings of granite stood about
morosely, preserving in mineral calm
a silent question, a reproach—
lost children of former mountains.

Behind a wire fence, zebras munching hay
peered, at a loss, into striped darkness.
Seals, poking their noses from the pool,
caught snow in mid-flight on their whiskers;
they gazed around them, quizzical, confused,
forsaken children of Mother Ocean
taking pity, in their slippery style,
on people—lost children of the Earth.

I walked alone. Now and then, in the thicket,
the crimson firefly of a cigarette
floated before an unseen face—
the staring pupil of Night's wide eye.

And I felt some stranger's feeling of being lost
was searching embarrassed
for a feeling of being lost like my own,
not knowing that this was what I longed for.

At night, beneath this snowfall,
its whispered secret having made us one,
America and I sat down together
in the place for lost children.

TRANSLATED BY JOHN UPDIKE
WITH ALBERT C. TODD

MONOLOGUE OF AN AMERICAN POET

to Robert Lowell

A loved one leaves
  like air from the lungs—
vapor amid the final dry snowflakes,
the black branches clicking and sagging
  with ice.
She can't be breathed back in.
A mere gesture, I abrade my cheek
  on the rust-scaled trunk
of a drain pipe.
  To no purpose, I weep.
    She departs.
Friends depart,
  fellow sufferers,
    peers,
as from the field of the young
we are led toward separate pens
away from the once-shared milk
In vain, like an unweaned whelp,
  I whine for friends;
they don't come back.
Hopes depart—
  such darling ladies,
whom I use on such useless occasions!

Only their petticoats stay in my hands;
hopes are meant to be held for a moment.
Certitude departs.
   I remember, I swore a sacred oath
to break my stupid head against the wall
  or the wall with my stupid head.
My head is scratched, true,
  but unbroken.
And what of the wall?
  The bastard smirks;
on its blankness they are blandly changing
the posters,
  the portraits of heroes . . .
Certitude,
  where are you?
New York,
  your dark sky circles above me
    like a hawk.
America, believe me,
  I'm finished,
    I'm finished,
      finished.
I am a ship
  where all the cabins smell of doom
and rats leap in terror from the clammy deck.
Hey, seagulls—don't weep!
  Don't,
    don't pity me!
My lovely leggy guests abandon me.
They take their places, as prescribed,
  the first in the lifeboat—

Farewell, my mistresses!
My apple-cheeked cadets abandon me.
They want to live.
    Fair enough,
        they are still young.
Farewell, lads!
    Row ahead.
        You are men.
Now the inane rumble of the engine shuts down.
Only talent
    like a drunken, unshaven captain
stands somberly on the bridge.
    The captain is the captain.
But he too, tears smearing his windburned skin,
he too abandons me,
    he too . . .
        he too . . .
Hey, lifeboats—stand away!
A ship, when it sinks,
    makes a maelstrom around it.
To be totally alone
    hurts worse than a knife,
but I won't suck anyone down with me.
I forgive you all.
    Robed in death's foam,
I bequeath it you to demolish that bastardly wall.
    My trumpet juts from the marble swirls:
        comrades, battle on.

1967

TRANSLATED BY JOHN UPDIKE
WITH ALBERT C. TODD

MONOLOGUE OF A POLAR FOX ON AN ALASKAN FUR FARM

I am a blue fox on a gray farm.
Condemned to slaughter by my color
behind this gnawproof wire screen,
I find no comfort in being blue.

Lord, but I want to molt! I burn
to strip myself of myself in my frenzy;
but the luxuriant, bristling blue
seeps through the skin—scintillant traitor.

How I howl—feverishly I howl
like a furry trumpet of the last judgment,
beseeching the stars either for freedom forever,
or at least forever to be molting.

A passing visitor captured my howl
on a tape recorder. What a fool!
He didn't howl himself, but he might
begin to, if he were caught in here!

I fall to the floor, dying.
Yet somehow, I fail to die.
I stare in depression at my own Dachau
and I know: I'll never escape.

Once, after dining on a rotten fish,
I saw that the door was unhooked;
toward the starry abyss of flight I leaped
with a pup's perennial recklessness.

Lunar gems cascaded across my eyes.
The moon was a circle! I understood
that the sky is not broken into squares,
as it had been from within the cage.

Alaska's snowdrifts towered all around,
and I desperately capered, diseased,
and freedom did a Twist inside my lungs
with the stars I had swallowed.

I played pranks, I barked nonsense
at the trees. I was my own pure self.
And the iridescent snow was unafraid
that it was also very blue.

My mother and father didn't love each other,
but they mated. How I'd like
to find a girl-fox so that I could
tumble and fly with her in this sumptuous powder!

But then I'm tired. The snow is too much.
I cannot lift my sticking paws.
I have found no friend, no girl friend.
A child of captivity is too weak for freedom.

He who's conceived in a cage will weep for a cage.
Horrified, I understood how much I love
that cage, where they hide me behind a screen,
and the fur farm—my motherland.

And so I returned, frazzled and beaten.
No sooner did the cage clang shut,
than my sense of guilt became resentment
and love was alchemized again to hate.

In you, Alaska, I howled in lost despair.
In prison now, I am howling in despair.
My America, I am lost,
but who hasn't gotten lost in you?

True, there are changes on the fur farm.
They used to suffocate us in sacks.
Now they kill us in the modern mode—
electrocution. It's wonderfully tidy.

I contemplate my Eskimo-girl keeper.
Her hand rustles endearingly over me.
Her fingers scratch the back of my neck.
But a Judas sadness floods her angel eyes.

She saves me from all diseases
and won't let me die of hunger,
but I know that when the time, set firm as iron,
arrives, she will betray me, as is her duty.

Brushing a touch of moisture from her eyes,
she will ease a wire down my throat, crooning.
BE HUMANE TO THE EMPLOYEES! ON FUR FARMS
INSTITUTE THE OFFICE OF EXECUTIONER!*

I would like to be naïve, like my father,
but I was born in captivity: I am not him.
The one who feeds me will betray me.
The one who pets me will kill me.

TRANSLATED BY JOHN UPDIKE

WITH ALBERT C. TODD

* Echoing typical signs on a Soviet collective farm.

FLOWERS & BULLETS

Of course: Bullets don't like people
                who love flowers.
They're jealous ladies, bullets,
                short on kindness.
Allison Krause, nineteen years old,
                you're dead,
for loving flowers.
When, thin and open as the pulse of conscience,
you put a flower in a rifle's mouth
                and said,
"Flowers are better than bullets,"
                that
was pure hope speaking.
Give no flowers to a state
              that outlaws truth;
such states reciprocate
              with cynical, cruel gifts,
and your gift, Allison Krause,
was the bullet
              that blasted the flower.
Let every apple orchard blossom black,
              black in mourning.
Ah, how the lilac smells!
              You're without feeling.

Nothing. The President said it:

                   "You're a bum."

All the dead are bums.

                   It's not their crime.

You lie in the grass,

         a melting candy in your mouth,

done with dressing in new clothes,

             done with books.

You used to be a student.

                 You studied fine arts.

But other arts exist,

             arts of blood and terror,

and headsmen with a genius for the axe.

Who was Hitler?

               A cubist of gas chambers.

In the name of all flowers

           I curse your works,

you architects of lies,

              maestros of murder!

Mothers of the world whisper

                "O God, God"

and seers are afraid

          to look ahead.

Death dances rock-and-roll upon the bones

              of Vietnam, Cambodia—

On what stage is it booked to dance tomorrow?

Rise up, Tokyo girls,

          Roman boys,

take up your flowers

          against the common foe.

Blow the world's dandelions
                    into a blizzard!
Flowers, to war!
                Punish the punishers!
Tulip after tulip,
            carnation after carnation,
rip out of your tidy beds in anger,
choke every lying throat
                    with earth and root!
Jasmine, clog
            the spinning blades of mine-layers!
Nettles, boldly block the cross-hair sights,
        drive your barbs into the lenses!
Of course:
                Bullets are stronger than flowers.
Flowers aren't enough to overwhelm them.
Stems are too fragile,
                petals are poor armor.
But if even flowers rise,
        then we've had enough
        of playing games with history.
Young America,
        tie up the killer's hands.
Let there be an escalation of truth
to overwhelm the escalating lie
                crushing people's lives!
Flowers, make war!
        Defend what's beautiful!

Drown the city streets and country roads
                    like the flood of an army advancing
and in the ranks of people and flowers
      arise, murdered Allison Krause,
the age's immortal,
                Thorn-flower of protest!

1970

TRANSLATED BY LAWRENCE FERLINGHETTI

WITH ANTHONY KAHN

FREEDOM TO KILL

The Statue of Liberty's color
Grows ever more deathly pale
As, loving freedom with bullets
And taking liberty with bullets,
You shoot at yourself, America.

You can kill yourself like that!
It's dangerous to go out
Into this nightmare world,
But it's still more dangerous
To hide in the woods.

There's a smell on earth
Of a universal Dallas.
It's frightful to live
And this fright is full of shame.

Who's going to believe false fairy tales,
When behind a façade of noble ideas
The price of gun oil rises
And the price of human life falls?

Murderers attend funerals in mourning,
And become stockholders later,
And, once again,
Ears of grain filled with bullets
Wave in Texas fields.

The eyes of murderers peer out
From under hats and caps,
The steps of murderers
Are heard at every door,
And a second Kennedy falls . . .
America, save your children!
Children in other countries turn gray,
And their huts
Bombed at night
Burn in your fire
Just like your
Bill of Rights.

You promised to be
The world's conscience
But, at the brink of bottomless shame,
You're shooting not at King
But at your own conscience.
You're bombing Vietnam
And also your own honor.

When a nation's going dangerously insane
It can't be cured of its troubles
By hastily prescribed peace.

Perhaps the only way is shame.
History can't be cleaned in a laundry.
There are no such washing machines
Blood can't ever be washed away!

O where's it hiding,
The shame of the nation,
As if it were a runaway slave?
There are slaves within slaves.

There are many murderers at large.
They carry out their mob justice
And pogroms,
And Raskolnikov wanders through America,
Insane,
With a bloody axe.
O, Old Abe,
What are people doing,
Sadly understanding only one truth:
That the greatness of a tree
Can be judged only after it's cut down.

Lincoln basks in his marble chair,
Bleeding.

They're shooting at him again!
The beasts!

The stars
In your flag,
America,
Are bullet holes.

Arise from the dead,
Bullet-holed Statue of Liberty,
Murdered so often,
And speak out
Like a woman and a mother
And curse the freedom to kill.

And without wiping the blood
From your forehead,
Oh, Statue of Liberty, raise up
Your green, drowned woman's face
Against this death of freedom.

1968

TRANSLATED BY LAWRENCE FERLINGHETTI
WITH ANTHONY KAHN

SMOG

·

I awake in the Chelsea Hotel.
Am I dreaming?
  Is it the heat?
    I seem to see
black streams,
  cloudy black worms,
slithering into the cracks across the floor.
Galia's nightgown has become a shroud:
soot is sprinkled
  on the pale cotton
like coal on sugar.
  Cruel as a rasp,
a cough tears her chest.
  "Zhenya, I'm frightened!"
In our cell of a room,
  the odor of Dachau.
"Zhenya, sweet Zhenya,
  I'm suffocating!"
Her face becomes a martyr's,
  imitated in wax.
"Air,
  air . . ."
The window opens wide and—
  I know I'm not dreaming—

a shaggy faceless beast is in the room,
  opaque as a nimbus cloud,
    surging . . .
"Zhenya, I cannot breathe!"
Galia, my love,
  I am already half dead.
The air I gulp
  is airless.
There's no vent!
Shall we perish on one another's lips?
Give respiration each to each?
Equally we're prisoners of the smog;
it's too late.
  Both of us are poisoned,
    both of us,
and a kiss in this stench
would be mutual poisoning.
There are framed instructions
  on maples and elms:
HOW TO KISS IN GAS MASKS.
In bars, they hang the brand-new slogan:
YOU CAN BREATHE BEST
  THROUGH VODKA.
And the uptown radio
doesn't give a damn,
blaring out joyously:
"And the smog rolls on . . ."

Who comes here,
  shambling along the sidewalks

with the childlike sadness of
Marcello Mastroianni?
Miller?
  Arthur?
    Slowly he whispers to me:
"It smells of fires,
  of a witch hunt . . ."
Miller coughs,
  emaciated,
    his face a handsome hatchet.
Harshly he speaks in a spirit of prophecy:
"More inquisitions will set further fires.
Smog—
  This is the smoke of burnings to come."
Awkwardly shielding himself with his wing,
thirsting for secrets
  and weary of secrets,
gaunt as a stork
  on a house of his own books,
anxiously stands Updike with his noble beak.
"Zhenya,
  men have been cruelly duped;
the earth has been set on
the backs of nonexistent whales.
Mankind, all of it,
  is overstrained
with tension,
  like a centaur.
Biune, it neighs and brays,
chafed by its own duality.

Possibly smog
   is the furious steam
from the centaur's distended nostrils!"
Wiping the smog from his glasses,
standing amid books as if among gravestones,
Lowell spoke to me, clearing his throat,
with a lofty professorial style:
"Only ghosts and books have a sense of honor.
Of what are we ashamed?
Only of ghosts am I ashamed.
And I am a product of ghosts. I am
Alyosha Karamazov and Saint-Just together.
I believe in the vengeance of history,
in the vengeance of heaven for depravity.
Possibly smog is an ectoplasm
descended for vengeance upon the world's baseness."
Allen Ginsberg—
   cagey prophet-baboon—
thumps his hairy chest
   as a shaman thumps a tambourine:
"Darkness is coming,
   darkness!
It reeks of deepest hell.
Those who can breathe this stench
are not worth keeping alive!
When the world is a cadaver,
a cesspool of fog and chaos,
it is a sign of excellence
to sink and drown.

False ideas,
   false morality,
fuming so many years,
   have soiled
     the sky.
Brahma lets fall this slime—
you can't suck it in."
But above the smog,
above today's exhausted vapors,
Whitman's basso thunders
   like the roar of Sabaoth:
"Listen!
   It is easy to lose your breath on a precipice.
But breathe deeply,
   breathe deeply!
     Give it a try!
Inhale all together!
   You will see—
     only inhale,
and the phantom smog
   by your breathing will be swept from the sky!"
And I felt the epoch
   standing still awaiting,
like a revolution of the universe,
   our common deep breath.

TRANSLATED BY JOHN UPDIKE
WITH ALBERT C. TODD

APPENDIX

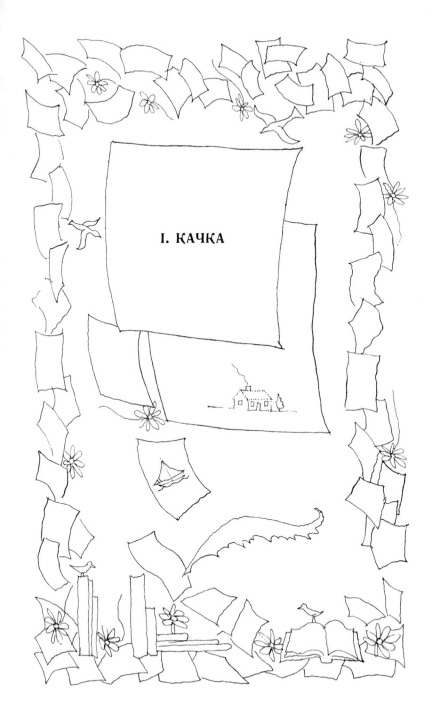

I. КАЧКА

ИЗБА

И вновь рыбацкая изба
меня впустила ночью поздней
и сразу стала так близка,
как та, где по полу я ползал.

Я потихоньку лег в углу,
как бы в моем углу извечном,
на шатком, щелистом полу,
мне до шершавинки известном.

Я здесь был свой, до боли свой,
и, возвышая, очищая,
здесь пахло рыбою, махрой,
детьми, котятами и щами.

Рыбак уже храпел вовсю.
Взобрались дети на полати,
держа в зубенках на весу
еще горячие оладьи.

И лишь хозяйка не легла.
Она то мыла, то скоблила.
Ухват, метла или игла —
в руках все время что-то было.

Печору, видно, проняло —
Печора ухала взбурленно.
«Дурит ...» — хозяйка про нее
сказала, будто про буренку.

В коптилку тусклую дохнув,
хозяйка вышла. Мгла обстала.
А за стеною — «хлюп да хлюп!» —
стирать хозяйка в кухне стала.

Кряхтели ходики в ночи —
они историю влачили.
Светились белые лучи
свеженащипанной лучины.

И, удивляясь и боясь,
из темноты неприрученно
светились восемь детских глаз
как восемь брызг твоих, Печора.

С полатей головы склоня,
из невозможно дальней дали
четыре маленьких меня
за мною, взрослым, наблюдали.

За них, молясь углами губ,
лежал я, спящим притворившись,
и вдруг затихло «хлюп да хлюп!» —
и дверь чуть-чуть приотворилась.

И ощутил я в тишине
сквозь ту притворную дремоту
сыздетства памятное мне
прикосновение чего-то.

Тулуп — а это был тулуп —
облег меня лохмато, жарко,
а в кухне снова — «хлюп да хлюп!» —
стирать хозяйка продолжала.

Сновали руки взад-вперед
в пеленках, простынях и робах
под всех страстей круговорот,
под мировых событий рокот.

И не один, должно быть, хлюст
сейчас в бессмертье лез, кривляясь,
но только это «хлюп да хлюп!»
бессмертным, в сущности, являлось.

И ощущение судьбы
в меня входило многолюдно,
как ощущение избы,
где миллионам женщин трудно,

где из неведомого дня,
им полноправно обладая,
мильоны маленьких меня
за мною, взрослым, наблюдают.

1964

ПОДРАНОК

А. Вознесенскому

Сюда, к просторам вольным, северным,
где крякал мир и нерестился,
я прилетел, подранок, селезень,
и на Печору опустился.

И я почуял всеми нервами,
как из-за леса осиянно
пахнуло льдинами и нерпами
в меня величье океана.

Я океан вдохнул и выдохнул,
как будто выдохнул печали,
и все дробинки кровью вытолкнул,
даря на память их Печоре.

Они пошли на дно холодное,
а сам я, трепетный и легкий,
поднялся вновь, крылами хлопая,
с какой-то новой силой летною.

Меня ветра чуть-чуть покачивали,
неся над мхами и кустами.
Сопя, дорогу вдаль показывали
ондатры мокрыми усами.

Через простор земель непаханых,
цветы и заячьи орешки,
меня несли на пантах бархатных
веселоглазые олешки.

Когда на кочки я присаживался, —
и тундра ягель подносила,
и клюква, за зиму прослаженная,
себя попробовать просила.

И я, затворами облязганный,
вдруг понял — я чего-то стою,
раз я такою был обласканный
твоей, Печора, добротою!

Когда-нибудь опять, над Севером,
тобой не узнанный, Печора,
я пролечу могучим селезнем,
сверкая перьями парчово.

И ты засмотришься нечаянно
на тот полет и оперенье,
забыв, что все это не чье-нибудь —
твое, Печора, одаренье.

И ты не вспомнишь, как ты прятала
меня весной, как обреченно
то оперенье кровью плакало
в твой голубой подол, Печора ...

[*Литературная Россия,* 1963]

ТЯГА ВАЛЬДШНЕПОВ

Приготовь двустволку и взгляни:
вытянув тебе навстречу клюв,
вылетает вальдшнеп из луны,
крыльями ее перечеркнув.

Вот летит он, хоркая, хрипя ...
Но скажи, — ты знаешь, отчего
тянет его, тянет на тебя,
а твою двустволку — на него?

Он летит, и счастлив его крик.
Ты, дрожа, к двустволке приник.
Он — твой безоружный двойник.
Ты — его бескрылый двойник.

Разве ты бескрылость возместишь
выстрелом в крылатость? Дробь хлестнет,
но ведь это сам ты летишь,
это сам себя стреляешь влет ...

[*Знамя*, 1963]

НЕВЕСТА

На Печоре есть рыбак
по имени Глаша.
Говорит с парнями так:
«Глаша,
            да не ваша!»
Ухажеров к ляду шлет,
сердится
            серьгами.
Сарафаны себе шьет
из сиянья северного!
Не красна она, наверно,
модною прическою,
но зато в косе

не лента,
а волна печерская!
Недоступна и строга,
сети вытягает,
а глаза,

как два сига,
из-под платка сигают!
Я ходил за ней,

робея,
зачарованный,
как черемухою,

ею
зачеремленный.
Я не знал, почему
(может быть, наветно)
говорили по селу
про нее:

«Невеста».
«Чья? —

ходил я сам не свой. —
Может, выдумали?»
Рыбаки,

дымя махрой,
ничего не выдымили.
«Чья она?

Чья она?
Чья она невеста?» —
спрашивал отчаянно
у норд-веста.
Вдруг один ко мне прилип
старичок запечный,
словно тундровый гриб,
на мокре взошедший:
«Больно быстр, я погляжу.
Выставь четвертиночку —
и на блюдце положу
тайну,

как чаиночку ...»
Пил да медлил, окаянный,
а когда все выкачал:

«Чья невеста?

    Океана ...

Того ...

    Ледовитыча ...»

Если б не был пьюха стар,

если б не был хилый,

я б манежничать не стал —

дал бы в зад бахилой!

Водят за нос меня.

Что это за шутки!

Аж гогочет гагарня,

аж хохочут шуки!

Ну, а Глаша на песке

карбас

   высмаливала,

и прорехи в паруске

на свету высматривала.

Я сказал ей:

    «Над водой

рыба вспрыгивает,

и, от криков став худой,

чернеть вскрикивает.

Хочешь — тундру подарю

лишь за взгляд за ласковый?

Горностаем подобью

ватник твой залатанный.

Пойду с неводом Печорой

в потопленные луга,

семгу выловлю,

     в которой

не икра,

   а жемчуга.

Все сложу я,

    что захочешь,

у твоих подвернутых

у резиновых сапожек,

чешуей подернутых.

В эту чертову весну,

сам себя замучив,

я попался на блесну
зубов твоих зовучих.
Но от пьюхи-недовеска,
пьяным-пьяного,
я слыхал,
                что ты невеста
океанова?!»

Отвечала Глаша:
                        «Да.
Я его невеста.
Видишь, как в реке вода
не находит места.
Та вода идет,
                идет
к седоте глубинной,
где давно меня он ждет —
мой седой любимый.
Не подав об этом вести,
веслами посверкивая,
приплыву к нему я
                        вместе
с льдинками-последками.
И меня он обоймет
ночью облачною,
и в объятьях обомнет,
разом обмершую.
На груди своей держа,
все забыть поможет.
В изголовье мне
                моржа
мягкого
                положит.
Мне на все он даст ответ,
всплесками беседуя ...
Что мои семнадцать лет?
С ним я,
                как безлетняя.
Все семнадцать чепушинок
с меня сыплются, дрожа,
как семнадцать чешуинок

из-под вострого ножа.
Океан
         то обласкает,
то грома раскатывает.
Все он гулом объясняет,
все про жизнь рассказывает.
Парень,
         лучше отвяжись.
Я твоей не стану.
Что ты скажешь мне про жизнь
после океана?
Потому себя блюду,
кавалер ты липовый,
что такого не найду,
как и он,
         великого ...»
И поднялся парусок
и забился влажно,
и ушла наискосок
к океану Глаша.
Я шептал —
              не помню что —
с опустелым взглядом.
Видно, слишком я не то
с океаном рядом.
И одно,
         меня пронзив,
сверлит постоянно:
что же я скажу про жизнь
после океана?!

[*Юность*, 1963]

БАЛЛАДА О ЛОЖНЫХ МАЯКАХ

... и оные огни неправдивые смущают буши
рыбацкие вселением набежды обманной ...

Из старинной лоции

Нам уже наворожили столько лжи
голубые ледяные миражи.
Врали метеопророки.
     Врал компас.
Бог,
  неверующих нас,
      видно, спас.
Сколько нищий в своей жизни медяков
столько видели мы ложных маяков!
И суденышко,
    зверея от ругни,
мы вели на эти подлые огни.
Но огни от нас давали стрекача.
Киль карябался о камни, скрежеща,
и с ладоней кожу клочьями срывал
вырывающийся спятивший штурвал.
Мы затерты.
    Льды суденышку-по грудь.
нам бы в бухту,
     нам бы малость отдохнуть,
зацепиться ржавым якорем за дно,
подремать с водой спокойной заодно.
Но мы тычемся опять о миражи
так, что ржут соленоусые моржи.
К порошковому привыкнув молоку,
мы не верим никакому маяку.
Можно сильно в этом деле прогадать —
настоящий,
    а не ложный проморгать.
Но надежней доверять не маякам —
доверять своей башке,
      своим рукам.
Вот опять биноклем бодро машет кэп:
«Эй, штурвальный, вон маяк,

ты что, — ослеп?»
но штурвальный,
        не впадая в его раж,
отвечает ему, хмыкнувши:
        «Мираж ...»

1964   [*Юность,* 1964]

КАЧКА

Качка!
    Застекленные инструкции
                срываются с гвоздей.
О башку «Спидола» стукается
           вместе с Дорис Дэй.
Борщ, на камбузе томящийся,
            взвивается, плеща.
К потолку прилип, дымящийся,
              лист лавровый из борща.
Качка!
    Уцепиться бы руками
              за кустарник, за траву.
Травит юнга.
       Травит штурман.
            Травит боцман.
                Я травлю.
Волны, словно волкодавы ...
           Ты такой, двадцатый век:
вправо-влево,
       влево-
          вправо,
            вверх-вниз,
               вниз-вверх.
Качка!
    Все инструкции разбиты,
            все портреты тоже-вдрызг.
Лица мертвенны, испиты.
        под кормой-крысиный визг,

а вокруг сплошная каша,
            только крики на ветру,
только качка,
            качка,
                  качка,
только мерзостно во рту.
Качка!
      Бочка прыгает но палубе,
бросаясь на людей.
Эх, ребята, и попали мы,
            а все же-не робей.
Вылезайте из кают,
            а не то, нам всем -каюк ...
Качка ...
А глаза у гарпунера,
            чумового горлодера
напряглись,
            и чуб-торчком.
Молча сделав знак матросам,
      к бочке мечущейся
                  с тросом
подбирается бочком
и бросается, что кошка,
            рассекая толчею,
ибо знает, сволочь-качка,
            философию твою.
Шкурой вызубрил он, рыжий,
                  навсегда в башку вдолбя:
или сам на бочку прыгнешь,
            или- бочка на тебя!
Качка!
      А бочка смирная лежит и не блажит.
Качка!
      Погода ясная от нас не убежит.
Качка!
      Пусть мы закачаны, и пусть в глазах темно-
            перекачаем тебя, качка,
                  все равн ...

[*Звезда востока*, 1966]

II. ТВИСТ НА ГВОЗДЯХ

Ты начисто притворства лищена,
когда молчишь со взглядом напряженным,
как лишена притворства тишина
беззвездной ночью в городе сожженном.

Он, этот город, — прошлое твое.
В нем ты почти ни разу не смеялась,
бросалась то в тряпье, то в забытье,
то бунтовала, то опять смирялась.

Ты жить старалась из последних сил,
но, отвергая все живое хмуро,
он, этот город, на тебя давил
угрюмостью своей архитектуры.

В нем изнутри был заперт каждый дом.
В нем было все недобро умудренным.
Он не скрывал свой тягостный надлом
и ненависть ко всем, кто не надломлен.

Тогда ты ночью подожгла его.
Испуганно от пламени метнулась,
и я был просто первым, на кого
ты, убегая, в темноте наткнулась.

Я обнял всю дрожавшую тебя,
и ты ко мне безропотно прижалась,
еще не понимая, не любя,
но, как зверек, благодаря за жалость.

И мы с тобой пошли ... Куда пошли?
Куда глаза глядят. Но то и дело
оглядывалась ты, как там, вдали,
зловеще твое прошлое горело.

Оно сгорело до конца, дотла.
Но с той поры одно меня тиранит:
туда, где неостывшая зола,
тебя как зачарованную тянет.

И вроде ты со мной, и вроде нет.
На самом деле я тобою брошен.
Неся в руке голубоватый свет,
по пепелищу прошлого ты бродишь.

Что там тебе? Там пусто и серо!
О, прошлого таинственная сила!
Ты не могла любить его само,
ну а его руины — полюбила.

Могущественны пепел и зола.
Они в себе, наверно, что-то прячут.
Над тем, что так отчаянно сожгла,
по-детски поджигательница плачет.

[*Нежность,* 1962]

□ □ □

Следов сырые отпечатки,
бульвар,
            заснеженный трамвай,
прикосновение перчатки
и быстрое:
            — Прощай!
Иду направленно,
                мертво,
и тишина,
        и снег витает.
Вот поворот,
            вот вход в метро,
и яркий свет,
                и шапка тает.
Стою на легком сквозняке,
смотрю в тоннель,
                набитый мраком,
и трогаю рукою мрамор,
и холодно моей руке.

И шум,
      и отправлений чинность.
И понимать мне тяжело,
что ничего не получилось
и получиться не могло ...

[*Обещание*, 1956]

МАША

Вдоль моря быстро девочка проходит,
бледнея, розовея и дичась.
В ней все восходит. Что с ней происходит?
В ней возникает женщина сейчас.

Она у моря тапочки снимает,
вступает, словно в музыку, в него,
и все она на свете понимает,
хотя не понимает ничего.

Рассудок трезвый, безрассудства масса,
взгляд из-под чуткой челки через всех
и — снова вниз ... Все это вместе — Маша,
серьезный большеглазый человек.

И у меня пересыхает нёбо,
когда, забыв про чей-то взрослый суд,
мальчишеские тоненькие ноги
ее ко мне беспомощно несут.

И на сыром песке у старой лодки
целую все призывней и властней
все то, что руки Машины, — от локтя
до розоватых лепестков ногтей.

Я надеваю трубчатую маску.
Плывет и Маша где-то надо мной.

Я сквозь стекло ищу глазами Машу
среди цветов и крабов, как хмельной.

И вижу я в зеленой толще светлой
над бурою подводною грядой —
колышутся, как беленькие стебли,
мальчишеские ноги под водой.

И я плыву, плыву в подводных чащах,
плыву я, воду ластами кроя,
и я несчастлив отчего, что счастлив,
и снова счастлив, что несчастлив я.

Что мне сказать? Пусть не боится мама —
тебе не причиню я, Маша, зла.
Мне от тебя немного надо, Маша,
и очень много — чтобы ты была.

В раздумиях о вечности и смерти,
охваченный надеждой и тоской,
гляжу сквозь твое тоненькое сердце,
как сквозь прозрачный камушек морской.

Коктебель, 1958

НЕ НАДО ...

Не надо ...
      Все призрачно —
              и темных окон матовость,
и алый снег за стопсигналами машин.
Не надо ...
      Все призрачно,
            как сквер туманный мартовский,
где нет ни женщин, ни мужчин —
                лишь тени женщин и мужчин.

Не надо ...
        Стою у дерева,
                молчу и не обманываю,
гляжу,
      как сдвоенные светят фонари,
и тихо трогаю рукой,
             но не обламываю
сосульку тоненькую с веточкой внутри.
Не надо ...
        Пусть в бултыхающемся заспанном трамваишке
с Москвой, качающейся мертвенно в окне,
ты,
    подперев щеку рукою в детской варежке,
со злостью женской вспоминаешь обо мне.
Не надо ...
        Ты станешь женщиной, усталой умной женщиной,
по слову доброму и ласке голодна,
и будет март,
        и будет мальчик, что-то шепчущий,
и будет горестно кружиться голова.
Не надо ...
        Пусть это стоит, как и мне, недешево,
с ним не броди вдвоем по мартовскому льду,
ему на плечи
           свои руки ненадежные
ты не клади,
      как я сегодня не кладу.
Не надо ...
        Не верь, как я не верю призрачному городу,
не то, очнувшись,
         ужаснешься пустырю.
Скажи: «Не надо ...», —
            опустивши низко голову,
как я тебе сейчас
      «не надо ...»
        говорю ...
1960

□ □ □

«Нет, нет,
         я не сюда попал.
Произошла нелепость.
                  Я ошибся.
Случаен и в руке моей бокал.
Случаен и хозяйки взгляд пушистый.
«Станцуем, а?
            Ты бледен.
                     Плохо спал ...»
и чувствую,
         что никуда не денусь,
но говорю поспешно:
                  «Я оденусь.
Нет, нет, —
         я не сюда попал ...»
А вслед:
      «Вот до чего вино доводит ...
Как не сюда —
            да именно сюда.
Расстроил всех собою и доволен.
С тобою просто, Женичка, беда.»

В карманы руки зябкие засовываю,
а улицы кругом снежным-снежны.
В такси ныряю.
            Шеф, гони!
                     За Соколом
есть комнатка.
            Там ждать меня должны.
Мне открывает дверь она,
                     но что такое с нею
и что за странный взгляд?
                        «Уж около пяти.
Не мог бы ты притти еще позднее?
Ну что ж, входи ...
                  Куда теперь итти»

Расхохочусь,

а может быть, расплачусь?
Стишки кропал,
                    а вышло, что пропал.
От глаз я прячусь.
                    Зыбко-зыбко пячусь:
«Нет, нет —
                    я не сюда попал.»
И снова ночь,
                    и снова снег,
и чья- то песня наглая,
и чей-то чистый-чистый смех,
и закурить бы надо ...
В пурге мелькают пушкинские бесы,
и страшен их насмешливый оскал.
Страшны ларьки,
                    аптеки и собесы ...
Нет, нет,
        я не сюда попал.
Как страшно жить,
                    как страшно жить, —
страшней —
                    уйти от жизни.
Бездомный, словно вечный жид,
эпохой я ошибся.
Нет, нет —
                    я не сюда попал.
Иду, сутуля плечи,
как будто что-то проиграл,
а расплатиться нечем ...

[*Знамя*, 1967]

А снег повалится, повалится,
и я прочту в его канве,
что моя молодость повадится
опять заглядывать ко мне.

И поведет куда-то за руку
на чьи-то тени и шаги,
и вовлечет в старинный заговор
огней, деревьев и пурги.

И мне покажется, покажется
по Сретенкам и Моховым,
что молод не был я пока еще,
а только буду молодым.

И ночь завертится, завертится
и, как в воронку, втянет в грех,
и моя молодость завесится
со мною снегом ото всех.

Но, сразу ставшая накрашенной
при беспристрастном свете дня,
цыганкой, мною наигравшейся,
оставит молодость меня.

Начну я жизнь переиначивать,
свою наивность застыжу
и сам себя, как пса бродячего,
на цепь угрюмо посажу.

Но снег повалится, повалится,
закружит все веретеном,
и моя молодость появится
опять цыганкой под окном.

А снег повалится, повалится,
и цепи я перегрызу,
и жизнь, как снежный ком, покатится
к сапожкам чьим-то там, внизу ...

[*Огонек*, 1966]

□ □ □

Я разлюбил тебя ... Банальная развязка,
банальная, как жизнь, банальная, как смерть.
Я оборву струну жестокого романса,
гитару пополам — к чему ломать комедь!

Лишь не понять щенку — лохматому уродцу, —
чего ты так мудришь, чего я так мудрю.
Его впущу к себе — он в дверь твою скребется,
а впустишь ты его — скребется в дверь мою.

Пожалуй, можно так с ума сойти, метаясь ...
Сентиментальный пес, ты попросту юнец,
но не позволю я себе сентиментальность.
Как пытку продолжать — затягивать конец.

Сентиментальным быть не слабость — преступленье,
когда размякнешь вновь, наобещаешь вновь
и пробуешь, кряхтя, поставить представление,
с названием тупым: «Спасенная любовь».

Спасать любовь пора уже в самом начале
от пылких «Навсегда!», от детских «Никогда!».
«Не надо обещать!» — нам поезда кричали,
«Не надо обещать!» — мычали провода.

Надломленность ветвей и неба задымленность
предупреждали нас, зазнавшихся невежд,
что полный оптимизм есть неосведомленность,
что без больших надежд — надежней для надежд.

Гуманней трезвым быть и трезво взвесить звенья
допрежь, чем их надеть, — таков закон вериг,
не обещать небес, но дать хотя бы землю,
до гроба не сулить, но дать хотя бы миг.

Гуманней не твердить «люблю», когда не любишь.
Как тяжело потом из этих самых уст
услышать звук пустой, вранье, насмешку, грубость,
и ложно полный мир предстанет ложно пуст.

218

Не надо обещать. Любовь — неисполнимость.
Зачем же под обман вести, как под венец!
Виденье хорошо, пока не испарилось.
Гуманней не любить, когда потом конец.

Скулит наш бедный пес до умопраченья,
то лапой в дверь твою, то в дверь мою скребя.
За то, что разлюбил, я не прошу прощенья,
прости меня за то, что я любил тебя.

[*Огонек*, 1966]

□ □ □

В самолетах, бесстрастно новейших,
набирая, как страсть, высоту,
я летал от надежды к надежде,
убивая и эту и ту.

А надежда была посредине
вне метаний и аэровех,
словно нерпа на крошечной льдине
с грустной мордочкой, задранной вверх.

Прижимал я к губам свои губы
с горькой сладостью взлетных конфет,
но пугал, разрываясь двулюбо,
как пустой прилетевший конверт.

И звала меня бездною нежность
в шелестенье спадавших одежд,
но ввергало опять в безнадежность
прикасанье к любой из надежд.

И метался я в панике жалкой,
с перекошенной маской лица,
как собака, побитая палкой,
у которой два ложных конца.

А однажды сквозь мчание мира
я в такси увидал из окна:
у дороги стонала, как лира,
раздвоившаяся сосна.

Значит, было не так уж нелепо,
что как вечный летающий жид,
даже небо-вы слышите? — небо
я втянул в свою личную жизнь.

И прямые полетов сквозь ливни
то туда, то сюда-хоть их режь,
словно струны на стонущей лире
между двух безнадежных надежд ...

[*Знамя*, 1967]

ТВИСТ НА ГВОЗДЯХ

Когда ты туфельки свои через плечо,
и в твист по сцене,
        и пошло,
            пошло,
               пошло,
пусть мальчик розовый тебя и круть и верть —
так не танцует жизнь,
            а так танцует смерть.
Танцуют бедра,
        плечи,
           груди,
              локотки.
Внутри танцуют пьяно
            воздуха глотки.
Танцует чье-то
         на руке твоей кольцо,
и не танцует лишь одно —
              твое лицо,

над жизнью тела так безжизненно летя,
как будто маска с мертвой снятая тебя.
И эта сцена —
          только часть того креста,
на коем некогда
          распяли Христа,
а гвозди вылезли с обратной стороны,
и танцевать на них,
          торчащих,
               стала ты.
И ты танцуешь на гвоздях,
            на гвоздях,
на ржавых сплетнях,
          на колючках-слезах,
и тем, что я тебя угрюмо полюбил,
я тоже гвозди в эту сцену
          криво вбил.
Ах, сволочь-музыка,
          ты все сильней, сильней?
Никто не видит —
          кровь сочится из ступней.
Омыть ступни водою чистой предпочту
тебе,
    Мария Магдалина, —
          не Христу.
Я их отмою от сегодня и вчера
не так, как брат — сестре,
          а как сестре-сестра.
Потом в руках тихонько ноги подержу
и поцелуями я их перевяжу ...

[Знамя, 1967]

□ □ □

Хочу того, чего сказать нельзя:
дерзя, с огнем играю без ферзя.

Мой ферзь-рассудок под ноги коню!
Какое счастье — проиграть огню!

Какой пожар в нечесаной ночи
от худенькой тебя, как от свечи!

Какого ты в понятие греха
лихого подпустила петуха!

Я корчусь, но блаженен смертный крик.
Огнем уже оправдан еретик.

В огне Гульрипш, Нью Йорк, Париж, Мадрид,
но кто-то в нем, любимый мне, горит.

А если от костра еретика
огонь скакнет на крышу бедняка, —

навеки будет проклято навзрыд
все то, за что тот еретик горит.

Ведь истина, — когда ты поджжешь
дом ближнего, — не истина, а ложь.

[*Знамя*, 1967]

Свет умер в зале ... Но пока играла
на сцене в главной роли темнота,
во мне была неслышимость хорала
по жилам леденяще разлита.

Я знал, что там, готовая к прологу,
и, видимая разве только богу,
как тоненький оттенок темноты,
стоишь живая, тоненькая, ты.

Мне не дал бог свой взгляд всевышний божий,
но рос хорал внутри, как божий глас,
и не глазами я смотрел, а кожей,
как тысячами слитых вместе глаз.

И в темноте, в прерывистых струеньях
дыханий чьих-то, в призрачных строеньях
теней бесплотных — чуть ли не крича,
определил я с яростным загадом
ту точку, где над раем и над адом
стояла незажженная свеча.

И ты зажглась, и свет воскрес, и хаос
чужих теней отпрянул от меня,
лишь золотая челка колыхалась,
как сбитый ветром язычок огня ...

[*Знамя*, 1967]

КРАДЕНЫЕ ЯБЛОКИ

Кренились от шторма заборы,
и крались мы в тенях озяблых,
счастливые будто бы воры
с рубахами, полными яблок.

Тяжелыми яблоки были,
и есть было страшно-престрашно,
но мы друг друга любили,
и это было прекрасно.

И нас, как сообщница пряча
от мира, где грязные волны,
шептала монахиня-дача:
«Не бойтесь любить … Вы не воры …»

Был дачи хозяин гуманный
футбольный на пенсии витязь,
и фото, мерцая туманно,
шептали: «Не бойтесь … Прорвитесь …»

И мы прорывались к воротам
в любовь, как в штрафную площадку,
и делали финт с поворотом,
и яблоками — в девятку.

И крошечны-снились нам будто —
игрушками-игрунами
качались футбольные бутсы
на ниточке тонкой над нами.

«Играйте … — шептали, как гномы … —
Играйте, и не понарошке …»
и били по шару земному —
такому же, в сущности, крошке.

И мы играли и били.
Игра была, может, напрасна,
но мы друг друга любили,
и это было прекрасно.

А море, лютея от рыка,
предупреждало о чем-то,
но, как золотая рыбка,
плескалась на лбу твоем челка.

И было не боязно думать,
что в будущем, штормом закрытым,
за жадность мою и за дурость
останусь с разбитым корытом.

Пусть буду я сплетнями загнан,
я знаю — любовь не для слабых,
и запах любви — это запах
не купленных-краденых яблок.

Что крик сторожей исступленных,
когда я под брызгами моря
лежал головой на соленых
двух яблоках, краденых мною!

[*Знамя*, 1967]

□ □ □

Мне снится — я тебя уже любил.
Мне снится — я тебя уже убил.

Но ты воскресла в облике ином,
как девочка на шарике земном
в изгибисто наивной простоте
у раннего Пикассо на холсте
и попросила, ребрами моля:
«Люби меня . . .» как «Не столкни меня . . .»

Я тот усталый взрослый акробат,
от мускулов бессмысленных горбат,
который знает, что советы-ложь,
что рано или поздно упадешь.

Сказать мне страшно: «Я тебя люблю.»,
как будто выдать: «Я тебя убью.»

Ведь в глубине прозрачного лица
я вижу лица, лица без конца,
которые когда-то наповал
или не сразу — пыткой-убивал.

Ты от баланса смертного бела.
«Я знаю все — я многими была.
Я знаю — ты меня уже любил.
Я знаю — ты меня уже убил.»
Но шар земной не поверну я вспять:
люби опять, потом убей опять.»

Девчонка ты. Останови свой шар.
Я убивать устал. Я просто стар.

Но, шар земной ножонками гоня,
ты падаешь с него: «Люби меня ...»
и лишь внутри — таких похожих! глаз
«Не убивай меня на этот раз ...»

[*Знамя,* 1967]

Качался старый дом, в хорал слагая скрипы,
и нас, как отпевал, отскрипывал хорал.
Он чуял, дом-скрипун, что медленно и скрытно
в нем умирал ты, и я в нем умирал.

«Постойте умирать!» — звучало в ржанье с луга,
в протяжном вое псов и в сосенной волшбе,
но умирали мы навеки друг для друга,
и это все равно, что умирать вообще.

А как хотелось жить! По соснам дятел чокал,
и бешал еж ручной в усадебных грибах,

и ночь плыла, как пес, косматый, мокрый, черный,
кувшинкою речной держа звезду в зубах.

Дышала мгла в окно малиною сырою,
а за моей спиной — все видела спина! —
с платоновскою «Фро», как с найденной сестрою,
измученная мной, любимая спала.

Я думал о тупом несовершенстве браков,
О подлости всех нас — предателей, врунов.
Ведь я тебя любил, как сорок тысяч братьев,
и я тебя губил, как столько же врагов.

Какая же цена ораторскому жару,
когда, расшвырян вдрызг по сценам и клише,
хотел я счастья дать всему земному шару,
а дать его не смог одной живой душе!

Да, стала ты другой. Твой злой прищур нещаден.
Насмешки над людьми горьки и солоны.
Но кто же, как не мы, любимых превращает
в таких, каких любить уже не в силах мы!!

Да, умирали мы ... Но что-то мне мешало
уверовать в твое, в мое небытие.
Любовь еще была. Любовь еще дышала
на зеркальце в руках у слабых уст ее.

Качался старый дом, скрипел среди крапивы
и выдержку свою нам предлагал взаймы.
В нем умирали мы, но были еще живы.
Еще любили мы, но были еще живы.
Еще любили мы, и, значит, были мы.

Когда-нибудь потом — не дай мне бог, не дай мне! —
когда я разлюблю, когда и впрямь умру,
то будет плоть моя, посмеиваясь втайне:
«Ты жив!» — мне по ночам нашептывать в жару.

Но в суете страстей, печально поздний умник,
внезапно я пойму, что голос плоти лжив,
и так себе скажу: «Я разлюбил. Я умер.
Когда-то я любил. Когда-то я был жив».

[*Огонек*, 1967]

ЗАКЛИНАНИЕ

Весенней ночью думай обо мне
и летней ночью думай обо мне,
осенней ночью думай обо мне
и зимней ночью думай обо мне.
Пусть я не там с тобой, а где-то вне,
такой далекий, как в другой стране, —
на длинной и прохладной простыне
покойся, словно в море на спине,
отдавшись мягкой медленной волне,
со мной, как с морем, вся наедине.

Я не хочу, чтоб думала ты днем.
Пусть день перевернет все кверху дном,
окурит дымом и зальет вином,
заставит думать о совсем ином.
О чем захочешь, можешь думать днем,
а ночью — только обо мне одном.

Услышь сквозь паровозные свистки,
сквозь ветер, тучи рвущий на куски,
как надо мне, попавшему в тиски,
чтоб в комнате, где стены так узки,
ты жмурилась от счастья и тоски,
до боли сжав ладонями виски.

Молю тебя — в тишайшей тишине,
или под дождь, шумящий в вышине,
или под снег, мерцающий в окне,
уже во сне и все же не во сне —

228

весенней ночью думай обо мне
и летней ночью думай обо мне,
осенней ночью думай обо мне
и зимней ночью думай обо мне.

[*Взмах руки*, 1960]

СЕНЕГАЛЬСКАЯ БАЛЛАДА

Lannie McNulty

I

Сенегал,
я ныряю на дно кабаков
                                без советчиков и стукачей,

в синяках
от чумных,
                начиненных нечаянностями ночей.
И плюю
на ханжей всего мира надводного —
                                этих и тех,

и плыву
среди стеблей подводных —
                                лилово мерцающих тел.

Голося,
две мулатки трясутся на сцене
                                и падают ниц.

Их глаза —
как актинии жадные
                с щупальцами ресниц.

Но, едва
колыхаясь в чаду,
                        меня тянут в себя сквозь века

твои два
карих глаза,
                как два необманных подводных цветка.

Мы вдвоем —
дети разных
                враждующих, как у Шекспира, семей.

Белый Дом,
Серый Дом*,
               мы прорвались друг к другу из ваших сетей.
Мы в ногах
у единой праматери — вечности,
                     гладящей головы нам.
Ланни,
     лань,
ты ко мне перепрыгнула через ракеты,
               эсминцы,
                    моря.
Где же грань,
где граница меж нами двоими? —
                 лишь кожа твоя и моя.
Так возьмись
перепрыгнуть и эту границу
               и губы бездонные дай мне до дна.
Так вожмись
кожей в кожу,
           и станут они как одна.
Ночь,
    визжи!
В тебе что-то по пьянке опять,
               словно атомный смерч, взорвалось,
и ножи
сумасшедшими рыбами пляшут
             над водорослями волос.
Скрежеща,
стулья в воздух взлетают,
             кастеты врезаются с хрустом под дых:
Страшно, а?
Режут белые — черных
        и черные — белых,
              а желтые — тех и других.
Рев зверья,
а над свалкой,
         как будто в библейских льняных облаках,
льдом звеня,
пляшет шейкер
        у бармена в цепких бесстрастных руках.

Финкой в бок
и мартелем по морде кому-то,
                              а бармен над хряском костей и когтей
«есть же бог!» —
наши души сбивает
                    в заказанный богом столетьями раньше коктейль.
Над ворьем,
над зверьем
            я за руку твою осторожно берусь.
Мы вдвоем.
«Не боишься?» — глазами вопрос,
                              и глазами ответ: «Не боюсь».

Что мне злость
всех бандитов на свете
                      и что приближенье конца,
если сквозь
эту страшную драку
                  ко мне приближенье лица?!

Отчего
эта драка?
          Какое нам дело!
                    А может, все эти ножи
для того,
чтобы сблизило нас
                  и прижало друг к другу
                                      в крутящейся смерчем ночи.

Что любовь?
Это ты,
      это я,
          над кастетами,
                      выстрелами,
                                надо всем.

Что любовь?
Это вечное НАД
              поножовщиной рас,
                          предрассудков,
                                    сословий,
                                          систем.

Что любовь?
Это вечное ВНЕ

всяких драк,
всяких свалок
Ромео с Джульеттой союз.
Что любовь?
«Не боишься?» — глазами вопрос,
и глазами ответ: «Не боюсь».

II

Я пришел провожать
с парой темных беспомощных рук —
не с цветами,
Мой ирландыш, прощай навсегда ...
Ну а может ...
А вдруг?
До свиданья!
Твое имя пребудет во мне
и в последний мой час
свято,
Ланни.
Хоть бы раз мы увиделись в жизни еще,
хоть бы раз ...
«До свиданья!»
«Самолет на Париж,
самолет на Париж, господа!»
... В каравеллу
чемоданчик плывет,
как по серой реке в никуда,
по конвейеру.
Мы прижались друг к другу
затерянно, как дикари,
в тарараме
спекулянтов гашишем,
идеями,
девками,

и

даже нами.
Мы бессильны с тобой,

ну а может, мы просто малы
и безвольны?
На руках у меня,

на ногах у меня — кандалы,
лишь

без звона.
Уступаю тебя,

да и ты уступаешь меня,

как в бою
отступая ...
Кандалы на руках

и сквозь белую кожу твою
проступают.
Мы — невольники века,

невольники

наших правительств

и рас.
Всюду —

путы.
Настоящей свободы —

ее ни у нас,

ни у вас —
лишь минуты.
Отпустив на минуту,

обмякшую жертву питон
дальше

душит.
Что любовь?

Это только минута свободы.

Потом
даже

хуже.
Нету прав у людей,

кроме древнего права страдать,
но и в этом
не хотят нам свободу по выбору нашему дать
кольца века.

Век сдавил наши души и, мнимой свободой дразня,
мнет их люто.
Если вечной свободы попавшему в кольца нельзя —
пусть
     минута!
А потом —
        меня можете вешать,
               ножами тупыми стругать —
что угодно!
Только раньше вы дайте мне право
             свободно страдать,
но свободно.
Пусть нам снова страдать,
           если снова мы будем вдвоем —
до свиданья!
Мыслим, — значит, живем?
            Нет, страдаем — и, значит, живем!
До страданья!

[Звезда востока, 1966]

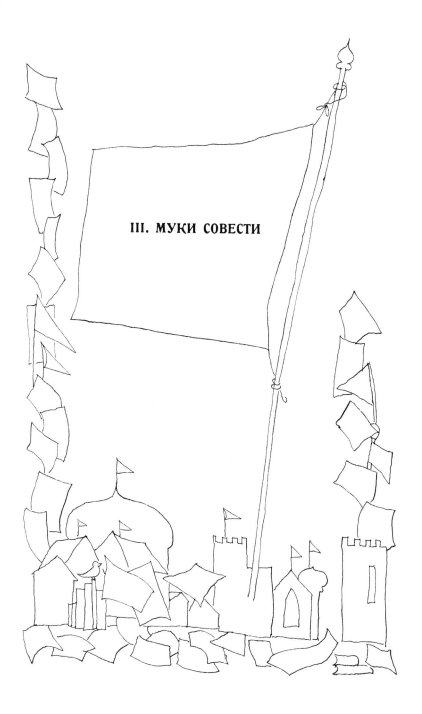

III. МУКИ СОВЕСТИ

КОРОВЫ

Все в чулках речного ила
помню-тихо шли стада,
а когда все это было,
не могу сказать когда.

Масти серой, масти пегой
шли коровы под горой ...
Год был, вроде, сорок первый
или год сорок второй.

Не в хлева, не для поправки
все в репейнике, в пыли
их к вагонам для отправки
молча школьники вели.

И со всеми я, усталый,
замыкающий ряды,
шел в буденовке линялой
с темным следом от звезды.

Ах, коровы, ах, коровы,
как вносили вы в луга,
словно царские короны,
ваши белые рога.

Вы тихонечко мычали,
грустно терлись о кусты,
или попросту молчали
и роняли с губ цветы ...

А теперь — коров к вагонам
подводили, и бойцы
с видом-помню-чуть смущенным
с них снимали бубенцы.

Рядом пили, рядом пели,
но открылся свет вдали,
и вагоны заскрипели,
заскрипели и пошли.

И какой-то оробелый
с человеческим лицом
в дверь глядел теленок белый
рядом с худеньким бойцом.

Он глядел, припав к шинели,
на поля и на леса,
а глаза его синели,
как Есенина глаза ...

[*Литературная Россия,* 1961]

□ □ □

Но лишь божественный глагол ...

А. Пушкин

Поэзия чадит,
да вот не вымирает.
Поэзия чудит,
когда нас выбирает.

Вот малый не дурак,
валидой сосущий,
в портфельчике несущий
отварной бурак.
Ему сейчас бы мусса
и ромовых баб,
но Муза —
            ай да Муза! —
его за шкирку
                цап!

И мысли лоб сверлят,
и он забыл о ложке,
и он гигант!
                Сократ!
... в обломовском обложке.
И вот не Аполлон —
тщедушный и невзрачный.
Весь как опенок он,
и зыбкий,
                и прозрачный.
Но вдруг какой-то свист
в ушах его —
                и точка!
И как боксерский свинг,
по морде века —
                строчка!
А вот —
        валится с ног
шалавая пичужка —
тряпичница,
                пьянчужка,
салонный клоунок.
Но что-то ей велит,
и —
        как зимою ветки,
бог
    изнутри
                звенит,
и —
    мраморнеют веки.
А вот
        пошляк,
                шаман,
впрямь —
            из шутов гороховых!
Ему —
        подай шампань,
и баб —
            да и не ромовых!
Но вдруг внутри приказ

прорежется сурово,
и он —
        народный глас,
почти Савонарола!

Поэзия чудит,
когда нас выбирает,
а после не щадит
и души выбивает.
Но кто нам всем судья?
Да,
      для мещан мы «в тлене»,
но за самих себя
мы сами —
          искупленье!

ПАНОПТИКУМ В ГАМБУРГЕ

Полны величья грузного,
надменны и кургузы,
на коммуниста русского
нахмурились курфюрсты.
Все президенты,
              канцлеры
в многообразной пошлости
глядят угрюмо,
           кастово,
и кастовость их —
               в подлости.
За то, что жизнь увечили,
корежили,
        давили,
их здесь увековечили —
верней,
      увосковили.
В среду заплывших,
             жирных
и тощих злобных монстров

как вы попали,
    Шиллер,
как вы попали,
     Моцарт?
Вам бы —
   в луга светающие,
вам бы —
    в цветы лесные ...
Вы здесь —
    мои товарищи.
Враги —
   все остальные.
Враги глядят убийственно,
а для меня не гибельно,
что я не нравлюсь Бисмарку
и уж, конечно, Гитлеру.
Но вижу среди них,
как тени роковые,
врагов,
   еще живых,
фигуры восковые.
Вон там —
    один премьер,
вон там —
    другой премьер,
и этот —
   не пример,
и этот —
   не пример.
Верней, примеры,
     да,
но подлого,
    фальшивого ...
Самих бы их сюда,
в паноптикум,
    за шиворот!
Расставить по местам —
пускай их обвоскуют.
По стольким подлецам
паноптикум тоскует!

Обрыдла их игра.
Довольно врать прохвостам!
Давно пришла пора
живых,
            залить их воском.
Пусть он им склеит рты,
пусть он скует им руки.
И пусть замрут,
                    мертвы,
как паиньки,
            по струнке.
Я объявляю бунт.
Я призываю всех
их стаскивать с трибун
под общих свист и смех.
Побольше,
        люди,
                злости!
Пора всю сволочь смаху
из кресел,
            словно гвозди,
выдергивать со смаком.
Коллекцию их рож
пора под резкий луч
выуживать из лож,
что карасей из луж.
Пора в конце концов
избавиться от хлама.
В паноптикум
            лжецов —
жрецов из храма срама!
Подайте,
        люди,
                глас —
не будьте же безгласны!
В паноптикум —
                всех глав,
которые безглавы!
И если кто-то врет —

пусть даже и по-новому,
вы —
        воском ему в рот:
в паноптикум!
                в паноптикум!
Еще полно дерьма,
лжецов на свете —
                войско ...
Эй, пчелы,
        за дела!
Нам столько надо воска!

ГЛУБИНА

Будил захвоенные дали
рев парохода поутру,
а мы на палубе стояли
и наблюдали Ангару.
Она летела озаренно,
и дно просвечивало в ней
сквозь толщу волн светло-зеленых
цветными пятнами камней.
Порою, если верить глазу,
могло казаться на пути,
что дна легко коснешься сразу,
лишь в воду руку опусти.
Пусть было здесь немало метров,
но так вода была ясна,
что оставалась неприметной
ее большая глубина.
Я знаю: есть порой опасность
в незамутненности волны —
ведь ручейков журчащих ясность
отнюдь не признак глубины.
Но и другое мне знакомо,
и я не ставлю ни во грош
бессмысленно глубокий омут,

244

где ни черта не разберешь.
И я хотел бы стать волною
реки, зарей пробитой вкось,
с неизмеримой глубиною
и с каждым
   камешком
     насквозь!

           [*Третий, снег* 1952]

МУКИ СОВЕСТИ

 Д. Шостаковичу

Мы живем, умереть не готовясь,
забываем поэтому стыд,
но мадонной невидимой совесть
на любых перекрестках стоит.

И бредут ее дети и внуки
при бродяжьей клюке и суме —
муки совести — странные муки
на бессовестной к стольким земле.

От калитки опять до калитки,
от порога опять на порог
они странствуют, словно калики,
у которых за пазухой — бог.

Не они ли с укором бессмертным
тусклым ногтем стучали тайком
в слюдяные окошечки смердов,
а в хоромы царей — кулаком?

Не они ли на загнанной тройке
мчали Пушкина в темень пурги,
Достоевского гнали в остроги
и Толстому шептали: «Беги!»

Палачи понимали прекрасно:
«Тот, кто мучится, — тот баламут.
Муки совести — это опасно.
Выбьем совесть, чтоб не было мук».

Но как будто набатные звуки,
сотрясая их кров по ночам,
муки совести — грозные муки —
проникали к самим палачам.

Ведь у тех, кто у кривды на страже,
кто давно потерял свою честь,
если нету и совести даже —
муки совести вроде бы есть.

И покуда на свете на белом,
где никто не безгрешен, никто,
в ком-то слышится: «Что я наделал?»,
можно сделать с землей кое-что.

Я не верю в пророков наитья,
во второй или в тысячный Рим,
верю в тихое «Что вы творите?»,
верю в горькое «Что мы творим?».

И целую вам темные руки
у безверья на скользком краю,
муки совести, светлые муки
за последнюю веру мою.

1966

[*Огонек,* 1967]

ПАМЯТИ АХМАТОВОЙ

I

Ахматова двувременной была.
О ней и плакать как-то не пристало.
Не верилось, когда она жила,
не верилось, когда ее не стало.

Она ушла, как будто бы напев
уходит в глубь темнеющего сада.
Она ушла, как будто бы навек
вернулась в Петербург из Ленинграда.

Она связала эти времена
в туманно-теневое средоточье,
и если Пушкин — солнце, то она
в поэзии пребудет белой ночью.

Над смертью и бессмертьем, вне всего,
она лежала, как бы между прочим,
не в настоящем, а поверх него,
лежала между будущим и прошлым.

И прошлое у гроба тихо шло
не вереницей дам богоугодных.
Седые челки гордо и светло
мерцали из-под шляпок старомодных.

Да, изменило время их черты,
красавиц той, когдатошней России,
но их глаза — лампады доброты —
ни крутоверть, ни мгла не загасили.

Шло будущее, слабое в плечах.
Шли мальчики. Они себя сжигали
пожаром гимназическим в очах
и в кулаках тетрадочки сжимали.

И девочки в портфельчиках своих
несли, наверно, дневники и списки.

Все те же — из блаженных и святых —
наивные российские курсистки.

И ты, распад всемирный, не убий
ту связь времен, — она еще поможет.
Ведь просто быть не может двух Россий,
как быть и двух Ахматовых не может.

II

Ну, а в другом гробу, невдалеке,
как будто рядом с библией частушка,
лежала в белом простеньком платке
ахматовского возраста старушка.

Лежала, как готовилась к венцу,
устав стирать, мести, скрести и штопать,
крестьянка по рукам и по лицу,
а в общем, домработница, должно быть.

Быть мертвой — это райское житье.
За ней так добро люди приглядели
и словно перед праздником дите
и вымыли и чисто приодели.

Цветами ее, правда, не почли,
но был зато по мерке гроб подогнан,
и дали туфли новые почти,
с квиточками ремонта на подошвах.

Была она прощающе ясна
и на груди благоговейно сжала
сухие руки, будто бы она
невидимую свечку в них держала.

Они умели в жизни все уметь
писали, правда, только закорюки,
тяжелые и темные, как медь,
ни разу не целованные руки.

И думал я: а может быть, а вдруг,
но все же существуют две России:
Россия духа и Россия рук —
две разные страны, совсем чужие?!

Никто о той старушке не скорбел.
Никто ее в бессмертные не прочил.
И был над нею отстраненно бел
Ахматовой патрицианский профиль.

Ахматова превыше всех осанн
покоилась презрительно и сухо,
осознавая свой духовный сан
над самозванством и плебейством духа.

Аристократка! Вся оттуда, где
под рысаками билась мостовая!
Но руки на цветах, как на воде,
покачивались, что-то выдавая.

Они творили, как могли, добро,
но силы временами было мало,
и, легкое для Пушкина, перо
с усмешкой пальцы женские ломало.

Забыли пальцы холодок Аи,
и поцелуи в Ницце, Петербурге,
и, на груди сведенные, они
крестьянскою усталостью набухли.

Царица без короны и жезла,
среди даров почтительности тусклых,
была она прощающе ясна,
как та старушка в тех дареных туфлях.

Ну, а старушка в том, другом гробу
лежала, не увидевшая Ниццы,
с ахматовским величием на лбу,
и между ними не было границы.

[*Юность*, 1966]

ШУТЛИВОЕ

Меняю славу на бесславье,
ну, а в президиуме стул
на место теплое в канаве,
где хорошенько бы заснул.
Уж я бы выложил всю душу,
всю мою смертную тоску
вам, лопухи, в седые уши,
пока бы ерзал на боку.
И я проснулся бы, небритый,
средь вас, букашки-мураши,
ах, до чего ж незнаменитый —
ну хоть «Цыганочку» пляши.
Вдали бы кто-то рвался к власти,
держался кто-нибудь за власть,
а мне-то что до той напасти, —
мне из канавы не упасть.
И там в обнимку с псом лишайным
в такой приятельской пыли
я все лежал бы и лежал бы
на высшем уровне — земли.
И рядом плыли бы негрешно
босые девичьи ступни,
возы роняли бы небрежно
травинки бледные свои.
. . . Швырнет курильщик со скамейки
в канаву смятый коробок,
и мне углами губ с наклейки
печально улыбнется Блок.

[*Огонек*, 1966]

ЭСТРАДА

Проклятие мое,
               души моей растрата —
эстрада ...

Я молод был.
            Хотел на пьедестал,
хотел аплодисментов и букетов,
когда я вышел
             и неловко стал
на тальке, что остался от балеток.
Мне было еще нечего сказать,
а были только звон внутри
                    и горло,
но что-то сквозь меня такое перло,
что невозможно сценою сковать.
И голосом ломавшимся моим
ломавшееся время закричало,
и время было мной,
                и я был им,
и что за важность,
                 кто был кем сначала.
И на эстрадной огненной черте
вошла в меня невысказанность залов,
как будто бы невысказанность зарев,
которые таились в темноте.
Эстрадный жанр перерастал в призыв,
и оказалась чем-то третьим слава.
Как в библии,
             вначале было слово,
ну, а потом —
              сокрытый в слове взрыв.
Какой я Северянин,
               дураки!
Слабы, конечно, были мои кости,
но на лице моем
              сквозь желваки
прорезывался грозно Маяковский.
И, золотая вся от удальства,

дыша пшеничной ширью полевою,
Есенина шальная голова
всходила над моею головою.
Учителя,
        я вас не посрамил,
и вам я тайно все букеты отдал.
Нам
      вместе
            аплодировал весь мир:
Париж, и Гамбург,
                и Мельбурн,
                        и Лондон.
Но что со мной ты сделала —
                    ты рада,
эстрада?!
Мой стих не распустился,
                    не размяк,
но стал грубей и темой
                и отделкой.
Эстрада,
        ты давала мне размах,
но отбирала таинство оттенков.
Я слишком от натуги багровел.
В плакаты влез
            при хитрой отговорке,
что из большого зала акварель
не разглядишь,
            особенно с галерки.
Я верить стал не в тишину —
                    в раскат,
но так собою можно пробросаться.
Я научился вмазывать,
                врезать,
но разучился тихо прикасаться.

И было кое-что еще страшней:
когда в пальтишки публика влезала,
разбросанный по тысячам людей,
сам от себя

я уходил из зала.
А мой двойник,
от пота весь рябой,
сидел в гримерной,
конченный волшебник,
тысячелик
от лиц, в него вошедших,
и переставший быть самим собой ...
За что такая страшная награда —
эстрада?
«Прощай, эстрада ...» —
тихо прошепчу,
хотя забыл я, что такое шепот.
Уйду от шума в шелесты и шорох,
прижмусь березке к слабому плечу,
но, помощи потребовав моей,
как требует предгрозье взрыва,
взлома,
невысказанность далей и полей
подкатит к горлу,
сплавливаясь в слово.

Униженность и мертвых и живых
на свете,
что еще далек до рая,
потребует,
из связок горловых
мой воспаленный голос выдирая.
Я вас к другим поэтам не ревную.
Не надо ничего — я все отдам,
и глотку
да и голову шальную,
лишь только б лучше в жизни было вам!
Конечно, будет ясно для потомков,
что я —
увы! —
совсем не идеал,
а все-таки,
пусть грубо или тонко,
но чувства добрые я лирой пробуждал.

И прохриплю,
   когда иссякших сил,
пожалуй, и для шепота не будет:
«Эстрада,
   я уж был какой я был,
а так ли жил —
    пусть бог меня рассудит».
И я сойду во мглу с тебя без страха,
эстрада ...

[Огонек, 1966]

ИДОЛ

Среди сосновых игол
в завьюженном логу
стоит эвенский идол,
уставившись в тайгу.

Надменно щуря веки,
смотрел он до поры,
как робкие эвенки
несли ему дары.

Несли унты и малицы,
несли и мед и мех,
считая, что он молится
и думает за всех.

В уверенности темной,
что он их всех поймет,
оленьей кровью теплой
намазывали рот.

А что он мог, обманный
божишка небольшой,
с жестокой, деревянной,
источенной душой?

Глядит сейчас сквозь ветви,
покинуто, мертво.
Ему никто не верит,
не молится никто.

Но чудится мне? ночью
в своем логу глухом
он зажигает очи,
обсаженные мхом.

И, вслушиваясь в гулы,
пургою заметен,
облизывает губы
и крови хочет он ...

[*Нежность*, 1955]

СТАРЫЙ БУХГАЛТЕР

Никакой не ведаю я муки,
ни о чем ненужном не сужу.
Подложив подушечку под брюки,
в черных нарукавниках сижу.

Вижу те же подписи, печати ...
На столе бумаги шелестят,
шелестят устало и печально,
шелестят, что скоро шестьдесят.

Ах, начальник — молод он и крепок!
Как всегда, взыскательно побрит,
он, играя четками из скрепок,
про футбол со мною говорит.

Ах, начальник! — вроде бы он ччстый,
вроде не похож на подлеца,
но я вижу все, что скрыть он тщится
под сияньем гладкого дица.

Ах, начальник! — как себя он холит!
Даже перстни носит на руках!
Только он не очень твердо ходит
в замшевых красивых башмаках!

Выйду я из маленькой конторы,
улыбнусь растерянно весне
и поеду в поезде, который
до Мытищ и далее везде.

Там живут четыре, тоже старых
женщины печальных у реки.
У одной из них, таких усталых,
попрошу когда-нибудь руки.

А когда вернусь в свою каморку,
в пахнущую «Примой» тишину,
из большого ветхого комода
выну фотографию одну.

Там, неловко очень подбоченясь,
у эпохи грозной на виду,
я стою, неюный ополченец
в сорок первом искреннем году.

Я услышу самолетов гулы,
выстрелы и песни на ветру,
и прошепчут что-то мои губы,
ну а что — и сам не разберу.

1958

[*Нежность*, 1958]

ТАЙНЫ

Тают отроческие тайны,
как туманы на берегах ...
Были тайнами — Тони, Тани,
даже с цыпками на ногах.

Были тайнами звезды, звери,
под осинами стайки опят,
и скрипели таинственно двери —
только в детстве так двери скрипят.

Возникали загадки мира,
словно шарики изо рта
обольстительного факира,
обольщающего неспроста.

Оволшебленные снещинки
опускались в полях и лесах.
Оволшебленные смешинки
у девчонок плясали в глазах.

Мы таинственно что-то шептали
на таинственном льду катка,
и пугливо, как тайна к тайне,
прикасалась к руке рука ...

Но пришла неожиданно взрослость.
Износивший свой фрак до дыр,
в чье-то детство, как в дальнюю область,
гастролировать убыл факир.

Мы, как взрослые, им забыты.
Эх, факир, ты плохой человек.
Нетаинственно до обиды
нам на плечи падает снег.

Где вы, шарики колдовские?
Нетаинственно мы грустим.
Нетаинственны нам другие,
да и мы нетаинственны им.

Ну, а если рука случайно
прикасается, гладя слегка,
это только рука, а не тайна,
понимаете — только рука!

Дайте тайну простую-простую,
тайну — робость и тишину,
тайну худенькую, босую ...
Дайте тайну — хотя бы одну!

1960

Играла девка на гармошке.
Она была пьяна слегка,
корка черная горбушки
иоснилась вся от чеснока.

И безо всяческой героики,
в избе устроив пир горой,
мои товарищи-геологи,
обнявшись, пели под гармонь.

У ног студентки-практикантки
сидел я около скамьи.
Сквозь ее пальцы протекали
с шуршаньем волосы мои.

Я вроде пил, и вроде не пил,
и вроде думал про свое,
и для нее любимым не был,
и был любимым для нее.

Играла девка на гармошке,
о жизни пела кочевой,
и шлепали ее галошки,
прихваченные бечевой.

Была в гармошке одинокость,
тоской обугленные дни
и беспредельная далекость,
плетни, деревья и огни.

Играла девка, пела девка,
и потихоньку до утра
по-бабьи плакала студентка —
ее ученая сестра ...

1955

КАИНОВА ПЕЧАТЬ

Памяти Р. Кеннеди

Брели паломники сирые
в Мекку
        по серой Сирии.
Скрюченно и поломанно
передвигались паломники.
От наваждений
        и хаоса —
              каяться,
                  каяться,
                     каяться.

А я стоял на вершине
грешником
        нераскаянным,
где некогда —
        не ворошите! —

Авель убит был Каином.
И — самое чрезвычайное
из всех сообщений кровавых,
слышалось изначальное:
«Каин,
          где брат твой, Авель?»
Но вдруг —
              голоса фарисейские,
фашистские,
              сладко-злодейские:
«Что вам виденья отжитого?
Да, перегнули с Авелем.
Конечно, была ошибочка,
но, в общем-то, путь был правилен …»
И мне представился каменный
угрюмый детдом,
              где отравленно
кормят детеныши каиновы
с ложечки ложью —
                      авелевых.
И проступает,
              алая,
когда привыкают молчать,
на лицах детей Авеля
каинова печать.

Так я стоял на вершине
меж праотцев и потомков
над миром,
          где люди вершили
растленье себе подобных.
Безмолнийно было,
              безгромно,
но камни взывали ребристо:
«Растление душ бескровно,
но это —
          братоубийство».

А я на вершине липкой

стоял,
           ничей не убийца,
но совесть библейской уликой
взывала:
           «Тебе не укрыться!
Твой дух растлеваешь ты ложью,
и дух крошится,
                     дробится.
Себя убивать —
           это тоже
братоубийство.
А скольких женщин
                     ты сослепу
в пути растоптал,
                     как распятья.
Ведь женщины —
           твои сестры,
а это больше, чем братья.
И чьи-то серые,
                     карие
глядят на тебя
                без пощады,
и вечной печатью каиновой
ко лбу прирастают взгляды . . .
Что стоят гусарские тосты
за женщин?
                Бравада, отписка . . .
Любовь убивать —
                     это тоже
братоубийство . . .»
Я вздрогнул:
                «Совесть, потише . . .
Ведь это же несравнимо,
как сравнивать цирк для детишек
с кровавыми цирками Рима . . .»

Но тень изможденного Каина
возникла у скал угловато,
и с рук нескончаемо капала
кровь убиенного брата.

«Взгляни —
                мои руки кровавы.
А начал я с детской забавы.
Крылья бабочек бархатных
ломал я из любопытства.
Все начинается с бабочек.
После —
        братоубийство ...»

И снова сказала,
                провидица,
с пророчески-горькой печалью
совесть моя —
            хранительница
каиновой печати:
«Что вечности звездной, безбрежной
ты скажешь,
            на суд ее явленный?
«Конечно же, я не безгрешный,
но, в общем-то, путь мой правилен»?
Ведь это возводят до истин
все те, кто тебе ненавистен,
и человечиной жженой
«винстоны» пахнут
                и «кенты»,
и пуля,
        пройдя сквозь Джона,
сражает Роберта Кеннеди.
И бомбы землю бодают,
сжигая деревни пламенем.
Конечно, в детей попадают,
но, в общем-то, путь их правилен ...
Каин во всех таится
и может вырасти тайно.
Единственное убийство
священно —
        убить в себе Каина!»

И я на вершине липкой
у вечности перед ликом
разверз мою грудь неприкаянно,
душа
      в зародыше
           Каина.
Душил я все подлое,
             злобное,
все то, что может быть подло,
но крылья бабочек сломанные
соединить было поздно.
А ветер хлестал наотмашь,
невидимой кровью намокший,
как будто страницы Библии
меня
      по лицу
         били ...

[*Огонек*, 1968]

БАЛЛАДА О СМЕРТНИКЕ

И я вздрогну,
         и я опомнюсь —
в стол зеленый локтями врыт,
бывший летчик-смертник —
              японец
о Раскольникове говорит.
На симпозиуме о романе
он,
    в свои сорок пять,
            старик.
Он,
    как вежливое рыданье.
Он,
    как сдавленный галстуком крик.
И сквозь нас и куда-то мимо,
сквозь шимозы и тень Лазо

желтым отблеском Хиросимы,
проплывает,
             кренясь,
                    лицо.
Ну а в горле его
              то ли комья слез,
то ли комья кашля ...
Император хотел, чтобы с детства он рос
смирным смертником —
                    комикадзе.
Хорошо по рукам и букетам плыть,
поздравляемым быть перед строем ...
Да,
    красиво народным героем быть,
но во имя чего —
              героем?
И бежал из героев он с горсткой друзей,
предпочтя свою славу покинуть
и остаться в живых ...
                    Это было смелей
чем во имя неправды погибнуть!
Ну а я —
        я слыву, что я смелый ...
Но о жизни и смерти моей
что я думаю,
            грешный и смертный,
среди грешных и смертных людей?
Все мы смертники.
                Все камикадзе.
Ветер смерти свистит в ушах.
Каждый шаг по планете комкастой
это к смерти невидимой шаг.
Пусть я буду разбитым и смятым —
не за то, что хотел бы тиран,
рычаги
      вырывая
            с мясом,
я пойду
      на последний таран.
Но тогда я хотел бы, потомки,

чтоб сквозь тело истлевшее,

                сквозь

моего самолета обломки
что-то доброе к вам прорвалось.
Но как страшно

           себе же казаться

погибающим в небе не зря,
а, погибнув уже,

             оказаться

обманувшимся смертником зла ...

                                      [*Звезда востока*]

ПОПЫТКА БОГОХУЛЬСТВА

Обращаясъ к вечному магниту
в час, когда в душе моей ни зги,
я всегда шепчу одну молитву:
«Господи, прости и помоги ...»

И господь прощает, помогает,
разводя руками оттого,
как людское племя помыкает
милостями столькими его.

Видно, бог на нас глядит со страхом.
Как бы его кто ни называл, —
Иеговой, Буддой и Аллахом —
он один, и богом быть устал.

Будь он даже некая бестелость
или портативный идолок,
как от поцелуев бы хотелось
спрятаться в укромный уголок!

Только ему прятаться негоже,
и, согбенный, будто в рабстве негр,
хочет бог поверить в бога тоже,
но для бога в мире бога нет.

И когда с просьбишками мы липнем,
забывая отдавать долги,
некому шептать ему молитву:
«Господи, прости и помоги . . .»

[*Знамя*, 1967]

У ВОЕНКОМАТА

Под колыбельный рокот рельсов
усталой смазчицей экспрессов
дремала станция Зима.
Дремал и шпиль на райсовете,
дремал и пьяница в кювете
и сторож у «Заготзерна».

Совсем зиминский, не московский
я шел и шел, дымя махоркой,
сквозь шелест листьев, чьи-то сны.
Дождь барабанил чуть по жести . . .
И вдруг я вздох услышал женский:
«Ах, только б не было войны! . . .»

Луна скользнула по ометам,
крылечкам, ставням и заплотам,
и, замеревши на ходу,
я, что-то вещее почуя,
как тень печальную ночную,
увидел женщину одну.

Она во всем, что задремало,
чему-то тайному внимала.
Ей было лет уже немало —
не меньше чем за пятьдесят.
Она особенно, по-вдовьи
перила трогала ладонью
под блеклой вывеской на доме:
«Зиминский райвоенкомат».

Должно быть, шла она с работы,
и вдруг ее толкнуло что-то
неодолимо, как волна,
к перилам этим ... В ней воскресла
война без помпы и оркестра,
кормильца, взявшая война.
Вот здесь, опершись о перила,
об эти самые перила,
молитву мужу вслед творила,
а после шла, дитем тяжка,
рукою правою без силы
опять касаясь вас, перила,
а в левой мертвенно, остыло
бумажку страшную держа.
Ах, только б не было войны!
(была в руках его гармошка ...)
Ах, только б не было войны ...
(... была за голенищем ложка ...)
Ах, только б не было войны!
(... и на губах махорки крошка ...)
Ах, только б не было войны!
(... Шумел, подвыпивший немножко:
«Ничо, не пропадет твой Лешка!»
Ну, а в глазах его сторожко
глядела боль из глубины ...)
Ах, только б не было войны!

□ □ □

Проклятье века — это спешка,
и человек, стирая пот,
по жизни мечется, как пешка,
попав затравленно в цейтнот.

Поспешно пьют, поспешно любят,
и опускается душа.
Поспешно бьют, поспешно губят,
а после каются, спеша.

Но ты хотя б однажды в мире,
когда он спит или кипит,
остановись, как лошадь в мыле,
почуяв пропасть у копыт.

Остановись на полдороге,
доверься небу, как судье,
подумай — если не о боге —
хотя бы просто о себе.

Под шелест листьев обветшалых,
под паровозный хриплый крик
пойми: забегавшийся — жалок,
остановившийся — велик.

Пыль суеты сует сметая,
ты вспомни вечность наконец,
и нерешительность святая
вольется в ноги, как свинец.

Есть в нерешительности сила,
когда по ложному пути
вперед на ложные светила
ты не решаешься идти.

Топча, как листья, чьи-то лица,
остановись! Ты слеп, как Вий.
И самый шанс остановиться
безумством спешки не убий.

Когда шагаешь к цели бойко,
как по ступеням, по телам,
остановись, забывший бога, —
ты по себе шагаешь сам!

Когда тебя толкает злоба
к забвенью собственной души,
к бесчестью выстрела и слова, —
не поспеши, не соверши!

Остановись, идя вслепую,
о население Земли!
Замри, летя из кольта, пуля,
и, бомба, в воздухе замри!

О человек, чье имя свято,
подняв глаза с молитвой ввысь,
среди распада и разврата
остановись, остановись!

1968

[*Огонек*, 1968]

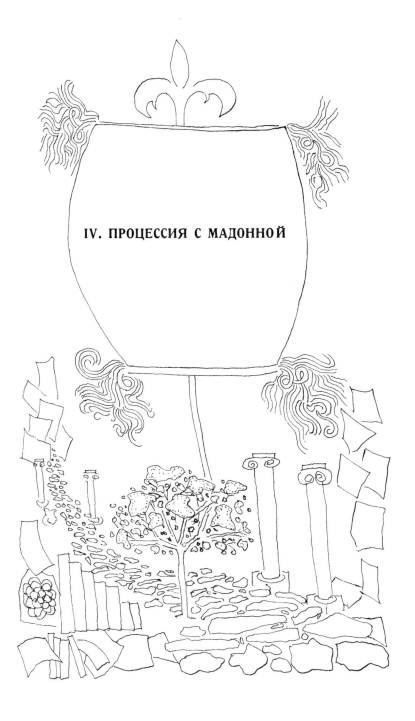

IV. ПРОЦЕССИЯ С МАДОННОЙ

ИСПОВЕДАЛЬНЯ

Окошечко исповедальни ...
Туда, во благостную тьму
потертый лик испитой дамы
с надеждой тянется к нему.

Дитя неапольских окраин
в сторонке очереди ждет,
раскрытой библией скрывая
свой недвусмысленный живот.

Без карабина и фуражки
карабинер пришел на суд,
и по спине его мурашки
под формой грозною ползут.

Несут хозяйки от лоханей,
от ипподромов игроки
и то, что кажется грехами
и настоящие грехи.

А где моя исповедальня?
Куда приду, смиряя страх,
с греховной пылью, с пылью дальней
на заблудившихся стопах?

Я позабуду праздность, леность.
Скажите адрес — я найду.
Но исповедоваться лезут
уже ко мне, как на беду.

Чему научит исповедник
заблудших, совестью больных,
когда и сам он из последних
пропащих грешников земных?

Мы ближним головы морочим,
когда с грехами к нам бегут.
Но говорят, что люди, впрочем
вовсю на исповедях лгут.

И проповедник, это зная,
и сам спасительно им лжет,
и ложь уютная, двойная
уютно нежит, а не жжет.

Но верить вере я не вправе,
хоть лоб о плиты разможжи,
когда почти как правда правде,
ложь исповедуется лжи.

Неаполь-Москва

ЖАРА В РИМЕ

Монахи,
            к черту все сутаны,
ныряйте в римские фонтаны!
А ну,
        синьор премьер-министр,
скорее к По
            и прямо — вниз!
И как ослы
            и как ослихи,
к воде — послы,
                к воде — послихи.
Миллионер,
            кричи в смятеньи:
«Подайте на кусочек тени!»
Объедини хоть раз господ
с простым народом
                        общий пот!
Все пропотело —
                даже чувства.
Газеты — липкое белье.
Мадонна плачет ...
                    Чудо!
                        Чудо!

Не верьте —
         катит пот с нее.
За сорок ...
         Градусники лопаются.
Танцует пьяно ртуть в пыли,
как будто крошечные глобусы,
с которых страны оползли.
Все расползается на части,
размякло все —
         и даже власти.
Отщипывайте
         мрамор храма
и жуйте
         вместо чуингама.

А бронзовые властелины,
герои,
      боги —
         жалкий люд,
как будто бы из пластилина:
ткнешь пальцем —
         сразу упадут.
На Пьяцца ди Индепеденца
тону беспомощней младенца.
Асфальт расплавленный —
         по грудь.
«Эй, кто-нибудь!
         Эй, кто-нибудь!»
Но нет —
         никто не отвечает.
Жить независимо —
         включает
и независимо тонуть.
А надо всем
        поэт-нудист
стихи пророчески нудит:
«Коровы на лугах протухли,
на небе Млечный Путь прокис.
Воняют люди и продукты.
Спасенье —

массовый стриптиз!
Не превращайтесь, люди,
                                в трупы,
не бойтесь девственной красы.
Одежду носят только трусы.
Снимайте радостно трусы!»

Дамы стонут:
              «Озона . . .
                        Озона!»
Объявили,
          портных окрыля,
наимодным платьем сезона
платье голого короля.

«Ха-ха-ха! . . . —
                    из веков раздается ответ. —
Оно самое модное —
                    тысячи лет . . .»

«О депутат наш дорогой,
вы в села —
            даже ни ногой,
а села обнищали . . .
Где все, что обещали?» —
«Я обещал?
          Ах, да,
                  ах, да! . . .
Забыл —
        простите, духота . . .» —
«Что ты слаб, мой миленький?
Подкрепить вином?
Ляжем в холодильнике,
может, выйдет в нем . . .»
Депутаты перед избирателями,
импотенты перед супружницами,
убийцы перед прокурорами,
адвокаты перед убийцами
все оправдываются добродушно:
«Душно . . .»

Душно,
      душно ото лжи …
Россия,
      снега одолжи!
Но ходят слухи — ну и бред! —
что и в России снега нет.
И слухи новые
         Рим облетели,
что и на полюсе нету льдин,
что тлеют книги
         в библиотеках,
в музеях
     краски
        текут
          с картин
И не спит изнывающий город ночей.
Надо что-то немедля решать,
если даже и те,
        кто дышал ничем,
заявляют:
     «Нечем дышать!»
Из кожи мира —
        грязный жир.
Провентилировать бы мир!
Все самолеты,
     ракеты,
        эсминцы,
все автоматы,
     винтовки,
        а с ними
лживый металл в голосах у ораторов,
медные лбы проигравшихся глав
на вентиляторы, —
        на вентиляторы,
на вентиляторы —
       в переплав!
Быть может,
     поможет …

[*Юность*, 1966]

РИТМЫ РИМА

Вставайте,
гигантским будильником Рим тарахтит у виска.
Взбивайте
шипящую пену пушистым хвостом помазка.
И — к Риму!
Отдайтесь рассветному стуку его башмаков,

                             молотков

и крику
молочниц, газетчиков, пекарей, зеленщиков.
Монашки,
хрустя белокрыльем крахмальным, гуськом семенят.
Медяшки
в их глиняных кружках, взывая к прохожим,

                                  звенят.

Путаны
идут с профилактики прямо — молиться в собор.
Пузаны
в кафе обсуждают, как вылечить лучше запор.
Монисты
бренчат на цыганках у выставки «Супер-поп-арт».
Министры
летят в «мерседесах». Ладони — в мозолях от карт.
Ладони
в рабочих мозолях плывут и не ждут ничего.
Лимоны
и люди в Италии стоят дешевле всего.
Куда вы
спешите, все люди? Куда вы ползете, куда
удавы
брандспойтов, где буйно играет, как мышцы, вода?
Все — к Риму,
как будто бы к храму, где вам отпущенье дадут,
и к рынку,
где, может, вас купят, а может быть, и продадут.
Урвал бы
я опыта Рима, чтоб в жизни потом не пропасть.
Украл бы
чуть-чуть его ритма, — да нет, ни урвать,

                                 ни украсть.

Есть Римы,
а Рима, наверное, просто физически нет.
Есть ритмы —
нет общего ритма, и в этом-то улиц секрет.
Но буду
старьевщиком лоскутов Рима, что порваны им.
Набухну,
как будто бы губка, всосавшая порами Рим.
До ночи
подслушивать стану, — и ночью, конечно, не спя,
доносчик
всему человечеству, Рим, на тебя и себя.
Напрячу
за пазуху все, что проулки твои накричат,
наплачут,
нашепчут, насвищут, налязгают и нажурчат.
Пусть гонка
за Римом по Риму мне кости ломает, дробя, —
как пленка,
я буду наматывать яростно Рим на себя ...

«Пожар! Пожар!
                Горит синьора Сильвия!»
«Да нет,
        дурак,
              квартира —
                        не она ...»
«В шкафу
        пошарь —
                там есть белье носильное,
и тот
    дуршлаг —
              скорее из окна!
Кидай
      диван
            и крышку унитаза!
... а все — горбом,
                  ну хоть о стенку лбом ...
Постой, болван,
              а где же наша ваза?
А где

альбом,
        семейный наш альбом? ...»
«Заткнись,
      жена,
          тут не поможешь визгом ...»
«... Зачем
      с греха
          пошла я под венец?!»
«Веревку
     на,
        спускай-ка телевизор ...
Повешен —
      ха! —
          проклятый, наконец!»
«Не плачь,
      все здесь —
           кастрюли и бидоны.
Очнись,
     жена,
        смотри — ты вся в пуху ...»
«Отстань,
      не лезь ...
             Постой, а где мадонна?
Горит
    она!
       Забыли наверху!!»
«Беда,
    беда ...
         Ты слышал это, сын мой?»
«Теперь,
     сосед,
        для них потерян рай.
Теперь
     всегда
        страдать синьоре Сильвии ...
Мадонны нет ...
Забыли ... Ай-яй-яй! ...»

«Кому дуче,
      кому дуче!

До чего хорош портрет!
Налетайте,
                люди,
                        тучей, —
лучше парня в мире нет!
Кисть художника —
                        ну что ж! —
не матиссова,
но ведь вам когда-то вождь
нравился мольтиссимо.
Налетай,
            блошиный рынок,
и торгуйся умненько.
Среди стольких птичек-рыбок
эта птичка —
                уника!
Покупателей открытых
нет сегодня на вождя,
но с достатком шитых-крытых:
по глазам их вижу я.
Посмелей —
            так будет лучше,
а то дуче трескается.
Кому дуче,
            кому дуче!
Никому не требуется?»

«Сюда подходите, синьоры, —
                        здесь продаются письма.
Самые настоящие —
                видите штемпеля?
Прошу не отклеивать марок —
                        читайте, не торопитесь ...
Писем на всех достаточно —
                    целые штабеля.
Пожалуйста, век восемнадцатый:
                        «... Я буду вас ждать хоть вечность».
Пожалуйста, век девятнадцатый:
                        «... Я буду вас ждать хоть сто лет».
А вот и двадцатый, синьоры:

«... Чего ты все крутишь и вертишь?
Уже я потратил два вечера,
                        а результата нет».
Вот первая мировая,
                а это уже вторая ...
(К несчастью, цензурные вымарки
                        временем не сняло ...)
А если третья случится —
                синьоры, я представляю,
и вы представляете, думаю, —
                        не будет писем с нее.
Синьоры, по-моему, письма
                дороже всяких реликвий,
но продают их дешево,
                        а я покупаю, старик.
Письма — странички разрозненные
                        книги, быть может, великой,
но нету такого клея,
                чтоб склеить все вместе их».
«Синьор, вам не кажется странным,
                        что вы — продавец писем?»
«Странным? А что тут странного?
                        Ага, угадал — вы поэт ...
А вам не кажется странным,
                что вы продавец песен?
В мире так много странного,
                а в сущности, странного нет ...»

«Мама Рома, мама Рома,
как тебе не совестно?
Тощ супруг, как макарона,
да еще без соуса.
Меня совесть не грызет —
кровь грызет игривая.
Дай,
        правительство,
                        развод,
или —
        эмигрирую!»

— Синьор доктор, объясните мне, какое я
                                    животное?
— Не понимаю вашего вопроса, синьора.
— Чего ж тут не понимать, синьор доктор!
Встаю и сразу начинаю штопать, гладить, готовить
завтрак мужу и детям — словом, верчусь, как
                                    белка в колесе.
Сама поесть не успеваю — остаюсь голодная,
                                    как волк.
Иду на фабрику и целый день ишачу.
Возвращаюсь в автобусе и шиплю на всех от злости,
                                    как гусыня.
Захожу в магазин и тащусь оттуда, нагруженная,
                                    как верблюд.
Прихожу домой и снова стираю, подметаю, готовлю, —
в общем, работаю как лошадь.
Падаю в кровать усталая, как собака.
Муж приходит пьяный, плюхается рядом и говорит:
                                    «Подвинься, корова».
Какое же я все-таки животное, синьор доктор,
                                    а синьор доктор?

«Исповедь кончается моя,
падре.
Нет волос, как прежде, у меня —
патлы.
Вы учили, падре, не грешить,
думать.
Я старалась, падре, так и жить —
дура.
Ничего не помню, как во сне.
Зряшно
так жила я праведно, что мне
страшно.
Согрешить бы перед смертью, но
поздно.
Лишь грехи, что были так давно,
помню.
Мне уже не надо ничего —
бабка.

Далеко до школьного того
банта.
Подойдите, что-то вам скажу,
внучки.
Истину, что крестик вам вложу
в ручки.
Вы не бойтесь, внученьки, грехов
нужных,
а вы бойтесь, внученьки, гробов
нудных.
Вы бегите дальше от пустой
веры
во грехи, как будто в лес густой,
вербный.
Вы услышьте, внученьки, тихи,
в стонах:
радость перед смертью — лишь грехи
вспомнить ...»

«Счастливые билетики,
                    билетики,
                            билетики,
а в них мотоциклетики,
                    «фиатики»,
                            буфетики.
Не верьте ни политике,
                    ни дуре-кибернетике,
а верьте лишь в билетики,
                            счастливые билетики ...
Сейчас на вас беретики,
                    а завтра вы — скелетики.
Хватайте же билетики,
                    счастливые билетики!»

«Если вы с неудач полысели,
                            то, синьоры, не будьте разинями —
вы купите себе полицейского
                            замечательного, резинового.
Бейте,
        плюйте,
                пинайте,

тычьте,
    а когда его так поучите —
облегченье хотя бы частичное
      в этой жизни треклятой получите ...»
«А резиновых членов правительства,
вы скажите,
   у вас не предвидится?»
«Обещать вам даже не пробую.
Сожалею, синьор, —
     все проданы».
"Руки прочь,
   руки прочь
     от Вьетнама!
Бросим стирку нашу,
    дочь,
как-никак,
   я мама.
Ну зачто они бомбят
Тех детишек —
    вьетнамят,
или все бездетны,
или врут газеты?"

А я — плевал я на Вьетнам!
Мне бы — тихо жить.
Мне —
   заплатку бы к штанам
новую пришить!»
«Синьор сержант,
     синьор сержант,
у Пьяцца ди Эспанья
искала я себе сервант
и секретер для спальни.
И вдруг — витрина,
    в ней кровать,
а на кровати девка,
в чем родила, конечно, мать,
лежит и курит дерзко.
А рядом с девкою лежат
кальсоны чьи-то сальные

и сверх того,
    синьор сержант,
пустые ...
    эти самые.
А над стыдобищем таким
написано:
    «Скульптура».
Синьор сержант,
    спасите Рим
и римскую культуру!»
«Рим спасти, синьора, сложно ...
Что поделать —
    молодежь ...
А что можно,
    что не можно —
в наши дни не разберешь ...»

«Стриптиз, наоборот,
    сейчас у нас в новиночках».
«Что это за штуковина?»
    «А делается так:
выходит, значит, дамочка —
    лишь бляшечки на титечках,
а после одевается,
    и в этом — самый смак».
«Старо ...
    На сцену жизни
    все выползают голыми,
а после одеваются
    в слова,
    слова,
    слова,
но под словами все-таки
    друг друга видят голыми.
Стриптиз наоборот — ля вита такова ...»
— Синьор, я хозяин бара, и, конечно, это не мое дело; но я хотел бы предупредить вас, что женщина, подсевшая к вашему столику, — извиняюсь, мужчина ...
— Что за странная шутка!
— К сожалению, это не шутка, а жизненный опыт, синьор. Обратите внимание на руки и ноги — они чересчур крупные и мускулистые. Расти-

тельность снята с лица специальной пастой. Длинные волосы — или парик, или свои, отпущенные. Вас, может быть, ввела в заблуждение выпуклая форма груди? Это следствие парафиновых инъекций. Болезненно, но действенно. Синьор, вы еще очень молоды и, видимо, неопытны, поэтому я счел своим долгом несколько неделикатно предупредить вас ...

— Значит, эта женщина — мужчина?

— Мужчина, синьор ...

— Черт знает что такое! Кстати, называйте меня не синьор, а синьорина. Я уже столько дней безрезультатно ищу себе хоть одну настоящую женщину ... Что поделаешь — не везет ...

«Синьоры!

От имени и по поручению президиума Клуба педерастов разрешите мне поднять первый тост за женщин. Пусть вас не удивляет этот тост, синьоры. При всех их физических и моральных недостатках женщины необходимы для того, чтобы рождать нас, педерастов. Итак — за женщин!»

«Мой друг, скажи, к чему писать стихи
среди распада страшного? Не знаю.
Как этот мир сурово ни стыди,
не устыдится. Предан стыд, как знамя.

Спасение в стыде, но он забыт,
и мне порою хочется воскликнуть:
«О, где же, человечество, твой стыд —
единственный твой двигатель великий?

Вокруг бесстыдство царствует в ночи,
а чувства и мельчают и увечатся, —
лишь пьяниц жилковатые носы
краснеют от стыда за человечество ...»

«Постой, постой ... Твой горький монолог
уже стихи ... Писать их, значит, стоит.
А не захочешь — так заставит бог,
который в нас, несовершенных, стонет.

Да, стыд забыт, — вернее, он притих,
но только сокрушаться не годится.
Ведь ты стыдишься! Почему в других
потеряна способность устыдиться?!

Бездейственно следить чужой разврат —
не лучше откровенного разврата,
и, проклиная свысока распад,
мы сами — составная часть распада.

Ну, а тебе не кажется, мой друг,
что, зренье потерявши от испуга,
мы в замкнутый с тобой попали круг,
не видя мира за чертою круга?

Но есть совсем другие круги, есть
и в этот миг — нетронуто, старинно, —
любовь, надежда, доброта и честь
идут, для нас незримые, по Риму.

Они для нас, как мы для них, — в тени.
Они идут. Как призраков, нас гонят.
И может, правы именно они
и вечны, словно Вечный этот город».

«Забыли нас, любимый мой.
Из парка все ушли домой,
и с чертового колеса
стекли куда-то голоса.

Механик, видно, добрый был —
на землю нас не опустил.
Остановилось колесо.
Забыли нас ... Как хорошо!

Внизу наш бедный гордый Рим,
любимый Рим, проклятый Рим.
Не знает он, что мы над ним
в своей кабиночке парим.

Внизу политики-врали,
министры, шлюхи, короли,
чины, полиция, войска —
какая это все тоска!

Кому-то мы внизу нужны,
и что-то делать мы должны.
Спасибо им, что хоть сейчас
на небесах забыли нас.

Чуть-чуть кабиночку качни
и целовать меня начни,
не то сама ее качну
и целовать тебя начну».

Постой, война, постой, война . . .
Да, жизнь, как Рим, — она страшна,
но жизнь, как Рим, она — одна . . .
Постой, война, постой, война . . .

[*Литературная газета*, 1965]

ПРОЦЕССИЯ С МАДОННОЙ

Людовико Коррао

В городишке тихом Таормина
стройно шла процессия с мадонной.
Дым свечей всходил и таял мирно,
невесомый, словно тайна мига.

Впереди, шли девочки — все в белом
и держали свечи крепко-крепко.
Шли они с восторгом оробелым,
полные собой и миром целым.

И глядели девочки на свечи
и в неверном пламени дрожащем
видели загадочные встречи,
слышали заманчивые речи.

Девочкам надеяться пристало.
Время обмануться не настало,
но, как будто их судьба, за ними
позади шли женщины устало.

Позади шли женщины — все в черном
и держали свечи тоже крепко.
Шли тяжелым шагом удрученным,
полные обманом уличенным.

И глядели женщины на свечи
и в неверном пламени дрожащем
видели детей худые плечи,
слышали мужей тупые речи.

Шли все вместе, улицы минуя,
матерью мадонну именуя,
и несли мадонну на носилках,
будто бы стоячую больную.

И мадонна, видимо, болела
равно и за девочек и женщин,
но мадонна, видимо, велела,
чтобы был такой порядок вечен.

Я смотрел, идя с мадонной рядом,
ни светло, ни горестно на свечи,
а каким-то двуединым взглядом,
полным и надеждою и ядом.

Так вот и живу — необрученным
и уже навеки обреченным
где-то между девочками в белом
и седыми женщинами в черном.

Сицилия

У РИМСКОЙ ЗАБЫТОЙ ДОРОГИ

У римской забытой дороги
недалеко от Дамаска
мертвенны гор отроги,
как императоров маски.

Кольца на солнце грея,
сдержанно скрытноваты,
нежатся жирные змеи —
только что с Клеопатры.

Везли по дороге рубины,
мечи из дамасской стали,
и волосами рабыни,
корчась, ее подметали.

В язвах богини Венеры,
панцирями одетых,
шагали легионеры
с лицами, как на монетах.

Еще не ставшие щебнем,
покачивались колесницы,
подобные гнутым гребням
в прическе императрицы.

Плиты дороги были
крепко рабами сбиты,
будто в дорогу вбили
окаменевшие спины.

Изнемогая от солнца,
мазью натершись этрусской,
с чашей лимонного сока
мыслил патриций обрюзглый:

«Пусть от рабочей черни
лишь черепа да ребра,
мы не умрем, как черви,
и не умрет дорога ...»

И мыслил араб-строитель,
покорно бивший кувалдой,

но все-таки раб строптивый,
но все-таки раб коварный:

«Думая лишь о плоти,
вы позабыли бога.
Значит, и вы умрете,
значит, умрет и дорога ...»

Сгнивали империи корни.
Она, расползаясь, зияла,
как сшитое нитками крови
лоскутное одеяло.

Опять применяли опыт
улещиванья и пыток,
кровью пытались штопать,
но нет ненадежней ниток!

С римского лицемерия
спала надменная тога,
и умерла империя,
и умерла дорога.

Пытались прибегнуть к подлогу.
Твердили, что в крови, когда-то
пролитой на дорогу,
дорога не виновата.

Но дикой травы поколенья
с ней счеты сводили крупно.
Родившая преступленья,
дорога — сама преступна.

И всем палачам-дорогам
и всем дорогам-тиранам
да будет высоким итогом —
высокая плата бурьяном!

Так думал я на дороге,
теперь для проезда закрытой,
дороге, забывшей о боге
и богом за это забытой.

Дамаск-Москва, 1967–1968

[*Огонек,* 1968]

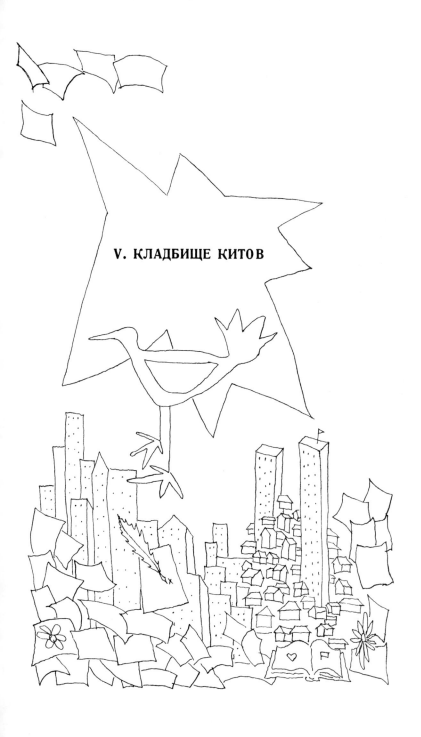

V. КЛАДБИЩЕ КИТОВ

В ДОМЕ СТАЛЕВАРА

Люблю Америку,
              которая плыла
по майской Эльбе,
                поднимая виски
в усталой правой,
                  подгребая левой,
ну а навстречу ей плыла Россия
по майской Эльбе,
                поднимая водку
в усталой левой,
                  подгребая правой,
и водка с виски —
                без! без перевода
так понимали —
              чорт возьми! —
                      друг друга
над вспененой водой победы обшей!

Люблю Америку,
              которая сейчас
сидит со мной в коттеджике стандартном
сталелитейщика,
              и на руках рабочих
натруженные жилы проступают,
как тайные притоки нашей Эльбы,
и между нами нет сейчас правительств.
Правительство невидимое наше
                    сейчас безмолвно выбранное нами, —
те самые усталые солдаты
ребята из Иркутска и Кентукки
которые невидимо к друг другу
по майской Эльбе до сих пор плывут.
Шумят,
        шумят невидимые волны
по братскому непышному столу,
и нами рюмки с плохоньким портвейном
качаются чуть-чуть на этих волнах,
алея, словно бакены надежды.

Мы говорим,
                как будто мы плывем
чтобы обняться, словно братья,
                                но
за двадцать лет так засорили Эльбу!
В нее спустили столько нечистот
заводы лжи —
                суперклоаки века.
Газеты, все пропитанные ядом,
                        окурки поджигательских речей,
плевки мерзавцев,
                грязный «kleenex» мятый,
брезгливо вытиравший жирный пот
с фальшивых лиц ораторов заядлых ...
А под водою нашей Эльбы скрыты
замшелейшие мины недоверья,
и новенькие гладкие подлодки,
брюхатые торпедами, как будто
детьми от брака страха
                        и науки ...
Ккогда,
        когда друг друга мы поймем
как водка с виски —
                без! без перевода
так понимали —
                чорт возьми! —
                        друг друга
над вспененной водой победы общей?
Неужто нужен новый Гитлер нам
чтоб мы объединились,
                        как когда-то?
Цена —
        похоже —
                слишком дорогая ...
Россия и Америка,
                ваш путь
к друг другу сложен,
                        но я верю,
                                верю
что через все отбросы или мины

мы доплывем к друг другу,
                    доплывем,
и мы обнимемся,
                    как в мае, в сорок пятом,
на этот раз —
            я верю —
                        навсегда!
Да,
    между нами океаны злобы,
Да,
    между нами океан Великий,
но поплывем,
            и превратитеся в Эльбу
любой великий самый океан!
. . . Люблю Америку,
                    которая сейчас
ножонками болтает в колыбельке,
светящими усталым грустным нам,
как тоненькие свечечки надежды.
Как ее имя —
            Джен?
                    А, может, Лара?
Ее глаза,
        большие,
                голубые,
как будто две доверчивые капли
той самой Эльбы,
                нашей обшей Эльбы,
которую не вправе мы предать.
. . . Россия и Америка,
                    плывите!

[*Литературная газета,* 1966]

МОНОЛОГ БРОДВЕЙСКОЙ АКТРИСЫ

Сказала актриса с Бродвея
                              разрушенно, будто бы древняя Троя:
«Нет роли!
Нет роли такой,
                   чтоб всю душу мне вывернуть!
Нет роли такой,
                   чтоб все слезы мне выреветь!
От жизни такой
                   хоть беги в чисто поле ...
Нет роли!
           Как шапка на воре пылает Бродвей ...
Нет роли,
           нет роли
                      средь сотен ролей.
Мы тонем в безролье ...
                          Где взять гениальных писателей!
А классики взмокли,
                      как будто команда спасателей.
Но что они знали
                   про Хиросиму,
про гибель безвинных,
                        про все наши боли?
Неужто все это невыразимо?
Нет роли.
Без роли —
           как будто без компаса.
Ты знаешь, как страшен свет,
когда в тебе копится,
                        копится,
а выхода этому нет.
Пожалте, гастроли,
пожалте, уют.
Отобраны роли.
Ролишки суют.
Я пью ...
           Понимаю, конечно, что это безвольно.
Но что же поделать,

когда так безлюдно, безрольно!
Пьет где-то рабочий
и грани стакана в нигроле ...
Нет роли!
Пьет фермер,
мыча от сознанья бессилья и боли ...
Нет роли!
Парнишку шестнадцати лет от безделья дружки
финкарем пропороли ...
Нет роли!
Молчавший о зверских убийствах,
истошно вопит на судью,
но где? —
на футболе ...
Нет роли!
Без роли вся жизнь — это тление.
Мы все гениальны в утробе,
но гибнут возможные гении
при невозможности роли.
Не требуя чьей-нибудь крови —
я
требую
роли!»

1967

[Знамя, 1967]

К ВОПРОСУ О СВОБОДЕ

Зола Дахау жжет мне до сих пор подметки.
Дымятся подо мной асфальт или паркет.
Как гвозди палачей, мне всажены под ногти
неправые штыки и острия ракет.

Поглажу я рукой любимой сонный локон,
а сам курю, курю, и это неспроста.
Я распят, как Христос, на крыльях самолетов,
летящих в эту ночь бомбить детей Христа.

Бросает кожу в дрожь от взрывов и от рева,
как будто бы она-вьетнамская земля,
и, хрупая хребтом, разламывая ребра,
берлинская стена проходит сквозь меня.

Вы о свободе мне? Досужее позерство
под сенью роковой, висящих в небе бомб.
От века своего свободным быть позорно.
Позорней во сто крат, чем быть его рабом.

Да, несвободен я и от ташкентских женщин,
и от далласких пуль, и от пекинских фраз,
и от вьетнамских вдов, и от российских женщин
с кайлами возле рельс, в платочках ниже глаз!

Да, несвободен я от Пушкина и Блока,
от штата Мэриленд и станции Зима.
Да, несвободен я от дьявола и бога,
от красоты земли и от ее дерьма.

Да, несвободен я от жажды мокрой шваброй
пройтись по головам среди грызни, резни.
Да, несвободен я от чести в морду шваркнуть
всем в мире сволочам, что сволочи они!

И, может буду тем любезен я народу,
что прожил жизнь, борясь, — не попросту скорбя,
что в мой жестокий век восславил несвободу
от праведной борьбы, свобода, за тебя ...

[*Литературная газета,* 1966]

РЕСТОРАН ДЛЯ ДВОИХ

Гонолулу,
на спине ты качаешься сонно в серебряно-черном нигде.
Гонит луны
вдоль зазывно-русалочьих бедер твоих ветерок по воде.
Всюду блестки.
По-дикарски ты любишь стекляшки витрин и реклам.
Словно брошки,
пароходы приколоты к влажным твоим волосам.
Ты тасуешь
австралийцев, японцев и янки в шальных шоколадных руках.
Ты танцуешь,
и звенят золоченые рыбки в стеклянных твоих каблучках.
Лорд-шотландец
в пестрой юбочке пляшет с тобою, пуская слюну,
и, шатаясь,
лезет мокро под юбку, и, кажется, не под свою.
Но, как гномик,
дотянулся до звезд на ходулях — на пальмовых сваях своих
                крошка-домик,
уникальный игрушечный храм — ресторан для двоих.
Без антенны
его крыша из листьев — зеленый смешной колпачок.
Его стены
из бамбука и тайны, а что там творится — молчок!
Бой-малаец
на подносе эбеновом вносит по лестнице в дом,
            ухмыляясь,
запеченный акулий плавник в ананасе насквозь золотом.
Два прибора.
Две свечи. Два лица. Два сообщника. Два беглеца.
Как в соборы,
от содома они убежали к друг другу в глаза.
Ненадежно,
как в фонарике елочном здесь, и, пожалуй, морально грешно.
В общем, ложно,
в общем, призрачно это, а все-таки так хорошо!
Трепет самбы,
лепет звезд и раскаты прибоя у дамбы — все только для них!

Я и сам бы
драпанул с удовольствием в тот ресторан для двоих!
        Подлым харям
закричал бы я, в пальцах обрыдлый бокал раздавив:
        «По-ды-хаю
от тоски среди вас. Я хочу в ресторан для двоих!»
        Надо делать
то и это, а этого — ни при каких?
        На-до-ело!
Я смертельно устал. Я хочу в ресторан для двоих.
        Надо думать
и бороться за что-то? Пытался я. Пробовал. Фиг!
        Надоумил
этот домик меня. Я хочу в ресторан для двоих!
        Пусть осудят —
удеру! Но бежать — это только для трусов, трусих.
        Что же будет,
если каждый запрячется в свой ресторан для двоих?!!
        Среди гнойных
всех нарывов эпохи не выход — бежать от тоски
        в домик-гномик,
в чьи-то волосы, губы, колени, ладони, виски!
        Шепот беса
нас толкает к побегам, а мы не умеем понять:
        после бегства
пострашней оказаться на каторге прежней опять.
        . . . В звездных безднах,
будто в хрупком кораблике, тихо сидят, нашалив,
        двое беглых,
а внизу ожидает с овчарками жизнь, как шериф.
        И малаец
на приступочке дремлет внизу — на заветной черте,
        умиляясь
так презрительно чьей-то святой и пустой простоте.
        Замечает,
что еще полчаса до закрытья, а после — катись! —
        и включает
для иллюзии рая — на пленку записанных птиц . . .

1967

[*Литературная газета*, 1967]

БАЛЛАДА О САМОРОДКАХ

Ночной Фербанкс притих, устав,
                                но всюду скрыты
по снежным улицам в унтах
                                гуляют скрипы.
В оленьей парке расписной
                                с лицом подростка
спешит работать в бар ночной
                                стрип-эскимоска.
Бухие летчики-дружки
                                с военной базы
швыряют в спину ей снежки,
                                томясь без бабы.
Ну а она несет впотьмах,
                                сквозь морды, хари,
как розу белую в зубах,
                                свое дыханье.

С морозу в двери кабака,
                                седы, как луни,
заходят шумно облака.
                                Внутри их — люди.
Охотники, и скорняки,
                                и парни с шахты
все на моржовые клыки
                                скидают шапки.
Кто представляет чей-то флаг?
                                Здесь не до флага.
Среди аляскинских бродяг
                                я свой, бродяга.
И нам превыше всяких благ
                                святая влага!
Ты пьешь со мною, старый Боб,
                                мой новый кореш.
Меня ручищами ты сгреб,
                                щетиной колешь.
Сверкает золотом оскал.

Ты худ и страшен.
«Всю жизнь я золото искал — ты слышишь? —
рашен!
Я был румяный — будь здоров! —
теперь я черен.
Аэродром для комаров —
мой лысый череп.
Я подвожу теперь черту —
остался рванью.
Сплошное золото во рту,
и медь в кармане.
У мерзлой ямы на краю
собаки выли,
когда я хоронил свою
старуху Виви.
Была девчонка первый класс, —
как на картинках!
Все тело белое, что кварц, —
чуть в золотинках.
Я молодой, глазастый был —
не из несчастных.
Сказал: «Тебя я застолбил.
Ты — мой участок».
Я мучил Виви сорок лет.
Я сумасбродно
всю жизнь хотел напасть на след —
на самородки!
Она хотела не тряпья,
а сына робко.
Ей снился сын такой, как я,
мне — самородки.
Я пил.
Но плыли на меня
из мутной водки,
как рыбы желтые, дразня,
те самородки.
И я закрыл свой личный трест,
банкрот хрипатый.
Я сколотил для Виви крест —
кирку с лопатой.

Я вез тот гроб — я не забыл! —

                                        на санках мерзлых.
Я не отрыл,

            а я зарыл

                        мой самородок . . .»
Сгребает центы Боб в горсти.

                                    Он пьян и мрачен.
«Без самородков я — прости.

                                    Поставь мне, рашен!»
Он открывает дверь пинком,

                            забыв про шапку,
ныряет в облако, и в нем

                            уходит шатко.
И я, как он, иду во тьме,

                            дитя шалмана,
и не оттягивает мне

                        ничто кармана.
Свой трест еще я не закрыл —

                                    я слишком робок,
но может быть, уже зарыл

                                свой самородок.
И рядом спутницей немой

                                с лицом подростка
бредет измученно домой

                                стрип-эскимоска.
Мороз. Сосульки у меня

                            на подбородке,
и звезды падают, звеня,

                            как самородки . . .

1967

[*Правда*, 1967]

КЛАДБИЩЕ КИТОВ

На кладбище китов
                     на снеговом погосте
стоят взамен крестов
                     их собственные кости.
Они не по зубам —
                     все зубы мягковаты.
Они не по супам —
                     кастрюли мелковаты.
Их вьюга, тужась, гнет,
                              но держатся-порядок! —
вколоченные в лед,
                     как дуги черных радуг.
Горбатый эскимос,
                     тоскующий о стопке,
как будто бы вопрос,
                         в них заключен, как в скобки.
Кто резво щелкнул там?
                              Ваш фотопыл умерьте!
Дадим покой китам
                     хотя бы после смерти.
... А жили те киты,
                     людей не обижая,
от десткой простоты
                     фонтаны обожая.
И солнца красный шар
                         плясал на струях белых ...
«Киты по борту! Жарь!
                         Давай, ребята, бей их!»
Спастись куда-нибудь?
                         Но ты-пространства шире.
А под воду нырнуть —
                     воды нехватит в мире.
Ты думаешь, ты бог?
                         Рисковая нескромность.
Гарпун получишь в бок
                         расплатой за огромность.
Огромность всем велит
                     охотиться за нею.

Тот дурень, кто велик.
                    Кто мельче-тот умнее.
Плотва, как вермишель.
                    Среди ее безличья
дразнящая мишень
                    беспомощность величья.
Бинокли на борту
                    в руках дрожат, нацелясь,
и с гарпуном в боку
                    Толстой бежит от «цейсов».
Китеныш, а не кит,
                    но, словно кит оценен,
гарпунным тросом взвит,
                    качается Есенин.
Кровав китовый сан.
                    Величье убивает.
И Маяковский сам
                    гарпун в себя вбивает.
Величью мель страшна.
                    На камни брошен гонкой,
обломки гарпуна
                    выхаркивает Горький.
Почти не простонав,
                    по крови, как по следу,
уходит Пастернак
                    с обрывком троса —
                              в Лету.
Хемингуей молчит,
                    но над могилой грозно
гарпун в траве торчит
                    проросший ввысь из гроба.
И, скрытый за толпой,
                    кровавым занят делом
даллаский китобой
                    с оптическим прицелом.
... Идет большой загон,
                    а после смерти-ласка.
Честнее твой закон,
                    жестокая Аляска.
На кладбище китов

у ледяных торосов
нет ханжеских цветов —
есть такт у эскимосов.
Эх, эскимос-горбун, —
у белых свой обычай:
сперва всадив гарпун,
поплакать над добычей.
Скорбят смиренней дев,
сосут в слезах пилюли
убийцы, креп надев,
в почетном карауле.
И промысловики,
которым здесь не место,
несут китам венки
от Главгарпунотреста.
Но скручены цветы
стальным гарпунным тросом.
Довольно доброты!
Пустите к эскимосам!

1967

[*Москва,* 1967]

НЬЮ-ЙОРКСКАЯ ЭЛЕГИЯ

В центральном парке города Нью-Йорка
Среди ночей, продрогнувший, ничей
я говорил с Америкой негромко —
мы оба с ней устали от речей.

Я говорил с Америкой шагами,
а это не слова — они не врут,
и отвечала мне она кругами
от мертвых листьев, падающих в пруд.

Шел снег. Себя он чувствовал неловко
у баров, продолжеющих гульбу,
садясь на жилы вспухшие неона

у города бессонного на лбу,
на бодрую улыбку кандидата,
пытавшегося влезть не без труда
куда не помню — помню, что куда-то,
но снегу было все равно куда.

А в парке здесь он падал бестревожно,
и как на разноцветные плоты
снежинки опускались осторожно
на тонущие медленно листы,
на шар воздушный, розовый и зыбкий,
о звезды сонно трущийся щекой,
прилепленный жевательной резинкой
к стволу сосны ребячьей рукой,
на чью-то позабытую перчатку,
на зоосад, спровадивший гостей
и на скамейку с надписью печальной:
«Здесь место для потерянных детей».

Олени снег потерянно лизали.
Мерцали белки у чугунных ваз
среди дерев потерянных лесами,
потерянными бусинками глаз

Храня в себе сурово и сокрыто
безмолвно вопрошающий укор
лежали глыбы грузные гранита —
потерянные дети бывших гор.

Жевали зебры за решеткой сено,
потерянно уставясь в темноту.
Моржи, вздымая морды из бассейна,
ловили снег усами на лету.

Моржи глядели горько и туманно,
по-своему жалея, как могли,
потерянные дети океана,
людей — детей потерянных земли.

Я шел один, и лишь вдали за чащей
как будто ночи пристальный зрачок,
перед лицом невидимым парящий
плыл сигареты красный светлячок,

и чудилось — искала угловато,
не зная, что об этом я молю,
потерянность неведомая чья-то
потерянность похожую мою.

И под бесшумным белым снегопадом,
объединявшим тайною своей,
Америка со мной садилась рядом
на место для потерянных детей.

[Знамя, 1967]

МОНОЛОГ АМЕРИКАНСКОГО ПОЭТА

Роберту Лоуэллу

Уходит любимая,
     будто бы воздух из легких,
навек растворяясь в последних снежинках излетных
в качанье ветвей с почернелою провисью льдышек ...
Обратно не вдышишь!
Напрасно щекою я трусь о шершавый понуренный хобот
трубы водосточной ...
     Напрасно я плачу —
        уходит.
Уходят друзья,
   кореша,
     однолетки,
как будто с площадки молодняка
нас кто-то разводит в отдельные клетки
от некогда общего молока.
Напрасно скулю по друзьям,
     как звереныш ...

Друзей не воротишь!
Уходят надежды —

        такие прекрасные дамы,
которых я выбрал в такие напрасные даты.
В руках остается лишь край их одежды,
но жалкое знамя —

        клочок от надежды ...
Уходит уверенность ...
Помнится —

      клялся я страшной божбою
о стену башку проломить

        или стену — башкою.
Башка поцарапана, правда, но, в общем, цела,
а что со стеной?

      Ухмыляется, сволочь-стена, —
лишь дворник на ней равнодушно меняет портреты ...
Уверенность,

      где ты?
Я словно корабль,

      на котором все гибелью пахнет,
и прыгают крысы ослизлые в панике с палуб.
Эй, чайки!

    Не надо Не плачьте —

        жалеть меня бросьте.
Меня покидают мои длинноногие гостьи.
Садятся они, как положено, первыми в лодки ...
Прощайте, красотки!
Меня покидают мои краснощекие юнги.
Им хочется жить.

     Справедливо.

        Они еще юны.
Прощайте, мальчишки!

     Гребите вперед.

        Вы мужчины.
А я выключаю бессмысленный рокот машины,
и только талант

     капитаном небритым и пьяным
на мостике мрачно стоит

      капитан капитаном.

Но, грязные слезы размазав по грубой обветренной

коже,

он тоже меня покидает.

Он тоже, он тоже ...

Эй, шлюпки,

а ну от греха отойдите в сторонку!

Корабль, если тонет,

вокруг образует воронку.

Остаться совсем одному —

это боль ножевая,

но втягивать я за собой никого не желаю.

Я всех вас прощаю,

одетый в предсмертную пену,

а вам завещаю

пробить ту проклятую стену

и вас призываю

торчащей в завертинах белых трубою

к бою ...

1967

МОНОЛОГ ПЕСЦА НА АЛЯСКИНСКОЙ ЗВЕРОФЕРМЕ

Я голубой на звероферме серой,
но, цветом обреченный на убой,
за непрогрызной проволочной сеткой
не утешаюсь тем, что голубой.

И я бросаюсь в линьку, я лютую,
себя сдираю яростно с себя,
но голубое, брызжа и ликуя,
сквозь шкуру прет, предательски слепя.

И вою я, ознобно, тонко вою
трубой косматой страшного суда,
прося у звезд или навеки волю,
или хотя бы линьку навсегда.

Заезжий мистер на магнитофоне
запечатлел мой вой. Какой простак!
Он просто сам не выл, а мог бы тоже
завыть, сюда попав, еще не так!

И падаю на пол, подыхаю
и все никак подохнуть не могу.
Гляжу с тоской на мой родной Дахау
и знаю: никогда не убегу.

Однажды, тухлой рыбой пообедав,
увидел я, что дверь не на крючке,
и прыгнул в бездну звездную побега
с бездумностью, обычной в новичке.

Вокруг Аляска высилась сугробно,
а я скакал, отчаянный, чумной,
и в легких танцевала твист свобода,
со звездами глотаемая мной.

Я куролесил. Я точил балясы
с деревьями. Я был самим собой.
И снег, переливаясь, не боялся
того, что он такой же голубой.

Мать и отец друг друга не любили,
а спаривались Как бы я хотел
найти подругу, чтобы в снежной пыли
я с нею кувыркался и летел!

Но я устал. Меня сбивали вьюги.
Я вытащить не мог завязших лап.
И не было ни друга, ни подруги.
Дитя неволи для свободы слаб.

Кто в клетке зачат, тот по клетке плачет.
И с ужасом я понял, что люблю
ту клетку, где меня за сетку прячут,
и звероферму — родину мою.

И я вернулся, жалкий и побитый,
но только оказался в клетке вновь,
как виноватость сделалась обидой
и превратилась в ненависть любовь.

Потерянно я выл в тебе, Аляска.
Потерянно я выл теперь в тюрьме.
Америка моя, я потерялся,
но кто не потерявшийся в тебе?

На звероферме, правда, перемены.
Душили раньше попросту в мешках.
Теперь нас убивают современно —
электротоком. Чисто как-никак!

Гляжу на эскимоску-звероводку.
По мне шуршит ласкательно рука,
и чешут пальцы мой загривок кротко,
но в ангельских глазах ее тоска.

Она меня спасет от всех болезней
и помереть мне с голоду не даст,
но знаю, что меня в мой срок железный,
как это ей положено, предаст.

Она воткнет, пролив из глаз водицу,
мне провод в рот, обманчиво шепча . . .
Гуманны будьте к служащим! Введите
на зверофермах должность палача!

Хотел бы я наивным быть, как предок,
но я рожден в неволе, я не тот.
Кто меня кормит, тем я буду предан.
Кто меня гладит, тот меня убьет.

[*Знамя*, 1967]

ЦВЕТЫ И ПУЛИ

Тот, кто любит цветы,
                    тот, естественно, пулям не нравится.
Пули — леди ревнивые.
                        Стоит ли ждать доброты!
Девятнадцатилетняя Аллисон Краузе,
ты убита за то,
                что любила цветы.
Это было —
            чистейших надежд выражение
в миг,
        когда, беззащитна, как совести тоненький пульс,
ты вложила цветок
                в держимордово дуло ружейное
и сказала:
            «Цветы лучше пуль».
Не дарите цветов государству,
                    где правда карается.
Государства такого отдарок циничен,
                            жесток,
и отдарком была тебе,
                    Аллисон Краузе,
пуля,
    вытолкнувшая цветок.
Пусть все яблони мира
                не в белое —
                        в траур оденутся!
Ах, как пахнет сирень,
                но не чувствуешь ты ничего.
Как сказал президент про тебя,
                        ты «бездельница».
Каждый мертвый — бездельник,
                    но это — вина не его.
Ты лежишь на траве
                с карамелькой, запрятанной за щеку.
Новых платьев тебе не надеть,
                    новых книг не прочесть.
Ты студенткой была.
            Изучала искусства изящные,

но другое искусство —
                               кровавое, страшное есть.
В том искусстве палаческом тоже, наверно,
                               есть гении.
Кто был Гитлер?
                  Новаторских газовых камер кубист.
От лица всех цветов
                  проклинаю я ваши творения,
архитекторы лжи,
                  дирижеры убийств!
Шепчут матери мира:
                  «О боже, о боже ...»
И гадалки боятся
                  загадывать наперед.
Рок-н-ролл на костях
                  смерть танцует сейчас во Вьетнаме,
                                            Камбодже,
и какую эстраду
                  она себе завтра найдет?!
Встаньте, девочки Токио,
                  мальчики Рима,
поднимайте цветы
                  против общего злого врага.
Дуньте разом на все одуванчики мира —
о, какая великая будет пурга!
Собирайтесь, цветы, на войну!
                       Покарайте карателей!
За тюльпаном тюльпан,
                  за левкоем — левкой,
вырываясь от гнева
                  из клумб аккуратненьких,
глотки всех лицемеров
                  заткните корнями с землей!
Ты опутай, жасмин,
                  миноносцев подводные лопасти!
Залепляя прицелы,
                  ты в линзы отчаянно впейся, репей!
Встаньте, лилии Ганга
                  и нильские лотосы,
и скрутите винты самолетов,

беременных смертью детей!
Розы, вы не гордитесь, когда продадут
подороже!
Пусть приятно касаться девической нежной
щеки, —
бензобаки
прокалывая
бомбардировщикам,
подлинней,
поострей отрастите шипы!
Если даже цветы восстают,
то негоже играться с историей в прятки.
Молодая Америка,
руки убийцам свяжи!
Нарастай,
нарастай,
эскалация правды,
против топчущей жизни людей
эскалации лжи!
Собирайтесь, цветы, на войну!
Защитите прекрасное!
Затопите шоссе и проселки,
как армии грозный поток,
и в колонны людей и цветов
встань, убитая Аллисон Краузе,
как бессмертник эпохи —
протеста колючий цветок!

1970

[*Правда*, 1970]

СВОБОДА УБИВАТЬ

Цвет статуи Свободы —
                            он все мертвенней
когда, свободу пулями любя,
сама в себя стреляешь ты,
                            Америка.
Ты можешь так совсем убить себя!
Опасно выйти
              в мире этом дьявольском,
еще опасней —
                    прятаться в кустах,
и пахнет на земле всемирным
                              Далласом,
и страшно жить,
                и стыден этот страх.
Кто станет верить в сказку лицемерную,
когда под сенью благостных идей
растет цена на смазку револьверную
и падает цена на жизнь людей?!
Убийцы ходят в трауре на похороны,
а после входят в дельце на паях,
и вновь
        колосья, пулями наполненные,
качаются в Техасе на полях.
Глаза убийц под шляпами и кепками,
шаги убийц слышны у всех дверей,
и падает уже второй из Кеннеди . . .
Америка, спаси своих детей!
Когда с ума опасно сходит нация,
то от беды ее не исцелит
спокойствие,
              прописанное наскоро.
Ей, может быть, одно поможет —
                                стыд.
Историю не выстираешь в прачечной.
Еще таких машин стиральных нет.
Не сходит вечно кровь!
                        О, где он прячется,
стыд нации,

как будто беглый негр?!
Рабы — в рабах.
                    Полно убийц раскованных.
Они вершат свой самосуд,
                    погром,
и бродит по Америке Раскольников,
сойдя с ума,
                    с кровавым топором.
Эй, старый Эйби,
                    что же люди делают,
усвоив подло истину одну,
что только по поваленному дереву
легко понять его величину.
Линкольн хрипит в гранитном кресле ранено.
В него стреляют вновь!
                    Зверье — зверьем.
И звезды,
                    словно пуль прострелы рваные,
Америка,
                    на знамени твоем!
Восстань из мертвых,
                    столько раз убитая,
заговори,
                    как женщина и мать,
восстань,
          Свободы статуя пробитая,
и прокляни свободу убивать!
Но к небу,
                    воззывая о растоптанности,
не отерев кровавых брызг с чела,
свое лицо зеленое утопленницы
ты,
          статуя Свободы,
                    подняла ...
1968

[*Правда*, 1968]

СМОГ

Я просыпаюсь в гостинице «Челси».
Чудится мне
        (Это бред?
                Это жар?) —
черные струйки,
           как черные черви,
в щели вползают на всех этажах.
Галя в рубашке ночной, словно в саване.
Кашель ей грудь раздирает,
                 как рашпиль.
А на рубашке,
         как уголь на сахаре,
черная копоть ...
           «Женя, мне страшно ...»
В комнате-камере
        запах Дахау.
«Женечка, милый,
         я задыхаюсь ...»
Лик ее мученический,
           как из воска.
«Воздуха,
      воздуха ...»
Настежь окно,
         но уже мне не чудится —
в комнату лезет косматое чудище,
движется облаком, черным, зыбучим ...
«Женя,
     задушит! ...»
Галя,
   я сам уже полузадушен.
Воздух глотаю,
         но он безвоздушен.
Нету отдушин!
В губы друг другу отчаянно рухнем?
Будем дышать, как спасеньем, друг другом?
Но не уйти от проклятого смога.
Поздно.
   Мы оба отравлены,

оба,
и поцелуй в этом смраде и тлене
как обоюдное отравленье ...
Рамки инструкций
                на кленах и вязах
«Как целоваться в противогазах»
В барах повесили лозунг-находку:
«Можно спокойно дышать
                   лишь сквозь водку».
И только радио
на все кладет,
горланя радостно:
«А смог идет ...»
Кто там,
        шатаясь, бредет по панели
с детским печальным лицом Паганеля?
Миллер?
      Артур?
             Он мне шепчет замедленно:
«Пахнет кострами,
             охотой за ведьмами ...»
Кашляет Миллер,
         худой,
               остролицый.
Миллер в пророчестве страшном суров:
«Будут еще костры инквизиций.
Смог —
        это дым от грядущих костров».
От смога неловко крылом заслоняясь,
жадный до тайн
            и усталый от тайн,
на домике собственных книг,
               словно аист,
тревожно стоит доброклювый Апдайк.
«Женя,
      людей так жестоко надули,
землю поставив на ложных китах,
и надрывается
        от натуги
все человечество,

                 будто кентавр.
И двуедино ржет и мычит оно
от двуединости делаясь злей.
Может быть, смог —
                      это бьющий мучительно
пар у кентавра из гневных ноздрей?»
Очки пытаясь протереть от смога,
у чьих-то книг, как у могильных плит,
с высокостью профессорского слога
мне Лоуэлл сквозь кашель говорит:
«Лишь у теней и книг — понятье чести.
Кого стыдиться? Лишь теней стыжусь.
И я продукт теней. Я — это вместе
Алеша Карамазов и Сен-Жюст.
Я верю в историческое мщенье,
в отмщенье неба за разврат, распад.
Быть может, смог — возвышенные тени,
которые за низость мира мстят?»
Ален Гинзберг —
                 лукавый пророк-павиан —
бьет в косматую грудь,
                     словно в бубен шаман:
«Темь надвигается,
           темь!
Пахнет кромешным адом.
Нет оправданья тем,
кто может дышать этим смрадом!
В мире моральных пустот,
в мире тумана и хаоса
стоит чего-то лишь тот,
кто задыхается ...
Все лжеидеи,
         все лжеморали
небо,
      чадя столько лет,
               измарали.
Небо обратно шлет эту нудь —
не продохнуть!»
Но где-то над смогом,
              над чадным вчера и сегодня

грохочет Уитмена бас,
                    будто рык Саваофа:
«Э-гей!
        Задыхаться — нехитрое дело у пропасти.
А вы продышитесь,
                а вы продышитесь!
                            Попробуйте!
Вздохните все вместе!
                Увидите —
                        только вздохнете,
и смог, словно призрак,
                    дыханием с неба смахнете ...»
И чудилось мне,
            замерев, ожидала эпоха,
как сдвига вселенского,
                    нашего общего вздоха.

[*Знамя*, 1967]

INDEX OF TRANSLATORS

DICKEY, JAMES

DUTTON, GEOFFREY

INDEX OF FIRST LINES